# LEE OF VIRGINIA

1642-1892

BIOGRAPHICAL AND GENEALOGICAL SKETCHES OF

# The Descendants of Colonel Richard Lee

EDITED AND PUBLISHED BY

EDMUND JENNINGS LEE

Arms of Lee, of Coton Hall
County Salop.

# LEE OF VIRGINIA

1642-1892

BIOGRAPHICAL AND GENEALOGICAL SKETCHES OF

# The Descendants of Colonel Richard Lee

WITH BRIEF NOTICES OF THE RELATED FAMILIES OF

ALLERTON, ARMISTEAD, ASHTON, AYLETT, BEDINGER, BEVERLEY, BLAND, BOLLING, CARROLL, CARTER, CHAMBERS, CORBIN, CUSTIS, DIGGES, FAIRFAX, FITZHUGH, GARDNER, GRYMES, HANSON, JENINGS, JONES, LUDWELL, MARSHALL, MASON, PAGE, RANDOLPH, SHEPHERD, SHIPPEN, TABB, TAYLOR, TURBERVILLE, WASHINGTON, AND OTHERS

---

EDITED AND PUBLISHED BY

EDMUND JENNINGS LEE, M. D.

MEMBER OF THE HISTORICAL SOCIETIES OF
PENNSYLVANIA AND VIRGINIA

Reprinted with Additions and Corrections



CLEARFIELD

Reprinted for
Clearfield Company, Inc. by
Genealogical Publishing Co., Inc.
Baltimore, Maryland
1999, 2000

Originally published: Philadelphia, 1895
Reprinted: Baltimore, 1974, by
Genealogical Publishing Co., Inc.
Reprinted with Additions and Corrections
furnished by The Society of the Lees of Virginia.
Baltimore: Genealogical Publishing Co., Inc., 1983.

Library of Congress Catalogue Card Number 73-18165
International Standard Book Number 0-8063-0604-1
*Made in the United States of America*

# PREFACE.

The purpose of this volume is to collect, and preserve in a permanent form, the history of a Virginia family and their kindred, believing that such a record will add something of interest to the general history of the glorious "Old Dominion." The volume had its inception in the youthful fondness of a boy for collecting letters and other original data concerning the early generations of his family. From his earliest boyhood the late Cassius F. Lee, Jr., evinced a passion for genealogical research, and during the many years he continued his investigations he had collected a large amount of original data, consisting of letters, wills, deeds, and such like records. In 1870, with the assistance of Mr. Joseph Packard, Jr., of Baltimore, he published in the *New England Genealogical and Historical Register* a brief "Record of the Descendants of Colonel Richard Lee of Virginia." This publication was merely tentative, with the hope of procuring additional information that would enable him to compile a complete family history at a later date. In this hope he was disappointed; little or no data were obtained. But Mr. Lee continued his personal efforts, and had secured considerable additions to his collection, when his untimely decease ended his work. A short time previous to his death, Mr. Packard had suggested to him that he put his collections into book form, and Mr. Lee was seriously considering the idea at the time of his death. The present editor of this volume has taken up and completed his brother's unfinished work, which he now offers to those interested in such records, hoping that the volume may not be found wholly lacking in interest and trustworthiness. The greatest care possible has been used to secure accuracy and certainty; nothing has been recorded that did not seem to be well established, and wherever any statement or any date was at all doubtful it has been so stated in the text.

The arrangement of the book is so simple that little explanation is needed. In order that something of the English ancestors of the Virginia Immigrant might be known, the valuable assistance of Mr. William Blackstone Lee, of Wiltshire, has been secured, and he has given a succinct account of his English line. Since many persons seem to think that every American who bears the same name must of necessity be of the same stock, a few sketches of the various English Lee families, to show the erroneousness of such an idea, have been given by Mr. J. Henry Lea, of Fairhaven, Mass., who is well equipped for such work. Coming now to the Virginia family, the life of the Immigrant has been traced as well as existing records would allow. Then each of his children has been treated in like manner; next, his grandchildren, and so on down to the present generation. As only three of the Immigrant's sons have been proven to have left surviving male issue in Virginia, and, as the issue of these three sons form three distinct lines of descent, they have been treated separately. Under the notice of each head of a family, the names of his children are given, numbered, in the order of their birth, by the Roman figures placed before their names. Those sons who married and themselves became heads of families have also Arabic figures placed after their names, to show where they are taken up in the next generation. Whatever is known as to unmarried sons, and as to all daughters, is given with their parents. The records upon which these sketches are based have been derived from wills, deeds, family Bibles, tombstone inscriptions, and such like authorities. All the wills, deeds, land grants, official commissions, etc., quoted in this volume are from duly attested copies. The official certificates have been omitted to save space.

The pictures given are photographic copies of old family portraits, miniatures, engravings, or photographs. Some of these were much defaced by time, and offered very poor subjects for copying. The general excellence of the prints given is due to the skill and attention bestowed upon them by the efficient employés of the Gutekunst Company of this city.

That equal prominence might be given to maternal ancestry, brief sketches of the parentage of wives of the Lees of the older generations are added; nearly all of the families so sketched have been for generations prominent in the social and political life of Virginia, and more or less complete records of them are given elsewhere. Consequently, it was felt that the merest outline of their family history would be sufficient in this connection. Wherever it has been possible to obtain an accurate representation of the coat-armor once actually used by these families, it has been given in as clear a copy as the original would allow.

The various spellings used in the old letters and documents have been followed; as far as possible their punctuation and use of capitals has also been preserved.

To those who have so kindly and efficiently rendered assistance in compiling this volume, the editor returns his most grateful thanks. Among those to whom he is especially indebted may be mentioned the following: Mrs. Mary Lee Gouverneur, of Frederick county, Maryland, the oldest living representative of the family, in spite of her advanced age, copied a large amount of the family records of the descendants of her grandfather, Gov. Thomas Sim Lee. To Miss Margaret H. Lee, of Richmond, the descendants of Hancock Lee owe the best part of the record of their line as given in this volume. Mr. W. G. Stanard, also of Richmond, has furnished much information, some of which has been acknowledged in the proper places throughout the text; but many dates, names of official positions, and such like data derived from him, have not been acknowledged in that way. Mr. R. A. Brock, who has rendered such efficient service in preserving and arranging Virginia history, as well as that of the South in general, has also given valuable assistance. Dr. A. G. Grinnan, of Madison county, Virginia, and Mr. Thomas M. Green, of Danville, Ky., have been very helpful, especially in sending information concerning the descendants of Hancock Lee. Mr. Alexander Brown, of Norwood, Nelson county, has been exceedingly kind in contributing material. In Baltimore, Mr. Wilson Miles Cary, and Mr. Joseph Packard, Jr., have been most helpful; to the latter especially many thanks are due for assistance in carrying the work through the press. From the Rev. Horace Edwin Hayden, and his invaluable *Virginia Genealogies*, much aid has been received. Miss Kate Mason Rowland, of Baltimore, has also sent some interesting data from the files of the old *Maryland Gazette*.

In conclusion, the editor desires to return thanks to the Franklin Printing Company of this city for the faithful manner in which they have prepared and printed this volume. The excellent proof-reading deserves special commendation.

Attention of readers is especially called to the Appendix, where some important and interesting additions and corrections are given.

PHILADELPHIA, 1st May, 1895.

# LIST OF ILLUSTRATIONS.

## PORTRAITS.

# OTHER ILLUSTRATIONS.

# CONTENTS.

## THE LEES OF ENGLAND.



## LEE OF VIRGINIA.

### FIRST GENERATION.



### SECOND GENERATION, STRATFORD LINE.



### THIRD GENERATION, STRATFORD LINE.

SIXTH GENERATION, STRATFORD LINE.

SEVENTH GENERATION, STRATFORD LINE.

## THE DITCHLEY LINE.

### FIRST GENERATION.



### SECOND GENERATION.



### THIRD GENERATION.



### FOURTH GENERATION.



### FIFTH GENERATION.

SIXTH GENERATION.



SEVENTH GENERATION.



## THE COBBS HALL LINE.

FIRST GENERATION.



SECOND GENERATION.



THIRD GENERATION.



FOURTH GENERATION.



FIFTH GENERATION.



SIXTH GENERATION.

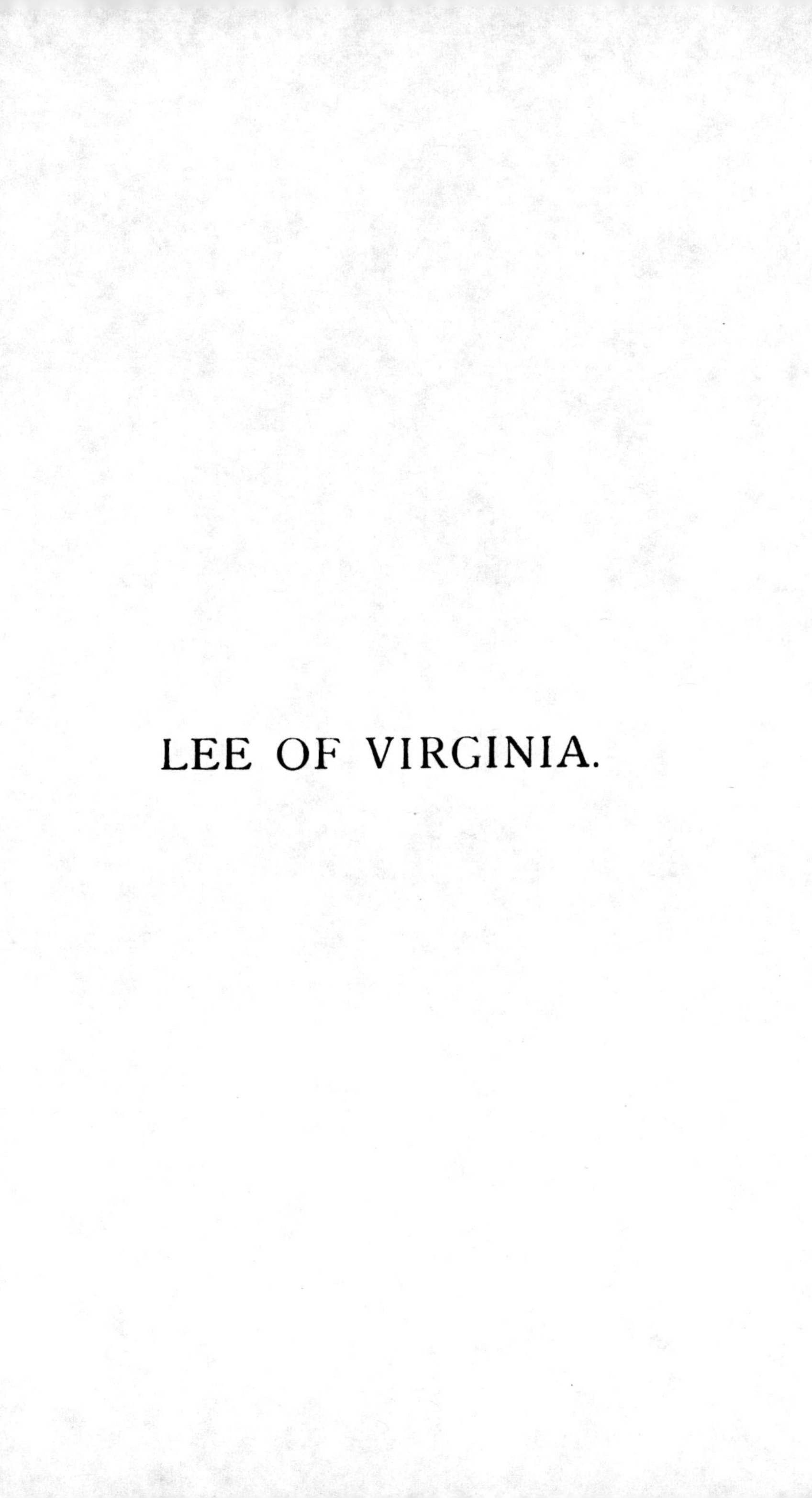

# LEE OF VIRGINIA.

# THE LEES OF ENGLAND.

THE earliest records of England contain references to many families of this name, though spelt in many different forms. The various counties of England have been from early times dotted with Lee villages, towns, and rivers; there was scarcely a county that did not contain several Lee seats, mansions, or manors. In view of the prevalence of this name, it will be readily acknowledged that the accurate tracing of the descendants of any special progenitor is no easy task. It can only be accomplished by a careful and thorough scrutiny of all reliable records; this Mr. William Blackstone Lee has done for the Lees of Langley and Coton, and gives here a summary of the reliable data he has gathered. The only addition to his accurate sketch that might be made, with interest to those not well versed in genealogy and heraldry, is a brief account of the other well-known Lee families of England. Such sketches will enable readers to discriminate between those having the same name, yet belonging to different families and bearing different arms. Families who lawfully bore similar arms were considered to have had a common parent stock.

The following sketches of ten of the principal Lee families in England are from the pen of Mr. J. Henry Lea, of Fairhaven, Mass., who has devoted considerable time to the study of the genealogies of the families of this name. His sketches may, therefore, be considered thoroughly accurate and reliable. They are necessarily very brief. These ten families are:

1. Leigh of West Hall, High Leigh, Cheshire.
2. Leigh of East Hall, High Leigh, Cheshire.
3. Lee of Lea Hall and Dernhall, Cheshire.
4. Lygh of Lanford and Corsley, Wiltshire.
5. Leigh of Flamberdstone, Wiltshire, and Isle of Wight.
6. Lee of De Lee Magna, Kent.
7. Lea of Halesowen, Salop, and of Kingsnorton, Worcester.
8. Ley of Bereferrers, Devon, and of Teffont Evias, Wiltshire.
9. Leigh of East Leigh, Kent, and of Addington, Surrey.
10. Lee of Hughley, Shropshire.

## 1. LEIGH OF WEST HALL, CHESHIRE.

Arms: Or, a lion rampant, gules. (ancient arms, Gules a pale fusillée argent, being the arms of Lyme).

This, the most ancient family of the name in England, traces its pedigree through Hamon de Leigh (temp. Henry II.) son of Gilbert de Venables, Baron of Kinderton, and great grandson of Gilbert de Venables of Normandy, who accompanied the Conqueror to England, and was a younger brother of Thibault (III.), Count of Blois, and a descendant of Thibault, brother of Rollo, the Viking, the first Duke of Normandy. Richard de Leigh, great grandson of Hamon, left issue Agnes, only daughter and heir, who married, first, Richard de Lyme, the younger son of Hugh de Lyme, and had issue a son, Thomas, who took the name of his mother, and became the ancestor of the Leighs of West Hall. This Agnes married, secondly, Sir William de Venables, Knt. (her fourth cousin in the male line), and had issue, John De Leigh, who assumed the name of his mother, but retained the arms of his father, *i. e.*, Azure, two bars argent. From him are descended the Leighs of Boothes, Stoneley, Lee of Hartwell, and many others.

The following ancient and noble families of the name trace their descent from the parent stock of High Leigh:—Boothes (arms: az. 2 bars arg., over all a bend gu.); Baguley (arms: az. 2 bars arg., over all a bend sa.); Adlington (arms: az. 2 bars arg., over all a bendlet gobony or and gu.); Berchington (arms: az. 2 bars arg., over all, on a bend gu., 3 phæons of the second); Lyme (arms: gu., a cross engrailed arg.); of the Ridge (same arms); Stoneley, Warw., Lords Leigh (same arms); Lee of Hartwell, Bucks. (arms: az. 2 bars or, over all a bend gobony or and gu.); Oughtrington (arms: arg. a bend fusillée sa., quartering or a lion rampant, gu.); Brownsover, Warw., Barts.; Annerley, co. Notts.; Egginton, co. Derby (arms: az., a plate betw. 3 ducal crowns or, within a bordure arg.); Birch, co. Lanc. (arms: az., 2 bars arg. a bend gobony or and gu., and sometimes 2 crowns in chief or); Rushall, co. Staff. (arms: gu., a cross engrailed arg., in dexter quarter an escutcheon of the last charged with 2 bars az. and debrused by a bend gobony or and gu.); Longborrow and Adlestrop, co. Glouc. (arms: gu., a cross engrailed arg., in dexter quarter a lozenge of the second); Newnham Regis, co. Warw., Earls of Chichester (same arms); Stockwell, co. Surry (arms: gu., a cross engrailed and bordure engrailed arg.); Isell, co. Cumb. (parent stock of Baguley); Townley, co. Lanc. (arms: arg., a fess and 3 mullets in chief, sa.); Middleton, co. York (arms: arg., 2 bars sa., over all a bend, gu.), and many other distinguished and gentle families. (*Omerod's Cheshire*, Helsby's Ed. I, 449.)

## 2. LEIGH OF EAST HALL, CHESHIRE.

Arms: Argent, a lion rampant gules.

Are descended from Efward or Oswald de Lega and were probably a co-armigerous family with the last named, the arms being identical except in tincture. The very strong probability of their descent from the Venables stock is recognized by Omerod and other authorities. Like the Leighs of West Hall, they have retained their estates and preserved a male succession. (*Omerod*, I, 457.)

## 3. LEE OF LEA HALL AND DERNHALL, CHESHIRE.

Arms: Argent, a Fess sable between three leopards' heads of the second. (A later grant 1583, gave a chevron instead of the fess.)

Are descended from John Lee, who married Isabelle, daughter of Sir Piers Dutton, of Dutton, and had a son, John, who married Elizabeth, daughter of Sir Thomas Fulleshurst, or Folhurst, and was succeeded by his eldest son, Thomas, who married Marjery, daughter of Sir John Aston, Knt., and had a son, John, who married Margery, daughter of Henry Hocknel, and had issue: 1, Thomas, his successor at Lea Hall; 2, John, of Aston, co: Stafford; 3, William; 4, Robert, of Aston; 5, Benedict, who married Elizabeth, daughter and heir of Sir John Wood, Esqr., of co: Warwick; his son, Richard, of Quarrendon, co: Bucks, altered his arms to, "Argent, a fesse between three crescents, sable;" he left, besides two daughters, Elizabeth and Katharine, four sons:

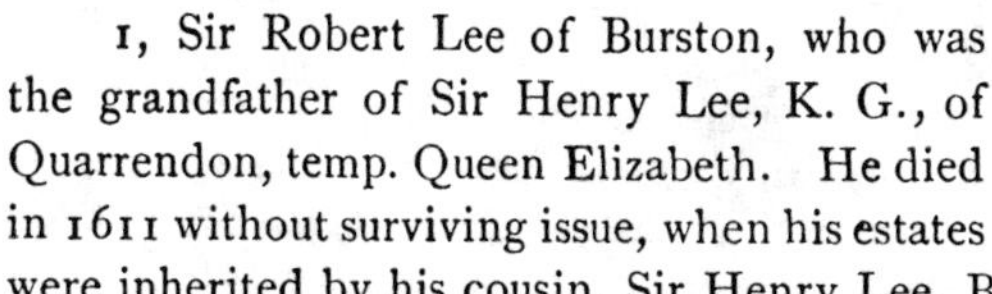

1, Sir Robert Lee of Burston, who was the grandfather of Sir Henry Lee, K. G., of Quarrendon, temp. Queen Elizabeth. He died in 1611 without surviving issue, when his estates were inherited by his cousin, Sir Henry Lee, Bart., of Ditchley.

2, Roger Lee of Pightlesthorne, co: Bucks., from whom the Lees of Binfield are descended.

3, Henry Lee (of Oxon. ?), left issue.

4, Benedict Lee of Hulcote, co: Bucks., was the father of Sir Robert Lee, Knt., of Hulcote, whose son, Sir Henry Lee, inherited the estates of his cousin, above mentioned, and became seated at Ditchley. From him was descended Sir Edward-Henry Lee, fifth Baronet, Colonel of the first Foot Guards, who was elevated to the peerage as Earl of Litchfield, by letters-patent, on the 5th of June, 1674; Robert, the fourth Earl died on the 4th of November, 1776, without issue; "when," says Burke, "the earldom of Litchfield and minor honors became extinct." The estates were eventually inherited by Lady Charlotte Lee, daughter of the second earl; she married on the 26th of October, 1744, Viscount Dillon, and has left descendants. From Thomas Lee, of Lea Hall, Cheshire, brother of the first Benedict, the male line of the elder branch of this family continued down in unbroken succession to Charles Lee, the General in the American Army during the Revolution. He was born in 1731; died at Philadelphia without issue, in 1782, and was buried at old Christ church in that city. At his death the elder branch became extinct in the male line.[1]

## 4. LYGH OF LANFORD AND CORSLEY, WILTSHIRE.

Arms: Argent, guttée de sang, a lion rampant, gules.

They were seated at Lanford as early as the reign of Henry III. (1216–1272), being then represented by James de Lygh, who held his lands by service of Albreda de Boterell. Perhaps cadets of the Leighs of High Leigh (compare arms), and became extinct in the direct line about 1515, when Robert Lygh, fourth of the name in succession, left two laughters, his co-heirs; Elizabeth, who married John Stanter of Horningon, Wilts., and Anne, who married William Beckett, of Wilton, co. Vilts. (*Hoare's Mod. Wilts.*, V, 82.)

[1] A genealogy of the Quarrendon Lees, by the writer, is now appearing in the *Genealogist*, 'ew Series, Vol. VIII, p. 226, *et seq.*, which will give, for the first time, a practically correct ıd complete account of this much abused and, in the male line, totally extinct family.

NOTE: As there has been for many years a tradition amongst the Lees of Virginia that ey were in some way descended from the Ditchley line, the arms borne by that family are ven above. As previously stated, Richard Lee, on becoming seated at Quarrendon, altered arms from "three leopards' heads" to "three crescents," retaining crest and motto. ough the Lees of Virginia cannot, as a family, trace any descent from the Ditchley stock, th re are some of them that can do so through the maternal line. Benedict Calvert, fourth Lord Baltimore, married in 1698 Lady Charlotte Fitzroy, daughter of Edward Henry Lee, first Earl of Litchfield; their great great granddaughter, Eleanor Calvert, married John Parke Custis, the grandfather of Mrs. Robert E. Lee, whose children are therefore descended from the Ditchley stock.—*Editor.*

## 5. LEIGH OF FLAMBERDSTONE, WILTS., AND OF THE ISLE OF WIGHT.

Arms: Argent, on a chief embattled sable, three plates.

This family, probably cadets of the last named, trace their descent from John Lye, of Flamberdstone (1368). A superb alabaster monument of Sir John Leigh, Knt., who died in 1522, is still remaining at Godshill church, in the Isle of Wight. They were long seated in the island, and are now represented by Edward Leonard Leigh, Esq., of Northcourt House, Charteris, Cambridgeshire. (*Hoare's Mod. Wilts.*, II, 4; *Berry's Hants. Genealogies.*)

## 6. LEE OF DE LEE MAGNA, KENT.

Arms: Azure, on a fess cotised or, three leopards' heads erased, gules.

Derive their descent from Symon Lee, "descended from ancestors in co: Worcester," whose son, John Lee, was of Wolksted in Surrey, and whose son, Sir Richard Lee, Knt., was Lord Mayor of London, 1461, and 1470. The last named purchased the estate of De Lee Magna, or Great Delce, in Kent. Edward Lee, Lord Archbishop of York (1531–44), was of this family; the elder line became extinct in the reign of Queen Anne. The Lees of Southwell, Notts., of Pinchinthorpe, Yorks., of Pinhoe and Totnes, in Devon., were cadets. (*Berry's Kent Genealogies*, 172. *Hastea's Kent*, I, 173; II, 55. *Harl. Soc.*, VI, 348. *Graves' Cleveland*, 434.)

## 7. LEA OF HALES OWEN GRANGE, SALOP, AND KINGSNORTON, WORCESTERSHIRE.

Arms: Argent, on a pale between two leopards' faces, sable, three crescents or.

Originally of Lea Green, Kingsnorton, where they appear in the 16th century. By the marriage of William Lea of Hales Owen, in 1709, with Frances, daughter of the Hon. William Ward, and sister and heir of Thomas, Lord Dudley, his son, Ferdinando Dudley Lea became heir (in 1740) to the Barony of Dudley, but died unmarried in 1757, when the title fell into abeyance. (*Her. and Gen.*, V, 213; VI, 363.)

## 8. LEY OF BEREFERRERS, DEVON., AND OF TEFFONT EVIAS, WILTSHIRE.

Arms: Argent, a chevron between three seals' heads, sable.

Of this family, who were also of Kempthorne in Devon., and of Morwinstow, Cornwall, was Henry Ley of Teffont Evias who, by his wife, Dyonisia, daughter of Walter de St. Maur, Esq., had issue six sons, of whom the youngest was Sir James Ley, Knt. and Bart., Baron Ley and Earl of Marlborough, and Lord High Treasurer of England; he died in 1628, aged 78. A splendid monument to his memory remains at Westbury in Wilts. He has been referred to by Milton (in a sonnet to his daughter Margaret) as,

> "That Good Earl, once President
> Of England's Council and her Treasury,
> Who lived, in both, unstained with gold or fee,
> And left them both, more in himself content."

William, fourth Earl, died without issue in 1679, when the earldom became extinct, to be revived later as a dukedom in the Churchill family. (*Hoare's Mod. Wilts.*, IV, 111; III, 35. *West. Antiq.*, IV, 175. *Complete Peerage*, V, 251. *Harl. Soc.*, V, 127.)

## 9. LEIGH OF ADDINGTON, SURREY.

Arms: Or, on a chevron sable, three lions' rampant, argent.

William a Lyghe was of East Leigh in Kent about 1327, from whom was descended John Leigh, Esq., sheriff of Surrey in 1469. He purchased Addington in 1447, and founded a flourishing family there and at Abingworth, whose elder line became extinct in 1732. They were Grand Masters of Sergeantry, and held Addington by service of carrying the first dish at the coronation feast of the king. (*Halsted's Kent*, II, 173. *Berry's Surrey Gen.*, 101. *Gent. Mag.*, VI, 632.)

## 10. LEE OF HUGHLEY, SALOP.

The first of this family was Renulf de Leges (1120), who was, perhaps, descended from Edric fitz Aluric, the Saxon feofee of the estate at the Conquest, or, more probably, from some usurping Norman, who replaced him in his fiefs after Doomsday. The family took their surname from the estate, which was at first called Lega or Lee, and afterward Hughley from the Christian name of one of the later lords of the manor (Hugo de Lee, occurs 1213 to 1262), presenting the curious result that while the family had taken its name from the manor, the manor, in its turn, took its distinctive name from a member of the family.

This Hugh Lee has been, by the Herald's College and, following their authority, by many others, placed as the prepositor of the Lees of Langley and Coton, an utter anachronism, as, when we examine the evidence, we find that while Hugh de Lee might have been a brother, or, still more probably, a nephew or cousin, of Sir Reyner de Lee, the real ancestor of the Lees of the latter line, it is preposterous to suppose that he was his father, as he occurs over forty years after Reyner's death, and the succession of his son to his estates. The documentary proof of this is conclusive and overwhelming. (*Eyton's Antiq. Salop*, VI, 302.)

## LEE OF HARTWELL, BUCKINGHAMSHIRE.

Arms: Azure, two bars or, a bend cheque or, and gules.

Among the dozen or more families that trace their descent from the parent stock of Leigh of High Leigh, Cheshire (as shown by Mr. J. Henry Lea), are the Lees of Hartwell, who settled in Bucks in the beginning of Henry IV.'s reign. William Leigh, of Moreton, in the parish of Dinton, died in 1486. Fourth in descent from him was Sir Thomas Lee, Knt., of Moreton, who married Eleanor, the daughter and eventually the heiress of Michael Hampden, Esq., of Hartwell, and had twenty-four chlldren. He was succeeded by his son, Thomas, and he, in turn, by a Thomas, whose eldest son, also a Thomas, was created a Baronet on the 16th of August, 1660. This Sir Thomas Lee served many years in Parliament, and "was much admired for his elegant speeches in the House of Commons, where he was a leader in the debates." His son, another Sir Thomas, also a member of Parliament, left four sons: 1, Thomas, his successor at Hartwell and in Parliament; 2, William, Privy Councillor and Lord Chief Justice of England; 3, John, a colonel in the Guards; 4, Sir George, LL.D., a privy councillor and treasurer to the Princess Dowager of Wales. Third in descent from this Sir Thomas was Sir George, rector of Hartwell, etc., who died in 1827, unmarried, when the Baronetcy expired. The Hartwell estate is said to have been in the possession of this family, *i. e.*, *the Hampdens*, since 1268. The present owner is Edward Dyke Lee, who recently inherited it from an uncle.

Hartwell was for some time the residence of Louis XVIII. while exiled from the throne of France, and became well known throughout Europe at that time as the headquarters of the Bourbon family. (*Lipscombe's Bucks*. I, 163, II, 303. *Dwinn's Visit. of Wales*, I, 199.)

## LEES OF LANGLEY AND COTON.

By William Blackstone Lee, Esq., Seend, Wilts.

Lee of Lea, Aldon, Alderton, Hadnall, Stanton, Roden, Pimhill, Berrington, etc., from about 1150 to 1380, and afterward of Langley, Lea Hall, Acton Burnell, Nordley Regis, and Coton Hall, all in Shropshire. Also of Ankerwycke and Wraysbury, Bucks. Also of Cholderton, Wilts, and Buriton, Hants.

Arms: Gu. a fesse chequy or and az. between ten billets arg. four in chief, and three, two, one in base. This is the form in which the arms were certified to each branch of the family (represented respectively by Richard Lee of Langley and Humphrey Lee of Coton) at the first visitation in 1569, and to this form the Coton branch has nearly always adhered, while the Langley branch has borne the fesse, sometimes chequy, sometimes counter-company, and has varied the number of billets. There is no heraldic distinction between the two branches, but it is shown by ancient seals that the earliest form of fesse was counter-company, and when Sir Humphrey Lee certified the pedigree for both branches of the family in 1623 the coat then allowed to him bore the fesse in that form. (The above statement is from an official report on the arms of the family by C. H. Athill, Esq., Richmond Herald.)

Crest: On a staff raguly lying fesseways a squirrel sejant proper cracking a nut (or acorn), from the dexter end of the staff a hazel (or oak) branch vert fructed or.

Motto: Ne Incautus Futuri.

Quarterings: *Langley branch:* Astley, azure a cinqfoil pierced erm. within a bordure engr. of the second. Burnell, az. a lion ramp. guard, arg. guttee de sang, crowned or. Peshall, arg. a cross fleury sa. on a canton gu. a lion's head erased of the first crowned or. Sprenchose, per fesse gu. and vert a fesse arg. in chief a chevron of the last. *Coton branch:* Astley az. a cinqfoil pierced erm. within a bordure engr. of the second.

The pedigree of this family, which is one of the oldest in England, is registered at the Herald's College, and covers a period of about 750 years, the representatives at the different visitations having been as follows:

1569. Richard Lee, Esq., of Langley, and Humphrey Lee, Esq., of Coton.

1584. John Lee, Esq., of Coton.

1623. Sir Humphrey Lee, Bart., of Langley, who certified the pedigree for both branches.

1663. Thomas Lee, Esq., of Coton.

From this last date the pedigree is certified by William Blackstone Lee, Esq., the present representative.

The late Rev. R. W. Eyton and the late Sir William Hardy, Keeper of the Records in the Office of the Duchy of Lancaster, two most able antiquarians and genealogists, have thrown a great deal of light on the early history of this family, and have brought that part of the pedigree to an unusual degree of fullness. The former in his History of Shropshire treats of every well-known family in the county; the latter made a special study of that of Lee. His MS. collections from the English Records are voluminous, while his correspondence with Eyton shows that with regard to this particular family the latter was greatly indebted to him. Their researches show that the Lee possessions in Shropshire were very large, and that many of the family were knighted in early times, the last being Sir Thomas de Lee or Atte Lee, Sheriff in 1395. One of them, Sir John de la Lee, was Knight of the Shire in the Parliament of York in 1322, and again at Westminster in 1324. From the time of Reigner de Lee's Shrievalty in 1201, the family have filled that office nine times. There are two or three instances of confusion in the early part of the pedigree; but it is remarkable, that in one going back to such remote times, it has been possible by satisfactory evidence to set right the only errors which have been actually proved. And here it may be as well to add a few words on the value of the Heralds' College records, as much misconception exists with regard to them.

In the first place, the College is the only existing authority on questions of coats of armour and descent. With regard to the former there is no appeal against its decisions, while as to the latter its testimony is in itself legal evidence, which can only be upset by better evidence to the contrary. In the second place, it must be remembered that the primary object of the Visitations was not to record pedigrees, but to ascertain who were entitled to bear arms. In early times the number of armigerous families in any given county was very small. They were people of distinction, and any impostor assuming the coat of arms of a well-known family would have been detected at once. Hence the bearing of a particular coat was most valuable evidence of descent, and this fact was recognized by the highest authority when the Visitations were instituted. They were taken under Royal Commission, and one of the instructions to the Heralds was that any person proving to their satisfaction that his ancestors had borne a particular coat before the date of the battle of Agincourt (1415) was to have his claim allowed. The proofs submitted to the Heralds would, of course, consist of all kinds of evidence, oral and documentary, and would include that derived from inscriptions on tombstones then existing, armorial devices, etc., etc. It is obvious that an immense mass of evidence must have been produced, much of which has now perished or is impossible to recover. Of its sufficiency the Heralds were the sole judges, and having once given their decision they were under no obligation to keep any record of the proofs upon which it was founded. They did, however, in most cases record more or less fully the pedigrees of those whose claims they allowed, but the means for securing the absolute accuracy insisted on at the present day did not then exist, and errors may no doubt be found in most pedigrees going back to very early times, and founded in great measure upon charters in the possession of the family. The Heralds made the best of the evidence before them, and having established the fact that the descent in the main was true, they "allowed," *i. e.*, acknowledged the right to the arms in question. Their "allowance" of the arms and the pedigrees recorded are legal evidence in any Court of Law in the Kingdom. And that evidence is two-fold. In the first place, the allowance of the arms is evidence of descent from a particular family. In the second place, the recorded pedigree is in any given case evidence of immediate parentage. The descent of any individual prior to the date of Agincourt from a family distinguished by a particular coat of arms having once been established by the Heralds, his claim and that of his descendants does not (to use the words of C. H. Athill, Esq., Richmond Herald) rest upon the accuracy of his description in the registered pedigree, but upon the fact of the heralds being satisfied that he bore those arms prior to 1415, the date of Agincourt. And the onus of proof does not lie on his descendants, but on any one who would dispute their claim. The allowance of the arms is legal evidence that their ancestor belonged to a particular family, and can only be upset by better evidence to the contrary.

To return to the Lee pedigree, the early part of which is chiefly founded on the charters or deeds belonging to Sir Humphrey Lee. The first name is that of Hugo de Lega, who is given as father of "Reginaldus de la Lee, cui Willus filius Willi filii Alani ad peticoem Fulconis filii Warini concesrt terras." This Reginald is the same with Reyner de Lee, who is given by Eyton as the first of the name known to him, and who "towards the close of the 12th century acquired Alderton from Fulke Fitz Warin, who held it under Fitz Alan." The actual wording of the charter compared with the description quoted above from the pedigree will show this identity. "Willus filius Willi filii Alani omnibus xp'i fidelibus ad quos præsens Charta pervenerit salutem. Sciatis me ad peticoem Fulconis filii Warini concessisse Reign'o de Le totam tram ipsius Fulconis, de Aluerton quæ est de feodo meo quam ipse Fulco dedit eidem Reign'o pro homagio suo et pro XX$^{ti}$ marcis argenti et uno palfrido, etc." The spelling of the name with a *g* and its abbreviation Reign'us might easily account for its appearing by a clerical error in the pedigree as Reginaldus. We find, however, in old documents that the same name was frequently spelt in a variety of ways, and there is certainly a strong resemblance between the names Reyner, Reigner, Rainald, Reignold, and Reginald. The transcriber of the pedigree may have taken the very reasonable view that they were essentially the same, and have used the form Reginald, not in error at all, but deliberately. The point, however, is not of importance, as the identity in this case is quite clear.

This Reginald or Reigner de Le was Sheriff, as FitzAlan's deputy, in 1201, and according to Blakeway, in his "Sheriffs of Shropshire," is the first of the family on record as bearing the fesse and billets which have been their coat-of-arms ever since, and which, carried by Richard Lee to his Virginian home and borne by generations of his descendants, are still to be seen there on ruined houses and old silver, giving witness to the race of which he came.

Eyton disputed the statement of the pedigree that Reigner was son of Hugo de Lega, but it does not appear that he gives any proofs in support of his opinion. Mr. J. H. Lea, who has devoted a considerable amount of time to the history of this family, quotes an instance in which Roger de Leg' appears as defendant with Reyner de Le in the suit of William de Wodston for lands, etc., in Culemere, anno 1203. These co-defendants may very likely have been brothers. In any case, it would be rash to attempt any hard and fast distinction between the names de Le, de Lega, and de Leg'. Indeed, one cannot doubt that Reigner de Le himself is identical with Reiner de Lega, who appears as one of the sixteen knights at the Salop assizes in 1203.

With regard to the deed from Fulke FitzWarin, the following are Eyton's words in a letter of April, 1852: "The deed is extremely important. It can be dated within two years, for Hugh de Say, the father of Helias the witness, was living November 12th, 1194 (*vide* Rot. Cur. Regis, Vol. I), and Mag$^{r}$ Rob$^{s}$ de Salop was consecrated Bishop of Bangor, 17th March, 1197. When I add that Reginald de Heding, who occupies a prominent position as a witness, was not entitled to such prominence by his possessions, but was under Sheriff to FitzAlan from September, 1195, to September, 1196, I think we have a fair presumption of the date of the deed."

It is clear from the date of the Bishop of Bangor's consecration that the deed was given before 1197, and the other particulars leave little doubt that it was not earlier than 1194. We know that Reigner was Sheriff in 1201 and he does not seem to occur after 1210. His date of birth may therefore fairly be taken as circa 1150–1170. His son is given in the pedigree as Sir John de la Lee and the son of Sir John as Sir Thomas. It appears, however, from the researches of Eyton and Hardy that two generations are here misplaced, and that Reigner's son was Sir Thomas, while John, given as Sir Thomas's father, was really his son. In proof of Sir Thomas being son to Reigner, Eyton writes, "Thomas de Lee was certainly son of Reyner, the two, as father and son, grant conjointly *2s.* rent in Weston to Haghmon, and another deed shews Thomas confirming his father Reyner's grant."

Sir Thomas (living circa 1221–1258) married Petronilla, daughter of Sir Thomas Corbet, Sheriff of Salop 38 Hen. III. (1253–4) and had two sons besides Sir John, viz.: Reyner (called again Reginald in the pedigree) and Sir Thomas, who is also given in the pedigree. The latter married Petronilla de Stanton, heiress of the Stantons of Stanton Hineheath, Acton Reynald, etc., through whom an unbroken descent is given by Eyton from Richard, Lord of Stanton Hineheath, in 1086. The identity of Reyner and Reginald is here again shown by comparing the description in the pedigree "Reginaldus cui pater ejus dedit villam de Lee subtus Pevenhull" with the wording of the charter "Thomas de la Lee miles dedit Reynero filio suo totam villam de Lee subtus Pevenhull." In the pedigree this Reyner or Reginald is called filius primogenitus, but this is clearly an addition made in error. He is not so described in the deed, while Eyton and Hardy give evidence that Sir Thomas's eldest son was John. The next step in the pedigree shows a second Sir John as son to Reginald or Reyner and married to Matilda de Erdington. Here again there seems undoubtedly to be confusion, and it is little to be wondered at, for on examining the pedigree by the light of Eyton and Hardy's researches we find the first Sir Thomas married to Petronilla Corbet; two of his sons, John and Thomas, married to Petronilla de Drayton and Petronilla de Stanton; and each of his three sons, Sir John, Sir Thomas, and Reyner, having a son John, two of these last three Johns being knighted. The one who married Matilda de Erdington seems to have been son of Thomas and of course nephew to Reyner, not son, as given in the pedigree. He again had an eldest son John, who was knighted, and a daughter Matilda, besides a second son, Sir Thomas de Lee of Okehirst, married (according to Hardy) to Sibilla. This last Sir John is shown in the pedigree as having a son Robert who married Margaret Astley, the heiress of another very ancient family (showing an unbroken descent from 1100–1135) and was the first Lee of Coton. It is quite certain from documentary evidence, including the Inquisition Post Mortem of Margaret herself, that her husband's name was Roger, not Robert, and Sir W. Hardy thought it most probable that he was younger son of Sir John Lee's brother, Sir Thomas of Okehirst, whose eldest son was, according to

Hardy, Sir Thomas Lee, Sheriff in 1395. One of the Harleian MSS. of about 1593 supports this view as follows: "Sir Thomas Lee Knight, temp. E. 3, had issue Roger Lee, Esq., a secound sonne whoe mar. Margaret daughter and heire of Thomas Aveley (Astley) sonne to Roger sonne to John (J$^{n}$ the 2 had another John to his sone) and had issue John Lee, Esq., whoe mar. J . . . so . . . e (Jocosa or Joyce) Packington, etc., etc., etc." (MS. Harl. 2163 fo. 40 b.) The date of this MS. is shown by its reference to the children of Thomas Lee of Coton. Only Richard (bapt. Oct., 1591) and Elinor are mentioned. Garret (bapt. Nov., 1593) and Launcelot, afterwards of Coton, (bapt. 1594) are not given. The MS. may therefore be taken as written between Oct., 1591, and Nov., 1593.

Eyton in writing to Hardy says he can throw no light upon the question and that the only thing clear is that Lee of Langley and Lee of Coton bore the same arms. Sir Wm. Hardy's opinion is of course entitled to great weight; but both he and Eyton, as their correspondence shows, had sometimes in constructing their pedigrees to satisfy themselves with the balance of probabilities, provided the main facts were established by direct evidence. In this case the main fact as to Roger Lee's descent is established by the Herald's allowance of arms at the first Visitation and their confirmation of the same at subsequent ones. Whether he was son, nephew, or cousin to Sir John Lee is not of vital importance. The statement in the Harl. MS. that he was son of Sir Thomas, though probable enough, is not supported by direct evidence, and the registered statement as to his immediate parentage is good evidence till disproved. There is indirect evidence showing that he was probably (as stated in the Harl. MS.) a younger son in any case; certainly he must have been so if he was son of Sir John.

We now come to a point where two important errors occur in the pedigree. The first Lee of Coton is there shown as having two sons by Margaret Astley, Roger the elder married to Joanna, heiress of Edward Burnell (of Acton Burnell and Langley), and John, the younger of Nordley Regis (and Coton). It is certain, from documentary evidence (including the Inq. P. M. on the death of Margaret and the livery of lands to John Lee), that the latter was son and heir to Roger and Margaret; while the evidence adduced by Eyton and Hardy shows that the first Lee of Langley was Roger, son of John de Lee of Pimhill and Lea Hall, descended from Reyner, younger son of Sir Thomas de Lee and Petronilla Corbet. Further, in the pedigree, Robert de Lee of Roden, married to Petronilla, is given as son of the above Roger and his wife Johanna Burnell, whereas the documentary evidence shows that Petronilla was daughter and heir to Roger and Johanna, while her husband, Robert, was son of John de Lee of Roden, Stanton, etc.

The evidence given by the Herald's allowance of arms as to the descent of the first two Lees of Langley is thus confirmed by the same documents which disprove the evidence of the pedigree as to their immediate parentage. The above-mentioned marriage of Robert de Lee of Roden, etc., with Petronilla de Lee of Langley united in their son Ralph all the estates, except Coton and Nordley, inherited or acquired by the family since the 12th century. For about 250 years longer this great inheritance was handed down from father to son till the death of Sir Richard Lee, in 1660. His father, Sir Humphrey, was a second son, and during his elder brother's life practiced as a barrister, having been admitted of the Inner Temple in 1578 (entered as H. Lea of Langley, Salop, gent.). He succeeded, however, in 1591, to the estates on the death of his father, who survived his eldest son. He was Sheriff in 1600, and was created a baronet by James I., May 3d, 1620, being the first Shropshire gentleman to receive that honour. He died in 1633 and was succeeded by his son Richard, second and last baronet. Sir Richard was a staunch Royalist, he attended the King at Oxford and suffered much in his cause, being reduced to compound for his estate.[1] He was M. P. for Salop and served as Sheriff in 1639. He died in 1660, when his estates were divided between his two daughters, Rachel, married to Ralph Cleaton, and Mary, married to Edward Smythe, who was created a baronet soon after the Restoration. Although the Langley branch thus came to an end and the chief possessions of the family passed into other hands at Sir Richard Lee's death in 1660, the Coton branch still continued to flourish. Fifth in descent from Roger and Margaret we find John Lee, born in 1528, as appears from the Inq. P. M. in March, 1588–9, on the death of his father, Humfrey. He married Joyce Romney and died in 1605, leaving directions in his will that he should be buried at Chesham, in Buckinghamshire, if he should happen to die there. He did die there, and there he was buried, having had eight sons, of whom Thomas, his heir, was his successor at Coton, and William, the second son, died young. The order of their birth is thus given by their father at the Visitation of 1584:—Thomas, son and heir; Gilbert, 4; Jasper, 5; Richard, 6; Edward, 3; William, 2, died young; Ferdinand, 7; Josias, 8. The only ones of these (except, of course, Thomas) of whom any subsequent trace has yet been found are Edward, whose death is recorded in 1616, and Gilbert, who seems to have

---

1 "Upon Saturdaye mornynme the XXIJ^nd of ffebruary, 1644, Colonell Mytton and Colonell Bayer on the p'liam^t side, w^th aboute fyfteene hundred horse and foote did very secretlie and cu'inglie enter Shrowesbury, etc.," "The names of the Knightes and men of noate taken p^rsone^rs in the same Towne weire, Sir Nicholas Byron, Sir Richard Lee," and many others. "Upon takinge of Shrowesbury the Kinges ptie burned and quytt Lea Hall, and Tonge Castle," etc. (Malbon and Burghall's *Civil War Memorials, Cheshire*, etc., p. 164–5.)—EDITOR.

settled in Essex. At least it is difficult to resist the conclusion that he must have been the Gilbert Lee of Tolleshunt Darcy, whose will was proved in 1621, leaving brothers Richard and Josias and nephew John. Jasper was probably dead when his father made his will, 17th May, 1605, as his name is not mentioned therein, but he may possibly have been married and left children. In the Visitation of 1623 Ferdinand, Josias, and William are marked s. p. What descendants may have been left by any of these brothers is at present unknown. Gilbert's will mentioning no child, of course makes it improbable that he left any, but what of Edward, Richard, and Jasper? The question is very interesting in view of the problem as to the immediate parentage of Colonel Richard Lee, the first of the Virginian branch, as either of the brothers might, in point of time, have been his father. The will of the eldest brother, Thomas of Coton, was proved October 9th, 1621, appointing as overseer "My well beloved kinsman, Sir Humphrey Lee Knight Barronnett," thus showing an affectionate intimacy between the two branches of Langley and Coton down to the time when the former was near its extinction.

Thomas Lee of Coton married Dorothy Oteley, and had two sons and six daughters. The second son, John, became a successful merchant, and purchased the estate of Ankerwycke, in Buckinghamshire. He married Mary Pollard, and had two sons, George of Stoke Milbro, Salop, and John, who in 1685 bought an estate at Wraysbury, Bucks. He had also a daughter, Elizabeth, married to Sir Philip Harcourt, M. P. for Oxfordshire, and in her descendants the Ankerwycke estate still continues. John Lee died in 1682, and was buried in the Harcourt Chapel at Stanton Harcourt. His coat of arms on his tombstone bears *fourteen* billets. His elder brother, Lancelot of Coton, married twice, and left a family by each wife. By the first, Jane Clemson, he had three sons: John, who died unmarried; Thomas, who succeeded him at Coton, and Richard, who is identified by E. C. Mead, in his *Genealogical History of the Lee Family*, with Colonel Richard Lee, the Virginian. There is no foundation whatever for this assumption, and it is disproved by the fact that Thomas Lee of Coton, Richard's own brother, in certifying the pedigree at the Visitation of 1663, gives Richard as being of the parish of St. Olave's, Southwark, and married to Elizabeth, daughter of Walter Langdon, of Cornwall; whereas Colonel Richard Lee, in his will of about the same date, names his wife Anna, who is also shown by the Land Patent Records of Virginia to have been his wife when he first settled there in 1641–2.

Thomas Lee, above mentioned, of Coton Hall, was J. P. for Salop, Surrey and Kent, and J. P. and D. L. for Middlesex. He married, 1st, Dorothy

Eldred, of a Norfolk family, and descended also from the family of William of Wykeham; 2d, Lady Mary, daughter of the Earl of Lindsey, K. G., and 3d, Charity, widow of his brother-in-law, John Eldred. He died in 1687, having had three sons and a daughter by his first and two daughters by his third wife. The second son, Thomas, married Elizabeth, daughter of Jonathan Hill, Esq., of West Cholderton and Winterbourne Dancey Wilts, and became ancestor of the Lees of Cholderton, Wilts and Buriton, Hants, now represented by the Rev. Lancelot John Lee, of Worthen, Shropshire, J. P. The third son, John, was rector of Crowmarsh, Oxon. The eldest son, Eldred Lancelot, of Coton Hall, J. P., married Isabella, daughter of Sir Henry Gough, of Perry Hall, Staffordshire. He died in 1734, having had three sons and eight daughters. The eldest son, Lancelot Lee, of Coton Hall, married, 1st, Elizabeth, daughter of Gervase Scrope, Esq., of Cockerington, Lincolnshire; 2d, Ann Elizabeth, daughter of John Michel, Esq., of Kingston Russell and Dewlish House, Dorset; and 3d, Catherine, daughter of Sir Joseph Danvers, Bart. By his second wife he left two daughters and one son, Harry Lancelot Lee, of Coton Hall, J. P., who married Jane, daughter of the Rev. E. Cox, and died in 1821, leaving an only child, Catherine Anne Harriet, by whose marriage with J. M. Wingfield, Esq., of Tickencote Hall, Rutland, the Coton estate passed to that family, and has since been sold. Thomas, the third son of Eldred Lancelot Lee, died unmarried. Harry, the second son, entered the Church and became Warden of Winchester College, from whose founder, William of Wykeham, he was, as we have seen, descended. He married Caroline, daughter of John Michel, Esq., of Kingston Russell, and Dewlish, and had two sons, Harry (Rev.), of Kingsgate House, Winchester, and Lancelot Charles, Rector of Wootton, Oxfordshire, who died unmarried in 1841. The elder son, Harry, married Philippa, daughter of Sir William Blackstone, and had two sons and a daughter. Harry, the elder son, of Kingsgate House, J. P., and Vicar of North Bradley, married Julia, eldest daughter of Gorges Lowther, Esq., formerly M. P. for Ratoath, and died without issue in 1880. William Blackstone, the younger son, Rector of Wootton, married Elizabeth, daughter of Charles Thomson, Esq., Master in Chancery, by his wife, Anne Dalzell Thomson, of Dalzells, St. Kitts, descended from the first Earl of Carnwath. They had five children, of whom two survive: Constance Anne, unmarried, and William Blackstone, present representative of the family. Mr. Lee is J. P. for Wilts, and married in 1874 Maud Ellen Legh, daughter of W. M. Bridger, Esq., of Halnaker House, Sussex and the Chantry, Bradford-on-Avon, J. P. for Sussex and Wilts, by his wife, Sophia, daughter of Gorges Lowther, Esq., formerly of Kilrue, co. Meath, and M. P. for Ratoath, and afterwards of Tilshead Lodge, Wilts.

The following members of the family have served as Sheriffs of Shropshire:

1201. Reigner de Le.
1387. Robert de Lee (or Atte Lee as given in Blakeway's list).
1395. Sir Thomas Lee, Knt.
1465. Ralph Lee, Esq.
1479. Richard Lee, Esq.
1496. Richard Lee, Esq.
1547. Thomas Lee, Esq.
1600. Humphrey Lee, Esq., created a baronet 1620.
1639. Sir Richard Lee, Bart.

Among the papers of the late Rev. Harry Lee of Kingsgate House and of his grandfather, the Warden of Winchester, are several of much interest with regard to the Virginian branch of the family, particularly, certain letters from William, son of Thomas Lee of Stratford House, and great-grandson of Colonel Richard Lee, the first settler in America. Also an account of the Virginian branch written by William Lee. It is clear from these papers that the Lees of Virginia always claimed descent from the Shropshire family. William Lee died in 1795, but the relationship was kept up till 1827 by Archibald Lee, who was very intimate with the family at Coton. Among the papers above referred to there is a letter from Mr. H. Lee Warner, who had lately been in America, (and whose family also claims descent from that of Coton Hall) to the Rev. Harry Lee of Kingsgate House, asking on behalf of the late General Robert Edward Lee for information as to the early ancestry of his family. The letter is dated 1868, and until General Lee's death no question seems ever to have arisen as to the origin of the Virginian Lees.

About that time there was published in America a book by E. C. Mead, entitled *Genealogical History of the Lee family of Virginia and Maryland.* This book contained a correct copy of the pedigree registered at the Visitation of 1623, two coats of arms correctly coloured, and some good prints of certain portraits in America. And it states that Colonel Richard Lee was of the Shropshire family. In other respects it is utterly worthless, and indeed too palpably so to do much mischief. Various families are mixed up in utter confusion, while the descriptions of armorial bearings show a total ignorance of the subject. The particular member of the Coton family identified (without evidence of any kind) with Colonel Richard Lee of Virginia is, as we have already seen, Richard younger brother of Thomas Lee of Coton, born in 1622 and married to Elizabeth Langdon of Cornwall.

Not long after this the Rev. Dr. F. G. Lee, of Lambeth, produced what he was pleased to call the *Lineal descent of the late General Robert E. Lee of Virginia.* Here the early part of the pedigree of the Lees of Ditchley is taken, and thereon is grafted from the Coton pedigree the above mentioned husband of Elizabeth Langdon, as the seventh son of Sir Robert Lee of Hulcott and brother to Sir Henry Lee of Ditchley. This arrangement was published by Dr. Lee in a well-known genealogical magazine, and probably has been accepted by many readers as a statement of ascertained fact.

The real facts, however, have at last been made known and the evidence published, first by Mr. J. H. Lea in the *New England Genealogical and Historical Register*, for January, 1890, and secondly by the present representative of the Shropshire family in the same magazine in which Dr. Lee's arrangement appeared, viz.: the "Miscellanea Genealogica et Heraldica," edited by Dr. J. J. Howard, in the numbers for July and August, 1892. The evidence produced by Mr. Lea that the seventh son of Sir Robert Lee died in youth is, as he justly says, convincing to any mind open to conviction, while that produced by the present representative is absolute proof that Colonel Richard Lee was either of the Shropshire family or an impostor. His descent from that family is attested by one who knew him intimately *and who was an officer of the College of Arms.* He claimed that descent himself and his descendants have done so for 200 years. He was a distinguished gentleman, a loyal Cavalier, and Secretary of State in Virginia. In the face of these facts, until his immediate parentage is proved, it is of course open to any one to argue that he was a gross impostor, but it is not too much to ask that any one who holds that belief should at least give some reason for it. None has hitherto been suggested. That, being an impostor, he should also be brother to Sir Henry Lee of Ditchley is, even if Mr. Lea had not produced his invaluable evidence, so monstrous a proposition that the mere statement of it is enough to refute it. The two families were alike in position and rank, the Lichfield peerage not having yet been created. Ditchley, which happily still remains in the hands of Lady Charlotte Lee's lineal descendants, a home worthy of an ancient race, has been made famous by a great writer, in whose pages the name of the beautiful old place and that of its knightly owner will live while the English language endures. On the other hand, though neither Langley, Lea Hall, Acton

Burnell, nor Coton, are celebrated places, still from the time of Reigner de Le, Sheriff in 1201, his descendants were represented by knights and gentlemen, serving their king as soldiers, or their country as Sheriffs and in Parliament, before families which now pride themselves on their antiquity had ever been heard of. It is incredible that a son of either house should try to hide his true origin, yet that is the assumption on which alone Dr. Lee's unsupported assertion must rest.

At the same time it is well that any one interested in this matter should know the evidence that exists, and therefore, by the kind permission of Dr. Howard, a reprint of the article in his magazine is here given:

In Volume I, Second Series, *Miscellanea Genealogica et Heraldica*, a pedigree was given assuming that Colonel Richard Lee, the ancestor of the Lees of Virginia, was seventh son of Sir Robert Lee of Hulcott, instead of being descended from the Shropshire family of Langley and Coton Hall, as had been generally believed.

I propose to shew—

1. That this assumption is *prima facie* so improbable as to require the strongest confirmation.

2. That no such confirmation exists.

3. That there is convincing evidence to the contrary.

Firstly, as to the improbability of the assumption, it is only necessary to point out that Sir Robert Lee of Hulcott married Lucy Pigott in 1561, *and that she was the mother of all his children*, whereas the Land Patent Records of Virginia shew that Colonel Richard Lee settled in America about 1641–2, and his will proves that his eldest son was under 18 in 1663. The will was made when the testator was starting for Virginia with a young family 102 years after the marriage of Lucy Pigott. Sir Robert Lee's third son, Benedict, was baptized in 1576, and would therefore have been 87 in 1663. There were only three sons and a daughter between him and Richard.

Secondly, as to the evidence necessary to outweigh the improbability shown above. Sir Robert Lee's nuncupative will describes him as of Stratford Langton, and shows that he died there, but desired to be buried at Hardwicke. His eldest son was Sir Henry Lee of Ditchley. Colonel Richard Lee describes himself in his will as "lately of Strafford Langton," and one of the family in America called his house Ditchley. That is all. As to any evidence such as one would expect in the way of wills or other documents, correspondence, or armorial bearings, there is absolutely nothing to confirm the original assumption.

Let us take the Stratford clue first. Colonel Richard certainly had a considerable estate in that neighbourhood. He mentions it in his will, and his great-grandson William (son of Thomas Lee of Stratford House) thus refers to it: "By his will he ordered an estate in England (I think) near Stratford by Bow in Middlesex, at that time worth £800 or £900 per annum, to be sold." Now if this estate had been left by Sir Robert Lee to his *seventh son*, such bequest must have appeared in his will, but there is nothing of the kind, or anything to show that he possessed land at Stratford. He seems to have resided there for some time, but was buried in Buckinghamshire, and the fact of Colonel Richard having possessed so considerable an estate rather tells against his having been one of the younger children of so large a family.

Search, however, has been made to ascertain whether there were other Lees in the neighbourhood of Stratford from whom Richard Lee might be descended. The records at Somerset House reveal the following:—

Richard Lee of Stratford Langton occurs 1578 in the will of Thomas Hitchcock.

Brian Lee of Stepney (the adjacent parish). Daughter married John Lott, 1590.

Gilbert Lee of Stepney. Died 1611.

Fulke Lee of Stepney. Died 1614.

Francis Lee of St. Peter's, Cornhill. Left "houses, lands, and tenements at Stratford Langthorne," 1618.

Sir John Lee of Stepney. Married Joan Lott, 1633.

Sir Robert Lee of Stepney. Granddaughter married William Cullum, 1635.

Humphrey Lee of Stratford Langthorne. Died 1645.

Sarah Lee of Stepney, widow. Died 1656.

It is remarkable that three of the names given above—viz., Gilbert, Fulke, and Humphrey—were in use in the Shropshire family at and before the period in question. See pedigree at the College of Arms. It is known also that Gilbert Lee of the Coton Branch settled in Essex. (Will proved 1621, Dale, 84.)

These records show that there were plenty of Lees in the neighborhood of Stratford, and the fact of the emigrant describing himself in 1663 as "lately of Strafford Langton" is therefore no reason for connecting him particularly with Sir Robert Lee who died there in 1616. Such a reason, however, is supplied by the reappearance in America of the name Ditchley, and if nothing more were known of the origin of the Virginian Lees the fact of one of them calling his house by that name would raise a strong presumption that they were connected with the Buckinghamshire family, and even if the connection were a distant one we should probably be able to find some other evidence of it. But if Colonel Richard was own brother to Sir Henry Lee of Ditchley, two things at least may be taken for granted. One is that he and his descendants would have continued to bear the Quarrendon arms; the other that any son or grandson of his coming to England would have looked to his uncle or cousin at Ditchley as the representative of his family. We shall presently see how far they did this. Meanwhile we have the fact that one of the American branch undoubtedly called his house Ditchley, though it seems doubtful which it was who did so. Mr. Alexander Brown of Norwood, Nelson Co., Va., F.R.H.S., who has taken much trouble with regard to the origin of the Virginian Lees, writes to me: "Philip Lee, grandson of Colonel Richard the emigrant, called one of his plantations 'Lee Langley.' Other seats of the Lees were 'Ditchley,' 'Stratford House,' 'Cobbs,' 'Paradise,' etc., etc., some of them evidently named for seats of the Lees in England." Now Langley was one of the best known seats of the Shropshire family, and if this information was correct, the argument based on the reappearance of Ditchley fell to the ground, the inferences to be drawn from names of places being evenly balanced. Compared with such evidence as will presently be mentioned, they are of little value. In answer to further inquiries, Mr. Brown repeated his statement as to Philip calling his estate Lee Langley, and gave as his opinion that Ditchley was built by Hancock, youngest son of Colonel Richard, about 1687. And in a subsequent letter he enclosed the following, written to himself:

"915 N. Charles Street, Baltimore.

"Dear Sir:—Pardon my delay in replying to your letter in regard to Lee Langley and Lee Hall. I have just been informed by Mr. Joseph Packard of Baltimore, a native of Fairfax Co., Va., that the two Lee seats are now known as 'Lee Hall' and 'Langley' in Fairfax, and that 'Lee Coton' or 'Coton' is another Lee mansion in Loudoun Co., Va., but that as to their present condition he can give little information, and he refers you to Mr. Cassius F. Lee of Alexandria.

"I am very truly, etc.,

"WILSON MILES CARY."

From the above it seems certain that different members of the family in America called their places "Ditchley," "Langley," and "Coton," and it appears from Colonel Richard's will, for a copy of which I have to thank General Fitzhugh Lee, that none of these names were given in the testator's lifetime. As to any inference which can be drawn from them, the presumption on either side is counterbalanced by that on the other, and nothing is left to outweigh the manifest improbability arising from the date of Lucy Pigott's marriage.

Thirdly, as to the evidence against the Ditchley theory.

In the *New England Historical aud Genealogical Register* for January, 1890, there is an article written by Mr. J. H. Lea to which I would refer any one interested in this question. Therein are cited the Inquisition Post Mortem of Sir Henry Lee, K. G., and the wills of the father, mother, three brothers, two nephews, and the great-nephew of the supposed Colonel Richard, not one of whom, though several had to provide for the succession to and entail of a large estate, ever mentions Richard's name! The conclusion drawn is, of course, that the seventh son of Sir Robert Lee died in youth. But further, Mr. Lea has taken a photograph of the monument at Hardwicke, showing Sir Robert with his wife and family of eight sons and six daughters. He says: "Of the sons, five are bearded men, and three are smaller and beardless figures, the first five representing Henry, Edward, Thomas, George, and Robert, who we know attained their majority; while the latter depict Benedict, Antony, and *Richard*, who, unnamed in all the wills, are thus still further proved to have died in infancy or early youth." N. B.—We know that Benedict, one of the three, would have been *forty* at his father's death, having been baptized in 1576. Mr. Lea justly says that his proofs "speak for themselves, and must be convincing to any mind open to conviction." But other evidence against the Ditchley theory exists. There are in my possession and that of my cousin, Miss Wingfield, of Market Overton, Rutland, original letters and papers which, together with other matters to be mentioned presently, prove beyond doubt that Colonel Richard Lee himself claimed descent from the Shropshire family, and that successive generations of his descendants did the same, certainly till the year 1827, and I believe up to 1868. The papers I refer to are, 1, a letter written in 1771 by William, son of Thomas Lee of Stratford House, and great-grandson of Colonel Richard, to the Rev. Harry Lee, Warden of Winchester College, and son of Eldred Lancelot Lee of Coton Hall; in the possession of Miss Wingfield. 2, a letter from the same to the same, also written in 1771; in the possession of the present writer. 3, an account of the Virginian branch, written by the same William Lee, and also in the possession of the present writer. 4, a number of letters from Archibald, fourth son, I believe, of Thomas Sim Lee of Maryland, to Harry Lancelot Lee of Coton Hall and his daughter, all in the possession of Miss Wingfield, the last being dated 1827.

The first letter to the Warden of Winchester begins: "Sir,—It gave me much pleasure to find from a conversation with Mr. Batson, my banker, that we were of the same family. He tells me that you are the second son of the late Eldred Lancelot Lee of Coton. . . . I know your father corresponded with mine, who was one of the King's Privy Council in Virginia . . . . and I remember when a little boy in Virginia to have seen and read a very sensible letter and well written from your father to mine giving an accurate genealogical account of our family from so old a date as the Saxon Government. . . . ." He also speaks of "Richard Lee my great-grandfather who went there (to Virginia) one hundred and thirty years ago to this very day;" and asks whether the Earl of Litchfield is of the same family, as he has the same name. The letter ends,

"I am with Respect, Reverend Sir,
"Your most obedient servant and Kinsman,
"WILLIAM LEE."

This letter is particularly interesting, as it proves a correspondence on family matters between the Coton family and Colonel Richard's grandson, Thomas Lee of Stratford House. How such a correspondence came about if Thomas Lee's grandfather was brother to Sir Henry Lee of Ditchley is for any one who holds that theory to explain.

The second letter encloses the account of the Virginian branch, and refers to a cup at Queen's College, Oxford, given by John Lee, the eldest son of Colonel Richard. It proceeds: "From further conversation with Mr. Batson I am inclined to think it must be your brother that corresponded with my father Thomas Lee of Stratford in Virginia, since the letter I mentioned was wrote about the time of the famous contest in Bridgnorth for a member of Parliament in the latter days of Sir Robert Walpole." It is signed,

"Your most obedient humble servant and Relation,
"WILLIAM LEE."

The account of the Virginian branch begins, "Richard Lee of a good family in Shropshire, and whose picture I am told is now at Coton near Bridgnorth, the seat of Lancelot Lee, Esq.," and deals chiefly with the second son, Richard, and his descendants. In speaking of this Richard (his own grandfather) the writer says: "He spent almost his whole life in study, and usually wrote his notes in Greek, Hebrew, or Latin . . . . *so that he neither improved nor diminished his Paternal estate.*" That estate appears from his father's will to have been the plantation Paradise. It has been thought that this Richard was the builder of Ditchley, but it seems improbable from his grandson's description of him. In any case he could have only taken the name as he might have done any other, or because he believed in some connection between the Shropshire and Oxfordshire Lees, for on his tomb may be seen to this day an inscription declaring his Shropshire origin: "Hic conditur corpus Ricardi Lee armigeri nati in Virginia fili Ricardi Lee, generosi, et antiqua familia in Merton Regis in comitatu Salopiensi oriundi."

John Lee, the eldest son, was at Queen's College, Oxford, and the cup referred to in William Lee's letter is still there. It bears the arms of Lee of Langley and Coton—viz., a fess chequy between eight billets—and the following inscription: "COLL. REGI. OXON. D. D. Johan'is Lee Natus in Capohowasick Wickacomoco in Virginia America Filius Primogenitus Richardi Lee Chiliarchæ Oriundi de Morton Regis in Agro Salopiensi, 1658." That the donor of a cup with the above arms and inscription was nephew to Sir Henry Lee of Ditchley, living within a ride of that very house, is incredible.

Now let us see what view Colonel Richard himself took of his origin. In a book by John Gibbon, Blue Mantle, dated 1682, and entitled *Introductio ad Latinam Blasoniam*, the following passage occurs at page 156: "A great part of Anno 1659 till February the year following I lived in Virginia, being most hospitably entertained by the Honourable Colonel Richard Lee, some time Secretary of State there; and who after the King's martyrdom hired a Dutch vessel, freighted her himself, went to Brussels, surrendered up Sir William Barcklaie's old commission (for the Government of that Province) and received a new one from his present Majesty (a loyal action and deserving my commemoration). Neither will I omit his arms, being Gul. a Fes chequy or, Bl. between eight Billets arg., being descended from the Lees of Shropshire who sometimes bore eight billets, sometimes ten, and sometimes the Fesse countercompone (as I have seen by our Office records)." It is difficult to conceive any reason why Gibbon, an official of the Heralds' College, should have made the above statement as to the arms borne by Colonel Richard Lee unless it were true, and the cup at Queen's makes assurance doubly sure. But there is yet another witness. In the E. D. N. Alphabet at the Heralds' College, a collection of arms made about temp. Chas. II., there is the following entry: "Salop—Lee—G. a fess chequy Or and Az. betw. 8 billets Arg. Colonel ·c^d Lee Secretary of State in Virginia Anno 1659. Descended from the Lees in Shropshire (who sometimes bore 8 billets, sometimes 10, and sometimes the fess countercompone)." The E. D. N. Alphabet is of no authority as to a *right* to bear arms, but is valuable as being probably the only work in existence which gives an account of the arms which were then or had been formerly made use of. The entry establishes the fact that Colonel Richard Lee *used* the arms of the Lees of Shropshire, but does not settle the question whether his claim to belong to that family had any foundation.

We have now, therefore, the following facts on which to base our judgment as to whether Richard Lee was brother to Sir Henry Lee, of Ditchley:

1. He claimed to belong to the Lees of Shropshire, as proved by his bearing the arms of that family.

2. His eldest son did the same, and recorded it at his college. Date on cup, 1658.

3. His second son's representatives did the same, as proved by the inscription on the tombstone (date of death, 1714); and one grandson—Thomas—corresponded with the head of the family at Coton about 1740.

4. His great-grandson, William, did the same, 1771; and another great-grandson, Richard Henry, is mentioned in Campbell's *History of Virginia* as bearing the motto of the Shropshire family.

5. After the death of William Lee in 1795, Archibald Lee kept up the relationship, staying at Coton and corresponding with the family till 1824; and, finally, within the last few years I have had the pleasure of meeting one of General Lee's children, who told me that until quite lately no doubt as to their Shropshire origin had ever existed among the members of the Virginia branch.

A letter now lies before me from a gentleman who was in America in 1867, and had some correspondence with General Lee as to his ancestry. He writes:

"I am afraid I have sent you all I have on the subject of General Lee. *I know that he said he was descended from the Shropshire Lees.*"

"Yours sincerely,

"H. LEE WARNER."

The italics are mine.

In his paper already referred to, Mr. J. H. Lea has shown good reasons for holding that the seventh son of Sir Robert Lee of Hulcott died in his youth, reasons which become the more convincing the more closely the evidence is examined. If, however, he survived, cut out of the succession, ignored by all his relations, not even mentioned in the will of father or mother, considered as one dead, and even represented as such on his father's monument, then I have shown—1st, the extreme improbability of his being the man who was going to Virginia with a young family in 1663; and 2d, that Colonel Richard Lee undoubtedly claimed descent from the Lees of Shropshire, and that successive generations of his descendants have done the same for two hundred years. His immediate parentage has not yet been proved. There are, however, besides collateral branches, nine persons named in the Shropshire pedigree any one of whom might in point of time have been his father. The nine are Walter, Francis, and Edward, brothers of Sir Humphrey, the first Baronet; and Edward, Gilbert, Jasper, Richard, Ferdinand, and Josiah, brothers of Thomas Lee of Coton. This Thomas had a son, John, and the will of Gilbert Lee, before referred to, mentions brothers Richard and Josiah and nephew John. The inference that the testator was the brother of Thomas Lee of Coton is almost irresistible, though the fact is not absolutely proved.

The following memorandum has been sent to me showing a natural connection between the founders of Virginia and the Shropshire Lees: "Sir Edmund Plowden, Knt., son of Francis Plowden of Plowden, Salop, had interests in America about 1632–42. John Eldred (1552–1632) of Great Saxham, was one of the leading founders of Virginia. Member of His Majesty's Council for the Virginia Company of London 1609–24." Now Maria Lee, aunt of Sir Humphrey, married Edward Plowden of Plowden, and Thomas Lee of Coton married Dorothy, John Eldred's granddaughter in 1649.

I believe that if the seventh son of Sir Robert Lee had been living when the Inquisitions Post Mortem of his cousin and eldest brother were taken, his name must have appeared with those of the other remainder-men, but in any case it is proved by the evidence of the Heralds' College and at Oxford, with the account given by Gibbon, that Colonel Richard Lee was either of the Shropshire family or an impostor. If an impostor, how could he be of Ditchley? At the period in question, the two families were alike in position and rank. Each had received a baronetcy from James I., and each was of great antiquity, claiming descent from knights and gentlemen of high position before the ancestors of half the present peerage had emerged from obscurity. Why should a member of either family try to pass himself off as belonging to the other? Yet this is the only hypothesis on which the Ditchley theory can any longer be upheld, and it is well to state it plainly for acceptance or rejection.

In conclusion, I have to thank the present owner of Ditchley for allowing me to quote the following sentence from a letter written to me in November, 1890, after considering the evidence given above:—

"I must admit that I think you have proved your case, and there is nothing more to be done except to place the whole series of proofs on record in a compact form. Yours very truly,

HAROLD DILLON."

Whether Colonel Richard Lee's immediate parentage can be determined it is as yet impossible to say. At any rate, the inquiry is being pursued, and the method now adopted is that of first searching out facts, and thence drawing conclusions. It is laborious, but in some respects seems preferable to the converse system, which has had a thorough trial.

NOTE.—The Richard Lee who married Elizabeth Langdon was the third son of Lancelot Lee of Coton. See the registered pedigree at the Heralds' College, certified in 1623 by Sir Humphrey Lee of Langley; in 1663 by Thomas Lee of Coton, brother to the above Richard; and in 1891 by the present writer. In the pedigree referred to at the beginning of this paper the account of the Virginian branch is full of errors; while not only is Col. Richard Lee's origin assumed without a shadow of proof, but his wife, the mother of all his children, is stated to have been the above mentioned Elizabeth Langdon. As a matter of fact his wife's name was Anna. Her surname is at present unknown.

## BURNEL OF ACTON BURNELL AND LANGLEY.

In view of the intermarriage of the Lees with the Corbet and Burnel families, the following is of great interest: The *Domesday Book*, or simply *Domesday*, is an ancient record, containing the survey of all the lands of England made in the time of William the Conqueror. It has been considered the final authority, from which no appeal could be taken.

"'The same Roger,' says *Domesday*, 'holds Actune, and one Roger [holds it] of him. Goldric held it [in Saxon times], and was a free man. Here iii and a half hides geldable. In demesne is one ox-team; ii serfs, one villain, iiii boors, and i radman, with a team and a half. In time of King Edward [the manor] was worth 30s. [annually]; afterwards 15s. Now [it is worth] 20s. One more team might be employed here.' (*Domesday*, fo. 255, b. i.)

"The Conqueror took the Saxon Goldric's manor from him, and gave it to the Norman Earl of Shrewsbury, who in turn conferred it on Roger Fitz-Corbet; accordingly, the seigneury over Actune remained with Fitz-Corbet's descendants, the barons of Caus.

"It is supposed that Roger, the *Domesday* tenant of Actune, was the ancestor of those Burnels, from whom afterwards the manor took its distinctive title of Acton Burnell. The first Burnel we hear of is William Burnel, who, previously to 1176, attested one of the Prior of Wenlock's

Charters. The family then appears as consisting of two distinct branches, both of whom claimed to have an interest in Acton Burnel. Thomas Burnel was the representative of the supposed elder branch: the Burnels of Acton Burnel and of Langley. Gerin, or Warin, was the representative of the younger branch. It is with the latter that we have more particularly to do.

"To Gerin Burnel succeeded Hugh, his son; after whom came Gerin Burnel II., who, with William Corbet and others, at the instigation of Thomas Corbet, robbed a monk of Buildwas. A list of Thomas Corbet's barony gives William and this Geryn Burnel as holding one knight's fee in Acton in 1240. William Burnel, here alluded to, slew two men, for which sentence of outlawry was pronounced against him, after which the King must have had his share of Acton Burnel for a year and a day, when, in the ordinary course, it would revert to the suzerain, Thomas Corbet of Caus.

"To Gerin succeeded Roger Burnel, after whom came Robert Burnel, who, purchasing the fee simple of the whole manor, eventually became sole lord of Acton Burnell. This extraordinary man enjoyed, in a remarkable degree, the favour and confidence of Edward I., and was his chief adviser in all his measures. Early betaking himself to civil and ecclesiastical employments, then generally combined, Burnel soon distinguished himself. While yet a young man, he was introduced to Prince Edward, who, pleased at his address, learning, and ability, made him his chaplain and private secretary. There is proof, that during the baron's wars, Robert Burnel was employed by the prince. It is uncertain whether or not he actually attended Edward to the Holy Land; but, on June 18, 1272, Prince Edward, then at Acre, in Palestine, made a will, in which he appointed Robert Burnel one of his executors. On September 21, 1274, King Edward, now on his father's throne, bestowed the Great Seal on Robert Burnel himself. When appointed to the office of Chancellor of England, Burnel had reached no higher ecclesiastical dignity than that of Archdeacon of York. Four months afterwards, however, he was raised to the See of Bath and Wells. He presided at the Parliament which met in May, 1275, and passed 'the Statute of Westminster the First,' the code rather than Act of Parliament, which has obtained for Edward I. the title of 'the English Justinian.' 'The chief merit of it,' says Lord Campbell, 'may be safely ascribed to Lord-Chancellor Burnel, who brought it forward in Parliament.'

"The advice which Burnel tendered his sovereign intimately connects him with the conquest of Wales. After the defeat of Llewellyn, the Chancellor was employed to devise measures for the pacification and future government of the conquered principality. He held courts of justice at Bristol, for the southern counties, and, giving general directions for the introduction of English institutions among the Welsh, he prepared a code under which Wales was governed till the reign of Henry VIII. In 1283, to gratify his faithful minister, King Edward summoned a Parliament, to meet at Acton Burnel, in the mansion of his favourite. Speaking of the gable ends shown at Acton Burnell, as those of the barn in which, according to tradition, the Commons met, whilst the Lords sat in Burnel's mansion, the learned historians of Shrewsbury contend that these did not belong to a barn. They add : 'We have little doubt that they belonged to a great hall erected by the munificent prelate for the entertainment of his sovereign ; and it is in the highest degree probable that the three estates of the realm, the Lords, spiritual and temporal, and the Commons, sat within its walls.'

"Here was passed the admirable statute, 'De Mercatoribus,' otherwise known as the 'Statute of Acton Burnel,' for the recovery of debts ; 'Showing,' says Lord Campbell, 'that this subject was as well understood in the time of Chancellor Burnel as in the time of Chancellor Eldon or Chancellor Lyndhurst.'

"A patent of January 28, 1284, allows that, 'Robert, Bishop of Bath and Wells, our chancellor, may, he or his heirs, strengthen with a wall of stone and lime, and also embattle their mansion of Acton Burnell.'

"While Burnel continued in office, the improvement of the law rapidly advanced. Various acts were passed, some of which have since become celebrated ; for instance, 'the Statute of Mortmain,' and the 'Ordinatio pro Statu Hiberniæ' (17 Ed. I.), for effectually introducing the English law into Ireland, and for the protection of the natives from the rapacity and oppression of the King's officers ; 'a statute framed in the spirit of justice and wisdom,' says Campbell, 'which, if steadily enforced, would have saved Ireland from much suffering and England from much disgrace.'

"Nor was King Edward's favorite a statute-framer only. As head of the law, Burnel exercised a vigilant superintendence over the administration of justice, and in the Parliament held at Westminster in 1290, the chancellor brought forward very serious charges against the judges, for taking bribes and altering the records, when, with two honorable exceptions, they were all convicted.

"Lord Chancellor Burnel conducted Edward I.'s claim to the superiority over Scotland, and pronounced the sentence by which the crown of that country was disposed of to be held under an English liege lord. He accompanied the martial monarch of England and his powerful army to Norham, and there addressed the Norman derived nobility of Scotland in the French language. The prelates, barons, and knights of Scotland having mustered on the green sward to the left of the Tweed, opposite Norham castle, in pursuance of the leave given them to deliberate in their own country, Burnel went to them in his master's name, and asked them 'whether they would say anything that could or ought to exclude the King of England from the right and exercise of the superiority and direct dominion over the Kingdom of Scotland, which belonged to him,' etc., to which the indignant but helpless Scots made no particular objection. Upon this, the chancellor recapitulated all that had been said at the last meeting relative to Edward's claim; and, a public notary being present, the right of deciding the controversy between the several competitors for the crown of Scotland was entered in form for the King of England. Then Burnel, beginning with Robert Bruce, lord of Annandale, asked him in the presence of all the bishops, earls, barons, etc., 'whether, in demanding his right, he would answer and receive justice from the King of England as superior and direct lord over the kingdom of Scotland?' Bruce answered, that 'he did acknowledge the King of England superior and direct lord of the kingdom of Scotland,' and that he would before him, as such, demand, answer, and receive justice. The same question being put to all the other competitors, each and all of them obsequiously replied as Bruce had done.

"Not satisfied, however, with having obtained their verbal assent to Edward's ambitious proposal, the crafty English Chancellor required the competitors to sign and seal a solemn instrument to the same effect, which they accordingly did, 'quickened by hints thrown out that the candidate who was the most complying would have the best chance of success.' One hundred and four Scottish and English commissioners were now appointed to take evidence and hear the arguments of all who were interested. They met at Berwick-upon-Tweed, and Burnel presided over them. King Edward, having been obliged to return south to attend the funeral of his mother, left Burnel behind to watch over the grand controversy. It was Robert Burnel who gave judgment in favour of Baliol.

"Lord Chancellor Burnel never returned southward, as he died on October 25, 1292. Summing up the character of this remarkable man, Lord Campbell says of him, 'As a statesman and a legislator he is worthy of the highest commendation. He ably seconded the ambitious project of reducing the whole of the British Isles to subjection under the crown of England. With respect to Wales, he succeeded, and Scotland retained her independence only by the unrivalled gallantry of her poor and scattered population. His measures for the improvement of Ireland were frustrated by the incurable pride and prejudices of his countrymen. But England continued to enjoy the highest prosperity under the wise laws which he introduced.'

"The inquisition taken after the decease of Robert Burnel shews that the deceased prelate had accumulated a vast possession in Shropshire; nor had the minutest gains of territory in this, his native, county been beneath his notice. His tenure of Acton Burnell, under Sir Peter Corbet, was by service of half a knight's fee. Philip Burnel, the Bishop's nephew, was his heir, who, a spendthrift, among other manors, gave that of Acton Burnell to certain merchants of Lucca in liquidation of his enormous debts." (John Corbet Anderson's *Shropshire: Its Early History and Antiquities*, p. 447, *et seq.*)

According to the "feodary" 1284, the bishop of Bath and Wells held "Langedon," of the king, in capite, for half a knight's fee, doing service of two foot soldiers in time of war for 40 days at his own cost.

## MORETON-CORBET.

"'The same Turold,' says *Domesday*, 'holds Mortune, and Hunnit, with his brother [hold the manor] of him. The same [Hunnit and his brother, in Saxon time] held it, and were freemen. Here i hide geldable. The [arable] land is for ii ox teams. Here are [ii teams], with v serfs and one boor. [Formerly] it was worth 10s. Now, 16s.'

"Amid the social revolution attendant on the Norman Conquest of England, the Saxon Hunnit and his brother lost their estates, some of which were given to their more fortunate countryman, Toret. 'Whatever,' says an authority [Eyton], 'were the misfortunes of Hunnit and his brother Uluiet, it is certain that the descendants of their contemporary and compatriot, Toret, succeeded to some of their estates, and this also is certain that a lineal descendant of the said Toret is at this day lord of Moreton-Corbet. These are terms in which very few Shropshire estates can be spoken of.' The lineal descendant alluded to is the present Sir Vincent R. Corbet, Bart.

"There is a tradition that, once upon a time, the heir of Moreton-Corbet went to the Holy Land, and was detained in captivity so long, that he was supposed to be dead, and his younger brother engaged to marry that he might continue the line. On the morning of the marriage, however, a pilgrim came to the house to partake of the hospitalities of that festal occasion, and, after the dinner, he revealed himself to the assembled company as the long-lost brother. The bridegroom would have surrendered the estate, but he declined the offer, desiring only a small portion of the land, which accordingly he received. This pilgrim was the ancestor of the Corbets of Moreton, whose primogeniture is established by their armorial bearings, the single raven. The real progenitor of all the Shropshire Corbets was Roger Fitz-Corbet, the Domesday baron, mentioned under Caus." (*Ibid.*, 431–32.)

Robert Fitz-Corbet, brother of this Roger held, says the *Domesday*, Languedune (Langley). His daughter, Alice, married Robert Boterell, of Cornwall, and through this marriage Langley came into possession of that family. "Sir William de Boterell, IV., alienated Langden to Robert Burnel, bishop of Bath and Wells, in exchange for lands in Somersetshire." Roger Lee, of Coton, married Joanna, heiress of Edward Burnell, of Acton Burnell and Langley. This Edward Burnell was (according to genealogy given in the Visitation of Shropshire, in 1623), the son of Sir Nicholas Burnell.

Roger and Robert Fitz-Corbet were sons of a Norman Corbet who came to Shropshire from the Pays de Caux, in Normandy. The Corbets were a very ancient and honorable family. They have settled in Spain, Flanders, and Scotland, as well as in England. The arms of the Shropshire family bore twenty-two quarterings.

COL. RICHARD LEE.

# LEE OF VIRGINIA.

## Colonel Richard Lee.

1. "Richard Lee, of a good family in Shropshire (and whose Picture I am told is now at Cotton, near Bridgenorth, the seat of Launcelot Lee, Esqr.), some time in the Reign of Charles the first, went over to the Colony of Virginia, as Secretary, and one of the King's Privy Council. . . . He was a man of good Stature, comely visage, an enterprising genius, a sound head, vigorous spirit and generous nature. When he got to Virginia, which was at that time not much cultivated, he was so pleased with the Country that he made large settlements there with the servants he had carried over; after some years, he returned to England, and gave away all the lands he had taken up, and settled at his own expense, to those servants he had fixed on them; some of whose descendants are now possessed of very considerable Estates in that Colony. After staying some Time in England, he returned again to Virginia, with a fresh band of Adventurers, all of whom he settled there."

These few lines, written by William Lee in 1771, give the earliest information (now to be found) of Richard Lee, the progenitor of the Lee family whose history this volume records. From his statement, it is learned that Richard Lee was descended from the Coton branch of the Lees of Shropshire. In the concise sketch of this Shropshire family already given, it has been shown that Langley and Coton are the two branches into which the parent stock divided near the end of the 14th century, when two members of the family, each named Roger, married two heiresses; one, Margaret, sister and heir of Thomas Astley, of Nordley, from whom are descended the Lees of Nordley-Regis and Coton; the other, Joanna, daughter and co-heir of Edward Burnell of Langley and Acton Burnell, from whom the Lees of Langley, Lea Hall, and Acton Burnell are descended.

As the early Colonial records of Virginia are scanty and incomplete, it is now almost impossible to substantiate all the statements of early writers. But sufficient data can be found to corroborate many points; much of William Lee's account of his ancestor can be readily verified. On the other hand, some of it cannot be proven: that Richard Lee came to

Virginia as Secretary, and member of the Council, or that he took up, at first, large tracts of land—cannot now be shown. But these items are of little importance; as he did all these things some time during his life, the actual date of doing them is of no consequence.

As to the portrait of Richard Lee ever having been at Coton, there is now no record of any such portrait. Mr. William Blackstone Lee has lately inspected the portraits that were formerly at Coton. "The two unknown Lee portraits," he writes, "are fine pictures, said to be by Sir Peter Lely. But I do not think either of them could have been Colonel Richard. I cannot say positively that the elder of the two (tradition says they are father and son) could not to my mind by *any possibility* have been the Colonel, but I should be very much surprised to find that it was." Whether or no his portrait was ever at Coton, the inference is plain that William Lee intended his reader to understand that Richard Lee was descended from the Coton branch of the Shropshire family. This line of descent seems well established by the coat of arms used by the earlier generations of the Virginia family. Probably the earliest example is the wood carving, which, tradition claims, ornamented for generations the front door of the old "Cobbs Hall" mansion. When, or by whom, it was placed there is not known; but, so far as tradition runs, it had been there for many generations. At the time the old mansion was torn down, or perhaps earlier, it was given by Mrs. Martha (Lee) Harvey to her cousin, Dr. Charles Lee Broun. On his death, in 1855, it passed into the possession of his brother, Judge Edwin Broun, the present owner. The print of it, given here, was made from a photograph taken in May, 1894. It will be observed that part of the ornamentation, on the right side, has been broken off and lost; the shield was once colored to properly represent the tinctures of the arms. This carving represents an old form of the Lee arms; the same, in fact, as were registered at the Herald's office at London, as borne by "Colonel Richard Lee Secretary of State in Virginia Anno 1659." The crescent (on the upper right-hand corner) has been very generally borne by the Coton family to indicate that they were the younger branch. Its use therefore on this carving would seem to indicate two things: first, that the owner was descended from the Lees of Coton; and secondly, that this owner was Richard Lee, the immigrant.[1] This latter inference is strengthened by the fact that neither of his eldest sons used the crescent. Another proof of this Coton descent is that the family in

---

[1] A strict interpretation of this coat of arms, would signify that its bearer was the eldest son of the "second house," and that his father was dead. Says a writer on heraldry: "The first brother of the second house beareth a Crescent with a Label during his father's life only."

Virginia, in the fourth generation, used the arms of Coton, quartered with Astley, as shown on the frontispiece.

An old tradition has stated that Richard Lee came to Virginia with a brother; that they settled in York County; that the brother became dissatisfied and desired to return home; that both of them gave up the lands they had settled and returned to England. A part of this tradition seems to be confirmed by a court record, which states that a patent was granted to Robert Lee for 540 acres in Gloucester County, "Beginning at a red oak by Mr. Thornton's path and to a white oak by Colonel Lee's Horse Path and to a branch by the said Robert Lee's plantation; 200 acres thereof formerly granted to Colonel Richard Lee, on the 17th of May, 1655, and by him assigned to the said Robert Lee, on the 5th of February, 1657, and the remaining 340 acres for the transportation of seven persons, &c." In the list of the vestrymen of old Petsworth Parish, Gloucester County, given by Bishop Meade, the name of "Rob't Lee" stands second.[1]

Whether or no Richard Lee was accompanied to Virginia by any relations of his name is not known. There were many of the name in Virginia from its earliest settlement; but what relationship, if any, existed between them cannot now be demonstrated. In 1646, Richard Lee sat on the York bench, as a magistrate, with a Dr. Henry Lee, who married one Marah Adkins, and has left descendants. Richard patented 1,250 acres in York County, in 1648, and named, amongst his head rights, Henry, Matthew, and George Lee, who may have been relatives. There was a Mr. Hugh Lee, Justice for Northumberland in 1655, who patented 100 acres there in 1650, and 288 acres in 1654.

That Richard Lee settled first in York County is proven by the grant of 1,000 acres, dated the 10th of August, 1642; the patent states that this land was due "unto the said Richard Lee by and for his own p'sonal Adventure, his wife Ann, and John Francis and by assignment from Mr. Thomas Hill, Florentine Paine and William Freeman of their right of land due for the transportation of Seaventeene p'sons." The term "head right" was derived from an ordinance of the "Virginia Company" of London, by which every person who permanently settled in the Colony was allowed 50 acres; the wife and each child were entitled to this allowance. This patent, therefore, proves that Richard Lee was married in 1642; but had no children, or they would have been named amongst his head rights. It

---

[1] "The Relict of Robert Lee" married Edward Porteus, the grandfather of Bishop Porteus, who was also a vestryman of old Petsworth parish. His residence still remains facing the York River, a little east of Poropotank Creek. It may have been built on this 540 acres. Edward Porteus' only son, Robert, married a daughter of Gov. Edmund Jenings. (W. & M. *Quarterly*, III, 38.)

also shows that this was his first home in Virginia, as it is stated that part of the land was due him "for his own p'sonal Adventure." This was the plantation he called "Paradise" in his will, and bequeathed to his second son, Richard. This name is frequently applied in subsequent records to this plantation; as on the 22nd of July, 1674, in a patent issued to "Major Richard Lee for 1,140 acres in Gloster, called Paradise, on a branch of Poropotank Creek; 1,000 thereof being due to the said Richard Lee by two former patents, and the residue now found to be within the bounds."

Virginia was originally divided into eight counties; of these, York was one. Gloucester was taken from York in 1652; all the land patented by Richard Lee between the years 1642–51, was situated in that part of York subsequently included in Gloucester. Richard Lee represented York as Burgess in 1647, and in 1651 "Mr. Lee" was paid for services as Burgess from Northumberland. As every Burgess was required to be a "freeholder in the place where he is elected from," it is probable that he had settled in Northumberland at that date.

According to a law of a later date (1705), "every Burgess coming by land, shall be paid by the county for which he serves, 130 pounds of tobacco and cask a day, besides the necessary charge of ferriage: And every Burgess that cannot come otherwise than by water, 120 pounds of tobacco and cask a day, over and above the following allowance for going and returning to and from the Assembly, viz: . . . For Stafford, Northumberland, Westmoreland, Northampton, and Accomack, four days for coming and four for returning."

It seems possible that Richard Lee was engaged in commerce as well as agriculture, and that he had an interest in vessels trading between England and Virginia, as had many of the large planters. In his will, he bequeathed to his son, Francis, his interest in two ships, which was one-eighth part in each vessel. He appears to have made frequent voyages to and fro; being in England in 1654–55, again in 1659, and later in 1661 and 1663.

The earliest settlements in Virginia were made along the banks of the rivers and navigable creeks; the object being to secure safe anchorage for vessels. So, Richard Lee's first plantation was on the York River, near the head of Poropotank Creek, where he had a store or warehouse. His next home was located on the Dividing Creeks in Northumberland, which afforded a very safe harbor. The main creek is only a mile or two long; then it divides into branches, which make the several small peninsulas or "necks," as they were formerly called. On two of these "necks" Richard Lee located his two plantations. The harbor was so well chosen that it is

A SECTION OF JEFFERSON'S MAP OF 1787, ENLARGED.

used to-day as the landing place for steamers from Baltimore. Grants for these two tracts were made him in 1651 and '56, and were for 800 and 600 acres respectively.

It has been a tradition that Richard Lee was the first white man to settle in the Northern Neck, and that he purchased his lands of the Indians. As early as 1646, the Assembly levied a tax upon the "inhabitants of Chicawane *alias* Northumberland, being members of this Colony," so it is not probable that the first part of this tradition is true. As to his buying lands of the Indians, it is probable that he gave them presents to secure their friendship. But the following order of the General Court does show that he must have settled in Northumberland before that country had been opened for general settlement:

WHEREAS, order for pattenting the land of the Wiccacomoco Indians[1] in Northumberland County vpon the said Indians deserting the said lands was granted to the honourable Samuel Matthewes, Esq., Governour, &c. the twenty-seaventh day of November, 1657, and confirmed by another order of the quarter court, dated the eleaventh of March, 1658, and that grounded vppon the desire of the said Indians to surrender the same to his honour, The Assembly hath thought fitt to ratifye the said grants, and do hereby confirme the same *Provided* that no intrenchment be made vpon any preceding rights of Coll. Richard Lee. (I, Hening, 515.)

The records of the general land office furnish a list, perhaps incomplete, of the various tracts of land taken up by Richard Lee; in some of them the official position held by him is stated. These patents, therefore, help to trace his movements after first settling in Virginia, and furnish, in a degree, a record of his official positions. They are also interesting as relics of the times, show the quaint methods then in vogue for describing boundaries, give many of the old forms of spelling, and other interesting data; therefore they are given in full:

Whereas &c. now Know yee that I the said S^r^ William Berkeley Kt. doe w^th^ the consent of the Councell of State doe accordingly give and grant unto Richard Lee gent his heirs or assignes for ever one thousand acres of Land situate on the North side of Charles river Called by the name of the Indian Spring on Poropotancke Creeke anglice vocatur fresh water Creeke running along the said Creeke . . . and halfe a point Southerly thence South East for altitude . . . hundred and sixtie chains along the marked trees of Francis Morgan thence for latitude twoe hundred and five Chaines thence North west one hundred and twentie Chaines to a . . . running to a little Creeke including the said little Creeke . . . to the great Creeke the said one thousand acres of Land being due unto him the said Richard Lee by and for his owne p'sonal Adventure his wife Ann and John Francis

[1] "In Northumberland," says Beverley, "the Wiccomocco [tribe] has but few men living, which yet keep up their kingdom, and retain their fashion; yet live by themselves, separate from all other Indians, and from the English."

and by Assignment from Mr. Thomas Hill, Florentine Paine and William Freeman of their right of land due for the Transportation of Seaventeene p'sons whose names are in the records mentioned under this pattent to have and to hold &c. To bee held &c. Yielding and paying unto Our Souveraigne Lord the King his heirs and Successors for every of the fiftie acres of Land herein by these p^rsents given and granted yearly at the feast of St. Michaell the Archangell the fee rent of one Shilling to his Maj'ties use which pay'mt is to bee made seaven yeares after the entry of this Claime being the twentieth sixth of July 1642 and not before according to the said Charter of Orders &c. ut in Aliis Given &c. dated the tenth day of August 1642. Richard Lee Ann Lee Florentine Paine twice Joane Pickering Thomas Hackett one hundred and fiftie acres rights of this pattent (yt is to say) the 3 first assigned to Mr. Dixon.

To all & Whereas and now Know yee yt I the said Richard Kemp Esqr[1] doe with the Advice and Consent of the Councill of State Accordingly give grant and Confirme unto Richard Lee Gent ninety one acres of Land Scituate lyeing and being in the County of Yorke lyeing upon the Ridge of the New Poquoson towards Yorke beginning at a Certain Marked white oake in the white marsh and running thence west by South Seventy Eight poles Sideing by the very Corner marked tree of Capt. Wormeleys unto a small red oake and thence South South East two hundred forty four poles unto a small White oake, and thence East North East fifty poles unto a Small White oake, and a Pcickery that stands in the Glade and then pararell to the Glade of white marsh unto the place where it begun w^ch Tract of Land contains Ninety one Acres the said Ninety one Acres of Land being due unto the said Richard Lee by and for the Transportation of two persons into this Colony whose names are in the records menconed under this Patent nine acres remayneing due upon the last name in his Certificate. To have and to hold and to Bee held &c. Yielding and payeing unto our Said Sovereign Lord the King his heirs and Successors for every fifty acres of Land herein and by these presents given and granted yearly at the feast of St. Michaell the Archangell the fee . . . rent of one Shilling to his Majesties Use, which payment is to be paide seven yeares after the Date and not before &c. Dated the Second of December 1644.

To all &c now Know yee that I the said Sr William Berkeley Knt. doe accordingly with ye advice and Consent of the Councell of State give, grant and confirm unto Richard Lee Gent twelve hundred and fifty acres of Land Scituate lyeing or being about six or seven miles up the Narrows in the Charles river alias Yorke or Pomunkey river being a neck of Land bounded between two branches or Creeke where the foot Company met with the Boats when they went pomunkey march under ye Comand of Capt. William Claiborne Upon the South side of the said river Extending itself for Length towards Warranye Town and for Breadth upon the said river between the said Gutt or Creeke if it will amount to the true proportion otherwise to bee made good in Length into the Woods, the said twelve hundred and fifty acres of Land being due unto him the said Richard Lee by assignment from William Freeman of his right and title to the Transportation of twenty five persons into this Colony whose names are in the records mentioned under this Patent. To have and hold

---

1 Richard Kemp, of "Rich Neck," came to Virginia in 1637, as Secretary; was long a member of the Council; during the absence of Berkeley, from June, 1644, to June, 1645, he was the acting governor; in his will (dated the 4th of January, 1649; probated at London on the 6th of December, 1656), he left 40 S. to "his beloved friend Richard Lee to buy him a ringe, to bee forthwith paid." Richard Lee may have been clerk of the Council under Kemp; Kemp was buried at Williamsburg.

&c. to be held &c Yielding and paying unto our said Sovereign Lord the King &c. Dated the 20: of August 1646.

This patent was surrendered and the names are inserted under a patent for 1,250 acres granted to Richard Lee the 21st of December 1648; given below.

To all &c Whereas now Know yee yt I the said Sr. William Berkeley Knt. doe with the advice and Consent of the Councill of State accordingly give and grant unto Richard Lee Gent. twelve hundred and fifty acres of Land lyeing on the North Side of Yorke River opposite to the poplar Neck on the South side of the river being the Land formerly possessed and belonging to John Bayles and George Knight and for want of an heir Devolved to his Majesties regent, the said Land being due to the said Richard Lee by and for the Transportation of twenty and four persons into this colony whose names are in the records mentconed under this Patent. To have and to hold &c to be held &c Yielding &c which payment is to be made Seven yeares after ye date hereof and not before &c. Dated ye 21st of December 1648.

(Head Rights.) Wm. Crawford, Henry Lee, Wm. Batchelor, Nich: Merron, Mathew Lee, John Farror, George Way, Chris: Feathergill, Edward Dicks, Wm. David, Joane Peayler, Elizabeth Peds, John Lyne, John Hunt, John Thomas, James Ware, Maryot Martins, Peter Parchmore, George Light, Fra: Newton, Geo. Lee, Tho: Kidd, Henry Kidd, John Permerter.

To all &c Whereas &c now Know yee that I the said Sr. William Berkeley &c give and grant unto Collo Richard Lee Esqre Secretary of State for this Colony five hundred and fifty acres of Land Scituate on the North side of Yorke river, three hundred and fifty acres thereof Bounded towards the head and South East Side of a Creeke which is the westward bounds of another Tract of Land of the said Collo Lees beginning at a marked oake and standing on a Poynt and from thence South East halfe a point Easterly two hundred and forty poles to a marked white oake on the North Side of a runne into the maine woods North East halfe a poynt Northerly two hundred and thirty poles North West halfe a poynt Westerly two hundred and forty poles till it meeteth with a swamp of the said Creeke and down the said swamp and Creeke to the place where it begann and two hundred acres the residue beginning at a marked white oake standing on the Westward side of a Runn or branch of a Creeke Called Bennetts Creeke and Extending West North West to a marked Ash tree Standing upon the Eastward side of a swamp Upon the head of the said Creeke and from thence North North East one hundred and Sixty poles East South East two hundred poles and South South west to the first Station where it begann the said Land being due unto the said Collo Lee by and for the Transportation of Eleven persons into the Colony &c To have and to hold &c To be held &c Yielding &c which payment is to be made seven yeares after the first grant &c Seating &c thereof and not before &c. Dated the 24th day of May, 1651.

[1] To all &c Whereas &c now Know yee that I the said Sr William Berkeley Knight &c Do with the Consent of the Council of State accordingly give and grant unto

---

[1] This patent was recorded at Northumberland Court-house 16th May, 1711. Following it is recorded a deed from Richard Lee, of Westmoreland, to his brothers, Hancock and Charles Lee, for the 800 acres. 600 were given to Hancock and 200 to Charles. This deed will be found in full under Hancock Lee [2].

Coll° Richard Lee Esq. Secretary of State for this Colony Eight hundred acres of Land Scituate in Northumerland County and uppon the South side of a Creeke Comonly called the Dividing Creek . . . abutting North East and Northerly uppon the said Creeke South-east and Southerly Upon a creek which issueth forth of the said Dividing Creek Which divideth his Land and the Land of Mr. Thomas Wilson Marriner, Southwest into the maine Woods West and Northwest upon a small creek which divideth this Land and the Land of Col° Richard Lee. The said Land being due unto the said Col° Richard Lee by and for the Transportation of Sixteen persons all whose names are in the Records mentioned under this Pattent &c To have and To Hold &c To be held of Our Sovereign Lord the King his Heirs and Successors forever as of his mannor of East Greenwich in free and Comon Soccage and not in Capite nor by Knights Service Yielding and paying unto our Sovereign Lord the King his Heirs and Successors &c Which payment & proveded & Given att James Citty under my hand and the Seal of this Colony the 21st day of May, 1651.

To all &c Whereas &c now Know yee that I ye said Richard Bennet[1] Esq &c Give and Grant unto Collonel Richard Lee Three hundred acres of Land scituated in ye County of Gloster upon ye north side of Yorke river bounded as followeth viz. abutting south west and southerly upon Yorke river north west and west north northwest upon ye land of Mr. Richard Jones dec'd now in possession of ye said Frances Jones ye relict of ye said Jones, northeast into ye woods three hundred and twenty po: East southeast and south east upon the land of Robert Todd. The said land being due unto ye said Coll. Richard Lee by and for ye Transportation of six persons into this Colony &c To have and to hold &c Yielding and Paying &c wch payment is to be made seven yeares after ye first grant &c sealing thereof and not before Provided &c Dated ye 20th March 1653.

To all & whereas &c now Know yee that I ye sd Richard Bennett Esq. do in ye name of ye Keepers of ye Liberties of England &c. Give and Grant unto Coll. Richard Lee Esq Three hundred acres of land scituated in ye County of Lancaster upon ye south side of Rappa: river bounded as followeth, vizt: from a mark'd oake wch standeth upon ye head of a southern branch of a Creek commonly known by ye name of Matchepungo Creek wch divideth this land and ye land of Dame Elizabeth Lunsford formerly Mr. Samuel Abbot extending along ye land of John Benton dec'd East by North to another branch of ye said Matchepungo Creeke South and by East into ye woods west by south upon a branch of Pyanketanck north by west upon ye land of Dame Elizabeth Lunsford and along her head line to ye place where this land first began. The said land being due &c by and for ye Transportation of six persons &c To have, Yielding &c wch payment &c Dated ye 14th of November 1653 ut in aliis Wm Flabian, Wm. Snapes, Wm. Muns, Theo: Carey, Ed: Hampton.

NOTE: The land contained in this patent was sold by Richard Lee (1st of March, 1656) to Miles Dixon, merchant. There is a deed from "Dame Elizabeth Lunsford" for 50

[1] Richard Bennett (said to have been a younger brother of Henry Bennett, Earl of Arlington, one of the celebrated "Cabal" temp. Charles II) was appointed one of their commissioners by the English Parliament, in 1651, "for the reducing of Virginia and Maryland to their due obedience to the Commonwealth of England." Later he organized the government of the Colony, and served as Governor from 1652–55. He was many years a member of the Council; was colonial agent at London, and major-general of the militia. His daughter, Anne, married Colonel Theodorick Bland, and his great-granddaughter, Mary Bland, married Henry Lee, of "Lee Hall," Westmoreland. Governor Bennett died in 1675, and was buried at Green Point, Md.

acres whereon "ye sd Lees servants now are" to her "loving friend Richard Lee," dated 28 April, 1656, which land was also sold by Lee on same date to same person as above mentioned land. (*Lancaster County Records.*)

To all &c Whereas &c now Know yee that I the said Edward Diggs Esqr &c give and grant unto Coll. Richard Lee two hundred Acres of Land scituated in the County of Gloucster bounded on the North East side and East with the land of Henry Corbell on the South East with a line of marked trees which divideth this land and the land of William Howard South and South West upon another tract of the said Coll. Lee's West upon the Dogwood Springe branch North West and North upon the Land of William Thorne. The said land being due by and for the Transportacon of four Persons &c To have and to hold &c Yielding and paying &c which payment &c Dated the Seaventeen of May 1655 ut in Aliis Cormanch O'Mally, Teague Slanny, Richard O'Harrat, Giles Paine.

To all &c Whereas &c now Knowe ye That I the said Edward Diggs Esq doe give and grant unto Col°. Richard Lee six hundred Acres of Land Scituate in Northumberland County and upon the South side of the Dividing Creek abutting East upon the said Creek South East southerly upon another Parcell of Land belonging to the said Lee divided from this by a small Creek Called Andrews Creek, South West Westerly upon the Glade and high land North West northerly upon a run and small Creek Called Freemans Ford. The said Land being due unto the said Col°. Richard Lee by and for the Transportation of Twelve Persons into this Colony &c To Have and To Hold &c Yielding and paying &c Which payment &c dated the 4th of March 1656.

To all &c whereas &c now Know ye that I the said Edward Diggs Esq &c give and grant unto Col°. Richard Lee Five acres of Land lying in the County of Gloucester towards the head of Poropotank Creek whereon the store of the said Col°. Lee standeth and is part of a Dividend of 700 acres granted unto Peter Knight Merch't bearing date the 25th day of August 1652 which is deserted for want Seating. The said Land being due unto the said Col°. Richard Lee by and for the Transportation of one person into this Colony &c 45 acres remaining due unto the said Col°. Lee To have and to Hold &c Yielding & paying & Which payment is to be made &c Dated the 4th day of June 1656. Morris Plummer.

To all &c Whereas now Know ye that I the said Edward Diggs Esqr. &c give and grant unto William and Hancock Lee sons of Col°. Richard Lee Eight hundred and Fifty acres of Land Situate in the County of Gloucester upon the branch of Peanketank Swamp bounded by marked trees Beginning at a Spanish Oake by the marsh swamp running South by East 80 perches to a Hickory Corner thence south west to a Corner tree thence North West to a Hickory Corner thence North East to a Hickory by Peanketank thence south East 183 perches to a White Oak thence to the place where it began. The said land being due unto the said William and Hancock Lee as followeth Vizt. Five hundred Acres part thereof by virtue of the Right of a Patent granted unto John Woodward the attorney of the said Col°. Lee bearing date the 17th of May 1655 & relinquished by the said Col°. Lee to make this good and Three hundred and Fifty acres the Residue by and for the Transportation of Seven persons into this Colony &c To have and to hold &c yielding and paying &c which payment is to be made, &c Dated the 2d of June 1656. Roger Sheely, John Leally, Patrick Graham, John Mathorn, David Mahone, Douny Casby, Richard Joy, Durmont O'Faine, land due for. Deserted by the said Wm. and Hancock Lee and granted to Thoms Brereton by Patent Dated the 28th March 1662. Test Fra Hickman.

To all &c now Know ye that I the said Samuel Matthews Esq &c give and grant unto Col[o]. Richard Lee One Thousand Acres of Land Situate upon the south side of Potomack River Beginning at the mouth of a Small Creek which issueth Out of a Matchoteck River up the said River dividing the said Land from the Land of Mr. Lewis Burwell East southeast 500 poles to Certain Dams being on the head of the said Creek into the Main Woods South Southwest 320 poles and from thence extending West Northwest 500 poles, North Northeast to the place where it began 320 poles. The said Land being due unto him the said Col[o]. Richard Lee by and for the Transportation of Twenty persons into this Colony &c To have and To Hold &c. To be held &c Yielding and paying &c Which payment is to be made seven years after the first entry of the bounds in the Office being the 18th day of October 1650, and not before dated the 11th of October 1657.

To all &c whereas &c now Know ye that I the said Samuel Matthews Esq &c give and grant unto Col[o] Richard Lee Two thousand Acres of Land Scituate upon the South side of Patomack River Beginning at a mouth of a small Creek which issueth out of Matchoteck River up the said River dividing this Land from the Land of Mr. Lewis Burwell East southeast 500 poles to Certain Dams lying On the head of the said Creek South southwest 64 poles into the main woods, thence North northwest 50 poles, thence North northeast 640 poles to the place where it Began. The said Land being due by and for the Transportation of Forty persons into this Colony To Have &c yielding &c Dated the 5th of June 1658.

[1] To all To whom these Presents shall come I send . . . Whereas &c now Know ye That I the Sd Sr. William Berkeley &c. . . grant unto Col[o] Richard Lee Esqr. Councillor of State Four Thousand Acres of Land situate and being in Westmoreland County and bounded vizt: 1000 acres part thereof behind the Land of Mr. Roger Isham beg. at a marked corner tree 320 poles Southwest from 1/4 of a mile ben. . . . the Dwelling House of the said Isham and running Northwest from the ——— 500 poles to another Corner Tree thence Southwest 320 poles ——— marked Red Oak thence Southeast 500 poles to a marked Hickory from thence Northeast 320 poles to the place where it first began on ——— acres. Another part thereof being in Potowmack Freshes on the Northeast ——— of a Creek below Piscataway, but on the opposite side the River Potowmacke bounding Southeasterly on the said River Southwesterly on a ——— called Hopkins's Creek running Northerly from the River 640 poles ——— the woods and Northeasterly from the Creek 250 poles towards the ——— Surveyed for Henry Vincent & 2000 acres the Remainder bou——— ——— Northerly on a Creek which issueth out of Patomack, Piscattaway Divideth this Land from a Tract of Land of 2000 acres appertaining ——— John Wood, Robert Smith and John Eyeres, Easterly upon the River, running from the Creek Southerly 320 poles and from the River ——— to the Creek Westerly 1000 poles. The said land being due to the said Col[o] Richard Lee Esq. as followeth Vizt: 1000 acres the first part formerly granted unto John Wood by Patent dated the 14th of January and 1000 acres the second part thereof formerly granted to Robert Cart— by Patent dated the 15th of July 1657 and 2000 acres the Residue being granted to Robert Clarke by Patent dated the 15th of July 1657 — Land for want of Seating according to the reservation the par——— to the said Col[o] Richard Lee Esqr by order of the General ——— bearing dated with these presents and is due by and for the Transportation of 8 persons &c To be Held &c Which payment to be made 7 years after the date hereof provided &c Dated the 26 of November 166–. This Patent was renewed by

[1] The blanks appearing in this copy are so in the record in Richmond, which was evidently copied from the original patent, not clearly legible.

Order of the General Court, dated the 26th of March 1663 and granted to the said Colo Lee by Sr. William Berkeley, Knight, his Majesties Governor &c the said 26th of March. Teste Ira Kirkman.

To all &c whereas &c now Know ye That I the said Sir William Berkeley Knight Governor &c give and grant unto Colo Richard Lee Esqr Two thousand Six hundred Acres of Land in the County of Northumberland on the south side of Potomack River bounded as followeth Viz: Two thousand two hundred acres part thereof, Beginning at the mouth of a Creek that issueth out of Machotick River East southeast up the said Creek and crossing the Beaver dams Five hundred poles to a marked Pockikory tree that stands on the West side of Pockatomes field, thence South Southwest Six hundred and forty poles to a marked White oak that stands upon the head of a swamp that issueth into the head of Nominy river, thence West Northwest Five hundred poles to a marked red —, thence North North East three hundred and twenty poles to a marked red Oak, thence North Northeast three hundred and twenty poles to Machotick River, thence East Southeast one hundred poles to the first specified place and four hundred acres the Residue at the mouth of a small Creek that issueth out of Machotick River and runneth up Machotick river West Northwest two hundred poles, thence South southwest three hundred and twenty poles thence East Southeast two hundred poles to a marked red oak, thence North Northeast to the first specified place. The Land being due unto the said Colo Richard Lee as followeth, Vizt: Two Thousand Acres part thereof being formerly granted to him by Patent bearing date the fifth of June one thousand six hundred and fifty eight, and six hundred Acres the residue being due by and for the Transportation of twelve persons &c To have and To hold &c To be held &c Yielding and Paying &c provided &c Dated the first of December one thousand six hundred and sixty four.

As shown by these land grants, Richard Lee held many offices in the Colony; having been Justice, Burgess, member of the Council and Secretary of State. He also served on various commissions. In the *Egerton MSS.* in the British Museum, there is a copy of the *Virginia Remonstrance* against granting lands in the Northern Neck to certain lords. It was dated the 28th of March, 1663, and signed by "Berkeley, Francis Moryson, Thomas Ludwell, Sect. Richard Lee, Nathaniel Bacon, Ab: Wood, John Carter, Edward Carter, Theodore Bland, Thomas Stegge, and Henry Corbyn." (Neil, *Va. Carolorum*, 421).

Hening states that in April, 1663, Governor Berkeley wrote to the governor of Maryland as follows: "I and the Councell here haue Considered of the means of Redresse [relative to the excessive planting of tobacco] and authorize the Gentlemen of the Councell, Coll Richard Lee, Coll Rob: Smith, Coll John Carter, and Mr. Henry Corbin our Commisrs to communicate our Results to you and appoynted the eleuenth day of May next to be the time and the County Courthouse of Northumberland the place of Conference." This commission met "at Mr. Aleston's[1]

[1] Probably intended for Allerton; Neil gives the place of meeting "at Major Isaac Allerton's." (*Va. Carolorum*, 305.)

in Wickacomoco in Virginia," and amongst the names signed on the 2nd of May, 1663, to their report was that of Richard Lee. (ii, Hening, 200.)

Richard Lee has always been represented as a most ardent royalist and supporter of the Stuarts; it has been claimed that he made a voyage to Holland expressly to visit Charles II., then in exile. Confirmatory of this journey, there is extant the testimony of a contemporary who visited Richard Lee in 1659, and left this record; its author, John Gibbon, was later an official of the Herald's office at London. In 1682 he published a book entitled, *Introductio Ad Latinam Blasoniam*. On page 158 of this work he wrote: "A great part of Anno 1659, till February the year following, I lived in Virginia, being most hospitably entertained by the Honourable Collonel Richard Lee, some time Secretary of State there; and who after the King's martyrdom hired a Dutch vessel, freighted her himself, went to Brussels, surrendered up Sir William Barcklaie's old commission (for the Government of that Province) and received a new one from his present Majesty (a loyal action and deserving my commemoration)." A copy of Gibbon's book, now in the possession of William Blackstone Lee, Esq., has this additional note, added by Gibbon himself: "The Collonell Lee mentioned page 156 of this Booke had a faire estate in Virginia. The product of his Tobacco amounted to £2000 per annum. Hee was willing to end his days in England and to send over some one to reside as generall Inspectour and overseer of his several plantations. I was recommended to him as a fitt and Trusty person, having beene a servant to Thomas, Lord Coventry, the Richest Baron of England &c. I accepted Collonell Lee's proffer—wee arrived in Virginia the last of October 1659 and 11br 2nd came to the Collonells house at Dividing Creekes. Before hee could settle Things for his final departure and settling in England, wee had newes from Newe England of ye Kings Restauration. The Collonell was willing to hasten to England and I was as willing as hee, having hopes to get some employment by means of John, Lord Culpeper, to whom my family had relation by mariage. But hee was dead before I reached England. Wee arrived at Mergate in Kent friday 22 March 1660–1. My leaving Virginia, I have sorely repented. He made mee proffers of mariage and offered mee 1000 acres of land."

In view of this statement of Gibbon, the following extract from English records shows Richard Lee in an entirely new light, that of one "faithful and useful to the interests of the Commonwealth" of England. But it is only fair to observe that this claim was made for him by a friend in his absence.

"The petition of John Jeffreys, of London, Merchant, in behalf of Col. Richard Lee, of Virginia, to the Lord Protector and Council. Certain plate brought from Virginia to London by Colonel Lee, about a year and a half ago, to change the fashion, has been seized, on his return to Virginia, by the searchers at Gravesend; every piece having the Colonel's coat of arms, and being for his own private use, who did not know but that plate manufactured might be transported to the English plantations. Colonel Lee being faithful and useful to the interests of the Commonwealth, the petitioner prays, in his absence, for an order to discharge the plate." Annexed to this petition was an affidavit from "Col. Richard Lee of Virginia," stating that his trunk had contained 200 ounces of silver plate, all marked with his coat of arms and intended for his own use, and that it had been seized at Gravesend aboard the ship Anthony of London; that he had had the most part of it many years together in Virginia. (Sainsbury Calendar of State Papers, Colonial Series, 1574–1660, p. 430.)

While in England in 1663, his wife and children being there also, probably for the education of the latter, Richard Lee made his will; the wording of this will indicates that he had given up his intention of settling permanently in England. For he ordered that his estate there should be sold, gave minute directions for the payment of his debts, and closing up of his interests in that country, and made arrangements for the settlement of his children in Virginia. It seems probable that he intended to return alone, for he requested that (in case of his death) "my good friends will with all convenient speed cause my wife and children (all except Francis if he be pleased) to be transported to Virginia and to provide all necessary for the voyage."

The account of his property given in this will shows him to have been possessed of considerable wealth—for that day. If his tobacco crop was actually worth £2000 a year, as Gibbon estimated, and his estate at Stratford-Langton, £800 a year, as stated by William Lee, then Richard Lee must have enjoyed an income larger than most of the early planters. The copy of his will, given here, was made by the late Cassius F. Lee, Jr., from one in the possession of Mr. Charles Campbell, of Fredericksburg, and is believed to be accurate:

IN THE NAME OF GOD, AMEN. I, Colonel Richard Lee, of Virginia. and lately of Stratford[1] Langton, in the County of Essex, Esquire, being bound upon a voyage to Virginia aforesaid, and not knowing how it may please God to dispose of me in so long a voyage, utterly renouncing, disclaiming, disannulling and revoking all former wills, either

---

[1] In a work entitled "*A Survey of the Cities of London and Westminster*," published in 1735, by Robert Seymour, he stated: "A mile from Stratford-Bow, in the Road into Essex, is Stratford-Langton or Langthorn, lying in the Parish of West-Ham, a place much frequented for the country-Houses of Wealthy Cittizens, and the Habitations of such other of them who cannot enjoy their Health in London, &c." (Book vi, 846.)

William Lee, in 1771, stated that this estate was worth about £800 or £900 a year, which would seem to represent quite a large property.

script, nuncupative or parol, and schedules or codicils of wills whatsoever, do make, ordain and declare this my last Will and Testament in manner and form following, first: I give and bequeath my soul to that good and gracious God that gave it me and to my Blessed Redeemer Jesus Christ, assuredly trusting in and by his meritorious death and passion to receive salvation, and my body to be disposed of whether by land or sea according to the opportunity of the place, not doubting but at the last day both body and soul shall be re-united and glorified.

Next, my will and desire is that all my estate aforesaid, both lease land, free land and copyhold land, and houses be, with all convenient speed that may be, sold for the payment of my debts to John Jeffries, Esq. and what the sale of that shall fall short of, to be made good out of my crops in Virginia, to be consigned to my good friends Mr. Thomas Griffith and John Lockey, or one of them in that behalf, and in case the estate of Stratford be not as speedily sold as I desire, that then the best improvement possible may be made from year to year of my said plantation, and my servants labour with such directions and appointments as the said Griffith and Lockey shall order, for the better and sooner payment of my debts, and that my number of servants be still kept up, and continued out of the labours by the said Griffith and Lockey, or one of them, for the better managing and effecting thereof.

Also my will and earnest desire is that my good friends will with all convenient speed cause my wife and children (all except Francis if he be pleased) to be transported to Virginia, and to provide all necessary for the voyage, and from time to time till my estate be disentangled and free of all my debts, to provide and allow for them, and every one of them, a competent and convenient maintenance according as the product of the estate will bear, relation being had to the payment of my debts and the annual supply of my several plantations, all of which I absolutely refer to the said Thomas Griffith and John Lockey, and after my debts are paid, I give and bequeath my estate as followeth:

To my wife, during her life, I give the plantation whereon I now dwell, ten English servants, five negroes, 3 men and 2 women, 20 sows and corn proportionable to the servants; the said negroes I give to her during her widowhood and no longer, and then presently to return to those of the five youngest children, also the plantation Mocke Nock.

Item. My will and earnest desire is that my household stuff at Stratford be divided into three parts, two of which I give to my son John, and bind him to give to every one of his brothers a bed, and the other part I give to my wife Anna Lee.

Item. I give all my plate to my three oldest sons, or the survivor or survivors of them, each to have his part delivered to him when he comes to the age of 18 years.

Item. I give to my son John and his heirs forever, when he comes to the age of 18 years, all my land and plantation at Machotick, all the stock of cattle and hogs thereupon, also 10 negroes, viz., five men and five women, and 10 English servants for their times, all the corn that shall be found there, all tools, household stuff, and utensils thereupon.

Item. To Richard and his heirs forever, when he come to the age aforesaid, I give my plantation called Paradise, with all my servants thereupon, all my stock of cattle and hogs, all working tools and utensils, and corn that shall be found thereupon to be for the provision of the said servants.

Item. To Francis and his heirs forever, when he comes to the age aforesaid, I give the Paper-makers Neck and the War Captains Neck, with five negroes, three men and two women, and 10 English servants, and the stock of cattle and hogs, corn, and tools and utensils upon the said several Necks.

Item. I give and bequeath to the five younger children, viz.: William, Hancock, Betsey, Anne, and Charles, the plantation whereon John Baswell now lives and so all along including Bishop's Neck and to the utmost extent of my land towards Brewer's and also 4,000 acres upon Potomack, also the two plantations before bequeathed to my wife, after her death to be divided between them or their survivors or survivor of them, also all the rest of my cattle, hogs, corn, household stuffs, tools, or whatsoever is or shall be found upon the said plantations at the time of my death, all which said estate so bequeathed to my younger children, after my debts are paid, I desire may be employed upon said plantations for a joint stock to raise portions of the said children against they come of age aforesaid or the females married. The said servants and what other products of their labours whether money or whatsoever, to be equally divided between them or their survivors or survivor of them, but the said land only to be divided between the male children.

Item. I give and bequeath unto my eldest son John, three islands lying in the Bay of Chesapeake, the great new bed that I brought over in the Duke of York, and the furniture thereunto belonging.

Item. My will is that my horses, mares, and colts be equally divided in two parts, one whereof to be and belonging to my three eldest children, and the other to my five youngest, and shall be sold as they increase toward raising money for their portions, and in case any of the three eldest children die before they come to the age of 18 years, that then his or their portion come to the survivors or survivor of them, and in case they all die that the whole personal estate equally to return to the five youngest children, but the land only to the male children, and if the five younger children die before they come to the age aforesaid, or the females married, then their parts to be divided among the three eldest or survivors or survivor of them.

Item. My will is that my son William Lee have all that land on the Maryland side, whereon George English is now seated, when he comes to the age aforesaid; also my will is that goods sufficient be set apart for the maintenance of the gangs of each plantation for the space of two years, and all the rest of my goods to be sold to the best advantage and the tobacco shipped here to Mr. Lockey and Mr. Griffith toward the payment of my debts.

Item. I give and bequeath unto my son Francis, after my debts are paid, my whole interest in the ship called Elizabeth and Mary, being one-eighth part, also one-eighth part in the ship called The Susan, and in case of the death of Francis, I give the same to Charles, and in the case of his death to the two girls Elizabeth and Anne.

But in case that by the blessing of God upon the industry and labour of my people upon the several plantations, my said debts be fully satisfied before the said land at Stratford be sold, nevertheless I will and entreat my good friends, Mr. Griffith and Mr. Lockey, or one of them, [that] it may be sold to the most and best advantage, and the produce thereof put out at interest, and the interest thereof be employed for and towards the better education of John and Richard, equally, to assist the one in his travels for the attainment of a reasonable perfection in the knowledge of Physick, the other at the University or the Inns of Court which he shall be most fit for, and the principal money to be equally divided between the two daughters when they come to age or be married, and that the said daughters be utterly debarred from all former legacies given to them as aforesaid, but in case of their death then the sale and produce of said estate at Stratford to be equally divided between my eldest son John and my youngest son Charles. Also I desire and order that my wife, my son John, and all my overseers, that either all or one, shall from time to time keep a correspondence with the said Griffith and Lockey, and order all my affairs in Virginia to the best advantage, as they or one of them shall direct them, and ship all my tobacco and what else shall be raised upon the said plantations to the said Griffith and Lockey for satisfaction of my debt and advantage of my children and do yearly give them an account of all horses, mares, negroes, goods, and all other things according as they shall receive directions and instructions from the said Mr. Thomas Griffith and Mr. Lockey.

Lastly: For the use aforesaid I make and ordain my ever loving friends, Mr. Thomas Griffith and Mr. Lockey, merchants, John and Richard Lee, my full and sole Executors of this my Last Will and Testament, but in respect to my son Richard, till he cometh of age, I do absolutely place all management of my will upon the care and trust of first mentioned executors till my said son, Richard Lee, comes to age as aforesaid, hoping the same friendship to mine after my death which they have always done unto me.

In witness thereof I have hereunto set my hand and seal this the Sixth day of February, in the 16th year of the Reign of our Sovereign Lord Charles II., King of Great Britain, &c., &c., and in the year of our Lord, 1663 [1664.]

[1] This will was probated in London, the next year:

"1664-5. Richardus Lee. Januarij. Decimo die probatum fuit Testamentum Richardi Lee nup de Stratford Langton in Com Essexiae sed apud Virginia in ptibus transmarinus ar. defunct hents, &c. Jurament Thomae Griffith et Johis Lockey duor Execut, &c., quih. &c., de bene &c. Jurat. Reservata ptate Similem Comnem faciend Johi ét Richo Lee alt Execut &c." Johis.

P. C. C. Probate Act Book fo 3.

The exact date of Richard Lee's death is not known. There is ample evidence to show that he returned to Virginia after executing his will in London on the 6th of February, 1663-4. The application of his son for land due his father, deceased, dated 20th of April, 1664, proves him to have died prior to that date. This order states that 4,700 acres were due to John Lee for the transportation of 94 persons into the Colony by "his ffather Coll°. Richard Lee, Esq., whoe is now deceased." His will was proven at London 10th of January, 1664-5; his widow remarried, as shown by this warrant:

24th of September, 1666, a writ was issued by Ira Kirkman, Clerk, to the Sheriff of Westmoreland County, requiring the arrest of Mr. John Lee, one of the Ex'rs of the Last Will and Testament of Colonel Richard Lee, to appear before the Governor and Council on the 3d day of next General Court, in the forenoon, to answer the suit of Edmund Lister, as marrying . . . Anne the relict of the said Colonel Lee (I, *Va. Cal. State Papers*, 7).

It also seems to be clearly proven that the later home of Richard Lee was at "Dividing Creeks," in Northumberland county. The testimony of Gibbon, who visited him there in 1659, and that of his son, Francis Lee, who stated, in 1677, that he had been "formerly an inhabytant at Dividing Creeks in Virginia," fully prove this assertion. But the time of his re-

[1] From an article on "Lee of Virginia," by Mr. J. Henry Lea, in *New England Hist. and Gen. Register*, January, 1892.

MRS. RICHARD LEE.

moving to Northumberland is not so certain; as he was a Burgess from that county in 1651, and patented land there in that year, it seems highly probable that he settled there about that date.

In 1798 Portia Lee, daughter of William Lee, wrote that Richard Lee "died at his seat upon Dividing Creeks in North'd County, where he is buried and his tombstone is there to be found." This statement is, of course, only traditional, unless it is to be supposed that she had seen the tombstone; but it shows, at any rate, what the family tradition was at that date, and had been, probably, ever since the death of the Immigrant. It has been constantly claimed that this home was the place known in later years as "Cobbs Hall;" but there is no direct evidence to substantiate this claim. The presence of the old carving of his arms over the front door is about the strongest bit of evidence yet found.

The only information as to the number and relative ages of the children of Richard and Anna Lee is taken from his will; the sons are probably named in the order of their birth; John and Charles are distinctly specified as the eldest and youngest sons. In naming his five younger children, he placed the two daughters between Hancock and Charles, so it may be fairly taken for granted that they were younger than Hancock and older than Charles. In the wills of olden time it was generally customary to name the sons first, whatever may have been the relative ages of the sons and daughters; but in this case the inference taken seems to be well justified. Their issue, then, were as follows:

i, JOHN [2], eldest son and heir at-law; died unmarried.
ii, RICHARD [2], after death of John, became heir-at-law; from him are descended the "Stratford" line, as designated in this work.
iii, FRANCIS [2], settled in London, died there and left issue.
iv, WILLIAM [2], married; probably left no male issue.
v, HANCOCK [2], married and left issue; from whom the "Ditchley" line are descended.
vi, ELIZABETH [2], no data.
vii, ANNE [2], married, and probably left issue.
viii, CHARLES [2], married, and left issue; from whom the "Cobbs Hall" line are descended.

## SECOND GENERATION.

### CAPTAIN JOHN LEE.

JOHN [2], the eldest son of Richard and Anna Lee, was born about 1645, "in Capohowasick Wickacomoco in Virginia," as he himself stated. It is difficult, with our present knowledge of these names, to understand clearly this description of his birthplace. The two Indian names seem to refer to two distinct localities; on a map[1] of America, made for James I. in 1610, "Capohowasick" is the name given to the peninsula which contains the present counties of Gloucester and Matthews, and "Wighcocomoco" is the name for the Northern Neck.[2] As Richard Lee's first home in Virginia was situated in the "Capohowasick" region and his later one at Dividing Creeks was in the "Wickacomoco" country, it would seem probable that John intended to name both his birthplace and his later home in Virginia.

John was educated at Oxford; he entered Queen's College, as an upper commoner, on the 2d of July, 1658, and graduated an A. B. on the 30th of April, 1662. He must have studied medicine later, for William Lee stated that "John took his degrees as Dr. of Physic." He was probably reading medicine at the date of his father's will, for in that will it was directed that the interest of invested funds "be employed for and towards the better education of John and Richard equally, to assist the one in his travels for the attainment of a reasonable perfection in the knowledge of Physick," etc. No mention is to be found of John Lee's ever have practiced his profession in Virginia.

While at Oxford he presented a silver cup to his college, a print of which is given, with a description of it, by the kind permission of Mr. J. Henry Lea, of Fairhaven, Mass.

"On a Silver Pint Cup, standing on a foot and weighing 14oz. 3dwt., now preserved in Queen's College, Oxford, is the following inscription—

COLL. REGI. OXON.

D. D. Johanis Lee Natus in Capohowasick
Wickacomoco in Virginia America Filius
Primogenitus Richardi Lee Chiliarchæ
Oriundi de Morton Regis in Agro Salopiensi.
1658.

---

1 See Plate CLVIII in the *Genesis of the United States*, p. 456, by Alexander Brown.

2 According to Beverly, the parishes in the Northern Neck, about 1705, were:
Lancaster, two, viz.: Christ and St. Mary-White-Chapel.
Northumberland, two, viz.: Fairfield and Bouthray, and Wiccocomoco.
Westmoreland, two, viz.: Copeley and Washington.
Standford (Stafford), two, viz.: St. Paul and Overworton.
Richmond, one, viz.: North-Farnham and part of another, viz.: Sittenburn.
King George, one, viz.: Hanover, and other part of Sittenburn.
(*Burke, Hist of Va.* 1805, Appendix, II.)

"Above are two shields, that to the right bearing the arms of Lee of Langley and Coton—A fess cheque between eight billets—that to the left with the arms of the College—Three Eagles displayed—To the left of the engraved work a Bishop's Mitre and Pastoral Staff appearing from behind a book, to the right the end of a staff appearing above a Book crossed by a pair of Compasses. Most of this detail appears clearly in the illustration from a photograph obtained by W. B. Lee, Esq., by permission of Rev. J. R. Magrath, D. D., Provost of the College."[1]

John probably returned to Virginia with his father in the spring of 1664; he was certainly in Northumberland in April of that year, when he obtained the order from the court for land due his father, then deceased. He was as certainly seated in Westmoreland in September, 1666, as shown by the writ already quoted. A year later, Captain John Lee was a member

[1] Copied from article in *New England Historical and Genealogical Register*, January, 1892.

of the "Committee of the Association of Northumberland, Westmoreland and Stafford" counties: this committee were for securing the defense of the Northern Neck from Indians, and were in some respects its local governors; he also was a Burgess from Westmoreland in 1673.

By the Govennor and Capt. Gennll: of Virginia, I doe Appoint Mr. John Lee high Sheriffe of Westmrland County, this next ensueing yeare and to be sworne the next County Court in case he Accepts thereof. But if Mr. Lee Be not willing to Accept thereof, then Mr. Clement Spillman is hereby Appointed to be high Sheriffe of the said County and bee Accordingly sworne and alsoe Before his swearing is to be one of the Comicons for the said County, dated this 28th day of March, 1672. (Signed) William Berkeley.

As an example of old official documents, this commission is perhaps worth preserving in its entirety:

To all to whom these presents shall come, I Sr William Berkeley Knt: Govenor and Capt : Gennll: of Virginia send Greeting—Whereas for ye More due Administracon of Justice in this Country and the greater ease of ye people and in obtaining the same, his Royal Matie: King Charles ye first, of ever Blessed memory was pleased by his Instruccons, directed to ye Honorable Governor and Councell of State here to require them to appoint in places Convenient Inferior Courts of Justice and Comiconrs: for ye same. In obedience thereto Itt was ordered by the Governor and Councell on the 25 of June, 1642, that Comiconrs: should be appointed in every County for ye keeping of Monthly Courts wch: hath been ever since continued and confirmed by Act of Assembly. And whereas by Act of Assembly bearing date the second day of March 1661 It was enacted that ye said Courts should continue in every County as formerly And that the said Courts should Consist of Eight of ye most Honest and Juditious psons in ye County, wch eight or any foure of them, where Allwaies one to be of ye Quorum, are to be Impowered by Comicon from ye Governor for the time being to act According to ye Lawes of England and this Country and to Impower them severally And out of Court to Act and doe all such things as by the Lawes of England are to be done by Justice of the peace there and that those psons soe Commiconated take ye oathe of Alleagianst and Supremacie, And the oath of a justice of the peace And that they be called Justices of ye peace, And whereas by a Late order of ye Gennll: Court, Itt was thought fitt and ordered for the better dispatch of all buiseness that two psons more Quallyfyed as aforesaid should be added to every Comicon, Now Know yee that I Sr William Berkeley Knt: Governor and Capt. Gennll: of Virginia out of the Confidence and Experience I have of the true Loyaltie, abilitie, Justice and Integritie of you Ltt: Coll: John Washington, Majr: William Pierce, Majr: Isaac Allerton, Capt: John Lee, Mr. John Appleton, Mr. John Lord, Capt. John Ashton, Capt. Thomas Philpott, Mr. William Storke, Mr. Robert Jadwin, have Assigned, And for the time Being Appointed you and every one of you to be present Justices of ye peace of Westmrland County, Giving and Granting unto you or any foure of you, whereof Ltt: Coll: John Washington, Major Wm. Pierce, Major Isaac Allerton, Capt. John Lee, Mr. John Appleton, and Mr. John Lord to allwaies one full power and Authoritie to heare and determine all suits and Controversies Between ptie and ptie According to the severall Lawes of this Collonie with power likewise to you and every one of you to take deposicons and Examinacons upon oath for the Clearing of the truth According to Law. And that you be carefull for ye Conservacon of the peace and the Quiett Govern . . . and safetie of the people, there residing or being. And that you Keepe or cause to be

Kept all orders of court and pclamacons directed to you or comeing to yo[r] hands from ye Governor and Councell and According to ye same and as neare as may be According to ye Lawes of England and this Country to Inflict punishment upon Offenders and Delinguents and to Doe and Execute whatsoever a Justice of the Peace or two or more Justices of ye peace may doe or Execute (such Offences only Excepted) as concerne taking Away Life or member, According to the Lawes of England and this Country. And further you are hereby required from time to time to Keepe or Cause ye Clearke of yo[r] Court to Keepe Records of all Judgments and matters of Controversies decided and Agreed upon by you or any foure of you as aforesaid, And this Comicon to be inforced to all Intents and purposes untill I shall signyfie ye Contrary under my hand and the seale of the Collony. Given under my hand and his Ma[ties]: seale of the Collonye this 29th day of March, In ye yeare of our Lord 1672. Signed, etc.

Among the Westmoreland records is an agreement, dated the 30th of March, 1670, between John Lee, Henry Corbin, Thomas Gerrard, and Isaac Allerton to build a banqueting hall at or near the head of Cherive's Creek, now called Jackson's, near the lines where their four estates cornered. This deed recites that each man or his heirs "shall yearly, according to his due course, make an honorable treatment, fit to entertain the undertakers thereof, their men, masters and friends yearly, and every year thereafter; to begin on the 29th of May, 1671. Corbin first, Lee next, Gerrard next, Allerton next, the year round. Every four years to have a procession to every man's land for re-marking and bounding by line-trees or other particular divident or seat in which no course hath been taking by the County Court of Westmoreland. This for the better preservation of that friendship which ought to be between neighbors, that each man's line, wherever any one of us is bounded, one upon another, may be re-marked and plainly set forth by trees," etc.

This banqueting hall did not long remain a centre of colonial hospitality. For Richard Lee (in his will of 1714) mentioned the "place where the Banqueting house had formerly stood." It had evidently been destroyed by fire. The cabin of a negro family at present occupies the position where it once stood. Nor did any of the four signers of this agreement long survive its enactment. Gerrard, Lee, and Corbin died a few years after its signing, and Allerton in 1702.

John Lee died late in the fall of 1673. The last mention of him occurs in these records: In 1673, Col: John Washington, Capt: John Lee, William Traverson, William Moseley, and Robert Beverley were appointed commissioners to arrange the boundary lines between Lancaster and Northumberland Counties. The records of Westmoreland show that John Lee sat as a magistrate as late as the 25th of June, 1673; about the same date he was mentioned, as living, in a deed from his brother-in-law,

Thomas Youell. On the 19th of 9$^{br}$ 1673, the will of "Thomas Garrard of Machotecks," &c., was proven by the oaths of John Waugh, Major Isaac Allerton, and Capt: John Lee. Isaac Allerton and John Lee owned a mill in partnership at Nominy; under date of the 26th of August, 1674, Richard Lee sold his share in this mill to Allerton. The deed states that "Whereas it hath pleased God of late to take ye sd John Lee unto his mercy, by whose decease the moiety of ye sd two acres of Land together with ye mill thereon erected descends unto me Rich: Lee," &c.

An inventory of John's personal estate was ordered on the 25th of February, was dated the 2d of March, and filed by Richard Lee, as administrator, on the 29th of April, 1674. This inventory contains some very curious items, and altogether furnishes strong presumptive evidence that his was the home of a bachelor. The house was evidently a small one, the hall having been, as customary in those days, furnished as a sitting-room. In "ye Hall chamber" were found, beside its usual furniture, "16 iron bound shovells, 2 frying panns;" in "ye parloure roome" (evidently also used as the dining room) were one "grey sute trimmed with silver buttons," one pair of "gloves with silver topps," silver plate of 145 ounces "habberdepoize." The books in "ye studdy" were appraised at 4,000 pounds of tobacco. In "Capt: Lee's chamber" were found "one pistoll, saddle and furniture for a horse," six quarts of hominy, and six of "oyle." A store room, with all the multitudinous articles needed on a large plantation, the blacksmith's shop, the tan-house, and other adjuncts of farm life, are named. In the "shoemaker's Shopp, William King, 3 years to learn and his tooles," were only valued at 2,000 pounds, while the "Negro boy ffranke and Livery sute" were placed at 4,000.

It may be of some interest to estimate the amount of land owned by John and later devised by Richard Lee. A fair estimate of the land owned by the Immigrant would place the acres at about 16,000. John received 4,700 after his father's death; it is, therefore, probable that Richard inherited about 20,000 acres.

By a comparison of several wills and other records it appears that the various old estates contained about the following number of acres. In the case of Stratford, it may be that Thomas Lee added to the original acreage. Mt. Pleasant, 2,600; Lee Hall, 2,600; Ditchley, 904; Cobb's Hall, 600; Stratford, 6,500. Philip Lee received probably 2,500 to 3,000 acres in Maryland, and 4,000 were bequeathed to Richard's daughter, Ann Fitzhugh. The rest of Richard's estate was left in a body, to be divided between his four sons; the number of acres cannot be estimated.

## FRANCIS LEE.

FRANCIS [2], the third son of Richard and Anna Lee, was probably born about the year 1648, and, from the data given here, it seems certain that he returned to England and died there in 1714. Francis was allowed the option, in his father's will, of remaining in England, if he so desired. The inference is that he was intended for a mercantile life. It is probable that he returned with his father to Virginia and went back to England, to establish himself in mercantile life, some years after his father's death. The Northumberland records contain a certificate from him, dated about 1670, stating that a servant had "served his full tyme to the Estate of Col. Richard Lee and myself." A "Mr. Francis Lee" was Justice for Northumberland in 1673. The Middlesex records give the following information concerning him:

Deed from Erasmus Welthers, Merchant, and Frances, his wife, to "Francis Lee of Buttolfe Lane, Merchant." Recorded 10 April, 1677.

Deed from "Francis Lee of Botolphe Lane in London, Cittizen and formerly an inhabytant at Dividing Creeke in Virginia." Recorded—April, 1677.

Power of attorney from "Francis Lee, Cittizen and Merchant, of St. Dionis Backchurch, London," to William Churchill, of Middlesex, in Virginia. Recorded 3d April, 1699.

The following is an abstract of his will (kindly furnished by Mr. William Blackstone Lee, of Seend, Wiltshire, England):

P. P. C. 1714, Ashton 224. Will dated 9 July, 1709; probated, London, 23 November, 1714. ffrancis Lee, of London, Merchant. I doe declare my sons Richard and Thomas Lee and my daughter Anne, wife of Henry Watson, to be fully advanced. Yet nevertheless I doe give unto them 5£ a piece for mourning. Unto my Honoured ffriends Sir Jeffery Jefferies, Knight, and John Jefferies, Esqr., Rings. Unto my Nephew Richard Lee, Merchant, and my ffriend Mr. Hanbury Walthall, of London, Haberdasher, Mourning. The Residue to my youngest son, Arthur Lee, his Executors, Administrators, and Assigns, at twenty-one years. The said Richard Lee and John Hanbury Walthall to be Executors in trust for said Arthur. They shall during his Minority Loan out the Moneys not expended in his Education and Maintenance for the increase of his ffortune. To my eldest Brother Richard Lee, Mourning. Witness. Edwd. Gilbert, Ser., Tho. Reason, Wm. Hodgdin.

23 Nov. 1714. Emanavit Commissio Arthuro Lee filio et Legatario Residuario ffrancisci Lee nuper Sancti Dionysii Backchurch, London, Mer-

catorio defuncti justa tenorem Testamenti (eo quod Richardus Lee et Hanbury Walthall Executors oneri renuntiaverint.)

The register of St. Dionis Backchurch has the following entries:

Abigail, daughter of Mr. Francis and Tamar Lee, Merchant, born and baptised, 9 July, 1694. John, son of Mr. Francis Lee, Merchant, buried in ye Great Vault, 9 June, 1694. Mrs. Tamar Lee, wife of Mr. Francis Lee, Merchant, buried in ye Great Vault, 1 May, 1694–5. Tamar, daughter of Mr. Francis Lee, Merchant, buried in Ye Great Vault, 18 January, 1699–1700. Mr. Francis Lee, Merchant, buried in Ye Great Vault in the Chancel, 19 Nov. 1714.

## Captain William Lee.

William [2], the fourth son of Richard and Anna Lee, was born about 1651; was named in his father's will as one of the "five younger children," and the first of them mentioned. Under date of the 25th of February, 1673–4, "Mr. Wm. Lee, aged about twenty yeares," made a deposition that "Mr. Rich: Cole did according to my apprehension of his words freely consent and agree to runn w^th: Jno: W^ms: of Ragged Poynt in my Bro^rs: pasture ye Raue w^ch: by agreem^t betwene ye sd Cole and Williams was to have bin on Machoatic Roade." Under date of "Aug^st: ye 26th 1674," Richard Lee wrote "Bro: W^m:" a letter requesting him to acknowledge a deed for him, &c., therefore William must have been over 21 at that date.

He was living as late as June, 1681, as mentioned by William Fitzhugh; from the records of Northumberland it is learned that Bartholomew Schrever and Mary, his wife, the executrix of Capt. William Lee, deceased, executed a deed on the 16th of February, 1697; in the same year Schrever made payments on the estate of William Lee. He died, therefore, prior to February, 1697–8. This Mary Schrever, his executrix, was either his widow or his daughter; probably the latter. In either case it may be inferred that he left no male heirs. Indeed, the following abstract is proof of this inference:

In an application for land Richard Lee stated that "George Colclough, Gent., owned the tract of land called Bishop's Neck by a patent of 3d of April, 1651, and died without will or heirs when the land escheated; that Richard Lee, deceased, father of the said Richard Lee, had died seized of the land (and was presumed to have had a title, though evidence does not remain), and by his will of the 6th February, 1663, gave this land to his son William Lee, but without any words of inheritance,[1] who held the

[1] Evidently refers to decisions of the English courts, that unless there were words of perpetuity added to a devise of land, the devisee would only have an estate for life, and that the fee would descend to the heir-at-law.

land until his death, and that Bartholomew Schrever, of Northumberland County, now holds the land under a devise of the said William Lee, who clearly had a title only for life; and that the land is now due to the said Richard Lee, the younger, as heir-at-law of his father, Richard Lee, deceased."

To William Lee was devised by his father's will "all that land on the Maryland side whereon George English is now seated." The tract, called "Bishop's Neck," was a part of the general bequest to the three younger sons, and was situated at Dividing Creeks. The records of Northumberland show that William Lee was a Burgess in 1680–93, and a Justice in 1690.

Bishop Meade has mentioned a tankard, "The gift of Bartholomew Shriver, who died in 1720, and of Bartholomew, his son, who died in 1727, for the use of the parish of Great Wycomico, in the county of Northumberland, 1728."—(*Old Churches, Families, &c., II. 134.*)

The will of Bartholomew Schrever (dated the 21st of March, 1720), mentioned his wife Mary and son Bartholomew; left "5£ to Wicomico Church, to be used towards buying Communion plate;" also 10£ to buy "tenn" mourning rings; for Mr. Richard Lee, Mr. Charles Lee and wife, Mr. Thomas Waddy and wife, Mr. Thomas Heath and wife, for "sister Bol," and for Sam'l Heath and wife. Residue of his estate to his son.

Bartholomew Schrever, Jr. (will dated 14 December, 1727; probated in April, 1728), gave 25£ to Mary Heath, daughter of his brother Sam'l Heath, to be paid when 16, or at marriage, whichever should first happen; to Elizabeth, daughter of his dec'd brother, Thomas Heath, also 25£ on same terms; To Wicomico Church, £5 to be added to the £5 already given by his father; 50 acres of land to his brother, Sam'l Heath. Residue of estate to the lawful male issue of his daughter, Elizabeth. In default of such issue, the estate to pass to brother, Sam'l Heath, who was appointed sole executor. (North'd County Records.)

ELIZABETH [2] and ANNE [2]. Of the two daughters of Col. Richard Lee, there are only data concerning one, Anne. "Thomas Youell of Nominy in Ye County of Westmoreland and Anne Youell, wife of Ye s^d^ Thomas, one of ye daughters of Coll: Rich^d^ Lee late of Stratford Langthorn in Ye Co: of Essex deceased," executed a deed of release unto "John Lee of Lower Machotocks in Ye County of Westmoreland son and heir apparent and one of Ye Exe's of Ye afr^sd^: Rich^d^: Lee deceased" in which they relinquished all claim to any share in the estate of Col. Richard Lee. Dated 23d June, 1673. The will of "Captain Thomas Youell of the parish of Cople, Westmoreland, Gentleman," named wife Anne, daughter Winifred English and her son Youell English, daughter Watts and her son Youell Watts, daughter Spence and her son Youell Spence. Dated 7th December, 1694; probated, Westmoreland, 29th May, 1695.

Having given all the data to be found concerning those children of Colonel Richard Lee, who did not apparently leave any male issue in America, the three sons, who have been proven to have left male issue, will be taken up *seriatim*. As each of these three sons has left a distinct male line, they will be sketched separately; thus avoiding confusion where similar names occur so frequently in each line. These three lines are called:

i, The Stratford. Including the descendants of Richard and Lætitia (Corbin) Lee, which embraces the Lees of Westmoreland, Stafford, Prince William, Loudoun, etc., in Virginia, and those of Maryland.
ii, The Ditchley. Embracing all the descendants of Hancock Lee.
iii, The Cobbs Hall. Embracing the descendants of Charles Lee.

## STRATFORD LINE, SECOND GENERATION.

### Colonel Richard Lee.

2. Richard [2], the second son of Richard and Anna Lee, was the eldest son to leave male issue in Virginia; he was born in 1647, most probably at "Paradise," in Gloucester County, and died on the 12th of March, 1714, at his home, "Mt. Pleasant," in Westmoreland. As mentioned previously, this estate, consisting of about 2,600 acres, had been bequeathed by the Immigrant to his eldest son, John, and was inherited by Richard as heir-at-law to their father.

An old manuscript has stated that "the eldest of the two sons [of the Immigrant] afterwards removed to Westmoreland and established himself at 'Mt. Pleasant' on the River Potomac. The large brick house, largely inclosed by a brick wall, was burned down and another was built on the surrounding heights of the Potomac." The date of this fire is not known, but it must have occurred between 1716 and 1730. Thomas Lee obtained a lease of this estate in 1716, and apparently lived there until he built the Stratford mansion. It seems likely that the loss by fire, mentioned by William Lee, occurred at "Mt. Pleasant," not at Stratford, as has been generally supposed. There is no record of a fire ever having occurred at the latter place; while frequent mention has been made "of the burnt house fields," at the former, evidently showing that the fire there had been so serious that the field had been named as a record of the disaster. The new

Rich^d Lee

house, built further back from the river and upon higher ground, was probably erected by George Lee when he came from England to settle in Virginia. It, too, has been burned. The present proprietor of "Mt. Pleasant" has built a very handsome mansion, not far from the old "Lee Hall," in all respects a complete and elegant house, with the most modern improvements. It is a pleasure to see an old estate, now past its two hundredth year, so well kept up, and still the seat of good old Virginia hospitality.

Richard Lee was educated at Oxford, and may have studied law at one of the London "Inns," but of this nothing is known. "He was so clever," said his grandson, "that some great men offered to promote him to the highest dignities in the Church if his Father would let him stay in England; but this offer was refused, as the old Gentleman was determined to fix all his children in Virginia. . . . Richard spent almost his whole life in study, and usually wrote his notes in Greek, Hebrew, or Latin . . . ; so that he neither diminished nor improved his paternal estate. . . . He was of the Council in Virginia and also other offices of honor and profit, though they yielded little to him."

A complete record of Richard's official positions is not obtainable, but sufficient data have been found to make it highly probable that he held important posts almost continuously from about 1675 to his death. He was certainly a member of the Council in 1676, 1680–83–88, 1692–98, and there does not appear to be any reason against the supposition that he was a member at later dates.[1] He was a Burgess in 1677, and probably earlier. In a list of officers, dated on the 8th of June, 1699, it was stated that "Richard Lee, Esqr., had been appointed by Sir Edm: Andros, Governor, &c., to be Naval Officer and Receiver of Virginia Dutys for the River Potomac, in which is included Westmoreland, Northumberland, and Stafford Counties." In 1680 mention was made of "Coll: Richard Lee, of the Horse in ye Counties of Westmoreland, Northumberland, and Stafford."

In a letter, dated the 10th of June, 1691, Governor Nicholson reported to the English government that Richard Lee, Isaac Allerton, and John Armistead, out of a scruple of conscience, had refused to take the oaths and had in consequence been dropped from the Council (Sainsbury's *Abstracts*). This scruple of conscience arose from their attachment to the Stuarts, and was a refusal to acknowledge the claim of William and Mary to the throne of England. Richard Lee apparently changed his mind, for he was soon after restored to his place in the Council.

[1] II *Hening*, 563, 569; III *Hening*, 557. I *Va. Cal. State Papers*, 21, 85.

Nathaniel Bacon, Jr., "the first Virginia rebel," as he has been called, issued a lengthy proclamation, in the name of "ye People,"giving a list of grievances of "ye Commonality" against Governor Berkeley and his faction. The proclamation concludes in these words: "And we doe further declare these ye ensueing p'sons in this list to haue beene his wicked and pernicious councell[rs] Confederates, aiders and assisters ag[t] ye Commonality in these our Civill comotions." Then follows a list of some sixteen prominent men, among them Philip Ludwell, John Page, Christopher Wormeley, Robert Beverley, Richard Lee, and others of like standing; all of whom were ordered to surrender themselves or be seized as "Trayters to ye King and Country" (Neil, *Va. Carolorum*, 365).

In a report to the English government (under date of the 15th of March, 1677–8) of those who had suffered by Bacon's rebellion, this was given: "Major Richard Lee, a Loyall Discreet Person worthy of the Place to which hee was lately advanced of being one of his Majesties Council in Virginia, and as to his loses wee are credibly informed they were very great and that hee was Imprisoned by Bacon above seaven weekes together at least 100 miles from his owne home whereby hee received great Prejudice in his health by hard usage and very greatly in his whole Estate by his absence."

In a letter to the justices of the Westmoreland Court, recorded on the 15th of August, 1677, he mentions his imprisonment and laments his poor health. "About this time twelve month, some three or four days before I was taken prisoner," and adds that he had not been "soe well in health as I could wish."

Beverley, the historian, mentions that "Col. Richard Lee, one of the Council, a Man of Note and an Inhabitant of the Northern Neck, privately made a Composition with the Proprietors [of the Northern Neck] for his own Land. This broke the Ice and several were induced to follow so great an Example" (*History of Virginia*, London, 1722, p. 84).

Patents for land in Virginia, were at first granted by the governor as representative of the Crown; later, when parts of Virginia had been given to certain Lords, favorites of the King, the settlers were required to pay the fees formerly due the Crown to the agents of these Proprietors. These grants to Proprietors caused much dissatisfaction in Virginia; it is this that Beverley refers to in the above quotation. By marriage with a daughter of Lord Culpeper, the proprietorship of the Northern Neck passed into the possession of Thomas, 6th, Lord Fairfax.

Governor Spotswood described Richard Lee, as "a gentleman of as fair character as any in the country for his exact justice, honesty and unexceptional loyalty. In all the stations wherein he has served in this government, he has behaved himself with great integrity and sufficiency; and when his advanced age would no longer permit him to execute to his own satisfaction the duty of Naval Officer of the same district, I thought I could not better reward his merit than by bestowing that employment on his son." (1 *Spotswood*, 178.)

Richard Lee married (it is said in 1674), Lætitia, the eldest daughter of Henry Corbin, and Alice Eltonhead, his wife; Lætitia was born in 1657, and died on the 6th of October, 1706. Their tombstone is still to be seen at "Mt. Pleasant;" it is a very large slab of hard white marble. The inscription has been almost effaced, which is not to be wondered at, as it has been exposed to the weather for almost one hundred and eighty years. It rested on a low brick foundation, which has partially fallen. The wall, which once surrounded this graveyard, can now be traced by removing a little earth; it enclosed a lot of about 20x25 feet, and was located some three hundred yards in the rear of the first mansion. Some bricks, scattered about, indicate where the old house once stood, and some remains of an old orchard are to be found.

Bishop Meade visited this spot many years ago, and wrote of it:[1] "From a tombstone in the Burnt House Fields, at Mount Pleasant, Westmoreland county, where are yet to be seen the foundations of large buildings, are the following:"

Hic conditur corpus Richardi Lee, Armigeri, nati in Virginia, filii Richardi Lee, generosi, et antiqua familia, in Merton-Regis, in comitatu Salopiensi, oriundi.

In magistratum obeundo boni publici studiosissimi, in literis Græcis et Latinis et aliis humanioris literaturæ disciplinis versatissimi.

Deo, quem, summa observantia semper coluit, animam tranquillus reddidit XII. mo. die Martii, anno MDCCXIV, ætat LXVIII.

Hic, juxta, situm est corpus Lætitiæ ejusdem uxoris fidæ, filiæ Henrici Corbyn, generosi, liberorum matris amantissimæ, pietate erga Deum, charitate erga egenos, benignitate erga omnes insignis. Obiit Octob. die vi, MDCCVI, ætatis XLIX.

"Translated, it reads:

"Here lieth the body of Richard Lee, Esq., born in Virginia, son of Richard Lee, Gentleman, descended of an ancient family of Merton-Regis, in Shropshire. While he exercised the office of magistrate he was a zealous promoter of the public good. He was very skillful in the Greek and Latin languages and other parts of polite learning. He quietly resigned his soul to God, whom he always devoutly worshiped, on the 12th day of March, in the year 1714, in the 68th year of his age.

---

[1] *Old Churches, Families, etc.*, II, 152.

"Near by is interred the body of Lætitia, his faithful wife, daughter of Henry Corbyn, Gentleman. A most affectionate mother, she was also distinguished by piety toward God, charity to the poor, and kindness to all. She died on the 6th day of October, 1706, in the 49th year of her age."[1]

This burying ground was certainly used for several generations as the family burying place. Thomas Lee in 1749, Arthur Lee in 1792, and Richard Henry Lee in 1794, all desired to be buried there. At present only the one tombstone is to be seen; but Mrs. Charles Calvert Stuart, who visited the spot many years ago, has stated that she looked over the brick wall and that the lot was then full of graves.

In the inscription on the silver cup which he presented to his college, John Lee stated that his family came originally from "Morton-Regis," in Shropshire. On Richard's tombstone, as just quoted, this place was spelt, "Merton-Regis." It is certainly reasonable to assume that both brothers referred to the same place. But what place? There has been considerable speculation on this point. Mr. J. Henry Lea, already so frequently quoted, thinks "Nordley-Regis," an old seat of the Coton branch, was the place referred to. This view is supported by the fact that Eyton, in his history of Shropshire, suggests the possibility of "the vill of Morton" having been intended for Nordley. In one of the Harleian MSS. Nordley is called "Mordley."

On the other hand, others, among them Mr. George William Montague, think "Merriton," as given on Camden's map of 1695, was the place. Mr. Montague quotes Camden: "At Langley in Shropshire, one mile from the castle of Acton-Burnel, lowly situated in a woody park, is the seat of the Lees, one of the most ancient and honorable families in these parts." Langley was south of the city of Shrewsbury, near Condover. Within the hundred of Shrewsbury, and a féw miles north of the city, was the village of Merton, spelled Merriton on Camden's map of 1695. Near this village was an ancient seat of the Lees, named Lea Hall. As to the various spellings, Mr. Montague says: "Both were correct at the time. The mode of spelling was a matter of no significance provided the initial letter of the word remained unchanged."

It is worthy of notice that John located his later home in Virginia by naming the nearest parish church "Wickacomoco."

Richard Lee's will, dated 3d of March, 1714; probated, Westmoreland, 27th of April, 1715, was as follows:

---

[1] NOTE. Depositions, concerning the nuncupative will of Captain Henry Creyk, who died at Col. Richard Lee's on the Potomac, were made on the 6th of Sept., 1684, by Lettice Lee, aged 26 years, and Matilda Lee, aged 50 years. Lettice was undoubtedly Richard Lee's wife; but who was Matilda Lee?

MRS. RICHARD LEE.

In the name of God Amen. I Richard Lee of Cople parish[1] in the County of Westmoreland & Colony of Virginia being weak of body but of sound & perfect sence & memory (blessed be God for it) doe make & ordaine & declare this to be my last Will & Testament in manner & form following hereby revoking & making void all former Wills & Testaments by me made dated in Virginia this third day of March in the year of our Lord one thousand seven hundred and fourteen, and in the first year of the reign of our Soveraign Lord King George over Great Britaine &c. Imprimis I bequeath my Soul unto God that gave it me hoping by his infinite mercy & by my dear Saviour Jesus Christ his intercession & the merits of his passion it shall at the last day be reunited to my body and glorified and I will that my body have Christian & decent burial in my garden by or near the body of my dear wife deceased. Item I will that all my just debts be truly paid & as for my goods with which it hath pleased my good God to bless me beyond any desert of mine I give & bequeath them together with my lands as follows (vig$^{t}$.) Item I give to my eldest son Richard & his heirs forever 2600 acres of land in Cople parish in Westmoreland being the land whereon I now live & to include my next quarter with all the low land and bounded as follows: Beginning at my landing upon a branch of Machotique river near the mouth of a creek which makes the head of the sd. branch, being the beginning of a patent for 1000 acres of land granted to my honoured father dec'd. in the year 1650 and from my said landing extending up the sd. creek or head of the Eastermost branch of the Machotique river which divides this land from the land of Col. Willoughby Allerton reduced to a strait line East South East 500 poles to the West side of Peccatones field to a locust post which stands by or nigh the place where the Banquetting house formerly stood and from hence South South West 640 poles thence the same cours 16 poles to the corner thence East South East 80 poles thence South by East 120 poles to the road that leads to Flints mill or very near it thence South five degrees East 88 poles to a stone which lies in the sd. road from thence West South West to a marked hickory tree (being a corner tree dividing this land from some land I doe by this Will give to my son Henry) from the aforementioned stone 162 poles & from thence along the sd. dividing line North 18 degrees West 410 poles from thence North North East 162 poles to a locust post standing to the northward of the main road which this line has crossed 40 poles thence West North West to the cross roads at the white oak thence along the road leading to my house North 41 degrees East 40 poles thence North 16 degrees East 30 poles and North 19 degrees East 36 poles thence West North West 30 poles to a branch & down it to a locust post & thence West 14 poles to another locust post, being the beginning of the aforementioned dividing line between my two sons Richard & Henry, and from thence West North West 300 poles to a corner & thence North North East to Machotique river & thence down that river to the first mentioned Eastermost branch & up that to the beginning at my landing. Item I give to my son Phillip Lee & to his heirs forever all my right title & claim to a tract of land at Cedar point in Maryland called Lee's purchase late in the possession of Phillip Lynes and for which I have been at law some time but in case neither I in my life time nor my son Phillip afterwards doe recover the possession of the sd. tract of land then & in such case only my will is that my sons Richard Francis Thomas & Henry doe pay to my sd. son Phillip one hundred and thirty pounds that is to say my son Richard thirty pounds my son Francis thirty pounds my son Thomas forty pounds my son Henry thirty pounds. Item I give to my son Phillip and his heires forever a tract of land in Dorchester

[1] At this date Westmoreland County was divided into two parishes: Cople, in the lower part, and Washington, in the upper part. Cople Parish had two churches, Yeocomico and Nominy; Washington Parish contained three churches, Round Hill, Old Pope's Creek, and Leeds, or Bray's.

County on the Eastern shoar in Maryland and on the North West fork of Nanticoke river containing 1300 acres more or less and bounded as follows, Beginning at the upper corner of a larger dividend of land I have there being a marked hiccory & red oak upon the side of said fork of Nanticoke & from E. by N. halfe Noly. 349 poles thence South 20 pole thence East 228 poles thence South 86 Do. East 410 poles thence South 274 poles thence W. by S. 300 poles thence N. 41 degrees West 290 poles thence N. 85 degrees West 180 poles thence N. 35 degrees W. 18 poles thence W. by S. 214 poles to the river or fork side which line divides my now seated plantation in two parts & from thence up the said river or fork its several courses to the beginning. Item I give to my son Francis and the heires male of his body lawfully begotten forever all my lands & tenements in Gloucester County called Paradice and for default of such issue I give the said lands to my sd. son Francis and the heires of his body lawfully beggotten and for default of such issue then & in such case I give the said land to my son Phillip & his heires forever. Item I give to my son Thomas and his heirs forever all my lands in the County of Northumberland at or near the dividing creeks. Item I give to my son Thomas & his heires forever the residue of all my lands in the North West fork of Nanticoke river in Dorchester County in the Province of Maryland, adjoyning to the land here before given to my son Phillip being in two parcells & containing 1300 acres more or less. Item I give to my son Henry & his heires forever the residue of all my lands in Cople parish in Westmo'l'd. County, adjoyning to a tract of land of 2600 acres here before given to my son Richard and divided therefrom by dividing lines which I have caused Mr. Thomas Thompson the Surveyour to make. Item I give to my daughter Ann Fitzhugh all my right title and claim to a tract of land of 4000 acres in Stafford County pattented by my honoured father deceased which said land I give to my daughter Ann & her heires forever. Item I give to my son Francis all the cattle & hoggs & horses & mares which belongs to me & shall be found on my Paradice plantation in Gloster County at the day of my death. Item I give to my eldest son Richard Lee eight cowes & calves which he or his order may chuse out of my stocks on this & my next quarter plantation with one fifth part of the hoggs that shall be found at both these places at the day of my death. Item I give unto my sons Phillip Thomas & Henry all rest & residue of my stocks of cattle hoggs horses and mares which shall be found upon any of my plantations or that doe belong to me at the day of my death and are not before disposed of by this will, to be equally divided betwixt them three. Item I give to my son Phillip these negroes (vig't.) Judith Somebody & Lawrence at home Harry Alice Sambo & Susan, Marion's girl at my next quarter, with Carpenter Jack & Ralph at the Eastern Shoar. Item I give to my son Francis these negroes (vig't.) Betty Judith Peter Lettice Dick Norman Charles Tony Alice Nan & Isabel at Paradice with Sambo at home. Item I give to my son Thomas these negroes (vig't.) Susan Tom Natt Young Pegg Doctor Bab Nanne Betty's girl at home, Charles at dividing creek with Mole Nan Ben & Numa at my next quarter. Item I give to my son Henry these following negroes (vig't.) Betty Phill Harry & Sarah Beck's children Prue Betty's girl & Ned all at home Sharp at Eastern Shoar & Will Sarah Jack & Frank Nan's children & George & Diana at my next quarter. Item My will is that where I have given any females to any of my sons that to such respective son I give the increase of such female whether born before or after the making of this will and not given particularly in this will or delivered into the possession of any of my sons or daughter before the making of this will. Item I give to my son Henry old Peg. Item I give to my son Thomas my chest of drawers in my hall. Item I give to my sons Phillip & Thomas my little Shallop & furniture. Item I give to my sons Francis Thomas & Henry all the sheets & table linnen now in my house that is marked with one or both letters of their names and to each of them one doz: new plates & four sizable dishes all of pewter. Item I give to my sons Francis and Henry the standing beds and furniture in the hall chamber.

Item I give to my daughter Ann Fitzhugh Tony and Kate negroe children which I have put into her possession which with what I had before given her I give her as her filial portion. Item I give to my sons Phillip Francis Thomas and Henry all and every portion of my real and personal estate that is not by this Will already given to be equally divided between them each to have one fourth part. Item my will is that my estate remain undivided for one year after my death the negroes to work upon the lands they work on at the time of my death and if my executors hereafter named in Virginia think it convenient that my estate remain in the same state for one year longer I doe hereby will the same and that such of the Tobacco made upon my plantations by my negroes during they are undivided as is fitt for the London markett be consigned to my son Richard Lee in London and the remainder of the cropps to be disposed of in such marketts as my Virginia Ex's thinks fitt my will and desire being that the whole produce of my negroes crops dureing the afores'd time be carr'd to the joynt acco't of my sons Phillip Francis Thomas and Henry and equally divided amonst them except what is necessary in the discretion of my Ex'rs for the use of my plantations and my will and desire is that noe part of my estate be appraised or valued and I doe hereby constitute and appoint my son Rich'd Lee Merch't in London and my sons Thomas and Henry Lee in Virg'a my Ex'rs of this my last Will and Testament. In witness whereof I have hereunto sett my hand and seale and published the same my last Will and Testament the day and yeare first menconed in the same.

Though no mention is made in this will of the furniture, books, portraits, and other household effects, it is probable they were all inherited by the eldest son. An inventory of the personal property, mentions "in the hall, Richard Lee's picture, frame and curtain, G. Corbin's picture, the Quaker's picture, T. Corbin's picture." Among some silver were "six large spoons, marked squirrel." In the library, a large number of volumes were named, among them the best authors of Roman, Grecian, and French literature, volumes of sermons, treatises on history, law, religion, medicine, botany, agriculture, and kindred subjects.[1]

Richard and Lætitia (Corbin) Lee had seven children, whose names are given in his will (with one exception). They were:

i, JOHN[3], The parish register of old Christ church, Lancaster, records the baptism of "John Lee, son of Major Richard Lee and Mad'm Lettice, his wife, on the 3rd day of Xber, 1678." As no such son was named in his father's will, he probably died in infancy.

ii, RICHARD[3], See 3.

iii, PHILIP[3], See 4.

iv, FRANCIS[3], nothing is known of his life, excepting the mere mention of him in the wills of his father, brother and nephew. He was living as late as 1749, for his nephew mentioned him, at that date, as being

[1] A full list of this library may be found in the *William and Mary College Quarterly*, II, 247, *et seq.*

"now in possession" of his estate, Paradise. He left no male heirs, for his brother, Philip Lee, of Maryland, willed the reversion to Francis' estate to his own sons, thus: To "sons, Thomas and Richard and their heirs forever, to be equally divided between them, that tract of land in Gloucester county, Paradise; the reversion left me by my deceased father, Col. Richard Lee, of Virginia." One of these sons, Thomas (in his will, dated in August, 1749) bequeathed his "moiety of a tract of land lying in Virginia, called Paradise, now in the possession of Francis Lee, left me by my honored father, Philip Lee, Esquire, to my son Thomas Sim Lee, and my daughter Sarah Brook Lee." Probably Francis never married; at any rate he had no male heirs as late as 1749, or the reversion to his estate could not have been devised.

v, THOMAS[3], See 5.

vi, HENRY[3], See 6.

vii, ANN[3], born ——; died in 1732; was twice married; first, to Col. William Fitzhugh, of "Eagle's Nest," King George county, by whom she had one son and two daughters: 1, Henry Fitzhugh, born ——; died the 6th of December, 1742; married Lucy, daughter of Robert Carter, of "Corotoman," and left issue; amongst others, a daughter, "Betsy," born the 20th of April, 1731, and married, on the 12th of February, 1747, Benjamin Grymes; they had a daughter who was twice married; first to William Randolph, and next, to Col. William K. Meade, and was the mother of the Rev. William Meade, Bishop of the Episcopal Church in Virginia. His son, William Fitzhugh of "Chatham," born the 24th of August, 1741; died some years after the Revolutionary war; was a near neighbor and trusted friend of Washington; he married Anne, only daughter of Peter and Lucy (Bolling) Randolph, of "Chatsworth," Henrico county, and left two daughters and one son; the eldest, Anne, married Judge William Craik[1] of Maryland; the second, Mary, married George Washington Parke Custis, of Arlington, and was the mother of Mary Anne Randolph Custis, who married Robert Edward Lee; the son, William Henry Fitzhugh, of "Ravensworth," Fairfax county, married on the 10th of January, 1814, Anna Maria Sarah, second daughter of the Hon. Charles Goldsborough (born 15th July, 1765; died 13th De-

---

1 The Hon. William Craik was the eldest son of Dr. James and Mariamne (Ewell) Craik; Dr. Craik was born in Scotland about 1730; came to Virginia in 1750; served on the expedition of General Braddock; was a life-long friend of Washington, and one of his physicians during his last illness. He died in Fairfax county the 6th of February, 1814. (Hayden, *Va. Genealogies*, 341.)

cember, 1834), and Elizabeth Goldsborough, his first wife; Mrs. Fitzhugh was born the 15th of November, 1796; died in April, 1874, without issue, when the estates passed to the children of Mr. Fitzhugh's niece, Mrs. Robert E. Lee. 2, Lettice Fitzhugh, born the 15th of July, 1707; died the 10th of February, 1732; married, on the 16th of March, 1727, George Turberville, of "Hickory Hill," Westmoreland; apparently left no issue. 3, Sarah Fitzhugh, who married, on the 5th of January, 1736, Edward Barradall, once attorney-general and judge of the Admiralty Court of Virginia.

Second marriage of Ann Lee: After the death of Col. William Fitzhugh, which occurred about 1713–14, his widow married Captain Daniel McCarty, of "the Parish of Cople in the Co: of West'd Esq[r]." He was born in 1679; died the 4th of May, 1724, his tomb is still to be seen at old Yeocomico Church; Captain McCarty was Burgess, Justice and Sheriff for Westmoreland; in 1715–20, he was Speaker of the Assembly. Ann (Lee-Fitzhugh) McCarty in her will (dated the 7th of November, 1728; probated at Westmoreland, the 31st of May, 1732) mentioned her son, Col. Henry Fitzhugh, her brother-in-law Henry Fitzhugh, her brothers, Thomas, Henry, and Richard Lee, her daughter Lettice, also Elizabeth, daughter of Major John Fitzhugh, her sons, Billington and Thaddeus McCarty, also her daughter Sarah Fitzhugh, Col. John Tayloe, and Sarah Beale. She appointed her son, Henry Fitzhugh, and her brothers, Thomas and Henry Lee, her executors. To her son, Henry, she left her "grandfather Corbyn's wedding ring." (Hayden, *Va. Genealogies*, 86, 87.)

## THE CORBIN FAMILY.

Arms: Sable, on a chief or, three ravens, proper.

The records of the "College of Arms" at London mention that one "Robert Corbin gave lands to the Abbey of Ealesworth between the years 1 and 7 Henry II., A. D. 1154–61." From this Robert, the record continues ten generations to one "Nicholas Corbin seized of Hall End and other Lands in the County of Warwick (*jure uxoris*), 1 Richard III., and 14 Henry VIII." Four generations afterwards is found, "Thomas Corbin of Hall End afores'd, born 24 May, 1594; died in June, 1637, bur'd at Kingswinford." This Thomas married in 1620, Winefred, daughter of Gawen Grosvenor, of Sutton Colfield co. Warwick. From this union, sprang Henry Corbin, the progenitor of the Virginia family; he was the third son, was born in 1629 (according to an affidavit), and died in Virginia, on the 8th of January, 1675. He came to Virginia about 1654 and settled first in the parish of Stratton Major, in King and Queen county; he appears to have taken up lands in Lancaster, Westmoreland, Middlesex and other counties; was a Burgess from Lancaster in 1659; a Justice for Middlesex in 1673; and a member of the Council as early as 1663; later he was seated at "Peckatone" in Westmoreland county. The patent for Peckatone was dated 26th of March, 1664. "Peckatom or Peckatone, an Indian name," says a writer on Westmoreland, "was a magnificent estate, owned by the Corbins. The house, built of imported brick, within a few yards of the river bank, shaded by old forest trees, grounds laid off on a large scale, it bore some years ago, more the appearance of a proud aristocratic residence than any other in the county. Since then the estate has been sold and the family scattered. Many wild stories were told, in my youth, of how a lady owner played the part of a petty tyrant among her overseers and negroes, confining the former in her dungeons beneath the house, and the latter sometimes whipped to death! How she traveled at night in her coach and four, armed with pistols and guns. How, in the last day of her recklessness, she, her coach and coachmen were borne aloft in a terrible hurricane, and lost to sight. From that day the house remained unoccupied for years. Then, in popular opinion, it was haunted; lights were seen passing from room to room, and awful groans and shrieks at night would assail the ear of the luckless traveler, who happened to be in its vicinity."

*Richard Corbin,*
*Laneville, Virginia.*

It has been a family tradition that Henry Corbin was married several times, but there is record only of one marriage; on the 25th of July, 1645,[1] he married Alice, daughter of Richard Eltonhead, of Eltonhead, co. Lancaster, England. It is said she was then the widow of Roland Burnham; after Henry Corbin's death, she married Captain Henry Creek, who died about August of 1684, "at the house of Col. Richard Lee on the River Potomac."

[1] If Henry Corbin was married only once, and that wife was the widow of Roland Burnham, first of York and later of Lancaster, then he could not have married before 1656. The records show that Capt. Roland Burnham was a Burgess in 1644-45-46-49. His will, dated the 12th of February, 1655; probated, in Lancaster, on the 14th of January, 1656, mentions children, Thomas, John, Eleanor, Francis, and wife, Alice. Several documents, recorded at Lancaster, show that Alice, the widow of Roland Burnham, married Henry Corbin, of Middlesex. (*Va. Mag. of History*, etc., I. 257, Notes.) But was she his first wife?

Henry Corbin, the Virginia immigrant, left three sons—Henry, Thomas, Gawin, and five daughters—Lætitia, Alice, Winifred, Anne, and Frances. The eldest son, Henry, died when two years old; the second, Thomas, settled at London, as a merchant, probably in partnership with his uncle, Gawin; for under date of the 22d of July, 1675, "Gawin Corbin Cittizen Leather Seller of London," appointed his "trusty and well beloved friend Richard Lee, Esq., of Virginia," his attorney to collect debts due him from John Frodsham, of Potomac River. He was living at London in 1722, and probably as late as 1732, for in that year a Thomas Corbin executed deeds; this latter Thomas might have been a cousin, the son of Gawin of London. Apparently Thomas Corbin never married, as his lands were eventually inherited and devised by his younger brother, Gawin of Virginia. Henry Corbin's daughters must have been older than the sons; were certainly so if he married only once. They married as follows: Lætitia, Richard Lee, of "Mt. Pleasant," Westmoreland, which estate adjoined "Peckatone;" Alice, Philip Lightfoot; Winifred, Le Roy Griffin; Anne, William Tayloe; Frances, Gov. Edmund Jenings, of Rippon in Virginia.

From Henry Corbin's youngest son, Gawin (possibly youngest child), are descended the Virginia family. He was a prominent man in the Colony; was Burgess in 1700, 1702, 1718, and probably in 1736; also a member of the Council. Richard of Laneville in a letter (preserved in his letter book) states that his "father Gawin Corbin died on the 1st of January, 1745." It is said that he was married several times; he was certainly married twice, and probably three times. His first wife was Catharine, daughter of Ralph Wormeley (probably by his first wife, Catharine Lunsford), no issue; he married, secondly, Jane, daughter and co-heir of John Lane, of York River, and widow of Willis Wilson—she was living as late as 1715; by this wife he had issue; possibly she was the mother of all his children. Bishop Meade has stated that "Gawin Corbin, the other son of Henry Corbin, and once President of the Council, married a daughter of William Bassett, and left seven children," etc.[1] The Va. *Gazette* gives notice of the death on the 12th of June, 1738, of Martha, wife of Col. Gawin Corbin of King and Queen county. William Bassett, second of the name in Virginia, had a daughter, Martha, born the 28th of December, 1694 (Keith). This Gawin certainly left three sons, Richard, John, and Gawin; as to the number of his daughters there is some uncertainty. Bishop Meade has stated that he had four, and that they married: Jenny, Col. John Bushrod,

---

[1] *Old Churches, Families*, etc., II, 146.

Burgess, Westmoreland, 1748–55, and had, among others, Hannah, who married John Augustine Washington; Joanna, Major Robert Tucker; Alice, Benjamin Needles; and Anne, Willoughby Allerton. His three sons, just named, married and (probably) had issue as follows:

i, Richard, "of Laneville in King and Queen county in Virginia, eldest son, President of the King's Council and Receiver General of the King's Quit Rents in Virginia, 1776. Living in 1783, aged about 75" (family chart). He married, in 1737, Elizabeth, daughter of John Tayloe, of Mt. Airy, Richmond county; she died in 1784, and left issue, three daughters and five sons; the eldest daughter married Carter Braxton; the other two, Alixia and Lætitia, died unmarried. The five sons married as follows: 1, Gawin, of "Buckingham House," Middlesex, was educated abroad, returned to Virginia about 1761, was a member of the Council 1775, Burgess 1769; married Joanna Tucker, probably his first cousin, and had three daughters, one of whom, Betsy, it is said, married George Lee Turberville; Felicia, Orris Chilton; Martha, —— Beale. 2, John Tayloe, was Burgess from King and Queen county 1769, 1772; married Mary, daughter of Benjamin Waller, and died in 1793, leaving issue, of whom later. 3, Richard, was unmarried in 1783, aged about 32. 4, Thomas, also unmarried in 1783, aged about 28. 5, Francis, of "The Reeds," Caroline county, who died on the 15th of June, 1821, aged 62 years; was educated at Canterbury School, Cambridge, and later studied law at the Inner Temple, and returned to Virginia about 1783; he was a frequent member of the House of Delegates and also of the Convention of 1788; he married Anna Munford, daughter of Robert Beverley, of "Wakefield," Culpeper county, and Maria Carter, his wife; they had issue: Robert, Francis Porteus, William Lygon, John Sawbridge, Washington Shirley, and Thomas Grosvenor; their daughter, Anna Page Corbin, married her first cousin, Benjamin Franklin Randolph.

ii, John, of "Portobago," Essex county, was born the 8th of July, 1715; died the 8th of August, 1757; married (about 1737) Lettice, eldest daughter of Richard and Martha (Silk) Lee, of London (see 3, ii), and had two daughters, Martha and Jane, and one son, Gawin, of "Yew Spring," Caroline county. John Corbin was the presiding justice for Essex in 1742, and member of the Council in 1775. His son, Gawin, married, in 1776, Betsy, daughter of Thomas Jones, of Northumberland county, and was the grandfather of Mr. Augustus G. W. Corbin, of that county. His sister, Martha, born the 19th of November, 1738, died the 8th of January, 1792; married her first cousin, John Turberville, of

"Hickory Hill," Westmoreland, and had ten children (see Turberville under 3).

iii, Gawin, of "Peckatone," Westmoreland, the third son of Gawin, inherited the property of his uncle, Thomas of London; he married Hannah, daughter of Thomas Lee, of Stratford, and left an only daughter, Martha, who married, on the 1st of June, 1769, George Richard Turberville, and had two sons, Gawin Corbin and Richard Lee. Gawin Corbin married a daughter of Col. John Daingerfield, and had a daughter, Mary, who married William F. Taliaferro, and left issue. The younger son, Richard Lee Turberville, married, about the 14th of December, 1794, his cousin, Henrietta, daughter of Richard Henry Lee, of "Chantilly," by his second wife, Anne (Gaskins) Pinkard (for their issue see Turberville). Gawin Corbin died about January, 1760; his will is given here in full; he names only brother Richard and sister "Tucker," but mentions "brothers and sisters."

In the name of God, Amen. I Gawin Corbin in the parish of Cople and County of Westmoreland, being weak of body but of sound sence and Memory, Blessed be God, do this twenty ninth day of October, . . . year of our Lord One Thousand Seven Hundred and . . . [fifty-nine?] . . . and publish this my last Will and Testament in manner following:

First, I desire to be buried privately and without pomp. Item, I lend all my Estate both real and personal to my dear wife during her widdowhood and Continence in this County, allowing my daughter Martha Corbin out of my Estate a Genteel Education and mentainance at the discretion of my Executors hereafter mentioned: but if my wife continues a widow until my Daughter Martha Corbin marries or comes to the age of one and twenty years, then it is my will and desire that she my said Daughter shall have one-half of my whole Estate, and if my wife marries again or leaves this County, then and in that case, my will and desire is that my said wife shall be deprived of the bequest already made her and in lieu thereof shall only have one third of my Estate real and personal, and the remaining two-thirds of my Estate shall immediately pass to my said Daughter Martha Corbin, and the heirs of her body lawfully begotten forever, and in default of such heirs, I give one half of my estate unto my brother Richard Corbin's two youngest sons and to their heirs forever and the other half of my Estate to the two youngest sons of my Dear sister Tucker, if it should so happen that she has more than two sons, but if not then I would have this half of my estate descend to her youngest son and his or their heirs forever, as the case may be. Item, my will and desire is that at the death of my dear wife that my whole estate both real and personal then in her possession shall descend to my Daughter Martha Corbin and the heirs of her body lawfully begotten forever, and for want of such heirs then to descend to the younger sons of my Brother Richard Corbin and . . . . . sister Tucker in manner as is before mentioned . . . . . . . .—rying again . . . . . . the County, or my Daughter's dying without heirs of her body lawfully begotten. Item, I give twenty pounds stirling to be sent for in Course goods to the Poor of the parish of Cople, such who have many children and use their utmost endeavors to support them by honest Labour and Industry, but still find themselves from their numerous family incapable; and this bequest

I will have distributed at the discretion of my Executors. Item, it is my Express desire that my Daughter Martha Corbin do not marry untill she arrives at the age of twenty one years and then not without the Consent of the Guardians or the majority of them, which if she does I desire that my estate may immediately descend to the youngest sons of my Brother Richard Corbin and my sister Tucker, as I have before directed and my Daughter Martha to have but one shilling of my Estate; this I desire that a prudent Choice may be made of a man of sense and Family—that she may live Happily in a matrimonial state. Item, I desire all my just debts may be paid as soon as possible. Item, my will and desire is that my Godson Thomas Lee, son of Richard Henry Lee, may be paid one hundred and fifty pounds sterling to be applied to accomplishing his Education when he is sent home. Item, my will is further that if my Crops should not be sufficient to pay my debts, then I would have my Caroline lands sold to pay them and it is my Express desire that Edy, Truelove and Cyrus, three of my negroes, be sent to the West Indies and sold, and the money arising from the sale of them to be applyed to the payment of my . . . . and this I will have done as soon as . . . opportunity . . . . . . decease. Item, I do hereby . . . . and appoint my wife, Colonel Richard Henry Lee, Thomas Ludwell Lee, Francis Lightfoot Lee and Richard Corbin, Executors of my will and Guardians of my Daughter Martha Corbin. Item, I give all my Brothers and Sisters, Nephews and Nieces a mourning ring apiece of a guinea value. Item, It is my desire that my Brother Richard Henry Lee may be one of my acting Executors. Item, my will and desire is that my Estate may not be appraised, as it may be attended with useless and unnecessary expense, trouble and Confusion.

[Probated, at Westmoreland, on 29th of January, 1760. In accordance with the requirements of this will, consent to the marriage of George Turberville and Martha Corbin were filed: from Thomas Ludwell Lee, R. H. Lee and Hannah Corbin, on the 23d of May, 1769; from Francis Lightfoot Lee on 16th of May, 1769.]

The later generations of this family in Virginia are descended from John Tayloe, second son of Richard and Elizabeth (Tayloe) Corbin; he married Mary, daughter of Benjamin Waller, of Williamsburg, and had four sons, and three daughters. His eldest son, Richard, inherited the family estates of Laneville, Moss Neck, Farley Vale, and others; served as a captain of artillery in 1812; died on 10th of June, 1819, aged 48 years; married Rebecca, daughter of James Parke Farley, and Elizabeth Byrd, his wife, and had three daughters and two sons. (The coat of arms, given above, was that used by him; it represents the arms of the Corbin family quartered with Tayloe bearing in an escutcheon of pretence the arms of Farley quartering Parke.) His second son, James Parke Corbin, born in 1808, died on the 28th of November, 1868; was twice married; first to Jane Catharine, daughter of John S. Wellford, of Fredericksburg, and next to Eliza Lewis Hoomes of Bowling Green; he had ten children; his second son, Spotswood Wellford Corbin (the present head of the family) was born the 22d of January, 1835; served in the Confederate navy, and is now the President of the Virginia State Board of Agriculture; he resides at "Farley Vale," in King George county. Mr. Corbin married Diana Fontaine, the second daughter of Com. Matthew F. Maury, the distinguished scientist, and has one surviving son, Matthew Maury Corbin.

## THE FITZ-HUGH FAMILY.

Arms: Azure, three chevrons brased in base, or, and a chief or.
Crest: A wyvern with wings expanded, argent.

"Although," says Burke, "the surname of Fitz-Hugh was not appropriated to this family before the time of Edward III., it had enjoyed consideration from the period of the Conquest: when its ancestor, Bardolph, was Lord of Ravenswath, with divers other manors, in Richmondshire." From this ancestor, the family is traced, from father to son, through the following generations: Bardolph was succeeded by his son Akaris Fitz-Bardolph; he by Hervey Fitz-Akaris; he by Henry Fitz-Hervey; then Randolph Fitz-Henry, Henry Fitz-Randolph, Randolph Fitz-Henry, who was succeeded by his brother Hugh Fitz-Henry; he died in 1304, and was followed by his son, Henry Fitz-Hugh, the first to bear the surname of Fitz-Hugh, which name has been adopted by his descendants to this day.

This Henry Fitz-Hugh followed the Edwards II. and III. in their Scottish wars; he was summoned by writ to parliament, as Baron Fitz-Hugh, in 1321, being the first to bear that title. He died in 1356, and was succeeded by his grandson, Henry; from whom the male line continued in unbroken succession till the death of George, the seventh Baron, when the barony "fell into abeyance." The Barons Fitz-Hugh took prominent parts in the political and military movements of their day; were summoned, generation after generation, to the various parliaments, and held other positions of trust and responsibility.

The progenitor of the well known Virginian branch of this family, was Colonel William Fitzhugh, who was the son of Henry, a lawyer of Bedford, England. He was born in the town of Bedford, on the 9th of January, 1651, and died at his home "Bedford," in Stafford county, in October, 1701. He came to Virginia about 1670; was a lawyer of prominence, a large planter, merchant and shipper. He married, on the 1st of May, 1674, Sarah Tucker, who was born in Westmoreland county on the 2d of August, 1663; she was therefore at the time of her marriage not quite eleven years old. It is said that her husband sent her to England, immediately after their marriage, to complete her education. Colonel Fitzhugh left six children, among whom he divided a very large estate. His children were:

i, WILLIAM, of "Eagle's Nest," who died in 1713–14; he married Ann, only daughter of Richard and Lætitia (Corbin) Lee, of "Mt. Pleasant," Westmoreland, and had issue as previously stated (p. 82).

ii, HENRY, born the 15th of January, 1686; died the 12th of December, 1758; married, on the 24th of February, 1718, Susanna, a daughter of Mordecai Cooke, of Gloucester county; she was born the 7th of December, 1693; died the 21st of November, 1749. They had a son Thomas, of "Boscobell," who was twice married; first, on the 18th of October, 1746, to Catharine Booth, who died in February, 1748; he next married Sarah, a daughter of the Rev. David Stuart, of King George county, and had two children: 1, Susannah, who married (1766) William Knox, of "Windsor Lodge," Culpeper county, the progenitor of that family in Virginia. 2, Thomas, of "Boscobell," who married Ann, daughter of Col. John Rose, of Amherst county; their son, William Henry, left a daughter, Ann Eliza Fitzhugh, who married Joseph Burwell Ficklen, of Fredericksburg, and their daughter, Ann Eliza Ficklen, married Captain Daniel Murray Lee (see 74).

iii, THOMAS, who married Anne, a daughter of Colonel George Mason, of Stafford county (second of the name and grandfather of the celebrated George Mason, of "Gunston"). He died in June, 1715.

iv, GEORGE, who married Mary Mason, a sister of his brother's wife; their son, William Fitzhugh, married Mrs. Martha (Lee) Turberville, the daughter of Richard and Martha (Silk) Lee, of London, and the widow of George Turberville, of Westmoreland; they had, at least, one son, George Lee Mason Fitzhugh, who has left descendants.

v, JOHN, born ——; died the 21st of January, 1733; he married Ann Barbara, a daughter of Capt. Daniel McCarty, of Westmoreland; they had issue: William, born the 13th of April, 1725; Daniel, born the 28th of June, 1733. His sister-in-law (Ann Lee Fitzhugh) mentioned in her will, a daughter, Elizabeth.

vi, ROSAMOND, who married a Colonel Allerton, or Ollerton, of Westmoreland, and died without issue.

The family seats of the Fitzhughs, in Virginia, were named after the ancestral estates in England; such as "Belle Air," "Boscobell," "Chatham," "Marmion," "Ravensworth," and "Ravenswood." The list of the grandchildren of Colonel William Fitzhugh, the progenitor of the Virginia family, is probably very incomplete; from these grandchildren a very numerous family has descended.

# STRATFORD LINE, THIRD GENERATION.

## Richard Lee, of London.

3. Richard, the oldest surviving son of Richard Lee[1] (Richard[2]) and Lætitia Corbin, his wife, was born about 1678–9, and died at London in 1718. Somewhere about 1710–11 he had gone over to London and settled there as a Virginia merchant in partnership with his maternal uncle, Thomas Corbin. Very little information can be found concerning him. By the kindness of William Blackstone Lee, Esq., the few items following were copied from the London records:

1719. Richard Lee died in the parish of St. Anne within the Liberty of Westminster, intestate. On the 8th of November, 1711, Wm. Ellins and Edmund Farrington sold to the said Ric. Lee all their wares, merchandises, &c. Ric. Perry of the parish of St. Catharine Creechurch, London, merchant, was appointed administrator of the goods of the said Ric. Lee as far as concerned the said merchandises. Given at London 2d January, 1718–19.

1724. On the 16th of November, 1724, there was issued a commission to John Crabb, creditor of the late Richard Lee, late of the parish of St. Olave, Hart Street, London, but who died in the parish of St. Anne Westminster in Co: Midd. Martha Lee, the relict and George, Martha, and Lætitia Lee, minors, children of the deceased, cited but not appearing.

On the 5th of November, 1716, "Richard Lee, of London, son of Richard Lee of Cople parish, in Virginia," leased to Reuben Welch, Thomas Lee and Henry Lee, of Essex, the 2,600 acres whereupon his father had lived. "Yielding and paying therefor the yearly rent of one peper corn only on the feast day of the birth of Our Lord God." This lease is mentioned in the will of Thomas Lee. In a petition from "Martha Lee, widow of the late Richard Lee, of London," dated the 19th of October, 1720, she mentioned this lease of 1716, and stated that her husband was the son of Richard Lee, Sen'r, &c.; gave her residence in "Goodman's Fields, parish of St. Mary White Chappel, Middlesex," England. William Lee (in 1771) stated that, "Richard married an heiress in England by the name of Silk, and by her left one son, George, and two daughters, Lettice and Martha; all of these children went to Virginia and settled. George married a Wormeley, who died leaving one daughter; he then married a Fairfax, nearly related to Lord Fairfax of Yorkshire, and died leaving by his last marriage three sons, that are now minors and are at school in England under care of Mr. James Russell. Lettice married a Corbin and her sister a Turberville; their eldest children intermarried, from which union, George Lee Turberville, now at school at Winton College, is the oldest issue." Richard Lee's wife was therefore named Martha Silk; they had three children:

i, GEORGE[4]. See 7.

ii, LETTICE[4], born at London about 1715; died the 15th of January, 1768, in Virginia, aged (it is said) 54 years; she married (probably about 1737) Col. John Corbin, of "Portobago," Essex county; they had two daughters—Martha and Jane—and one son, Gawin, of "Yew Spring," Caroline county. Martha Corbin, born the 19th of November, 1738; died the 8th of January, 1792; married her first cousin, John Turberville, and had ten children (see Turberville); Jane was probably the "Miss Jane Corbin" mentioned as having stood sponsor for George Lee Turberville in 1761.

iii, MARTHA[4], born at London about 1716; was twice married; first, to Major George Turberville, of "Hickory Hill," Westmoreland, and had a son, John Turberville, who was born the 14th of September, 1737; died the 10th of July, 1799; married, in 1759, his first cousin, Martha Corbin, as previously stated, and had ten children (see Turberville). After George Turberville's death, in 1742, Martha (Corbin) Turberville married Captain William Fitzhugh, of Maryland, and had one son, George Lee Mason.

NOTE.—Mr. Augustus G. W. Corbin, of Northumberland county, has some very interesting portraits of the Corbins. An account of them, sent by a lady of that county, is as follows:

Hon. John Corbin, in British uniform, with sword in hand, full-size portrait.

Wife of above, who was a Lee (Lettice?), taken in full dress, brocade silk, with much lace.

Gawin—a boy—with his sister Jane, said to be children of above.

Bettie Tayloe Corbin, married a Turberville, in full evening costume, brocade silk, handsome lace, decollete, an English face, full and florid, an exquisite arm and hand, which she displays to the best advantage by pointing to an imaginary object. (Painted by John Hesselius, 1755.)

## THE TURBERVILLES.

Arms: Ermine, a lion rampant, gules, crowned or.
Crest: A castle, argent, portcullis or.

The Virginia Turbervilles are said to be descended from the English family of Bere Regis, Dorset. On the "Battel-Abbey Roll" appears the name of a Sir Payne Turberville, who was a companion of the Conqueror, and is supposed to have been the progenitor of this family in England. The manor of Bere Regis was sold to Robert Turberville, for £608, 16s. 8d., in 38 Henry VIII., and was for years the seat and sepulchre of generations of this family. The hall of the manor house was adorned with the arms of Turberville, impaling those of the various families with whom they had intermarried. In the year 1633, a John Turberville died, aged 77, leaving a grandson, John, his heir, of whom no account is given in the family pedigree; he may have been the ancestor of the John Turberville who died in Virginia in 1728. As the family in Virginia used the arms of the Turbervilles of Bere Regis, it is most probable they were descended from them. The print, given here, is a copy of the book-plate of George Lee Turberville.

John Turberville, of Lancaster county, was a Justice in 1699, Burgess in 1703–4, Sheriff in 1705–7, and died in 1728. In a deed of 1726, he mentioned his son, George, as his sole heir. A daughter probably married Francis Kenner, as the latter mentioned in his will of 1725, his brother-in-law George Turberville.

George Turberville, of "Hickory Hill," Westmoreland, was a Justice in 1720, Sheriff in 1722–23, Clerk in 1726–42; he was married three times; first, to Elizabeth, a daughter of Henry Ashton, of Westmoreland, by whom he had, at least, one daughter, Elizabeth, as mentioned in the will of Henry Ashton. He married, secondly, on the 16th of March, 1727,

Lettice, the daughter of William and Ann (Lee) Fitzhugh; she was born the 15th of July, 1707; died the 10th of February, 1732, and was buried near "Hickory Hill;" her tombstone states that she "died great with child," but mentions no children. George Turberville married, thirdly, Martha, the daughter of Richard Lee, of London, and Martha Silk, his wife; after his death, which occurred in 1742, she married William Fitzhugh, of Maryland, a captain in the English army and had a son, George Lee Mason.

George Turberville's daughter by his first wife probably married Gowry Waugh, and had a son, George Waugh. The records of the Va. Court of Appeals show that Mrs. Waugh had a half-brother, George Fitzhugh. The will of George Turberville, probated at Westmoreland on the 30th of March, 1742, mentioned his wife, Martha, a daughter, his "dear little son John," and an unborn child, who was named George Richard. The eldest son, John, was born the 14th of September, 1737; died the 10th of July, 1799; married, in 1759, his first cousin, Martha, daughter of Col. John Corbin, of "Portobago," and Lettice Lee, his wife; they had these ten children:

i, George Lee (a copy of whose book-plate is given) was born the 7th of September, 1760; died in 1798; married Betty Tayloe Corbin (probably a daughter of Gawin Corbin, of "Buckingham House") and had issue John and two daughters, who married two Beales; George served for some time as captain on the staff of General Charles Lee; later with Steuben in the south, as the following letter shows:

Under date of 21st of March, 1781, Col°: Geo: Lee Turberville wrote to Gov: Jefferson.

"Dear Sir, I cannot express myself in terms sufficiently strong to convey to you an Idea of my Gratitude in return for your obliging Letter relative to Baron Steuben. I follow'd precisely its advice, altho' subsequent ill-treatment from the Baron has obliged me to act differently since, the whole of which I will make known to you the first favorable opportunity. I have only to solicit you at present to let me know by the first opportunity whether you or the Council have ever informed the Baron that you *highly disapproved of my conduct whilst I had the honor to command at Sandy Point;* as that Major-Genl: has given information to the Marquis that it was from the Executive very much disapproving of my conduct that occasioned him to some steps with me that have been highly prejudicial to my reputation, health and peace of mind" (I, *Va. Cal. State Papers*, 585).

After the war he was a delegate to the Virginia Assembly in 1785–86–87; a member of the Convention of 1788, and Sheriff of Richmond county in 1798.

ii, Lettice Corbin, born the 7th of January, 1763; married, about 1778, Major Catesby Jones, of Westmoreland, and had these seven children:

Roger, Thomas ap Catesby, Philip Catesby, Eusebius, Elizabeth Lee, Martha Corbin, and Sally Skelton Jones. (See Jones Family under 36, i.)

iii, John Corbin, born the 10th of October, 1765.

iv, Jane Lane, born the 1st of May, 1767.

v, Ann Silk, born the 1st of April, 1769.

vi, Lucy Silk, born the 11th of May, 1770.

vii, Rebecca Lee, born the 21st of September, 1772; died the 1st of April, 1785 (tombstone near "Hickory Hill").

viii, Charles Lee, born the 16th of December, 1775.

ix, Martha Corbin, born the 4th of November, 1778; married, on the 25th of January, 1800, Dr. Mottrom Ball (1767–1842), second son of Captain Spencer Ball, of "Coan," Northumberland county; she died the 26th of March, 1865, and left four children (Hayden, *Va. Genealogies*, 136).

x, Troilus Lewin, born the 29th of December, 1780; died without issue.

The second son of George Turberville, by his third wife Martha Lee, was born some time after his father's death, about 1742, and was named George Richard; he married, on the 1st of June, 1769, Martha, the only child of Gawin Corbin, of "Peckatone," Westmoreland, and Hannah Lee, his wife, and left two sons, Gawin Corbin and Richard Lee. There was probably a daughter also, as a Hannah Turberville, who was said to be engaged to a Mr. Tomson, is mentioned in the *Journal of a Young Lady of Virginia*, p. 32. Of the sons, Gawin Corbin married a daughter of Col. John Daingerfield, of Essex county, and had a daughter, Mary, who married William F. Taliaferro, and left issue.

The younger son, Richard Lee Turberville, married about 14th of December, 1794, his cousin, Henrietta, daughter of Richard Henry Lee, of "Chantilly," by his second wife, Anne (Gaskins) Pinkard, and had issue: Cornelia Lee, George Lee, and Richard Henry Turberville (see 18, vi). Of these, Cornelia Lee, born the 6th of September, 1797; died the 4th of March, 1883, and married, in 1814, Charles Calvert Stuart, who was born the 9th of February, 1794, and died the 2d of September, 1846; he was the youngest son of Dr. David Stuart[1] and Eleanor (Calvert) Custis,

---

[1] Dr. David Stuart (born 3d of August, 1753) was the son of the Rev. William Stuart and Sarah Foote, his wife, and the grandson of the Rev. David Stuart, who married Harriet Gibbons, sister of Sir John Gibbons, Bart., and M. P. for Essex; the Rev. David Stuart was Rector of St. Paul's Parish, King George county, 1722–49, when he was succeeded by his son, the Rev. William Stuart, who died in 1796 (Hayden, *Va. Genealogies*, 732).

his wife, who was the widow of John Parke Custis, and the second daughter of Benedict Calvert, of "Mt. Airy," Prince George's county, Md.; she was born about 1756, and died the 28th of April, 1811; Mr. Custis died on the 5th of November, 1781, and she married Dr. Stuart in the autumn of 1783; they resided for some years at "Abingdon," on the Potomac River between Washington and Alexandria (see, also, Custis Family, under 50). They had seven children: Ann Calvert, Sarah, Ariana Calvert, William Skolto, Charles Calvert, Eleanor, and Rosalie Eugenia Stuart. George Lee Turberville married a Miss Dobell, and left issue. Richard Henry Turberville died without issue.

## Hon. Philip Lee.

4. Philip[3], third son of Richard Lee[2] (Richard[1]), and Lætitia Corbin, his wife, was born in Westmoreland county, about 1681[1]; he died in 1744, about April of that year. As he moved to Maryland in 1700, he may have been born earlier than the date given here. He was a member of the Council in Maryland, and a Justice; no further data concerning his career has been discovered. He lived at "Blenheim," in Prince George's county, in that State.

Philip was twice married; first to Sarah, daughter of Hon. Thomas Brooke, Esq. (1632–1676), of "Brookefield," and Barbara Addison, his wife; Thomas and Barbara Brooke deeded land to her, as wife of Philip Lee, in 1713; she died in November, between 16th and 28th, 1724. By her will (dated 16th and probated 28th of November, 1724), she left her "younger son Arthur Lee and his heirs forever all that tract or parcell of Land which my Honored Father Thos. Brooke, Esq., gave me the said Sarah Lee, . . . lying at Rock Creek, and I do by these presents Constitute ordain and appoint my Loving Brother Mr. Thomas Brooke, Gentleman, to be Executor of this my Last Will and Testament, &c." Philip married, secondly, about 1725–6, Elizabeth, the widow of Henry Sewall, Gent., who survived him. In the Maryland *Archives* Council Proceedings, 5th of July, 1728, it was stated that the Hon. Philip Lee, member of the Council, claimed the care, education, and estate of his stepson, Nicholas Sewall, son of his wife by her first husband, Henry Sewall, Gent., late of St. Mary's county. The stepson, Nicholas Sewall, being then about seven years old, was, it is stated, sought to be "Romanized" by his uncle, Nicholas Sewall.

---

[1] Col. William Fitzhugh, under date of 8th June, 1681, wrote to the "Hon'ble Col. Richard Lee." At the end of his letter he expresses this wish: "I wish you much joy in your young son now and hereafter" (*Va. Magazine*, etc., I, p. 41). This son *may* have been Philip.

Philip Lee's will, dated the 20th of March, 1743, and recorded in Charles county, the 1st of May, 1744, was as follows:

In the name of God Amen. I Philip Lee of Prince George's County in the Province of Maryland Gentleman being Sick and Weake in Body but of sound and perfect memory Thanks be to Almighty God for the same and Considering the uncertain State of Mankind and that it is appointed for all men to die and reflecting that I am possessed of Sundry Lands Tenements and hereditaments Goods and Chattells by the Blessing of God Almighty far beyond my deserts. I have thought Proper and Convenient to make this my Last Will and Testament in the manner and forme following to wit: First, I give and bequeath my Immortall Soul to the Omnipotent God that gave it Trusting Through his Great Merrits and the Sufferings and Merrits of my Lord and Saviour Jesus Christ Crusified on the Cross for the Sins of All Mankind that my Sins of Commission and Omission will Receive Pardon at the great Tribunal when Every man shall be Judged by his Faith and works.

Secondly, As to what Goods Chattells Lands Tenements &c. I am possessed of as before I give and Bequeath as followeth: But First my Desire is that all my Just Debts be paid but as many pretenses and claims may be exhibited against my Estate after my Decease not really due from me I do hereby Direct and Order my Executor or Executrix or if more than one Executor in all cases Except the Debt Appears as clear as the Sun at noonday to plead the act of Assembly of Limitation in barr of all such Claims. Secondly, I give to my Son Richard Lee after his mother in Laws decease (to her I give During Life if she continues a protestant) all that Tract of Land I bought of Thomas Smith, also that Tract of Land I bought of Daniel Dulaney Esquire, on the Other Side the Great Branch, provided that he, the said Richard Lee, do make over the Tract of Land at Rock Creek of 500 acres left by his mother to Arthur Lee, and on refusal to do so, Then I give to Arthur Lee the aforementioned Two Tracts of Land, after my present Wife's decease, to him the said Arthur Lee and his heirs Forever. Item, I give to my Son Hancock Lee my moiety of the Tract of Land I took up at Rock Creek called———, The other half I Give to Corbin Lee, to them and their heirs forever. The Land so bequeathed Joyns on part of ——— 500 acres Given my first [wife] Sarah Lee, Deceased. Item, I give to my Son Hancock Lee that plantation I bought of Widow Joseph and James Brooke with the addition I bought of James Brooke, to him and his heirs Forever. Item, I give to my Son Corbin Lee 200 acres of Land, part of the Land Called Rehoboth, Given me by my hon'd Father, to him and his heirs Forever. Item, I give to my Son John and George Lee and their heirs forever 600 acres of Land out of the Land Called Rehoboth, in N. West fork of Nanticoake to be equally Divided between them. Item, I give to my Son Francis Lee and his heirs, 200 acres of Land, part of the Tract Called Rehoboth aforesaid. Item, I give to my Grandson Philip Lee 200 acres of Land, part of Rehoboth, to him and his heirs Forever. Item, I give to my said Wife during her life, if she continues a Protestant, that Tract of Land Called Barthope and the addition (I bought of Maj'r or Capt. Samuel Perry) for raising a Stock for support of my younger Children. Item, I give to my Son George Lee and his heirs forever that Tract or parcell of Land I bought of John Ashmar Joyning on the Tract left by my hon'd Father deceased, Called Lee's Purchase or Stump Dale, near Cedar point on Potomack river. Item, I give to my Son Richard and Thomas Lee and their heirs for Ever, to be equally Divided between them, that Tract of Land in Glorcester County, Paradise, the Reversion left me by my Deceased Father Col. Richard Lee, of Virginia. Item, I give to my Beloved Wife during the term of 15 years if she continues [a widow ?] and a Protestant, all that Tract and parcell of Land Called Lee's Purchase or Stump Dale, Whereon I have built a fine Bake House and . . . mill in order to Carry on the Baking and Gris Trade, for the Support of my Children hereafter name during the said space and my Grandson [son of] Philip Lee, Jun'r, Deceased, in trust for the use of the following Children &c., Amongst whome the Clear or nett proceeds is to be divided, the charges being first deducted, and my Wife to have her one or two shares if she so pleases for her Trouble, the Children are Letticie unless she marries well, Elizabeth, Alice, Hancock, Corbin, John, George and Margarett, also my Grandson Philip Lee, son of Philip Lee Deceased, aforesaid. Item, My Will is that for the Term of Ten years after said Fifteen the profits of the said Land, I mean the Bake house and the Mill shall goe to the support of my Grand Children, now Born and to be Born as descendant from Richard Lee, Francis Lee, Philip Lee, Thomas Lee and Arthur Lee, the said Land to be in the occupation of my son Thomas Lee and George for the aforesaid share they to be Accountable for the profits, taking to themselfs Each one share. Item, my Will is that the remaining or remainder of the said Lands shall descend to my Son Thomas & George Lee and their heirs for Ever, and the profits thereon arrising. Item, I Give unto my Beloved Daughter Eleanor Lee five pounds to buy her mourning which with what I Give her by marriage Contract Shall be in full of her filial portion. Item, I Give to my Daughter Ann Russell five pounds to Buy her mourning which said five pounds with what I have before Given her shall be in full of her Fillial portion. Item, I Give to my Son Francis Lee two negroes, which with what I have before Given him shall be in full of his Filial portion. Item, I Give to my son Thomas two negroes with what I have before Given him shall be in full of his Filial portion. Item, I Give to Each of my Grandchildren decendants from Philip Lee Jun'r, Late Son of Philip Lee, Each one young negroe Boys or Girls at the discretion of my Ex'r. Item, I Give to my Grand Children, decended from Richard Lee, my Eldest Son and his Wife Grace each one Small negro Girl.

Item, I Give to my Grand Son Philip Lee son of Philip Lee and Grace, my fluted or Scolloped montif. Item, I Give to my Wife Elizabeth three negro men, three negro Women, Vizt. Charles, Harry and Quicke, also Lettice, Agitha and Judith. Also I Give to my Said Wife the Best Bed and furniture and all her apparell. I also Give to her the new skreen, cost five Guineas, and her horse America Saddle and furniture, Twenty head of Cattell, a tenth part of my hoggs, and sixth part of my Sheep also one eighth part of my household furniture upon condition that she renounces her right and title to her thirds of my personal Estate or Else the above devises to be void and of none effect. I Give to my Daughter Potts Wife of Will Potts three negroes two women, one man, vizt. Langress a lad, Phildo now a large Girl and Rose at Rock Creek. Item, I Give to my Daughter Alice Lee two negro Girls vizt. Phillis and Prise. Item, I Give to my Daughter Hannah Lee two negro Girls vizt. Jane and Fido. Item, I give to my Daughter Peggy Lee one negro Girl named Venus. Item, I Give to my Son George Lee one negro boy Ignatius. Item, I Give to my Son Corbin one negro boy named Giles. Item, I Give to my Son Hancock Lee two negroes named Quitchee and Nathaniel. I Give to my Son John Lee two negro boys vizt. Chesshire and Charles. Item, I Give to my Daughter Lettice Lee one negro Girl named Clare. Item, I Give to my Daughter Elizabeth Lee one negro Girl called Kate.

I Do order and Direct my Executors hereafter named not to suffer any part of my Estate to be Divided untill two years after my death and I do nominate and appoint my Loving Wife Elizabeth Lee, and my Son Thomas Lee to be my Executors of my Estate, Given under my hand and Seal, as the Law Directs, this Twentieth day of March in the year of our Lord Christ Seventeen hundred and Forty Three-four and I do hereby revoke and make Null and Void all other Wills or Testaments or Codicils by me heretofore made.

There is considerable doubt as to the proper order in which the children of Philip Lee should be placed; little assistance can be had from his will. He named Richard as his eldest son; also mentioned two of his daughters as already married: Anne Russell and —— Potts, wife of William Potts. It is said that her name was Sarah, and she is so named here. As the other daughters, Eleanor, Hannah, Lettice, Elizabeth, Alice, and Margaret, were mentioned by their maiden names, it is to be supposed they were unmarried at date of will. A trust was made, to continue fifteen years, for the support of the following named children: Lettice, Elizabeth, Alice, Hancock, Corbin, John, George, and Margaret. This would imply that they were the youngest children all under age at that date. At the expiration of this fifteen years, the same property was to be placed in trust again, for the support of grandchildren, "now born or to be born," issue of Richard, Francis, Philip, Thomas, and Arthur Lee; this would indicate that these five were his oldest sons and already married or of a marriageable age. It seems probable that the eight oldest children were by his first wife. Hancock Lee, in 1759, mentioned Hannah, Lætitia, Corbin, Alice, Margaret, John, and George as his brothers and sisters, evidently meaning his full brothers and sisters. Guided by these statements, the children of Philip Lee have been placed in the following order:

i, RICHARD[4], See 8.
ii, FRANCIS[4], See 9.
iii, PHILIP[4], See 10.
iv, THOMAS[4], See 11.
v, ARTHUR[4], See 12.
vi, ANNE[4], married James Russell, merchant of London.
vii, SARAH[4], mentioned in her father's will as wife of William Potts; they had issue, names unknown.
viii, ELEANOR[4], said to have married Philip Richard Fendall, and to have died the 22d of April, 1759. There was a P. R. Fendall, Justice for Charles county, in 1790, and also one residing at Alexandria, at same date. They were probably father and son; if so, the father married this Eleanor, and the son was married twice; first, to the widow of Philip Ludwell Lee, and, secondly, to Mary, daughter of Henry and Lucy (Grymes) Lee, of Prince William, by whom he had a son and a daughter.
ix, HANNAH[4], was twice married; first to (Daniel?) Bowie, and secondly, to Joseph Sprigg, issue by both marriages. By her first husband, she had, at least, one son, Daniel, as mentioned in her brother Hancock's

will; she had also two daughters, one of whom married Thomas Belt, then residing at Hagerstown, Md., and had issue. The other daughter, Barbara Bowie, was born the 13th of November, 1756; died the 21st of February, 1805; married twice; first to —— Hall, and had, at least, Thomas Belt Hall, who left issue, and a daughter, Lætitia Hall, who married —— Stull, and had ten children. Barbara (Bowie) Hall married, secondly, about 1789, Major Ignatius Taylor (born the 11th of September, 1742; died the 21st of September, 1807), of Hagerstown, Md., she was his third wife; they had issue: Hannah Lee, Jane, and Lucretia Taylor. Of these daughters, Hannah Lee, born the 9th of January, 1791; died the 11th of November, 1832; married, on the 29th of October, 1807, Gov. John Chambers, being his second wife; they had twelve children (see Chambers' Family).

Jane Taylor married Judge Samuel Treat, of Missouri, and left issue. Lucretia Taylor married (14th of June, 1814) Arthur Fox, of Mason county, Ky., and left twelve children. (Data from the will of Ignatius Taylor, probated 31st December, 1807, and the family Bible of Gov. Chambers.)

After the death of (Daniel?) Bowie, Mrs. Hannah (Lee) Bowie married, secondly, Joseph Sprigg, and had issue: Joseph, Osborn, Thomas, Corbin, William Sprigg. The latter was Judge of the Supreme Court of Ohio, then of the Territorial Court of Indiana, and lastly of Illinois. After Hannah Lee's death, her husband married and had a son, the Hon. Samuel Sprigg, of Prince George's county, Md. Mrs. Charles Carroll, of Bellevue, was also one of their descendants.

x, LETTICE[4], said to have been married three times; first to James Wardropp, of "Ampthill," Chesterfield county, Va.; next to Dr. Adam Thompson, and lastly to Col. Joseph Sims. She had issue only by her second husband, two daughters: Mary Lee Thompson, who married Col. Williams, of Maryland; and Alice Corbin Thompson, who married Capt. John Hawkins, an officer in the Revolutionary army, serving with the Virginia troops, and had a daughter, Maria Love Hawkins (1789–1826), who married J. A. W. Smith, a lawyer of Fauquier county (*Marshall Family*, 89). There seems to be considerable doubt as to the third marriage of Lettice Lee. In 1759, she was named as "Lætitia Wardropp;" in 1790, her nephew mentioned in his will a brooch left him as a legacy by his "Aunt Lettice Thompson," which would imply that she had died the wife of Mr. Thompson.

xi, ELIZABETH[4], died the 19th of September, 1752, æt. 22 years.

xii, ALICE[4], married twice; first, Thomas Clark, by whom she had a daughter, who married John Rogers, Chancellor of Maryland; she was mentioned as "Alice Clark," in 1759, by her brother Hancock Lee. She married, secondly, about 1760, Meriwether Smith; their son George William Smith, Governor of Virginia, was among the victims burned in the old Richmond theatre, 26th December, 1811.

xiii, HANCOCK[4], See 13.

xiv, JOHN[4], See 14.

xv, CORBIN[4]; lived at "'The Adventure,' an estate of 1,000 acres, lying on the Great Falls of Gunpowder River, six miles from Joppa; with a large elegant brick house," etc. Was a member of the House of Burgesses from Baltimore county, Md., in 1761; died between 27th of November and the 9th of December, 1773. Wife's name was Elinor ——. No issue.

xvi, GEORGE[4], See 15.

xvii, MARGARET[4], called "Margaret Symer," by her brother Hancock Lee, in 1759. Said to have had a daughter, who married —— Phenix and left a son, Thomas Phenix.

## THE CHAMBERS FAMILY.

About 1720, Randle, or Rowland Chambers, of Scotch-Irish descent, emigrated from county Antrim to Pennsylvania, where he died in 1747–8, leaving wife, Elizabeth, and children, Joseph, Benjamin, John, Arthur, James, and Robert. Of these sons, Benjamin was the most prominent, having been well known throughout western Pennsylvania as "Col. Ben." Chambers; with his brother Joseph he laid off and founded the town of Chambersburg in 1764. His son, General Benjamin Chambers, served with distinction during the Revolution. James, next to the youngest son of the Immigrant, married Sarah ——; their grandson, Gov. John Chambers, has stated that her name was Sarah Lee, and that she was nearly related to Gov. Thomas Sim Lee, and to a Mr. Potts, of Frederick, Md. Unfortunately, this statement has not been verified, and her parentage has not been discovered. This James died the 13th of March, 1758, leaving wife, Sarah, and children, Ann, Elizabeth, Roland, James, Benjamin, Joseph, and Sarah. Of these, Roland, born in 1744, settled in New Jersey, finally moved to Kentucky, where he died in 1821, leaving several children, among them Gov. John, who was born at Bromley Bridge, N. J., on the 6th of October, 1780, and died near Paris, Ky., on the 21st of September, 1852; he was twice married; first, on the 16th of June, 1803, to Margaret, daughter of Major Ignatius Taylor, of Hagerstown, Md., who was born the

22d of May, 1781, and died the 4th of March, 1807, without surviving issue; he married, secondly, on the 29th of October, 1807, Hannah Lee, a half sister of his first wife, and daughter of Major Ignatius Taylor, by his third wife, as stated.

John Chambers studied law and was admitted to the bar in 1800; in 1812 and 1815 he was elected to the Kentucky legislature; in 1813 he served as a volunteer aide-de-camp on staff of General William Henry Harrison; in 1827 was elected to Congress, but declined a renomination, preferring to serve in the State legislature, 1830–32. Was appointed Judge of the Kentucky Court of Appeals in 1835, from which he resigned to take his seat in the 24th Congress, where he served from 1835 to 1839; in March, 1841, President Harrison appointed him governor of the Territory of Iowa, 1841–45. By his second wife, Gov. Chambers had twelve children: Margaret Taylor, Joseph Sprigg, Hannah Lee, James, Matilda, Francis Taylor, Jane, Mary, Laura, John, James, Henry, and Lucretia. Of these children, the eldest, Margaret Taylor, was born the 2d of December, 1808; died the 8th of July, 1863; married, the 12th of September, 1826, Hugh Innes Brent (born the 31st of August, 1803; died the 2d of September, 1845), son of Hugh Brent and Elizabeth Trotter Langhome, his wife, of Paris, Ky. They had issue (Brent) as follows:

i, Elizabeth Langhome, born the 27th of July, 1827; died the 9th of September, 1846; married, in June, 1843, Dr. George Esten Cooke, of Louisville, Ky., son of Dr. John Esten and Lucy (Beale) Cooke, of Lexington, Ky., and had two children, Hugh Innes Brent and John Esten Cooke.

ii, John Chambers, born the 15th of May, 1829; died the 2d of March, 1877; married, the 25th of October, 1859, Lucy Beale, of Fredericksburg, Va., no issue; after his death his widow married Frederick W. Page, of Charlottsville, Va.

iii, Hugh Innes, born 21st of August, 1832; died the 20th of March, 1852.

iv, Thomas Young, Major C. S. A., born the 29th of December, 1835; was killed at the battle of Green River, Ky., the 4th of July, 1863, while commanding the 5th Kentucky Cavalry; he married, the 21st of June, 1860, Mary Moore, daughter of Capt. Charles Chilton and Mary Harrison (Stone) Moore, of "Forest Retreat," Fayette county, Ky., and left two children, Mary Chilton (who married Prof. Charles W. Dabney) and Margaret Thomas Brent, who is unmarried.

v, James Henry, born the 11th of August, 1842; married, the 16th of October, 1866, Elizabeth Durrett (a cousin), daughter of Francis T.

Thomas Lee.

Chambers and Elizabeth Durrett, his wife; they have issue: Gabriella Durrett, Margaret Chambers, Mary Porter, Hugh Innes, Frances Christine Brent. James Henry Brent has recently been Judge of the Superior Court of Kentucky.

vi, MARGARET CHAMBERS, born the 3d of January, 1846; married, the 18th of November, 1868, the Hon. William Hardia Mackoy, M. A., son of John and Elizabeth Gravit (Hardia) Mackoy, of Covington, Ky. Mr. Mackoy was a member of the Kentucky Constitutional Convention of 1890. They had issue: Daisy (born 25th and died 26th February, 1870); Lewis Dixon (born 17th May, 1872), Henry Brent (born 18th July, 1874), and Elizabeth Cary Mackoy (born 3d June, 1879). To the kindness of Mrs. Mackoy most of these notes are due.

Brigadier-General Benjamin Chambers, who commanded the Maryland Militia in 1814 was of this family; his son, Ezekiel Forman Chambers, was U. S. Senator, 1826–34 and Judge of the Court of Appeals of Maryland, 1834–51. (Hanson's *Old Kent*, 192.)

## "PRESIDENT" THOMAS LEE.

5. THOMAS[3], the fifth son of Richard Lee[2] (Richard[1]) and Lætitia Corbin, his wife, was born at "Mt. Pleasant," in Westmoreland county, in 1690; died at "Stratford," in same county, on the 14th of November, 1750. Of his early days his son has written: "Thomas, the fourth son, though with none but a common Virginia Education, yet having strong natural parts, long after he was a man, he learned the Languages without any assistance but his own genius, and became a tolerable adept in Greek and Latin. . . . This Thomas, by his Industry and Parts, acquired a considerable Fortune; for, being a younger Brother, with many children, his Paternal Estate was very Small. He was also appointed of the Council, and though he had very few acquaintances in England, he was so well known by reputation that upon his receiving a loss by fire, the late Queen Caroline sent him over a bountiful present out of her own Privy Purse. Upon the late Sir William Gooch's being recalled, who had been Governor of Virginia, he became President and Commander in Chief over the Colony, in which Station he continued for some time, 'til the King thought proper to appoint him Governor of the Colony, but he dyed in 1750 before his commission got over to him."

That Thomas Lee possessed "strong natural parts" seems well attested by the important positions confided to him during an epoch in which the Colony was strong in men of marked ability. Besides being for many years a member of the House of Burgesses, a member of the Council and later its president, he became after the death of John Robinson, on the 5th of September, 1749, the acting Governor of the Colony, and held that position until his death. He served also upon various commissions for arranging boundaries, for making treaties with the Indians, and held other similar positions of trust and responsibility.

In May, 1744, Thomas Lee and William Beverley were appointed by the Governor his commissioners to treat with the Iroquois Indians for the settlement of lands west of the Alleghany Mountains. Governor Gooch wrote: "Whereas of late some misunderstandings and differences have arisen between His Majesty's Subjects of this Dominion and the Six United Nations of Indians, and being induced by several Representatives and Messages interchanged, to believe that they are desirous to enter into Treaty with this Government, &c. &c. . . . Know Ye that I reposing special Trust, &c. in the experience, Loyalty, Integrity and Abilities of Thomas Lee Esqr. a member in Ordinary of His Majestys hon'ble Council of State, and one of the Judges of the Supreme Court of Adjudication in this Colony, and of William Beverley Esqr. Col: and County Lieutenant of the County of Orange and one of the Representatives of the People in the House of Burgesses of this Colony and Dominion of Virginia, &c., . . . Have, &c. nominated and Constituted the said Thomas Lee and William Beverley Commissioners &c. to meet the Six Nations or such Sachems &c. as shall be deputed to them. &c. . . . at Newtown in Lancaster Co. Province of Pennsylvania." (I, *Va. Calendar State Papers*, 238.)

William Black, a Scotchman, accompanied this commission as secretary, and left a diary, in which he gave a very spirited account of their journey from Stratford to Philadelphia. Mr. Black wrote in part: [1]

"Thursday, May the 17th (1744). This Morning at 9 of the Clock, in Company with the Hon'ble Commissioners, and the Gentlemen of their Levees, Colonel John Taylor, Jun'r, Presley Thornton, Warren Lewis, Philip Ludwell Lee, James Littlepage, and Robert Brooke, Esquires, I Embarked on Board the Margaret Yacht lying off Stratford on Potomac, and about 10 minuetes after, was under sail with a small Breeze of Wind at S. W. One Jack Ensign and Pennon flying. After the Vessel had got way, with the Trumpet we hailed the Company (who came to the waterside to see us on Board) with Fare-you-well, who returned the Complement, wishing us a Good Voyage and Safe Return, for which, on the part of the Company, I gave them Thanks with the discharge of our Blunderbuss. As

---

[1] *Penna. Mag.*, I, 117, *et seq.*

farr as I could observe the Gentlemen and Ladies on the Sandy Bank, we had full Sails, but on loosing the Sight of them, or on their retiring, we lost our Wind, which made me conclude, the Gentle Gale we had then was nothing else but the tender Wishes of the Women for their Husbands and the affectionate Concern of the Mothers for thair Sons, Breath'd after Us in Gentle Sighs."

On reaching Annapolis, the next day, the festivities began: "The Commissioners, &c., went on Shoar, and was very Kindly Received at the Landing Place, by several Gentlemen of Distinction of that Province, and Conducted to the first Tavern in Town, where they welcomed the Commissioners, and the Gentlemen of their Levee to Annapolis, with a Bowl of Punch and a Glass of Wine, and afterwards waited on us to the House of the Honourable Edward Jennings, Esq., Secretary of the Province, where we Din'd very Sumptuously." . . . The next day they dined with the Governor: "We were Received by his Excellency and his Lady in the Hall, where we were Entertained by them, with some Glasses of Punch in the intervals of the Discourse; then the Scene was chang'd to a Dining Room, where you saw a plain proof of the Great Plenty of the Country, a Table in the most Splendent manner set out with Great Variety of Dishes, all serv'd up in the most Elegant way, after which came a Dessert no less Curious; Among the Rarities of which it was Compos'd was some fine Ice Cream which, with the Strawberries and Milk, eat most Deliciously. After this Repast was over, which (notwithstanding the great variety) show'd a face of Plenty and Neatness, more than Luxury or Profuseness, We withdrew to the Room in which we was first Received, where the Glass was push'd briskly round, sparkling with the Choicest Wines, of which the Table was Replenished with Variety of Sorts."

On the 21st, "At Night his Excellency the Governor and some other Gentlemen, for the Entertainment of the Commissioners and the Gentlemen of the Levee, gave a Ball in the Council Room, where most of the Ladies of any Note in the Town was present, and made a very Splendent Appearance. In a Room back from that where they Danc'd, was Several sorts of Wines, Punch, and Sweet Meats; in this Room, those that were not Engag'd in any Dancing Match, might either Employ themselves at Cards, Dice, Back-Gammon, or with a cheerful Glass; the Commissioners amus'd themselves till about 10 o'clock, and then went home to their Lodgings.

"The Ladies was so very Agreeable, and seem'd so Intent on Dancing that one might have Imagin'd they had some Design on the Virginians, either Designing to make Tryal of their Strength and Vigour, or to Convince them of their Activity and Sprightliness. After several Smart Engagements, in which no Advantage on either side was Observable, with a Mutual Consent, about 1 of the clock in the morning, it was agreed to break up, every Gentleman waiting on his Partner home."

And so on; the journey being marked at each stopping place by these receptions and entertainments, too numerous to give a full account of them. After leaving Chester, they were welcomed by "Several Gentlemen of Philadelphia, who Received us very kindly, and Welcomed us into their Province with a Bowl of fine Lemon Punch big enough to have Swimm'd half a dozen of young Geese; after pouring four or five Glasses of this down our throats we cross'd the River about two hundred yards over, and riding three short miles on the other side brought us into the sight of the famous City of Philadelphia."

Mr. Black mentioned visiting a friend, in Philadelphia, who "Kept Batchellor House, and Consequently had more Freedom, than when a Wife and Children is to be Conformed to. I staid till after 11, and parted, he making me Promises to be no Stranger while I staid in Town, of which there was no great fear, as he kept a Glass of Good Wine, and was as free of it as an Apple-tree of its Fruit on a Windy Day in the month of July."

Sunday, June 3d. After attending morning service at Christ Church, "Colonel Taylor, Mr. Lewis, etc., of the Levee went to the Commissioners' Lodgings, where we found Colonel Lee ready to go to Mr. Andrew Hamilton's, where we were Invited to Dine this Day; about a Quarter after 1 O'Clock we had Dinner, and I do assure you a very fine one, but as I am not able to draw up a Bill of Fare, I shall only say, that we had very near 18 Dish of Meat, besides a very nice Collation; after this was over, it was time for to think of going to Church for Afternoon; accordingly, most of our young Company with my Self, went in order to Visit the Reverend Mr. Gilbert Tennant, a Disciple of the Great Whitefield, whose followers are Call'd the New Lights; we found him Delivering his Doctrine with a very Good Grace, Split his Text as Judiciously, turn'd up the Whites of his Eyes as Theologically, Cuff'd his Cushion as Orthodoxic, and twist'd his Band as Primitively as his Master Whitefield could have done, had he been there himself."

The conferences with the Indians were begun at Lancaster, the 22d June, 1744. A record of the meeting states that wine and punch, as well as the customary pipe, were handed around. After the Indians had partaken, the conference was opened by a speech from the governor of Pennsylvania.

During these conferences, one of the Indian chiefs (showing they were not behind their pale face brother in liking "the fire water") said: "You tell us you beat the French, if so, you must have taken a great deal of Rum from them, and can better spare us some of that Liquor to make us rejoice with you in the Victory." "The Governor and Commissioners ordered a Dram of Rum to be given to each in a *small* Glass, calling it, *A French Glass*." The next day the Indians demanded more of the rum, this time in *large English Glasses*. "The Indians gave, in their Order, five Yo-bahs; and the honorable Governor and Commissioners calling for some Rum and some middle sized Wine Glasses, drank Health to the Great King of England and the Six Nations and put an end to the Treaty by three loud Huzzas, in which all the Company joined."

Mr. Whitham Marshe, secretary for the Maryland Commissioners, wrote an account of these conferences (at Lancaster on the 28th of June, 1744), stating: "The Commissioners of Virginia had a private treaty with the Chiefs, in the Court house, and Col. Lee made them a speech, which see in printed Treaty fol. 20, 21, 22." An account of the proceedings and the treaty were printed by Benjamin Franklin, Philadelphia, 1744; from which rare work the following copy of Thomas Lee's address has been taken:

The Commissioners of Virginia desired the Interpreter to let the Indians know that their Brother Assaragoa was now going to give his Reply to their answer to his first Speech, delivered the day before in the forenoon.

"Sachims and Warriors of the Six United Nations,

"We are now come to answer what you said to us Yesterday, since what we said to you before on the Part of the Great King, our Father, has not been Satisfactory. You have gone into old Times, and so must we. It is true that the Great King holds Virginia by Right of Conquest, and the Bounds of that Conquest to the Westward is the Great Sea.

"If the Six Nations have made any Conquests over Indians that may at any Time have lived on the West-side of the Great Mountains of Virginia, yet they never possessed any Lands there that we ever heard of. That Part was altogether deserted, and free for any People to enter upon, as the People of Virginia have done, by Order of the Great King, very justly, as well as by an ancient Right, and by its being freed from the Possession of any other, and from any Claim even of you the Six Nations, our Brethren, until within these eight Years. The first Treaty between the Great King, in behalf of his Subjects of Virginia, and you, that we can find, was made at Albany by Col. Henry Coursey, Seventy Years since; this was a Treaty of Friendship when the first Covenant Chain was made, when we and you became Brethren.

"'The next Treaty was also made at Albany, about fifty-eight Years ago, by the Lord Howard, Governor of Virginia; then you declared yourselves Subjects to the Great King, our Father, and gave up to him all your Lands for his Protection. This you own in a Treaty made by the Governor of New York with you at the same Place, in the Year 1687, and you express yourselves in these Words:

"'Brethren, you tell us the King of England is a very Great King and why should not you join with us in a very just Cause, when the French join with our Enemies in an unjust Cause? O, Brethren, we see the Reason of this; for the French would fain kill us all and when that is done, they would Carry all the Beaver Trade to Canada, and the Great King of England would lose the Land likewise; and therefore, O, Great Sachim, beyond the Great Lakes, awake, and suffer not those poor Indians, that have given themselves and their Lands under your Protection, to be destroyed by the French without a Cause.'

"The last Treaty we shall speak to you about is that made at Albany by Governor Spotswood, which you have not recited as it is; For the white People, your Brethren of Virginia, are in no Article of that Treaty prohibited to pass and settle to the Westward of the Great Mountains. It is the Indians, tributary to Virginia, that are restrained, as you and your tributary Indians are from passing to the Eastward of the same Mountains, or to the Southward of the Cohongorooton, and you agree to this Article in these Words: 'That the Great River of Potowmack and the high Ridge of Mountains, which extend all along the Frontiers of Virginia to the Westward of the present Settlements of that Colony, shall be for ever the established Boundaries between the Indians subject to the Dominion of Virginia, and the Indians belonging and depending on the Five Nations; so that neither our Indians shall not, on any Pretence whatsoever, pass to the Northward or Westward of the said Boundaries, without having to produce a Passport under the Hand and Seal of the Governor or Commander in-chief of Virginia; nor your Indians to pass to the Southward or Eastward of said Boundaries, without a Passport in like Manner from the Governor or Commander-in-chief of New York.'

"And what Right can you have to Lands that you have no Right to walk upon, but upon certain Conditions? It is true, you have not observed this part of the Treaty, and your Brethren of Virginia have not insisted upon it with a due strictness, which has occasioned some Mischief.

"This Treaty has been sent to the Governor of Virginia by Order of the Great King, and is what we must rely upon, and being in Writing is more certain than your Memory. That is the Way the white People have of preserving Transactions of every Kind, and transmitting them down to their Childrens Children for ever, and all Disputes among them are settled by this faithful kind of Evidence, and must be the Rule between the Great King and you. This Treaty you Sachims and Warriors signed some years after the same Governor Spotswood, in the Right of the Great King, had been, with some People of Virginia, in possession of these very Lands, which you have set up your late Claim to. . . .

"Brethren, This Dispute is not between Virginia and you; it is setting up your Right against the Great King, under whose Grants the People you complain of, are settled. Nothing but a Command from the Great King can remove them; they are too powerful to be removed by any Force of you, our Brethren; and the Great King, as our common Father, will do equal Justice to all his children; wherefore we do believe they will be confirmed in their Possessions.

"As to the Road you mention, we intended to prevent any Occasion for it, by making peace between you and the Southern Indians, a few years since, at a considerable Expense to the Great King, which you confirmed at Albany. It seems by your being at War with the Catawbas that it has not been long kept by you. However, if you desire a Road, we will agree upon the Terms of the Treaty made with Col. Spotswood, and your People, behaving themselves orderly like Friends and Brethren, shall be used in their Passage through Virginia with the same Kindness as they are when they pass through the Lands of your Brother Onas. This, we hope, will be agreed to by you, our Brethren, and we will abide by the Promise made to you Yesterday.

"We may proceed to settle what we are to give you for any Right you may have, or have had, to all the Lands to the Southward and Westward of the Lands of your Brother, the Governor of Maryland, and of your Brother Onas; Tho' we are informed that the Southern Indians claim these very Lands that you do. We are desirous to live with you, our Brethren, according to the old Chain of Friendship, to settle all these Matters fairly, and honestly; and, as a Pledge of our Sincerity, we give you this Belt of Wampum."

Which was received with the usual Ceremony.

As a result of this conference, a treaty was made by which the Indians, in consideration of £400 paid and a promise of further payments, granted the Virginians the right to settle the land west of the mountains to the Ohio River. The two following letters from Thomas Lee, then acting as Governor of the Colony, to Governor Hamilton, of Pennsylvania, are in relation to the settling of these lands:

"STRATFORD, 22d November 1749.

"SIR,

"I had the Pleasure to congratulate You on your arrival to your Government by the Favour of my Friend Mr. Strettell; I had great satisfaction when I heard of your being advanced to that Honourable Station, because I had a very great Esteem for You ever since I had the Honour to know You.

"Upon Sr. William Gooch's leaving this Colony the Government here has devolved upon me as eldest Councellor, and I hope the good Agreement that will subsist between us will be of service to both Governments.

"I am sorry that so soon I am obliged to complain to You of the insiduous behaviour, as I am informed, of some traders from your Province, tending to disturb the Peace of this Colony and to alienate the Affections of the Indians from Us.

"His Majesty has been graciously pleased to grant to some Gentlemen and Merchants of London and some of both sorts of this Colony, a large Quantity of Land West of the Mountains, the design of this Grant and one condition of it is to Erect and Garrison a Fort to protect our trade (from the French) and that of the neighboring Colonies, and by fair open Trade to engage the Indians in Affection to his Majestie's Subjects to supply them with what they want so that they will be under no necessity to apply to the French, and to make a very strong Settlement on the Frontiers of this Colony, all which his Majesty has approved and directed his Governor here to assist the said Company in carrying their laudable design into Execution; but your Traders have prevailed with the Indians on the Ohio to believe that the Fort is to be a bridle for them, and that the roads which the Company are to make is to let in the Catawbas upon them to destroy them, and the Indians naturally jealous are so possessed with the truth of these insinuations that they threaten our Agents if they survey or make those roads that they have given leave to make, and by this the carrying the King's Grant into execution is at present impracticable. Yet these are the Lands purchased of the Six Nations by the Treaty of Lancaster.

"I need not say any more to prevail with you to take the necessary means to put a stop to these mischievous practices of those Traders. We are informed that there is Measures designed by the Court of France that will be mischievous to these Colonys which will in Prudence oblige Us to unite and not divide the Interest of the King's Subjects on the Continent. I am with Esteem & Respect," &c.

"Stratford, 20th December, 1749. Sir, Since the Letter I had the Pleasure to write You I have found it necessary to write to the Lords of the

Treasury desiring their Lordships to obtain the King's Order for running the dividing Line betwixt this Colony and Yours, else many difficultys will arise upon the seating the Large Grants to the Westward of the Mountains. In the case of the Earl of Granville and Lord Fairfax this method was taken and Commissioners appointed by his Majesty and those noble Lords. I thought it proper to aquaint you with this Step that there might be no Surprize and that a matter of such Consequence may meet with as little Delay as the Nature of it will admit. I am with all possible Esteem," &c.

The grant referred to was that of 500,000 acres situated in the present counties of Jefferson and Columbiana in Ohio, and in Brooke county, West Virginia. This was probably the first effort of the English to settle any of the territory "Westward of the Mountains." It is said that Thomas Lee was the originator of the project;[1] he was certainly the first president of the company; at his death, he was succeeded by Lawrence Washington.

The "order of the Committee of the Council, referring to the Lords of Trade, the petition of John Hanbury et als, incorporators of the Ohio Company, 9 Febr. 1748, B. T. Va. vol. 20," reads:

Whereas His Majesty was pleased by His Order in Council of the 11th of last month to referr unto this Committee the humble Petition of John Hanbury of London, Merchant, in behalf of himself and of Thomas Lee Esq. a Member of His Majesty's Council and one of the Judges of the Supreme Court of Judicature in His Majesty's Colony of Virginia, Thomas Nelson Esqr. also a Member of His Majesty's Council in Virginia, Colonel Cressup, Colonel William Thornton, William Nimmo, Daniel Cressup, John Carlisle, Lawrence Washington, Augustus Washington, George Fairfax, Jacob Gyles, Nathaniel Chapman and James Woodrop Esq[res], all of His Majesty's Colony of Virginia and others for settling the Country upon the Ohio and extending the British Trade beyond the Mountains on the Western confines of Virginia, &c. (See *Ohio Valley in Colonial Days*, by Berthold Fernow, Albany, 1890.)

The Ohio Company sent out, as their agent, one Christopher Gist, who established his first trading post not far from the site of the present city of Pittsburg. He was the first Englishman to settle beyond the Allegheny Mountains.

Though Thomas Lee may have been a person of some influence in his day, he is known rather for his many distinguished sons than for his own individual merit. For it has seldom fallen to the lot of any man to rear six sons who took an active and patriotic part in the service of their country, at least four of whom were distinguished for their unselfish patriotism during the Revolutionary struggle. Of these sons Mr. Campbell has written:[2]

---

[1] "Mr. Thomas Lee, president of the Council of Va., took the lead in the concerns of the company at the outset, and by many has been considered its founder." (Irving, *Life of Washington*, I, 46.)

[2] *Introduction to the History of Va.*, 1847.

"As Westmoreland, their native county, is distinguished above all others in Virginia as the birthplace of genius, so perhaps no other Virginian could boast of so many distinguished sons as President Lee."

President John Adams (who was not usually lavish in his praise of any one) wrote in after years to Richard Bland Lee:

"Quincy, 11 August, 1819.

"I thank you for your oration on the red-letter day in our national calendar, which I have read with mingled emotions. An invisible spirit seemed to suggest to me, in my left ear, 'Nil admirari, nil contemnere;' another spirit, at my right elbow, seemed to whisper in my ear, 'Digito compesce labellum.' But I will open my lips, and will say that your modesty and delicacy have restrained you from doing justice to your own name, that band of brothers, intrepid and unchangeable, who, like the Greeks at Thermopylæ, stood in the gap, in the defence of their country, from the first glimmering of the Revolution in the horizon, through all its rising light, to its perfect day.

"Thomas [Ludwell] Lee, on whose praises Chancellor Wythe delighted to dwell, who has often said to me that Thomas Lee was the most popular man in Virginia, and the delight of the eyes of every Virginian, but who would not engage in public life; Richard Henry Lee, whose merits are better known and acknowledged, and need no illustration from me; Francis Lightfoot Lee, a man of great reading well understood, of sound judgment, and inflexible perseverance in the cause of his country; William Lee, who abandoned an advantageous establishment in England from attachment to his country, and was able and faithful in her service; Arthur Lee, a man of whom I cannot think without emotion; a man too early in the service of his country to avoid making a multiplicity of enemies; too honest, upright, faithful, and intrepid to be popular; too often obliged by his principles and feelings to oppose Machiavellian intrigues, to avoid the destiny he suffered. This man never had justice done him by his country in his lifetime, and I fear he never will have by posterity. His reward cannot be in this world." (*Life and Works of John Adams*, X, 382.)

Thomas Lee was married, in May, 1722, to Hannah, second daughter of Colonel Philip Ludwell, of Greenspring, James City county, an associate of the Council. She was born at "Rich Neck," in Bruton parish, James City county, the 5th of December, 1701; died at Stratford, 25th of January, 1749, and was buried in the old family burying-ground, called the "Burnt House Fields," at Mt. Pleasant. Her tombstone is now to be seen at

MRS. THOMAS LEE.

Stratford, whither it was removed for preservation, probably by General Henry Lee, who built the new vault at that place. The following is a copy of a bond given by Thomas Lee on the eve of his marriage. The original bond is in his writing:

Know all men by these presents that Thomas Lee of Westmoreland County in Virginia, Gentleman, and Francis Lightfoot of Charles Citty County, Gentleman, doe owe and stand indebted to Philip Ludwell of Greenspring in James City County in Virginia, Esq., in the Sum of twelve hundred pounds of Lawfull money of England to the payment whereof well and truely to be made to the said Philip, his Execut's, Administrators or Certain Attorney at Greenspring upon demand, we bind ourselves and either of us, our and either of our heirs, Execut's and Administrators, jointly and Severally firmly by these presents sealed with our Seals and dated this twenty third day of May, Anno Domini one thousand Seven hundred and Twenty two.

The Condition of this Obligation is such that whereas a Marriage is intended to be had and Solemnized betwixt the Above bound Thomas Lee and Hannah, the Daughter of the above said Philip, with whome the said Thomas is to have and receive in Marriage six hundred pounds sterling money of England which was given to her by Philip Ludwell and Benjamin Harrison, Esqrs. her grandfathers: now if the said Marriage shall be had and Solemnized and the said six hundred pounds sterling shall be paid to the said Thomas and he shall depart this life leaving the said Hannah Surviving, then in that Case if the heirs, Execut's or Administrators of the said Thomas or one of them shall pay and deliver to the said Hannah upon Demand the Sum of six hundred pounds of good and Lawfull money of England or Such part of the Estate of the said Thomas as the Law appoints for Widows dowers, which she the said Hannah shall Choose which Choice shall be made within one Month after such decease, if thereunto required and not sooner, then this obligation to be void otherwise to remain in full force. Signed &c.

In this bond it is stated that the marriage "is intended to be had," but evidently had not then been solemnized; in his receipt for the £600, he mentioned "Hannah my wife." So it would seem evident that the marriage took place at Greenspring between the 23d and the 30th of May.

Virg'a Greenspring May ye 30th, 1722. Received of Philip Ludwell Esq'r. one set of bills of Exchange drawn by him on Mr. Micajah Perry, merch't in London for Six hundred pounds payable to me which is in full payment (when paid) of one Legacy of one hundred pounds given by Benja: Harrison Esq'r to Hannah my wife and also of five hundred pounds sterl: given to my s'd wife by the last will of Philip Ludwell Esq'r her grandfather and I do hereby Requit ye first named Philip the father of my wife from ye same and every part thereof. Witness my hand the day and year above written.

The following letter, evidently written to Philip Ludwell, is interesting; this copy is from the original; part of the date is torn:

"COLO. TAYLOES 16 Aug. 172–.

"Hon[d] Sir, I lately rec'd a letter from Mr. Robertson to send Mrs. Drysdale what was due from the ships and clerks to the late Governor and by my Unkle T. Corbin I have sent her bills for the ship dues tho' I Have not rec'd them, because they are under my collection as Naval off'r; but what is due from the clerks I cou'd not pay, because they have not sent mee an acc't what is due, tho' I have wrote them Mrs. Drysdales desire and the necessity of their speedy Answer upon the occasion of her Going for England. Mr. Cocke indeed writes mee he is out of cash not Expect'g to be called on, untill October and I don't think it safe to pay money for the clerks before I receive it. I suppose the Gov'r made a will soe yt. Mrs. Drysdales rents will be good for the money I pay.

"The lower hous of Assembly purs't to the Gover' of Maryl'ds speech (here inclosed) did pass a bill to lessen the q'ty of Tob: but clogg'd soe y't the Council cou'd not pass it without amendments, which would not goe down with them below. Then the Coun'l prepared and pas'd a bill to prevent the tending seconds and regulating the time of ship'g Tob: w'ch the lower hous threw out upon once reading. This last draft is to be sent over to the councel here, and soe all their projects for to mend the Tob: trade are come to nothing. The dry weather has done great hurt both there and here to the crops especially of Corn.

"I hope this will find ye all in good health, my wife writes to Mad'm Ludwell, whom I pray Give my duty and accept it yourself very heartily presented by Dear Sir. Y'r most Obed't dutyfull son and ser't."

Where Thomas Lee lived during the first years of his married life is a matter of some doubt. It seems most probable that his first home was at "Mt. Pleasant," and that the loss by fire, of which his son William wrote, was the destruction of that mansion. It is certain that the house at "Mt. Pleasant" was burned early in the last century, but there is no evidence of a fire ever having occurred at Stratford. If Queen Caroline gave Thomas Lee a "bountiful present out of her own privy purse," while she was Queen, she must have given it between 1727 and 1737, as she became a Queen in the former year and died in the latter. As Princess of Wales, she would hardly have possessed sufficient means to make a large present. It seems, therefore, highly probable that the Stratford house was erected about 1725–30, hardly later, as it is said that all of Thomas Lee's sons were born in that mansion.

An old mansion has been declared to be a history in itself; its rooms being the chapters; its stories, volumes; its furniture, illustrations, and its inmates the characters. Such a mansion is certainly an illustration of the customs, habits, and mode of life of the period in which it was built and inhabited. And this thought seems to be applicable to Stratford for many reasons. Since it was erected upon the banks of the historic Potomac, American history has been made, and some prominent actors in that history were born under its roof. At the time of its building, the American Colonies were few in number, and weak in strength, hardly able to defend their homes from the marauding Indian. Spotswood and his daring followers had only recently crossed "the Great Mountains," and looked upon the beautiful valley of Virginia. The imagination of to-day can hardly realize that there was ever a time when such a trip could be considered a daring venture, and the suggestion of such an idea seems a joke. "Early in his administration," writes Howe, "Spotswood, at the head of a troop of horse, effected a passage over the Blue Ridge, which had previously been considered an impenetrable barrier to the ambition of the whites, and discovered the beautiful valley which lies beyond. In commemoration of this event, he received from the king the honor of knighthood, and was presented with a miniature golden horse-shoe, on which was inscribed the motto, *Sic jurat transcendere montes*—Thus he swears to cross the mountains." Since that time a new nation has been born and grown to manhood; from infantile dimensions, a narrow strip of inhabited land, hugging the Atlantic as if afraid to loosen its hold on the mother country, its habitations have extended from ocean to ocean, from the great lakes to the gulf. The war of the Revolution, with its heroes and patriots, has come and gone. All these changes has Stratford witnessed, yet it remains to-day solid and strong, a monument of the past age in which it was erected, and had it no other claim to distinction, it might surely rank as one of America's historic mansions. But it possesses much greater claims than mere age; as the birthplace of two signers of the Declaration of Independence, and of two others who represented their country at the courts of Europe, during the earlier years of that struggle, it is hallowed by memories which no other mansion in America can share. There, too, on the 19th of January, 1807, was born Robert Edward Lee, an event well worthy of being the last act in the great drama, of which Stratford has been the stage.

Bishop Meade wrote many years ago: "Some mournful thoughts will force themselves upon us when considering the ruins of churches, of mansions, and of cemeteries, in Westmoreland. By reason of the worth, talents, and patriotism which once adorned it, it was called the Athens of Virginia. But how few of the descendants of those who once were its ornaments are now to be found in it? Chantilly, Mt. Pleasant, Wakefield are no more. Stratford alone remains. Where now are the venerable churches? Pope's Creek, Round Hill, Nomini, Leeds, where are they? Yeocomico only survives the general wreck. Of old men, mansions, churches, etc., we are tempted to say, 'Fuit Ilium, et ingens gloria Dardanidum.'" (*Old Churches, Families, etc.*, II, 171.)

Stratford house, with its solid walls and massive, rough-hewn timbers, seems rather to represent strength and solidity than elegance or comfort. Its large rooms, with numerous doors and windows, heated only by the large open fireplaces, would to-day scarcely be considered habitable. Nor would the modern housewife care to have her kitchen placed out in the yard some fifty or sixty feet from her dining room. The house was built in the shape of the letter H, the cross line being a large hall room of some twenty-five by thirty feet, serving as the connecting link between the two wings; these wings are about thirty feet wide by sixty deep. The house contains some eighteen large rooms, exclusive of the hall. The view given here represents the rear, the small stairway leads up to the rear door of the hall room. The room to the right, as one faces the picture, is the bed room in which tradition states that Richard Henry Lee and his brothers were born; also, General Robert E. Lee. The hall room was, in those days, used as the library and general sitting room, especially in summer, being large, airy, well lighted and ventilated. The ceiling is very high, dome shaped, the walls are panelled in oak, with book cases set in them; back and front are doors, leading into the garden, flanked on either side by windows, as shown in the illustration. On the other two sides of this hall, between the book cases, are two doors, opening into the wings. Outside, at the four corners of the house, are four out-houses, used as storehouses, office, kitchen, and such like purposes. At the corner of the house, to the right of the picture given here, but too far off to be seen, was the kitchen, with its immense fireplace, which by actual measurement was found to be twelve feet wide, six high, and five deep, evidently capable of roasting a fair-sized ox. Lying on the grass, there is seen a large, old fashioned shell or cannon ball, which tradition says was once fired at the house by an English war-ship. In recent years it has served the more useful purpose of a hitching block for horses.

The portions of the stable yet remaining show it to have been very large; the kitchen garden was surrounded by the usual brick wall, much remaining at the present time. At the foot of the kitchen garden are the remains of the large brick burial vault, of which Bishop Meade wrote: "I have been assured by Mrs. Eliza Turner, who was there at the time, that it was built by General Henry Lee. The cemetery [vault] is much larger than any other in the Northern Neck, consisting of several apartments or alcoves for different branches of the family. Instead of an arch over them there is a brick house, perhaps twenty feet square, covered in. A floor

STRATFORD HALL

covers the cemetery. In the centre is a trap door, through which you descend by a ladder to the apartments below." This brick house having fallen into ruin, a late proprietor of Stratford had it torn down and the bricks heaped up into a mound, which, covered with earth and surmounted by the tombstone of Thomas Lee, would serve as a fitting mark for the unknown dead reposing underneath.

Thomas Lee Shippen, a grandson of Thomas Lee, visited Stratford in 1790, and wrote his father these interesting letters, telling of his trip and giving his impressions of the places he visited:

"Alexandria, 15 Sept., 1790. My dear Sir, I arrived here late at night before yesterday, and yesterday I was so engrossed by the Lees, who abound here, that I could not find time to write to you. My journey was a delightful one from Chestertown to Georgetown, whether spoken of for the excellence of the society, my fare, the weather, or the roads. For I overtook, as I told you I expected I should, my two valuable friends Messrs. Jefferson and Madison. At Rock Hall, 12 miles from Chestertown, we waited all that day for want of a vessel to take us over, and I never knew two men more agreeable than they were. We talked and dined and strolled and rowed ourselves in boats, and feasted on delicious crabs. A six hours passage over the bay for us, and one of eighteen for my poor Baptist. I had made him go with my horses and carriage in a different boat from that we went in, as there was not room for all, and, wonderful to tell, although at one time they had got before us on the passage, we arrived 12 hours before them. . . . Dined at Georgetown, and at quarter past seven at night I left my companions, who accompanied me in the boat to this side of the Potomac; they returned to Georgetown, and I came on to Alexandria, eight miles; I travelled in the night, a new road, but arrived without any adverse accident, at a little after eight, at my Uncle's house on the banks. My horses performed wonders, my carriage is delightful.

"Yesterday, I passed at Ludwell's seat, a mile from Alexandria, with my Uncle Fendall, Flora, Ludwell and Molly of Chantilly. The place is called Shuter's Hill, and is infinitely handsomer than the one in England of that name. The house is handsome and spacious. Today they dine with us. Tomorrow I pass at Mt. Vernon, and on the day after hope to set off on my tour. My Uncle accompanies me throughout the whole of it. Had I room I would tell you our plans, but I will write again soon, and tell you all. My love to all my friends, my dear Mamma and yourself in particular."

(It may be well to explain some points in this letter. The Chestertown mentioned was in Maryland; to reach Washington, in those days, one drove to Chestertown, took a boat to Annapolis, and then drove on to Washington. The uncle mentioned as his host and his companion on his tour, was probably Arthur Lee, as he then lived in Alexandria and on the "banks" of the Potomac. Ludwell and Molly were children of Richard Henry Lee; Flora was wife of Ludwell and daughter of Philip Ludwell Lee, whose widow had married the Mr. Fendall mentioned.)

"Mount Vernon, 16 Sept., 1790. My dear Father and Friend, This is to be sure a delightful place. Nothing seems wanting to render it the fit residence of its owner, worthy to employ and amuse the leisure of so great a man as our President.

"I have been here two days, and have seen most of the improvements which do honour at once to the taste and industry of our Washington. I have been treated as usual with every most distinguished mark of kindness and attention. Hospitality indeed seems to have spread over the whole place its happiest, kindest influence. The President exercises it in a superlative degree, from the greatest of its duties to the most trifling minutiæ, and Mrs. Washington is the very essence of kindness. Her soul seems to overflow with it like the most abundant fountain and her happiness is in exact proportion to the number of objects upon which she can dispense her benefits. I have some difficulty in leaving them so soon.

"But I must leave them to talk of the Lees; you know my partiality and attachment to them too well to be surprised at my passing my time at Alexandria most happily. They are everything I could wish. My cousin Flora, who is to be sure a most amiable sweet cousin, has just given us another image of herself in a little daughter. Nancy of Chantilly [daughter of R. H. Lee] is married to Charles Lee, has her father's sense and her mother's beauty. Molly [also daughter of R. H. Lee] is like her father and only wants affability to make her engaging. Lucinda of Bellevue [daughter of Thomas Ludwell Lee] has her brother Tom's sprightliness and is a charming girl.

"I dine with them all tomorrow at Charles Lee's, and in the evening go as far as Col. Mason's [Gunston Hall, on the Potomac, just below Mt. Vernon]. Our mode of travelling is as follows. Uncle and Nephew in Uncle's phaeton; John the Baptist in Jones' sulky, and Philip the African on horse back with the portmanteau. We go from Col. Mason's to Richland, Mrs. Thomas Lee's [the widow] seat, thence to Bellevue, the seat of Mr. Thos. L. Lee; to Chatham, to Mansfield, the former the seat of Mr. Fitzhugh, the latter of Mr. Mann Page; to Chantilly, to Nomini, to Manokin, to Richmond, to Nesting, to Westover, to Cawson, to Petersburgh, to Greenspring, my Uncle William's, to Williamsburgh, and then according to my time my route will be further determined.

"My having joined those charming men, Jefferson and Madison, though it gave me infinite pleasure, cost me money, so that when I arrived here I found that I was by thirty dollars poorer than when I left you. This, added to the necessity, which I find still exists, of giving money to servants, and much money too, occasions that of my asking you the favour of a bill for $50, or a bank note to that amount, to me here, to be enclosed in a letter to the care of Ludwell Lee, Esqr., Shuter's Hill near Alex'a.

"Give my love to my dear Mamma, Sister, Uncle, Aunt and cousins, and know me unchanged and unchangeably yours."

"Menoken, 20th September, 1790. My very dear Sir: Altho' your request, to give you the news as soon as possible from Westover, seemed to urge my speedy departure for that place and to dispense with my writing until I arrived there, I cannot deny myself the pleasure I always feel when communicating to you my feelings and thoughts. This apology I hope will satisfy you for my writing before I arrive at Westover. And now I am to speak of Stratford, Chantilly and Menoken! Stratford, the seat of my forefathers, is a place of which too much cannot be said; whether you consider the venerable magnificence of its buildings, the happy disposition of its grounds, or the extent and variety of its prospects. Stratford, whose delightful shades formed the comfort and retirement of my wise and philosophical grandfather, with what mixture of awe and pious gratification did I explore and admire your beauties!! What a delightful occupation did it afford me, sitting on one of the sofas of the great hall, to trace the family resemblance in the portraits of all my dear Mother's forefathers, her father and mother, her grandfather and grandmother, and so on upward for four generations. Their pictures, drawn by the most eminent artists of England and in large gilt frames, adorn one of the most spacious and beautiful halls I have ever seen. There is something truly noble in my grandfather's picture. He is dressed in a large wig, flowing over his shoulders (probably his official wig as President of the Council), and in a loose gown of crimson sattin, richly ornamented. I mention the dress, as it may serve to convey to you some idea of the stile of the picture. But it is his physiognomy that strikes you with emotion. A blend of goodness and greatness; a sweet yet penetrating eye, a finely marked set of features, and a heavenly countenance. Such I have almost never seen. Do not think me extravagant; my feelings were certainly so when I dwelt with rapture on the portraits of

Stratford, and felt so strong an inclination to kneel to that of my grandfather. It was with difficulty that my Uncles, who accompanied me, could persuade me to leave the hall to look at the gardens, vineyards, orangeries and lawns which surround the house.

"Colonel Harry was not at home, so we returned to Chantilly to dinner. Chantilly is upon the same river with Stratford, at a distance of about three miles, and commands a much finer view than Stratford by reason of a large bay into which the Potomack forms itself opposite to Chantilly, and a charming little creek whose windings spread across and water the space which lies before Chantilly and the river. Besides, there is a fine island called Blackstone's that adds to the landscape. At Chantilly, you have everything that is most excellent in fish, crabs, wild fowl, and exquisite meats, the best of liquors, and a most hearty welcome. The house is rather commodious than elegant. The sitting room, which is very well ornamented, is 30 x 18 feet, and the dining room, 20 x 24. My Uncle has a charming little daughter, whom you remember he mentioned to us, his little beauty. Her name is Sally, and she is everything her friends could wish. The pleasures which so many agreeable circumstances necessarily afforded us at Chantilly were not a little interrupted by the extreme indisposition of the family. Excepting Sally, there was not one of them perfectly well. You were frequently wished for; we never sat down to a fine rock-fish, soft crab or wild duck without my Uncle Richard's wishing for you to partake of it. But I must reserve a more particular description of them until we meet. Else I should not have room to say a word of Menoken. I find my Uncle and Aunt Frank as happily situated as it is possible in this world, except their want of society, which they have in themselves, only. They are prodigiously kind to me and to poor Baptist, who has the fever and ague. I have escaped only by taking a dose of bark every day. My Aunt is both Baptist's nurse and mine. She often talks of you and Philadelphia. What a favourite you are in Virginia! Attribute it not to flattery, when I say what I really think, that you ought to be so everywhere. God bless you, my dear Father. I pray you, Sir, always to remember me most affectionately to all my dear relations, and friends. My dear Mama, and Sister in particular. My Uncles and Aunts all desire me to remember them particularly to you."

The last will and testament of Thomas Lee, though very long, is interesting and gives a fair idea of the man. It also shows him to have acquired quite a large estate. The will was dated 22d February, 1749, and probated in Westmoreland 30th July, 1751.

In the name of God, Amen. I, Thomas Lee of Stratford in the County of Westmoreland in Virginia, Esquire, President and Commander-in-chief of the said Colony being thanks be to God of sound Perfect and disposing sence and memory; do make and declare this my Last Will and Testament, all written in my own hand this twenty-second day of February in the year of Our Lord God one thousand seven Hundred forty and nine, 1749–50. First, my soul I doe resign with all Humility and Sincerity to the Lord God of the Heavens, my Creator, from whom my sinfull flesh received it in steadfast hope of mercy and forgiveness of all my sins and offences by the sufferings and merits of his beloved son Jesus Christ, the Saviour and Redeemer of all men. Amen. Amen. Amen. As to my Body, I desire if it Pleases God that I dye anywhere in Virginia if it be Possible I desire that I may be buried between my Late Dearest wife and my honoured Mother and that the Bricks on the side next my wife, may be moved, and my Coffin Placed as near hers as is Possible, without moving it or disturbing the remains of my Mother. Having observed much indecent mirth at Funerals, I desire that Last Piece of Human Vanity be Omitted and that attended only by some of those friends and Relations that are near, my Body may be silently intered with only the Church Ceremony and that a Funeral sermon for Instruction to the living be Preached at the Parish Church near Stratford on any other Day.

In the next place I desire my Ex'ors to pay all my just Debts without delay or Trouble, all but Trifles may be found on my Book.

Item. I give and devise to my Eldest son all my Lands in the Countys of Westmoreland and Northumberland to my Eldest son and the heirs male of his body lawfully begotten forever, and for want of such Issue to my second son and the heirs male of his Body Lawfully begotten forever, and for want of such Issue to my Third son and the heirs male of his Body Lawfully begotten forever, and for want of such Issue I give the said Lands to my Eldest son and his Heirs forever, and my will is, and upon this Express Condition it is that I have Entailed these Lands on my second and third sons, in Case of Failure of heirs male, that my second or third sons to whom these Lands shall descend do Pay respectively to the Heirs Female of my Eldest or Second son as the Case may be two Thousand Pounds sterling which either the second or third sons failing to doe I revoke those gifts and then as Heirs it will descend to the Female Issue of my Eldest son as I desire it shou'd.

Item. I give and bequeath to my Eldest son and his heirs forever all my Lands on the Eastern Shoare of Maryland and called Rehoboth, my two Islands, Moreton and Eden in Cohongaronto or Potomack, 3,600 on the broad run of Potomac and to include half the good Land on Cohongaronto or Potomac, which is my first Patent, Survey by Thomas Stooper Surveyor and all my Land at or near the falls of the Potomac in three Patents or deeds Containing in the three Patents above 3,000 acres, all these Lands, I give my Eldest son in fee simple and I give my said son all the Utensils on the said Lands.

Item. I give and bequeath to my second son and the male Heirs of His Body Lawfully begotten forever, the remainder of all my Lands between Goose or Lee Creek and broad Run joining to the Land I have given my first son, all the Lands I hold on Difficult run except 800 acres hereafter given to my fourth son, all my Land in the County of Stafford all wch Lands I give to my second son in Tail male as af's'd, and in Case of failure of such Issue then I give all the said Lands to my Eldest son in tail male, and for want of such Issue to my third and other sons in tail male upon this Express Condition that which ever of my sons these Lands Descend on for want of male Issue of my second son, that such son shall before he enters on the said Lands pay to the Female Issue of my said second son fifteen hundred pounds sterling, otherwise this gift to all but my second son to be void.

Item. I give and bequeath to my third son and the heirs male of his Body Lawfully begotten forever, all my Lands in Prince William County Containing by deed from the Prop'rs Office 4,200 acres more or less, and in case of Failure of such Issue to my fourth and other younger sons in Tail male, and whichever of my sons shall take by virtue of this Gift, I will and direct shall pay Female Issue of my said third Son one thousand pounds Sterling before entry into the said Lands, which if he fails to doe then I declare my gift to him to be void.

Item. I give and bequeath to my fourth son and the heirs male of his Body Lawfully begotten forever all my Lands on Horse Pen run and Stallion Branch and 800 acres of Land his choice in any one Place out of my Lands on Difficult run in Fairfax County, but my meaning is that he shall chuse it on any one side of the Land, and not in the middle, my design being to give him a Conven't Place to live on with a good Spring and high Ground, and for want of Issue as above I give the said Lands on horse pen Run to my third son in tail male, and to my other younger sons in tail male, but with this Proviso that whichever son takes these Lands other than my fourth shall before he enters Pay to the Female heirs of my Fourth son Eight Hundred Pounds Current money and in case he fails the Gift to be void, and for want of such Issue male as af'r'd I give the 800 acres on difficult to my second son in tail male and for want of such Issue to my Eldest son in fee. Item. I give to my Daughter Alice one thousand Pounds Sterling to be paid her at twenty-one years of age or day of marriage and till such time I desire her a reasonable maintenance, board and education out of my Estate. Item. Whereas I have a long Lease of Land in Cople Parish in which the fee is in my Nephew George Lee, my will and desire is that my Eldest son do Convey to ye said George Lee all my right to the said Land to the said George Lee in tail male for the consideration of three hundred Pounds Sterling first to be paid by the said George Lee to my said Eldest son, and in Case of failure of male Issue of the said George Lee that the said Lands return to my Lawfull Heir male he paying to the Heirs Female of the said George Lee a proportion of the said three hundred pounds Sterling as shall be with relation to the time to Come in the said Lease from the time of the said Purchase money being paid, but one acre where my Hon'd Father is Buryed is not to be in this Purchase and sale, but remain as on the first sale to me, not to be disposed of upon any pretense whatsoever.

Item. To my fifth son, I give one thousand Pounds Sterling to be paid at Twenty one years of age, and till then to be maintained and Educated out of my Estate. Item. To my sixth son, I give one thousand Pounds Sterling to be paid at twenty one years of age, and till then to be maintained and educated out of my Estate. Item. I desire and impower my Ex'ors who I appoint Guardians to my children to educate my children in such manner as they think fitt Religiously and virtuously and if necessary to bind them to any profession or Trade, soe that they may Learn to get their Living honestly. Item. I give my stock in Trade in Company with Col. Tayloe and Mr. Anthony Strother to which of my two youngest Sons my Ex'ors shall think fitt, such son paying to my two Daughters Hannah Corbin and Alice and the other Brother to each a fourth Part of the Stock in money or Bills and in such time as my said Ex'ors shall think fitt. Item. I give my share in the Stock in trade and the Profit of the Land to be granted by Virtue of the King's Warrant to my second son he paying on every Division made by the Company one equal third part of the Profitts of his share to my third and fourth sons to each an equal Part with himself, or this gift to be void and he only to come in for one third to be paid by the Comp'y and one third to each of his two Brothers af's'd. Item. Whereas I have given to my Eldest son one Share in the said Company both Trade and Land which I paid for him in the Stock in Trade I hereby Confirm my said Gift Absolutely.

Item. I give to my Eldest son one hundred Negroes above ten years old and all of and under that age on the Lands I have given him but what above a 100 yt are above ten yrs old to be divided as hereafter is mentioned, and in this Gift to make up the numbers, I give all my Tradesmen, all which Negroes young and old I annex to the Land given my Eldest son to pass and Descend with the said Lands as the Law Commonly Called the Explanatory Law directs. Item. I give to my second son, Fifty Negroes above Ten years of age and all the young ones of and under that age that are on the Lands I have given him annexed and to descend as the Land I have given him does. Item. I give to my Third son Forty Negroes above ten years of age and all of yt age and under yt are upon the Lands, I have given him annexed and to Descend as the Lands I have given him. Item. I give to my Fourth son Thirty Negroes above Ten years of age and all of that age and under that are on the Lands I have given him to be annexed and descend as the Land I have given him. Item. The Profits of the Naval Office according to my Contract w$^{th}$ Col. Richard Lee, I give to my two youngest sons equally and to the survivor of them.

Item. My Will is and I accordingly desire yt my whole Estate be kept together till all my debts and Legacies be settled and Paid. Item. I will and Devise yt if any of my younger children dye before twenty one yt in such case that Legacy be p'd in equal parts to such other as live to be twenty one, that is my two daughters and my youngest sons. Item. I give to my Second Son my Gold watch and seal. Item. I Give all the Rest and Residue of my Estate to my Eldest son and his heirs forever, and the several Bequests and Legacies heretofore given I give in lieu and full satisfaction of their Filial portions and so I desire it may be taken and understood, and I hope I have Expressed so plainly that a Lawyer will not find room to make Constructions prejudicial to my Family. Item. I devise and Bequeath to my Five younger sons two hundred pounds each towards building and Finishing each a house and this legacy I design and order to be paid before my Estate is Divided. Item. I hereby appoint my Friends and Relations, Richard Corbin, Esqr, my Eldest son Philip Ludwell Lee, my son-in-law Gawin Corbin, Esqr, and my second son Thomas Ludwell Lee, my Ex'ors and Guardians to my children. Item. I give to each of my sons and Daughters a mourning ring of five pounds Sterling value. Item. I give to my second son the mourning ring I had for Col. Grymes. Item. I give to my third son the mourning ring I had for Col. Lightfoot. Item. I give to my Eldest Son the ring Col Custis gave me in his life time. Item. I give to my third son the mourning ring I had for Col Tayloe.[1]

There has been some uncertainty as to the burial place of both Thomas Lee and his son, Richard Henry; the former has always been thought to have been buried at Old Pope's Creek church, and the latter at Chantilly. But an examination of their wills and other data proves most conclusively that both of them were buried in "the Old Burnt House Fields," at "Mt. Pleasant." It requires no proof to show that Richard Lee and Lætitia Corbin, his wife, were buried at this place, as their tombstone is still to be seen there. Thomas Lee's wife died about a year before her husband, and of course had been duly buried; in his will he desired to be "buried between

---

[1] John Tayloe, Esq., of Richmond county, in his will (dated the 3d of January, 1744) left his "friend and kinsman," Col. Thomas Lee, a mourning suit, a ring, and £100; in a codicil (dated 31st of January, 1744), he gave him £150 additional, also a mourning ring to Mrs. Hannah Lee, and to the testator's kinsman, Col. Henry, Lee of Westmoreland, £50.

my Late Dearest wife and my Honoured Mother, and that the bricks on the side next my wife may be moved and my coffin Placed as near hers as is possible, without moving or disturbing the remains of my Mother." This request proves his wife had been buried very near the grave of his mother. There can be no doubt that Thomas Lee was buried, as he desired, beside his wife, for *one slab* covered the two graves, and has on it the following inscription, recently copied. The slab, now at Stratford, is in perfect condition, and the inscription as legible as when first cut:

Here lies Buried the Hon'ble Col. Thomas Lee, Who dyed 14 November, 1750; Aged 60 years; and his beloved wife, Mrs. Hannah Lee. She departed this life 25 January, 1749-50. Their monument is erected in the lower church of Washington Parish, in this County; five miles above their Country Seat, Stratford Hall.

Westmoreland was then divided into two parishes; Cople (once written "Copeley") occupied the lower part of the county and Washington the upper. Cople parish had two churches, Yeocomico and Nominy. Washington parish had three: Round Hill, on the *upper* border, near King George county; Pope's Creek, *lower down*, on the main road from Westmoreland court-house to King George; and Leeds or Bray's church, on the Rappahannock river. Yeocomico alone remains of all these churches.

As Old Pope's Creek church stood about five miles above Stratford, and was *the* lower church of Washington parish, it was evidently the one alluded to in the above quoted inscription. And it is probable that persons in after days, seeing the monument at this church, very naturally supposed Thomas Lee had been buried there also.

Bishop Meade has stated that Thomas Lee was buried at Old Pope's Creek church, but gave no reasons for the statement; it is most probable he had been informed by persons who had seen the monument. Though he visited the church and held services there in 1812, he saw no tombstones; on the contrary, he expressly stated that there "the remains of not a few were interred, although no tombstones have preserved their names. Among those whose bodies were deposited around this church is to be numbered the Hon. Thomas Lee," &c. He then gives the epitaph from his tombstone, and gives an erroneous one: "I take the following inscription from his tombstone, which I saw some years since, lying against the wall of the family vault at Stratford,

'In memory of the Hon. Thomas Lee, whose body was buried at Pope's Creek Church, five miles above his country seat, Stratford Hall, in 1756.'"

A comparison of this inscription with the correct one, just quoted, shows many errors. The tombstone states that "their monument is erected in the lower church of Washington Parish, in this County, five miles above their Country Seat, Stratford Hall." Fortunately, a copy of the inscription once on this monument has been preserved, in the writing of Richard Henry Lee; but, unfortunately, a part of the manuscript is torn, so that the name of the "family burying place" is lost:

> This Monument is erected to the Memory of the Honourable Col^o. Thomas Lee, Commander-in-chief and President of His Majesties Council for this Colony, descended from the very ancient and Honourable Family of Lees in Shropshire in England, who dyed November 14, 1750, aged 60 years; and of the Hon^ble Mrs. Hannah Lee, his Wife, by Philip Ludwell Lee, their eldest son, as a just and dutyfull Tribute to so excellent a Father and Mother, Patterns of Conjugal Virtue. They are buryed eighteen miles from this in the family burying place, called the old ——— in Cople Parish, in this County.

No one can well doubt that the "family burying place" was in the old Burnt House Fields, at "Mt. Pleasant." This was the "one acre where my Hon'd Father is Buryed" that Thomas Lee, in his will, desired should not "be disposed of upon any pretense whatsoever." It was the "family burying place at the burnt House, as it is called," where Richard Henry Lee desired to be buried.

Thomas and Hannah (Ludwell) Lee had the following issue; names and dates were copied from the family Bible of Richard Henry Lee, who stated he had copied from that of his father at Stratford:

i, RICHARD [4], born 17 June, 1723; died unmarried, before his father.
ii, PHILIP LUDWELL [4]. See 16.
iii, HANNAH [4], born 6 February, 1728; married Gawin Corbin (who died prior to 1760), and left a daughter, Martha, who married George Richard Turberville. Philip Ludwell Lee, writing to his brother William, under date of 31 May, 1769, said: "Tomorrow Patty Corbin and George Turberville are to be married." They had two sons: Gawin Corbin and Richard Lee; the latter married his cousin, Henrietta, daughter of Richard Henry Lee, and left issue. (See Turberville, under 3; also 18, vi.)
iv, JOHN [4], born 28 March, 1729, and died the same day.
v, LUCY [4], born 26 September, 1750, and died unmarried.
vi, THOMAS LUDWELL [4]. See 17.
vii, RICHARD HENRY [4]. See 18.
viii, FRANCIS LIGHTFOOT [4]. See 19.
ix, ALICE [4], born the 4th of June, 1736, at Stratford; died at Philadelphia, on the 25th of March, 1817; married at London, in 1760, Dr. William Shippen, Jr., and had several children, only two of whom

lived to marry. They were: 1. Anne Hume, born in 1763; died at Philadelphia, the 23d of August, 1841, æt. 78 years; she married, on the 11th of March, 1781, Col. Henry Beekman Livingston, son of Robert R. Livingston, Sr., of Clermont, N. Y.; they had a daughter, Margaret Beekman, who died unmarried. 2. Thomas Lee Shippen, born in 1765; died near Charleston, S. C., on the 4th of February, 1798; he married, at "Nesting," Va., on the 10th of March, 1791, Mrs. Elizabeth (Farley) Bannister, the widow of John Bannister, Jr., of Virginia. (Elizabeth, daughter of John and Elizabeth (Hill) Carter, married Col. William Byrd[3], of "Westover," Charles City county, and had, among others, Elizabeth Byrd, who married James Parke Farley; their daughter, Elizabeth Carter Farley, married John Bannister, Jr., and after his death, Thomas Lee Shippen, as stated.) Thomas Lee, and Elizabeth (Farley-Bannister) Shippen had two sons; only one of whom left issue: William Shippen, M. D., born at "Farley," Bucks county, Pa., the 19th of January, 1792; died at Philadelphia, the 5th of June, 1867; married at Petersburg, on the 14th of February, 1817, Mary Louise, daughter of Thomas and Jane Gray (Wall) Shore, of Petersburg; she was born the 17th of March, 1798; they had ten children, of whom the following five lived to be married: 1. Jane Gray (born in 1818) married (1843) Edward Wharton, of Philadelphia, and left a daughter, who died unmarried. 2. Alice Lee, born 5th of March, 1821; died 27th of January, 1862; married (1847) Dr. Joshua Maddox Wallace, of Philadelphia, and had three children. 3. Thomas Lee, born 27th November, 1822; married, on the 11th of January, 1860, Jane Gray, daughter of Dr. John and Elizabeth S. (Shore) Gilliam, and had one son, William Shippen, born 21st of May, 1861. 4. William, born 21st of May, 1825; died the 3d of April, 1858; married at Baltimore, Achsah Ridgley, daughter of Charles R. and Rebecca Ann (Pue) Carroll, and had one son, Dr. Charles Carroll Shippen. 5. Edward, M. D., U. S. A., born the 23d of June, 1827; married, on the 3d of December, 1878, Mrs. Rebecca Lloyd Post, the widow of Capt. John Eager Howard Post (a great-grandson of the famous Col. John Eager Howard, of Md.), and the second daughter of James Macon Nicholson, of Baltimore, and Arinthea Darby Parker, his wife; Mr. Nicholson was a son of Judge Joseph Hopper Nicholson, of Md. Mrs. Shippen is also a great-granddaughter of Col. Edward Lloyd, of "Wye House," Talbot county, Md., and Elizabeth Tayloe, of "Mt. Airy," Virginia, his wife. Dr. and Mrs. Shippen have one son, Lloyd Parker Shippen, born the 18th of October, 1879. Dr. Shippen resides at Baltimore, Md.

x, WILLIAM[4]. See 20.

xi, ARTHUR[4]. See 21.

## THE LUDWELLS.

Arms: Gules, between two towers on a bend, arg., three eagles displayed, sable.
Motto: I pensieri stretti edil viso sciolto.

The Ludwells are believed to have come originally from Germany and to have settled in the county of Somersetshire, England, from whence two brothers, Thomas and Philip, came to Virginia. They were the sons of Thomas Ludwell, and Jane Cottington, his wife; she was the daughter of James Cottington, of Discoe, in the parish of Bruton. This James was the son of Philip Cottington, Gent., of Godminster, Somersetshire, and a brother of Philip, Lord Cottington, prominent as a statesman and diplomat in the reign of Charles the Second.

Thomas, the elder brother, apparently came to Virginia some years before Philip; he was secretary of the Council in Virginia, and long a prominent supporter of Berkeley; his tombstone, at Williamsburg, surmounted by the Ludwell arms, has this inscription:

"Under this Marble lieth the Body of Thomas Ludwell, Esqr., Secretary of Virginia, who was born at Bruton in the County of Somerset in the Kingdom of England: and who departed this Life in the year 1678: and near this place lye the bodies of Richard Kemp Esqr., his Predecessor in ye Secretary's Office, and Sr. Thomas Lunsford Kt, in Memory of whom this Marble is placed by Order of Philip Ludwell, Esqr., nephew of the said Thomas Ludwell, in the year 1727."

About 1660, Philip, the brother of this Thomas Ludwell, came to Virginia; he was soon chosen deputy secretary under his brother, and finally succeeded him in that office, which he held for many years. He was, also, a firm adherent of Sir William Berkeley, and appears to have been a strong backer of the governor during the troublesome times of Bacon's rebellion; in 1689, he went to England to present a petition to the King for redress of certain grievances against Effingham; and was so successful in this mission that the House of Burgesses voted a gift of £250, with their hearty thanks; in 1793, he was appointed governor of the Carolinas, and appears to have been very aggressive in his administration, especially against the pirates that infested the coast, many of whom he hanged. He returned to England, died there sometime after 1704, and was buried in the Ludwell vault at Bow Church, then near London. This Philip Ludwell was twice married; first, to Lucy, the daughter of Robert Higginson, and the widow (successively) of Major Lewis Burwell and of Col. William Bernard; by this union, Philip had a son and a daughter. He married, secondly, Lady Berkeley, who had also been twice married; her first husband was one Samuel Stephens, of Warwick county, and her second, Sir William Berkeley; she was the daughter of —— Culpeper, and evidently "a high dame," with considerable notion of her own importance; while the wife of Philip Ludwell, she always styled herself "Lady Berkeley." So far as known Lady Berkeley had no issue by any of her husbands.

Sir William Berkeley, in his will, left his estate, "Greenspring," to his wife in these words: "*First,* I make my deare and most virtuous wife, Lady *ffrances Berkeley,* my full and whole executrix of all the goods God has blessed me with in this world. *Next,* with my goods, I give her all my lands, houses and tenements, whatsoever; and not only to her, *but to avoid all cavil,* to her and her heires forever." (II Hening, 559.) At her death, this property apparently passed into the possession of the Ludwells.

Philip, son of Philip Ludwell, and Lucy Higginson, his wife, was born at "Carter's Creek, in the Parish of Abingdon, in Gloucester County, in Virginia, on the 4th day of February, Anno Dom. 1672, and died January 11, Anno Dom. 1726–27." He was married on the "eleventh day of November, being Thursday, Anno Dom. 1697, to Hannah, the daughter of Benjamin Harrison of Southarke Parish, in Surry County in Virginia, Esquire, and Hannah, his wife, who was borne at Indian Fields in the said Parish, on the 15th day of December, 1678, and died April 4, Anno Dom. 1731." The inscription on her tombstone, in Jamestown churchyard, reads:

"Under this Stone lies interred The Body of Mrs. Hannah Ludwell, relict of The Hon[ble] Col. Philip Ludwell Esqr., By whom she has left one son and two daughters. After a most exemplary Life spent in Cheerful innocence and the Constant Exercise of Piety, Charity and Hospitality, she Patiently Submitted to Death on the 4th day of April, 1731, in the 52d year of her age."

Philip Ludwell and Hannah Harrison had three daughters and two sons, two of whom died in infancy: 1, Lucy, born "at Rich Neck, in Bruton Parish, in James City County, the second day of November, Anno Dom. 1698, about 8 of ye clock in the morning, being wenesday." She married Colonel John Grymes, and left issue; she died on the 2d of November, 1748. 2, Hannah, born "at Rich Neck, aforesaid, on the 5th day of December, anno Dom. 1701, being fryday, about nine of the clock at night, and died at Stratford on Potowmack, January 25, 1749." She married Thomas Lee, and had issue, as previously stated. 3, Sarah, born "at Rich Neck, aforesaid, the 29th day of July, anno Dom. 1704, being Saterday, about 8 of ye clock at night. She died January, 6, 1704–5." 4, Philip, born at "Greenspring, in James City Parish and County, on the 19th day of January, Anno Dom. 1705–6, being Saterday, about 10 in ye morning; he died the 9th of March following. He was a very pretty boy, like his mother." 5, Philip, "borne at Greenspring aforesaid, in the night betwixt fryday the 28th and Satterday the 29th of December, about 12 of ye clock, Anno Dom. 1716." He married Frances "the daughter of Charles Grymes of North Farnham Parish in the county of Richmond, in Virginia, Esquire, and Frances his wife, daughter of the Hon'ble Edmund Jenings of Rippon, in Yorkshire, in England, Esquire, who was born at Morattico, in the aforesaid County and Parish, on ye 19th day of November, An. Dom. 1717. The marriage took place at Morattico afores$^{d}$, A. D. 1737." Philip Ludwell died on the 25th of March, 1767, in England, and was buried at Bow Church. With his death the male line of the Virginia Ludwells became extinct. He had been a member of the Council in Virginia, and in 1695 the Speaker of the House of Burgesses. He left three daughters: 1, Hannah Philippa, who was born "at Greenspring on Wednesday, Dec., 21, 1737, at 52 min. past 4 in the morning, being St. Thomas Day, and was christened the Tuesday following by the Rev. Wm. Lehein." She was married, at St. Clement Dane's, in the County of Middlesex, on the 7th of March, 1769, to William Lee. (See 20.) 2, Lucy, who married, in 1769, John Paradise, Esqr., of Charles Street, Berkeley Square, London, who died in England in 1796; she returned to Virginia in 1805, and died there in 1814, intestate. Their daughter, Lucy, born in England about 1770, married, in 1787, Count Barziza, a Venetian subject, by whom she had two sons; one was born at Venice in February, 1789; the other in August, 1796; both sons were living in 1819. Countess Barziza died at Venice in August, 1800. 3, Frances, born in 1750; died on the 14th of September, 1768, unmarried.

## THE SHIPPEN FAMILY.

Arms: Argent, a chevron between three oak leaves, gules.
Crest: A bird, close, sable, in its beak an oak leaf, vert.

Edward Shippen, son of William Shippen, of Yorkshire, England, was born in 1639; he emigrated to America in 1668, settling at Boston. Entering mercantile life, he speedily amassed a large fortune; was a member of the "Ancient and Honorable Artillery Company" of that city. In 1671 he married one Elizabeth Lybrand, a Quakeress, and joined that sect; he had been previously of the English Church. On account of the "jailings, whippings, and banishments, fines, &c.," meted to the Quakers by the Puritans, he was finally compelled to leave Massachusetts. Consequently, in 1693, he closed up his affairs and removed to Philadelphia, where he died in 1712. Edward Shippen was evidently a man of much ability, as well proven by the position accorded him in his new home. For shortly after taking up his residence in Philadelphia he was chosen a member of the Provincial Assembly and soon elected its Speaker (1695). A few years later he was appointed by Penn the first Mayor of Philadelphia under the new charter (25th of October, 1701). Previous to that appointment he had been placed in the Council, and continued a member until his death, having served as its President in 1702–4. On remarrying he withdrew from the Society of Friends, and shortly afterward from public life. Mr. Shippen built himself a very handsome house in Philadelphia, which was generally known as the "Governor's house." He was characterized as having the "biggest person, the biggest house, and the biggest coach in the city." His son, Joseph Shippen, prominent in political and educational affairs, was born in 1679 at Boston, and died in 1741 at Philadelphia. He married Abigail Gross and had quite a large family, only three of whom survived him: Edward, Anne, and William. Edward (1703–1781) removed to Lancaster, and held many important positions there. He left a son, also an Edward (1729–1806), known as "the jurist," who studied law at home and at the Temple in London. Returning to Philadelphia, he was appointed, in 1752, a Judge of the Court of Vice-Admiralty, and (in 1770) a member of the Council. During the Revolution he appears to have sympathized with England; yet, in 1784, he was appointed President Judge of the Court of Common Pleas of Philadelphia, and in 1791 an Associate Justice of the Supreme Court of the State; in 1799 the Governor nominated him as Chief Justice, which position he held until 1805. His brother, Joseph Shippen (1732–1810), was educated at Princeton, became a Colonel in the Provincial army, and later (1762) a member of the Council. He, too, removed to Lancaster, and was a Judge of the County Court. Anne, daughter of Joseph and Abigail (Gross) Shippen, married Charles Willing. Their third child, William Shippen (known as "the Elder," to distinguish him from his son, William Shippen, Jr., both being physicians of renown at the same time in Philadelphia), was born at Philadelphia on the 1st of October, 1712; died at Germantown on the 4th of November, 1801. William gave evidence early in life of an aptitude for medicine, by which he later acquired both fame and fortune. Though devoted to his profession, he was closely identified with many public interests; was instrumental in aiding to establish the Pennsylvania Hospital, and one of its attending physicians for many years; was a member and Vice-President of the American Philosophical Society; in 1778 he was elected by the Pennsylvania Assembly a member of the Continental Congress and again the next year.

Scarcely less noted was his son, Dr. William Shippen, Jr., who was born in Philadelphia, 21st of October, 1736, and died at Germantown, on the 11th of July, 1808. After graduating at Princeton in 1754, he began the study of medicine under his father; later, he went to London and studied there under the celebrated surgeons, William and John Hunter. Next he read at the University at Edinburgh, where he received the degree of M. D. in 1761. After his settling at Philadelphia, he opened the first systematic course of lectures on anatomy (1762), which were very successful and were really the beginning of the medical department of the University of Pennsylvania. Dr. Shippen was thoroughly patriotic during the Revolutionary struggle, and held various positions as surgeon in the army. He was appointed chief physician to "the Flying Camp of the Continental Army," 15th of July, 1776, and later director-general of the military hospitals. He married, in 1760, Alice, daughter of Thomas Lee, and had issue, as stated.

## Henry Lee.

6. Henry[3], fifth son of Richard Lee[2] (Richard[1]) and Lætitia Corbin, his wife, was born about 1691; and died between the 13th of June and 25th of August, 1747; he lived at "Lee Hall," on the Potomac, adjoining "Mt. Pleasant." It is probable that he took little or no part in public affairs, for no records exist of his having done so. He married, about

1723–24, Mary, daughter of Colonel Richard Bland, of "Jordans," Prince George's county; she was born the 21st of August, 1704; died —— 1764. On the opposite page is given a *fac simile* copy of Henry Lee's commission as lieutenant-colonel of the Westmoreland county militia.

Henry Lee made his will the 30th of July, 1746, and added the last codicil the 13th of June, 1747: it was probated, at Westmoreland, the 25th of August, 1747:

In the name of God, Amen. I Henry Lee of the parish of Cople, in the County of Westmoreland, Gent. being sick and weak of body, but of perfect sense and memory, Do make this my last Will and Testament. First and principally I recommend my Soul to Almighty God and my body to the Earth to be decently Bury'd, there to rest in hopes of a Joyful resurrection and Union with my Soul at the last day through the merits and mediation of our Blessed Mediator and Redeemer Jesus Christ. And as for what Worldly Estate, which it hath pleased God to bestow on me, I give and Dispose of the same in manner and form following.

Imprimis I do Order that all Just Debts which I do owe be paid first out of my Estate. And whereas I have a Suit at law with Mr. John Crawley of Northumberland County for my lands in the said County which I purchased of the Heir of Thomas Matthews dec'd, as by Deeds from Westard and Lessingham assignees of the said Matthews may fully and at large appear. It is my Will Intention and desire that the said Suit be Continued and if Occasion that other Suits be brought ag'st the said Crawley for to obtain the s'd Lands, which he unjustly detains from me, and that the charges thereof be born and Defrayed out of my whole Estate.

It is my Will and desire that my Estate be only Inventory'd and not to be appraised. And it is also my Will and desire that my Estate be kept whole and entire for three years after my decease before any Division or any part be taken by any, to whom it is bequeathed. I give and bequeath to my Son John and to his heirs forever, the plantation and Tracts of Land in Machotique Neck, that I now mention, Viz't. the Lands called King Copsco on Potomac river, which I bought of John Wright and William Chandler and Deliverance, his Wife, and of Susanna Appleyard and the Land and Plantations I bought of Col°. Henry Fitzhugh, and all the several Tracts or parcels of Land I bought of Samuel Attwell, as by the several Deeds will more plainly and at large appear. I give and bequeath to my Son John and to his Heirs, One hundred acres or more of Land in Machotique Neck, as contained in a Lease from the late Daniel McCarty Gent. dec'd. to Francis Attwell, which I purchased of the said Francis Atwell.

I give and bequeath to my Son John and to his Heirs forever, Eighteen slaves, Viz't. Old Will, Absalom, Solomon, Ceasar, Peter, Howels, Jack, Toney, Sue, Sue's Sarah, Sue's Letty, Sue's Winney, Lucy, Davey, Joe, Siss, and Cyruss now are on the aforesaid Lands, and from my Dwelling plantation Ben and Winney's Nan, and after my Wife's death, I give to my Son John and to his Heirs forever two more slaves, Viz't. Old Betty and Cupid, I give to my Son John a servant man called Smith. I give and bequeath to my Son Richard and to his Heirs forever all the Lands, Plantations and Houses where I now live, being all the Lands given and bequeathed to me by my Honoured Father Col. Richard Lee dec'd., as by his last Will and Testament will more plainly appear, and all the several plantations and Tracts of Land which I have at Sundry times bought of Joseph Chandler, John Chandler, John Byard, James Byard, William Oxford and Frances, his Wife, by the several Deeds will

William Gooch Esq. His Majesty's Lieutenant Governour & Commander in Ch[ief]
of the Colony and Dominion of Virginia.

To Henry Lee Gent.

By virtue of the Power and Authority to Me Given by His Majesty as Commander in Chief of this Colony I do hereby Constitute and Appoint you the said Henry Lee to be Lieutenant Colonel of His Majesty's Militia in the County of Westmoreland whereof Thomas Lee Esq. is County Lieutenant: You are therefore carefully & Diligently to Discharge the Duty of Lieutenant Colonel by duly Exercising and Disciplining the Soldiers under your Command, and by taking that they be provided with Horses Arms & Ammunition as the Law requires. And I do hereby Command them to Obey you as their Lieutenant Colonel, and you are to follow all such Orders and Directions from time to time as you shall receive from Me, your County Lieutenant, or any other your Superior Officer, according to the Rules and Discipline of War.

Given under My Hand and the Seal of the Colony at Williamsburgh this 2d day of June — 1737 in the Tenth Year of His Majesty's Reign.

William Gooch

more plainly appear. And also One hundred and one acres of Land more or less in Machotique Neck, which I bought of Richard Kenner. I give and bequeath to my Son Richard and to his Heirs forever all my Lands and Plantations in Northumberland County which I bought of the Heir of Thomas Matthews dec'd. as by Deeds from Westard and Lessingham assignees of the said Matthews may more fully appear. I give and bequeath to my son Richard and to his Heirs forever One Acre and a half of Land at the Turks Swamp which I bought of Cap't. Richard Bushrod with design there to build a mill. My Will and desire is that a mill be there built at the charge of my Estate, which mill I give to my Son Richard and to his Heirs forever.

I give and bequeath to my Son Richard and to his Heirs forever fifteen slaves now at my dwelling plantation, Viz't. London, Boatswain, little Will, Old Phill, Prue's Tom, Prue's Sam, Frank Nugent, Dick, Natt, little Betty, Eave, Patty, Belinda, her child Maread and old George, and after my Wife's death, I give and bequeath to my Son Richard and to his Heirs forever, thirteen more slaves, now at my dwelling plantation, Viz't. Jack, Harry, Black Sarah, Phillis, Tom, Daniel, little Phill, little Sarah, Prue, Prue's George, Beck, young Prue, and Nell,—I give and bequeath to my Son Richard thre Servants men, Viz't. the Shoemaker, the Piper and a servant named Cook. I give and bequeath to my Son Richard and to his Heirs all the pictures in my House and my Clock and a Escreture made of mahogany. I give and bequeath all my Stocks of Cattle, Hoggs, Sheep and Horses, which are at my River Side quarters unto my two Sons John and Richard to be equally divided between them.

I give and bequeath to my Son Henry and to his Heirs forever, all my Plantations and Land in Prince William County which I have at Free Stone point and at Neapsco and Powells Creeks, which was granted by Pattent to Gervas Dodson for two thousand acres, and by my Grandfather, Henry Corbin Gent. given to his Daughter Lettice who was my Mother and afterwards descended to my Brother Mr. Richard Lee as Heir at Law to her and by my said Brother given to me as by deeds Recorded in Stafford County may more fully appear. And whereas I sold to John Wright One thousand Acres, a part of the said Land, and since have purchased the same again, Viz't. 666½ acres of Francis Wright, son of the aforesaid John, and 333½ acres of Mr. Benjamin Grayson to whom the said Francis had sold: whereby I am now invested of the whole Two thousand acres of Land in fee simple as aforesaid given and bequeathed to my Son Henry and to his Heirs forever. I give and bequeath to my Son Henry and to his Heirs forever all that my 3111 acres of Land and Plantation thereon in Fairfax County, at or near Salsbury plain and Flatt lick, as by a proprietors Deed for the said Land may more plainly appear. Also the land I bought of James Walker for three hundred acres more or less, adjoining to the last mentioned Land in the said county of Fairfax. I give and bequeath to my Son Henry and to his Heirs forever Twenty slaves, Viz't. Tom, Dinah, Hannah, Moll, Daniel, Frank, little Dinah, Dick and Cato, now at Neapsco Quarter and Titus, Cain, Westminster, Eava, Harry, Joe, Sabina her child, Joe and Harry, now at Salsbury plain Quarter, and at my dwelling plantation Prue's Frank and Winney's Moll. I give and bequeath to my Son Henry and to his Heirs all my Stocks of Cattle and Hoggs and all other my personal Estate which I have in the said County of Prince William and in the said County of Fairfax, excepting Debts due to me, which are to come into my Estate. My Will and desire is that my Son Henry be Continued at the College two years from the date hereof and afterwards to be a writer in the Secretary's Office, till he be twenty one years of age.

I give and bequeath to my Daughter Lettice and to her Heirs Seven hundred pounds sterling to be paid her as soon, and as conveniently as my Estate can do it, after she attain to the age of twenty one years or the day of her marriage, which shall first happen. I give and bequeath to my said Daughter two slaves named Letty and Peg and their increase to my said Daughter and to her Heirs forever. I give to my said Daughter a Chest of Drawers made of Oak, as is now called her chest of Drawers, and a new Chest of Drawers made of Mahogany. I lend to my beloved Wife Mary, in full consideration of her Dower, thirds or childs part of my Estate, both real and personal, and for no other intent whatsoever as I hereafter mention, in every particular, Viz't. I lend to my said wife the use of my dwelling plantation and the use of my dwelling House, Out Houses, Garden, Orchards, and all other appurtenances to the same belonging, and Land adjoining, making in the whole 600 acres during her life, also I lend to my said wife the use of my Land at Kingcopsco in Machotique Neck during her life, which I bought of William Chandler and Deliverance, his wife, and of Susannah Appleyard as by Deeds will more plain appear. And my Will and desire is that for the use of the said Land and Plantation at Kingcopsco, my Wife shall at all times, when occasion, have free liberty on any of my Land next adjacent to have Timber for Framing, Rafters, Posts, Studs, Culs bords, Tob: sticks, fencing and fire wood or for any other necessary use for the service of the said Plantation. Also I lend to my said wife the use of fifteen slaves during her life, Viz't. Jack, Harry, Black Sarah, Phillis, Tom, Daniel, little Phill, little Sarah, Prue, George, Beck, young Prue, and Nell, who are now at my dwelling plantation, and Old Betty and Cupid who are now at my River Side Quarter, and I lend to my wife the use of all my House hold furniture and Utensils in the Kitchen, Dairy, Meat house, and in all other Houses and places belonging to my dwelling plantation, also the chaise, the chair, the Horses and Harness during her life. And I give to my wife all my stocks of Cattle, Hoggs and Sheep belonging to my plantation where I live, and I give to my Wife three casks of the best Cyder from my Quarters at the River Side, every year during her life. It is my will and desire that all times when my Wife has Occasion for Tob: Casks and Cyder Cask, that Frank Nugent and Dick get the Timber and make the cask and that they mend and repair all the houses on my dwelling plantation, and they to do any other Coopers or Carpenters Work for my Wife as she may have occasion, and when she requires it, and that without any charge to her for the same.

After my Estate has paid all my Debts and the Charges of my Suit or Suits, with Mr. Crawley, and paid my Daughters fortune of Seven hundred pounds Sterling as aforementioned, and paid the Charges of building the mill for my Son Richard,—what Tob: and money shall then happen to remain belonging to my Estate I give and bequeath the same to my Wife and three Sons to be equally divided between them, and after my Wifes death, I give and bequeath all my Household furniture and all other moveables and personal Estate whatsoever, not already given or bequeathed, I give to my three Sons, John, Richard and Henry, to be equally divided between them.

It is my desire that my Wife and three Sons do in the management of their Estate take advice of my two Brothers The Hon'ble Thomas Lee Esqr. and Col^o. William Beverley. My Will and desire is that my body have a private a decent Interment, without any funeral Sermon, and that the buryal Service for me to be performed by the parish Clark or some other fitt person. Lastly I do hereby appoint my two Brothers The Hon'ble Thomas Lee Esqr. and Col. William Beverley, also my two Sons, John Lee and Richard Lee, Executors of this my Last Will and Testament, and hereby revoke and make void all former Wills heretofore made by me, either by word or Deed, and declare this to be my last Will and Testament, and hereunto I set my hand and Seal this thirtieth day of July in the year of our Lord One thousand Seven hundred and forty six.

1st. Codicil. Westmoreland, July thirtieth, 1746. It is my Will that my Executors above named Lease to Adam Mitchell for his own and his Wifes life, One hundred and fifty Acres of Land adjoining to the House in which he now lives, and likewise that one of his Children which he pleases to put in, may hold the same for his life, he or they or any of them paying yearly during the terms mentioned the Sum of six hundred and thirty pounds of Tob

A further Codicil. Westmoreland County, August 10th, 1746. I do hereby Constitute and appoint my two Brothers The Hon'ble Thomas Lee Esqr. and Col°. William Beverley Guardians to my Son Henry and to my Daughter Lettice till each of them respectively attain to the age of twenty-one years.

Third Codicil. In the name of God Amen. I Henry Lee of Westmoreland County in Virginia and now at the Warm Springs in Frederick County, being sick and weak but perfect in sense and memory thanks be to God for the same, do add this as a Codicil to a former Will by me made, which will is still to stand absolute, the two following clauses only excepted, to wit: Imprimis, it is my Will that the Carpenters which I have heretofore employed in building certain Houses for the use of my son John Lee that is to say a Dwelling House, a kitchen and an Office, shall be continued in such Employment untill such time as the said Houses shall be compleated: The aforesaid Houses to be of the following dimensions: the Dwelling House thirty-six feet by twenty four, the kitchen Eighteen feet by Sixteen, and the Office Eighteen feet by Sixteen.

Item, That the Gift made in my former Will of a negro Woman named Pegg to my Daughter Lettice Wife of William Ball of Lancaster County Gentleman be hereby revoked and made Null; and I bequeath the said negro Pegg with her increase unto my Son John Lee and his heirs forever, he or they paying unto the aforesaid Lettice Ball, or to her Heirs, the sum of Forty pounds Current Money. In witness whereof I hereunto set my hand, and affix my Seale as a Codicil to my former Will, this thirteenth (13th) day of June, in the year of our Lord One thousand Seven hundred and forty-seven.

(Another codicil, without date.) I give my—Saddle and furniture to my Son John Lee, I give to my aforesaid Son my new Gun with a silver sight, and my ould Gun. I give to my aforesaid Son my blew Cloath Suite and my new mourning Gound and Sword, which is gone to England. I give to my Son Henry Lee a new Gun which came in for him and a Gun called Hawells and my Watch. I give to my Son Richard Lee my long Gun which cost three Geanes and a Gun called Watson which is now sent to England by Capt. Jno. Johnson and I give my aforesaid Son my wriding Horse. I give to my Daughter Lettice Ball a bed, bolster and two pillows, a pair of Blankets, a quilt and a pair of sheets.

Henry Lee's widow survived him many years, dying in 1764. Her will was dated 19th of October, 1762, and probated, Westmoreland, 29th of May, 1764.

In the name of God, Amen. I Mary Lee of Lee Hall in the parish of Cople and County of Westmoreland, Widow, being of perfect sence and memory, for which I thank God, after recommending my Soul into the hands of that Almighty God who gave it and declaring my trust through the merrits and intercession of my Blessed Redeemer and Saviour to receive pardon and remission of all my sins, do make and ordain this my last Will and Testament in manner and form following. Imprimis, I direct my body shall be buried at the discretion of my Executors hereinafter named. Item, I desire my just debts may be paid as soon as they conveniently can after my death. Item, I give and bequeath unto my beloved Daughter Lettice Ball all my wearing apparel, Books and whatsoever other things of mine that may be in the house at the time of my decease excepting the Legacies hereafter mentioned. Item, I give and bequeath unto my Dear Son Richard Lee my Charriot and horses and all my stocks upon his paying to my Grand-Daughter Mary Ball One Hundred pounds current money of Virginia to be put out at interest on good security untill my said Grand-Daughter arrives at the age of twenty-one years or is married, when she is to have the whole principal and interest. Item, I give and bequeath unto my Daughter Lettice Ball all the money that my son Richard Lee may owe me at the time of my decease after deducting the price of the mourning Rings hereafter mentioned and paying all my just debts which said money I order to be paid to my said Daughter as soon as possible after my decease. Item, I give to each of my children John Lee, Richard Lee, Lettice Ball and Henry Lee and my Daughters-in-law Mary Lee and Lucy Lee and my Grand Daughter Mary Ball a mourning Ring of a guinea value. Item, I give unto my son John Lee my Weding ring. Item, I give unto my Granddaughter Mary Ball my old mourning ring, my Bible and Common Prayer Book. Item, I lend unto my said Daughter Lettice Ball during her natural life to use them in whatsoever manner she thinks proper without paying any compensation whatsoever the following slaves, . . . together with all the rest and residue of my estate both real and personal, not before given and after the Death of my said Daughter I give and bequeath unto my Grand Daughter Mary Ball and her heirs forever the following slaves . . . provided the said Mary Ball shall marry with the consent and approval of her said Mother Lettice Ball but if she should not marry with such consent and approbation then I give all the said negroes and their increase and all the rest of my estate to my Grandsons William and Henry Lee Ball in such parts and proportions as my said Daughter Lettice Ball shall direct by her last will and Testament in writing or by Deed Executed in her life time before two credible witnesses, and if my said Daughter should fail to make such will or deed then to be equally divided between them the said William Ball and Henry Lee Ball after the decease of my said Daughter. Item after the decease of my said Daughter Lettice Ball I give and bequeath to my two Grandsons William Ball and Henry Lee Ball and their heirs forever the following slaves . . . to be divided between or wholly given to either of my said Grandsons William Ball and Henry Lee Ball as my said Daughter Lettice Ball shall direct by her last Will and Testament or by Deed executed in her life time before two credible witnesses and if my Daughter should fail to make such will or Deed, then to be equally divided between the said William Ball and Henry Lee Ball. Item, I constitute and appoint my son Richard Lee sole Executor to this my last Will and Testament. In testimony whereof I have hereunto set my hand and seal this 19th of October, 1762, and do hereby revoke every other will heretofore by me made and Executed.

Henry and Mary (Bland) Lee left four children, three sons and one daughter, named in their wills as follows:

i, JOHN[4], See 22.
ii, RICHARD[4], See 23.
iii, HENRY[4], See 24.
iv, LÆTITIA[4], born about 1730–1; married in 1746–7, Col. William Ball, of Lancaster county; she was his second wife. She died in 1788, and left two sons, William and Henry Lee Ball, and one daughter, Mary Ball; so given in their grandmother's will.

Col. William[5] Ball (William[4], William[3], William[2], William[1]) of "Millenbeck," Lancaster county, was a cousin of the James Ball who, about the same time, married another Lettice Lee, a daughter of Richard and Judith (Steptoe) Lee, of the Ditchley line; as there were several intermarriages between the Balls and the Lees of Ditchley, a more extended notice of them will be giving when sketching that branch of the Lee family.

## THE BLAND FAMILY.

ARMS: Argent on a bend, sable, three phaeons of the field.
CREST: Out of a ducal coronet, or, a lion's head ppr.
MOTTO: Sperate et vivite fortes.

The Blands of Virginia are descended from Sir Thomas Bland, of "Kippax Park," near Leeds in England, who was created a baronet by Charles I., in 1642; he was the representative of an ancient and honorable family. Of this family was John Bland, grocer, of London, who was early interested in the Colony of Virginia; he was born in 1573 and died in 1632, leaving a large family and a very great personal estate. Four of his sons emigrated to Virginia:

i, Adam, who died on the voyage.

ii, John, a merchant, trading to Virginia and the West Indies, probably made his first voyage about 1635. On the 20th of March, 1674–5, his nephew, Edward, son of his brother, Edward, conveyed to him 3,000 acres, called "Kymages," in the parish of Westover, Charles City county, in Virginia. His son, Giles, settled on this land, was collector of the lower James River, took part in Bacon's Rebellion, and was hanged, in 1676, under a decree of Berkeley's court-martial. John Bland died in 1680, leaving "Kymages" to his wife, and Thomas Povey, whose daughter, Frances, was the widow of his son, Giles. This branch of the family is extinct.

iii, Edward, the third son to emigrate, married his cousin, Jane, daughter of Gregory Bland; he came to Virginia before 1652; died in 1653, leaving an only son, Edward. This son married and left a son, John, who died unmarried; also a daughter, Sarah, who married and left issue.

iv, Theodorick, the fourth son to emigrate to Virginia, was the fifteenth child; he was baptized at St. Antholin's (London) on the 16th of January, 1629–30; was first a merchant with his brother, Edward, at St. Luca, in Spain, then in the Canary Islands, and shortly after his brother's death in 1653, he came to Virginia. He purchased "Berkeley" and "Westover," where he lived; was Speaker of the House of Burgesses, 1659–60; member of Council, 1666, "and was both in fortune and in understanding inferior to no person of his time in the country." He was buried at Westover. (Alexander Brown, *Genesis of the United States*, 829–30.) His tombstone, at Westover Church, had this inscription:

J. S. H. Prudentis et Eruditi Theodorici Bland, Armig: qui Obiit Aprilis 23d A. D. 1671. Ætatis 41. Cujus Vidua Mœtissima, Filia Richardi Bennett, Armig: Hoc Marmor Posuit.

Theodorick Bland married Anne, daughter of Richard Bennett, and was the progenitor of the Virginia family. Richard Bennett deserves a passing notice in this connection, as he acted a prominent part in the affairs of the Colony of Virginia. He was a member of the House of Burgesses in 1629; of the Council in 1639–42–44–45–46–58–59–60–75, and probably at other dates; was appointed by the Council of State in England one of their commissioners to "reduce the plantations within the bay of the Chesapeake to their due obedience to the Parliament of the Commonwealth of England," which the commissioners did in 1652; was governor of Virginia 1652–55; commissioner to England in 1655; and was appointed a major-general of the Virginia troops, 1662–72; died in 1675, and left a son, Richard of Bennett's Point, Queen Anne's county, Md. Gov. Bennett is said to have married Mary Ann Utie, who was probably a daughter of the Col. John Utie, who settled at Chiskiack in 1632, and was an early member of the Virginia Council.[1]

Anne (Bennett) Bland died at Wharton's Creek, Kent county, Md., in 1687; they had issue two sons:

i, Theodorick, of "Westover," who was also a member of the Council; he died in 1702, and left Theodorick, John (who returned to England), and Scarborough.

---

[1] *W. & M. Quarterly*, III, 206–207.

ii, Richard, of "Jordans," James River, born at "Berkeley," the 11th of August, 1665; died the 6th of April, 1720, and was buried at "Westover;" he was twice married; first to Mary, the daughter of Col. Thomas Swan; secondly (in 1701), to Elizabeth, the daughter of Col. William Randolph, of "Turkey Island," the progenitor of the Randolph family in Virginia;[1] she died the 22d of January, 1719; several children by his first wife died young; by the second wife he left these five children: 1, Mary, born the 21st of August, 1704; married about 1723–4, Henry Lee, of Westmoreland, as stated. 2, Elizabeth, who married Col. William Beverley, of "Blandfield," Rappahannock River. 3, Col. Richard Bland, of "Jordans," a member of the House of Burgesses, of the first Continental Congress, of the Virginia Convention of 1775; he married Anne, daughter of Peter Poythress, the "Antiquary," by whom he had issue. 4, Anne Bland, who married Capt. Robert Munford. 5, Theodorick Bland, born in 1720; married (1739) Frances, daughter of Drury Bolling, and had, among others, Col. Theodorick, M. D., statesman, soldier, and poet; he was born the 21st March, 1742; through his mother he was descended from Pocahontas; received his degree in medicine at Edinburgh; practiced for a short time in Virginia; later distinguished himself as a leader of volunteers against Lord Dunmore, and also wrote, under the *nom de plume* of "Cassius," some very spirited letters against him; he was captain of the First Troop of Virginia cavalry; later became colonel, and distinguished himself greatly by his services in the field; he served in the old Congress, in 1780–3; opposed the adoption of the new Constitution, but later accepted a seat in Congress. Theodorick and Frances (Bolling) Bland had also a daughter, Frances, born 24th September, 1752; died 18th January, 1788; married twice; first (in 1769) John Randolph, nephew of the above mentioned Elizabeth Randolph, whose son was the famous John Randolph, of "Roanoke;" she married, secondly (in 1777), St. George Tucker, whose son, Judge St. George Tucker, was the father of the Hon. John Randolph Tucker, and others.

The famous "Westover" estate, so frequently mentioned in these notes, is said to have contained about 2,000 acres, originally patented by Captain Thomas Pawlett in 1637. At his death, in 1648, he left the land to his brother, Sir John Pawlett, who sold it, in 1665, to Theodorick Bland for £170 sterling. His eldest son, also Theodorick, divided it with his

---

[1] See sketch of Randolph Family, under 48.

brother Richard ; they sold the estate, in 1668, to the first Colonel William Byrd for £300 sterling and 10,000 pounds of tobacco.

## STRATFORD LINE, FOURTH GENERATION.

### Colonel George Lee, of Mt. Pleasant.

7. George[4], the eldest child and only son of Richard Lee[3] (Richard[2], Richard[1]) and Martha Silk, his wife, was born at London, on the 18th of August, 1714; came over to Virginia some years after the death of his father and settled at "Mt. Pleasant," in Westmoreland county, where he died the 19th of November, 1761. The probabilities are that George Lee was educated in England, and did not come to Virginia until a year or so before his first marriage. He was married, on the 30th of September, 1738, to Judith, daughter of John and Elizabeth Wormeley, of "Rosegill," Middlesex county. The parish register of old Christ Church states that "Sarah and Judith, daughters of John and Eliza Wormeley, were born the 20th of June, and baptised the 27th of June, 1714." Elizabeth Wormeley, of Middlesex, by her will (of the 3d of March, 1743), gave her daughter, Judith, the wife of Mr. George Lee, £200 sterling. Mrs. Lee died on the 8th of June, 1751, leaving a daughter, Elizabeth. George Lee married, secondly, on the 16th of December, 1752, Mrs. Anne (Fairfax) Washington, the widow of Lawrence Washington, of Mt. Vernon, and the daughter of the Hon. William Fairfax, of "Belvoir," Fairfax county. Lawrence Washington was the half-brother of George Washington, to whom he bequeathed Mt. Vernon after his widow's death. General Washington occupied Mt. Vernon after her second marriage and paid a yearly rental of some £82 from 1752 to 1761.[1] Mrs. Lee died the 14th of March, 1761, only a few months before her husband. (The above data are taken from the family Bible of George Lee, which has the name "Judith Wormeley," and the date, "1736," on the fly-leaf. It is probably the same "great Bible" that George Lee devised to his daughter, Elizabeth, "which were her mother's.")

---

[1] The "Little Hunting Creek" or Mt. Vernon estate was first devised by John Washington, the immigrant, to his son Lawrence, who left it to his daughter, Mildred, in these words: "I give and bequeath my Daughter Mildred Washington all my Land in Stafford County, lying upon hunting creek, where Mrs. Elizabeth Minton and Mrs. Williams now lives by estimation 2,500 acres to her and her heirs forever." On the 17th of May, 1726, Roger Gregory, and Mildred Washington, his wife, executed a deed of release for this property to her brother, Augustine Washington, "for divers good causes and conciderations him thereunto moving but more especially for and in concideration of the sum of one Hundred and eighty pounds Sterling money of Great Britain." Augustine devised the estate to his second son, Lawrence, who, in turn, left it to his wife for her life and at her death to go to his younger brother, George Washington. Lawrence Washington desired to be buried there beside his three children, and mentioned also a daughter, Sarah who must have died shortly after her father.

George Lee was deputy clerk of Westmoreland, under his brother-in law, George Turberville, from 1740 to 1742, at which date he succeeded him in the office, and held it until his own death. He also represented the county as Burgess in 1748, 1751, and perhaps at other times; was a Justice for Westmoreland in 1737; a vestryman of Cople parish in 1755. His will, dated the 13th of September, 1761, and probated, at Westmoreland, the 26th of January, 1762, was as follows:

In the Name of God, Amen. I George Lee of the parish of Cople in the County of Westmoreland, gentleman, being sick and weak but of perfect mind and memory (thanks be to God) do make this my last Will and Testament in manner and form following: First, I desire I may be buried decently but without any pompt, in my garden, as near to my wife as possible. Item, I desire that all my just debts be punctually paid and as soon as may be after my decease. Item, I give and devise unto my eldest son George Fairfax Lee and to his heirs forever besides the tract of land I live on,[1] which is entailed on him, the three several tracts or parcels of land which I hold in fee simple, adjoining to the said Entailed land, for one of which tracts I have an Escheat Deed, for another I bought of Henry Garner and the third is known by the name of the Burnt House tract, which was held by the late President the Hon^ble. Thomas Lee Esquire, and which was conveyed to me by the Hon^ble. Philip Ludwell Lee Esquire, agreeable to the Will of his Father, upon this condition, nevertheless that my said son George Fairfax Lee suffer the negroes hereinafter given to my two sons, Lancelot Lee and William Lee, and the increase of the said negroes, to work on his Lands aforesaid with his own negroes, untill the said Lancelot arrives to the age of twenty-one years, when a Division of the slaves given to my said two sons, Lancelot and William, is to be made, and the said Lancelot is to be possessed with his dividend of the same, and after my said son Lancelot arrives at the age of twenty-one years, that the said George Fairfax Lee also permit my said son William Lee's slaves to work on the said lands with his own, until the said William Lee arrives to the age of twenty-one years, and untill all my said sons arrive to their respective ages they are to be suitably maintained and educated, at the discretion of my Executors hereafter named, out of the profits of the whole of the negroes as well of those of my son George Fairfax Lee's as of my said other two sons, working on the said Land, and what profits remain over and above what are to be applied as aforesaid, to be to the use of my said son George Fairfax Lee, and his heirs forever. But if my said son George Fairfax Lee should refuse to let my said two sons Lancelot's and William's slaves work on his lands as aforesaid or should after they have worked on the same refuse to suffer my Executors to apply the profits as is before directed, I then revoke the Devise of the three tracts or parcels of land which I hold in fee simple and which I have given to my said son George Fairfax Lee on the Condition aforesaid, and do devise the same unto my son Lancelot and his heirs forever, also upon this Condition that he the said Lancelot shall suffer my said son William Lee's negroes to work on the same land untill my said son William arrives to the age of twenty-one, and permit him to receive the profits of his said negroes during the whole time, but if my said son Lancelot Lee should refuse to permit the same then I give the said three tracts or parcels of land aforesaid unto my son William Lee and his heirs forever. Item, I give and devise unto my son Lancelot Lee and his heirs forever one-half of a

---

[1] George Lee had built himself a residence on the hill-side, about quarter or half-mile from the side of the old mansion, which had been on the lowland nearer the water front.

tract or parcel of land lying as I believe in Loudoun County, containing nineteen hundred acres, which said tract or parcell of land was granted by Deed from the Proprietor's office, bearing date the first day of July one thousand seven hundred and forty-one to Miss Ann and Sarah Fairfax jointly and afterwards the joint tenancy was severed by Deed Executed by the said Ann and Sarah; since which the said Ann whom I intermarried hath by joint Deed with me, recorded in the general court, conveyed her half part to Richard Lee Esquire, in trust to the use of me and my heirs in fee. Item, I give and devise unto the said Lancelot Lee and his heirs forever, a tract or parcel of land, containing five hundred and seventy acres, in Frederick County, which was granted to Lawrence Washington, Gent., deceased, and by him devised to his widow the said Ann, who after her intermarriage with me, executed a Deed for the same with several other tracts of land, to the said Richard Lee in trust to the use of me and my heirs. But if my said son Lancelot should die under age without issue, I give all the said lands hereinbefore devised to him, to my son William Lee and his heirs forever. Item, I give and devise unto my son William Lee and his heirs forever, a tract of land containing eighteen hundred and forty acres, lying in Loudoun County on the north side of Elk licking run, of Cub run, granted to the said Ann Fairfax by Proprietor's Deed, bearing date the twelfth day of June one thousand seven hundred and forty-one, also a tract of land, containing fourteen hundred acres, lying in Loudoun County, on the branches of Bull Run and the broad run of Potomac, also granted to the said Ann by Proprietor's Deed, bearing date the sixteenth day of June one thousand seven hundred and forty-one, also a tract of land, containing three hundred and three acres, lying on or near the branches of Goose Creek, granted by Proprietor's Deed to the said Lawrence Washington and by him devised to his widow the said Ann, all which said several tracts or parcels of land the said Ann jointly with me after our intermarriage, conveyed to the said Richard Lee, in trust to the use of me and my heirs, as by a Deed for that purpose of record in the Secretary's office of this Colony may more fully appear.

But if my said son William Lee should die under age without issue, I give the said several tracts or parcels of land to my son Lancelot Lee and his heirs forever. Item, I give and devise unto my two sons Lancelot and William and their heirs twenty two slaves, . . . to be equally divided between my said two sons Lancelot and William, when Lancelot shall arrive at the age of twenty one years. But if either of my said two sons die before they arrive to the age of twenty one years without issue then I give the share of such son so dying to the Survivor. Item, the following thirty four slaves, . . . being entailed they descend to my son George Fairfax Lee, and it is my will he have them. Item, if it should so happen that my son George Fairfax Lee should die without issue, by which means his entailed estate, both land and negroes, will descend to my son Lancelot, then and in such case I revoke the several bequests to him the said Lancelot made of lands and slaves aforesaid and do devise the same to my son William Lee and his heirs forever. Item, I give and bequeath to my dear Daughter, Elizabeth Lee, one thousand pounds current money of Virginia, to be paid to her by my Executors when she arrives to the age of twenty one years or is married, which ever shall first happen, upon condition she relinquish, before the said one thousand pounds are paid to her, all right or title she may have or claim to a negro wench called Judy's Alice, which wench I bought of one Minor and formerly promised to give to my said Daughter Elizabeth. But, if my said Daughter Elizabeth, refuses to make such relinquishment of her right to the said negro Alice and her increase, I then revoke the legacy of one thousand pounds before given and give her only eight hundred pounds current money in lieu thereof. Item, I give unto my good friend Col°. Richard Henry Lee my Staunton gun. Item, I give to my son George Fairfax Lee one hundred head of neat cattle and such other stock as my Ex'ors. shall think necessary for his plantations. I also give my said son the Quilt worked by his Mother, all his Mother's and my books, my Grandfather's Picture and my Father's Picture set in gold, the mourning ring I expect from England for his Mother, all the plate in the house, Col. Fairfax's Snuff Box, and George's Mother's stone buttons set in gold which are in the said Snuff Box. Item, I give to my Daughter Elizabeth the Mourning Ring which I wore for her late Mother, as also the great Bible and Common Prayer-Book which were her Mother's. Item, I give to my son Lancelot Lee a seal set in gold with the family coat of arms cut thereon which was given to me by my friend Col. Richard Lee. Item, I desire that my charriot and charriot horses and all blooded horses, mares and colts may be sold, but that in order to have them sold to the greatest advantage the time and place of sale be advertised in the Virginia Gazette. Item, I desire that all my household furniture and other personal estate except what is specially given by this my last Will, and Except such stock as my Executors shall think proper to keep for the use of my said sons plantations, may be sold for the most that can be got for them. Item, I give to my son William Lee two guineas to purchase him a mourning ring for his Mother. Item, such stocks as my Executors shall think proper to be kept for my sons Lancelot and William and all the rest of my personal estate, after my debts and legacies are paid, I give to my sons Lancelot and William, to be equally divided between them, when Lancelot shall shall arrive to the age of twenty-one years, but if either of my said two sons die before they arrive to the age of twenty one years without issue, then I give the whole to the Survivor.

Item, it is my earnest will and desire that my Executors as soon after my death as conveniency will admit of, send my son George Fairfax Lee to England to the care of my friend Mr. James Russell, to receive his Education there. Item, if my Executors think they can have my two sons Lancelot and William well Educated cheaper in England than in Virginia, I do give them the power of sending them, but leave the sending them or not to their discretion, not doubting they will take the necessary care of their Education. Item, I do Impower my friends Col°. George William Fairfax, Col°. Richard Henry Lee, Col°. Richard Lee, Mr. Bryant Fairfax and Capt. John Turberville, whom I hereby appoint guardians to all my children, to lease out or sell any of back lands that are hereinbefore given to my two sons Lancelot and William (before they arrive to their respective ages of twenty one) and whatever sum or sums of money arrise from the sale of such lands or any part thereof, I desire may be put out at interest on good security and that the same be paid to such son that the land so sold is devised to by this Will, when he shall arrive to the age of twenty one years. Item, I desire my Daughter Elizabeth may be suitably maintained out of my Estate untill she arrives to the age of twenty one or is married, whichever shall first happen. Item, I request of my Executors that they will not put the wench, called home house Kate, to the hoe or any hard labour but keep her whilst it is necessary, to wait on and take care of the children, and when there shall be no need of such service that she be kept to making the negroes cloathes or such like business I likewise request of my Executors that they never permit any other kind or sort of Tobacco than sweet scented to be tended on the old house plantation or the Lower plantation under the Hill and that they ship all my Tobaccos and do not sell them in the Country and I recommend it to them to consign such Tobaccos to my friend Mr. James Russell as long as he continues in the Tobacco Trade. I also desire that the goods, Cloaths and tools wanted for the use of the negroes and plantations may be yearly sent for to England and none purchased in the Country but what there is an absolute necessity for, and lastly I do nominate and appoint my good friends the said Richard Henry Lee, Richard Lee, and John Turberville Executors of this my last Will and Testament hereby revoaking every other Will and Testament heretofore by me made. In Witness whereof I the Said George Lee have to this my last Will and Testament set my hand and Seal th thirteenth day of September 1761.

Richard Henry Lee, one of the executors of this estate, kept an account of receipts and payments in the neatest and most clerk-like manner; from this account, in his own writing, a few extracts are given:

1762, 9th March, received by cash of Mr. Lane for prizes in the Northern Lottery, £1,3. 1st June, "By 4 hhds. Tob: received from Mr. Pierce for Clerks fees, 4004 llbs." 29th. July, "By 4 hhds. Tob: from Mr. Pierce for Clerks fees, 4045 llbs." 24th. November, "By Cash from Col°. George Washington for rent, £82.10." On the side of payments there are frequent entries of a guinea or several guineas to "Miss Betty Lee for pocket money." But the boys fared rather better, for he gave "Mr. Geo. Lee for pocket money, £12. The doctors also did well, even in "ye olden time," for "Dr. Steptoe's medical account of £27.10," was a good one for those days, when a guinea was of considerable value. Nor did the executor fail to keep an exact account; consequently he charged up "postage on Mr. Lancelot Lee's letter, 8d."

Of the two children by his first wife, only the daughter survived him; all three sons by his second wife survived, as named in his will:

i, RICHARD [5], born 13th of August, 1739; died in infancy.

ii, ELIZABETH [5], born on the 21st of November, 1750, and died, unmarried, on the 19th of May, 1828, in her 78th year.

iii, GEORGE FAIRFAX [5]. See 25.

iv, LANCELOT [5]. See 26.

v, WILLIAM [5], born the 17th of November, 1758; died, unmarried, on the 19th of May, 1838.

## THE WORMELEYS.

The first members of this family, in Virginia, appear to have been two brothers, Christopher and Ralphe Wormeley, who were descended from "Sir John de Wormele, Hadfield, county York, England, Knt., 1312."[1] Captain Christopher Wormeley was the acting governor of Tortugas Island in 1631–35, when, owing to some negligence of his, the Spaniards captured the island, and he was compelled to flee. He reached Virginia in 1635, and received grants for some 1,450 acres in Charles River county, the 27th of January, 1638; he was a member of the Council in 1637. His death

[1] This account of the Wormeleys is taken, almost entirely, from that given by Mr. Hayden (*Va, Genealogies*, pp. 230-31), with a few changes suggested by Mr. W. G. Stanard, of Richmond,

occurred about 1649, whether with or without heirs is not clearly proven, but he devised land to his brother, Ralph. (The Christopher given below as his nephew might have been his son.)

Captain Ralph Wormeley, of "Rosegill," Middlesex county, was born about 1620, and died about 1665; "he was a member of the Council as early as 1649, and was re-appointed in 1650 by Charles II., then at Breda" (W. G. Stanard); he married, about 1640–45, Agatha, a daughter of Richard Eltonhead, of Eltonhead, county Lancaster, England (whose younger sister married Henry Corbin); after his death, the widow married Sir Henry Chicheley, Knt., and deputy governor of Virginia in 1678, being his second wife. Ralph Wormeley received 3,000 acres in Virginia, 2d of October, 1649, a part of which had been formerly granted Capt. Christopher Wormeley, on the 27th of January, 1638, and the rest had been assigned by Ralph Read and Francis Carter to Robert Todd, who sold to Ralph Wormeley, and 1,545 acres due to the latter as executor and heir to Capt. Christopher Wormeley (which would seem to imply that the testator had left no male issue). Ralph Wormeley also received (23d of March, 1640) a grant for 237 acres on Rappahannock River, at the mouth of Nimcock Creek, for five persons. His children were, probably, as follows: i, Col. Christopher was a member of the Council, 1666, and later; he was one of those proscribed by Bacon in his proclamation against Governor Berkeley and his friends; he married a Mrs. Aylmer, for, in 1671, he brought suit as the husband of the relict of the Rev. Justinian Aylmer (of Jamestown, and minister of Hampton Parish, 1665–7, æt. 26). "Frances Wormeley, wife of Col. Christopher Wormeley, died the 25th of May, 1685, and was buried in the garden the next day." He had a daughter, Judith, born in May, 1683, and probably others. ii, Ralph, of whom later. iii, "Aylmer, son of Hon. Ralph Wormeley, died the 16th of January, 1669–70."

Col. Ralph Wormeley, of "Rosegill," second son, was born about 1650, and died on the 5th of December, 1703; he matriculated at Oriel College, Oxford, the 14th of July, 1665; according to a published list of members of the Council, Ralph Wormeley, 1670, and Ralph Wormeley, Jr., 1673, were members.[1] The son was Secretary of State in 1693, and President of the Council; he was also Collector of Naval Duties, etc., for the Rappahannock River. He was twice married; his first wife was the widow of Capt. Peter Jenings, attorney-general of Va., and a daughter of Sir Thomas Lunsford; in 1674, Captain Ralph Wormeley brought suit as the husband of the relict of Captain Peter Jenings; "the Hon. Lady Madame Catharine Wormeley," died on the 17th of May, 1685; their daughter, Catharine, married Gawin Corbin, and died without issue. Ralph Wormeley's second wife was Elizabeth, daughter of Col. John Armistead, "the Councillor," who was a son of William Armistead, the Immigrant; her younger brother, William, married, Anna, the daughter, of Hancock and Mary (Kendall) Lee. The record gives the marriage "at Col. Armistead's Feb'y 16, 1687, Madame Elizabeth Armistead of Gloucester;" Ralph Wormeley had issue: i, Elizabeth, who married, in 1703, John Lomax (1674–1729), the son of the Rev. John Lomax. ii, Ralph, who died unmarried, at William and Mary College, in 1700. iii, John, of whom later. iv, Judith, who married, in 1712, the Hon. Mann Page, of "Rosewell," Gloucester county, a grandson of Col. John Page, the Virginia Immigrant; she was his first wife, and left issue two sons and a daughter, at her death on the 12th of December, 1716, aged 22.

John Wormeley, of "Rosegill," Middlesex, was born in 1689, and died in 1726; his will (dated the 15th of April, 1725) names his wife Elizabeth, to whom he gave one-half of his real estate. She died in 1743, and by her will (dated the 3d of March, 1743) gave her son, John, 650 acres in York county; he was also the heir to 2,000 acres of entailed land, "Portobago," held formerly by his sister, Elizabeth Lomax, which entail he broke (Nov., 1762) to fulfill his father's will (Hening, V, 85; VIII, 452). He had issue: Ralph, Elizabeth, Sarah, Judith, Agatha, and John. Of these, Judith married George Lee, as stated. This John held land in Middlesex, Gloucester, King William, York and Caroline counties.

Ralph, the eldest son, was a member of the Council in 1764, and Burgess, 1743 to 1764, with but few interruptions; he was twice married; first, to Sally, daughter of Col. Edmund Berkeley, of "Barn Elms," Middlesex, and, secondly, to Jane, daughter of Jeoffrey Bolles. He had issue: i, Ralph (1744–1806), member of Council, 1771, of the Convention of 1788, and of the House of Delegates, 1787–90; he married Eleanor, daughter of John Tayloe, of "Mt. Airy," and had issue; she

---

[1] See *W. and M. College Quarterly*, III, 67.

died the 23d of February, 1815, in her 60th year (*Old Churches, Families*, &c., II. 371). ii, James, who married twice; first, Ariana Randolph, and was the father of Ralph Randolph Wormeley, Admiral, R. N.

John, the second son, Burgess from Middlesex, married Elizabeth, daughter of William Tayloe, and had a daughter, Elizabeth, who married William Digges, and also a son, John Wormeley. William Tayloe, of Lancaster (will dated 5th February, 1767), devised 800 acres to William Digges, who had married Elizabeth, daughter and heir of John Wormeley, and granddaughter of testator (VIII, Hening, 452).

"Rosegill, where," wrote Bishop Meade, "the Wormeleys lived in English state," was situated high upon the banks of the Rappahannock River, a few miles from old Christ Church. It was a large and handsome specimen of old colonial mansion. Bishop Meade also stated that a piece communion service of five pieces had been presented to Christ Church by the Hon. Ralph Wormeley, and in his list of the vestrymen of this parish, dating from 1663 to 1767, he named five Wormeleys, who were probably of successive generations.

## THE FAIRFAX FAMILY.

This family traces its descent from Richard Fairfax, Lord Chief Justice of England in the reign of Henry VI., whose third son, Sir Guy, also bred to the law, was Attorney-General, and, later, Justice of the King's Bench, in the reigns of Edward IV., Richard III., and Henry VII. Sir Guy built Steton Castle, in the county of York; married Margaret, daughter of Sir William Ryther, and had Sir William, his heir, and Thomas, who married Cecily, daughter of Sir Robert Manners, ancestor of the Duke of Rutland. Sir William, who succeeded, was Sheriff, a Justice of the Common Pleas in the time of Henry VIII.; his son, also Sir William, was Sheriff of Yorkshire in same reign. He, in turn, was succeeded by his son, Sir Thomas, who accompanied the Earl of Essex into France, where he was knighted by him for his bravery in the camp before Rouen. On the 4th of May, 1627, he was created a Baron of Scotland by Charles I.

His son, Ferdinando, 2d Baron, was a General in the Parliamentary army, as was also his own son and successor, Sir Thomas Fairfax, who was for some time the Commander-in-Chief of the Parliamentary army and a very successful officer. He became dissatisfied with the courses of Parliament, resigned in 1650, and was succeeded by Oliver Cromwell. He later assisted General Monk in effecting the restoration of Charles II., and was until his death in favor with that monarch. He died in 1671 without male issue, when the title passed to his cousin, Henry, 4th Baron, and grandson of Thomas, 1st Baron. Thomas, 5th Baron, married Catharine, only daughter and heir of Thomas, Lord Culpeper, the Proprietor of the Northern Neck. Their eldest son, Thomas, 6th Baron, inherited the grant and became the Proprietor. He died in 1738, and was succeeded by his brother, Henry, who died in 1782. Of him Bishop Meade has written: "Lord Fairfax was a man of the most perfect English education, Oxford being his *Alma Mater*. . . . In 1739 he visited his estates in Virginia, and was so pleased with the country that he determined to settle there. During this visit he became acquainted with and attached to young George Washington, then only sixteen years of age. The affection was returned on the part of Washington, and he readily accepted the proposition of Lord Fairfax to become surveyor of all his lands. Washington continued for two or three years in the service of Lord Fairfax, and as public surveyor for Western Virginia. At the death of Henry, Lord Fairfax, the title fell to his only surviving brother, Robert, in England, and at his death, which occurred soon after, to the Rev. Bryan Fairfax."

The Rev. Bryan Fairfax, who thus inherited the title, was the youngest surviving son of William Fairfax, of "Belvoir," in Fairfax county, and his wife, who was a Miss Gary. William was the son of Henry, the second son of Henry, 4th Baron. He was President of the Council and for a long time the manager of the Fairfax estates in Virginia. His daughter, Anne, married first, Lawrence Washington, of Mt. Vernon, and, secondly, George Lee, as previously stated. Another daughter, Hannah, married Warner Washington, of "Fairfield."

The title is now held by John Contee Fairfax, of Prince George's county, Md. He was born on the 13th of September, 1830; has one son and three daughters.

### "Squire" Richard Lee, of Maryland.

8. Richard [4], eldest son of Philip Lee [3] (Richard [2], Richard [1]) by Sarah Brooke, his first wife, was born ——; died intestate about the year 1787. He was a member of the Proprietors' Council in 1755; he married Grace Ashton, daughter of Col. Henry Ashton, of Westmoreland county. On the

28th of May, 1745, Richard Lee, of Maryland, and Grace, his wife, executed a deed to Thomas Lee of Virginia. (Westmoreland records.) Heretofore it has been erroneously stated that Grace Ashton married Philip, not Richard, Lee. A comparison of the wills of Col. Henry Ashton and Grace Lee shows that the latter devised land given by the former to his daughter, Grace Ashton.

Col. Henry Ashton, of Westmoreland, was a son of John Ashton by Grace, his wife. He was "born in Westmoreland, the 30th day of July, 1670," and died in 1731; was Sheriff of that county, 1717–18. Henry Ashton was twice married; first to "Elizabeth, daughter of William Hardidge, Gent., by Francis, his wife, by whom he had four daughters: Frances, Elizabeth, Ann, and Grace. The last only survived him." (Ashton family records.) His second wife was Mary (Watts?), by whom he apparently had two sons: Henry and John. Mr. Hayden gives this abstract of his will:

The will of "Mr. Henry Ashton, Gent," of Cople Parish, Westmoreland, dated the 26th of February, 1730; probated 24th of November, 1731, names his wife Mary, executrix, with Capt. Geo. Turberville, Capt. Burdett Ashton, Mr. Andrew Monroe and Richard Watts; gives daughter, Grace Ashton, 1,000 acres, called "Poore Jack," granted Col. Wm. Hardidge, 15th of September, 1651–3, and 1,200 acres of "Peyton's Level," granted Col. Valentine Peyton, 22 July, 1662; the said Grace to make over to Eliza'h and Ann Aylett, daughters of his daughter, Anne Ashton, dec'd, and her husband, Capt. Wm. Aylett, Jr., the land called "Sturmans," which he gave Anne at marriage; also to granddaughter Elizabeth Turberville, 850 acres of "Peyton's Level," and to granddaughters Eliza'h and Anne Aylett the rest, 400 acres of Peyton's Level; also his land "Nominy," 1,000 acres granted to Col. Thomas Speke, 16 September, 1651. To sons Henry and John Ashton lands and copper mines in Stafford Co., and lands in Westmoreland Co. To cousin Burdett Ashton, 1,000 acres in Stafford. To godson, John, son of Mr. Charles Ashton, 1,700 acres in Stafford. To his sister, Mrs. Sarah Macgill, a ring. (*Va. Genealogies*, 489.)

Compare with this abstract, the following will of Grace Lee; it was dated the 18th of November, 1787, and probated, in Charles county, Md., on the 22d of October, 1789:

In the name of God, Amen. I Grace Lee, of Charles county, in the State of Maryland being sick and weak in body but of sound mind and memory and understanding considering the certainty of death and the uncertainty of the time thereof, and being desirous to settle my worldly affairs, and thereby be the better prepared to leave this world when it shall please God to call me hence, do therefore make and publish this my last Will and Testament in manner and form following, that is to say:

First, and principally I commit my Soul into the hands of Almighty God and my body to the earth to be decently buried at the discretion of my Executors hereinafter named, and after my debts and funeral charges are paid, I devise and bequeath as follows. I give and devise unto my well beloved daughters Elinor Ann Lee and Alice Lee all my lands lying in Richmond county in the State of Virginia commonly called and known by name of Paytons Levels, containing by estimation about 1400 acres, be the same more or less, to them the said Elinor Ann Lee and Alice Lee and their heirs in fee simple, to be equally divided between them.

Item. I give and devise unto my said daughters Elinor Ann Lee and Alice Lee all my land lying in Westmoreland county in the State of Virginia (one of which tracts or parcels of land is commonly called and known by the name of Poor Jack containing about 600 acres be the same more or less, and the other is commonly called and known by the name of Sturman containing by estimation about 60 acres be the same more or less) which said two tracts or parcels of land I give and devise to them the said Elinor Ann Lee and Alice Lee, and their heirs in fee simple to be equally divided between them.

Item. I give and devise unto my said daughters Elinor Ann Lee and Alice Lee my other Lands, which I now have or may hereafter claim interest or estate in of what nature or kind soever lying and being in either of the aforesaid countys and State aforesaid to them and their heirs and assigns forever, in as full ample and extensive manner as the nature of the lands will or may admit of, to be equally divided between my said daughters their heirs and assigns and to their sole and simple use respectively without let or molestation of any person or persons claiming or may claim by from or under me.

Item. I give and bequeath unto my Grandson Russell Lee one full half of all the negroes I may in any manner be entitled to or have in possession at the time of my death, to him the said Russell Lee, his heirs and assigns forever. Item. I give and bequeath to each of my Granddaughters, Sarah Russell Lee, Ann Lee, Elinor Lee, and Margaret Russell Lee, a Negro girl to be from twelve to fifteen years of age each, to my said Granddaughters respectively, and to their heirs and assigns forever.

Item. The residue and remainder of the negroes I shall be possessed of or in any manner entitled to at the time of my death and which are not herein given or intended to be given or bequeathed, I give and bequeath unto my daughters Elinor Ann Lee and Alice Lee, to them and their heirs and assigns forever, to be equally divided between them. Item. All the remaining part of my personal estate goods and chattels of any and every nature or kind soever not herein before bequeathed or disposed of by me, I give and bequeath unto my son Richard Lee, my daughters Elinor Ann Lee and Alice Lee, my grandson Russell Lee, my granddaughters Sarah Russell Lee, Ann Lee, Elinor Lee and Margaret Russell Lee, to them their heirs and assigns forever, to be equally aportioned, distributed and divided amongst them share and share alike.

And Lastly I hereby ordain constitute and appoint my much esteemed son in law Philip Richard Fendall Esqr. and my beloved daughters Elinor Ann Lee and Alice Lee to be my executors of this my last Will and Testament, revoking and annulling all former wills by me heretofore made, ratifying and confirming this and none other to be my last Will and Testament. In testimony whereof I have hereunto set my hand and affixed my seal, this eighteenth day of November Anno Domini Seventeen hundred and eighty seven,—signed, sealed, published and declared by Grace Lee the above mentioned testatrix as for her last Will and Testament in the presence of us, who at her request and in her presence, have subscribed our names as witnesses thereto.

Indorsed on the back of this will was the following:

BLENHEIM, 25th October, '89.

SIR:—The right of administration, De bonis non, on the estate of my honored father being in me, and also the joint executorship of the last will and testament of my dear deceased mother; but as I do not intend to interfer in either of these cases, it may be necessary to inform you that I relinquish my title to the administration and Executorship above mentioned and I do this in behalf of my trusty friend P. R. Fendall Esquire, who is so kind as to undertake the unfinished administration of my father's estate and also the Executorship of my mother's will. It is my request that he should be appointed to both these duties and that letters may be taken out in his name.

(Signed) ELINOR ANN LEE.

A comparison of these wills proves conclusively that "Grace Lee," the testatrix, was the daughter of Henry Ashton; and the certificate of the Register of Wills for Charles county shows that she was the wife of Richard Lee. His certificates were:

"On the 2d day of October 1789, Letters Testamentary on the Estate of Grace Lee were granted and committed unto Philip Richard Fendall, the acting Executor and his bond with Benjamin Contee and Matthew Blair, his sureties, was taken in the sum of £2000 current money for due administration."

"Letters *de bonis non* on the Estate of the late Richard Lee, were also granted unto Philip Richard Fendall, with £10,000 security."

Elinor Ann Lee asked that Mr. Fendall be appointed administrator of her father's estate; the court records show that he was appointed administrator of the estate of "the late Richard Lee."

It will be observed that Grace Lee made no mention of her second son, Philip Thomas Lee, who was dead; property was bequeathed to his children. She also referred to Philip Richard Fendall as her "son-in-law;" but made no bequest to his wife nor to any children. This can only be explained on the theory that Mrs. Fendall was dead and without issue; or it may be that "son-in-law" was an error for brother-in-law; for it has been stated that a Fendall married Eleanor, sister of Grace Lee's husband and that she died in 1759.

From Grace Lee's will, the following issue are given as the children of Richard and Grace (Ashton) Lee:

i, RICHARD[5], said to have died in 1834, and without issue. Had evidently been an invalid for many years prior to his death, for his sister, Elinor Ann Lee, in her will of 1805, requested that "the Rev. Mr. Contee's and his wife's attention may be extended towards their afflicted Uncle, my said Brother, as far as his remote situation may admit, and I do also authorize and empower them fully to transact all his concerns."

It is possible that this was the brother whose full name was Philip Richard Francis, that he was the officer who served as a captain in the Continental Line, was wounded at the battle of Brandywine, and to whose representatives the following (Virginia) land warrants were issued; if so, he must have served from Virginia:

No. 3175, 21st of July, 1784, to the representatives of Philip Richard Francis Lee, for 4,000 acres, due for three years' service as a captain.

No. 4867, 1st of October, 1798, for 4,000 acres, "for services for the war."

No. 9127, 6th of November, 1845, for 164⅔ acres to Alice A. Kent and Benjamin Contee.

No. 9128, for 184⅔ acres to E. A. Contee, Eliza Lyson, and Sarah E. Fendall.

No. 9129, for 174⅓ acres to all before mentioned as heirs of Capt. P. R. F. Lee for seven years and eight months' service, less amounts already received.

In 1845, in establishing claim for bounties, it was proven that the heir of P. R. F. Lee was Richard Lee, whose son, Philip Thomas Lee (the only son to leave issue) had these children: 1, Sarah Russell, who married the Rev. Benj. Contee. 2, Margaret Russell, who married James Clerklee (and had issue: Eleanor Russell, who married Edward Henry Grette; Caroline R., who married Josias Hawkins, of Charles county, Md.; Eliza, who married —— Lyson; Emily, who married Thos. D. Fendall, of Charles county, Md.). 3, Eleanor, who married William Dawson. 4, Ann, who married William Gamble.

As all these heirs of Philip Richard Francis Lee inherited from him through their grandfather, Richard Lee, it seems evident he must have been the father of this Capt. P. R. F. Lee.

ii, PHILIP THOMAS[6]. See 27.

iii, ELINOR ANN[6]. Died, evidently, unmarried, on 17th May, 1806. She left a lengthy and intricate will, detailing minutely the provisions for her various bequests. An abstract only is given here. It is signed by her maiden name, thus showing her to have died unmarried; dated the 19th of October, 1805, and a codicil was added on the 7th of November; probated in Charles county, Maryland, 12th of August, 1806. She desired some lands in Kentucky and "Sturmans," in Virginia, to be sold for the payment of her debts; "Peytons Levells" and "Poor Jack," in Virginia, were left to her niece, Sarah Russell Contee, during the term of natural life of her brother, Richard Lee; at his death the land called "Poor Jack" was to be divided between her nieces, Ann Lee, Margaret Russell Clerklee, and Elinor Dawson; to her "niece Sarah Russell Contee, her heirs and assigns, all which I hold of a tract of land in Virginia, whether lying in Westmoreland or Richmond countys . . . called and known by the name of Peytons Levells;" at her niece's death the land was to go to her children, "Elinor Contee, Alice Lee Contee, Philip Ashton Lee Contee and Edmund Henry Contee," all living in 1805. To the same niece, Sarah Russell Contee, was given "a certain tract of land at Nominy, which was conveyed to me, on the fourth of July Seventeen hundred and ninety eight by Richard Henry Lee, Richard Lee and George Washington . . . for the term of my Brother Richard's natural life," and at his death to be divided as the laws of Virginia should order. Two Maryland negroes were left to her goddaughter and great niece, Caroline Clerklee; to great nephews Philip Ashton Lee Contee and Edmund Henry Contee, some silver; to great nieces Sarah Elinor Contee, Alice Lee Contee, some silver; the Rev. Benjamin Contee was appointed sole executor. No mention was made of her sister, Alice Lee, or of Philip Richard Fendall, nor of any heirs of the same.

(NOTE.—The date given above for the deed signed by Richard Henry Lee, etc., must be an error; he died on the 19th of June, 1794.)

iv, ALICE[5]. The *Maryland Journal,* under date of 1st of April, 1788, gives this: "Married a few days ago at Blenheim in Charles county, John Weems, late resident of the State of Delaware, to Miss Alice Lee, daughter of the Hon. Richard Lee, deceased." "Miss Alice Lee of Md." stood sponsor, on the 10th of October, 1777, for Cassius, son of R. H. Lee; probably this was the Alice so mentioned.

## FRANCIS LEE.

9. FRANCIS[4], (second) son of Philip Lee[3] (Richard[2], Richard[1]) by Sarah Brooke, his first wife, was born ——, and died in Cecil county, Md., in 1749. He had been clerk of that county since 1746, and had been also a deputy from Dorset county, for in 1746 an election was held to choose a successor to "Mr. Francis Lee, Esq." (*Md. Archives*). He probably moved from Dorset to Cecil in that year. Mr. Francis Lee offered for lease his "late Mansion House on the Northwest fork of the Nanticoke River" (Md. *Gazette,* 30th January, 1747–8).

Francis Lee married Elizabeth Hollyday, as stated in his will, and left three children. She was probably the daughter of Col. Leonard Hollyday, of "Brookfield," who is said to have married a Semmes,[1] but may have been twice married. In his will Francis Lee mentions his brother-in-law, Thomas Hollyday, and a James Hollyday. This Elizabeth had a brother, Thomas, and an uncle, the Hon. James Hollyday; these are the only clews which connect his wife with the daughter of Dr. Leonard Hollyday.

His will, dated the 15th of September, and probated the 21st of November, 1749, was as follows:

In the Name of God, Amen. I Francis Lee, late of Checil County in the Province of Maryland in the [first] place do give and bequeath my soul into the Almighty God that gave it to be bery'd in a decent manner according to rightious Institution hoping a blessed Mansion of eternity, &c. Item. I give unto my beloved Wife Eliz'a Lee all the Right and Interest she had in marriage with me for which her jointure made her; she had a jointure made her for two Negro with her to sell they not being very likely Viz: James son of Peter and Pegg Daughter of Kate and the Interest I bought of Philip Cakeor in Cecil County and all the Tobacco Debts due me for Clks fees in said County and elsewhere. Item. I give and bequeath unto my daughter Amelia Lee the negro Girl I gave her a good while Whesst by way of Bill of Sale Viz Silver. Item. I give to my son Francis Leonard Lee two negroes called Darby and Moll. Item. I give to the said Francis Leonard Lee all my dwelling Plantation in Dorset County called Rehoboth to him and his heirs forever. Item. I give to my son Lancelot Richard Thos. Lee a Tract of land called Lee's first Purchase containing 317 acres lying on the North East Fork of Nanticoke River, to him and his heirs forever. Item. I give to the said Lancelot several tracts of land lying on Broad Creek in Somerset and Worchester Countys to him and his heirs forever. Item. I give to my wife Elizabeth Lee a Track of Land in Dorset County where the ship was built containing 50 acres to her and her heirs forever. Item. I give to my son Francis Leonard Lee two tracts of Land bought from John Smith joining to Rehoboth to him and his heirs forever—and I also bequeath to the said Francis Leonard all Tracts of Land whatsoever that I have any right to except those Lands willed as above. I give to my wife Eliz. Lee my large riding Horse a little gray mare, a bob'd tail bay Horse and the chair, and all my household Furniture of what kind so ever except my Plate w^ch^ properly belongs to my Daughter Amelia Lee which is to belong to my said Wife till my Daughter Amelia Comes to age. Item. I give to Doct^r^. Benj. Bradford my bay Horse w^ch^ I bought from Peter Commerford. Item. I give to my son Lancelot two Negro Boys named Tony and Peter to him and his heirs forever. Item. I give to my daughter Amelia two negroes call'd Pompey and Dan to her and her heirs forever. Item. It is my will that my Estate shall not be separated for the space of two years till my Debts are paid and the Tob: and Debts due to me are collected. Item. I do will and appoint my well beloved wife Elizabeth my sole Executrix of this my last Will and Testament and none other. And I appoint Mr. James Holliday and Doct^r^. Benj. Bradford to assist my Wife in making up the above Estate w^th^ the Comisary and all other things needfull. Item. I leave unto Mr. James Holliday my riding Pistols. And I will after all my just debts are paid that the residue of my personall Estate be equally divided between my wife and children. Amongst w^ch^ Debts I doe declare the debts due to Edmund Jennings Esqr. and Robert Swan are not justly claimed and several others too teadious to name. And I request it of my Brother in Law Tho^s^ Holliday and Mr. Francis Warrim in Company w^th^

[1] *Old Kent*, by George A. Hanson, 247.

John Cook Esqr. to settle my affairs concerning the ship Paglo and Ann w[th] James Russell and Henry Red Crab in Company, and to see my Estate has justice done it. As to the Debts due to Capt. Allen and Davis I left in the hands of Edmund Jenings Esqr. twenty Thousand Wt. of Tob: to pay them; the overplus to be returned to me—and I have ordered my Attorney in Dorset Capt. Charles Dickinson to pay Benj. Fisher Esqr. the Sterling money I owe him. I order Capt. Charles Dickinson to pay his Excellency Sam'l Ogle Esqr. the money due him for Licenses w[ch] money I was disappointed of by two Gentlemen when last at Annapolis tho' they faithfully promised. Signed, &c., &c., 15th September, 1749.

As named in this will, the issue of Francis and Elizabeth (Hollyday) Lee were two sons and a daughter. From the wording of the will it is probable that the two sons were of age in 1749; but the daughter was not.

i, FRANCIS LEONARD [5].

ii, LANCELOT RICHARD THOMAS [5].

iii, AMELIA [5].

## PHILIP LEE.

10. PHILIP [4] (third) son of Philip Lee [3] (Richard [2], Richard [1]), and Sarah Brooke, his first wife, was born ——, and died in the summer of 1739; he lived in Charles county, Maryland. His will, dated 17th of April, and probated 3d of July, 1739, was as follows:

In the name of God, Amen. I Philip Lee Jun[r] of Charles County being weak of body but sound of memory, blessed be God, do this 17th day of April, in the year of our Lord Christ 1739 make and publish this my last Will and Testament in manner following, First I bequeath my Soul to Almighty God who gave it me and my body to the earth whence it came, after such manner as my executors hereafter named shall think fit, that is to say after my just debts and funeral expenses are paid, I dispose of my worldly goods as follows. Imprimis I give to my dearly beloved Wife Bridgett Lee, during her widowhood, one negro man called Tom, which said negro is now an apprentice to Joel Andrew Mimistree Joiner but at the death or marriage of her my said wife my will and pleasure is that the same negro man be the property of my son Philip Lee, his heirs and assigns. Item. My will and pleasure is that when a certain tract of Land called Lee Langley is recovered out of the hands of a certain William Wilkinson of Charles County that then the same be immediately sould by my Ex'rs hereafter named and the produce thereof be equally divided amongst my three daughters namely, Sarah, Elizabeth and Lettice Lee or the survivors of them, their heirs and assigns, which said part of my Daughters Portion my will and pleasure is shall be paid to them at the day of their marriage or at twenty one years of age. Item. My desire is that all the remaining part of my personal Estate after debts paid and rec'd be div'd as the law directs. I make and ordain my dear and honoured Father Philip Lee Esqr. my dear Brothers Francis Lee, Henry Lee and Thomas Lee, Executors of this my Last Will and Testament. In witness whereof, &c., &c.

On the 3d of July, 1739, Henry Lee, one of the executors named in this will, renounced his executorship, as he was "determined to goe directly to England;" this renunciation was witnessed by Philip, the father, and Hancock, the brother. No mention was made in the will of Philip Lee, Sr., of a son, Henry; he may have settled permanently in England or have died without issue, before the date of his father's will. The children of Philip and Bridget Lee, as named in his will, were:

i, PHILIP[5].
ii, SARAH[5].
iii, ELIZABETH[5].
iv, LETTICE[5].

## THOMAS LEE.

11. THOMAS[4] (fourth), son of Philip Lee[3] (Richard[2], Richard[1]) by Sarah Brooke, his first wife, was born ——, and died in August or September, 1749; of his life there is no record. He married Christiana Sim, daughter of Dr. Patrick Sim, of Prince George's county, Md., and Mary, his wife, who was a daughter of the Hon. Thomas Brooke, of "Brookefield;" she was probably his first cousin. After his death, Mrs. Lee married Capt. Walter Smith. Thomas Lee's will was made in August and probated in October, 1749. The will was without date; these are from the probate act.

In the name of God, Amen. I Thomas Lee of Prince George County in the province of Maryland Gent. being Sick and Weak in body but of sound and perfect Memory thanks be to Almighty God for the same and considering the Uncertain State of Mankind and that it is appointed for all Men once to dye do make this my last Will and Testament in manner and form following that is to say. First, I commend my Soul to Almighty God that gave it trusting through the merits of my Saviour Jesus Christ forgiveness of my Sins. 2ndly, As to what worldly Estate it has pleased Almighty God to bless me with I give and bequeath the same as followeth:

First, I desire all my Just debts be paid. 2ndly, I give my Moiety of a Tract of Land lying in Virginia Called Paradise now in the possession of Francis Lee the reversion left me by my Hon'd Father Philip Lee Esqr. to my son Thomas Sim Lee and my Daughter Sarah Brooke Lee to be equally Divided between them to them their Heirs and assigns forever and in case of either of their Deaths to the Survivor his or her heirs or assigns forever and in the case of the Death of both my son and daughter without legal Heirs of their body or that they arrive to full age then I leave the Said Land to be equally Divided between my nephews Philip Lee son of Philip Lee and Arthur Lee, son of Arthur Lee, their Heirs and assigns forever. 3rdly, I give my Moiety of a Tract of Land Called Lees purchase or Stump Dale on Potomack the Reversion me left by my Hon'd Father to my dear and Loving Wife her Heirs and assigns forever. 4thly, I Will that my Land on Seneca Creek in Frederick County and an Island purchased of Thomas Beall be sold for Payment of my Debts by my Executor, hereafter named and if need not be then I Will that the same be sold and the Money thereby Raised to be equally divided between my children.

Lastly, I appoint my dear and Loving Wife and Major Joseph Sim full and Sole Executors of this my last Will and Testament. And I also appoint Mrs. Mary Sim and Major Joseph Sim Guardians to my Children. I hereby Revoke and make void all Wills &c., &c.

The issue of Thomas and Christiana (Sim) Lee were two; both minors in 1749:

i, THOMAS SIM[5], See 28.

ii, SARAH BROOKE[5]; married twice; first Archibald Buchanan, no issue; secondly, —— Turnbull, and left issue.

### CAPTAIN ARTHUR LEE.

12. ARTHUR[4], (fifth) son of Philip Lee[3] (Richard[2], Richard[1]) and Sarah Brooke, his first wife, was born ——; died, probably in 1760; on the 26th of December, 1760, there was a new election for a delegate from Charles county, Md., "in room of Capt. Arthur Lee, deceased." (*Md. Archives.*) Arthur Lee married Charity Hanson, who was a daughter of Samuel and Elizabeth Hanson, of "Greenhill," Charles county, Md.; she seems to have been the widow of a Mr. Howard, when she married Arthur Lee. In her will (dated the 2d of January, and probated the 21st of March, 1755–6) she appointed her "dear husband Arthur Lee to be guardian to my said daughter Chloe Howard till she arrives at the age of sixteen;" also mentioned her own mother, Elizabeth Hanson, and her brother, Walter Hanson. The will of Arthur Lee has not been found, so there is no record of any children; but his brother, Thomas Lee, left the reversion of some land to his "nephew Arthur Lee son of Arthur Lee."

## THE HANSON FAMILY.

JOHN HANSON, of London, son of John and Frances Prichard Hanson, visited Sweden, fell in love with a Swedish lady, married and settled in that country. From this union are descended the Hansons of Maryland. His son entered the Swedish army. Being of the same age as the renowned Gustavus Adolphus, they became intimate and devoted friends; he rose to be a colonel in the army, and was killed at the battle of Lutzen, 6th of November, 1632, while defending his royal friend, with whom he died on that sanguinary field. His sons, Andrew, Randal (or Randolph), William and John, came over to Delaware, with Lieutenant Colonel John Printz, the governor of "New Sweden." The family finally became seated in Charles county, Maryland, where they have been prominent ever since. Col. John Hanson was authorized by the Swedish authorities to bear arms; he adopted a

modification of those borne by the English branch of his family, which have been used by his American descendants. An illustration of them is given here.

It appears that only the youngest of these sons left issue; the family is therefore descended from John Hanson, who was born about 1630; settled in Charles county and died about 1713; he left issue: Robert, Benjamin, Mary, Anne, Sarah, John, and Samuel Hanson. Robert, the eldest, represented Charles county in the (Md.) Assembly in 1719–20–28–32–34–39–40; he died in 1748, and left issue: Samuel, William, Dorothy, Mary, Sarah, Violetta, and Benjamin Hanson. Samuel, the youngest son, also represented Charles county, 1716–28; was county clerk in 1739. In his will (dated 22d of October, 1740), he mentioned his wife, Elizabeth, and children: Judge Walter, of "Harwood;" William; Samuel, of "Greenhill;" John, of "Mulberry Grove;" Elizabeth, Charity (who married Arthur Lee); Jane, and Chloe Hanson, then a minor; she afterward married Philip Briscoe, of St. Mary's county, Md., and has a line of descendants. "This Samuel Hanson was buried at 'Equality,' an estate then owned by his son-in-law, David Stone, 'the inheritor of Paynton Manor, with Court Leet and Court Baron,' a lineal descendant of Governor William Stone (of Md., 1649–54), the great-grandfather of the Hon. Frederick Stone, of Port Tobacco, Md." His eldest son, Judge Walter Hanson, of "Harwood," was Commissary of Charles county, 1740; he married —— Hoskins; his daughter, Elizabeth, married Daniel Jenifer, and died in November, 1757, aged 25 years. His son, Hoskins Hanson, married Sarah Thompson, and had Richard Thompson Hanson (who moved to Georgia), Sarah Hanson (who married Major William Penn, of Charles county), and Catharine Hanson. The third son, Samuel, of "Greenhill," Charles county, was "noted for his patriotism; it is related of him that he presented General Washington with £800 sterling to aid in covering the bare feet of his soldiers with shoes." His brother, John Hanson, of "Mulberry Grove," was a staunch friend of the Colonies; it is said that in the early part of the Revolutionary struggle, some very decided resolutions were introduced into the Maryland Assembly, of which he was a member; when the motion for their adoption was put, there was an awful pause; the members hesitated to take overt action, which might place their heads and fortunes in jeopardy; thereupon rose John Hanson, and said: "Mr. President, these resolutions ought to pass; it is high time," etc. They were then promptly passed "amidst much enthusiasm." He was born in 1715 in Charles county, which he represented almost continuously from 1757 to 1773; he then moved to Frederick county, which he also represented till

1781; was very active in opposition to all Parliamentary measures; signed the "Non-Importation Agreement of Maryland," 22d of June, 1769; was chairman of the "Committee of Observation" for Frederick, from 1775 to the formation of the State government; he held continuously the most important positions in county and State; entered the Continental Congress, 22d of February, 1781, and was chosen its President the next November, to act for the coming year. He had the honor of welcoming General Washington, when he came to Philadelphia, after the surrender of Cornwallis at Yorktown. Signed the articles of Confederation, 1st March, 1781. This John Hanson "was a man of great moral intrepidity and decision of character, and but few men, in the exciting times of the Revolution, and prior thereto, enjoyed in a greater degree the confidence of the community, as is fully evinced by the fact that he was elevated by his countrymen to the very highest and most responsible offices, and was in the service of the State almost without intermission from 1757 to 1782. He was a member of the Episcopal Church and zealous in its interests." He married Jane, daughter of Alexander Contee; she died on the 21st of February, 1812, aged 84 years; they had issue: Alexander Contee Hanson, Chancellor of Maryland, who died on 22d of November, 1783, aged 68 years, at "Oxon Hill," Prince George's county, while on a visit to his nephew, Thomas Hanson. He was, in early life, assistant private secretary to General Washington; later, was one of the first judges of the General Court of Maryland, under the Constitution of 1776; in 1789, he was appointed Chancellor of Maryland, and held the position until his death; at the request of the Legislature he compiled the laws of the State, known as "Hanson's Laws;" he married Rebecca Howard, of Annapolis, and left: Charles Wallace, Alexander Contee, and a daughter, who married Thomas Peabody Grosvenor, a member of Congress from New York. Charles Wallace Hanson was a judge; he married Rebecca, daughter of the Hon. Charles Ridgeley, who was governor of Maryland, 1815–18; but had no children. The second son, the Hon. Alexander Contee Hanson, U. S. Senator, 1816–19, was the editor and proprietor of the *Federal Republican*, a Baltimore paper of influence; he was mobbed and nearly killed, at Baltimore, in June, 1812, because he opposed the war with England. At the same time, General Lingan was killed, and General Henry Lee seriously injured. He married Priscilla Dorsey and had issue: Charles Grosvenor Hanson, who married (1840), Annie Maria, daughter of T. H. Worthington, of Baltimore county, and had: John Worthington, Priscilla, Charles Edward, Murray, Samuel Contee, Grosvenor, Nannie, Florence, Alice, and Bessie Hanson. (Hanson's *Old Kent.*)

## Hancock Lee.

13. Hancock Lee[4], (sixth) son of Philip Lee[3] (Richard[2], Richard[1]) was probably by his second marriage; he was born ——, and died the latter part of October, 1759; apparently he was never married, no mention being made of wife or children. His will, dated 10th October and probated 5th November, was as follows:

In the name of God, Amen. I Hancock Lee of Prince George's County in the Province of Maryland being weak and infirm of body but of sound and disposing mind and memory do make and ordain this my last will and testament in manner and form following. Imprimis, I bequeath my Soul into the hands of my Redeemer and my body to be decently buried without pomp or show and in the presence of a few friends only.

Item. I will direct and appoint that all my just debts be paid and satisfied by my Ex'rs hereafter named. Item. Whereas I have heretofore been jointly concerned with Mr. James Russell of London Merchant w[ch] Concern or Partnership has been lately settled but several mortgages of the sd. Concern yet remaining unpaid not foreclosed or taken in being the profits of the sd. Concern or Partnership as by bonds books bills of sale and mortgages will appear. I therefore will desire and direct that my sd. Ex'rs shall as soon as may be collect and receive all the said debts so outstanding foreclose all the mortgages convert the same into and raise all the money or Tob: which the bills of sale af[sd] or other deeds may produce and to make remittances of one moiety or half part thereof to him the said James Russell and the other moiety to be applied to my own account to be disposed of in my Estate and to be applied as is hereafter directed. Item. Whereas I past a bond to the said James Russell in England conditioned for the payment of Eleven hundred and odd pounds and whereas I have since remitted to him the said James Russell (exclusive of one hundred and eighty Pounds sterling upon my own proper account) one hundred eighty and three hogsheads of tobacco and two hundred and odd Pounds in bills of Exchange wh[ch] being part of the profits of the sd. old Concern I have directed the sd. James Russell to applye and appropriate one half part of the proceeds of the said Tob: and one half of the bills of Exch. af[sd.] to his the said James Russell's own proper use and acc't. and that the other half or moiety of the sd. Tob: and bills of Exchange should be placed to the credit of my said bond. But if there should yet remain anything due and owing on my sd. bond I hereby order direct and appoint that the same may be paid off and discharged as soon as may be. Item. I will direct and appoint that all the effects w[ch] shall appear to be my own private property excepting what is hereafter particularly mentioned shall be sold by my Ex'rs hereafter named and converted into money with all convenient speed. Item. I give and bequeath to my sd. Br. Corbin Lee a gold watch with the chain and seal belonging to it w[ch] I usually wear myself. I also give unto my Br. John Lee a sword and to his my sd. Brothers wife a neat sett of china which were presented to me by my sister Ann Russell. I give unto my sister Alice Clark all my shirting and wearing stockings. I also give unto my sister Bowie's son Daniel Bowie all my waring apparel. To my sister Alice Clark two feather beds and to my sister Margaret Symer two feather beds and to each of my Brothers and Sisters vizt. to my Brother Corbin Lee to my Brother John Lee to my Brother George Lee to my Sister Lætitia Wardrop, Alice Clark, Hanna Bowie and Margaret Simer one hundred pounds Sterling to be paid to each of them. Item. I give and bequeath to Hancock Lee son of my Br. John Lee in Virginia two hundred pounds sterling to be paid to his father my sd. Br. John Lee for the use of his sd. son Hancock Lee,

Item. All the rest and residue of my Estate be it of what kind or nature soever I give and bequeath to my sister Lætitia Wardrop to be paid to my Br. George Lee and by him to be paid over to her for her sole use and maintenance. Item. Whereas I brought out this year from London a large assortment of goods on the joint account of the afors[d] James Russell and myself great part of which are yet on hand and unsold it is my will and desire and I hereby direct that my Ex'rs shall dispose of the same and make up the accounts thereof as soon as may be and remit the produce thereof to the sd. James Russell in order to reimburse him for what he has been or may be in advance for the said goods which are now divided into two cargoes one being at the town of Nottingham in Prince George's County and the other at George town in Kent County on the Eastern Shore unless Mr. James Russell's attorney in fact shall take all the sd. cargoes or concerns on the proper acc't of for the use of the sd. James Russell; in which case it is my will and desire and I hereby direct and appoint that all the said goods books and other things in any way relating to the sd. Concern shall be delivered up unto him the said James Russell's attorney in fact and I hereby constitute and appoint Mr. Charles Graham of Calvert County Merch't, Theodore Contee, my Brother George Lee Executors of this my last Will and Testament, desiring them to accept of such commission as they may think proper for their trouble. In witness, &c., &c.

It will be observed that Hancock, in this will, made bequests to each of his father's younger children, Elizabeth excepted, who died in 1752; they were probably his full brothers and sisters, that is, the children of the second marriage.

## John Lee.

14. John[4], (eighth) son of Philip Lee[3] (Richard[2], Richard[1]), born in Maryland, moved to Virginia and settled in Essex county; he succeeded his cousin, Col. John Lee, of "Cabin Point," as county clerk in 1761. (This John was the eldest son of Henry and Mary (Bland) Lee, of "Lee Hall," Westmoreland; he married Mrs. Mary (Smith) Ball, and had succeeded Captain William Beverley as clerk in 1745.) John Lee (of Maryland) married Susannah Smith, a sister of his cousin's wife; he had been given some land in Essex by his cousin, which place he named "Smithfield." John Lee (of Maryland) was in turn succeeded in the clerkship, in 1777, by his son, Hancock Lee, who held the position until 1792, when his brother, John P. Lee, became clerk and continued in office until 1814.

John Lee's will was dated 24th of April and was proved on the 19th of May, 1777:

In the name of God, Amen. I John Lee of the county of Essex being sick and weak but of sound and disposing mind and memory do make and ordain this my last will and testament in manner and form following. Imprimis: I lend unto my beloved wife Susanna Lee during her life the land conveyed to me by John Lee gent. deceased, containing about 300 acres being part of the tract purchased by the said John Lee last mentioned of John Nail. Item. I give and devise unto my son Hancock Lee and his heirs forever the said 300 acres of land after my wife's decease in lieu of and as a satisfaction for £200 sterling given him by his uncle Hancock Lee of the Province of Maryland, but if my son Hancock should refuse to accept of the said land as a satisfaction for the said sum of £200 sterling then I direct that the interest in the said land hereby devised to him shall be sold by my executors hereafter named and the money arising from such sale be divided amongst such of my younger children as shall be living at the time of my wifes death.

Item. I direct that all the rest and residue of my estate of what nature or kind soever or so much of it as my executors shall find necessary shall be sold for the discharge of my debts and the surplus I devise to my said wife Susanna and my younger children equally to be divided between them, my said wife to enjoy her proportion of such surplus so long as she shall continue my widow and no longer. Lastly, I constitute and appoint my friends Muscoe Garnett and William Young, executors of this my Will. In witness, etc.

This will mentions by name only one child, Hancock, but alludes to "my younger children." The names of these children are found in the wills of John Lee, the cousin of the testator, and in those of his sons, Hancock, John Pitt, Baldwin Matthews, and George W. Lee. The daughter, Mary, married a Micou, probably a Paul Micou, as a nephew, Paul Micou, Jr., is mentioned; Lettice married John Whiting; apparently neither Hancock, Baldwin, or George left any issue; it is said that Philip married Mary Jacqueline Smith (the sister-in-law mentioned by Baldwin), who was a daughter of Dr. John A. Smith, as stated by his daughter, Mary D. Smith. The widow, Mrs. Susannah Lee, was living on the 28th of December, 1793, as mentioned by her son, Philip. Abstracts of the wills of these brothers are given here together for easier comparison.

The children of John Lee and Susannah Smith, his wife, were:

i, HANCOCK[5], born ——; died in August or September, 1792; married Anne Smith. His will was written the 8th of February, 1790, and probated the 17th of September, 1792: "I Hancock Lee being sick and weak but of perfect sense and memory do make and ordain this my last will and testament in manner following. Imprimis: I give and bequeath to my beloved wife Anne Lee two thirds of my slaves . . . also one third of my household and kitchen furniture. My land at Makeshift and the other third of slaves and two thirds of my stock to be sold for payment of my just debts. I give to my Brother John Lee my seal left me as a legacy by uncle Hancock. I give to my Brother Phill my silver . . . which was left me as a legacy by my Aunt Lettice Thompson. I also give to my beloved wife the silver spoons left her by her Mother Ann Smith. I appoint my brothers Phill Lee, Jno. Lee, and Jno. Smith Executors," etc.

ii, JOHN PITT[5]. Nothing is known concerning this John P. Lee excepting what is contained in his will, which was written on the 1st of August, and probated, in Essex, the 15th of August, 1814. Left to his "sister Whiting, of Middlesex, all my Middlesex property, Land, negroes, stocks, &c., during her life and at her death I give the same to her four daughters;" the money paid to Henry Gaines for John Micou to be considered a gift to said John Micou; gave to his "brother Baldwin M. Lee and his heirs forever my Mount Landing property with all the negroes, stocks, &c., upon it . . . and do confide to his Trust and care and particular attention Catherine, Flora, Wm. and John and my faithful servant Jonathan;" to Baldwin M. Lee and George W. Lee he left "the residue of my Estate, the Gloster and Matthews lands."

iii, BALDWIN MATTHEW[5], born ——; died the 7th of February, 1822; his will contains all now known about him, apparently he never married. "This is the Last Will and testament of Baldwin M. Lee of Leesville in the County of Westmoreland and State of Virginia. First I give that part of the Smithfield tract of land in the County of Essex, which I shall be entitled to at the death of my Mother Susanna Lee, to my Brother John P. Lee, to him and his heirs forever. 2ndly. I give all the rest of my property, lands and negroes and every other kind and description of property Interest, and Estate, to which I am entitled, to my sister in Law Mary J. Lee, to her and her heirs forever, incumbering her with the payment of all my just debts, and do give her full and ample power to sell and dispose of the same if she thinks proper. I do appoint Mrs. Mary J. Lee, John P. Lee, and George W. Lee, my Ex'ors, &c., &c." This was dated 27th September, 1804; in a codicil of the 10th September, 1821, his brother George W. Lee was excluded from the executorship; "it is very much my desire to do something for the four children recommended to my care by my brother John P. Lee, to wit: Catharine Smith, Florinda, John and William Smith, but I find some difficulty in doing so at this time, but having the most implicit and unlimited confidence in my Sister in Law Mrs. Mary J. Lee, I shall leave them to her care, believing she will do them Justice and also do Justice with whatever estate may be left after paying my just debts," &c., &c. This will was probated 25th February, 1822.

iv, GEORGE W.[5], will dated 3d October and probated 15th November, 1824, in Essex county. Mentioned his sister "Mary Micou," to whom he lent his Smithfield lands for life and at her death one-fourth to nephew John Hancock Micou; of the balance of his estate he gave one-fifth each to Albert Micou, Susannah Micou, and Felicia Micou; to his niece Maria Micou one-fifth for life, and at her death to her children; the remaining fifth to the children of nephew, Paul Micou, Jr. Nephews John Hancock and Albert Micou, executors.

v, PHILIP[5], See 29.

vi, LETTICE[5], died 8th August, 1838, aged 84 years; married, in 1783, Captain John Whiting, of Gloucester, and had: 1, Susannah Smith, who died 3d April, 1845, unmarried. 2, Lettice Lee, who died 28th January, 1828; married, 22d January, 1820, Richard Woodward, and had one son, John Pitt Lee, still living. 3, Mary Anna Edwards, who died 3d April, 1845, unmarried. 4, Elizabeth Hancock, who married James Chowning. Her brother, John Pitt Lee, left to his "sister Whiting of Middlesex all my Middlesex property, Land, negroes, stocks, &c., and at her death I give the same to her four daughters."

vii, MARY[5], from her brother George W. Lee's will it is learnt that she married a Micou and had: Paul, John Hancock, Albert, Susannah, Felicia, and Maria Micou. (This Paul Micou, whom Mary Lee married, was probably a grandson of the Paul Micou, the Huguenot refugee, who lived on the Rappahannock at a place called "Port Micou." He died there the 23d of May, 1736. His daughter, Margaret, married Moore Fauntleroy. A Paul Micou, Jr., was Justice for Essex county from 1740 to 1790; his son, of same name, held the office from 1780 to 1800, and was probably the husband of this Mary Lee.)

viii, ELIZABETH[5].

## GEORGE LEE.

15. GEORGE[4] (seventh) son of Philip Lee[3] (Richard[2], Richard[1]), by his second wife, Mrs. Elizabeth Sewall, was evidently very young at the time of his father's death; he was probably the youngest son, if not the youngest child. There is no record to be found of his life; from his will, it is discovered that he was married, but to whom is not known. From the desire to be buried at "Green Hill," in Charles county, and from mention of the Hansons, it may be surmised that he married one of that family. "Green Hill," later known as "Hanson's Hill," had been a seat of that family for many years. It was bequeathed by Samuel Hanson, Sr., to his son, Samuel, in 1740. George Lee spoke of the family burying-ground at this place, probably meaning of his wife's family. He desired to be "remov'd hence [from Washington] to the family burying Grounds at Green Hill in Charles county and there be interred without pomp or considerable expense by the side of my beloved wife. On whom as well as myself I desire a monumental slab of plain free stone to be laid with some short and appropriate inscription thereon."

In this will, he styled himself George Lee, of the City of Washington, gave minute directions for the disposal of his slaves, many of whom were to be freed after various terms of service; those that were to be sold were to have time to look for kind purchasers, and none to be sold to any dealer in slaves. He left legacies to Nancy H. Baker, George Lee Magruder, Chloe Ann Lingan, Chloe Lee Carr, and to "Thomas Sphenix son of my niece." Gave $500 to Rebecca Hanson, the daughter of Thomas Hanson; but mentioned no relationship. Henry H. Chapman, John R. Magruder, Jr., and Nicholas Lingan were appointed his executors. The will was dated the 15th of May, and probated on the 30th of September, 1807. George Lee's sister Margaret married a man by the name of "Symer," and had a daughter who married a Phenix; this Thomas Phenix was her son. Chloe Lee Carr was the wife of Overton Carr, of Prince George's county, whom she married on the 21st of April, 1807. Her maiden name was Baker, probably a sister of the above-mentioned Nancy H. Baker. Mr. G. G. Eaton, of Washington, thinks they were both granddaughters of Chloe Howard, daughter of Mrs. Charity Lee, wife of Arthur Lee. George Lee Magruder died at Annapolis, Md., on the 13th of June, 1863, aged 62 years. The Nicholas Lingan mentioned was probably of the same family as General James M. Lingan, of Revolutionary fame, who was killed by the mob in Baltimore, in 1812, at the same time that General Henry Lee was injured.

## HON. PHILIP LUDWELL LEE.

16. PHILIP LUDWELL [4], eldest surviving son of Thomas Lee [3] (Richard [2], Richard [1]) and Hannah Ludwell, his wife, was born on the 24th of February, 1726–7, and died on the 21st of that month in the year 1775. Whether he was born at Stratford or Mt. Pleasant is not known; tradition has always claimed that all the sons of Thomas Lee were born at Stratford. As to his death, there is the letter of his cousin, "Squire" Richard Lee, to William Lee, in London: "I wrote the 23d of February [1775] you that your Brother, the Honourable Philip Ludwell Lee, Esq., departed this Life the 21st of that month; he was interred on the 24th of February, his birthday, and a son was born the same day and at the time of his Interment. No will has been found." Mr. Lee was educated in England, but at what institution is not known. Studied law at the "Inner Temple," London.

As heir-at-law of his father, Philip Ludwell inherited the larger share of his estate, and was charged with the care and education of his younger brothers. These lands were in Westmoreland, Northumberland, on the eastern shore of Maryland, two islands in the Potomac, and some land up the river above the Falls of the Potomac. It has been said that Thomas Lee, many years before, had taken up land on the upper Potomac, above the site of the present location of Georgetown, believing that some day the Colonies would become independent of Great Britain, and that the new nation would locate its capital on the Potomac near these falls! This story seems rather improbable; one might have prophesied that the growing Colonies would one day form themselves into a new nation, but that one could so far in advance predict the location of its capital is rather unlikely. At any rate, prophet or no prophet, Thomas Lee did locate a claim only a few miles above the present city of Washington.

In 1757, Loudoun county was formed from Fairfax, and included in its borders some of Philip Ludwell Lee's lands; "Leesburg, the county seat, . . . was named from the Lee family, who were among the early settlers of the county; it was established in September, 1758, in the thirty-second year of the reign of George II. Mr. Nicholas Minor, who owned the sixty acres around the court-house, had them laid off into streets and lots, some of which, at the passage of the act, had been built upon. The act constituted the Hon. Philip Ludwell Lee, Esqr., Thomas Mason, Esqr., Francis Lightfoot Lee, James Hamilton, Nicholas Minor, Josiah Clapham, Aeneas Campbell, John Hugh, Francis Hague, and William West, gentlemen, the trustees for the town." (Howe's *History of Virginia*, 353.)

Philip Ludwell Lee was a member of the House of Burgesses (30th March, 1756), and succeeded his father as member of the Council; apparently he was the secretary of the Council on the 18th of June, 1770, when a "list of Books necessary for the Council Chamber" was made out by him; the list included reports of Parliament, histories, philosophical transactions, Demosthenes' orations, and the like.

After his brother William's marriage he wrote him this gossipy letter:

"Dear Brother: Though you wd not write me of your good tidings amongst others you wrote, yet I shall be amongst the first to wish you joy very heartily; one of the most amiable women in the world you have possession of and I hope and Don't doubt you will do everything in yr. power to make her as happy as mortals can be, in gratefull return. I suppose you will hear from R. H. Lee that the Executors have refused to divide the estate 'til October; I wonder you shd. not know they wd. refuse; by the will if the young ladies dye under particular circumstances, they get the Estate; had I been concerned for that reason I wd. have made them done it instantly. How cd. you appoint yr. two Brothers, who know nothing of surveying or good land from bad and one of the Executors who I have heard you talk of you know how, to divide it? Something shd. be speedily done for the Estate, tho' fine, does not make enough to bare the Expenses of it; I wonder you don't come in to see it divided and to live on it, if you do not it will always bring you in debt, remember I tell you so.

"Mrs. Lee and Matilda wish you joy. I enclose a letter from Miss Galloway. Our Bro. Franc: Lee was married to Miss Rebec: Tayloe last Thursday; to-morrow Patty Corbin and Geo: Turberville are to be married; Davenport is married to Miss Ransdell, Miss Betty Washington to Alex'r. Spotswood, Nancy Washington to Burdet Ashton, Miss Cate Vaulx to young Banhead, Thos. Turner to Miss Jane Fauntleroy, Dr. Fauntleroy of Leeds to Miss Fauntleroy of Essex, Landon Carter, son of old Charles, is to be married in a little while to Miss Molly Fauntleroy of Naylor's Hole; Merriwether Smith is to marry in a few days Miss Daingerfield of Essex with £1,500 fortune; Widow Rust at Rusts Ferry to Corrie, Hobs Hole, mar'd some months, and sundry others; so you see this has been a marrying year. . . . . Miss Bushrod is mar'd to Phil: Smith; the Widow Lee of Jno: Lee to old Jno: Smith the inoculator. . . ."

"Virg'a Stratford, 31 May, 1769."

Philip Ludwell Lee married (about 1761–2) Elizabeth, second daughter of James Steptoe, of Westmoreland, and left three children. His widow married Philip Richard Fendall, and died about June, 1789, probably without issue by her second marriage.

On 19th of April, 1782, the report of the appraisement and division of Philip Ludwell Lee's estate was filed; the land consisted of 6,595 acres, mentioned as "the Clifts, Stratford, and All Hallows;" the mansion house, with its offices, and 1,800 acres were allotted Mrs. Fendall; the remaining two-thirds reserved for the two daughters, the son having died. On the 30th of May, 1780, £1,352, currency, one-third dower, was paid to Philip Richard Fendall, for "Mrs. Fendall."

The children of Philip Ludwell and Elizabeth (Steptoe) Lee were:

i, MATILDA[5], married her cousin, Henry Lee (35, q. v.).
ii, FLORA[5], married her first cousin, Ludwell Lee (33, q. v.).
iii, PHILIP[5], born on the 24th February, 1775; died in infancy.

The will of James Steptoe (dated 10th May, 1755; probated, Westmoreland, 28th September, 1757) mentioned wife, Elizabeth; sons, George, James, Thomas, and William; daughters, Ann and Elizabeth; sister Carrell to have charge of daughter Elizabeth; estate to be kept intact until children were 21 years old. Wife Elizabeth, Richard Lee, Philip Ludwell Lee, and George Lee, Ex'rs. Richard Lee filed an account, as administrator, 28th

September, 1762, in which payments were credited to Philip Ludwell Lee, "on account." In a division of slaves, recorded 26th March, 1771, the two daughters were mentioned; Elizabeth as the wife of Philip Ludwell Lee and Ann as the wife of Samuel Washington. (Westmoreland records.)

The following note was written by the housekeeper at Stratford; it is quite unique:

"To Miss Martha Corbin, Potobac. Stratford, September the 27. Dear Miss. I gladly embrace this opportunity of writing to you to put you in mind that there is such a being as my Selfe. I did not think you two would have slited me so, your Little cosen matilda was made a cristan the 25 of September the godmothers was mrs. washington miss becy taloe miss molly washington miss Nancy Lawson Stod proxse for miss nelly Lee and I for mrs. Fauquer, godfathers was col. Taloe mr. Robert Carter mrs. washington Col. Frank Lee, the Esqr [Squire Richard Lee], mrs washington and your ant Lee Dessers there Love to you I am your very humble Servant, Elizabeth Jackson."

## Thomas Ludwell Lee.

17. Thomas Ludwell[4], fourth son of Thomas Lee[3] (Richard[2], Richard[1]) and Hannah Ludwell, his wife, was born the 13th of December, 1730, and died at his home, "Bellevue," in Stafford county, on the 13th of April, 1778. His brother, R. H. Lee, writing to Arthur Lee, then in London, under date of the 12th of May, 1778, said: . . . "It is with infinite pain that I inform you our dear brother of Belleview departed this life on the 13th of April last, after sustaining a severe Rheumatic fever for six weeks. Dr. Steptoe attended him the whole time, and I was also with him. Both public and private considerations render this loss most lamentable. He had just been appointed one of our five judges of the General Court, in which station he was well qualified to do his country eminent service. He has left behind him a numerous family (7 children) and a very disconsolate widow."

Of the school days and earlier life of Thomas Ludwell nothing is known. It is highly probable that he was sent to England for his education, as were most of his brothers. It is also likely that he read law at one of the London schools. John Adams, quoting Chancellor Wythe, said of him: "Thomas Lee was the most popular man in Virginia, and the delight of the eyes of every Virginian, but . . . would not engage in public life." This latter statement, that he "would not engage in public life," is susceptible of two interpretations. First, that Thomas Ludwell was averse to public positions, or that he would accept none outside of Virginia. He certainly did hold many positions in the State, but may have been, like his brother, Francis Lightfoot, averse to public life. He was, at the time of his death, one of the judges of the General Court, and had been a frequent member of the Assembly as well as of the Conventions.

Mr. Grigsby, in his *Discourse on the Virginia Convention of* 1776, has said of him: "Among the patriotic names distinguished in our early councils none is invested with a purer lustre than the name of Lee. It is radiant with the glory of the Revolution. It has been illustrated by the sword, by the pen, and by the tongue. And in the Convention, now sitting, were two brothers[1] who bore the name, and who impressed upon it a dignity, which, prominent as it had been for more than a century of Colonial history, it had never borne before.

"Thomas Ludwell Lee and Richard Henry Lee were brothers. Thomas Ludwell, the elder of the two, held a conspicuous position as a patriot and lawyer, and died before the close of the war, but not until he had filled the most responsible trusts with fidelity and honour. He had been a member of the House of Burgesses, was a member of the Convention of July and December, 1775, and was chosen a member of the Committee of Safety. He took his seat in the Convention now sitting as a member from Stafford, and was placed on the committee appointed to draft a declaration of rights, and a plan of government. On the organization of the new government under the Constitution, he was appointed one of the five Revisors, and later elected one of the five judges of the General Court."

Thomas Ludwell Lee was an ardent supporter of the Colonies against the encroachments of the British ministry, as the following extract from a letter to his brother, Richard Henry Lee, then attending Congress at Philadelphia, shows. Writing from Williamsburg, under date of the 18th of May, 1776, he said:

"Enclosed you have some pointed resolves which passed our convention to the infinite joy of the people here. The preamble is not to be admired in point of composition, nor has the resolve for independency that peremptory and decided air which I could wish. Perhaps the proviso, which reserves to this Colony the power of forming its own government, may be questionable as to its fitness. Would not a uniform plan of government prepared for America by the Congress and approved by the Colonies be a surer foundation of increasing harmony to the whole? However such as they are, the exultation here was extreme. The British flag was imme-

---

[1] And two others of the family, Henry Lee, of Prince William, and Richard Lee, of Westmoreland, were also members of this Convention.

diately struck on the Capitol, and a Continental hoisted in its room. The troops were drawn out, and we had a discharge of artillery and small arms. You have also a set of resolves offered by Col: M. Smith; but the first, which were proposed the second day by the President, for the debate lasted two days, were preferred. These he had formed from the resolves and preambles of the first day, badly put together. Col: Mason came to town yesterday after the arrival of the post. I showed him your letter, and he thinks with me that your presence here is of the last consequence. He designs to tell you so by letter to-day. All your friends agree in this opinion. Col°: Nelson is on his way to Congress, which removes the objection respecting a quorum of delegates. To form a plan of just and equal government would not perhaps be so very difficult; but to preserve it from being mar'd with a thousand impertinences, from being in the end a jumble of discordant, unintelligible parts, will demand the protecting hand of a master. I cannot recollect with precision the quantity of lead which we have received from the mines, though I think it about ten tons.

"The works are now carried on by the public on a large scale, and no doubt is entertained here that a full supply for the continent may be had from thence, by increasing the number of hands. In my next you shall have a more accurate acc't. The fast was observed with all due solemnity yesterday. The delegates met at the Capitol and went in procession to hear a sermon by appointment of the convention. Corbin and Wormeley . . . the first to an estate his father has in Caroline, the other to his plantation in Berkley. Adieu my dear Brother, give my love to Loudoun,[1] and let us have the satisfaction to see you assisting in the great work of this Convention."

The "resolves," which did not have the "peremptory and decided air" that Mr. Lee desired, were passed by the Virginia convention, on the 15th of May, 1776, and were as follows:

> Resolved, that the delegates appointed to represent this Colony in General Congress, be instructed to propose to that respectable body, to declare the united colonies free and independent states, absolved from all allegiance to, or dependence on the crown or parliament of Great Britain; and that they give the assent of this Colony to such declaration, and whatever measures may be thought necessary by Congress for forming foreign alliances, and a confederation of the colonies, at such time and in the manner that to them shall seem best: provided, that the power of forming governments for, and the regulations of the internal concerns of each colony, be left to the colonial legislatures.

Thomas Ludwell Lee married Mary, daughter of William Aylett, probably of Prince William; they had the following issue:

---

[1] F. L. Lee, frequently so called by his brothers.

i, THOMAS LUDWELL[5], See 30.
ii, WILLIAM AYLETT[5], died young and unmarried.
iii, GEORGE[5], See 31.
iv, ANNE FENTON[5], born ——; died ——; married, on the 3d of January, 1782, Daniel Carroll Brent, of "Richland," Stafford county, and had twelve children; of whom, only six grew up: 1, William, born 13th of January, 1783; died 13th of May, 1843; married his first cousin, Winifred Beale, daughter of Thomas Ludwell, and Fanny (Carter) Lee (see 30, iv). 2, Thomas Ludwell Lee, born the 9th of August, 1784. 3, Adelaide Brent, born the 25th of December, 1786. 4, Eleanor, born the 11th of October, 1787. 5, George Lee, born —— August, 1793. 6, Mary Aylett, born the 3d of October, 1795.
v, LUCINDA[5], born ——; died ——; married Dr. John Dalrymple Orr, of Prince William county, and had issue: Mary Aylett, Eleanor Lee, Thomas Ludwell Lee, John Dalrymple, Arthur Lee, and Ann Fenton Brent Orr, all of whom died young or without marrying, excepting Eleanor; she married, on the 5th of May, 1829, General Asa Rogers, of Loudoun county, and had: John Dalrymple, Arthur Lee, Lucy Lee (who married on the 9th of August, 1859, the Rev. O. A. Kinsolving, and dying at the early age of twenty-eight years, left two sons: the Revs. Arthur B. Kinsolving and Lucien Lee Kinsolving, the latter now of the Brazilian Mission), Laura Frances (who married, on the 27th of June, 1860, her cousin, George Lee, of Loudoun, son of Dr. George and Eveline Byrd (Beverley) Lee), and Hugh Hamilton Rogers. Lucinda Lee was the writer of the *Journal of a Young Lady of Va.*, published at Baltimore, 1871. (This journal was evidently written about 1787.)
vi, REBECCA[5], died unmarried.

This obituary notice was written by Joseph Gales, then editor of the *National Intelligencer*, of Washington, D. C.:

"On Friday, the 31st ult., at the residence of his brother, Col. Orr, Mayor of the City of Washington, after some weeks of severe suffering, Dr. John Dalrymple Orr, of Frederick county, aged forty-four years. The character of Dr. Orr, as a gentleman and philanthropist, is too well known to require our testimony. Having perfected in Scotland, the education of which the foundation was laid in this, his native country, he practiced medicine for several years in Alexandria; but relinquished it after his removal over the Blue Ridge, and devoted himself to the calls of society, the education of his children, and the cultivation of his farm. The disease, which deprived his children of an affectionate parent, his friends of a beloved and respected associate, had preyed upon his health for several years, and at length triumphed over the best medical and surgical aid."

Henry Lee, of "Lee Hall," Westmoreland, had a daughter, Lætitia, who married Col. William Ball, of Lancaster county; their daughter, Mary Ball, married, on the 2d of March, 1765, her cousin, John Ball, of Fauquier county, whose sixth child, also named Mary Ball, married Col. Alexander Dalrymple Orr.

## THE AYLETTS.

"The Aylett family of England is a very old one, claiming descent from a companion of the Conqueror, whose sons obtained grants of land in Cornwall. The etymology of the name, Aylett, is a sea-cow, Cornish Chough." In 1656, it is said, a Captain John Aylett emigrated from Essex county, England, to Virginia, and later took up large tracts of land in the present county of King William. This Captain Aylett left a son, Philip, who settled in King William in 1686; he was succeeded by his son, William, who represented that county as Burgess in 1723–26. This William Aylett married Anne —— and left three sons, and many daughters, who are said to have married the eldest sons of the neighboring gentry.

The Anne Aylett who married Richard Henry Lee, in 1759, was born in 1738, and may have been one of these daughters, or more probably the child of one of their brothers. Thomas Ludwell Lee married a Mary Aylett, who was certainly the daughter of a William Aylett. Captain William Aylett, Jr., of Westmoreland, married Annie Ashton, who died prior to 1750–1, leaving two daughters, Elizabeth and Anne.[1] The former married George Turberville; the latter, it is said, married Augustine Washington.

Philip Aylett, son of the above-mentioned William, of King William county, married (about 1739) Martha Dandridge, the daughter of Hon. William and Unity (West) Dandridge, by whom he had Col. William Aylett, the assistant commissary general of Virginia during the Revolution, also a son John, and two daughters, Unity and Anne. Thus, there were in the Aylett family at nearly the same date three Annes; just which of them married R. H. Lee, is at present difficult to decide.

## Richard Henry Lee.

18. Richard Henry[4], the fifth son of Thomas Lee[3] (Richard[2], Richard[1]) and Hannah Ludwell, his wife, was born at Stratford, Westmoreland county, the 20th of January, 1732, and died at his home, Chantilly, in the same county, on the 19th of June, 1794.

---

[1] Hayden, *Va. Genealogies*, 489.

Richard Henry Lee

After a course of private tuition at home, Mr. Lee was sent to the Wakefield Academy, in Yorkshire, England; on leaving that school, he made a brief tour of northern Europe, and returned to Virginia, being then only nineteen years old. For some years, probably until his marriage, he resided with his eldest brother, at Stratford, and passed the time, it is said, in diligent reading of the ancient classics and modern histories. Such a range of study seemed to be chosen, as if by intuition, to prepare him for the part he was destined afterward to take in the struggle between England and her American colonies. His taste for the classics was constantly displayed in after life by the frequent and appropriate quotations he made from them to enrich his diction or to fortify his argument.

The greater part of the estate left Mr. Lee by his father was located in Prince William county, but he continued after his marriage to reside in Westmoreland. It is said his eldest brother was so devoted to him that he would not consent to having him settle far away from Stratford. So, when Richard Henry was about to establish a home for himself, his brother insisted that he should build near Stratford, and leased him, for the purpose, the estate called "Chantilly." It appears this name was given it by Richard Henry, and that the estate was formerly known as "Hollis' Marsh;" it was situated about three miles below Stratford, and also on the Potomac River. Later in life, Mr. Lee paid a rental for it to General Henry Lee, and mentions in his own will that he only held the estate on a lease.

When about twenty-three, Mr. Lee raised a company to join General Braddock in his ill-fated expedition against the French and Indians; their aid was declined by the haughty Englishman, who had no use for provincials. So, perhaps, Braddock preserved Mr. Lee's life for a future of greater usefulness. A few years later, when about twenty-five, Mr. Lee was appointed a Justice for Westmoreland, a position of influence and much sought after in those days. He so impressed his colleagues on the bench with his special fitness for the duties of the position, that they petitioned the governor to antedate his commission that he might be chosen their presiding officer. It was about this date (1757) that he made his first appearance in the political arena, by being chosen a member of the House of Burgesses; he continued a member of that body, when not in Congress, until 1792, when he finally retired from active public life.

"Like his brother, Thomas Ludwell, he was oppressed with a natural diffidence, which was heightened by a contemplation of the dignified intellects who surrounded him, and for one or two sessions he took no part in their debates." His first effort in that body was a speech against the importation of slaves into the Colony; the proposition was "to lay so heavy a tax upon the importation of slaves as effectually to put an end to that iniquitous and disgraceful traffic within the Colony." This trade was continually the object of repressive legislation by the early Virginians. Mr. Lee's speech on this proposition proved him to possess keen foresight, and to have thus early discovered this dangerous rock, upon which the future Republic was destined to be so nearly wrecked. His opening words were:

"Sir, as the consequences of the determination we must make in the subject of this day's debate will greatly affect posterity, as well as ourselves, it surely merits our most serious attention. And well am I persuaded, Sir, that if it be so considered, it will appear, both from reason and experience, that the importation of slaves into this Colony has been and will be attended with effects dangerous both to our political and moral interests. When it is observed that some of our neighbouring colonies, though much later than ourselves in point of settlement, are now far before us in improvement, to what, Sir, can we attribute this strange, this unhappy truth? The reason seems to be this: *that with their whites they import arts and agriculture, whilst we with our blacks exclude both.*" After alluding to the dangers of servile wars, etc., he added: "Nor, Sir, are these the only reasons to be urged against the importation. In my opinion, not the cruelties practised in the conquest of Spanish America, not the savage barbarity of a Saracen, can be more big with atrocity than our cruel trade to Africa. There we encourage those poor, ignorant people to wage eternal war against each other; not nation against nation, but father against son, children against parents, and brothers against brothers, whereby parental, filial, and fraternal duty is terribly violated; that by war, stealth, or surprise we *Christians* may be furnished with our *fellow-creatures*, who are no longer considered as created in the image of God as well as ourselves, and equally entitled to liberty and freedom by the great law of nature; but they are to be deprived, forever deprived, of all the comforts of life, and to be made the most wretched of the human kind. I have seen it observed by a great writer that Christianity, by introducing into Europe the truest principles of humanity, universal benevolence, and brotherly love, had happily abolished civil slavery. Let us, who profess the same religion, practise its precepts, and, by agreeing to this duty, convince the world that we know and practise our truest interests, and that we pay a proper regard to the dictates of justice and humanity."

When the proposed Stamp tax was under discussion and before its full purport was understood, Mr. Lee applied for the position of collector under it. For this he was afterward censured; he defended himself in these words, 25th July, 1766: "Early in November, 1764, I was, for the first time, informed by a gentleman of the intention of Parliament to lay a stamp duty in America, with a friendly proposition on his part to use his influence to procure for me the office of stamp collector. I call it friendly because I believe the gentleman, no more than myself, nor perhaps a single person in this country, had at that time reflected the least on the nature and tendency of such an act. Considering this only in the light of a beneficial employment, I agreed the gentleman should write, and I wrote myself. It was but a few days after my letters were sent that, reflecting on the nature of the application I had made, the impropriety of an American being engaged in such an affair, struck me so strongly that I determined to exert every faculty I possessed, both in private and public life, to prevent the success of a measure which I now discovered to be in the highest degree pernicious to my country. I considered that to err is certainly the portion of humanity, but that it was the business of an honest man to recede from error as soon as he discovered it, and that the strongest principle of duty called upon every citizen to prevent the ruin of his country, without being restrained by any consideration which could interrupt the primary obligation. But it did not appear to me that a promulgation of my application was necessary, as I considered that my actions would be the strongest proofs of the rectitude of my intentions. That such was the conduct held by me in public, I desire not to be credited on my bare assertion, but with confidence I appeal to the many worthy gentlemen with whom I served in the General Assembly. They know who first moved, in the House of Burgesses, for the address to his majesty, the memorial to the Lords, and the remonstrance to the House of Commons; they also know what part I took in preparing those papers."

This letter was published in the *Virginia Gazette;* as stated in it, Mr. Lee was the one to bring before the Assembly the Act of Parliament, claiming their right to tax America, and he served on the special committee appointed to draft an address to the King, a memorial to the House of Lords, and a remonstrance to the Commons. He was selected to prepare the first and last of these three papers. Mr. Lee happened to be absent from the sitting of the Assembly, when Patrick Henry introduced (in May, 1765) his famous resolution; but he concurred most heartily in its sentiment; shortly afterward he organized the "Westmoreland Association" of patriots and wrote their resolutions. In these it was declared (February, 1766) that "We, who subscribe this paper, have associated, and do bind ourselves to each other, to God, and to our country, by the firmest ties that religion and virtue can frame, to support and maintain, and defend each other in the observance and execution of these following articles." The articles were chiefly a direct protest against the Stamp Act, and expressed their determination to "exert every faculty to prevent the execution of the said Stamp Act in any instance whatsoever within this Colony."

When a draft of the "Boston port bill" reached Virginia, the Assembly was in session; an animated protest was made against it, which caused the royal governor to dissolve the Assembly. Nothing daunted by this action of the Governor, some members met the next day at the "Raleigh Tavern," and in the "Apollo" room, drew up a manly and vigorous address to their constituents. They recommended that every county should send delegates to a convention, which should be held in Williamsburg on the 1st of August, 1774. This advice was followed. The convention met, discussed in detail their grievances, declared their rights, and ended by electing delegates to a general Congress of all the Colonies, which met in Philadelphia, on the 4th of September, 1774.

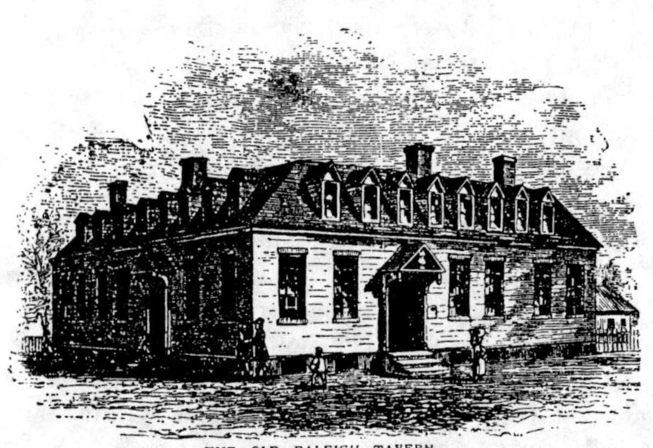

THE OLD RALEIGH TAVERN.

The following memorandum, in General Washington's writing, doubtless gives the result of the balloting in this Convention for these delegates. The original paper is in the possession of the Pennsylvania Historical Society: Peyton Randolph, 104; R. H. Lee, 100; Geo. Washington, 98; Pat. Henry, 89; Rich[d] Bland, 79; Ben. Harrison, 66; Edm[d] Pendleton, 62.

The first Continental Congress met in Carpenters' Hall, on Chestnut Street, Philadelphia; its convening had been in many ways prepared for by correspondence between the leading patriots in the different colonies.[1]

[1] NOTE.—Thomas Cushing, writing from Boston to Arthur Lee, under date of 22d of April, 1773, said: ". . . The house of burgesses of the government of Virginia, as you will find by the enclosed paper, have upon this occasion passed a number of resolves, appointing a standing committee of correspondence and enquiry, to correspond and communicate with their sister colonies in America, respecting the acts and resolutions of the British parliament; and have directed their speaker to transmit them to the speakers of the different assemblies through the continent, and request them to appoint similar committees. There is no doubt that most of the colonies, if not all, will come into like resolutions; and some imagine if the colonies are not soon relieved, a congress will grow out of this measure."

It seems that Arthur Lee was instrumental in having his brother and Mr. Dickinson correspond. The latter wrote to Arthur Lee, under date of 26th of June, 1769: ". . . I return you many thanks for procuring me the honor of your brother's correspondence. I cannot tell you how much I esteem it."

Mr. Lee had been an early advocate of this correspondence; he wrote (under date of the 25th of July, 1768) to John Dickinson, of Pennsylvania, suggesting not only that select committees should be appointed for this purpose, "but that private correspondence should be conducted between the lovers of liberty in every province." In 1773, the Virginia Assembly (Massachusetts took similar action about the same date) appointed a "Committee of Correspondence," of which Mr. Lee was a member. The first voice raised in this Congress was that of Patrick Henry; who, in a speech, it is said, of impassioned eloquence, unfolded to his anxious listeners the perils and the duties of the hour. The second speaker was Richard Henry Lee, who supplementing and enlarging upon Henry's words, impressed the members with his wisdom and sagacity. Such evidently was the result of his eloquence, for he immediately took a leading place in that body, composed as it was of the ablest and wisest of all America.[1] Joseph Read, a fellow-member, wrote of the Virginians: "There are some fine fellows come from Virginia, but they are very high. The Bostonians are mere milk-sops to them. We understand they are the capital men of the Colony, both in fortune and understanding."[2] Some one has said that the delegates from Virginia were "carefully selected, and represented in Richard Henry Lee and Patrick Henry, oratory and eloquence; in George Washington, the soldier; in Richard Bland, the finished writer; in Benjamin Harrison, the wealthy and influential planter; in Edmund Pendleton, the man of law; in Peyton Randolph, solidity of character."

Mr. Lee was an active and energetic member of many of the leading committees of this Congress; from his pen emanated the memorial of Congress to the people of British America, which has been generally considered a masterly document. Being a member of the next Congress, he wrote their address to the people of Great Britain, also a masterly state paper. As chairman of the committee, he drew up the instructions of Congress to General Washington upon his assuming command of the army. His most important, and distinguished service was rendered on the 7th of June, 1776, when, in accordance with the instructions of the Virginia Con-

---

[1] Of the men of this time and their work, Mr. Everett has said:

"The various addresses, petitions, and appeals, the correspondence, the resolutions, the legislative and popular addresses, from 1764 to the Declaration of Independence, present a maturity of political wisdom, a strength of argument, a gravity of style, a manly eloquence, and a moral courage, of which unquestionably the modern world affords no other example. This meed of praise, substantially accorded at the time by Chatham, in the British Parliament, may well be repeated by us. For most of the venerated men to whom it is paid, it is but a tribute to departed worth. The Lees, Henry, Otis, Quincy, Warren, and Samuel Adams, the men who spoke those words of thrilling power, which raised and ruled the storm of resistance, and rang like the voice of fate across the Atlantic, are beyond the reach of our praise." (Edward Everett, in an address commemorating the Fiftieth Anniversary of the Declaration of Independence.)

[2] *Life of Joseph Read*, I, 75.

vention, and at the request of his colleagues, he proposed the resolution for the independence of the colonies; of which resolution a *fac-simile* is given on opposite page.

This motion was seconded by John Adams, of Massachusetts; the discussion upon its adoption continued until the 10th of June, when a committee was appointed to prepare a declaration, in accordance with this motion. Mr. Lee's speech, advocating his resolution, has not been preserved; but tradition states that it was an effort worthy of the occasion. His biographer [1] has given these concluding sentences: "Why then, Sir, do we longer delay? Why still deliberate? Let this happy day give birth to an American Republic! Let her arise, not to devastate and conquer, but to re-establish the reign of peace and of law. The eyes of Europe are fixed upon us. She demands of us a living example of freedom, that may exhibit a contrast, in the felicity of the citizen, to the ever-increasing tyranny which desolates her polluted shores. She invites us to prepare an asylum, where the unhappy may find solace and the persecuted repose. She entreats us to cultivate a propitious soil, where that generous plant, which first sprung and grew in England, but is now withered by the poisonous blasts of Scottish tyranny, may revive and flourish, sheltering under its salubrious and interminable shade, all the unfortunate of the human race. If we are not this day wanting in our duty to our country, the names of the American legislators of '76 will be placed by posterity at the side of Theseus, of Lycurgus, of Romulus, of Numa, of the three Williams of Nassau, and of all those whose memory has been, and forever will be, dear to virtuous men and good citizens."

It is the uniform rule of all deliberative bodies to appoint the member who has offered a resolution the chairman of any committee selected to report upon that motion. In this case, therefore, Mr. Lee would have been chosen chairman of the committee for the drafting of the Declaration of Independence, had he been present. On the evening of the 10th of June, he received word of the serious illness of his wife; he left Philadelphia to visit her on the very day this committee was appointed. Thus an accidental sickness in his family probably deprived him of the signal honor of being the author as well as the mover of the Declaration of American Independence. It is said that the English papers, which gave the first intelligence of the adoption of the Declaration of Independence, headed their columns with this line:

"Richard Henry Lee and Patrick Henry have at last accomplished

---

1 *Life and Correspondence of R. H. Lee*, 1825, pp. 171 *et seq.*

Resolved

That these United Colonies are, and of right ought to be, free and independent States, that they are absolved from all allegiance to the British Crown, and that all political connection between them and the State of Great Britain is, and ought to be, totally dissolved.

FAC-SIMILE OF THE ORIGINAL RESOLUTION AS OFFERED BY RICHARD HENRY LEE.

ORIGINAL PAPER IS PRESERVED IN THE ARCHIVES OF THE STATE DEPARTMENT AT WASHINGTON.

their object: The colonies have declared themselves independent of the mother country."

Mr. Lee's grandson stated that Governor Johnson, of Maryland, told him "that shortly after the war, he heard from an English gentleman of great respectability who had lived in London during the Revolution, and who had had opportunities of hearing a good deal of the plans and intentions of the ministry, that they had intended, in the event of the reduction of the colonies, to have demanded the delivery of General Washington and Richard H. Lee, and to have them executed as principal rebels."

Mr. Lee continued to serve in Congress for many years, being a member in 1778–80–84–87, and was one of the signers of the articles of confederation in 1778. During the sessions of 1784, he occupied the chair as President, being, it is said, the unanimous choice of all the delegates present. Some idea of his activity and of his almost incessant labors, may be gathered from the fact of his having served upon nearly one hundred committees during the sessions of 1776–77. But it is not the purpose of this sketch to give a history of Mr. Lee's public services; the active part he took in the Revolutionary struggle is too well known, is too much a part of the common history of this country, to need further notice in this sketch.

Every man who has taken important parts in public affairs has made enemies, nor was Mr. Lee any exception to this common fate. At the election of delegates from Virginia, in 1777, he was defeated; a result effected by his enemies in an underhand manner, by circulating reports injurious to his reputation. On hearing of this he instantly withdrew from Congress, returned to Westmoreland, and was promptly elected to the Assembly; he hastened to take his seat, and at once demanded an investigation into these charges. His request was granted. It is said that he defended himself most eloquently; he was triumphantly acquitted, and a resolution was passed instructing the Speaker to publicly thank Mr. Lee. The venerable George Wythe was Speaker. He addressed Mr. Lee in these words:[1]

"Sir:—It is with peculiar pleasure that I obey this command of the House, because it gives me an opportunity, whilst I am performing an act of *duty* to them, to perform an act of *justice* to yourself. Serving with you in Congress, and attentively observing your conduct there, I thought that you manifested in the American cause a zeal truly patriotic; and, as far as I could judge, exerted the abilities for which you are confessedly distinguished, to promote the good and prosperity of *your own country* in par-

---

[1] *History of Virginia*, by Burk, p. 225.

ticular, and of the United States in general. That the tribute of praise deserved may reward those who do well, and encourage others to follow your example, the House have come to this resolution :

"'Resolved, That the thanks of this House be given by the Speaker, to Richard Henry Lee, Esq., for the faithful service he has rendered to his country, in discharge of his duty, as one of the delegates from this State in general Congress.'"

It is said that Mr. Wythe shed tears while addressing Mr. Lee.

Mr. Lee responded:

"MR. SPEAKER:—I thank the House for this instance of candor and justice, which I accept the more willingly, as my conscience informs me it was not undeserved. I consider the approbation of my country, Sir, the highest reward for faithful services, and it shall be my constant care to merit that approbation by a diligent attention to public duty. My thanks are particularly due to you, Sir, for the obliging manner in which you have been pleased to signify the vote of the House, and I pray you, Sir, to receive my grateful acknowledgments accordingly."

Col. John Bannister, in writing to Theodoric Bland,[1] has described this scene: "You have no doubt heard of Mr. R. H. Lee's having been superseded in his appointment to Congress. This measure was adopted in an early part of the session, in his absence, which (though I am not very fond of that gentleman) I considered a most flagrant act of injustice, and as a precedent dangerous in its nature, and might (if not guarded against in time) be carried to lengths the most unwarrantable, and in the end be destructive of every principle of rectitude and impartiality in the trial of offences. The accusation was that Mr. Lee had, in the year 1776, directed a change of rents from money to tobacco, on a supposition that the large emission of paper money (the inevitable consequence of an expensive war) would depreciate the one and raise the other. To this charge was added another, of a more criminal nature, importing that Mr. Lee had engaged his tenants to pay (in case they failed to make good their rent in tobacco) during the continuance of their leases, in gold and silver money, at its then value, or as much paper as would purchase gold and silver to the amount of their yearly rent. . . . This being the state of what was imputed to him as criminal, I leave to you to form your own opinion of his conduct, and to determine whether the Assembly were right in his amotion from office. But if they were right in that, what will you say to their consistency and uniformity of opinion, when I tell you that the very body of men who but a few days before had disgraced, have returned him the thanks of their

[1] *Bland Papers*, 57.

house? Certainly no defense was ever made with more graceful eloquence, more manly firmness, equalness of temper, serenity, calmness and judgment, than this very accomplished speaker displayed on this occasion, and I am now of the opinion that he will be re-elected to his former station, instead of Mr. George Mason, who has resigned.—Williamsburg, 10 June, 1777."

Mr. Lee opposed the adoption of the Constitution of 1787; in this opposition, he was in agreement with George Mason, Patrick Henry, Benjamin Harrison, Thomas Jefferson, and others, in Virginia, and many of the ablest patriots of the time in other States. But, after the ratification of the Constitution, he consented to serve as one of the Senators from Virginia, mainly for the purpose of urging some amendments which he believed to be needed; many of these he was instrumental in securing. After many years of active service in Congress, and all the while a member of the Virginia Assembly, he finally, in 1792, retired from public life. Both branches of the Virginia Assembly gave him a vote of thanks for his patriotic services.

Richard Henry Lee, with his brothers, was a devoted personal, as well as political, friend of Washington; and, if one may judge by the tenor of the correspondence which passed between Washington and the Lees, this affection and friendship were cordially returned by Washington.[1] Something of the friendly intimacy that existed between Washington and Richard Henry Lee may be shown in a brief extract from the diary of an Englishman, who visited Washington at Mt. Vernon in 1785. This gentleman, a Mr. John Hunter, wrote:

"Wednesday 16th of Nov., 1785.—After breakfast I waited on Colonel Fitzgerald. A fire that had broke out in the town hindered us from getting off so soon as we intended. However, after some trouble it

---

1 An exception to this statement, as far as it concerns the friendly feeling that generally subsisted between General Washington and Mr. Lee may be made, for at one period of their lives there seems to have been some coolness between them. This was during the time the adoption and ratification of the new Constitution was under discussion. Washington at first refused to attend the convention, which met at Philadelphia for the framing of the Constitution; but later was persuaded to attend, became its presiding officer, and eventually the leading champion for its ratification by the several colonies. On the other hand, Mr. Lee was most decidedly and emphatically opposed to its ratification. And Washington does not appear to have been in a mood to brook opposition. Writing to James Madison on this subject, he mentions George Mason and R. H. Lee, two earnest opponents of the new Constitution, and adds:

"The political tenets of Col. M. and Colonel R. H. L. are always in unison. It may be asked, which of them gives the tone? Without hesitation I answer the latter, because I believe the latter will receive it from none. He has, I am informed, rendered himself obnoxious in Philadelphia by the pains he took to disseminate his objections among some of the leaders of the seceding members of the Legislature of that State. His conduct is not less reprobated in this country. How it will be relished generally is yet to be learned by me." After the Constitution was ratified, and Washington became President, the friendly feeling, usually subsisting between these two patriots, seems to have been fully restored (Bancroft, *History of the Constitution*, II, 443.)

was extinguished and at half past eleven we left Alexandria with Mr. Lee, the President of Congress, his son and servants. . . . When Colonel Fitzgerald introduced me to the General I was struck with his noble and venerable appearance. It immediately brought to my mind the great part he had acted in the late war. The General is about six feet high, perfectly straight and well made; rather inclined to be lusty. His eyes are full and blue and seem to express an air of gravity. His nose inclines to the aquiline; his mouth small; his teeth are yet good and his cheeks indicate perfect health. His forehead is a noble one and he wears his hair turned back, without curls and quite in officer's style, and tyed in a long queue behind. Altogether he makes a most noble, respectable appearance, and I really think him the first man in the world. . . . After tea General Washington retired to his study and left us with the President, his lady and the rest of the Company. If he had not been anxious to hear the news of Congress from Mr. Lee, most probably he would not have returned to supper but have gone to bed at his usual hour, nine o'clock, for he seldom makes any ceremony. We had a very elegant supper about that time. The General with a few glasses of champagne got quite merry, and being with his intimate friends, laughed and talked a good deal. Before strangers he is generally very reserved, and seldom says a word. I was fortunate in being in his company with his particular acquaintances. . . . We had a great deal of conversation about the slippery ground (as the General said) that Franklin was on, and also about Congress, the Potomac, improving their roads, etc. At 12 I had the honor of being lighted up to my bedroom by the General himself." (*Penna. Mag.*, etc., *XVII*, 76 *et seq.*)

Previous to this visit, under date of 12th of June, 1781, Mr. Lee had written to Washington: "Although our correspondence has been long interrupted, I hope our friendship will never be, notwithstanding the arts of wicked men, who have endeavored to create discord and dissension among the friends of America. For myself, having little but my good wishes to send you, it was not worth while to take up your attention a moment with them. The contents of this letter will, I am sure, require no apology, because you always approve that zeal which is employed in the public good." . . .

Under date of 15th of July, Washington replied: "Dear Sir, The moving state w[ch] the army was at the time your letter of the 12th ulto. came to hand, the junction of the allied troops at that period, and a variety of matters which have occurred since that period consequent of this junction, rather than a disinclination to continue a correspondence, the benefits of which were in my favor, must plead as an excuse for my silence till now.

Unconscious of having given you just cause to change the favorable sentiments you have expressed for me, I could not suppose you had altered them; and as I never suffer reports, unsupported by proofs, to have weight in my mind, I know no reason why our correspondence should cease, or become less frequent than heretofore, excepting on my part, that, as our affairs became more perplexing and embarrassed, the public claimed more of my attention and consequently left me less leizure for private indulgences." . . . (Ford's *Writings of George Washington*, IX, 304–5.)

One of the last letters upon public affairs written by Mr. Lee was to Washington; in it he most cordially and heartily indorsed the administration of the President. Mr. Lee's correspondence was immense; not only with his fellow-patriots in all parts of America, but also with many of the brightest minds of Europe. And the idea conveyed to the reader of the letters addressed to him is that the writers entertained great esteem for the man as well as unbounded admiration for the patriot.

The Virginians seemed especially anxious that Mr. Lee should attend their convention, when it met to frame a constitution. Jefferson wrote (8th July, 1776): "I shall return to Virginia after the 11th of August. I wish my successor may be certain to come before that time: in that case, I shall hope to see you, and not Wythe, in convention, that the business of government, which is of everlasting concern, may receive your aid."

John Page, of "Rosewell," wrote: ". . . I would to God you could be here at the next Convention. . . . If you could I make no doubt you might easily prevail on the Convention to declare for Independency and establish a form of government."

George Mason, of "Gunston," wrote: ". . . I need not tell you how much you will be wanted here on this occasion. I speak with the sincerity of a friend when I assure you, that in my opinion, your presence cannot, must not be dispensed with. We cannot do without you."

Mr. Lee had been most urgent in the demand that no treaty should be made with England that did not allow to America the free navigation of the Mississippi and the right of fishing, etc., on the banks of Newfoundland, etc. For this the New England States were very grateful to him, as shown in this letter:

"Portsmouth, N. H., 17th April, 1783. My dear Sir:—I cannot omit an opportunity that offers by a vessel bound to Virginia, to congratulate you on the happy event which, for many years, has been the great object of your labours and anxious cares. The very unequivocal part you, my dear friend, have taken, in this great revolution, must furnish your hours of retirement with the most pleasing reflections. Though the terms may not be, in all respects, exactly conformable to our wishes, they are, perhaps, equal to what we had a right to expect, all things considered.

"My happiness is greatly increased by this joyous event, as it opens a prospect of seeing you here. I already anticipate the pleasure of recapitulating with you those private as well as public consultations, in which you took so eminent a part, and which have produced such happy effects. This country, my dear sir, is very particularly obliged for your exertions to secure the most valuable branch of her trade, the fisheries. As a small token of my sense of the obligation, I must beg your acceptance of a quintal of fish, which, I think, is of the best quality. With very particular attachment, and the greatest respect, I am, my dear sir, your most affectionate friend and humble servant.

(Signed) WM. WHIPPLE."

Both Samuel and John Adams expressed themselves frequently in a similar manner; indeed, such was the common tenor of the letters received by this patriot. No man of the period appears to have been held in greater esteem by those whose good opinion was at once a tribute to merit and an honor to be coveted. John Adams noted in his "diary" his impressions of the various men he met at different times, and had this to say of his first meetings with Mr. Lee—and time seems rather to have increased than diminished his good opinion of the Lees.

Saturday, 3d of September, 1774. "Breakfasted at Dr. Shippen's; Dr. Witherspoon was there. Col. R. H. Lee lodges there; he is a masterly man. This Mr. Lee is a brother of the sheriff of London, and of Dr. Arthur Lee, and of Mrs. Shippen; they are all sensible and deep thinkers. Lee is for making the repeal of every revenue law—the Boston Port Bill, the bill for altering the Massachusetts Constitution, and the Quebec Bill and the removal of all troops—the end of the Congress, and an abstinence from all dutied articles, the means; rum, molasses, sugar, tea, wine, fruits, etc. He is absolutely certain that the same ship which carries home the resolution will bring back the redress. If we were to suppose that any time would intervene, he should be for exceptions. He thinks we should inform his Majesty that we never can be happy while the Lords Bute, Mansfield, and North are his confidents and counsellors. He took his pen and attempted a calculation of the numbers of people represented by the Congress, which he made about two millions two hundred thousand; and of revenue, now actually raised, which he made eighty thousand pounds sterling. He would not allow Lord North to have great abilities; he had seen no symptoms of them; his whole administration had been a blunder. He said the opposition had been feeble and incomptent before, that it was time to make vigorous exertions."

"Mrs. Shippen is a religious and a reasoning lady. She said she had often thought that the people of Boston could not have behaved. through their trials, with so much prudence and firmness at the same time, if they had not been influenced by a superior power. Mr. Lee thinks that to strike at the Navigation Acts would unite every man in Britain against us, because the kingdom could not exist without them, and the advantages they derive from these regulations and restrictions of our trade are an ample compensation for all the protection they have afforded us. . . . Spent the evening at Mr. Mifflin's, with Lee and Harrison from Virginia, the two Rutledges, Dr. Witherspoon, Dr. Shippen, Dr. Steptoe, and another gentleman; an elegant supper, and we drank sentiments till eleven o'clock. Lee and Harrison were very high. Lee had dined with Mr. Dickinson and drank Burgundy the whole afternoon. . . . Galloway, Duane, and Johnson are sensible and learned, but cold speakers. Lee, Henry, and Hooper are the orators; Paca is a deliberator, too; Chase speaks warmly; Mifflin is a sprightly and spirited speaker."[1]

Henry Lee, the eldest son of General Henry Lee, is responsible for this story concerning Mr. Lee. "During the War of the Revolution, and, I believe, while Mr. Jefferson was Governor of Virginia, a British squadron which had been scouring the waters and wasting the shores of the Chesapeake, taking advantage of a favorable breeze, suddenly came-to off the coast of Virginia, where the majestic cliffs of Westmoreland overlook the stormy and sea like Potomac. Mr. Lee was at that time on one of those visits to his family, with which, from the permanent sitting of Congress, the members were of necessity occasionally accommodated. He hastily collected from the nearest circle of his neighbors a small and ill-armed band, repaired at their head to the point on which the enemy had commenced a descent, and without regard to his inferiority of means and numbers instantly attacked them. He drove the party on shore back into their barges, and held them aloof until ships were brought to cover the landing with round shot and shells, which he had no means of returning. Then as he was the first in advance so he was the last to retire; as the men who were with him have, since his death, often said. Several of the hostile party were killed or wounded, among them an officer, whom they carried off. One man they buried on the shore. In a grove of aged beech-trees, not

---

[1] *Life and Works of John Adams*, Vol. II, p. 362, *et seq.*

far from Mr. Lee's residence, rest the remains of this unknown and unforgotten foe."

At the present time there is shown at Stratford one of these round shot, which tradition says was fired at the house by an English warship; how much of truth there is in this tradition cannot be ascertained. The iron missile now performs the useful and harmless service of a hitching-block for horses.

Bishop Meade has left his estimate of Mr. Lee's character and public services in these words:[1]

"In looking over the two volumes containing the life and correspondence of Richard Henry Lee, of Chantilly, in Westmoreland, the reader cannot fail to ask himself the question, 'Was there a man in the Union who did more in his own county and State and country, by action at home and correspondence abroad, to prepare the people of the United States for opposition to English usurpation, and the assertion of American independence? Was there a man in America who toiled and endured more than he, both in body and in mind, in the American cause? Was there a man in the Legislature of Virginia, and in the Congress of the Union, who had the pen of a ready writer so continually in his hand, and to which so many public papers may be justly ascribed, and by whom so much hard work in committee-rooms was performed?' To him most justly was assigned the honourable but perilous duty of first moving in our American Congress, 'That these United Colonies are, and of right ought to be, free and independent States.' Nor is it at all wonderful that one who was conversant with the plans and intentions of the English ministry should have declared that, in the event of the reduction of the Colonies, the delivery of General Washington and Richard Henry Lee would be demanded, in order to their execution as rebels. Although the great principles of morality and religion rest on infinitely higher ground than the opinion of the greatest and best of men, yet it is most gratifying to find them sustained in the writings and actions of such men as Richard Henry Lee. Mr. Lee advocated private education as being better calculated for impressing the minds of the young 'with a love of religion and virtue.' His biographer says that he had early studied the evidences of the Christian religion, and had through life avowed his belief in its divine origin. He was a member of the Episcopal Church in full communion, and took a deep interest in its welfare. He proved the sincerity of what has been quoted from him, in favour of private education, by having a minister, or candidate for the ministry, in his family as private

---

[1] *Old Churches, Families*, etc., II, 140, *et seq.*

tutor. Mr. Balmaine was sent over to him by his brother, Arthur, from London, as both a staunch friend of America and a pious man. I have often heard Mr. Balmaine speak in the highest terms of Mr. Lee as a Christian and a patriotic statesman. His attachment to the Church of his fathers was evinced by the interest he took in seeking to obtain consecration for our Bishops, immediately after the war, and when he was President of Congress. Twice were thanks returned to him by our General Convention for his services. Mr. Lee was a decided advocate of the appointment of public acts of supplication and thanksgiving to Almighty God in times of adversity and prosperity. When all was dark and lowering in our political horizon, and when it was proposed that, as one means of propitiating the favour of God, it should be recommended to the different States to take the most effectual means for the encouraging of religion and good morals, and for suppressing 'theatrical entertainments, horse-racing, gaming, and such other diversions as are productive of idleness, dissipation, and a general depravity of manners,' while some voted against the measure, Mr. Lee was found in company with the most pious men of the land in favour of it, and it was carried by a large majority. Again, when by the capture of Burgoyne's army the hearts of Americans were cheered, we find Mr. Lee one of a committee drafting a preamble and resolution, which is believed to be from his own pen, in the following pious strain:

"'Forasmuch as it is the indispensable duty of all men to adore the superintending providence of Almighty God, to acknowledge with gratitude their obligation to Him for the benefits received, and to implore such further blessings as they stand in need of; and it having pleased Him in His abundant mercy, not only to continue to us the innumerable bounties of His common providence, but also to smile upon us in the prosecution of a just and necessary war for the independence and establishment of our unalienable rights and liberties; particularly in that He hath been pleased in so great a measure to prosper the means used for the support of our arms, and crown them with the most signal success; it is therefore recommended to the Legislature and the executive powers of these States, to set apart Thursday, the eighteenth of December next, for solemn thanksgiving and praise; that with one heart and one voice the people may express the feelings of their hearts, and consecrate themselves to the service of their Divine Benefactor; and, together with their sincere thanks, acknowledgments and offerings, they may join the penitent confession of their manifold sins, whereby they have forfeited every favour, and their earnest and humble supplication that it may please God, through the merits of Jesus Christ, mercifully to forgive and blot them out of remembrance; that it may please God, etc.'

"Mr. Lee, though entirely opposed to any Church establishment, was, together with Henry, an advocate for the proposition to make every man contribute to the support of the Christian religion, as the only sure basis of private and public morality. In this, however, they failed. When the question about paying debts in depreciated currency came on, Mr. Lee evinced his high and honorable sense of morality in the earnest and eloquent opposition made to it. He declared that nothing so deeply distressed him as a proposition which he regarded as a violation of honesty and good faith among men, and said that it 'would have been better to have remained the honest slaves of Britain, than dishonest freemen.'"

Of Richard Henry Lee's personal appearance and of his style of oratory one or two descriptions by contemporaries may be given. William Wirt wrote: "His face was on the Roman model; his nose Cæsarean; the port and carriage of his head, leaning persuasively and gracefully forward; and the whole contour, noble and fine. He had studied the classics in the true spirit of criticism. His taste had that delicate touch which seized with intuitive certainty every beauty of an author, and his genius that native affinity which combined them without an effort. Into every walk of literature and science he had carried this mind of exquisite selection, and brought it back to the business of life, crowned with every light of learning and decked with every wreath that all the muses and all the graces could entwine. Nor did these light decorations constitute the whole value of its freight. He possessed a rich store of historical and political knowledge, with an activity of observation and a certainty of judgment which turned that knowledge to the very best account. He was not a lawyer by profession, but he understood thoroughly the Constitution, both of the mother country and of her colonies; and the elements also of the civil and municipal law. Thus, while his eloquence was free from those stiff and technical restraints which the habits of forensic speaking are apt to generate, he had all the legal learning which is necessary to a statesman. He reasoned well, and declaimed freely and splendidly. The note of his voice was deep and melodious. It was the canorous voice of Cicero. He had lost the use of one of his hands, which he kept constantly covered with a black silk bandage, neatly fitted to the palm of his hand, but leaving his thumb free; yet, notwithstanding this disadvantage, his gesture was so graceful and highly finished that it is said he had acquired it by practising before a mirror. Such was his promptitude that he required no preparation for debate. He was ready for any subject as soon as it was announced; and his speech was so copious, so rich, so mellifluous, set off with such bewitching cadence of voice and such captivating grace of action that, while you listened to him, you desired to hear nothing superior, and indeed thought him perfect. He had a quick sensibility and a fervid imagination."

Dr. Rush said of him: "I never knew so great an orator whose speeches were so short. Indeed, I might almost say that he could not speak long.

Richard Henry Lee

He had conceived his subject so clearly, and presented it so immediately to his hearers, that there appeared nothing more to be said about it. He did not use figures to ornament discourse, but made them the vehicles of argument."

John Adams wrote, 24th February, 1821, to a grandson of R. H. Lee: "With your grandfather, Richard Henry Lee, I served in Congress from 1774 to 1778, and afterward in the Senate of the United States in 1789. He was a gentleman of fine talents, of amiable manners and great worth. As a public speaker, he had a fluency as easy and graceful as it was melodious, which his classical education enabled him to decorate with frequent allusion to the finest passages of antiquity. With all his brothers, he was always devoted to the cause of his country."

It has been the purpose of this sketch to give a brief outline of the public services of Richard Henry Lee, together with a few comments, chiefly from the pens of his contemporaries who had ample opportunity of judging fairly of him. Perhaps another, and a better method of judging him may be found in his correspondence. The few letters given here are mostly to relatives, or dear friends, and many of them have never been printed.

Alluding to his ill-treatment by the Assembly, he wrote a friend: "Dear Sir:—I have but a moment to return you my thanks for your friendly and obliging letter. It was impossible for me to avoid feeling the unmerited ill-treatment that I had received, but I have now the pleasure to inform you that the two houses have removed all bad impressions by their favourable approbation of my conduct; and they have directed me to return to Congress as one of their Delegates. This latter is a most oppressive business, and therefore, unsought by me, but having put my hand to the plough, I am bound to go through. Not much important business has yet been done, but they propose to crowd a good deal into this week, at the end of which they talk of rising." (No superscription. Dated, Williamsburg, 28th of June, 1777.)

Under date of 14th January, 1764, he wrote from same place, to an unknown friend:—"By the Governor's speech, which you have inclosed, you may perceive that considerable business was markt out for us. But our glorious resolution of yesterday, to be defended by Militia, and to have no further concern with Regulars, will put a short period to the session, which now we expect will rise by Wednesday next. Two addresses that are ordered by the House have not yet been presented."

Writing from "Chantilly," 22d June, 1766, also to an unknown correspondent, he said:

"Dear Sir:—Is it true that one of the best friends, as well as one of the most able of the community, intends to quit the service of the country at this most important crisis? when every mental, every corporeal faculty that America possesses should be strained in opposition to preserve the most palpable privileges of human nature, the legal rights of America, and the constitutional freedom of British subjects?

"I yet hope, my friend, that you have only thought, not determined on declining to take a poll at the coming election. When the cause of our dissolution is known, will Ministerial cunning fail to suggest, that the people of Virginia disavow their Burgesses' claim to freedom, if a considerable change is made by them, in their choice of new representatives?

"Let us remove from despotism every show of argument, and let us endeavor to convince the world that we are as firm and unanimous in the cause of liberty, as so noble and exalted a principle demands. The inclosed pamphlet is said to be written by the first minister of Britain. If no better reasons can be assigned to support the measure he contends for, a strong proof is to be drawn from thence of its intrinsic vileness. It shows, indeed, that systems calculated to destroy human liberty, can only be maintained by vain sophistry, and an idle affectation of wit, without one single ray of wisdom; and that such doctrines are as far remote from true policy, as they are closely connected with the futile genius of a dealer in expedients, who never is able, and seldom willing to draw the necessary supplies of Government from such sources only as are consistent with the end of all government, the safety, the ease, and the happiness of the people.

"I would recommend the pamphlet to your attention, not for its merit, but that it may receive proper answer, and such an one it easily admits of, as would make its author blush, if it is possible for a minister to blush. But though an answer might fail to do this, it will certainly have weight with the cool and sensible part of mankind, and thereby perhaps prevent the extension of arbitrary, unconstitutional power."

Baltimore, 1st Jan., 1777, to Dr. Wm. Shippen, Jr., at Bethlehem, Pa.:

"My dear Sir, A happy new year is my wish for you and your family; that it will be a year of freedom, our brave troops appear determined on, and whilst they are so, the instruments of tyranny and the perpetrators of devilish deeds will not, cannot face them. The removal from Philadelphia was not a measure of mine, but had my hearty disapprobation so long as disapproving availed anything; but when go they would, I endeavoured to put the best face on it. The Congress have lately invested General Washington with complete powers to displace, place, and direct everything relative to the Military Hospitals. To him therefore, let me advise you to make your application by laying your plan before him and prove, as you have done to me, the propriety of adopting it. No doubt can remain but that it will meet with his approbation and support. As for Morgan, the very air teems with complaints against him. If all charged against him be true, I would not have my conscience so burthened for Mountains of Gold. Reasons for expecting the strongest friendship from France and Spain multiply upon us every day. If they can be prevailed with to make war, farewell the glory of England, and it may then be said, as formerly it was of Rome, '*Sævior armis luxuria incubuit victumque ulcissitur orbem.*'

"Had it not been for the vile appendages of Luxury, we should not have been abused nor Britain overwhelmed by France. It will give us great pleasure to hear from you but greater still to see you."

To the same, dated, 18 April, 1779, from Shippen Hall in Fourth Street: "My dear Sir: Possession is eleven points of the Law, and there are in this city profligates enough, who would, for a good fee, secure the twelfth part. Thus you seem to be more at mercy now than when Mrs. ——— the Tory's Doctor's wife had residence here. How I came to get possession is another thing, and it may be accounted for in this way. On my Brother's departure for Virginia last Friday, I was obliged to decamp from Market Street, and it not being easy to find a lodging quickly, my most worthy friend, the old Doctor [Dr. Wm. Shippen, Sr.] proposed that I should have a room here. The bargain was soon made; I am in your chamber, and we propose to club for our marketing. The old gentleman drinks nothing but water, and small beer contents me. The Barrack Master furnishes us with wood, and I assure you we live with great happiness and content, whilst we exhibit an example of the truest republican economy. After quitting the irksome business of Chestnut street, I have the pleasure of contemplating in my old friend, what Man should be, but what, alas, he seldom is, temperate, wise and honest. I am much obliged to you for your favour of the 15th, but I do not despair. I am well satisfied, however, that we must suffer very considerably before the States in general will feel the necessity of sending wiser and better men to this Assembly. Where a man by being honest is sure to be oppressed; where disgrace and ruin are to reward the most faithful services; when the discharge of duty raises up the angry and malignant passions of envy, malice and all uncharitableness, it is best to retire until necessity has pointed out proper men and proper measures. The party seem long since to have abandoned all thoughts of supporting Deane, but they are determined to sacrifice the Messrs. Lee and Mr. Izard to the manes of their dear unprincipled friend.

"The doctrine is that it is too expensive and not necessary to have any minister at Vienna, or Berlin or Tuscany, and that it will never do to try a man in his absence; therefore we will damn his reputation with a recall, and let him recover it if he can; in the meantime our Junta will be supplied with places. It is in vain to say that thus to destroy the reputations of men, against whom no shadow of offence appears, and who on the contrary, have honestly and ably served the public at every risk to themselves, merely to gratify the wishes and accomplish the views of avaricious and ambitious men, will exhibit such an example as must deter every man, who has character to lose, and means to be honest, from entering into the public service. So the public business must of necessity be committed to unprincipled men and avaricious plunderers. By the aid of a certain little great whispering politician this point of sacrifice will, I think, be carried. Fine reward, excellent encouragement to give up all *pro patria*.

"On a late motion to give a million to the Hospital department, much violent debate took place, and it was insisted on that infinite abuses prevailed and demanded immediate enquiry. It was alleged that great quantities of stores were charged for geese, ducks, chickens, &c., &c. That the wine was all drunk by the well and not by the sick. All this ended in reducing the sum to $500,000. The Southern Chief, who you know is a most excellent character, said that he hoped soon for an inquiry into the conduct of the Director General and all the rest. Therefore a prospect of encountering so great a personage makes it necessary to say, '*Cave quod agis*.' The Dutch having lately taken off the prohibition from the exportation of military stores, which they had imposed to oblige Great Britain, proves clearly that the interest of England is waning in Holland. There have arrived 7 vessels here lately from the West Indies, which has terrified the Specs and lowered the price of sugar £20 in the hundred. It is said that many more vessels are expected. Trade seems to thicken along the wharfs and Marine business is recovering its former countenance. I shall go to Virginia in a fortnight, where I hope to rest from public toil for sometime at least. I think you are with Mr. Blair and his Lady, if so, I pray you to remember me to them and present my love to my sweet sister and cousins. I am yours sincerely and affectionately.

"Dr. William Shippen, Jr., Esquire, Director General of the Hospitals of the United States at Raritan in New Jersey."

The following letters written by Richard Henry Lee to his nephew, Thomas Lee Shippen, son of the Dr. William Shippen, Jr., are very interesting. They are in a lighter vein, and contain more of family concerns:

"Trenton, 19 Nov., 1784. My dear Cousin. This morning's post put into my possession your favour of the 17th inst., and I thank you for it with great sincerity. I am very happy to hear that Mr. Read is in your delegation, and I should have been much more so if your worthy father had been there likewise. It greatly soothes the rugged paths of politics to travel them with men of ability, integrity and candour. We are as remote from having a Congress as we were 19 days ago; with the Southern delegates at Philadelphia and those of your State inclusive, we have but six and an half States represented. But one delegate from the eastward, whence formerly proceeded the most industrious attention to public business. I do not like this strange lassitude in those who are appointed to transact public affairs.

"I am here placed in the house of a Mr. Howe, where I have a good warm chamber and other conveniences to my satisfaction. The streets of the village in this rainy season are most disagreeably wet and muddy. How long we shall remain here it is not in my power to say. Mr. Wolcot, one of the Commissioners for the Indian treaties, has come here with a treaty concluded very satisfactorily with the Six Nations. He says that the other Commissioners are gone to Pittsburgh to treat with the Western Indians, and he apprehends that they will accomplish their business in that quarter with facility.

"I am a good deal distressed about my horses; if they go to vendue, they will sell for nothing. . . . At Alexandria they are to be delivered to Mr. Fendall, with the enclosed letter, who lives about an half mile from the town and is well known there. If Mr. Lee will undertake the affair for me I shall certainly succeed and my horses will not be injured in going back, which latter may happen by over-driving, not properly resting and properly feeding. Will you be so kind as to try your talents at negotiation with Mr. Lee? Julius Cæsar showed his ambition as much when he preferred being the first man in a small village to the second in Rome, as when he grasped the imperial purple. So evidence may be given in small negotiations of superior fitness for great affairs. I will enclose you a letter for Mr. Fendall to go with the horses, upon a presumption that your address will be surely successful. Present my best love to your Father, Mother, and Sister, and when you see the old Gentleman, do not forget me with him. I am, my dear Cousin, Your affectionate Uncle and Sincere friend."

"New York, 17 January, 1785. How has it happened that my dear Cousin hath not yet informed me how he and his companion, the good Doctor, escaped the perils of that dreadful frost that enveloped all nature, when they left Trenton? I suppose that contemplating the Belles of Philadelphia kept the heart in such vigorous action as to counteract all the severity of winter! I have twice seen my sweet cousin, Peggy Livingston, since my arrival here. She is very pretty and very chatty and loves her Uncle mightily. She promises to come and see me often when I get into the Presidential House, which will be this week; having hired Mrs. Franklin's house in the street where little Peggy lives. It is a very elegant house and provided with every convenience.

"I think that little Peggy is very much like her picture in your Father's house. Mr. De Barthold has by this time, I suppose, rigged me out in such a manner as to convert the old President into a young Beau! Very well, if for the good of the country I must be a Beau, why I will be a Beau. Colonel Monroe is returned and is now in the City, and so is Colonel Straight; so that I shall probably not get my clothes soon, unless the kind Doctor is so good as to bring them. My best love attends your Father, Mother, and Sister. God bless you."

"New York, 3rd March, 1785. My dear Cousin. I had made such effectual enquiry after my dear Cousin's stock buckle that I have found it, and safely delivered it to my Brother, A. Lee. The world has assigned to you politeness equal to the good sense that distinguishes you. By what strange fatality then has it happened that the charms of a lady have been neglected by you? I learn from Chantilly that a young lady of that place had a pair of set shoe buckles committed to your care by her Brother, Thos. Lee, some years ago to get repaired. And that to this day the workman has not made the necessary reparation. I thought that the tradesmen in Philadelphia were more punctual; but this fellow has taken the advantage of your engagement in law study to neglect this business, which he would not have dared to do, if your piercing eye had been upon him. Will you be pleased to recollect this matter and inform me in what train it is? I suppose that our good friend, Mr. Prager, has delivered you the guineas that I sent by him. How proceeds the leather covering for the top and sides of my chariot or have you yet met with an opportunity of sending it to Virginia.

"In the month of April, I suppose the chairmaker will commence his operations upon my most elegant and strong and every way complete chair, trunk box, etc. I rely a good deal upon yours and my good friend, the doctor's admonitions to the artist, that he may be induced to exert his *honest* art most fully upon this little machine. My gun and sword cannot forget that they are under your protection, and much want repair. God knows when I shall get away from this place; but I know that if your worthy father would but honor me with his company here, that the best Champaign should be plentifully at his call. God bless you and the whole family, prays sincerely, my dear cousin, Your affectionate uncle and friend."

"New York, 14 October, 1785. I hope my dear Cousin has returned to Phila. brim full of health and law. But, say, is it law, or is the study of law alone, that is inconsistent with the duties of friendship? There must be something in the way, or it never could have happened that I should not have received a letter from you in so great length of time. My silence could not be the cause, as your humanity would readily find an apology for me in my very ill state of health. The Holker cause was not tried it seems, but the Election strife is over, and I wish to know the event as well in other places as in Phil'a. Nor will it be uninteresting to know something of the maneuvers of the contending parties. Curse and doubly curse the Algerines, for these Pirates, I fear, have too certainly made war on our Commerce. Paul Jones from L'Orient informs us that Mons. Soulanges' letter was there and its contents believed. These Infernals, having put all the Commercial nations of Europe under contribution, except Portugal, the trade of Portugal with ours is all that remains for them to plunder.

"Several years ago your worthy Father sent me to Virginia, a Dutch fan, and now the skreens of it are all worn out. I shall thank you exceedingly for getting a new sett of the different fineness made for me, by the best hand according to the enclosed measure; that I may take it with me to Virginia, as I pass through your city on the 11th or 12th of next month. My Mrs. Lee writes me that she must and will have a handsome Bread Tray for serving bread to Table; also a Basket proper for holding clean plates and one for foul plates. Now you must be informed that this demand comes from too high authority for me to venture neglecting it; therefore I must again put your friendship to work to find these out, genteel ones, and that they may be ready to go by Mr. Crump, who I expect will return to Phil'a. early next month, by water. I hope to see my Gun and Pistols here handsomely repaired before the 5th of next month. My best wishes attend the whole family, and that at Germantown, and I pray God to have you in his holy keeping; farewell."

"Chantilly, 4th December, 1785. My dear Nephew: The Saturday night after I left you brought me safe to this place, where I have the happiness to find all well. Our felicity would be complete indeed if our Philadelphia friends made part of our circle. I am not without hopes that it may one day or other be the case. Already I treasure up your promise of visiting these parts before you cross the Atlantic. You have numerous friends here, who will rejoice to see you, and the fine sparkling black eyes of my little Frank will glisten wonderfully at the beautiful blue eyes of his fair cousin,

Peggy Livingston. Whether or not my health will permit my return to Congress next year is a question that I dare not undertake to answer yet. Neither my favourite little Boat or the Box that I left at your house with part of my baggage are yet arrived here; nor have we heard a tittle of the vessel (Mr. Wyncoop's and Seamen's) that was to have sailed with them the Sunday after I left you. Where is the vessel, and where are my things? if they yet remain in Phil'a., the vessel commanded by Capt. Stewart, that lays at Arch Street Wharf, will bring and land them for me at Zachary Weaver's, where he landed the Plaster of Paris.

"The plate and the Bread Baskets, bless me, the most important of all, because commanded by the highest authority, as all married men know, which pleasing influence will in due season be felt by my friend to whom I write. The non-arrival of these baskets has been imputed to accident, for says she, Mr. Shippen is polite and exact, so that no omission can possibly have arisen from him. I agree that it is so, and we resolve to expect them by the first fair wind. The Skreens too for my Dutch fan, that I was at such pains to send the measure of, I unfortunately forgot in my haste. And now my fan is quite useless for want of the Skreens. I pray you, my dear Cousin, to let these things be sent expeditiously, together with two or three ounces of the Butter Nut Syrup that your worthy Father promised to procure for me. By means of Mr. Thomson, Merchant here from your City, I can and will order you payment for these things the moment that I know their cost. The roll or two of narrow pink ribbon for Molly's Tambour is also much wanted. We all here join most cordially in love and compliments to your whole family. And I pray you not to forget my best affection for the old Doctor, when you see him. God bless you; farewell."

"Chantilly, 17 April, 1787. My very dear Cousin: Since I parted with you and my other very dear friends in Philadelphia, in the fall of 1785, I have been agreeably employed in family cares and domestic concerns. This pleasant life, with much attention to my health, has restored it beyond my hopes; but yet not so firmly as to promise the power of again engaging largely with public affairs. Perhaps I may venture to Congress during the course of the coming summer. I feel and see the unhappy state of public affairs that you describe; but I hope for amendment.

"In May next a Convention is to meet at Philadelphia for the purpose of amending our Federal Constitution. From this source perhaps we may derive some good. We have everywhere young men coming forward with worth and talents.

"From the Herald's office, in London, you may get the most perfect information concerning our family before some of them came here, and I think my eldest Brother did lodge with the office an account of that part of the family that came here. Your Uncle, A. Lee, who is now here, tells me that Mr. Wm. Lee did get from the Herald's Office a very complete account of the family. The book you allude to is in the possession of Mr. Fendall, who married my brother's widow, and he is at present not in the country. The elder branch of our family lives now in Shropshire, near Shrewsbury, and possesses undiminished the old original family estate. I dare say he will be glad to see you when you travel that way, and he becomes acquainted with your extraction. •I received the stockings and socks, that you were so good as to send me, with double pleasure because they gave me additional proof of your friendship and because they are so admirably fitted for the purpose they were intended. I have worn them ever since with great satisfaction. I hope, my dear friend, that you will continue your agreable correspondence; it will be a great comfort to me in my retirement. But above all I hope you will not forget your promise of coming to see us on your return to America. I assure you that I contemplate that time with great delight. Will you give my best respects to the worthy Bishop of Chester, when you see him, and inform him that I never received the letter he was pleased to write me by Mr. Beverley. The gentleman took such measures as did indeed seem secure for conveying the letter, but it miscarried by accident. I wish also to be affectionately remembered to my friend, Edmund Jennings, Esqr. If any very valuable and well-approved Books, in any science (if they be not very dear indeed), shall make their appearance, be so good as to send them to me, and on your application to my Merchant in London, Mr. Thomas Blane, he will pay you the money for them.

"Farewell my dear Cousin, and that you may be happy and return to yr. native Country, is the prayer of your affectionate Uncle and Friend."

"New York, 22 July, 1787. My Dear Cousin: Having recovered my health much better than I ever expected to have done, I have again taken my seat in Congress. I arrived in this city a fortnight ago, having stayed a week in Philadelphia, where I saw your friends all in good health, and your father as usual in high spirits. I was extremely happy to find that you were so well placed for improvement, and to see under your own hand such strong proofs that you had greatly profited by your situation.

"The Federal Convention at Philadelphia is proceeding slowly but I hope surely in a practical improvement of our Federal Constitution. Experience seems to have proved that our governments have not tone enough for the unruly passions of men, and so far as I can judge the general wish is for a balanced government where the powers shall be placed independently as in England, and of a duration somewhat longer than at present. Congress is proceeding with the ordinary business until the Convention shall report their plan for consideration and recommendation to the different States. I suppose it will be recommended to the States to call conventions for the special purpose of approving the new system, that it may rest on the broad base of the people's choice rather than on the more feeble opinion of the ordinary legislatures.

"In my last to you from Virginia, I requested you to send me a few of the newest books, if there were any published of high character, and to apply to Mr. Thomas Blane, Merchant in London, for the cash to pay for them, and to deliver them to him that they might be forwarded to me. If you have not already complied with this request, you need not now trouble yourself about it; because I have written to Mr. Blane for as many books as my finances will allow me to devote in one year to that article. But you will very much oblige me by getting for me some one of the most approved modern lamps of polished tin, such as Doctor Franklin brought over with him, for giving great splendor of light to a parlor where company sit. If, in order to use this lamp any explanation is necessary, let such explanation accompany it. Mr. Blane will receive and forward the lamp with my other goods that he sends me the ensuing Fall; and he will, on your application, supply the money necessary to pay for it, as I have directed him.

"I pray you to remember me affectionately to Mr. Adams, and inform him that I will shortly write to him. Congress have not yet determined on complying with his request to be permitted to return home; but when they do so, I will certainly do my endeavor to have Col. Smith appointed Charge des Affairs at the Court of London, if such should be the plan fixt on. My compliments, if you please, to Col. Smith. I hope to hear from you ere long, because I am always happy to do so, being with the most unfeigned affection and the truest regard, my dear Cousin, yours forever."

"P. S., 30 July. The want of nine States prevented a determination on Mr. Adams' business by this packet, so that we do not know the future arrangement. I enclose you, my dear Cousin, a letter for our relation, the Bishop of Chester.[1] It may bring you acquainted with a learned and worthy man. Remember me to Dr. Cutting. Mr. Blane may be met with on the Royal Exchange, the Virginia Walk. Seal the Bishop's letter before delivery. Farewell."

"Chantilly, 21 Sept., 1791. My dear Nephew: The letter that you

---

1 Bishop Porteus, of Chester, was the son of Col. Robert Porteus, of Virginia, who married a daughter of Governor Edmund Jennings. Governor Jennings married Frances, youngest daughter of Henry and Alice (Eltonhead) Corbin; her eldest sister, Lætitia, married Richard Lee[2], and was the grandmother of Richard Henry Lee[4].

had the goodness to write to me on the 11th inst., I received last evening. We all here join in thanking you for the happiness created among us by your information of the health of your Lady, yourself and my dear Sister and Brother, your Father and Mother. It was but one copy of Anderson's History of Commerce that I desired, having no possible occasion for more. And this copy may remain at Philadelphia until I come there, which now I expect will be about the 10th of November, when I suppose forms will have subsided into business; the first day of the session being the last day of October, it may be hoped that 10 days will be sufficient for the important negociation of compliments. I am now to beg a favour of you which I hope you will have the goodness to execute for me. To engage decent Lodging and as convenient to the State House as possible, that my gouty feet may sustain no injury from the wintry weather. If it can well be done, I should prefer getting my meals where I lodge, and you will please to remember that Charles is to be provided for also. The time of entering to be when I arrive, which I desire to be about the 10th of November.

"I shall thank you very much for sending me a line to be left at Charles Lee's in Alexandria, until I pass there, informing me where my lodgings are that I may go there directly on my arrival. It will suit me well if I can hire room for 2 horses and find provender myself. And if you think that this last can be better procured now than when I come, you will greatly oblige me by engaging both oats and hay for two horses for the probable length of the session; the cash shall be paid immediately on my arrival.

"How are the mighty fallen indeed! It is not easy for a mind of sensibility not to feel for the King and Queen of France, for the latter especially. I think with you that few traces of wisdom are to be found in that attempt, but it is difficult to judge without knowing all the circumstances. I must confess that I am not yet so *hardened* with *politicks* as to have lost humanity. Nor am I ashamed to own that I begin to be heartily sick of politicks and politicians. I think that generally speaking the former may be called the science of fraud and the latter the professors of that science.

"We are not here behind my dear Niece in love of her and her sociable and amiable manners. To her, to your good Father, Mother, and Sister, we present our best affections. I am, with the truest affection, yours always."

Mr. Lee's will, dated the 18th of June, 1793, and probated, Westmoreland, the 24th of June, 1794:

In the name of God, Amen. I Richard Henry Lee of Chantilly in the county of Westmoreland, being of sound and disposing mind, do make this my last Will and Testament, revoking all others, this eighteenth day of June, one thousand seven hundred and ninety three. First, I desire to be decently, privately and frugally buried in the family burying ground at the Burnt House, as it is called, and as near to my late ever dear wife as 'tis possible to place mine without disturbing her remains, and upon her left, so that my present dear Mrs. Lee may be laid, when she dyes, on my right; and so my body may be laid between those of my dear wives. Secondly, I desire my Executors, who will be hereafter named, to pay as soon as possible, all my just debts. But I do earnestly recommend to my Executors not to pay any demand made against my estate but such as are supported by evidence strictly legal, or such demands as they or any of them know to be just. This desire is founded on long observation of great injury being done to the estates of persons deceased, by fictitious, false demands and accounts trumped up and sworn to upon a mistaken supposition that such oaths give legal validity to accounts and demands so partially supported. Item. My will and desire is that my Executors have my dear wife's dower assigned to her, with as little trouble to her, and as soon after my death as possible. Item. I give to my dear wife over and above her dower my two leases for the plantation of Chantilly and the Marsh plantaion, which leases were made to me by my brother Philip Ludwell Lee and my son Ludwell Lee, and afterwards confirmed by Col. Henry Lee, under whom they are now holden, and she is to be charged with the payment of one third of my debts. Item. I give and bequeath unto my three sons, Thomas Lee, Ludwell Lee and Cassius Lee, and to their heirs forever, all my lands in the County of Fauquier to be equally divided between the three according to quantity, quality and value taken together, so that each son may have as equal part as possible, and this division I desire may be made by three disinterested men or the majority of them, to be appointed by the County Court of Westmoreland, who in assigning to each son his part will have regard to the future falling in of my wife's dower, after her death, and regulate both quantity and situation so that each son during my wife's life may have a third part only of the remaining two thirds, and each a third part of my wife's third part, when she shall dye. And my will is further upon this point that the parts of my sons Thomas Lee and Ludwell Lee (to be circumstanced as mentioned) may be assigned to them respectively as soon after my death as it can conveniently be done. And that the part assigned to my son Cassius may be delivered to him at 21 years of age. And the profits in the meantime to maintain Cassius. Item. I give to my son Cassius Lee my negro bricklayer named Phil, to him and his heirs forever. Also I give to my said son Cassius Lee my gold watch that I have sent to London for, with the triangular gold seal, given to me by Mrs. Fendall and hanging to my watch. Item. I give to my said son Cassius Lee my books, Encyclopedia or dictionary of arts and sciences in ten volumes quarto, and Millots elements of general history, in five volumes octavo. Item. I give to my son Francis Lightfoot Lee all my Law books of every kind and nature whatsoever, and two hundred pounds sterling to be paid him by my Executors out of my personal estate so soon as he comes of age, in order to procure for him a good Law Library. Item. I give to my said son Francis Lightfoot Lee and his heirs forever my negro blacksmith, named Anthony, to be delivered to my son at twenty-one years of age and in the meanwhile, during the minority of my said son Francis, the said smith Anthony to work at Chantilly gratis for the benefit of my wife's two plantations of Chantilly and Hallows's Marsh. Item. I give to my said son Francis Lightfoot Lee my gold watch and sleeve buttons of gold that I now wear, and the triangular gold seal that was his Uncle Arthur's. Item. I give to my said son Francis the four silver plates, silver spoons, silver pronged forks, with the knives that belong to the travelling case, and the three silver Tumbrils belonging to the same case, all which appropriated to travelling by my late brother Arthur Lee, Esqr., seem not to be included in the bequest of household furniture by him given to my son Francis Lightfoot Lee all which together with the travelling case, I give to my said son Francis. Item. I give to my dear daughter Mary Washington as specific legacies the mulatto girl Letty that has usually waited on her, and the gold watch that came to me by my brother Arthur. Item. I give to my dear daughters Harriot and Sally Lee the sum of eighty two pounds ten shillings current money, to be equally divided between them, the same being the amount of Col. Turner's bond to Mrs. Richards, and also I do give to my said daughters, Harriot and Sally, all the money of Mrs. Richards that was found in this house at her death, amounting to forty pounds two shillings currency, and given by Mrs. Richards in her will to my two said daughters, subjecting this legacy always to the deduction of six pounds nine shillings and six pence paid by me for funeral expenses, and other charges on account of Mrs. Richards as will appear on my ledger. Item. All the rest of my Estate both real and personal and of what nature and kind soever that I may dye possessed of, or in any manner entitled to, not herein before given, I do hereby give and bequeath to my dear daughters Mary Washington of Haywood, Hannah Washington of Walnut Farm, Anne Lee of Alexandria, Henrietta Lee and Sarah Lee, to them and their heirs forever, share and share alike, and I do hereby constitute these my five daughters aforesaid my Residuary Legatees, always subjecting the clause just preceeding to the following exceptions. Item. I give to my dear son Thomas Lee all the negroes, men, women and children, that came to me by his mother my first dear wife, except Jonas who is excepted in a deed of gift made for these negroes to my said son Thomas lately and who is to go into the residuum given to my said daughters in place of Newman one of my paternal negroes given to my son Thomas in the said deed of gift aforementioned, which said negroes so coming to me by my first wife, I give to my said son Thomas Lee and his heirs forever, excepting as is before excepted. Also, whereas I have already given property as part of their fortunes to my two first married daughters, as appears on my Ledger to the amount of ——— to my daughter Hannah Washington and to the amount of ——— to my daughter Anne Lee and have not yet made such provision for my daughter Mary Washington of Haywood my will and desire is that a sum equal to what is mentioned on my Ledger as above stated furnished to each of my said daughters, Hannah and Anne, be first deducted, and a sum equivalent thereto be provided out of the residuum (devised as above) for each of my daughters Mary Washington, Henrietta and Sally Lee, and the remainder to be shared among the five Daughters aforesaid, Mary, Hannah, Anne, Henrietta and Sarah. Item. My will is that if my son Thomas should disturb my estate by making any claim against it by or for reason of any Legacy left him by Gawen Corbin deceased that then and in that case I revoke and absolutely annul the Legacy of land left him in this my will, and desire that the said land so left to Thomas may be equally divided between my two sons Ludwell Lee and Cassius Lee and their heirs forever.

This my last Will and Testament all written with my own hand upon six pages of paper at Chantilly, this eighteenth of June in the year of our Lord one thousand seven hundred and ninety three. And for my last Will and Testament I humbly pray that it may be taken by all Judges Justices and Courts before whom these presents shall come.

Codicil, 18 June, 1793. I do hereby constitute and appoint my dear Wife Anne Lee, my dear brother Francis Lightfoot Lee and my much valued friends and sons-in-law William Augustine Washington, Corbin Washington and Charles Lee of Alexandria, Esquires, my Executrix and Executors of this my last Will and Testament, and guardians of my infant children. This my codicil is also all written with my own hand at Chantilly the day and year above mentioned.

Codicil, May, 1794. Whereas it has always been my intention to make the fortunes of my single daughters, Harriot and Sally Lee, equal to their marryed sisters; I have for that purpose lent to Mr. George Lee, of Loudon County, the sum of five hundred and forty-three pounds thirteen shillings and four pence, current money of Virginia, for which he has given his Bond bearing date the first day of October, 1793, to William Augustine Washington, Corbin Washington and Charles Lee, in trust for my use, or to such person or persons as I shall under my hand and seal, or by my last Will and Testament direct. Now my will and desire is that the money lent to Mr. George Lee, for which he has given his Bond as aforesaid. be equally divided between my two daughters, Harriot Lee and Sally Lee, but should either of them die before marriage, in that case the part of the one so dying to be divided equally between my Daughters Mary Washington, Hannah Washington, Anne Lee and the survivor of the two before named. And whereas I have lent to Mr. William Augustine Washington and Mr Corbin Washington the sum of $4,911.30 in six per cent. stock of the United States, and the sum of $833.39 in three per cent. stock of the United States, for which they have given their Bond bearing date the fourth day of May 1794 to my sons Thomas Lee, Ludwell Lee, and my son-in-law Charles Lee, in trust for my use or to such person or persons as I shall under my hand and seal, or by my last Will and Testament direct. Now my will and desire is that the sum of $1,507.33 of six per cent. stock of the United States, lent as above, be equally divided between my two daughters, Harriot Lee and Sally Lee, and that the sum of $3,403.97 of six per cent. stock of the United States, and the sum of $833.39 of three per cent. stock of the United States, lent as above aforesaid, be equally divided between my five Daughters, Mary, Hannah, Anne, Harriot and Sally; but should either of my Daughters Harriot or Sally die before marriage, in that case the part left to them I direct to be equally between my daughters Mary, Hannah, Anne, and the survivor of them. Be it remembered that this my codicil is not written by me but I desire it may be received and considered as a part of my last Will and Testament, in witness whereof I have hereunto set my hand and seal, this fourth day of May in the year of our Lord 1794.

Mr. Lee died two years after retiring from public life; his constitution had been enfeebled by his long and arduous labors. He was troubled much with the gout, which attacked the abdominal viscera, and caused him great suffering, but, though his body had become feeble, his mind retained its vigor. He breathed his last at Chantilly on the 19th of June, 1794, and was buried in the old family burial-place, at the "Burnt House Fields," Mt. Pleasant, as he desired in his will.

As in the case of his father, Thomas Lee, tradition has given Richard Henry the wrong burial-ground. Both he and his father were buried at Mt. Pleasant. Richard Henry Lee expressly desired to be buried there; saying he wished "to be decently, privately, and frugally buried in the family burial ground at the Burnt House, as it is called, and as near to my late ever dear wife as 'tis possible," etc. There can be no reason for supposing his request was denied, especially as there is the corroborative testimony of one who was at the funeral. The late Mrs. Charles Calvert Stuart, of "Chantilly," Fairfax county, wrote many years ago to the late Cassius F. Lee, Sr., of Alexandria:

"Our grandfather, R. H. Lee, was buried near the old burying-ground at Mount Pleasant, Westmoreland county. I visited the spot many years ago; the gentleman who went with me pointed out the spot, just outside of the brick wall, and under a cluster of splendid shade trees; they told me the graveyard was full and consequently this was considered the best place. Aunt Henry Lee told me she well remembered the appearance of your dear mother and mine when they came to their father's burial; Aunt Lee was visiting at Lee Hall at the time. I looked over the tombstones. They were those of the first Lees who came to this country, the Richards, etc." The Lee Hall mentioned here was the adjoining estate to Mt. Pleasant; in fact, the old mansion of Lee Hall must have overlooked this graveyard.

In an article, "On the Northern Neck" of Virginia (*American Gentlemen of the Olden Time*), by Benjamin Ogle Taylor, 1851, there is given an extract from a letter written by an old lady; it is dated "Locust Farm," Westmoreland, and says: "I am now away down here in the Northern Neck of Virginia, and not far from the spot on which Washington was born; scattered here and there all around me are the birthplaces of Madison,[1] Monroe, and Richard Henry Lee. Yesterday I was on the ground on which rest the ruins of the residence of Richard Henry Lee. All that stands upright of that (once) imposing mansion is the kitchen chimney. In front scarce a half mile distant is the shore of the lordly Potomac, here about nine miles across. Lee is gone, his house is in the dust, his garden a wild; but here are the same sky, the same lands, the same Potomac, and the same dirge that of yore broke in murmurs on the shore. The remains of Lee lie in the midst of a corn-field, some five miles distant, and on which, I am told, is a stone with his name engraved upon it."

Of the home of Richard Henry Lee, little is known. Thomas Lee Shippen, when describing his visit to Westmoreland, wrote his father that Chantilly "commands a much finer view than Stratford by reason of a large bay into which the Potomack forms itself opposite Chantilly. . . . The house is rather commodious than elegant. The sitting-room, which is very well ornamented, is 18x30 feet, and the dining-room, 20x24." From the inventory and appraisement of the furniture, etc., at Chantilly, it is learned that there were a dining-room, library, parlor, and chamber on the first floor. The hall being, as was usual, furnished as a sitting-room, contained: a mahogany desk, twelve arm chairs, a round and a square table, a covered walnut table, two boxes of tools, and a trumpet. On the second floor there were four large chambers, and a smaller one at the head of stairs; two rooms in third floor; store rooms, and closets. The out

---

[1] Alluding, doubtless, to the tradition that Madison had been born at Port Conway; his mother, it was said, was there on a visit.

buildings mentioned were: kitchen, dairy, blacksmith shop, stable, and barn. The enumeration of the books in the library showed about 500 separate works, on science, history, politics, medicine, farming, etc., etc., which were appraised at £229 10s. 7d. Of money in the house at the time of his death, there were $54 silver, valued at £16 4s.; in bank at Alexandria, £181 19s. 7d; "Tobacco notes" for 13,907 pounds, nett.

Richard Henry Lee was twice married; first, on the 3d of December, 1757, to Anne Aylett, who was probably a daughter, or maybe granddaughter, of William and Anne Aylett, of King William county; she died on the 12th of December, 1768, leaving four young children, and was buried, as stated in her husband's will, at Mt. Pleasant. But a monument was placed in the old church at Nominy, to her memory—another instance of a person, buried in the old family burying-ground, while the tablet to her memory was placed in a church some miles off. The old Nominy Church stood upon a slight hill overlooking Nominy creek, and was about five miles from Mt. Pleasant, and about the same distance from Stratford, being situated between the two estates. The old church was burned many years ago; another building has been built near the former site. This copy of the inscription on the tablet is from a manuscript in his writing:

"Description of my dear Mrs. Lee's monument in Nominy Church."

Sacred to the Memory of Mrs. Anne Lee, wife of Col. Richard H. Lee. This monument was erected by her afflicted husband, in the year 1769.

Reflect dear reader on the great uncertainty of human life, since neither esteemed temperament nor the most amiable goodness could save this excellent Lady from death in the bloom of Life. She left behind her four children, two sons and two daughters. Obiit 12th December, 1768, æt. 30.

"Was then so precious a flower
But given us to behold it waste,
The short lived blossom of an hour,
Too nice, too fair, too sweet to last."

Richard Henry and Anne (Aylett) Lee had these four children:

i, Thomas[5], See 32.

ii, Ludwell[5], See 33.

iii, Mary[5], "was born on Saturday, the 28th day of July, 1764, in the night. She was christened by the Rev. Archibald Campbell, the 11th of March, 1765, and her proxies were Mr. Francis Lightfoot Lee, Mr. Joseph Lane and James Davenport, with Miss Elizabeth Steptoe, Miss Betty Washington, and Miss ——" (paper torn). She married on the 5th of July, 1792, Col. William Augustine Washington, the son of

Augustine and Anne (Aylett) Washington, and died early in life, leaving no issue.

iv, HANNAH[5], the record of her birth, etc., in the family Bible cannot be deciphered. She was probably born in 1766; she died about 1801; married on the 10th of May, 1787, Corbin Washington, of "Walnut Farm," Westmoreland, son of John Augustine and Hannah (Bushrod) Washington, and had six children. (See Washington Family.)

Richard Henry Lee[1] married, secondly, about June or July, 1769, Mrs. Anne (Gaskins) Pinckard, who was the widow of Thomas Pinckard (by whom she had, at least, one child, a son) and the daughter of Col. Thomas Gaskins, Sr., of Westmoreland, and the sister of the Col. Thomas Gaskins who was prominent during the Revolution. In 1783 Thomas Gaskins, Sr., executed a gift deed to his "daughter Anne Lee, now intermarried with Richard Henry Lee" (North'd records). Mrs. Lee survived her husband. By his second marriage, Mr. Lee had issue two sons and three daughters, whose names and ages are taken from his Bible:

v, ANNE[5], "born the first day of December, 1770, and was christened the first day of January, 1771; her sponsors were Mr. Francis Lightfoot Lee, Dr. Steptoe, Mrs. Richard Lee and Miss Sarah Gaskins. She was christened by the Rev. Thomas Smith." She died the 9th of September, 1804; married, her cousin Charles Lee (36, q. v.), on the 11th of February, 1789, and left issue.

vi, HENRIETTA[5], "born on the 10th day of December, 1773. She was christened by the Rev. Thomas Smith, the —— day of January, 1774, and her sponsors were Capt. John Lee, Richard Lee, George Lee, and James Steptoe, Esqrs., Miss Eliza Gaskins, Miss Matilda Lee, and Miss Mary Lee." She died in 1803-4; was twice married; 1st, about the 14th December, 1794, to Richard Lee Turberville,[2] and left: 1, Cornelia Lee, who married Charles Calvert Stuart, of "Chantilly," Fairfax county. 2, George Lee, who married a Miss Dobell and had issue. 3, Richard Henry, who died without issue. Henrietta (Lee) Turberville married, secondly, the Rev. William Maffit, of South Carolina, and had two children: 1, Anne Lee, who died unmarried. 2,

---

[1] Arthur Lee to R. H. Lee: ". . . My letters by Johnstone brought me an account of your marriage; on which I give you and Mrs. Lee joy with all my heart."—4th of August, 1769.

". . . I may now I hope congratulate you on your marriage with Mrs. Pinckard; the small acquaintance I had with her gives me great reason to believe she will make you happy; and I most ardently pray that her goodness may prevent both you and the poor little ones who survive, from feeling the loss of the tender and amiable wife and mother that is gone."—15th of August, 1769.

[2] At the request of "Anne Lee" a marriage license was granted at Westmoreland, on the 13th of December, 1794, between Richard Lee Turberville and Henrietta Lee, spinster.

Harriotte, who married the Rev. Reuben Post, and left issue. (See Turberville.)

vii, SARAH[5], "born the 27th of November, 1775, and was christened by the Rev. Mr. Smith; her proxies were, Thomas Ludwell Lee, and Henry Lee, Esqrs., Miss Eliza Lee, Miss Mary Lee, Miss Nancy Lee, and Miss Hannah Lee." She died at Alexandria, the 8th of May, 1837; married her cousin Edmund Jennings Lee (39, q. v.), of Alexandria, and left issue.

viii, CASSIUS[5], "born at 3 o'clock at night on the 18th of August, 1779; was christened 10th of October, 1779, by the Rev. Thomas Smith; his proxies were, Rev. Mr. Smith and Mrs. Armistead, Miss Alice Lee of Maryland, and Miss Nancy Lee of Chantilly and Miss ——" (record torn).

> "May every Cæsar feel,
> The keen deep searching of a Patriot's steel."

"Dyed at Princeton on the 8th of July, 1798, in the 19th year of his age Cassius Lee (son of R. H. Lee, Esqr.) a student of Nassau College, New Jersey. Let not the voice of sorrow be repressed, let it teach those who knew him not, to appreciate the loss the community has sustained in the death of this amiable young man. He was endowed with feelings the most ardent and philanthropic, united to a superior intellect, assiduously cultivated, combined with sentiments of Liberality and Benevolence. But, alas! the hopes formed of such a youth were never to be realized, he was received by the Grave, almost at the time he was to leave the place of his education, and bestow his talents on his Country. From the short period of his life, his acquaintance was confined to a few! but while one of that few remains, he will be respected, beloved and lamented.

> "'Some messenger of God from Earth returning
> Saw this beauteous flower, transported gathered it
> And in his hand bore it to Heav'n rejoicing.'"

(Signed) CORNELIA LEE.

ix, FRANCIS LIGHTFOOT[5], See 34.

## GASKINS WILLS.

Thomas Gascoyne, dated the 20th of June, 1663; probated on 9th of November, 1665; legatees: Josias, John, and Henry Gaskoyne; will signed "Thomas Gaskin."

Thomas Gaskins received a grant of 300 acres on the 9th of September,

1636, for the transportation of Thomas Gaskins, Elizabeth Gaskins, Josiah Gaskins, Mary Gaskins, Alice Gaskins, and Josiah Gambling, and for his own "adventure." There is recorded a deed, dated the 29th of July, 1657, from Thomas Gaskins to his cousin, Elizabeth, daughter of John Gambling. On the 26th of May, 1653, Thomas Gaskins made a deposition, and stated his age to be 52 years.

Will of Isaac Gaskins, dated the 22d of October, 1709; probated the 18th of January, 1712; legatees: sons Isaac and Samuel, wife's son Thomas; mentioned daughters, Sarah, Elizabeth, and Hannah; Thomas Gaskins and Bartholomew Schrever, overseers of will.

Thomas Gaskins, dated the 28th of April and probated the 20th of September, 1726; mentioned wife Martha; granddaughter Elizabeth Gaskins; grandsons, Thomas and Edwin Gaskins; son Thomas residuary legatee. On the 17th of June, 1713, Thomas Gaskins executed a gift deed to his granddaughter, Sarah Hull, daughter of Richard Hull.

On the 8th of August, 1737, the will of a Thomas Gaskins was ordered to be recorded, but no record of it exists. But on the 12th of March, 1738, Mary Gaskins, widow of Thomas Gaskins, received her share of his estate, also the wife of Richard Hull, and on the 9th of November, 1741, shares were allotted to his children: Thomas, Edwin, Sarah Ann, John, and Annie, each one-fifth part. Elizabeth Schrever (will dated on the 17th of July, 1737; probated on the 11th of 7br, 1737) left her estate to "aunt Mary Gaskins, uncle Richard Hull, and cousins, Elizabeth, Thomas, Edwin, Sarah-ann, Anne, and John Gaskins, the children of uncle Thomas Gaskins."

Thomas Gaskins, no date to will; probated on the 12th of April, 1785; mentioned wife Sarah; children: Thomas, Anne, Sarah, Elizabeth, and Henry Lee Gaskins; sons-in-law, Richard Henry Lee, Edward Diggs and John Hull, Ex'rs. Also mentioned Thomas Pinckard, as late husband of daughter, Anne Lee. In 1769 Thomas Gaskins, Sr., deeded 391 acres to Thomas Gaskins, Jr., which had been devised to him by his father, Thomas Gaskins. In 1770 Col. Thomas Gaskins and Capt. Thomas Gaskins were both vestrymen of old Wycomico Church. (*Old Churches*, &c., II, 468.)

In 1783, "Thomas Gaskins, Sr., executed a gift deed to his daughter Anne Lee, now intermarried with Richard Henry Lee." (Northumberland records.)

## THE WASHINGTON FAMILY.

An enthusiastic genealogist once traced the descent of this family from Odin, the mythical King of Scandinavia. It is needless to add that no one ever credited such a claim. Yet, until very recently, no exact data had been discovered to prove their true descent. This problem has been finally solved through the careful and painstaking researches of Mr. Henry F. Waters, whose numerous contributions to American genealogy are so well known. He has shown that the two Virginia immigrants, John and Lawrence, were descended, in the eighth generation, from John Washington, of Whitfield, County Lancaster, England. Lawrence, grandson of this John of Whitfield, died in 1584; on his tomb at Sulgrave Church was a fine cut-in brass of his arms. Lately a deed has been found, dated 1601, with the signature and a very clear wax impresion of the arms of his son, Robert.[1] Still another representation of their arms was on the tomb of Lawrence, son of Robert, who died in 1616. Thus there are accurate representations of the Washington arms, as used in England by three successive generations—Lawrence, Robert, and Lawrence. These are the same arms as always used by the Virginia branch, and are said to have been the origin of the stars and stripes of the American flag. A copy of the well-known book-plate of General Washington is given here, showing these arms.

John, the elder of the two immigrants, is supposed to have settled in Virginia some years prior to 1655. In a commission to the military officers of Westmoreland, dated on the 4th of April, 1655, he was styled "Major."[2] He was a Justice in 1662; Burgess, 1666, 1676 (II, Hening, 250). John was twice married, but nothing is known about his first wife. He remarried before 1659, for on the 1st of May, 1659, a deed was executed by Nathaniel Pope to his daughter, "Ann Pope *als* Washington." On the 13th of June, 1661, "Mrs. Ann Pope *alias* Washington" patented 700 acres in Westmoreland. John Washington probably died in the latter part of 1676; his will was dated the 11th of September, 1675, and was probated on the 10th of January, 1677. He mentions his children in this order, Lawrence (stated to be the eldest), John and Ann. The document is a very curious one. To

[1] This very interesting document has lately been acquired by James J. Goodwin, Esq., of Hartford, Conn., through whose liberality Mr. Waters was enabled to prosecute his researches amongst the English records that finally led to the tracing of the true ancestry of the Virginia Washingtons.

[2] *William and Mary College Quarterly*, IV, 139, *et seq.*

the lower church of Washington parish he left "ye ten Commandments & the Kings armes wch is my desire be sent for out of wt mony I have in England." Desired to be buried on his plantation, beside his deceased wife and two children.[1] Lawrence, son of the immigrant, mentioned that his father, mother, brothers, sisters, and some of his own children had been buried at Bridge's Creek, Westmoreland, before the date of his will, 11th March, 1697–98. From these children of John Washington a numerous family has descended.

The eldest son, Lawrence, married Mildred, daughter of Col. Augustine Warner, of Gloucester county, by whom he had two sons and a daughter. Of these, 1, John married Catharine Whiting, of Gloucester, and had Warner, Henry, and three daughters. 2, Augustine (died the 12th of April, 1743, aged 49) was twice married; first, on the 20th of April, 1715, to Jane, daughter of Caleb Butler, of Westmoreland, by whom he had three sons—Butler, Lawrence, and Augustine—and a daughter; of these sons Lawrence married Anne, daughter of the Hon. William Fairfax, of "Belvoir," Fairfax county, and died without surviving issue, leaving his estate, Mount Vernon, to his younger and half-brother, George Washington; his widow married Col. George Lee, of "Mt. Pleasant." Augustine (the youngest son of Augustine and Jane Butler) lived at Wakefield, Westmoreland; he married Anne, daughter and co-heir of William Aylett, of Westmoreland. (This William Aylett was probably the "Capt. Wm. Aylett, Jr.," who married Anne, the daughter of Henry Ashton, of Westmoreland; his will mentioned two daughters, Elizabeth and Anne.) They had issue, three daughters and one son: Elizabeth, Jane, Anne, and William Augustine Washington. The son (born the 25th of November, 1757; died at Georgetown, in October, 1810) was married three times. First, to his cousin, Jane, daughter of John Augustine and Hannah (Bushrod) Washington, and had several children; he next married Mary, the eldest daughter of Richard Henry Lee, by his first wife, but had no issue; his third wife was Sally, daughter of Col. John Tayloe, of "Mt. Airy," Richmond county, by whom he had two or three children.

Augustine, the elder, after the death of Jane Butler, married on the 6th of March, 1730–1, Mary, daughter of Col. Joseph Ball, of "Epping Forest," Lancaster county, by whom he had four sons and two daughters: George, Elizabeth, Samuel, John Augustine, Charles, and Mildred. Of these sons, John Augustine, born the 13th of January, 1736; died in February, 1787; married Hannah, daughter of Col. John Bushrod, and had

---

[1] *N. E. Hist. and Gen. Register*, XLV, 200, *et seq.*

issue: Jane (who married her cousin, as just stated), Mildred, Bushrod, Corbin, and William Augustine. Of these children, Mildred, born at "Bushfield," about 1760, married, about 1780, Thomas, son of R. H. Lee. Corbin, of "Walnut Farm," Westmoreland, married Hannah, daughter of R. H. Lee, as stated, and had issue (as named in Hannah Bushrod Washington's will): 1, Richard Henry Lee. 2, John Augustine, born the 26th of May, 1789; died ——; married on the 14th of November, 1811, Jean Charlotte, eldest daughter of Capt. Richard Scott Blackburn, U. S A., and Judith Ball, his first wife; she was born ——; died in 1856; they left three children, Anna Maria, John Augustine, and Richard Blackburn Washington. 3, Bushrod Corbin, born the 25th of December, 1790; died 28th of July, 1851; married in 1810, Anna Maria Thomasina, second daughter of Capt. R. S. Blackburn, and sister of his brother's wife; they had two children: Hannah Lee, who married William P. Alexander, and Thomas Blackburn, who married Rebecca J. Cunningham. 4, Mary Lee, born ——; died in 1877; married in 1819, Noblet Herbert, and left two sons. 5, Jane Mildred. 6, A son, Corbin, who was mentioned in his grandmother's will as "now an infant;" he probably died young.

The children of John Augustine, and Jean Charlotte (Blackburn) Washington, mentioned above, married as follows:

i, Anna Maria, their second child, (the eldest George, having died young), was born 5th November, 1817; died on the 29th of March, 1850; married on the 15th of May, 1834, Dr. William Fontaine Alexander, and had seven children.

ii, John Augustine, born on 3d of May, 1820; was killed at Cheat Mountain, in West Virginia, on the 13th of September, 1861; he married in February, 1842, Eleanor Love Selden, and had seven children: 1, Louisa Fontaine, born 19th of February 1844; married Col. R. P. Chew, C. S. A., and has issue. 2, Jean Charlotte, born 16th of May, 1846; married Nathaniel P. Willis, and has issue. 3, Eliza Selden, unmarried. 4, Anna Maria, born 17th of November, 1851; married, 22d July, 1873, the Rev. Beverly Dandridge Tucker (son of Nathaniel Beverly, and Jane Ellis Tucker), and has issue. 5, Lawrence, born 14th of January, 1854; married, on the 14th of June, 1876, Fannie, daughter of Thomas Lackland, of Charlestown, West Virginia, and has issue. 6, Eleanor Love, born 14th of March, 1856; married on 5th of May, 1880, Julian Howard, of Richmond county. 7, George, born 22d of July, 1858. This Col. John Augustine Washington was the last of his family to own Mt. Vernon. He sold it in 1860, to the "Mt. Vernon Ladies Association."

iii, Richard Blackburn Washington, born 12th of November, 1822; die ——; married, on the 20th of November, 1844, Christine Maria, daughter of Samuel Walter, and Louisa (Clemson) Washington, of "Harewood;" they had issue: 1, Elizabeth Clemson, born 21st of August, 1845. 2, John Augustine, born 27th of May, 1847. 3, Ann M. F. Blackburn, born 1st of November, 1849. 4, Louisa Clemson, born 17th of November, 1851. 5, Samuel Walter, born 1st of November, 1853. 6, Richard Blackburn, born 21st of March, 1856. 7, Christine Maria, born 13th of June, 1858. 8, George Steptoe, born 7th of June, 1860; is married.

iv, William de Hertburn, born 14th February, 1864.

3, Mildred (born 1695–6), the only daughter of Lawrence and Mildred (Warner) Washington, was married three times; first a Gregory, "Mrs. Mildred Gregory" was one of General Washington's sponsors; she married, secondly, Col. Henry Willis, whose daughter, Mary Willis, had married (1733) Hancock Lee.

Lawrence, the other Virginia immigrant, is supposed to have arrived some years after his brother John. He was the ancestor of "the Chotank branch" of the Washington family, which has not been thoroughly traced out. Lawrence was born in Bedfordshire, England, in 1635; died, in Virginia, in 1677. He left a son, named John, who was mentioned in the wills of his uncle Major John and of his cousin, Lawrence Washington. He married Mary, daughter of Richard Townshend, and left, amongst others, Henry (1695–1747), of Stafford county; his youngest son, Bailey Washington, of "Stafford Co. Gent.," married Catharine Stork and had: Baily, of "Windsor Forrest," Stafford, who married Euphan, daughter of James and Elizabeth (Westwood) Wallace; their eldest son was Dr. Bailey Washington, U. S. N., born in Westmoreland in 1787; died in District of Columbia, 4th of August, 1854; he married Ann Matilda, daughter of Richard Bland and Elizabeth (Collins) Lee; she was born at "Sully," on the 13th July, 1799; died on 20th December, 1880, leaving one son and three daughters (see 37, iii).

(Information concerning Washington family, etc., from Ford's Washington Wills; Hayden's *Va. Genealogies.*)

The will of Hannah Bushrod is worth preserving; an abstract of it is given. The portions omitted are simply enumerations of furniture, etc., given to the legatees named.

"In the name of God, Amen. I Hannah Washington of Bushfield in the parish of Cople and County of Westmoreland, being sound in mind though weak in body and health make this my last Will and Testament. I am very conscious of my great inability in drawing up any instrument of writing yet as none except my dearest friends will be at all concerned about it, I trust that they will make every allowance for the defects which they may meet with here. I shall try to explain my desire which I hope will be sufficient. The cruel custom in this country of hurrying a poor creature into a coffin as soon as the managers of the business (who are generally indeed people quite indifferent about the deceased or the most ignorant) suppose them dead; the friends at that awful moment quit the room and leave their dear friend to the discretion of these creatures who tired of setting up and confinement have them hurried into the coffin. No physician in the world can possibly tell whether or not a person is dead until putrifaction takes place and many have most assuredly been hurr'd away before they were dead. As I ever had a most horrid idea of such usage I most earnestly entreat my friends to act with me in the following manner, and that when it is thought I am dead that I remain in my bed quite undisturbed in every respect, my face to be uncovered not even the thinnest thing to be laid over it also I do request that not one thing shall be attempted about washing or dressing me. No laying out as it is called I beg. I therefore most earnestly pray that I may be allowed to remain in my bed just as I did whilst living until putrifaction by every known sign justifies my being put into the coffin; it is my will to be laid by my ever dear husband. It is my will and desire that after all my just and lawfull debts are paid, which indeed are but few, that my estate shall be disposed off in the following manner. In the first place I give and bequeath to my dearest and most tenderly beloved son Bushrod Washington all my stock, horses, &c., &c., not hereafter disposed of . . . on this plantation." Then follows a long list of furniture given to same son, part of which belonged "to Mrs. Hannah Washington of Selby." . . . "I give and bequeath to my Dearest and greatly beloved grand-Daughter Ann Aylett Robinson the whole of my Drawing room furniture," &c., &c. . . . "In the next place I give and bequeath to my ever darling grandson Richard Henry Lee Washington" some silver plate. Part of which "was sent for to the Federal City to cost £30, being a legacy from my worthy Brother in Law General Washington." To the same grandson she left a negro woman, who "was a very good Cook, her age I suppose to be about forty and a very healthy hearty woman, she also spins, washes and Irons Extremely well." If this grandson died before coming of age, the property left him was "to be the property of my truly beloved (now an infant) Grandson Corbin Washington of Selby, in case of my grandson Corbin Washington's death his brothers John Augustine and Bushrod Corbin Washington to have it. I give to my dearest daughter-in-Law Hannah Washington all my spun and unspun cotton," and some furniture described at length. . . . "I direct to my dearest daughter in law Anne Washington a mourning ring to cost ten pounds current money of Virginia, and one half of my little library, the other half to Anne Aylett Robinson." Horses to be given to "Daughter in Law Hannah Washington" and "dearest son Bushrod Washington." To "dear good friend Mrs. Mary Harrington wife to Doctor Timothy" some furniture. . . . "I give my mahogany dressing table and the small cabinet which stands on it with a looking glass door to my dearest grand-daughter Jane Mildred Washington. I give my beloved Mary Lee Washington my handsome Chamber table and the dressing glass with three small drawers which stands on it." . . . "I give my dear grand-daughter Anne Aylett Washington the miniature of my ever darling Mildred Lee. My other trinkets I desire may be equally divided between my three granddaughters Vizt. Anne Aylett Robinson, Jane Mildred and Mary Lee Washington;" to the same three were given her clothing, &c. A "mourning

Francis Lightfoot Lee

ring of five pounds value currency of Virginia to my beloved grandson Bushrod Washington son of William Augustine Washington and my dear daughter Jenny. My hand is so very well known that I trust this my last Will and Testament needs no vouchers. I constitute my Darling son Bushrod Washington and William Robinson, the latter who married my Dear granddaughter Anne Aylett Washington, my Executors." No date; was probated at Westmoreland on the 26th of April, 1801.

## FRANCIS LIGHTFOOT LEE.

19. FRANCIS LIGHTFOOT[4], the sixth son of Thomas Lee[3] (Richard[2], Richard[1]) and Hannah Ludwell, his wife, was born at Stratford, the 14th of October, 1734, and died at his home, "Menokin," Richmond county, about January of 1797. Francis Lightfoot Lee was educated at home by a private tutor, the Rev. Mr. Craig, who not only made him a good scholar but imbued him with a genuine fondness for the study of the classics, and for literature in general. Mr. Lee, on arriving at manhood, first settled in Loudoun county, the lands left him by his father being in that county; he and his brother, Philip Ludwell, are mentioned as among the founders of the town of Leesburg; as early as 1765, he appeared in public life, being chosen a Burgess from that county. A few years later, on his marriage, he moved from Loudoun to Richmond county, and built himself a home which he called Menokin, from the Indian name, Manakin. Being chosen a Burgess from Richmond county, he was acting in that position when the first rumblings of the coming storm were heard, and seems to have promptly taken his stand by the side of his brothers as an earnest patriot. When in August, 1775, Col. Bland resigned his position as a representative in the Continental Congress, George Mason, himself refusing the position, recommended Francis Lightfoot Lee, and he was chosen.[1] It is not recorded that he held any position as a speaker; his usefulness, therefore, lay in the quieter and less ostentatious forms of public service, and it may be safely assumed that he was useful, for he was successively re elected in 1776–77–78; in the spring of 1779 he retired from Congress, being averse to a public life and hoping to be allowed to live henceforth a quiet country life. But not so; he was soon called again to the front, this time to serve in the Senate chamber of the Virginia Assembly.

Mr. Lee's chief public services, while in Congress, were to assist in framing the articles of the old confederation, and later in his vigorous demand that no treaty of peace should be made with Great Britain which did not guarantee to the Americans the freedom of the northern fisheries and the free navigation of the Mississippi river; subsequent events have amply

[1] *Calendar Va. State Papers*, I, 268.

proven the wisdom of his foresight in making this demand. Mr. Lee was also with his brother, Richard Henry, a signer of the Declaration of Independence.

At one period of the Revolutionary War, some of their enemies tried to prove that "the Lees of Virginia," as they called them, were secretly, if not openly, hostile to General Washington. This charge has been completely refuted; in fact, that great patriot had no warmer personal friends, nor any more sincere political supporters than Richard Henry Lee, Francis Lightfoot Lee, Henry Lee, and others of the family. A perusal of their private letters amply sustains this assertion. An anecdote is told of Francis Lightfoot Lee, which well illustrates his admiration for Washington. Being one day at the county court house, just after the new federal Constitution had been adopted at Philadelphia, and was, of course, the subject of general interest, some one asked his opinion of it. He replied that he did not pretend to be a good judge of such important matters, but that one circumstance satisfied him in its favor;[1] this was that "General Washington was in favor of it and John Warden was against it." Warden was a Scotch lawyer of the county, who had just been making a speech against the ratification of the new Constitution.

A writer on the Signers of the Declaration of Independence has said of him: "In the Spring of 1779, Mr. Lee retired from Congress, and returned to the home to which both his temper and inclination led him, with delight. He was not, however, long permitted to enjoy the satisfaction it conferred; for the internal affairs of his native State were in a situation of so much agitation and perplexity, that his fellow-citizens insisted on his representing them in the Senate of Virginia. He carried into that body all the integrity, sound judgment, and love of country for which he had ever been conspicuous, and his labors there were alike honorable to himself and useful to the State.

"He did not long remain in this situation. His love of ease, and fondness for domestic occupations now gained the entire ascendency over him, and he retired from public life with the firm determination of never

[1] General Washington to James Madison, 10th January, 1788. . . . "That the opposition should have gained strength at Richmond, among the members of the Assembly, is not, if true, to be wondered at, when we consider that the great adversaries to the Constitution are all assembled at that place, acting conjointly, with the promulgated sentiments of Colonel Richard Henry Lee as auxiliary. It is said, however, and I believe it may be depended upon, that the latter, (though he may retain his sentiments,) has withdrawn, or means to withdraw, his opposition; because, as he has expressed himself, or others have done it for him, he finds himself in bad company such as with M[erce]r, Sm[i]th, etc., etc His brother, Francis L. Lee, on whose judgment the family place much reliance, is decidedly in favor of the new form, under a conviction, that it is the best that can be obtained, and because it promises energy, stability, and that security, which is, or ought to be, the wish of every good citizen of the Union."—Ford's *Writings of George Washington*, XI, 207-8.

again engaging in its busy and wearisome scenes; and to this determination he strictly adhered. In this retirement, his character was most conspicuous. He always possessed more of the gay, good humor, and pleasing wit of Atticus, than the sternness of Cato, or the eloquence of Cicero. To the young, the old, the grave, the gay, he was alike a pleasing and interesting companion. None approached him with diffidence; no one left him but with regret. To the poor around him, he was a counsellor, physician, and friend; to others, his conversation was at once agreeable and instructive, and his life a fine example for imitation. Like the great founder of our Republic, he was much attached to agriculture, and retained from his estate a small farm for experiment and amusement.

"Having no children, Mr. Lee lived an easy and a quiet life. Reading, farming, and the company of his friends and relatives, filled up the remaining portion of his days. A pleurisy, caught in one of the coldest winters ever felt in Virginia, terminated the existence of both his beloved wife and himself within a few days of each other. His last moments were those of a Christian, a good, honest, and virtuous man; and those who witnessed the scene were all ready to exclaim, 'Let me die the death of the righteous, and let my last end be like his.'"

Mr. Lee, married, about the 21st of April, 1769, Rebecca, second daughter of Col. John and Rebecca (Plater) Tayloe, of "Mt. Airy," Richmond county; both he and his wife died within a few days of each other and without issue, in the winter of 1797, having taken cold from exposure to the severe weather then prevailing.

TAYLOE.—John Tayloe was descended from William, who came to Virginia about 1650, and married Anne, daughter of Henry Corbin, whose sister had married Richard Lee, grandfather of F. L. Lee; William Tayloe had a son, John, who married a Mrs. Elizabeth (Gwynn) Lyde, and left three children: John, Betty, and Anne Corbin. This John Tayloe, of Mt. Airy, married Rebecca, daughter of Gov. George Plater of Maryland, and had, it is said, twelve children; of these one son and eight daughters survived him. The eight daughters, above mentioned, all married into prominent families: 1, Elizabeth married Gov. Edward Lloyd, of Maryland, in 1767. 2, Rebecca, Francis Lightfoot Lee, as above stated. 3, Eleanor, Ralph Wormeley, of Middlesex, in 1772. 4, Anne Corbin, Thomas Lomax, of Caroline, in 1773. 5, Mary, Mann Page, of Spottsylvania, in 1776. 6, Catharine, Landon Carter, of Richmond county, in 1780. 7, Jane, Robert Beverley, of Essex, in 1791. 8, Sarah, Col. William Augustine Washington, of Westmoreland, in 1799. John, son of John and Rebecca (Plater) Tayloe, and brother to these eight daughters, was born in 1771, and married, in 1792,

Annie, daughter of Gov. Benjamin Ogle,[1] of Maryland, and died in Washington city, in 1828, having had, it is said, fifteen children; amongst whom was a son, also named John, and fourth of the name, who entered the navy and was distinguished in the battles of the old frigate "Constitution," against the "Guerriere," and with the "Cyane and Levant." After the first action, the State of Virginia presented him with a sword. (*Old Churches, Families, etc.*, II, 181.)

His will was dated the 30th of December, 1795, and probated in Richmond county the 6th of February, 1797. It was written by himself, and reads:

In the name of God, Amen. I Francis Lightfoot Lee of the County of Richmond in Virginia being in pretty good health and of sound memory do make and Constitute this my last Will and Testament Vizt.

First I give to my beloved wife Rebecca Lee, forever, a mulatto woman named Cate, who is at present my wife's maid, and all the said Cate's female issue. 2dly. I give my dearest wife all the furniture in the room we lye in, called the Chamber, and also the following pieces of silver plate, to wit, a coffee pot, a Chamber Candlestick, two tea Canisters, a Milk pot, and a sugar sifting spoon.

3dly. I Lend my dearest wife during her life all the furniture not before given, all the Liquors and family necessaries in the house and offices, all my negroes on the Menokin Plantation, with the utensils of Husbandry, all the stocks of every kind on the plantation, all the Grain and provisions in hand and growing at the time of my death, and the post Chaise or other carriage I may have and Horses and also whatever family goods and necessaries I may have ordered from Europe or elsewhere, and not arrived before my death. I mean hereby a comfortable provision for my dearest wife during her life. After her death, I give all the said negroes, furniture and what may remain of the other articles mentioned in this clause to my nephew Ludwell Lee, second son of my Brother Richard Henry Lee, forever.

4thly. It is my will and desire that if at any time my dear wife should be of the opinion that it would contribute to her ease and Comfort to have any or all of the negroes at Menokin Sold, in such case, my Executors shall sell them, on reasonable credit or for ready money if they see fitt, and the money arising from such sale, to be, at her option, laid out in the purchase of other negroes, for her use during her lifetime or to be put to Interest on good landed security, and the interest paid to my said wife during her life. The negroes so purchased or the money at Interest, I give to my nephew Ludwell Lee forever, after the death of my wife.

5thly. I give my dearest wife Two hundred and fifty pounds a year during her life, and my will is that the said Two hundred and fifty pounds be always rated according to the present value of Gold and silver Coins legally Current, and as it may be more convenient to my dearest wife, I desire my Executors, if she should desire it, to pay the said £250 half yearly, that is to say, £125 at the experation of each six months.

---

[1] Ogle. Samuel Ogle, Esq., of Northumberland county, England, had a son, his eldest, the Hon. Samuel Ogle (died the 3d of May, 1752, æt. 52,) who was three times Proprietary Governor of Maryland. His son, the Hon. Benjamin Ogle, also Governor, (1798–1801), left a son, Benjamin, who married Anna Maria Cooke, daughter of William and Elizabeth (Tilghman) Cooke.

6thly. I give to my dearest wife £250 to be paid to her as soon after my death as may be, independent of the £250 yearly before Given to her.

7thly. I direct that the taxes on the land and negroes at Menokin, for which my wife may be liable during her widowhood, shall be paid out of the Estate hereafter given to my nephew Ludwell Lee, and that two able well broke young horses may be furnished for her use during her life, occasionally as she may call for them, at the expense of my estate given to Ludwell Lee. It is also my will and desire that in case my dear wife should chuse to remove from Menokin that then all the furniture, necessaries and provisions that she shall not reserve for her use shall be sold with her consent and the principal and interest issuing from such sale shall be applied in the same manner as is directed in the 4th clause of this will with respect to the Principal and Interest arising from the sale of the negroes.

7thly. The provision herein made for and the bequests herein given to my dear wife I mean and declare to be in lieu of dower, but if she should prefer her dower, in that case, I do revoke them all and declare them void, Except her maid Cate, the furniture in the Chamber and the Six pieces of silver plate. 8thly. I give to my nephew Thomas Lee of Loudoun all my lots in the town of Matildaville to him and his heirs forever. 9thly. I give to my nephew George Lee my Tract of Land near Colchester in Fairfax to him and his heirs forever. 10thly. I give my Gold enameled snuff Box and the picture set with diamonds belonging to it, which was given to me by my ever lamented brother Arthur Lee, to my nephew Francis Lightfoot Lee. 11thly. I give to my much esteemed friend Doctor William Shippen, Jr., of Philadelphia, fifty guineas to be laid out in a piece or pieces of Silver plate, as he may chuse, as a small testimony of my gratefull sense of the many Civilities shown to me and Mrs. Lee when in Philadelphia.

12. I give to my nephew Thomas Lee Shippen of Pennsylvania a ring of two guineas value. 13. I give and bequeath all the rest of my Estate real and personal and of whatever kind soever to my nephew Ludwell Lee, to him and his heirs forever. And I do hereby make Constitute and appoint him the said Ludwell Lee my heir and residuary legatee.

And it is my meaning and intent that all the monies and annuities given my wife and my Debts be paid out of the Estate which I have given to my nephew Ludwell Lee. 14. It is my desire that in case my dearest wife shall accept the provision herein made for her that then there be no Appraisement made nor Inventory taken of the furniture, family necessaries &c. lent her herein, but that she may at any time convenient to herself deliver a list of them to my Nephew Ludwell Lee. Lastly, I do Constitute and appoint my much beloved wife Rebecca Lee, my nephews Ludwell Lee, Thomas Ludwell Lee of Loudoun and George Lee, Executors of this my will, all written with my own hand and each page signed with my name and this last page with my Seale affixed to it. On the 30th day of December in the year of our Lord, 1795.

As so few of Francis Lightfoot Lee's letters have been preserved, these given here will be of interest. They throw some additional light upon the interesting period of the Revolution; very few of them have ever appeared in print.

To Col. Landon Carter, Sabine Hall, Richmond county:

"Philadelphia, 21st October, 1775. My Dear Colonel: I received your Letter with great pleasure, tho' contrary to your expectation it paid postage to the *hated* Post Office; the Continental post now goes regularly, so we may with a safe conscience say how d'ye to each other. It gives me concern to hear that you are withdrawing from public business; upon my word, this is not a time for men of abilities with good intentions to be only spectators; if we can't do all the good we could wish, let us at least endeavour to prevent all the mischief in our power. Your good friend Lord Dunmore is endeavouring to raise all the powers on earth to demolish poor Virginia. We have advice that at his earnest solicitation a fleet may be expected this fall to ravage our defenceless plantations and burn our little Towns; and we have lately discovered a plot of his and Connolly's, which is to be executed in the following manner; Connolly despairing of getting up the country through Virginia, or the Carolinas, is to go to St. Augustine from thence to the Creeks and Cherokees, and through all the tribes to Detroit; by Gen. Gage's commission he is to have the Garrison and Cannon of that place and the assistance of the French of that settlement, with all these he is to form an army in the spring and march to Pittsburgh, from thence to Alexandria, proclaiming freedom to all servants who will enlist; there he is to be joined by Dunmore with the fleet, and troops from England and to march through the Country. He has Captain's commissions from Dunmore for Cornstalk and White Eyes.

"We have given the earliest intelligence of these schemes to our Committee of Safety, and hope with their endeavours, assisted by the Carolinas and Georgia, that Connolly may be intercepted this fall or winter. Our military operations this campaign have been very languid, from the want of powder; but we still hope our success in Canada will be such as to cut a figure for our first essay. Such measures have been taken as give us good reason to expect a plentiful supply of that necessary article before the next spring, and then we shall be in readiness to receive the very warm attack, which from all our advices, the Ministry are preparing for us. But lest we should fail in being supplied from abroad, every man should assert himself in making saltpetre; your several plantations would furnish a good deal, and you know the process is easy. With plenty of powder, the victory is surely ours.

"22nd October. Here I was interrupted yesterday evening by an express for Dr. Shippen to see our worthy Speaker;[1] he went out to dine with Wm. Hill and while at dinner, was suddenly seized with a dead palsy, and this morning, we are informed that he died last night. You know his virtues and will lament the loss of the friend and Patriot. I am so concerned that I can't think of politicks.

---

[1] Peyton Randolph.

"My best respects to my good friend Mr. Carter; I have got a man to work at his wool cards, and we are in possession of Miss Betsey's musick, which shall be sent by the first opportunity. Mrs. Lee joins me in every good wish to Mrs. Carter and Miss Lucy. We have no doubt of Miss Lucy's happiness in the married state, as so much depends on herself, and knowing the worth of Mr. Colston. Remember me to all friends, when I shall see them, God knows. Believe me, my dear Colonel, Your sincerely affec't friend and respectfull Servant."

To William Lee at London.

"Dear Brother, I wrote to you by the Anne, Capt Sinclair, who sail'd the 9th of this month inclosing bills of Exchange and other papers, and directed it to the care of Mr. Molleson, as you had forgot to mention where your Letters shou'd be directed, but I have heard since that the Capt. is a very worthless fellow, therefore it may be necessary you shou'd make some inquiry after him; he is in a ship of Glasford's consigned to Rob't Bogle & Scott, this comes by Capt Walker he I suppose will sail in 3 or 4 weeks, but I am oblig'd to write this early because I set off to day for Loudoun to the election, which will be in 8 or 10 days. The people are so vex't at the little attendance I have given them that they are determined it seems to dismiss me from their service, a resolution most pleasing to me, for it is so very inconvenient to me that nothing shou'd induce me to take a poll, but a repeated promise to my friends there, enforced by those here who consider me as a staunch friend to Liberty; for the ruin of which our Governor seems to be taking some very subtle measures, supported by the Att'y Gen'l who is pushing hard for the Govr's favor, and to succeed the honest worthy Ned Ambler, who is dead, as a representative for James Towne. What a change! Lord Botetourt, in the opinion of everybody is a polite, very agreeable man, and it is probable from his universal character that we shou'd be very happy in a Governor, if it was not for our unhappy dispute with G. Britain, in which he must no doubt think and act with the ministry. Indeed he honestly says so and from what little he speaks about it, it appears the Ministry are determined to enforce. We have not heard any thing from Boston since I wrote last, the post did not bring in the last Northward papers, why we do not know. The Pennsylvania Assembly has adjourned to the Spring without taking the least notice of the damn'd acts. Oh, I forget, by some private acct's from Boston, they are enveigling the soldiers, who desert in crouds dayly; our Assembly will meet in the spring when I hope you will have something worthy Virg'a.

"I was miserably disappointed in my expectations from Williamsburgh, altogether owing to my having employ'd the Esquire and which I did contrary to my own opinion of things in general, but because I knew you usually employ'd him in such affairs; now you must not expect any remittances till after the Oyer Court, and then by the first ship you cannot fail. You have enclosed Hector Ross's second Exchange for £40 to purchase for me things necessary for our fulling mill, such as screw, or Press, Paste boards, shears and dyes, the quantities and kinds of which I leave to you and if you can recollect any other thing necessary, send it, you have also Armstead's and Claiborne's seconds, the first of which were sent in my last, they are for the Misses quota's of B. Moore, and Armstead, I am informed we can get good Jamaica spirit cheaper from London than the W. Indies, for the duty is drawn back there and none paid here, do inquire about it and let us know, my love to the Doct'r, I shall certainly write to him soon, no offer for his chair and Horses yet and Col. Phil. says Griffin will not take the things at William'bg. Harry, you'll repent having desired me to write often. Adieu."

To Robert Wormeley Carter, Esquire, at the Convention, Richmond, Virginia:

"November, 1775. Dear Sir: We have had nothing new since the reduction of Montreal, which I suppose you must have heard of. It is supposed Arnold must be in possession of Quebec by this time if he shou'd be too weak to affect it Montgomerie will join him fromMontreal. At all events we have got the most valuable part of Canada, as it cuts off all communication with the Indians and prevents inroads on our frontier. It wou'd give me infinite pleasure, if our affairs to the Southward wore as favorable an aspect, it will require very vigorous efforts to put a stop to the proceedings of Lord Dunmore. We are extreamly alarmed by an express from the Com'tee of Northampton County to Congress informing that he has issued a Proclamation, declaring military law in Virg'a and offering freedom to all servants and slaves who shall repair to the King's standard which he has erected; that the inhabitants of Norfolk and Princess Ann Counties have taken an oath to oppose to the last drop of their blood any of their countrymen who shall come in arms into their Counties. The Com'tee asks for assistance, being apprehensive that their people from their exposed situation and the number of their slaves will thro' fear be induced to follow the example of the other Counties. We have got the Proclamation. I have been fearfull lest the letters from Northampton to our Com'tee of safety, shou'd be intercepted, which they were apprehensive of. This intelligence gives great concern to all the friends of America and subjects your countrymen to the sneers of its disguised Enemys and the lukewarm. Fatal consequences may follow if an immediate stop is not put to that Devil's career. I shou'd think a sufficient force of Militia or Minute men, shou'd immediately be sent, to drive him and his adherents on board the ships; the estates of the inhabitants of Norfolk, or elsewhere, who have taken arms, ag'st the Country shou'd be sequesterd for its defence. The proclamation burnt by the hangman, heavy penalties inflicted on those who disperse them thro' the Country; the patroles shou'd be very diligent; will it not be necessary for the convention by a short ordinance to establish the present Laws and judges? It would contribute more than anything to the quiet and safety of the people, and security of our commerce in the spring; if the Convention wou'd exert themselves in fitting out small armed vessells, to prevent small tenders from infesting the bay and rivers, if it cannot be done in Virg'a they might be procured here, probably Virg'a might spare powder for this purpose, but without very bad fortune we shall soon have it in. It is inconceivable what good effects have been produced from such a measure to the Northward, not a tender dares to come from under the guns of the large ships, and the vessells employed by the Army in Boston to procure wood and provisions are every day falling into our hands, there are small guns in several parts of Virg'a; a few at Hobbs' hole and Col. Fauntleroys. The furnaces shou'd be set to casting them, God prosper your deliberations."

To Landon Carter of Sabine Hall, Richmond County, Virginia.

"Philadelphia, Nov. 20, 1775. My dear Colonel: I wrote to Col. Taylor two or three days agoe, from whome I suppose you have had the news, and intended by Mr. Colston to answer your last letter; but an express from the camp last night having bro't fresh intelligence I take the advantage of to morrow's post to communicate it to you. The transports from Ireland with five Regiments, compleat, have arrived at Boston; a fishing boat with 6 muskets took a schooner belonging to the fleet, loaded with provisions for the Officers, in her were many letters by which we learn that the Roman catholic Lords Bishops and Gentry are extremely active in procuring recruits. The Protestants very averse to the business, many recruiting parties driven out of their towns, and even the lower class of catholics, show great dislike to it, but with the high premiums given by the Popish towns &c many recruits are raised, and it is expected as many will be raised as will compleat the number intended for the next campaign, which they say is 22,000. 5,000 Hanoverians are to garrison Gibraltar and Portmahon, the British regiments there to go to England and Ireland. I will not anticipate your reflection upon the infamous proceedings of the Ministry, but I think he must be blind indeed who does not see the design of establishing arbitrary Government in America, and be unworthy the name of man who does not oppose it at all hazard. The establishment of Popery will no doubt be the reward of the exertions of the Roman Catholics. We do not think the whole of these raw Irish will make a dinner for our troops, our only fear is the want of ammunition ; but we hope to be relieved from that before next spring, our cutters have taken two more of their caitering vessels, one loaded with wood, the other with provisions. 6,000 of the Enemy made a sally out of Boston to carry off some cattle but a few of our men quickly repulsed them, with the loss of two of their men. We have heard of Arnold's being in Canada and rec'd with open arms by the inhabitants, so we expect that Quebec, and of course the whole province is ours by this time, so much for news. I am glad to find that amidst all the breeches, button making in Virg'a and in spite of the Cholic you keep up your spirits and therefore hope you have defeated all the party schemes in Richmond. Lord Dunmore seems to be a little quiet since the taste of Virg'a prowess at Hampton, we expect that Col. Woodford will keep him to his good behaviour at Norfolk. Pray remember me to all my friends, present my best respect to my friend, Mr. Carter and his lady and believe me always y'r aff't h'b'l serv't."

To THE SAME.

"Philadelphia, Dec. 12th 1775. Dear Colonel: Before you receive this, Mr. Colston will have given you all the news of this place when he left it ; since which one of our little men of war, called the Lee, Cap't Manly, has taken a storeship, loaded with 2,000 stand of arms, a great deal of artillery, 30 tons of shot, a quantity of shells and shot for the bombs and Cannon ; and a very great quantity of all kinds of artillery stores ; to the amount of 20,000£ Str., as 'tis tho't.

"We make no doubt but Quebec and Carlton with his powder are in our possession by this time. If we are supply'd with powder from that or any other quarter this winter, we shall certainly make Boston too hot for Howe, as the ministry has kindly supplied us plentifully with artillery ; these successes to the Northward, and the former reputation of Virg'a, make the present proceedings with you appear in a very odd light. The real friends of liberty are under great concern, and your delegates are mortified with the sneers and reflections of the lukewarm, but that is trifling to the uneasiness we suffer, from the apprehension of the consequences, that may follow, from L'd Dunmore's being allowed to get to such a head.

"It does not appear to me, that Woodford is sufficient to effect anything decisive. In my opinion, our safety depends upon an immediate and effectual stop being given to that infernal Demon, and his Tory associates at Norfolk. The Congress are giving the greatest attention to a Navy and I hope we shall have ships enough by the spring to oblige the ministerial fleet to consult their safety by keeping close together, and of course will not be able to do us much injury. I am surprised at not receiving Letters from my friends in Richmond by the Cont'l post. The Postmaster assures me there is a post established from Fredericksburg to Portroyal, Hobbs' hole, and Urbanna; the County Com'tees were to direct where the offices shou'd be kept. I wish it was enquired into and the obstruction mentioned; that they may be removed, if in the Postmaster's power. I hope the County chose a Com'tee to your liking and that everything is quiet. Is it not necessary that the convention shou'd establish some kind of Government as Lord D. by his proclamation, has utterly demolished the whole civil Government? I believe the Congress will adjourn before Christmas, but whether long enough to allow me to see Virg'a. is uncertain. In the meantime my best wishes attend my friends in Richmond."

### To the same.

"Philadelphia, March 19, 1776. My Dear Col.: Before this I suppose you have rec'd a copy of *Common Sense*, which I sent you sometime ago; if not, I now send a parcel to Col. Tayloe, of whome you may have one.

"Our late King and his Parliament having declared us Rebels and Enemies, confiscated our property, as far as were likely to lay hands on it; have effectually decided the question for us, whether or no we sh'd be independent. All we have to do now is to endeavour to reconcile ourselves to the state it has pleased Providence to put us into; and indeed upon taking a near and full look at the thing, it does not frighten so much, as when viewed at a distance. I can't think we shall be injured by having free trade to all the world, instead of its being confined to one place, whose riches might allways be used to our ruin; nor does it appear to me that we shall suffer any disadvantage by having our Legislatures uncontrolled by a power so far removed from us, that our circumstances can't be known; whose interest is often directly contrary to ours, and over which we have no manner of control. Indeed great part of that power being at present lodged in the hands of a most gracious Prince, whose tender mercies we have often experienced; it must wring the heart of all good men to part; but I suppose we shall have Christian fortitude enough to bear with patience and even cheerfullness the decrees of a really most gracious King. The danger of anarchy and confusion, I think altogether chimerical; the good behaviour of the Americans with no government at all, proves them very capable of good Government. But my dear Col. I am so fond of peace that I wish to see an end of these distractions upon any terms that will secure America from future outrages; but from all our intelligence I really despair. There is such an inveteracy in the ——— and his advisers that we need not expect any other alternative than slavery or separation, is it not prudent therefore to fit our minds to the state that is inevitable. Virginia, it seems, is considered at home as most liable to deception and seduction; and therefore the Commissioners are to bend their chief force that way, backed by a considerable detachment of the Army. I hope it will turn to the honor of my Country, as it will afford an opportunity of showing their virtue and good sense. Col. Tayloe has the news. I wrote yesterday to my friend Col. R. Carter by the post, letting him know that Gen'l Lee, who has the Southern command, was furnished with the two aides-de-camp paid by Congress, before my application, but agreed to take your Grandson as a supernumerary aid, he bearing his own expenses. If this is agreeable you will perhaps see the Gen'l as he had some thoughts of passing through Richmond. Best respects to Sabine Hall."

### To the same.

"Philadelphia, Sep. 15, 1776. My Dear Col.: I acknowledge myself greatly indebted to your goodness for which, tho' I despair of ever making full returns; yet I shall endeavor to show my gratitude by such partial payments, as my time and abilities will admit of.

"I cannot think the apprehensions of our Council, without foundation, for whether the Enemy is successfull or not at N. York, there is reason to believe, they will make some attempts upon some of the southern states, and we know that our people upon the least removal of danger, are too apt to relapse into supineness and inattention. We find from experience that regulars only can effectually be opposed to the British troops; therefore we are collecting our regular batallions to resist the efforts of the Enemy at N. York, and if any sudden attack should be made upon any state we must depend upon the Militia to impede their progress, untill they can be opposed by some regular troops.

"The Militia is not only ineffectual, but beyond measure expensive, such a number of regulars will therefore be raised for the next campaign, that we shall not have recourse to the Militia, but upon extraordinary occasions; six new Regiments will be raised in Virginia.

"You have no doubt before this, been informed that our General upon finding Long Island not tenable, have quitted it, after a smart engagement between a party of between 2 and 3000 of our men, and the greater part of the Enemy's Army, in which tho' we were out-generaled yet the troops behaved so exceedingly well, that Howe has been very cautious in all his movements since; all of which indicates his intentions of getting upon the back of our Army and with their shipping on the front and each side cut off all communication with the country, in which case we must either fight to a disadvantage or surrender for want of provisions. Our gen'l is taking measures to prevent this; for which purpose the City of N. York must be evacuated; which is by no means tenable, if the Enemy choose to direct their efforts ag't it.

"As the Court of G. B. has ever accompanied violence with deception; Lord Howe their agent since his arrival has constantly endeavored to make the people believe that he has great powers, and earnestly wished for peace, and at length carried the matter so far, as to desire a conference with some members of Congress, in their private capacities. The Congress to show they were not averse to peace, sent a Com'tee of their body to confer with him, they had the honour of three hours conversation with his L'dship and returned here last Fryday. He acknowledged he had no power to suspend the operations of war, or to offer any terms; but said, he had waited two months in England to prevail with the Ministry to empower him to *converse and confer* with Gen't'n of influence in America, that he was sure of the good intention of the King and the Ministry, if we would return to our allegiance, they would revise the late instructions to Gov'rs and the Acts of Parliament, and if there was anything in them that appear'd unreasonable to *them*, he did not doubt but they wou'd make them easy. The whole affair will soon be published by Congress which I will send to my friend in Richmond and shall be glad of your remarks.

"All well at Ticonderoga. Every advice from all parts of the French dominions give us hope of a speedy rupture with G. B.—That event will make us somewhat easy. My best respects to the Ladies and my friend Mr. Carter."

TO THE SAME.

"Philadelphia, Feb. 12, 1776. My Dear Colonel: I intended to have devoted yesterday to answering your kind letters by last monday's post, but unexpected business intervened, which prevented me, and this day I find my obligation increased by the receipt of yours of the 1st inst. I must now content myself with assuring you that I am very sensible of your friendship, and acquainting you with the occurrences in this part of the world; the only return in my power for your kindness. Gen'l Washington having intelligence that Gen'l Clinton with a body of troops had sailed from Boston and suspecting their intention was to make a lodgement in N. York, dispatched Genl. Lee to prevent it. Lee arrived there last week with 1100 men; and on the same day in pops Clinton, who had been separated from his fleet in a snow storm; finding Lee there, he and Tryon assured the town upon their honor that the troops were not destined for N. York and nothing hostile was intended ag't them. Lee knowing the cue of the Ministry and all their agents, continued to call in more forces; this day he sent us an express that one of the transports full of soldiers was arrived and several others seen at the Hook, however as Lee had 4000 men, it is imagined Clinton will comply with part of his *honorable* engagement, and attempt nothing at N. York, but proceed to Virga., which place, some Gentlemen (in pretended confidence) were assured, was the original destination of the fleet, so that perhaps old Bess will not long remain clear, Clinton's pretended rendezvous is at Hampton road, where he is to be joined by a fleet from England with 5 regiments, his present force is supposed to be 6 or 700 men. I fear your want of arms and good Gen'ls will make this little Army very formidable to you. We have not yet applyd to Congress for y'r Genr'l Officers, nor do we know where they will be got; those that are good for anything seem to have their hands full to the North and Eastward, whenever they are appointed, you may be assured I will not fail to put in a good word for my young friend Landon. Had we not been deceived in our intelligence respecting the 30 tons of powder, Boston in all probability would now be in our possession; but alas for want of that necessary, the favorable season has passed away, without anything being affected and now the rest must remain probably until next Winter; however we have now in hand 117 tons of saltpetre, 13 of powder and 300 stand of arms; the utmost dispatch is using to manufacture the saltpetre, which will soon enable us to answer all demands w'ch are now very great from all quarters; but we expect in the present scramble for the B'tons to get one or two for Virga. Our affairs in Canada are in as good a situation as we could expect, since our unfortunate attempt on Quebec; we have no doubt of having a sufficient force there to render good acct's of Carlton before he can be reinforced. Capt'n Manly, formerly of the Lee, now of the Hancock, is daily taking some of their supply transports; in return for which two ships loaded by the Congress with flour to procure military stores, have fallen into the Enemy's hands. I find L'd D. is endeavoring to persuade the settlers on the Rivers to remain quiet, and not remove their stock and provisions, no doubt till he is enabled to come and ease them of them all. 'Tis strange that this monster and the rest of his infernal tribe should expect to be credited by a single person, after the innumerable instances of cruelty and rapacity and perfidy, fresh in every one's mind, which they have exhibited in every part of the world. The Ministerial scheme against Sayre, Lee and others was this: The workmen leaving the docks, demanding higher wages, applying to the American friends to supply them with money to convey them out of the Kingdom; was all under the direction of L'd Sandwich, in order to bring the Americans under the penalty for inveigling the King's workmen out of the Kingdom. It was about to take effect, when one more honest than the rest of his fellows, disclosed the whole affair to the Alderman. This failing, their next plan is to make one Richardson, a native of this City, whome they have made an officer in the Guards, swear away the life of Sayre and it is apprehended of the others also. Is it possible that any one can expect anything from such abandoned villains. From them and their hellish plots, good Lord deliver us! Our best respects to Sabine Hall and believe me, dear Colonel, your aff't friend and very humble servant."

The following joint letter explains itself; it was written after the vote in the Virginia Assembly, by which Richard Henry Lee was defeated for Congress, with its implied censure of his conduct.

"To the Hon. George Wythe, Speaker of the H. of D.'s of Va."

"Sir: We shall be much obliged to you to inform the House of our warmest desire to have leave to return home immediately and that other gentlemen may be sent to fill our places. What passed in the House, previous to the last election of Delegates, is well known. We do not presume to judge of the proceedings of the House other than as they affect ourselves; in which case we hope to be excused if we are determined by our own feelings. From what then passed, and our long and intimate acquaintance with Col. Lee, we are sorry to be obliged to think that however upright our conduct may be, we may, while absent and engaged in a very painful service, in an instant be deprived of what we esteem most valuable, our reputation. It is impossible we could do our full duty, as we could wish, while our minds labour under such melancholy impressions. We love our Country and will cheerfully share its fate, whatever may be the issue of the present contest; but we must be content to serve it in a more humble station, less exposed to envy, hatred and malice."

(Signed)

MANN PAGE, JR.
FRANCIS LIGHTFOOT LEE.

PHILADELPHIA, 10 June, 1777.

To Richard Henry Lee.

"Philadelphia, June 30, 1776. Dear Brother: Our affairs in Canada are at length bro't to a conclusion, and we have now to contend with all the bad consequences, which have been apprehended from the Enemy's being in possession of that Country.

"You will see by the papers that Gen'l Thomson was sent with 2000 men to dislodge a party of the Enemy at Trois Rivieres, but Gen'l Burgoyne having arrived with a considerable body of troops, our men were obliged to retreat with the loss of 150; leaving the Gen'l and a few others in captivity. Burgoyne pursued his advantage, and our Generals found it absolutely necessary to retire out of the Country with their sick and dispirited army. The accounts of Burgoyne's force are from 8000 to 10,000. We cou'd not muster above 3000, all the rest being ill with the Small pox.

"Our army, being 7000 bro't off all their artillery, stores, baggage and provisions, having destroyed all the forts and bridges behind them they are now at Crown Point, where they propose to make a stand against Burgoyne's army, assisted by Canadians and Indians; by keeping the mastery of Lake Champlain, if possible, which is much to be doubted, as he has bro't with him a great number of vessels ready framed. At New York General Washington has not 10,000 men, and 50 of Howe's fleet are now at the hook. None of the militia is yet come in, and Gen'l Washington is apprehensive they will not, till it is too late. And there is reason to fear they will never join the army at Crown Point for fear of the small pox, or if they do, that they will be rendered useless by it, add to all this, that it is certain great numbers in the province of N. York will join the Enemy; a horrid plot was lately discovered in the City to deliver up our army to the Enemy by spiking the cannon and blowing up the Magazine and some say to assassinate the Gen'l. We have not yet the particulars, but many are in goal; they had debauched two of the Gen'ls guards, one of whom is executed. Thus you have a full view of the situation of our affairs; from which I dare say you will agree with me, that we are in a most perilous state, from which nothing but some extraordinary event can extricate us. We have advice, that the crew of one of the ships that sailed from this port last winter, loaded by the Congress, confined the Cap't and carried her into Bristol, and discovered the signals by which all the other ships were to distinguish their friends from their Enemies upon their arrival on this Coast. I have nothing to ballance this dismal acc't, but that we have taken about 700 of Frazer's highlanders; and that depending on the goodness of our cause, we have not lost our spirits.

"1st July. This day the resolve for independency was considered and agreed to in Com'tee of the Whole, two [States] dissented—S. Carolina and Pennsylvania. N. York did not vote, not being empower'd; to-morrow it will pass the house with the concurrence of S. Carolina; the Pennsylvania delegates indulge their own wishes, tho' they acknowledge, what indeed every body knows, that they vote contrary to the earnest desires of the people.

"This morning an unanimous vote of the Maryland Convention was bro't to Congress, empowering their delegates to concur in all points with Congress. All the colonies have declared their sense, except N. York, whose new Convention, now chusing is to do the business. We expect you will join us in August, as soon as Government is settled; indeed it will be necessary as Col. Braxton talks of going away in 3 weeks, and I suppose Col. Harrison will go early in August, which will leave us a bare representation. 3 or 4 months will in a great measure decide the fate of America—Tho' I think, if our people keep up their spirits and are determined to be free, whatever advantage the Enemy may gain over us this summer and fall, we shall be able to deprive them of in the winter, and put it out of their power ever to injure us again. I confess I am uneasy, lest any considerable losses on our side, shou'd occasion such a panick in the Country, as to induce a submission.

"The evil is coming, which I always dreaded, at the time when all our attention, every effort shou'd be to oppose the Enemy, we are disputing about Government and independence."

To Dr. Walter Jones, Richmond county, Va.

"Baltimore Febr'y 3d 1777. My dear friend: I this evening rec'd your Let'r by Mr. Sebastian, who I understand intends to leave this to-morrow morning, tho' it is without date, yet by the contents I find it was wrote before you had heard of the change of our affairs: which I hope will something forward the recruiting business. I agree with you that bad management has had a greater share in our bad success than fortune; but is it to be wondered at, plunged at once into an immense system, without anybody possessed of the knowledge requisite for the proper conducting the different departments, which other nations have acquired by the experience of ages; continually pressed by a powerfull Enemy, so that the present emergency necessarily engrossed all our attention; every necessary for a large Army immediately to be procured in a Country which had depended for almost everything on foreigners. A number of internal enemies exerting all their faculties to frustrate our endeavours. All things considered, the wonder, I think, is that we have succeeded so well. Yet if to these difficulties, short enlistments had not been added, I think we should have finished the war this campaign; how that happen'd, I have before informed you. We are now much better provided with necessaries than we were this time twelve months, and expect additional supplies, tho' many will fall into the hands of the Enemy, who are well informed, and are now keeping a sharp lookout. I hope the frigates in our bay will not throw Virginia into a panic. This day we rec'd a copy of the Tyrant's speech to his venal Parliament; he at length acknowledges that he has an arduous task on hand, and demands large supplies; says, he is assured of the amicable disposition of all the powers of Europe, but which seems to give him the lie, urges them to put the Kingdom into a posture of defence: pities us for preferring the tyranny of factious leaders to wholesome laws and liberty. You will soon see the curious piece in the papers. Nothing has happen'd of consequence, since the date of the inclosed: frequent skirmishes, which for the most part are much in our favor, indeed it is pretty certain the Enemy's Army is mouldering fast with sickness, desertion and captures, which will prevent their attempting anything of consequence, till reinforced; if Gen'l W. can keep enough of the Militia together till part of the new Army is raised.

"Our Gen'l thro' the whole campaign, has shown himself vastly superior in abilities to the Enemy; and I am convinced if he now had 8,000 regulars, Howe wou'd soon have reason to wish himself at Halifax. Such of your medicines as cou'd be got here I send by Mr. Crump, I hope you have rec'd them long e'er this: I need not tell you how happy it wou'd make me to see you here. Morgan is displaced and Shippen is in his room, the sick in a much better way."

"*To his Excellency President Wharton, President of the E. Supreme Council of Penna., Lancaster.*"

"War Office, Dec. 30, 1777. Sir: Congress have received such unexpected and distressing accounts from the General relative to the situation of the Army, that they have appointed a committee to fall upon immediate methods for supplying them with provisions. They are so much in want of an instant supply owing to delay and Embarrassments in the Commissary's Department and other unexpected causes that however plenty we shall have them in future, at present at least a Removal out of this State must be the immediate Consequence of even a short Continuance of their present Circumstances.

"An instant supply must be procured from this State for the support of the Army until the Supplies expected from the neighboring States arrive, as it may give Umbrage to the Inhabitants the Committee deplore the necessity *they* are under of sending Officers with Parties to collect such Cattle, Flour and Grain as the Army wants, without the least delay, as the crisis is too alarming to admit of the business being postponed on any consideration.

"It will be improper to communicate the real Situation of the Army but with the utmost Prudence and caution. Your Excellency will therefore judge in what manner the Concurrence of this State is to be procured as their vigorous Exertions are necessary in Cooperation with those of the Committee, who will, at least, till they see the Business properly conducted as doubtless it will be by the Government of this State, be obliged to give Orders for the Taking, conveying and driving all Cattle, Hogs, Pork, Flour and Grain fit for their consumption to the Army, the Persons employed for this Purpose giving Certificates to the Owners expressing as nearly as possible the Weight and Quality of them and agreeing to pay for them at such Prices as shall be settled by the Convention of Committees from the several States who are to meet at New Haven the 15th of Jan. next agreeable to a Resolution of Congress of the 22d Nov. last.

I have the honor to be with great Respect

Your very obedient Servant

FRANCIS LIGHTFOOT LEE

for the Committee."

"The Committee requests you will be pleased to inform them whether the Proclamation ordering the Inhabitants of York and Cumberland Counties to thresh out their Grain has been issued."

"Richmond, 13 Nov., 1780. My Dearest Love: I, this moment, had the pleasure of your letter by Jupiter. You are wrong indeed my Love, to confine yourself so much at home. I beg you will endeavour to amuse yourself, so much anxiety and gloomishness is enough to give you headache, which for my sake pray avoid; for nothing can compensate to me, for your want of health. Sutton's behaviour vexes me much; I cannot conceive what the fellow can mean. I now write to him. The small quantity of peas really surprises me, there were several bushels in the field when I left home; they have certainly let the fowls and other things eat them up. As Garland cannot supply oil for the leather, tallow, with a very little butter, will answer the purpose; please to weigh what you furnish that I may know whether it is properly used. Your supply of cash, gave me pleasure, as it was one more instance, added to thousands, of your affection; but upon the whole I could not help being a little angry at your having disfurnished yourself; small as it was it might have been of some little use to you, here it is as a drop in the ocean. Indeed, my dear, you must not suppose that I can have any enjoyment in which you have not a share.

"Mr. Joe Jones, R. H. L. and myself are in pretty good lodgings. Mr. Page left us a few days agoe, having received advice that his father, who had got home, was in a very dangerous way. I suppose he will not return. I am now well, the cold in my head being nearly gone. There is no prospect of the Assembly rising till Christmas, but you may be assured I will get off as soon as possible. I cannot say at present when that may be, for we have not yet a senate; but I hope we shall soon have some members to spare. As soon as I see a prospect I will inform you of it. In the meantime, let me again intreat you to fall upon some method of deverting yourself, either by going abroad or inviting others to join you at Menokin, or both.

"We have nothing new since my last; by the motion of the Enemy below, it looks as if they meant to winter there; in which case, they will give us a good deal of trouble; but at the same time, they give us an opening for a good stroke in our favour, if the French force should come upon our coast, which is not improbable. Love to Miss Sally and other friends, I am dearest Becky your ever affectionate," etc.

P. S.—"The milch cows will have the fresh gathered corn-fields to run in, where I expect they will have plenty of good food; therefore it will be better not to stall them yet, as we have a long winter to go thro."

"Menokin, 30 April, 1795. My Dear Brother [William]: I can readily conceive, and it is with very great concern, the distressed situation you must be in; and it gives me pain when I reflect how little it is in my power to assist you. Mrs. Lee and myself are little fitted for the fatigues of travelling; she, thank God! seems recovering from her long ill state of health; but I have no reason to expect otherways than a regular decline of the small portion of bodily powers that I at present possess; for the last twelve months, I feel the decline very sensibly. Were we ourselves in a proper situation we have at present no conveniency for travelling.

"I can't but still flatter myself that the good weather of May will enable you to bear easy travelling, which would probably contribute much to restore you to a tolerable state of health. As to worldly matters, I think you should make your mind easy on that score; you will at all events leave a sufficiency to your children, to make them happy, unless they are much wanting to themselves; in which case millions would be insufficient.

"It gives me comfort that there is a prospect of procuring you a housekeeper, who will remove many of your domestic inconveniences. Mr.

William Lee

Aylett Lee is seriously very confident that he can procure one against whom there is no objection; but that she is high spirited and keeps very strict hand upon the servants; the excess of which may, I think, with a little prudence be qualified; tho' a Scotch woman, he says, from particular acquaintance, he knows her to be very cleanly. He has just left us for the district court at Fredericksburg, where he is to make the necessary inquiries, settle matters and write you by post.

"I am so very little in the world and find it so impossible to get anybody to do any business for me, that I am obliged to have recourse to Mr. Wilson for a bill for Mr. Thorp; but I have reason to hope it will not fail a second time. The world seems crazy, and we old people must scuffle with it, as well as we can, for our few days of existence. With the warmest wishes that you may recover a better state of health, I am, my dear Brother, yours most affectionately."

P. S.—"I thank you for having settled the duties on my goods at Norfolk, and intended to have sent you the £17 10s. 9d. by Mr. Greenlaw, but he has sent for our letters, it not being convenient to call himself."

## William Lee.

20. William[4], the seventh son of Thomas Lee[3] (Richard[2], Richard[1]), and Hannah Ludwell, his wife, was born at Stratford on the 31st of August, 1739; his daughter Cornelia has recorded his death in these words: "Greenspring, Virginia, Saturday 27 June, 1795, at 20 minutes after six in the afternoon, my dearest Father was taken from this turbulent and mortal state, after a lingering Illness of ten months, æt. 55 years 9 months and 27 days. On the 28th June at 6 o'clock the precious remains were interred in James Town Church Yard at the south end of the graves of my Great Grandfather and Grandmother Ludwell."

While residing at London, Mr. Lee had married his cousin, Hannah Philippa, daughter of Philip Ludwell and Frances Grymes, his wife; she was born at "Greenspring," the 21st of December, 1737; and died as stated by her daughter, Cornelia, on "the 18th of August, 1784, My dear Mother Hannah Philippa Lee resigned her pure unspotted Soul into the hands of her Merciful Creator at the house of Mr. Edward Brown in Ostend, in Austrian Flanders, æt. 46 years 8 months, where she had gone on her way from Ostend to England. Her remains were deposited in the family Vault of the Ludwells in Bow Church Yard near London. She was the eldest daughter and co-heiress of the Hon'ble Philip Ludwell, Esq., of Greenspring, Virg'a, and was married on Tuesday the 7th of March, 1769, to William Lee, fourth son of the Hon'ble Thomas Lee of Stratford

Virginia, in St. Clements Dane Church in the City of Westminster, G. B."

The Greenspring mansion, once famous in the history of early Virginia, was built by Sir William Berkeley; probably just previous to his marriage with the beautiful widow, Mrs. Stephens. Greenspring was situated about five miles from Jamestown, and about two from the James River. During Berkeley's life, Greenspring was practically the seat of the government, and his party were known as the "Greenspring faction." After his death, his widow married Philip Ludwell, a widower, who lived near-by, and again the mansion became the centre of political manœuvering. Mrs. Ludwell always called herself "Lady Berkeley;" she left this estate to her husband, and he, in turn, to his son. So it descended until it came into the possession of the two daughters of the third Philip Ludwell; one of whom married William Lee, as stated; the other married John Paradise, of London, and lived there. (For further notice of the Ludwell family see under sketch of Thomas Lee, number 5.)

Of the early life and education of William Lee nothing is known; presumably he was educated at home, as was his brother, Francis Lightfoot Lee. He first appeared on record as one of the signers, in February, 1766, of the famous resolutions of the patriots of the Northern Neck. Very shortly after this, he must have gone to settle in London as a Virginian Merchant; his brother Arthur accompanied him to study law at the Temple. The two brothers appear to have soon become interested in the political questions of the hour, which were of the most exciting nature; to the general questions of political character, were, there, added those of a local nature, and the two combined kept the London merchants greatly excited. For an American, the mercantile business appears to have been simply the selling of tobacco and buying manufactured goods to send out in return for the tobacco; in the royal exchange there was "the Virginia Walk," where merchants, interested in Colonial trading, chiefly conducted their business. William Lee seems to have divided his time between mercantile and political pursuits; for he had not been long in London before he was engaged very actively in its local politics. His numerous letters, home, were about equally divided between politics and business, and it is probable that these letters kept Americans well informed as to the trend of opinion in England. From the earliest date, he warned them they could not expect any redress from the British ministry; that their only alternatives were surrender or war.

"In May, 1775, the alderman of Aldgate ward, John Shakespeare, died, and a ward-mote was held at Iron-mongers' Hall to elect a successor.

. . . Mr. Lee was elected, and made a 'spirited speech' to the electors, summarized by the *London Chronicle* as follows:—'He assured them, that though he was elected for life, he should always think himself accountable to them for the discharge of the trust reposed in him. That as a public magistrate, he should attend the dispensation of justice with care and assiduity; and as their particular magistrate, he should endeavor to promote and maintain harmony, peace, and good order in the ward. He said that as to his public principles, he held the free constitution of this country sacred and inestimable, which, as the source and security of all our happiness, it was the duty of every honest man to defend from violation; that therefore it should ever be his care, by every exertion and at every hazard, to resist the arbitrary encroachments of the Crown and its Ministers, upon the rights of the citizens, and the liberties of the people.'

" 'As an American, he declared it was his wish that the union between Great Britain and the colonies might be re-established, and remain forever, but that constitutional liberty must be the sacred bond of that union. He considered the attempts of the present administration against American liberty, as a plain prelude to the invasion of freedom in this country; but he trusted, that the virtue of the Americans, aided by the friends of freedom here, would teach the tories of this day, as their ancestors had been happily taught, how vain a thing it is to attempt wrestling their liberties from a people determined to defend them.'

"Mr. Lee was sworn in on the 14th of June, and after the meeting was over 'went in the state coach with the Lord Mayor to the Mansion House, where he was elegantly entertained by his Lordship, with a number of other guests.' " (From the *Letters of William Lee*, edited by W. C. Ford, 1891, 26–7.)

Thus, the beginning of the Revolution found Mr. Lee holding the office of sheriff in London, yet bound by all ties of kindred and by his business interests to the cause of the Colonies. "His connections and opinions were well known in the city and to the government, and he, with his brother Arthur, were soon objects of suspicion to the ministry. It was not surprising, therefore, to find in the English Records Office some letters from William to his brothers in Virginia that the administration had intercepted; and the contents of these missives fully justified the suspicion of the ministry of his disloyalty, and arouse in us a feeling of surprise that the writer was not seized or his usefulness as an agent of America repressed." (*Ibid.*, 44.)

In 1775, Alderman Lee accompanied the Lord Mayor and other city dignitaries to St. James to present to the King "an humble address and petition," praying for the suspension of all "operations of force," etc.

About the 21st of April, 1777, Mr. Lee received notice of his appointment as commercial agent for the Continental Congress in France; subsequently, in September, 1777, he was appointed to represent the Colonies at the courts of Berlin and Vienna; to the latter city he went on a fruitless errand; his brother, Arthur, going in his place to Berlin, and was likewise unable to gain any substantial results from that court. Later on, William Lee accepted the position of representative at The Hague, where he was able to conclude a treaty with the Dutch, which exerted some moral influence, though not of practical value. It is claimed that Mr. Lee was one of the earliest originators of the move which finally secured the treaty of "armed neutrality," which was to protect the freedom of commerce against the exactions of England. This treaty was of considerable value to America, as it enabled them to secure supplies from friendly nations in Europe, and if Mr. Lee was instrumental in gaining this treaty he rendered his country a valuable service.

Both William and Arthur Lee soon became involved in disputes with their colleagues, and were antagonized in their efforts by these quarrels. This unfortunate antagonism greatly enfeebled the commissioners in their efforts to serve their country. Finally the quarrel grew so bitter that the Congress recalled them and sent other agents abroad. It is not within the purpose of this work to discuss political questions, therefore the various causes which led to these quarrels cannot be considered here; it is, however, only just to the Lees to state that they were supported in their views by many of the truest patriots of the time, and subsequent disclosures would seem to prove the justness of their contentions. Though he felt himself to have been most unjustly treated, William Lee maintained a dignified silence, being "so patriotic as to submit his plea to Congress and then remain inactive," as the evidently prejudiced editor of his "Letters" puts the case. He remained in Europe until about 1784, when he returned to America, and resided on his estate, Greenspring; the last years of his life were saddened by poor health and almost total blindness. A three-volume edition of the *Letters of William Lee* have recently been published by Mr. W. C. Ford, of Brooklyn. A perusal of these letters (and they are only a small part of his letters remaining, preserved in his letter-books) show the writer to have been a true, honest and very energetic patriot.

As so many of his letters are in print now, only a few of them are given in this sketch. One to his kinsman, Thomas Sim Lee of Maryland, is interesting. Writing under date of 10th December, 1780, from Brussels, he said:

"Dear Sir,—I embrace the earliest opportunity of congratulating you on the signal honor done, by your country, to your merit and abilities, by appointing you their governor; and, though the period is trying and difficult, I have no doubt of your acquitting yourself in the important station to the advantage of your country and credit of yourself. . . .

"You have been frequently advised of the enemy's plan against North Carolina, Virginia, and Maryland, which was adopted since receiving advice of the capture of Charleston; and, to facilitate the business, many suspicious characters, natives of those States, that have been in England, doing no good to us, for some years past, have been ordered to their respective countries to aid the enemy's designs by creating division, confusion, and disturbance in your councils and operations. Should any such characters now come among you, especially if they have passed through the enemy's quarters, you cannot be too attentive to their motions and conduct. It is said that they have permission from the British ministry to take the oaths to their respective States, for reasons obvious. By Leslie's expedition to the Chesapeake, part of the enemy's grand plan has begun to be executed; and if Leslie succeeds in making any establishment in Virginia or North Carolina, next spring's campaign will be opened with the greater part of the British force against Virginia and Maryland, in which case your country will act with sound wisdom and policy by affording every powerful assistance to Virginia, which will surely prove the most effectual method to prevent the horrors of war from waging in their own country, and the flames from seizing their own homes. Every State will show its wisdom in choosing the most able and honest men among them, and who have interest of their own to lose, to represent them in Congress. The system of general and long-continued embargoes on the export of grain and provisions appears to be bad policy, as they naturally tend to produce scarcity, and, in bad seasons, even a famine, by discouraging agriculture. Your operations seem to have been much distracted by the depreciation of your paper currency: the only solid remedy seems to be in the power of Congress; and perhaps it has hitherto been neglected because it is plain and simple. A fund established in Europe (which might be established by a loan, until by the export of your commodities, it might be supported on easier terms to America), and sacredly appropriated to the sole use of paying the interest annually of the paper money, would, in a little time, establish the credit and currency of your paper on as solid a basis as the bank-notes of England or Holland; and by this means, with your paper, you would be enabled to procure supplies for your army on much better terms than you have done hitherto. The plan of conducting such a business is so plain, that I shall only add my sincere wishes that it may speedily be adopted.

"The British ministry have certainly promised Gen. Clinton to send him in the spring a re-enforcement of ten thousand men, including the recruits for the German corps now in America. Perhaps some may flatter you that the enemy will not be able to procure such a number to send; but I request you not to deceive yourselves, and be inattentive to your true interests, by relying on such rumors, or the foreign aid that may be promised you from Europe; no people can be in safety that rely on another for protection. France is indeed very powerful, both by sea and land, and will, no doubt, act vigorously against the common enemy; but so many accidents and untoward circumstances have intervened to render abortive all the attempts they have hitherto made to assist us, that, in common sense and prudence, you ought not to trust to aid that must come from Europe. If it does come, so much the better, as you may then finish the war at once; but place your confidence on yourselves alone, and then you cannot be essentially hurt.

"The Dutch have at last formally acceded, and so has the King of Prussia, to the treaty of armed neutrality, as proposed last spring by the Empress of Russia, and since entered into by Sweden and Denmark. The object of this great and powerful league is to support the freedom of general commerce and navigation against the unwarrantable pretensions of Great Britain; therefore she must now quietly permit France and Spain to be supplied with naval stores for the support of their navy, or enter into a war with this tremendous confederacy. It is, however, impossible for her to resist, which must finally give the superiority to France and Spain. I feel no little pleasure in communicating to you the completion, so far, of this confederacy, as the first traces were laid by myself two years ago; and if Congress had now in Europe ministers properly authorized to negotiate with those powers, it would not be difficult to obtain a general acknowledgment from them of the independence of America, which was my ultimate object in forming the outlines of this scheme.

"The public news in England you will see in all the papers that go by this conveyance; so that I have only to recommend to you, in the most pressing manner, a vigorous exertion, unanimity, and confidence in yourselves, which may, in all probability, end the war this year in your favor.

"We humbly present our respectful compliments to your worthy lady, and beg you to believe me to be, at all times, dear sir, your affectionate relation, and most obedient, humble servant."

To his brother, Arthur Lee, he wrote from Ostend, under date of the 22d of June, 1783:

"My Dear Brother: I have been here with my son ten daies waiting to embark in the *Virginia*, Capt. Robinson, p$^{r}$ James River in Virginia. We shall sail in two daies certainly if the wind permits, but as we are to call at Madeira this is sent by a vessel from this port to Baltimore; and if she has a quick passage this may reach you some time before we arrive. Therefore wish you to write immediately to R. H. L. to prepare to côme down to Green Spring, with his son Tom, to meet me, for I shall have great occasion to see them and our brother Loudoun[1] immediately on my arrival. Therefore shall send an express to them for that purpose the moment I get on shore. Can I get three or four carriage horses in Virginia, or are they to be got cheaper or better at Philadelphia? If they are, can you purchase two good ones for me, and contrive them to Green Spring by the middle of September at farthest? If you can, I shall be obliged to you for doing so, but remember I can't afford to give above 30 or 35£ Virginia currency apiece for stout, good, and young carriage horses from four to six years old. In August last I sent you some papers. They were directed under cover to the President of Congress, then by Mrs. Izard put up in a packet with her own letters, directed to her husband, and delivered into the hands of Gen'l DuPortail. If you have not received these letters, may inquire of Mr. Izard and Gen'l DuP. about them.

"English and French news you will have more authentic and fresh from England and France than this could carry to you. It seems pretty certain that war is by this time commenced between Russia and the Turks. The Emperor will certainly join Russia, and in this case many think that France and even England will assist the Turks. If so, the war will be general in Europe. I have just received your favor of the 19th of April from Alexandria with its inclosures, for which I greatly thank you. Adieu till I see you."

Mr. Lee sailed from Ostend on the last day of June, and arrived at Greenspring, after a tedious voyage, on the 25th of September. (*Letters of William Lee*, 946.)

Under date of 24th of April he had written to John Adams: "I propose to embark for Virg$^{a}$ in three weeks from this time, but in order to make my passage convenient I have been obliged to purchase a ship" (*Ibid.*, 944).

The correspondence between William Lee and his kinsman, the Rev.

---

[1] His brother, F. L. Lee.

Henry Lee, warden of Winchester College, England, will be read with interest, as it is chiefly on family history:

To Dr. H. Lee, dated 9 September, 1771. "Sir: It gave me much pleasure to find from a conversation the other day with Mr. Batson, my banker, who spoke very highly in your praise, that we were of the same family. He tells me that you are the 2d son of L. Lee, Esqr., late of Cotton in Shropshire, and that your elder Brother Lancelot, is now abroad at Aix, for the recovery of his health. I know your father corresponded with mine, who was of the King's privy Council in Virginia, and when he died President and Commander-in-chief over that Colony; and I remember, when a little boy in Virginia, to have seen and read a very sensible letter, and well written, from your father to mine, giving an accurate genealogical account of our family from so old a date as the Saxon government in this country; from which people, I am sure, he traced the descent of our family. From that account, it appeared that the Cotton family was the eldest branch and his immediate predecessor, who went to Virginia about one hundred and thirty years ago as Secretary and of the King's Privy Council, was a younger brother. I remember one observation he made, which struck my young mind very forcibly. He said, ''Tis worthy of remark, that, in so long a period, there has been neither spendthrift nor usurer in the family; the children moderately using the patrimony left them, without adding much to the store, by which means they have always continued independent; and, not being ambitious, they have kept nearly the same rank in life through so many centuries as the original stock was in, which is more than can be said of most families in the kingdom': which remark is surprisingly verified by the family in Virginia, which has continued from father to son, to be placed in the highest offices of honour in the colonies ever since the first Richard Lee, my great-grandfather, who went over there one hundred and thirty years ago to this very day; and I believe every inch of property left at his death (which was considerable) is now in the possession of his immediate descendants. As your father was a gentleman of learning and observation, I do not doubt his having left behind him some historical account of our family, and I shall be particularly obliged to you for giving me what information you can about it, as I am most anxious to know all the different branches in this country. Pray, is not the Earl of Litchfield of our family? For he has the name, and, I think bears our arms, or have we any relations in or near London, as I find there are many of our name? I shall be glad to hear of your brother's recovery; and, if he comes through London on his return, I shall be happy to see him on Great Tower Hill, where I shall hope for the honour of a visit from you when you come to

Town; and I shall with pleasure render you any services here that are in my power.

"I am, with great respect, Reverend Sir, Your most obedient servant and Kinsman."

Rev. Henry Lee to William Lee:[1]

"Sir, I return you Thanks for your civil and polite Letter and likewise my good Friend Mr. Batson for making me known to you. I wish it was in my Power to give you that Intelligence which you so earnestly desire of y^e^ Genealogy of our Family. The Pedigree which my Father left behind him is now in the Possession of my elder Brother, which to the best of my Remembrance traces our Family from the Saxon Government. As he is abroad, I cannot procure it from him, but I have sent to another Relation, who I believe has a copy of it. As to myself, being a younger Brother, I never made a deep Inquiry into the Origin of our Family. As far as my knowledge extends I will reveal to you. My Grandfather, Thos. Lee who was a Barrister of Law, Lincolns Inn, married a Daughter of John Eldred of Great Saxham in Norfolk, from which Alliance I'm related to William of Wykeham. He left several children, the eldest was my Father, another son who settled in Wiltshire and has left children behind him. The third, a clergyman, who had Issue, but are now dead. The Heir to the Lee in Wiltshire is a young man in the Army. He has two Brothers and several sisters. The second is a Linen Draper in London, and the youngest is now at school here and upon the Foundation as a Founders Kinsman. He is one of the Senior Boys of the school and I hope will soon succeed to New College in Oxford. My own Family are numerous, one Brother and seven Sisters, who are married and dispers'd. As soon as I can get a perfect account of our Family you shall hear from me. In the mean Time, if you shou'd have a Desire of seeing your young Relation whom you have been so kind as to send to Winchester School, you will make my Wife and me extremely happy by favouring us with your Company. You may depend upon it, I shall not fail paying my Respects to you the first Time I go to London. My Brothers Wife is now with me, she leaves me Friday next in order to go to her Husband. He gives but a very indifferent Account of himself in his Letters. I shall desire my Sister to communicate the Contents of your Letter to him. We are not related to the Earl of Litchfield. There is a Doctor Lee in London, a Physician and I'm inform'd bears our Arms. Whether he is related to us, or not, I know not. My Sister and

[1] Dated Win; Coll; 12 September, 1771.

Wife join me in Compl[ts]. to you. With Dear Sir, Your most obedient Servant and Kinsman, (Signed) Harry Lee."

William Lee to Rev. Henry Lee:

"London, 26 October, 1771.—Sir, I am afraid you will hardly forgive me for not answering sooner, your very kind and obliging favour of the 12th ulto.; but the true reason is, that my friend being out of Town, I waited his return to get a Frank, to inclose you a short account of our Family, since the first Richard Lee went to Virginia, in return for the account you so obligingly promise to procure for me. What I have written is all from memory, tho' I believe pretty accurate; but after it was written I have found in an old manuscript, this inscription taken from a cup in the University of Oxford: 'Coll: Reg: Oxon. Inscript: Cyath: Johann: Lee. Coll: Reg: Oxon. D. D. Johann: Lee natus in Capahowasick Wickacomoco in Virginiâ Americæ, filius primogenitus Richardi Lee Chiliarchæ oriundi de Morton Regis in agro Salopiensi: 1659.' This John Lee was the eldest son of my Great Grandfather, Richard Lee, who dyed as I have mentioned in Virginia and unmarried, before his Father. The Dr. Lee in London, whom you mention, is I presume my younger brother. It perhaps may be in my way to be of some service to the Mr. Lee who is in London, therefore should be glad to know the street he lives in. From some further conversation with Mr. Batson, I am inclined to think it must be your Brother that corresponded with my Father, Thomas Lee of Stratford in Virginia: since the letter I formerly mentioned was wrote about the time of the famous contest in Bridgenorth for a member of Parliament in the latter days of Sir Robert Walpole.

"I have no doubt of Master Turberville's receiving all the benefit that can be desired from your College as he has good parts and I hope good dispositions; any countenance you show him will always be thankfully acknowledged by me. I am well convinced that London is an exceeding improper place for boys or young men, more especially when not under the immediate control of their parents, for which reason it will give me much concern if there should be a necessity of Master Turberville's coming up at the two vacations. I some time ago wrote to Dr. Warton on this subject, but he has never yet favoured me with an answer. It appears to me a very eligible plan, if it can be executed, at those periods to procure a master for him, either in Winchester or some neighboring Clergyman, who might instruct him in Geography, Mathematics or Arithmetic; or to amuse him with the reading of History and country exercises.

"You will oblige me much by giving me your sentiments on it, or by proposing some other plan that you more approve of, that will answer the ends of improving his understanding and keeping his morals untainted.

"It will give me much pleasure to hear of your Brother's recovering his health and whenever you and your Lady pay a visit to this Metropolis, Mrs. Lee and myself will be very happy to see you on Tower Hill. During the Winter my time will be too much taken up with necessary business to admit of the pleasure I should receive in kissing your hands at Winchester but I will flatter myself with that happiness next Summer. I beg my respectfull Compliments may be presented to your Lady and that you will believe me to be with great regard, Dear Sir, Your most Obedient, Humble Servant and Relation."

While residing in London, William Lee wrote, as he mentioned in the preceding letter, an account of the Virginia family; this paper has never been published in full, or accurately. The following copy is taken from William Lee's original manuscript, now in the possession of William Blackstone Lee, Esq., of Seend, Wiltshire, who has kindly furnished it.

Dated London, September, 1771.—"Richard Lee, of a good family in Shropshire (and whose Picture, I am told is now at Cotton, near Bridgenorth, the seat of Launcelot Lee, Esqr.), some time in the Reign of Charles the first, went over to the Colony of Virginia, as Secretary and one of the King's Privy Council, which last post will for shortness hereafter be called of the 'Council.' He was a man of good Stature, comely visage, an enterprising genius, a sound head, vigorous spirit and generous nature. When he got to Virginia, which was at that time not much cultivated, he was so pleased with the Country that he made large settlements there with the servants he had carried over; after some years, he returned to England and gave away all the lands he had taken up, and settled, at his own expense, to those servants he had fixed on them; some of whose descendants are now possessed of very considerable Estates in that Colony.

"After staying some time in England, he returned again to Virginia, with a fresh band of adventurers, all of whom he settled there. During the civil war here Sir William Berkeley was Governor of Virginia, he and Lee, being Loyalists, kept the Colony to its allegiance; so that after the death of Charles the 1st Cromwell was obliged to send some Ships of War and Soldiers to reduce the Colony, which not being well able to resist, a Treaty was made with the Commonwealth of England, wherein Virginia was styled an independent dominion. This Treaty was ratified here, as made with a foreign Power, upon which Sir William Berkeley (who was of the same family with the present Earl of Berkeley) was removed and another Governour appointed in his room. When Charles the 2d was at Breda, Richard Lee came over from Virginia and went there to him to know if he could undertake to protect the Colony if they returned to their allegiance to him; but finding no support could be obtained, he returned to Virginia and remained quiet until the death of O. Cromwell: when he, with the assistance of Sir William Berkeley, contrived to get K. Charles the 2d proclaimed there King of England, Scotland, France, Ireland and Virginia, two years before he was restored here; and Sir William Berkeley was reinstated as his Governour, in which station he continued till some time after the Restoration, when he came over here and dyed presently. It was in consequence of this step that the motto to the Virginia arms always till after the Union, was 'En dat Virginia quintam,' but since the Union it was changed to 'En dat Virginia quartam,' that is King of Great Britain, France, Ireland and Virginia.

"Here by the way I cannot help remarking the extreme ingratitude of this Prince, Charles the 2d. Oliver Cromwell to punish Virginia, and some other parts of America, for adhering so firmly to the Royal Cause, after he had got himself quite fixed in his Supreme Authority both here and there, contrived the famous Navigation Act, upon a model he borrowed from the Dutch; by which the American Colonies were deprived of many of their ancient and valuable privileges; upon the Restoration, instead of repealing this act, it was confirmed by the whole legislature here, and to add to the ingratitude, at two other periods in his reign, Taxes were imposed on American commodities under the pretext of Regulations of Trade, from which wicked source have flowed all the bitter waters that are now likely to overwhelm America, or this country and most probably will be in the end the ruin of both.

"But to return. This Richard Lee had several children; the two eldest, John and Richard, were educated at Oxford. John took his degrees as Doctor of Physic, and returning to Virginia, dyed before his Father.[1] Richard was so clever and learn'd that some great men offered to promote him to the highest dignities in the church if his Father would let him stay in England; but this offer was refused, because the old Gentleman was determined to fix all his children in Virginia, and so firm was he in this purpose that by his will he ordered an Estate he had in England, (I think) near Stratford-by-Bow in Middlesex, at that time worth 8 or £900 per

[1] As clearly shown elsewhere (see page 69), this statement is erroneous. John evidently died about nine years after his father. But he apparently died without issue, and so left Richard heir to his father and head of the family. It was probably knowledge of this latter fact that led to the statement that John died before his father.

annum to be sold, and the money to be divided among his children. He dyed and was buried in Virginia, leaving a numerous progeny, whose names I have chiefly forgot. His eldest son, then living, was Richard, who spent almost his whole life in study and usually wrote his notes in Greek, Hebrew, or Latin, many of which are now in Virginia; so that he neither improved or diminished his paternal Estate, though at that time he might with ease have acquired, what would produce at this day a most princely revenue. He was of the Council in Virginia, and also in other offices of honour and profit, though they yielded little to him. He married a Corbin, into which family his Predecessors in England had before married, but the name was then spelt Corbyn or Corbyne, I think of Staffordshire. From this marriage he had, and left behind him when he dyed, in Virginia, which was some time after the Revolution, five sons, Richard, Philip, Francis, Thomas, Henry, and one Daughter. Richard settled in London, as a Virginia merchant, in partnership with one Thomas Corbin, a brother of his mother's; he married an heiress, in England, by the name of Silk, and by her left one son, George, and two daughters, Lettice and Martha; all of these three children went to Virginia and settled. George married a Wormeley there, who dyed leaving one daughter; then he married a Fairfax, nearly related to Lord Fairfax of Yorkshire, and dyed leaving, by his last marriage, three sons, that are now minors, and are at school in England under the care of Mr. James Russell. Lettice married a Corbin and her sister married a Turberville; their eldest children intermarried, from which union George Lee Turberville, now at School at Winton College, is the oldest issue. Philip, the second son, went to Maryland, where he married and settled. He was one of the Proprietor's Council; and dyed leaving a very numerous Family, that are now branched out at large over the whole Province, and are in plentiful circumstances. The eldest son, Richard, being now a member of the Proprietor's Council. Francis, the third son, dyed a Batchelor. Thomas, the fourth son, though with none but a common Virginia Education, yet having strong natural parts, long after he was a man, he learned the Languages without any assistance but his own genius, and became a tolerable adept in Greek and Latin. He married a Ludwell, of whose genealogy I must give a short account, being materially interested therein.

"The Ludwells, though the name is now extinct, are an old and honourable family of Somersetshire in England; the original of them, many ages since, coming from Germany. Philip Ludwell and John Ludwell, being brothers and sons of a Miss Cottington, who was heiress of James Cottington, the next brother and heir to the famous Lord Francis Cottington, of whom a pretty full account may be seen in Lord Clarendon's *His-*

*tory of the Rebellion*, were in Court favour after the Restoration of Charles the 2d. John was appointed Secretary and one of the Council in Virginia, where I believe he dyed without issue. Philip, the eldest brother, went to America Governour of Carolina, and from whence he went to Virginia and married the widow of Sir Willliam Berkeley, by whom he had a daughter[1] that married a Col. Parke, who was afterwards Governour of the Leeward Islands in the West Indies, and dyed in Antigua, the seat of his Government, and one son named Philip. After some time old Philip Ludwell returned to England and dying here was buryed in Bow church near Stratford; his son, Philip, remained in Virginia, where his father had acquired a very capital estate, and married a Harrison, by whom he had two daughters: Lucy, the eldest, who married a Col. Grymes, who was of the Council in Virginia, and Hannah, who married the before mentioned Thomas Lee, and one son, Philip. This Philip was, as his father had been, of the Council in Virginia. He married a Grymes by whom he had several children, most of whom dyed in their infancy, and in the year 1753, his wife dyed; in 1760, he came over to England for his health and in 1767, he dyed here, when the male line of Ludwell became extinct; he left heiresses three daughters, Hannah Philippa, Frances, and Lucy. The second daughter is since dead, unmarried.

"This Thomas Lee, by his Industry and Parts, acquired a considerable Fortune, for being a younger Brother, with many children, his Paternal Estate was very small. He was appointed of the Council, and though he had very few acquaintances in England, he was so well known by reputation, that upon his receiving a loss by fire, the late Queen Caroline sent him over a bountiful present out of her own Privy Purse. Upon the late Sir William Gooch's being recalled, who had been sometime Governor of Virginia, he became President and Commander-in-chief over the Colony; in which station he continued for sometime 'til the King thought proper to appoint him Governor of the Colony; but he dyed in 1750, before his commission got over to him. He left by this marriage with Miss Ludwell six sons, Philip Ludwell, Thomas Ludwell, Richard Henry, Francis Lightfoot, William, Arthur, and two daughters, all well provided for in Point of Fortune. Philip Ludwell is now of the Council in Virginia, is married, has two daughters and lives at Stratford on Potomack River, Virginia; Thomas Ludwell is married, has several children and lives at Bellevue on

---

[1] This seems to be an error, for, so far as is known, Lady Berkeley never had any issue. This Philip Ludwell was twice married; his first wife had been twice married before she married him. She was Lucy, daughter of Robert Higginson, and had married successively Major Lewis Burwell and Col. William Bernard. (*Va. Magazine*, etc., I, 178.) Philip Ludwell's brother was *Thomas*, not *John*, as given by William Lee.

Potomack River, Virginia; Richard Henry is married, and lives at Chantilly, Potomack River, Virginia, and has several children; Francis Lightfoot, two years ago, married a daughter, and one that will be a coheiress of the Hon. John Tayloe of Virginia; he has no child, and lives at Menokin on Rappahanoc River in Virginia. William, the writer of this account, in 1769, married in London Miss Hannah Philippa Ludwell. He has no children and is settled as a Virginia merchant on Tower Hill, London. Arthur studied Physic at Edinburgh, where he took his degrees, but disliking the profession, he entered about two years ago as a student of law at Lincoln's Inn and is now at No. 3 Essex Court in the Temple, prosecuting his studies. The two daughters, Hannah and Alice, were both well married, and are settled in America. Henry, the fifth brother, and next to Thomas, married a Bland, and left John, Richard, Henry and Lettice. John is dead without issue; Richard is still living, and unmarried, though 45 years old, which is a great age in Virginia to be single, and his seat is called Lee Hall on Potomack River Virginia. Henry is married and has several children; his seat is called Leesylvania, on Potomack River, Virginia. The only sister of these five brothers, married a Fitzhugh, a considerable family in Virginia, and left several children. Her descendants are still living."

William Lee's will was dated the 24th of February, 1789; two codicils were added at later dates; it was probated at Richmond, on the 11th of June, 1796.

In the name of God Amen. I William Lee of Virginia late alderman of London being of sound disposing sense and memory do make publish and declare this instrument or written paper to be and contain my last will and Testament hereby revoking annulling and rendering void to all intents and purposes all former wills or testaments by me heretofore made. First my soul I commit to our Gracious God and Heavenly father stedfastly hoping that through his infinite mercy and the precious merits of our blessed redeemer Jesus Christ it will enter into eternal salvation—Amen. Item, I desire that my body may be committed to the earth wherever I may chance to die without any pomp or parade, or any unnecessary expense whatever. Item, my will and desire is that my executor herein after named, do pay as soon after my decease as may be consistent with the good of my estate all my just debts that is to say all demands not debarr'd by any act or acts of limitation and which shall be supported by indifferent testimony and no others; the various affairs in which I have been concerned in the variety of Countries in which my transactions have been, and the circumstances of the late revolution which have necessarily occasioned the loss of many material papers and vouchers together with the misfortune of losing my eyesight which has caused my accounts to be more imperfect than they otherwise would have been, render this precaution absolutely necessary. Item, I give and devise and bequeath to my dearly beloved son William Ludwell Lee and his heirs forever all that estate real personal and mixed lying being and situate in James City county James Town and the City of Williamsburg which descended to his mother my late dear wife Hannah Philippa Lee as coheiress and legatee of her late father the Honourable Philip Ludwell and as coheiress to her late sister Frances Ludwell with all the Horses, Mares, colts, mules, asses, Horn'd cattle, sheep Hogs and stocks of every kind and all the plantation utensils that may be on said estate at the time of my decease, and also all my Books plate and furniture that may be in my house at Greenspring or in the hands of any other persons or person at the time of my decease, except such particular Books and pieces of plate or furniture which I shall herein after bequeath to either of my two daughters Portia and Cornelia. Item, I give devise and bequeath unto my dear daughter Portia Lee and her heirs forever all that tract or parcell of Land lying and being on the waters of Bull run and in the County of Prince William or Loudoun which I purchased of John Page Esq$^{r}$. of Rosewell in the County of Gloucester containing by estimation twelve hundred and fifty acres more or less which tract of land was conveyed to me and my heirs forever by the said John Page by deed bearing date on the twelfth day of October in the year one thousand seven hundred and eighty seven and by him acknowledged in the General Court on the twenty sixth day of the said October in the said year and then and there ordered to be recorded together with all houses and improvements advantages and hereditaments and appurtenances to the said tract of land in any wise belonging when she shall arrive at the age of twenty one years or on her day of marriage provided she doth not marry without the consent of a majority of her Guardians herein after appointed who shall act in that capacity, to be obtained in writing and not before she shall arrive to the age of sixteen years, for my will and meaning is that if she shall marry before she shall be of the age of sixteen years or after that before she shall be of the age of twenty one years without the consent in writing previously obtained of a majority of her guardians aforesaid as aforesaid in either of the above cases the devise herein made of the land aforesaid shall be void and of no effect but the said land shall pass and go to my son William Ludwell Lee and his heirs forever. Item, I give and bequeath to my said dear daughter Portia Lee twelve hundred and fifty pounds sterling money of Great Britain, to be paid to her at the age of twenty one years or on her day of marriage, but upon the same condition and proviso which hath been herein before annexed to the devise of the land herein before given to her, and in the mean time my will and desire is that the profits of the land herein before devised to her and the interest of the legacy of twelve hundred and fifty pounds sterling aforesaid shall be applied from the time of my decease to her maintenance and education or so much thereof as my executors herein after mentioned or a majority of them shall think proper and the overplus if any there be shall be paid as before mentioned with regard to the said money legacy to my said daughter Portia Lee. Item, I give and bequeath unto my said dear daughter Portia Lee a Mahogany desk and bookcase which stands in my chamber and was used always by her late dear Mother together with all the printed and manuscript Books therein at the time of my decease. Item, I give and bequeath to my dear daughter Cornelia Lee two thousand pounds sterling money of Great Britain to be paid to her when she shall arrive to the age of twenty one years or on the day of her marriage, provided she doth not marry without the consent of a majority of her Guardians herein after appointed who shall act in that capacity to be obtained in writing and not before she shall arrive to the age of sixteen years for my will and meaning is that if she shall marry before she shall be of the age of sixteen years or after that before she shall be of the age of twenty one years without the consent in writing previously obtained of a majority of her Guardians aforesaid as aforesaid in either of the above cases the bequest herein made to her shall be void and of no effect but the said legacy shall pass and go to my son William Ludwell Lee forever and in the mean time until the said legacy shall be payable to her my will and desire is that the profits or interest of the said two thousand pounds sterling from the time of my decease shall be applied to her maintenance and education or so much thereof as my Executors herein after mentioned or a majority of them shall think proper and the overplus if any there be shall be paid as before mentioned with regard to the legacy itself to my said dear daughter Cornelia Lee. Item, My will and desire is that my property in the British Funds which is placed there in the names of Thomas Rogers and George Welch Bankers of London shall not be applied either to payment of debts due from me or of any of the legacies herein bequeathed until after my other personal Estate not herein before given shall have been applied and found insufficient. Item, I hereby nominate constitute and appoint the Honorable John Blair of the City of Williamsburg, Benjamin Harrison, Esq[r.] of Brandon in Prince George County and my two dear Brothers Francis Lightfoot Lee and Arthur Lee Esq[r.] to be executors of this my last Will and Testament and guardians to my children and I also appoint my dear sister Rebecca Lee of Menokin guardian of my two dear daughters Portia and Cornelia Lee particularly desiring they may be under her sole care and direction respecting their education. Item, I give to each of my above mentioned executors a mourning ring of five guineas value as a testimony of my esteem and in full of every claim that they might or may have against my estate as being executors thereof, and my meaning is that my executors or any of them shall not be discharged by virtue of this will or any clause thereof from the payment of any debt or debts that they or any of them now owe or at the time of my decease may be owing to me. Item, I give to my dear sister Rebecca Lee of Menokin a mourning ring of ten guineas value. Item, My will and desire is that my son William Ludwell Lee may henceforth omit the name of Lee and take and bear the name of William Ludwell only that the family name of Ludwell so ancient and honorable both in England and America, from which he is lineally descended, may be revived. Item, It is my will and desire and earnest request to my executors that they take special care that no woodland be cleared and that no timber or other trees be cut down on any part of my estate in James City County on any pretext whatever except for the necessary purposes of my said estate that is to say for firewood to be used on my plantations for the necessary building and repairing of the houses for making and repairing the fences on my lands, for tobacco Hogsheads and tight casks for the use of my plantations and for wheelwright timber to be worked by my own people and for coal for my blacksmith's shop. Item, I desire that my Executors may have two women servants at least to be occupied in and about my house Greenspring and a man and a boy to work in the gardens to take care of the fruit trees on my several plantations and to take [care] of my stables. Lastly, I give devise and bequeath to my son William Ludwell Lee and his heirs forever all the rest and residue of my Estate not herein before devised whether the same be real personal or mixed. In Witness whereof I have hereunto this twenty fourth day of February in the year one thousand seven hundred and eighty nine subscribed my name and fixed my seal.

I William Lee of Greenspring in the Parish and County of James City and Commonwealth of Virginia do make and publish and declare this writing to be a codicil to my last Will and Testament dated (I think) in February 1789 which is now in the possession of my Brother Francis Lightfoot Lee Esq[r.] of Menokin in the County of Richmond and Commonwealth aforesaid: Whereas in my said last Will and Testament I have given and devised to my only son William Ludwell and his heirs forever all my lands both freehold and leasehold in the s[d.] County of James City all my Household lots in Williamsburg and James Town which I hold in right of his late dear Mother Hannah Philippa eldest daughter and coheiress of the late Honorable Philip Ludwell, also all my lands in Loudoun or Prince William County which I purchased of John Page Esq[r.] of Rosewell in the County of

Gloucester also all my negro slaves, horses, horn'd cattle, sheep, goats, hogs, asses, mules and stock of every kind with all my plantation utensils which may be on my said lands and furthermore have made him my said son my residuary legatee whereby he will be entitled to and inherit all that Tract or Parcel of Land adjoining to Green Spring being part of the Land commonly called and known by the name of the Main or Governor's Land which I have lately bargained for with the Professors of William and Mary Colledge and with the approbation of the Visitors of the said Colledge. Now I do hereby declare and make known that my intention by the before mentioned legacies and devises was and is to give and bequeath all the said before mentioned lands houses lots negro slaves with their increase, and all the other property therein mentioned to my said son William Ludwell and his heirs forever when he shall arrive at the age of twenty one years and in the meantime so much of the produce or profits thereof as my executors shall think proper shall be applied to his maintenance and education and the remainder of such profits or produce if any there be to go and descend to him with the other real and personal Estate. But if my said son William Ludwell should depart this life before he arrives at the age of twenty one years then and in that case I give and bequeath to my eldest daughter Portia and her heirs forever when she shall arrive at the age of twenty-one years if she be then unmarried, or at the age of eighteen if she be then married or at any time thereafter when she shall be married before she arrives at the age of twenty one years provided always that she marries agreeably to the restrictions pointed out in my said last Will and Testament all that tract or parcel of land lying and being in the said Parish and County of James City commonly called and known by the name of Green Spring whereon are the plantations called Green Spring Scotland and Verneys and several tenements, also all that tract or parcel of Land adjoining Greenspring being part or parcel of the tract of land commonly called and known by the name of the Main or Governor's land which I have lately bargained for with the professors of William and Mary Colledge and with the approbation of the Visitors of the said Colledge, also all my Lots in James Town also half of my negroe slaves respecting quantity and quality in which half all the tradesmen are to be included together with one half of all my Horses, horn'd cattle, sheep, Hogs and stocks of every kind and all my plantation utensils that may be on the said lands and the produce and profits of the said lands and personal estate from the time of my decease or that of my said son William Ludwell whichever shall last happen shall go and descend to my said daughter Portia together with the real and personal estate herein given to her. Item, In case my said son Wm. Ludwell departs this life before he arrives at the age of twenty one years then and in that case I give and devise to my daughter Cornelia and her heirs forever when she shall arrive at the age of twenty one years if she be then unmarried or at the age of eighteen years if she shall be then married or at any time thereafter before she arrives at the age of twenty one years when she shall be married provided she marries agreeably to the restrictions mentioned in my said last Will and Testament all those two tracts or parcels of land lying and being in the said County of James City commonly called and known by the names of Hotwater and New Quarter all my Houses and lots in the City of Williamsburg and all my lands in Loudoun or Prince William County which I purchased of John Page Esq$^{r.}$ of Gloucester County and also the remaining one half of all my negro slaves of all my horses, horn'd cattle, sheep, Hogs and stock of every kind and all the plantation utensils that may be on the lands herein given to her the produce and profits of the said real and personal estate from the time of my decease or that of my son William Ludwell which ever shall last happen shall go and descend to my said daughter Cornelia, together with the real and personal estate herein before given to her. Item, I hereby nominate and appoint Mr. Robert Andrews of the City of Williamsburg

Mr. William Wilkinson Junr. of the Main executors of this Codicil and of my last Will and Testament jointly with those gentlemen mentioned as my executors in my said last Will and Testament. Item, I give to the said Robert Andrews and William Wilkinson Junr. to each of them a mourning ring of five guineas value as a mark of my esteem and compensation for their trouble as my Executors. Item, I desire that this codicil may be proved and recorded in the same Court with my said last Will and testament. Given under my hand at Green Spring this twenty first day of April in the year of our Lord one thousand seven hundred and ninety.

Know all men that I William Lee of Greenspring in James City County and Commonwealth of Virginia being of sound disposing sense and memory do make ordain publish and declare this to be a Codicil to my last Will and Testament to which I shall subscribe my name at the bottom this fourth day of February in the year of our Lord Jesus Christ seventeen hundred and ninety five, Whereas I did on the sixth day of October last at a public sale of the lands and other property of John Warburton deceased purchase of his Ex'ors one tract of land in the Main containing by a late survey three hundred acres whereon the late John Harriss some time since lived and dyed and one other tract of Land lying in the pine woods between the land of Wm. Wilkinson Junr. and John D. Wilkinson containing between fifty and sixty acres more or less for which two tracts or parcels of land the said Executors of John Warburton deceased have made and passed deeds of conveyance to me which are recorded in the County Court of James City, Now I do by this Codicil give and bequeath the said two above mentioned tracts or parcels of land with all their appurtenances to my son William Ludwell and his heirs forever exactly in the same manner that I have given to him my other land in James City County with this further condition that he is in consideration of this devise to pay to my two daughters Portia and Cornelia Lee the sum of seven hundred pounds current money to be equally divided between them their respective portions or moieties of the said seven hundred pounds to be paid to each of them when they shall arrive at the age of twenty one years or be married which ever event shall first take place but in case my said son William Ludwell should depart this life before he arrives at the age of twenty one years then I give and bequeath the said two before mentioned tracts or parcels of land with all their appurtenances to my daughter Portia Lee and her heirs forever she or they in consideration of this devise paying to my daughter Cornelia Lee the sum of five hundred pounds current money when she the said Cornelia Lee shall arrive at the age of twenty one years or be married which ever event shall first take place. In witness whereof I have hereunto set and subscribed my name the day and year above written.

William and Hannah Philippa (Ludwell) Lee had four children, two sons and two daughters.

i, WILLIAM LUDWELL[5], born at London the 23d of January, 1775; died at "Greenspring" the 24th of January, 1803. He was buried in the old Jamestown church-yard, near his father. In his will he asked that he be buried there, saying: "I desire that my body may be committed to the earth near the grave of my dear respected father in the church yard at James Town. The spot where I wish to be interred is designated by two pegs of Sycamore on the south side of the grave of my late father." He also desired that the lot be inclosed with a substantial brick wall five feet high and an iron gate. He bequeathed all his library, excepting the family Bible, to Bishop Madison; set all his slaves free and provided for them; gave 500 bushels of corn per annum to William and Mary College; remainder of estate to his two sisters.

ii, PORTIA[5], born in 1777; died the 19th of February, 1840; married William Hodgson, formerly of White Haven, England, who died at Alexandria the 7th of November, 1820; they had eight children: 1, William Ludwell, who died the 27th of September, 1841, aged 42 years. 2, Cornelia Ludwell, who died the 4th of June, 1846; 3, Caroline Octavia. 4, Charles Henry. 5, Augustus Henry. 6, Julia Augusta. 7, Elizabeth Augusta, who died on the 6th of June, 1825, aged 11 years. 8, Sydney Ludwell Hodgson, who died in 1869.

iii, BRUTUS[5], born in November, 1778; died in June, 1779.

iv, CORNELIA[5], was born at Brussels the 3d of March, 1780; died in 1815; married on the 16th of October, 1806, John Hopkins, Esq., of Richmond; their issue were: 1, Portia Lee, born at "Bellevue" the 30th of August, 1807; married Dr. Robert T. Baldwin, of Winchester, and left issue. 2, Hannah Philippa Ludwell, born at Alexandria the 3d of August, 1811; married her cousin, Cassius Francis Lee (57, q. v.), and left issue. 3, Mary Anna, born at Alexandria on the 8th of January, 1814; married the Rev. William M. Jackson on the 23d of April, 1835, and left issue; she died in 1843; he in 1855. 4, Henrietta Lee Hopkins, born at Alexandria the 2d of April, 1819; died the 14th of February, 1839; married on the 24th of August, 1837, the Rev. Richard K. Meade, who died the 19th of November, 1892, and left one son, the Rev. W. H. Meade, D. D.

## DR. ARTHUR LEE, LL. D., F. R. S.

21. ARTHUR[4], youngest son of Thomas Lee[3] (Richard[2], Richard[1]) and Hannah Ludwell, his wife, was born at Stratford the 21st of December, 1740, and died at his home, "Lansdown," in Middlesex county, the 12th of December, 1792. After a course of private tuition Arthur was sent to Eton, from thence to Edinburgh, where he studied "general science and polite literature," and, later, medicine. He obtained a diploma, approving him as a general scholar and conferring the degree of M. D. He was always fond of botanical studies, a subject frequently mentioned in his letters; for his thesis, upon graduation, he wrote on "Peruvian Bark," and obtained the prize given each year for the best thesis on a botanical topic.

Arthur Lee

His essay was so much approved that it was "decreed" to be published under the direction and authority of the university.

Before returning to Virginia Dr. Lee traveled through Holland and parts of Germany. Soon after his return he commenced the practice of medicine at Williamsburg, at that time the chief town of the State. Like many others, who find the study of medicine agreeable enough, but its practice very unsatisfactory, he soon gave it up and turned his attention to law and politics, pursuits that suited his restless, energetic disposition much better than medicine. Early in 1767 he returned to England in company with his brother William, the one to study law,[1] the other to enter a mercantile life. Both soon interested themselves in the political questions of the hour. These were in an agitated condition; many in England were dissatisfied with the ministry in both its domestic and colonial policies. It was the endeavor of the Lees to unite this element of opposition in favor of the Colonies by a shrewd combination of colonial with domestic affairs. Mr. Lee was admitted to the bar in April, 1775, and began the practice of the law in London. In 1776 he left London for Paris and other Continental cities to act as a commissioner for the American Colonies. Previous to his departure he had been acting as agent at London for the Colonies of Massachusetts and Virginia. He had also been instrumental, by means of a vast correspondence, in bringing the American cause to the attention of many in England and on the Continent. By his letters to friends in America, he had been keeping them in touch with the trend of political events in England. Thus, on the one hand, he aroused public sympathy in Europe; on the other, he warned the Americans of their danger. It is not doubtful that he was able, by this correspondence, to effect much for the cause of the Colonies. Few writers of that period wielded a more vigorous pen than Arthur Lee.

In the spring of 1775, the Mayor, Aldermen, and Livery of London desired to present a petition to the King as a remonstrance against the measures of his ministry in their colonial policy; at their request, Dr. Lee wrote this remonstrance. A copy of it was also sent to the American Congress, who ordered a suitable reply to be made. Richard Henry Lee, as chairman of the committee, drafted this reply. Neither of the brothers were aware of the part the other had acted in this matter until they met years after its occurrence. Besides the correspondence, already alluded to,

---

[1] It appears from some of his letters that Arthur Lee went to England with the intention of practicing medicine there, but later turned to the law. A list of "American Templars" (*Pa. Magazine of History*, XIV, 97) gives "Arthur Lee of Virginia" as entered at "Lincoln's Inn" in 1770 and at "The Middle Temple" in 1773.

Dr. Lee published his "Monitor's Letters," addressed to the people of the Colonies, and an "Appeal to the English Nation," which was greatly admired and for some time attributed to Lord Chatham. Under the signature of "Junius Americanus," he published a series of letters. They were so bright, so able, that Junius wrote to Wilkes: "My American namesake is plainly a man of abilities. . . . You may assure Dr. Lee that to *my* heart and understanding the names of American and Englishmen are synonymous; and that as to any future taxation upon America, I look upon it as near to impossible as the highest improbability can go.

"*I hope, that since he has opposed me, where he thinks me wrong, he will be equally ready to assist me, where he thinks me right.*" [1]

Before his death, Dr. Lee had commenced a memoir of the Revolution, but did not live to complete it. Much of the part he did write has been lost, a fragment only being preserved. Some extracts from this will give a better idea of him and of his work than anything from the pen of another: "It is to aid in placing the history of the American Revolution in its true light, that the following memoirs are written. The author of them was concerned in its events from its commencement to its conclusion. He was employed generally in the highest stations, and in the most secret and confidential transactions. He always preserved the original papers and letters, on which he founded the journal from which the following memoirs are extracted. He is therefore sure of their authenticity, as well as of his determination, *ne quid falsi dicere; ne quid acre narrare.*

"The writer of these memoirs was in London when the repeal of the stamp-act was agitated in both houses of parliament. He heard Mr. Pitt and Lord Camden deliver those celebrated speeches on this question, which would have immortalized them as orators and statesmen. Though the obnoxious act was repealed, yet he was persuaded that the spirit which dictated it and was still resting near the throne was not changed. With this impression he returned to Virginia.

"It was not long before my apprehensions were realized, by the passage of an act of the British Parliament for imposing duties on tea, paper, glass, etc., exported to the colonies. This was changing the mode but preserving the principle of the stamp-act. This was soon and ably pointed out in some periodical letters, under the signature of a 'Pennsylvania Farmer.' These letters were written in a popular style, were universally read and as universally admired.

"I endeavoured to aid their operation in alarming and informing my

---

1 *Life of Arthur Lee*, I, 25.

countrymen by a series of letters under the signature of 'Monitor.' In the course of a few months it was manifest that the people of this continent were not disposed to be finessed out of their liberties; and as I knew the British cabinet was determined to enforce rather than abandon the usurpation, I was persuaded that a very serious contest was approaching. To prepare for that was the next object in my mind. The most effectual way to accomplish this, it seemed to me, was to form a correspondence with leading patriotic men in each colony. I wrote myself to London, where the acquaintance I had would enable me to obtain speedy and accurate information of the real designs of the British ministry, which being communicated to leading men in the several colonies, might enable them to harmonize in one system of opposition, since on this harmony the success of their opposition would depend. In pursuance of this plan I went to Maryland, to Philadelphia, and New York. The men I had in contemplation were Mr. Daniel Dulany, who had written some able pieces, styled 'Considerations on the Stamp-Act;' Mr. John Dickinson, who was the author of the celebrated 'Farmer's Letters,' and the leader of the Livingston party in New York, who is at present the governor of New Jersey.

"I found Mr. Dulany so cold and distant that it seemed in vain to attempt anything with him. Mr. Dickinson received me with friendship, and the contemplated correspondence took place. Mr. Livingston, of New York, was absent from the city in the country, lamenting the death of a child, so that I did not see him. The time I was to sail for England now approached; I could not therefore proceed farther eastward. Embarking with one of my brothers, we arrived safely in London.

"The proceedings against Mr. Wilkes at this time agitated the nation. Mr. Wilkes was the idol of the people, and the abhorrence of the king. All the power of prerogative, all the influence of the crown, and every practicable perversion of law, were employed to subdue him. Of courage, calm and intrepid, of a flowing wit, accommodating in his temper, of manners convivial and conversible, an elegant scholar, and well read in constitutional law, he stood the Atlas of popular opposition. Such was the man against whom the whole powers of the crown were mustering their rage; and whom, to use the words of Junius, 'the rays of royal indignation collected upon him, served only to illuminate, but could not consume.' Mr. Wilkes was then confined in the King's Bench, as the printer and publisher of the 'Essay on Woman.' The city of London was the stronghold of popular opposition, and the Society of the Bill of Rights the most active in conducting it. This society consisted of real or pretended personal friends of Mr. Wilkes; but some insinuated themselves with very different views.

"Having taken this view of the political condition of England, I formed the plan of connecting myself with the opposition; and the grievances of America with those of England. For this purpose I became a member of the Bill of Rights, and purchased the freedom and livery of the city of London. By these means I acquired a voice and influence in all the measures of that society, and in the proceedings and elections of the city. An acquaintance with Mr. Wilkes soon grew into intimacy and confidence. The arbitrary views of the crown originated in the same spirit on both sides of the Atlantic. To sensible men, therefore, the combining of the complaints of the people of America and England appeared just and politic. I procured the introduction of the grievances of America into the famous Middlesex Petition; and to keep them alive in the popular mind I commenced and continued a periodical paper, under the signature of Junius Americanus. My brother established himself in London, was elected an alderman and one of the sheriffs. Our footing was now strong, and the American cause was firmly united with that of England. During these transactions I studied law in Lincoln's Inn and the Middle Temple, and being called to the bar, practiced in the King's bench and on the home circuit. This situation increased my opportunities of serving my country. . . .

"Of the disposition and intentions of the administration I kept my correspondents in America constantly informed, with this constant opinion, that they must prepare to maintain their liberties at all hazards. My conduct in England had reached America in so favorable a light that the house of Representatives in Massachusetts elected me their agent, in case of the absence or death of Dr. Franklin. At that time I was not personally known to any member of the house. . . .

"My political progress had made me acquainted with many of the leaders of all parts of the opposition, such as Lord Shelburne, Mr. Beckford, Lord Temple, Mr. Dunning, Sergeant Glynn, Col. Barré, Mr. Wilkes, the Aldermen Sawbridge, Townsend, and Oliver. It was by constantly comparing the different ideas of those gentlemen with one another, and with the plans and proceedings of the ministers, that I was able to form a pretty accurate judgment, both of the real intentions of the latter and how far America was warranted in relying on the support of the former. These were the two principal objects of my pursuit. The dearest rights and interests of my immediate country were at hazard. It would not have been wise to have trusted these to the mere issues of political intrigues and party opposition for place and preferment. Some, however, of the above leaders appeared to me hearty in the cause of America, as well as of England.

Their advocation of liberty was general. Among these the most illustrious was the Earl of Shelburne. Him had I long known, long studied, and found his conduct uniform and unimpeachable. But the private life of this nobleman was no less the subject of my esteem and admiration."[1]

In November of 1775 Congress appointed a committee to secretly correspond with the friends of America in Great Britain "and other parts of the world." The committee chose Dr. Lee their secret agent in London; this letter from them was copied from the original MSS.[2]

"Philadelphia, 12th December, 1775. Sir: By this conveyance we have the pleasure of transmitting to you sundry printed papers, that such of them as you think proper may be immediately published in England. . . . It would be agreeable to Congress to know the disposition of foreign powers towards us, and we hope this object will engage your attention. We need not hint that great circumspection and impenetrable secrecy are necessary. The Congress rely on your zeal and abilities to serve them, and will readily compensate you for whatever trouble and expense a compliance with their desire may occasion. We remit you for the present £200. Whenever you think the importances of your dispatches may require it, we desire you to send an express boat with them from England, for which service your agreement with the owner there shall be fulfilled by us here."

In the winter of 1776 Dr. Lee went to Paris, in pursuance of this commission; and at various times thereafter he visited other capitals on the same errand—seeking supplies and making friends for the Colonies. He wrote his brother, R. H. Lee, in 1777: "I have within this year been at the several courts of Spain, Vienna, and Berlin, and I have found this of France is the great wheel that moves them all." It was in February, 1777, that Dr. Lee was selected as the commissioner from Congress to proceed to Madrid, and endeavor to interest the Spanish court in the struggle between England and the Colonies. As soon as the British ministry heard of his appointment they instructed their minister at Madrid to protest against his reception. In consequence, Dr. Lee was stopped at Burgos, by an order not to proceed further. He returned so spirited a protest that the Spanish government finally allowed him to proceed to Madrid; once there, he exerted himself with great zeal to influence that court, but with no definite result. The Spanish, being afraid to provoke the English ministry, were plentiful in promises and assurances of the good-will of the king and people. Finally Dr. Lee was granted permission to make contracts with any mer-

---

[1] *Life of Arthur Lee*, I, pp. 243, *et.seq.*
[2] *Ibid.*, I, 53.

chants, etc., for arms and ammunition; and the Spanish ambassador at Paris was instructed to keep up a friendly intercourse with the American commissioners at that capital. From this intercourse they finally obtained a large loan.

William Lee, his brother, then stationed at The Hague, was selected by Congress to act as their agent at Berlin. When this appointment was received at Paris, the commissioners there decided that William should remain in Holland, as his services there were too valuable to make it advisable for him to go to Berlin. Consequently, they desired that Dr. Lee should take his commission, and proceed to Berlin, in his place. This he did, but he found the difficulties in the way of accomplishing any good for America were very great, as Frederick the Great was under treaty obligations to England, and was not bound in any way to America. The objects of his mission were to establish communication between Prussia and America; to prevent any further raising of German auxiliaries for the English army, and to gain permission to purchase supplies. In these designs, Dr. Lee succeeded partially; Frederick refused to receive him officially, and thus recognize the United States, but he authorized his minister to conduct secret correspondence with him. While residing at Berlin, some one stole his private papers from his room at the hotel; Dr. Lee immediately complained to the King. An answer was returned by the King that the police would investigate the affair, which resulted in the prompt return of the papers. At the request of Frederick, the English government recalled their envoy, it being proven that he was concerned in the theft of the papers.

Dr. Lee continued to correspond with Baron Schulenberg, the Prussian minister, after his return to Paris. In one letter, Schulenberg wrote:

". . . The events of this war become every day more interesting. I again pray you to communicate to me regularly all the news you may receive. The King seems much interested in it. His Majesty wishes that your efforts may be crowned with success, and as I told you in mine of the 13th of December, he will not hesitate to acknowledge your independency as soon as France, which is more immediately interested in the issue of the contest, shall set the example."

Shortly after the news of the surrender of General Burgoyne, at Saratoga, was received, the French court began negotiations for signing a treaty with America; in these negotiations, Dr. Lee took a prominent part, and was one of the signers of that treaty on the part of America. Soon after this event, he was recalled, and John Adams was appointed in his place. This recall was due to violent dissensions between the commissioners; especially between Dr. Lee on the one part, and Dr. Franklin and Silas

Deane on the other.[1] The two latter accused Dr. Lee of being quarrelsome, captious, and dishonest in his professed loyalty, etc., while he wrote to his brother, R. H. Lee, under date of 9th of January, 1778, "Things are going on worse and worse every day among ourselves, and my situation is more painful. I see in every department neglect, dissipation, and private schemes. Being in trust here I am responsible for what I cannot prevent, and these very men will probably be the instruments of having me one day called to an account for their misdeeds."[2]

Of this quarrel, much has been written, and in fact is still being written. To give the reader a fair idea of Dr. Lee's part therein, a few quotations from some of the most prominent and patriotic actors in those scenes are given. It is certain that Dr. Lee held until his death the esteem and friendship of the purest and ablest men of the Revolutionary period; the friendship of such men should be ample vindication against slanders from any source. His biographer has written:[3] "A brief attempt has been made to give the reader a general idea of the value of his services during the period which elapsed from October, 1778, until the end of the year 1779. He who shall read his correspondence during this time, will perceive that it has been thought better to leave the reader to form a due estimate of the zeal and disinterestedness of Mr. Lee's services from the materials of this memoir, than from an elaborate effort of his biographer to present here a full statement of his labors.

"Great and undeniable as has been the patriotism and services of Mr. Lee, he did not escape the malicious insinuations and false charges of detected peculation and conscious infidelity to public trust; while he experienced the inevitable consequence of an honest performance of duty, the persecution of a bating faction. A short period of his life afforded another instance, in addition to the many furnished by the history of all times, that

---

[1] John Adams, after investigating on the spot the causes of these dissensions, wrote his impressions concerning them to James Lovell. On the one side he found the capricious temper of an ardent patriot, Arthur Lee, on the other the egregious vanity of Franklin played upon and controlled by Deane, who was even more "than complaisant to interested adventurers." Writing from Passy, France, under date of the 20th of February, 1779, Mr. Adams said:

. . . "Our old incidental agent is an honest man, faithful and zealous in our cause. But there is an acrimony in his temper, there is a jealousy, there is an obstinacy, and a want of candor at times, and an affectation of secrecy, the fruit of jealousy, which renders him disagreeable often to his friends, makes him enemies, and gives them infinite advantage over him. That he has had great provocation here, I never doubted, and since the appearance of the address less than ever. . . ."

"On the other hand, there was a monopoly of reputation here, and an indecency in displaying it, which did great injustice to the real merit of others, that I do not wonder was resented. There was an indolence, there was a dissipation, which gave occasion of complaint, and there was complaisance to interested adventurers." (*Life and Works of John Adams*, IX, 477.)

[2] *Life of Arthur Lee*, II, 127.

[3] *Ibid.*, I, 152.

active virtue never passed along its whole career without detraction and injustice. To posterity, and not to contemporaries, patriotism and virtue have ever been most indebted for a just estimate of their claims to admiration and gratitude. . . ."

"It was of necessity that Congress employed many commercial agents; and an equal necessity obliged them to authorize their commissioners to employ sub-agents to attend to details of business which it was impossible for the commissioners themselves to transact. . . . Such is the desire for gain, such is the *sacra auri fames*, that in almost every instance the agents employed by Congress and by the commissioners, and the merchants with whom contracts were made, proved regardless of principle, and amassed wealth for themselves at the expense of the United States. . . . Against this abuse Mr. Lee uniformly, actively, and with an uncompromising spirit, opposed all the authority and restraint he could exercise. This course excited against him, as he was aware it would certainly do, the most intense dislike. The most desirable object to these faithless agents was to procure his dismission from the public service, and his recall to the United States. He was a subject of their constant abuse and complaint. . . . Mr. Lee continued during the period of two years, notwithstanding the malevolence of the public defaulters, and the injuries they were constantly inflicting on his feelings and character by their misrepresentations, to pursue, detect, and denounce them. He acquainted Congress with their peculations, and pledged himself to make good his charges against them. Upon his arrival in America, *he redeemed the pledge* he had made to Congress, and proved to their conviction, and to the satisfaction of the country, the defalcation of many of the public agents. He broke down the hostile faction and triumphed over its machinations."

Arthur Lee, on his return to America, presented to Congress a written paper, vindicating his actions while abroad as their commissioner. Of this paper, the opinions of several prominent members of Congress may fitly be given here. Perhaps a fuller investigation would discover many more of the same favorable tenor.

Joseph Read to R. H. Lee:[1] "Philadelphia, 15th April, 1780. Sir—I am to acknowledge and thank you for your obliging favour of the 17th February, enclosing Mr. Lee's vindication, which has been published in our papers. To some collateral parts, there have been replies by Mr. Conyngham and Mr. Joseph Wharton. The multitude and enormity of public abuses one would have thought should have excited general atten-

---

[1] *Life of R. H. Lee*, II, 175.

tion and alarm; but attempts to detect and prevent them have generally been retorted in such a manner as almost to sanctify unfaithfulness and dishonesty. I cannot help considering it as one of the most unfavourable symptoms, that, while we are all complaining against abuses, as soon as the offender is detected, he finds friends and advocates even in the most respectable assemblies. . . ."

Thomas M'Kean to R. H. Lee:[1] "Philadelphia, 25th March, 1780. Dear Sir—Your much esteemed favour of the 15th of last month, with the extracts from your much injured brother's letter to the President of Congress, and the copy of Dr. Berkenhout's letter to yourself, enclosed, came safe to hand. Next to the approbation of my own conscience, it has always been my wish to obtain that of the wise and good, and I confess I am happy in having yours. I flatter myself the time will shortly come when the honest labourers in the cause of freedom and their country will at least meet with the reward of being known; and when, also, the double dealing, artful pretenders will be discovered. There has been a virtuous band in Congress from the beginning of the present contest, but they were never so few, or so much opposed, as just after you and your good brother left us. In the winter and spring of 1779, there was a cabal whose views I could not fathom; there were some possessed of restless spirits, and who endeavoured to set member against member, and Congress against states, particularly Pennsylvania and those of New England; and the states against Congress. Every artifice was used to instil prejudice against all our foreign ministers and commissioners, particularly your brothers (Dr. Arthur Lee and William Lee), and I really believe, if I had not in April last, gone off the bench into Congress, in the face of a vote of the Assembly of Pennsylvania, that they would have been recalled without exception. . . . When I reflect upon the assiduity, the zeal, the fidelity, the abilities and patriotism of Dr. A. Lee, I cannot help deploring his fate, and reprobating the ingratitude of Congress; but, sir, it is with pleasure that I can assure you, that he has many unshaken friends still remaining in that body, who have never seen him, and who esteem him only for his public virtues. I profess myself one of these, and he has at least my warmest thanks for his substantial services rendered to my country. . . ."

William Whipple to R. H. Lee:[2] "Philadelphia, 18 September, 1779. . . . I much approve of Dr. Lee's intention to come to this country, when the Spanish business is concluded. I think it necessary he should have a fair opportunity of putting to shame those base assassins, whose malice is

[1] *Life of R. H. Lee*, II, 176.
[2] *Ibid.*, II, 113.

wrought up to the highest pitch, by a consciousness of their own inferiority. If he lands in New Hampshire, I am confident he will be received with the respect due, and, in some measure, proportioned to his merit. I shall be particularly happy in having an opportunity of manifesting my gratitude for his services to America."

Samuel Adams to R. H. Lee:[1] "Philadelphia, 15th January, 1781. My dear Sir—Your second letter came to hand in due season. My much esteemed friend, Mr. Arthur Lee, will take charge of this. I will say to you, as I have said to my Boston friends, who were solicitous to know what treatment he meets with here: the more I have conversed with him, the more I have been confirmed in a good opinion of him, and lamented the mistakes and prejudices of some men and the wickedness of others. His enemies, I think, dare not openly attack his reputation or conduct, but the whispers of envy and malice have sometimes influence enough to prevent the justice due to the virtuous citizen; when this is the case, it affords a symptom of the decay of public spirit, more threatening to the liberties of a commonwealth than hosts of foreign enemies. Monarchs have their favorites, who serve as pimps on their honest subjects, but republics should examine the conduct of their servants with an impartial eye. And it discovers the want of public virtue, as much to withhold their smiles from the wise and good as to bestow them on the wicked and unfaithful. Mr. Lee, as yet, had neither smiles nor frowns. I am still in hopes he will meet with the rewards, which I am sure he would receive if he had returned a few years ago; he will have them when the trustees of the public shall have fortitude enough to be uninfluenced by great names and characters, given to men of base and depraved minds. You will ask, when will that be, perhaps not in this age; but the historian will in some future time draw forth the proofs of his patriotism, and unprejudiced posterity will acknowledge that Arthur Lee has borne a great share in defending and establishing the liberties of America. I say posterity, for I believe a wiser generation will enjoy the fruits of patriots and heroes in the present day. . . ."

On a later occasion Mr. Adams paid this tribute to Dr. Lee: "As an inhabitant of Massachusetts Bay, I should think myself ungrateful not to esteem Arthur Lee most highly, for his voluntary services to that state, in times of her greatest need, to the injury of his private interests and at great risk of his life."

John Adams to Count de Vergennes:[2] "Passy, 11th February, 1779.

---

[1] *Life of R. H. Lee*, II, 126.
[2] *Life of Arthur Lee*, I, 157–8.

. . . It is my indispensable duty upon this occasion to inform your excellency without consulting either of my colleagues, that the honourable Arthur Lee was as long ago as 1770 appointed by the house of representatives of the Massachusetts Bay, of which I had then the honour to be a member, their agent at the court of London, in the case of the death or absence of Dr. Franklin. This honourable testimony was given to Mr. Lee by an assembly in which he had no natural interest, on account of his inflexible attachment to the American cause, and the abilities of which he had given many proofs in its defence. From that time to the year 1774 he held a constant correspondence with several of those gentlemen who stood foremost in the Massachusetts Bay against the innovations and illegal encroachments of Great Britain. This correspondence I had the opportunity of seeing; and I assure your excellency, *from my own knowledge*, that it breathed the most inflexible attachment to, and the most ardent zeal in the cause of his country. From September 1774 until November 1777, I had the honour to be in Congress, and the opportunity of seeing his letters to Congress, to their committees and to individual members. *Through the whole of both those periods he communicated the most constant and certain intelligence which was received from any individual within my knowledge.* And since I have had the honour of being joined with him here, I have ever found in him the same fidelity and zeal; and I have not a glimmering of suspicion that he ever maintained an improper correspondence in England, or held any conference or negotiation with anybody from thence, without communicating it to your excellency or to his colleagues. I am confident therefore that every insinuation and suspicion against him, of infidelity to the United States, or to their engagements with his majesty, are false and groundless, and that they will assuredly be proved to be so.

"The two honourable brothers of Mr. Lee, who are members of Congress, I have long and intimately known; and of my own knowledge I can say that no men have discovered more zeal in support of the sovereignty of the United States, and in promoting, from the beginning, a friendship and an alliance with France. There is nothing of which I am more firmly persuaded than that every insinuation that is thrown out to the disadvantage of the two Mr. Lees in Congress is groundless. . . ."

Writing to Samuel Cooper, John Adams expressed himself even more forcibly.

"Passy, 28 February, 1779. Dear Sir,—Your letter by the Marquis de Lafayette I have received, and it contains so handsome a testimony to the merit of that gallant nobleman, as well as so many judicious observations on other subjects, that I have ventured to permit it to be translated and published.

"The complaint against the family of Lees is a very extraordinary thing indeed. I am no idolator of that family or any other; but I believe their greatest fault is in having more men of merit in it than any other family; and if that family fails the American cause, or grows unpopular with their fellow-citizens, I know not what family or what person will stand the test.

"There is reason, however, to be upon our guard against the power of a family of so much merit; and if the complaint had only been, that one of the family was minister at the Courts of Versailles and Madrid, another at Vienna and Berlin, I would have joined in that with all my heart. But this, to my certain knowledge, was not the fault of the family, but partly owing to accident, and partly because other gentlemen refused or declined to undertake so dangerous a voyage and so difficult a service.

"If the complaint had been confined to want of figure, dignity and address, I should have left the discussion of such important questions to those who think so much of them, and these might have determined whether the complainers or complainees have the most to boast of in this kind.

"If the complaint had been confined to the subject of temper, I should not have thought it worth while to have consider long, in order to determine which was the most inconvenient to the State, a little too much asperity, or a little too much good nature, a little too much acid, or a little too much oil.

"But when the complaint becomes so outrageous as to throw about the world insinuations of infidelity and breach of trust against some of the most faithful and inflexible men in the community, it becomes the cause of every virtuous man, and such injured characters must be vindicated, or the State undone." . . . (*Life and Works of John Adams*, IX, 478–9.)

John Dickinson to Arthur Lee: "Kent, 30 March, 1780. Sir— . . . Do not imagine that the 'arts of' your 'enemies' have erased from my mind those favourable sentiments I have ever entertained of you since I had the pleasure of your acquaintance. Your friends can witness that throughout the debates in Congress relating to you, I always bore open and faithful testimony to the ability, zeal, courage, integrity, and diligence manifested by you in the support of our cause; and that, in confirmation of what I said, I mentioned your correspondence with me in very dangerous circumstances, on points of the last importance. . . . But while I thus interested myself in what concerned my friend, the conduct you object to was influenced by two reasons, that, leaving the qualities of your head and heart unimpeached, would have led me to the same conclusion if you had been my brother. These were, a coolness in the court of Versailles towards you, and the difference with Dr. Franklin. When it was considered that the connexion between the branches of the house of Bourbon is so intimate, and that harmony between ministers who are to negotiate with them, especially on the same subject, and those most momentous ones, is so necessary, all private regards gave way to the superior force of public obligations. To wound and mourn, falls to the lot of more than 'Brutus.'"[1]

That General Washington esteemed Dr. Lee, and valued his communications, is evident from this note to him:

"Newburgh, 15th April, 1782. Dear Sir,—I have received your favour of the 2nd instant, and thank you for the several articles of European intelligence contained in it. Permit me to solicit a continuation of such advices as you may think interesting respecting the military or political manœuvres of foreign powers. Such communications will not only be a private gratification, but may produce public good; as a perfect knowledge of these matters will enable me to decide with more certainty and precision on doubtful operations, which may be had in contemplation, than I could possibly do without. With great esteem and regard I am my dear sir, your most obedient, humble servant."[2]

Whatever "coolness" may have existed between Arthur Lee and the court of Versailles, it did not prevent the King from paying him a very handsome compliment, which he explained in this letter to the President of Congress:

"Mr. President,—I return to you, in consequence of the resolution with which I engaged in this cause, to see the liberty of my country established, or to perish in her last struggle.

"When I took leave of the court of Versailles as one of your former commissioners, his excellency the Count de Vergennes presented me with a gold enamelled snuff-box, containing the picture of the king of France, set with diamonds. The minister accompanied it with an assurance that he delivered it to me as a mark of the esteem of his sovereign. In my opinion no period ever produced a prince whose esteem was more valuable. His portrait is engraven on my mind by the virtue and justice which form his character; and gold and jewels can add nothing to its lustre.

"This testimony of his majesty's esteem, however flattering to me, I received with the resolution of holding it at your disposal only. I therefore now beg leave, agreeably to what I think my duty, to deposit it with Con-

---

[1] *Life of Arthur Lee*, II, 313, *et seq.*

[2] *Ibid.*, II, 171.

gress; for I esteem it of dangerous consequence, that any republican should receive presents from a foreign prince or retain them without the knowledge or consent of the republic. Still more dangerous and unbecoming is it to measure the merits of those employed in the public service by them, or to make their characters depend on complimentary letters and praises from the followers of the court where they have resided. It is the most sure of all possible methods, to make them subservient where they ought to be independent, and lead them to substitute intrigue in the place of a due discharge of their duty, or sacrifice the interests of their country to the inclinations of a foreign minister. If they do their duty to their country, their constituents ought best to know it; and the reward they are pleased to bestow upon them, is the sole and sufficient recompense becoming the dignity of a free citizen to possess."

In reply this report was made: "In the Continental Congress: The committee to whom were referred the letter of Arthur Lee, Esq., etc., submit the following report: Arthur Lee having deposited with the President of Congress a picture of the king of France, set with diamonds, and presented by the minister of that monarch on his taking leave of the court of Versailles as a mark of his majesty's esteem; and having intimated that as the picture was presented to him in consequence of his having been a commissioner of Congress at that court, it did not become him to retain the same without the express approbation of Congress:

"*Resolved*, That he be informed that Congress approves of his retaining the picture.

"*Resolved*, That Mr. Lee be further informed, in answer to his letter, that there is no particular charge against him before Congress, properly supported; and that he be assured his recall was not intended to affix any kind of censure on his character, or on his conduct abroad."

As a further mark of their confidence, Congress requested Dr. Lee to give them the benefit of his knowledge of and views upon foreign affairs. He rendered a strict and satisfactory account of all the funds expended by him.

After his return to Virginia, Dr. Lee was elected a deputy from Prince William to the Virginia Assembly, and later, by the Assembly, to the general Congress. He was one of the signers of the treaty for the cession of the northwestern territory by Virginia to the general government. In 1784 he was appointed by Congress one of the commissioners to make a treaty with the Indians on the northwest frontier; Lafayette accompanied this expedition. On their return Dr. Lee was appointed to the "board of treasury," with Samuel Osgood and Walter Livingston, in which position he continued from 1784 to 1789. In 1786 he was chosen one of the commissioners to revise the laws of Virginia. From the board of treasury he retired to private life, and lived upon his estate in Middlesex county. During the years spent in this retreat he carried on a very extensive correspondence with many of the prominent persons to whom his official career had made him known.

A writer has said: "The career of Arthur Lee, though undistinguished by any connection with the great and prominent events, such as catch the public eye, was one of the most important and useful to his country, which the history of that day records. At a time when the new-born republic was struggling for existence, and carrying on a war against a powerful country with which the nations of Europe were at peace, and to which they were bound by treaties, he represented his country with a zeal and efficiency which accomplished the greatest and most valuable results. His mind seems to have burned with a restless ardor, and he never rested in his attempts to conciliate the courts of Europe in favor of America, and to induce them to furnish her with material aid."

As a mark of their approbation for his services as their agent abroad, the states of Massachusetts and Virginia both granted him large tracts of land. Harvard College conferred upon him the honorary degree of LL. D.; the Academy of American Arts and Sciences, and the American Philosophical Society elected him an honorary member.

While upon the expedition to the western Indians, already mentioned, Dr. Lee penned these thoughts, which are very interesting: [1]

"Being this day indisposed, and obliged to keep my room, I could not avoid meditating on my future prospects. Should I settle and remain among my friends in Virginia; should I retire to Kentucky; or return to England, and enjoy in retirement there all that a country great in arts and sciences affords. I entered life glowing with sentiments of liberty and virtue. The seeds of the American Revolution were then sowing, in the acts of Parliament for imposing taxes on the Colonies. I embraced the opposition with a double degree of enthusiasm, which the love of liberty and my country inspired. I devoted myself to the cause from its very infancy. From that time my life has been a continued scene of agitation and commotion. No calm, no repose has refreshed me. To live in Virginia without a wife is hardly practicable. But in Virginia boys and girls only marry, and they marry from almost every motive but love. A man at thirty, a woman at twenty, is old in Virginia; and with my sentiments of love and marriage I am not likely to find a wife there. . . .

---

[1] *Life of Arthur Lee*, II, 389, *et seq.*

"Shall I retire to Kentucky, and try my fortune in a young country and a rising region? The soil and climate are fine. I have lands there, which would become very valuable by residence; and it would be easy, with a little money, to acquire a princely territorial property. Ambition and avarice seem therefore to join in their invitation. But after the scenes through which I have passed such an ambition seems *low*, and the avarice, without an incentive. For whom should I sacrifice present enjoyment to secure a future fortune? He who pursues ambition in that country must expect no repose. He must first agitate its *separation* and *independence*, then control the various turbulent spirits which are gathered there from different States; he must court those whose lives and manners are little removed from those of savages. He must be in perpetual action, as nothing else can promote his purposes, or even prevent him from repining at the loss of everything that can engage the cultivated mind or gratify the senses. He must submit to the wretched accommodations which an almost savage country can afford; and not only be content without luxuries, but even without the necessaries of life. What is there then that can tempt a sober man, in my situation, to Kentucky?

"A single man, intent upon gratifying his taste, might accomplish this purpose with great certainty, and at a moderate expense, in London. Secure of £600 a year, he might live in style perfectly genteel, and see and hear everything worth seeing and hearing. But then he must live for himself only. He must forget that he has relations in another land, *near* and *dear*, whom he has sacrificed forever. All the charities of blood and country must be forgotten. His hours of retirement must be sad and solitary. Should ill-health overtake him, he must not only be cut off from the enjoyments he promised himself, but he must expect no tender hand to soothe his pillow, no sympathising soul to mitigate with nameless gentle offices the anguish of disease, and minister to the troubled and desponding mind. And why indeed should he, who lives for himself only, expect that society will feel for him, or furnish him with aid or solace, beyond the influence of his money?

"Those, too, with whom I was immediately connected in friendship and politics, when a fellow-subject, would regard me now with cold indifference, if not with aversion. Many would consider me as having contributed to wound and dishonor that country which is the dearest object to every good Englishman. Could I be restored to the situation that I enjoyed before the Revolution, unless the tumult of political commotion may have unparadised it, I might be happy. That is, as happy as man without domestic cares, domestic anxiety, and domestic love, could be. I was placed in chambers in the Temple, which looked into a delightful little garden on the Thames, of which I had the key ; I could go in and out at all hours, and have what company I pleased, without being questioned or overlooked. I was near the Royal Society, of which I was a fellow, where, every week, whatever was new and ingenious in literature was communicated. Not far from me was the hall of the Society of Arts and Agriculture, of which I was an honorary member, and where I had access to all the new discoveries in arts, agriculture, and mechanics.

"The play houses and the opera were equally convenient, where I could select the opportunity of seeing the best tragedies and comedies represented, and of hearing the most exquisite music. I was a subscriber to Bach's and Abel's concert, where the most masterly performers of the world (Bach, Abel, Fishar, Tassot, Ponto, and Crosdal), played to a most polite and fashionable audience, in one of the most elegant concert rooms in the world. In the field of politics, from the politician in the cider-cellar to the peer in his palace, I had access and influence. At the Bill of Rights, the city of London, the East India House, and with the opposition in both houses, I was of some consideration. Among my particular friends, to whom I always had access, were Lord Shelburne, Mr. Downing, Col. Barré, Mr. Wilkes, Serjeant Glynn, and several others. I was so well with several of the nobility and gentry that I could spend all my leisure time at their country seats. At Bath I had a very extensive acquaintance ; and there is not in the world a more agreeable place to one so circumstanced. As one of the law, I enjoyed the protection and distinction of that body, with the prospect of rising to place and profit, which all of that body, who have moderate abilities, enjoy. So circumstanced, nothing but the peculiar and extraordinary crisis of the times prevented me from being entirely happy, and pursuing the fortune which sat with golden plumes within my reach. But everything was absorbed in the great contest which I saw fast approaching ; and which soon called upon me to quit London, and take an open part in the Revolution, as a representative of the United States at the court of France."

Perhaps nothing will convey a clearer idea of the character of Arthur Lee than some of his letters written to his intimate friends or near relations. In such a correspondence, he appears to have frankly spoken his inmost thoughts. It is believed that few of these letters have ever been in print.

To Richard Henry Lee.

"Glasgow, 21 October, 1761. My dear Brother, In pursuance of my Husbandry Scheme, I am now in Glasgow. I find the Drill Plow, as used for sowing wheat, will not answer your Purpose, but I have conceived one which I think may be applicable to your Grain, as this is to Wheat. I communicated the Plan to the mechanical Gentleman with whom I live, and received his approbation. But I shall put it in practice, before I trouble you any further with it, for I am sensible that ideal Machines are worked with much more ease than real ones.

"I spent all yesterday with Mr. Smyth, Author of the moral sentiments, who is a very agreeable companion, and am this day to go with him to the Farmer I mentioned in a former letter; who has pursued the new Husbandry with such success. This Town is by far superior to any in Scotland, in Regularity, Beauty and Magnificence; the Inhabitants are mostly Traders in Tobacco and are said to import ⅓ of the whole produce of America. Their strict attention to Business has rendered them an uncivil, unsocial People, and utterly strangers to Politeness, so that the Gentlemen of the Colledge are the only sociable People in Town.

"The River Clyde runs smoothly by the Town, and is navigable for small Craft. They have many manufactories, which they carry on with success. I saw the shattered ruins of a Palace, which was once the Residence of the Arch Bishop of Glasgow, and near it stands an old Cathedrall of vast Magnitude. The Colledge has lately built a fine Astronomical Observatory, which is well furnished with the necessary instruments, by the best Makers.

"I have been really unfortunate in not finding the farming Gentleman at home; I had only the opportunity of viewing his grounds and examining the Instruments with which he tills them. I was satisfied of the Truth of what I had heard, that he had drawn ten yearly crops from the same Field, cultivated agreeably to the Principles of the new Husbandry, without the least assistance of Manure of any kind, and that every succeeding crop had excelled its Predecessor. I saw the same Field bearing its eleventh Crop, and from one Acre of this, he last year received 56 Bushels of wheat; from this Day's Observation and Intelligence, I am convinced, of which indeed I wanted no conviction, that the new Husbandry is the most rational and profitable method. In a former Letter, I mentioned my opinion that ploughing between the Rows of your Tobacco would be of infinite advantage to it, but I did not observe that this was the most effectual means of destroying the weeds; but this must be the consequence of many years Culture, which will almost utterly eradicate and destroy them; but at first they flourish with much more strength and vigour, so that the only method of succeeding is to persevere in it for some years.

"I have had a strong proof of the unsociable Disposition of the

Inhabitants here; for, tho' I made a point of getting acquainted with some of the Merchants, so as to settle some sure method of Correspondence with you, I have not been able to accomplish it; so that we must still continue the same uncertain manner of Corresponding. I would only beg you to write always by the Glasgow ships, as by others the Letters are long before they reach me, and are then burdened with Intolerable Charges.

"The pacific Disposition of the new ministry is so much confided in that the Stocks rose considerably, since their appointment, in Expectation of an immediate peace. Mr. Pitt's Acceptance of a Pension has given a mortal stab to his Reputation. It pleases his Enemies to have such a fair Opportunity of aspersing his character with the most severe Reflections, whilst his Friends are dejected, and see with sorrow their high Expectations of his Integrity and disinterested patriot Spirit uttterly deceived. Forget not to remember me to all with you and believe me to be, as I really am, my dear Brother, Yours most affectionately."

To William Lee.

"Bristol Wells, 17 June, 1769. Dear Brother, Tho' I have delayed thanking you for your favour from Ipswich, yet I did not neglect the commands it contained; but executed them immediately as directed. Capt. Walker I had before seen and informed of what you desired.

"I am happy to hear you are well and much pleased with your situation, particularly Mrs. Lee. To please the wife is all in all; 'tis the husband's duty to labour at this with all his mind, soul, and strength. A'nt I a good creature Mrs. Lee? for preaching this wholsome doctrine? I hope neither your approbation of me nor your situation find any change. Three whole days was Eve satisfyd with Paradise, and without flattery, I believe her daughters are equally content. Much more could I say, with truth, in your praise, fair daughter of Eve, but you would call me flatterer, and I desist. I lay my life now you will say, one can never make out my meaning. Now then I'll be explicit. Have you found out for me the fair one you promised? young, innocent, accomplished, sweet-tempered, well-bred, playful and rich?

Excelld by none, equall'd by few,
Or in a word, resembling you.

"But by all means let her hate flattery; for as I abominate it myself, I could not be offering this forced incense to the goddess I ador'd. Besides you know, my dear Mrs. Lee, that all sensible and pretty Ladies regard it as odious and hateful. Go find out the fair one that's form'd on my plan and I'll love her forever—I mean if I can. This forever is a fine thing, if it would but last.

"Well, best to be serious and grave too, for a young lady told me at the Assembly last night, that I must put on a great wig; pray now by the bye (for had I gone strait on I should have been at Bristol Wells) is there any probability she meant to typify matrimony, under this same figure of a great wig? Nay don't laugh, 'tis a serious matter, for if she did, 'tis meet that I answer it; not by putting it on, I assure you, for I have a notion it would prove rather warm, especially in the summer months. A light wig or a night cap which one can throw on or off at pleasure, seems better accommodated to feverish heads. Now (as I shou'd have said before, had I not been interrupted by this matrimonial wig, of which I conceive, *en passant*, Tristram Shandy would have made a good joke. But the Ladies never touch Tristram Shandy, his nose was so long, he frightened them; not one, however desirous, had the courage to approach it), I am safe at Bristol Wells, snug in a garret, which is the manner in which they treat all new Comers; and you are exalted by descending to a better berth. This bull in practice, is perhaps imported from Ireland; with which you know there is a great intercourse from here. I arrived on Saturday evening only, therefore, cannot yet form any judgement of the place. There is not much company, but more is expected; the height of the season is not 'till July. I have touched two guineas already since I came here; I mean in paying my subscription for the rooms. I must be very particular, Mrs. Lee so often quarrels with me about the ambiguity of my expression.

"Mrs. Dinwiddie and Family are well and offer up their warmest wishes for Mrs. Lee's happiness. Ten to one but I shall occasion another misapprehension, you will imagine I have seen or heard of them; but that will be a mistake, not mine indeed, for I know better. They are neither at the Wells nor at Clifton and as I only passed thro' Bath, I had not an opportunity of inquiring after them.

"Take care of indulging too much in Fish and Flesh; it is sometime before the Lungs recover their proper vigour after such a shock as yours have lately undergone. Oppressing them suddenly, as a precipitate return to such diet will do, may endanger the fixing imperceptibly an obstruction in them detrimental if not destructive. I can assure Mrs. Lee too, that it is not the best way of accomplishing, what is every good Wife's most earnest wish, the renewal of her husband's strength.

"Farewell, my blessing season these things in you."

## To Richard Henry Lee.

"Bristol-Wells, 4th August, 1769. My dear Brother,—I am sorry you have so much reason to complain of my neglect; for which I must rely on your goodness to pardon me. My letters by Johnston brought me an account of your marriage; on which I give you and Mrs. Lee joy with all my heart. The union which crowns a mutual affection long tried, promises the most permanent felicity; and I hope every succeeding moon will find you equally happy with the first. I am now the only unhappy or single person of the family; nor have I any prospect of being otherwise. I have spent this season at the Bristol Wells in pursuit of practice and to make acquaintances, and shall remain the winter at Bath with the same views. In the latter it is easy to succeed, in the first not quite so easy here as at Williamsburg. Perseverance, of which unhappily I have very little, is absolutely requisite to accomplish this business. I often feel so home sick that I cannot bear the thoughts of living forever from you; so that if I am not very short lived I feel I must make another trip to see you.

"Contrasted with that of this country, how illustriously eminent does the patriotic conduct of Virginia appear. I had my fears, my anxieties about Virginia, but my countrymen have fulfilled my most sanguine wishes and acquired an honour which can never be tarnished. Here the spirit of liberty is very languid, and all attempts to rouse it meet with very little success. Corruption has spread its baneful influence so universally, that this country seems now to be nearly in that state in which Jugurtha found Rome when he exclaimed,

'*O venalem urbem, et citò perituram, si emptorem invenies.*'

"However, the utmost endeavours are used to awaken a proper resentment of the atrocious injuries which have been offered to the constitution. And though I believe they will obtain petitions enough to awe the ministry, yet I do not hope to see all the grievances fully redressed, and the authors of them brought to condign punishment. With respect to us the ministry speak in a conciliating tone, but they are so void of all virtue that no credit is due to them, especially as their principles are most notoriously arbitrary. Persevere in the plan of frugality and industry, encourage and confirm a spirit never to submit or yield, and you will compel them to be just—*hæ tibi artes, hæc arma;* and may heaven render them invincible. The town of Bristol, which is very near the wells, is immersed in the turtle and venison feasting, and therefore seems to apprehend little from the revolutions you have made; but they will feel presently, and then I will answer for their justice being awakened, and their feeling how cruel it is to oppress us. We have much company here, besides invalids, dancing, card playing every day, so that time passes agreeably enough though idly. My Lord Bute having lately arrived from abroad, it is expected his advice will make some change in administration; but from so impure a fountain no good can be expected. The Mississippi scheme must lie dormant till Lord Hillsborough is removed, for he will never suffer it to be executed."

To John Hopkins, Esqr., Richmond, Va.

"New York, 13 June, 1786. Dear Sir, I this day received your favour of the 3rd. I shall attend to your desire of having leave of absence. But to pay your salary here is an absolute impossibility, not one State in the Union having remitted one dollar to the Treasury for two months past, nor is any one likely to do it. This, together with anticipations already made on the Treasury, precludes any hope of its being able to furnish, for the next quarter, the salaries of those immediately about Congress, including the President's household. And, if any money is obtained for this purpose, it will be from this State only. There never was so total desertion of federal support as has been for sometime past.

"This situation makes it particularly distressing to me, that neither the Certificates nor Indents have produced any Cash, of which I am proportionally more in want, as this place is more expensive than Virginia, and strangers have very little credit. As to Pierce's notes, if they can be exchanged for Military Certificates drawing interest in the state, I should wish them to be so disposed of. If Mr. Duncomb should come to this place before you, I entreat you to send me what money you can collect on the Indents by him for I am much in want of it."

To his nephew, Thomas Lee Shippen.

"New York, 1 March, 1786. My dear Tom. You reason like Bacchus himself upon the superiority of Ch. J. Blake's system of study to that of C. J. Coke! But there is a time for all things. I rejoice that you have translated yourself to the sober regions of Philadelphia. . . . I want your opinion of the conduct of a nephew of mine, who shall be nameless. You must know that I left some clothing and other things in a trunk at his father's house, which this same nephew is charged with having tumbled out and packed away, God knows where, taking the trunk for his own use. Was this handsomely done? Your Father maintains towards me the most solemn silence. What am I to augur from it? The silence of great politicians is always ominous!

"As to Cousin Frankey's demand, I can answer it in a few words. I opposed the Congressional Claims, four years ago, as dangerous innovations, without giving the States an opportunity in peace of supporting federal demands, conformably to the confederation. The trial has been made, and the States have proved shamefully defective. So that they have brought it to a question now whether we shall continue a confederate nation or not. I still think the system is not good; but it is better than a dishonest bankruptcy—better than that we should be degraded from the rank of Nations—better than that we should violate all public faith, and much better than that we should see hostile Squadrons before our Towns, demanding, with bitter and merited reproaches of violated faith, a payment of our just debts and fulfilment of solemn engagements."

"To Thomas Lee Shippen, Esqr., No. 3 Church-yard Court, Inner Temple, London.

"New York, 2 January, 1787. My dear Nephew, Many happy New Years to you. The Packet is arrived but no letter from you, which I much lament. Yours by Mr. Voss came safely. I am afraid that our own conduct will soon render us objects of pity and contempt, instead of resentment. Great, no doubt will be the triumph, where you are, when they see us sacrilegiously pulling down the glorious name we had raised among the nations of the Earth. The formidable insurrections in the State [of Massachusetts] where we supposed government was best established, and the general reluctance in them all to support the federal government with effect, banishes all hope of our maintaining the dignity of national character which we had acquired. I am in doubt whether a majority of the States will concur with Virginia in sending Delegates to a National Convention. Most of them seem to think that the proposition for amending the Constitution, and the mode, should originate with Congress, and be proposed to the States. Diversity of opinion will leave us where we were. In this situation of inaction and incertitude, it requires more sagacity in political events than I possess to determine what will be the issue. It is unpleasing to conjecture even, because conjecture covers it with confusion, shame and horror to us as a Nation.

"I wish you to enquire whether Lands in the Province of Maine or in Kentucky will sell in London. I have a grant in the former of excellent Land, six thousand acres, for which I would take 5*s*. sterling per acre; and 10,000 in Kentucky at the same price. The titles are unquestionable, and certainly to one that would provide for young children, no plan can be more eligible. I would engage to furnish the original Patents to any Agents here on the deposit of the money in a Banker's hands in London, subject to my disposal, when such agent's certificate of the original patent and deed from me, are delivered to him, for the purchasers.

"We have no Congress, at present, nor any certainty of one. I forward you Letters from Phil'a. which will furnish you all the news there. Remember me to all inquiring friends, and do not forget me to Mrs. Adams and Mrs. Smith and their husbands. It is most true that I have not written to Mr. and Mrs. Paradise; but it is not so, that I do not remember them affectionately, and of this, I beg you will assure them. I am from my situation more a stranger to their affairs in Virginia than they are; otherwise I should have written to them on that subject."

To SAME, WITH SAME ADDRESS.

"2 May, 1787. Your favours of 19th Jany., 6th Feby., and 6th March, are all before me. My absence in Virginia accumulated them for one reading. I had before attended to the expense of postage and therefore forwarded some letters by a private ship instead of the Packet. This and not inclosing is all that can be done, because the Captains are not only enjoined by Law, but tempted by receiving 1d. on each letter to commit the Letters they bring to the post at the first port. It is therefore to particular friends only that they will do the favour of delivering letters or packets in London. I could not have agreed in the opinion that Mr. Pitt's administration would not survive this parliament. By the best accounts his abilities and integrity deserve permanency, and will have it unless royal jealousy, which is the intolerable principle of his Master, and has been the misfortune of the present reign, should take alarm and determine his fall. *When* that will happen is not calculable upon the principles of reason; but when it does, Mr. Pitt will fall the victim of a narrow and even envious sentiment in the royal breast, however great his abilities may be or unblemished his administration. In the duplicity and littleness of the King's mind, courtiers and anti-courtiers all agree. The ministers, therefore, who hang on this Prince's favour are in an eminent degree exposed to those sudden court frosts which nip their honours, even in their fullest bloom.

"I am sorry that your observation on the minority of the people are not graced with that liberality which I wished. We are certainly ourselves the chief cause of that asperity which you have observed in their sentiments and conduct towards us. We have not conducted ourselves with that modesty which manifests true dignity; we have not managed the wounded spirit of a great nation. But we have aggravated their mortification by violence and insolence and vain boasting. At the same time, we exposed ourselves to their contempt by the dishonesty of our conduct, the dissensions of our Councils, and the weakness of our governments. Is it their fault that we have rendered ourselves at once hated and contemptible? Is it surprising that they should seize the commercial advantages which our intolerance of all wise and honest regulations gave them; when we had vainly threatened the extermination of their commerce and boasted of our superiority? We had no right to expect commercial favours from them, when our behaviour was by no means calculated to obtain as a favour what we could not demand as a right. We have not considered that we are an infant nation and required nursing; that our governments were yet experimental, unknit and unestablished, and therefore requiring much wisdom and temper in management, both at home and abroad. We have sported with our national character as children do with baubles; and have nearly inclined the world to believe that we are incapable of self government. All this is our own fault, and we must not expect that a nation we have so sorely wounded will see it without rejoicing, and not take advantage of our follies.

"Lord Lansdowne says it is not his fault if he does not see you frequently; 'that you may depend on his attention and services.' Where he forms an attachment, he is constant in his friendship. What he most admires is manliness of character. You will, I hope, visit him often and cultivate his good opinion. But I warn you that a little more liberality in your sentiments of the government and people of England will not hurt you in his estimation. Nor, indeed, do I think it will be any impeachment of your candour and judgment. I beg you will always assure his Lordship of my unalterable respect, and that you will not forget to remember me to his son, Lord Wycombe. I am mistaken if he does not possess a mind of great nobleness and worth. His age and yours are more likely to assimilate into friendship than that of his Father, and therefore you will permit me to wish that you would be very attentive to him. There is hardly anything more lovely than friendship formed in youth between worthy minds. It is always a pleasing reflection thro' life and often extremely useful.

"It is painful to me to write on the people and politics of the U. S. The utmost that charity can say is that they do not improve. The same unprincipled pursuit of private speculations, the same sacrifice of the public honour and interests to the selfish objects of individuals, the same antipathy in the dishonest to the payment of public and private [debts?], the same open and sometimes studied violation of their faith pledged in the confederation by their respective Assemblies. The most baneful of all luxuries, the luxury of the common people, who are more extravagant than any people in the world of the same rank. All these conspire the dissolution of government, the corruption of manners, the insecurity of property and the destruction of national faith, character and confidence.

"For remedy of these evils the Convention is now meeting in Philadelphia. Gen'l Washington, Mr. Henry, your Uncle R. H. Lee have refused to attend it. I do not hope anything from this meeting; because, in fact, the evil is rooted in the very Assemblies, who are to confirm the acts of the Convention. This renders it too probable that a plan of dignity and effect will not even be proposed, and, if proposed, will not be accepted. It is plain to me that what is doing is tempering with the disease, deceiving the people and endangering some violent commotion. It is most manifest that we have not the public virtue and private temperance which are necessary to the establishment at least of free Republics; but that we have courage, enterprise, and high-mindedness to make a great and even illustrious people under one sovereignty, consisting of an Imperial head, a Senate for life and an elective house of Commons. All things short of this appears to me the frippery of little politicians, whose minds are incapable of deep reflection and bold execution."

To SAME.

"29 May. Since I wrote the above, Mr. Adams' defense of the Constitution of America has fallen into my hands. The work is anything but what the title imports, because there is not one State in the Union whose Constitution is balanced as his Book proves they ought to be. It is very much read and will do a great deal of good. Had M. Turgot read a single chapter in Bulstrode Whitelock on Parliament, he would have been convinced that the balance in the English Constitution is essential to the preservation and prosperity of it, and it would have weaned him from his preference to Franklin's defective Bantling. Mr. Adams has fully illustrated Whitelock's balance, and in his preference for the English Constitution, I do most heartily concur. In your letter by the Bishop and that by Mr. Randall, you mentioned having sent packets of pamphlets and papers to me. But I have neither received any such, nor with all my inquiry can I learn anything of them. Yr. sister writes me that the Millinery, which she supposes you sent her by Mr. Randall, is not received. There seems to be some equivoque in all this."

To SAME.

"4th June. I am to thank you for yours of 6th April, by Mr. Harrison who was very careful of all you sent. Reynolds is truly an Attorney, therefore put no confidence in him. The unpopularity of Mr. Adams gives me pain. I am afraid he has appeared too much to associate with men in opposition to the government, which may have soured the minds of the King and his Ministers. At the same time I am much inclined to believe that both these personages are inimical to America, and therefore must hate a man of Mr. Adams' integrity and real patriotism. I shall endeavour to improve by the rebuke of Mr. Adams, and I sincerely pray that the judgment I have formed of our fellow citizens and our affairs may be altogether unfounded.

"Ten States are now represented in Convention, and in general, very well represented. Gen'l Washington, having altered his mind, attended and is its President; your Uncle R. H., would not attend because, being a member of the Congress, who are to receive new powers and to determine upon the Acts of the Convention, he thought there was manifest impropriety in it; and that it would be a very popular argument with the anti-federalist men in the several Assemblies against ratifying the Acts of the Convention. There are however several members of Congress attending in Convention, and I wish it may not have the consequence my Brother apprehends.

"As yet the Convention has done nothing material. Many and various are the plans of different members. Some are for two estates, executive and legislative, with a negative on the acts of the several legislatures. Some for adding an Executive to the present Congress. Others are for giving more powers to Congress; others for changing the Constitution of Congress, as well as adding powers, and some are for not giving any additional powers. Amendment, by some additional powers, and the alteration of others, seems to have been the object of the appointment and no more will the Assemblies grant at present. But, if I can effect it, there shall be a Convention every 5 years, so that by gradual amendments we may get right at last. For I do not expect that a total reformation would be adopted, and by attempting too much, at once, we may lose all. The Democracy have such prevalence that great management is necessary to reduce them to order and establish a proper balance. I do not know the exact number of Emigrants to Pennsylvania, but it has certainly been very great.

"Since the election of Mr. Hancock as Gov'r the Insurgents have again put themselves in motion and things wear an alarming aspect. How he will act is yet to be seen. But I apprehend he will temper with them 'till they have augmented their force, so as to raise a convulsion in the State, that will shake him like a catter-pillar from the tree he is destroying. It seems to me that this man's unbounded vanity and extravagance, accompanied with both want of sense and principle, is the curse of that happy State. He is supported, as I am told, by Sullivan, Hitchborne, and Morton, three Lawyers of daring character and not too squeamish conscience. The ingratitude of the people to Mr. Bowdoin is among the sins which their own calamities will make them repent of.

"I will send you some newspapers by Carper or any other private opportunity that I can find. By that time perhaps something of consequence may transpire from the Convention. They have determined not to open their doors. You see how I have economised my paper. If the Venetian Count is not an impostor, Miss —— is very well off.

"6 Jany. Nothing of any consequence has occurred since the last date, and the mail closes in a few hours, therefore I have only, my dear Nephew, to bid you most cordially Adieu."

"To Thomas Lee Shippen, Esqr., No. 4, New College, Oxford." Postmark, "New York, 1st. August, 1787."

"I received your favour of the 6th ult., my dear Nephew, but not the Magazines &c. Probably Mr. Joy sent it on to your father, for he told me he had none for me. It surprises me that you should complain of not having heard from me for some time. I have written once a month by the Packet or by some private ship, so that I must fear that all of my letters have miscarried. Mr. Richard Penn carried many letters to you by the last Packet. Our affairs rest much as they were. Nothing material escapes of what passes in the Convention. Much is expected from the deliberation of their debates, and it is hoped that something will at last be produced worthy of such a Body and of such mature discussion. The present possessors of State powers are in general against any alteration. But the People, at large, appear anxious for change and more efficient general Government. And this sentiment, I think, must at last prevail. The Science of Government is no trifling matter. It requires education and experience, it requires the habits of great worlds and of great men, it requires the leisure which independent fortune gives and the elevation of mind, which birth and rank impart. Without these, you might as well attempt to make sevres china out of common earth as Statesmen and Politicians out of men bred and born in the sordid occurrences of common life. This is an evil remediable, indeed, by time, and in that we must put our trust. In the interim, if we have the prudence to be sure we can walk before we attempt to run; we may escape the shame and injury of falling. By slow degrees the liberal arts were won, and Hercules grew strong. The mighty oak was first an humble plant, and some Shepherd's cottages swelled by long and gradual steps into Imperial Rome, the nurse of Heroes, the delight of the Gods. By the same gradual progress must we arrive at imperialism.

"Not, my dear Nephew, not by that vanity and pride of opinion which seem to possess us merely, and which, I confess, puts me too much in mind of the frog in the fable. What ideas must that Governor have had of the character of sovereign states and of the dignity of the diplomatic corps, who would recommend such an animal as Mr. Lamb to be a negotiator of treaties, and who would have believed it possible that such a creature should have visited Europe and Africa as a Minister from the United States of America. In all probability had he missed this appointment, the same sage Governor would have recommended him to be the Skipper of a New England schooner.

"This is an odious subject to think on, and I wish it was the only one of that complexion. My sentiments on these matters will be condemned by the very pride I have censured, for pride and dignity are seldom allied. But what I mean by it is, that instead of being proud in words, we should be dignified in acts, not vain in speculation but prudent in conduct.

"How did it happen that you said nothing about our noble relation, when you enclosed his letter? Is he assuredly noble, with £2,000 per annum, and if so what could be the Father's objection? Mr. Wilkes is a man of high political discernment. He must therefore see with disappointment and anxiety the falling off of those whose virtue he always professed to admire, and in whose success he so avowedly interested himself. I beg you will remember me to him most affectionately. It pleases me much that Lord Lansdowne corresponds with you. I again exhort you to cultivate his friendship and that of Lord Shelburne. Remember me to them both, particularly to Lord Lansdowne. Whenever the Convention shall have settled and announced their plan for our future government, I shall write to him. What are his politics touching Hastings and Holland?"

"30th July. The Convention has adjourned for ten days, leaving Gov. Randolph, Mr. Rutledge, Mr. Ellsworth, Mr. Wilson and Mr. Gorman a committee to arrange what has been agreed upon for the final decision of the whole. It is therefore to be conjectured that we shall soon be gratifyed with the plan they mean to recommend. . . ."

"1st August. I waited to see whether the post would bring any letters from our friends in Phil'a, but it has not. Your Uncle Richard is here, lives with me, and is in better health than I have seen him since I came to America. He remembers and loves you. I answered Count Barziza's letter, but directed it to Mr. Paradise[1] for want of his address. We shall cer-

[1] Lucy Ludwell, sister of Mrs. William Lee, and second daughter of Philip Ludwell and Frances Grymes, his wife, married, in 1769, John Paradise, of London; their daughter, also called Lucy Ludwell (born about 1770), married, in 1787, Count Barziza, a Venetian nobleman; she died in August, 1800, and left two sons.

tainly receive Mrs. Paradise with cordial love whenever she comes, which I do not expect will happen; however much she may talk of it. Give my love to them, if you please. Your Father talked of your travelling for a year; write me your plan, in your next, that I may assist you with recommendations. Remember me to Dr. Price, if you see him. I will write him by the next Packet. Adieu."

Dr. Arthur Lee's will was recorded in the county court of Middlesex, at the court-house of Urbanna, on December 24th, 1792, and Richard Henry Lee qualified as executor:

I, Arthur Lee of Lansdown in the county of Middlesex, being of Sound and disposing mind, do make this my last will and testament, revoking all others: this twenty seventh day of July, one thousand seven hundred and ninety two.

1st My will is, that all of my just debts be paid, and that my Remains be interred in the Vault of my dear parents; unless I should die at an inconvenient distance.

2nd I give to my most dear brother Richard Henry Lee, for his life only all my lands and Negroes, houses, Stocks and furniture, except as hereafter shall be excepted, in the county of Middlesex.

3rd I give the said lands, houses, furniture, Negroes and Stock at the death of my said brother to his son Francis Lightfoot Lee, together with all my lands in Kentucky, with my lots in the town of Richmond, to him and his heirs forever.

4th I give to my said Nephew, F. L. Lee, the tract of land in the province of Maine granted to me by the State of Massachusetts, to him and his heirs forever.

5th I give to my said nephew fifteen acres of Land, being a lot in the Parish of Passyunk, near Philadelphia, to him and his heirs forever.

6th I give to my said nephew my stock in the Bank of North America.

7th I give to my nephew Cassius Lee my lots in Norfolk, my lands on the north side of the Ohio, consisting of my shares in the Ohio Company and my purchases from the United States on the seven ranges, and also my purchase from Col. Henry Lee of his Military rights, consisting of eight thousand five hundred acres, to him and his heirs forever.

8th I give to my nephew Cassius Lee my postponed 6 per cents in the funds of the United States.

9th I give to my nephew Ludwell Lee all my French Books and Manuscripts.

10th I give to niece Flora Lee my set of white tea China of Sevres, together with the red and white Sevres China Coffee Cups, Tea pot, Milk pot and bowl.

11th I give to my niece Hannah Washington, one half acre lot in Alexandria lying on Washington and Oronoko Streets and lett on ground rents, to her and her heirs forever.

12th I give to my niece Ann Lee, a half acre lot in Alexandria lying on Princess and St. Asaph streets which I purchased of Col. Henry Lee, to her and her heirs forever, also my silver desert knives with pearl handles.

13th I give to my niece Harriet Lee the six lots in Alexandria sold to me by Col. Henry Lee and which by his agreement with me were to yield fifty pounds per annum ground rents, to her and her heirs forever.

14th I give to my niece Sally Lee one half acre lot in Alexandria No. 76 on Duke and Royal Streets, to her and heirs forever.

15th I give to my niece Lucinda Lee one half acre lot in Alexandria lying on Duke and St. Asaph Street and lett on ground rents to her and her heirs forever.

16th I give to my niece Ann Brent a piece of plate as she may choose of the value of twenty Guineas.

17th I give to my dear sister-in-law Rebecca Lee of Menokin my diamond ring and my gold sleeve buttons with pictures in them.

18th I give to my dear sister-in-law wife to Richd. Henry Lee a piece of plate of the value of ten guineas.

19th I give to my dear brother Francis Lightfoot Lee, my gold enamelled Snuff Box set with diamonds.

20th I give all the residue of my estate real and personal to my dear brother Richard Henry Lee, if he should survive me, if not, then to his son Francis Lightfoot Lee.

21st I constitute and appoint my brother Richard Henry Lee, my sole executor and if I should survive him, then I request my friend Ralph Wormley of Rosegill to accept of that charge and of a piece of plate worth thirty guineas for his trouble.

October 25th 1792. Codicil—I give to my nephew Cassius Lee five thousand dollars in lieu of the deferred six per cents, which I give to my nephew Francis Lightfoot Lee and it is my will that the aforesaid 5,000 dollars should be paid out of my stock (No 6) to my nephew F. L. Lee.

## Colonel John Lee.

22. John[4], eldest son of Henry Lee[3] (Richard[2], Richard[1]), and Mary Bland, his wife, was probably born at "Lee Hall," Westmoreland, about 1724; he died in the year 1767. It appears to have been the usual custom to bequeath to the eldest son the family homestead; but, in the case of John Lee, this custom does not seem to have been observed, for Richard, the second son, inherited "Lee Hall." The apparent cause of this was that John had settled in Essex county, where he was clerk of the courts as early as 1745, which was two years before his father died. He held the office until 1761, when he was succeeded by his first cousin, John, son of Philip Lee, of Maryland; it appears they married sisters.

John Lee represented Essex county in the House of Burgesses in 1762–63–64–65. There is no information as to any other positions filled by him.[1] He married, on the 20th of December, 1749, Mrs. Mary (Smith) Ball. (She is said to have been a daughter of the Rev. Thomas Smith, a rector of Cople parish.) After Mr. Lee's death, she married, for the third time (30th of August, 1768) "old John Smith, the inoculator," as he was called in a letter from Philip Ludwell Lee to his brother William, under date of 31st of May, 1769. John Lee lived at "Cabin Point," on the Potomac River, where he died. His widow died in 1802. They had no children; conse-

[1] Note. In a court record, this John Lee was given the title of "Colonel," which would indicate that he held some position in the county militia. The exact meaning of these titles has not been clearly shown; yet they were very exact, in those days, in giving these military titles only to persons who held certain positions.

quently he left the larger part of his estate (after his wife's death) to the male heirs of his brothers, Richard and Henry, the reversion being in favor of his nephew, Henry (afterward General Henry) Lee; and as Richard Lee left no male heirs, almost all of this estate came eventually to General Henry Lee. The family portraits, mentioned in John's will, were all destroyed by fire many years ago.

John Lee's will was dated the 23d of September, 1765, and probated, at Westmoreland, on the 24th of February, 1767. It reads:

In the name of God, Amen. I John Lee of the County of Essex, gentleman, being sick and weak in body but of sound memory and understanding (praise God for it) do make this my last Will and Testament hereby revoking and disannulling all former Wills by me heretofore made first and principally I commend my soul into the hands of Almighty God my Creator hoping for free pardon and remission of all my Sins and to enjoy Everlasting Happiness in his Heavenly kingdom through the sole merits of Jesus Christ my Saviour. My body I commit to the Earth at the discretion of my Executors hereinafter named and as to such worldly estate as it hath pleased God to intrust me I dispose of as followeth: Item, I lend unto my wife Mary Lee all my estate both real and personal excepting the lands purchased by me of John Miller and Thomas Ayres, during her natural life. Item, I lend unto John Lee, Junr, and Susanna, his wife, during their natural lives, the land purchased of John Miller and Thomas Ayres aforesaid, and I give and devise the remainder in said Lands to my Cousin Hancock Lee (son of the said John Lee, Junr.) to him and his heirs forever. Item, I give and bequeath unto the said Hancock Lee all the rest of my lands in the County of Essex to him and his heirs forever. Item, I lend (after the death of my wife) unto my brother Henry Lee for and during his life my lands in Westmoreland County called King Capsicoe, which my father purchased of John Wright, William Chandler and Deliverance, his wife, and Susanna Appleyard and the lands I purchased of Francis Wright and Molly, his wife, and after the death of my said brother Henry, I give and devise the said Lands unto my nephew Henry Lee and his heirs forever, provided my said nephew live to the age of twenty-one years, remainder to my said brother Henry and his heirs forever. Item, after the death of my wife, I lend all the rest of my lands in Westmoreland unto my brother Richard Lee for and during his natural life, the remainder I give and devise to the issue male of my said brother Richard Lee but for want of such issue I give and devise the said lands to my nephew Henry Lee and his heirs, provided my said nephew lives to the age of twenty one years, remainder to my brother Henry and his heirs. Item, I lend unto my sister Lettice Ball during her life the negroes I purchased of Col°. William Ball's estate, Vizt. Letty and her child Frank, George and Betty and their increase and after the death of my Sister I give the said negroes and their increase to my niece Mary Ball and Nephew Henry Lee Ball to be equally divided between them and their heirs forever. Item, I give unto my wife Mary Lee my negro fellow Abel, Moll (the daughter of Yellow Nan) my chariot Harness and six chariot horses to her and her heirs forever. Item. After the payment of my debts I give unto Mary Smith and Fanny Smith Daughters of Baldwin Mathews Smith one young negro woman each to them and their heirs forever. Item. After the life of my wife my will is that my negroes be divided into three equal parts, one third whereof I lend to my brother Henry Lee during his life and after his death I give the same to my nephew Henry Lee and his heirs, provided he live to the age of twenty one years, otherwise I give the same to my brother Henry Lee and his heirs. Item, I lend one other third part of my said negroes to my brother Richard Lee during his life, the remainder to the issue of my said brother Richard Lee but for want of such issue, I give the same to my brother Henry Lee and his heirs. Item, I give the other third and residue of my slaves to in manner following, that is to say, one moiety thereof to Hancock Lee, son of John Lee Junr., and his heirs, the other moiety I give to be equally divided amongst Lettice Lee, Philip Lee, Mary Lee and Elizabeth Lee, the other children of the said John Lee and their heirs. Item, I give and bequeath unto my nephew Hancock Lee my negro fellow Peter (carpenter) exclusive of his part of the other slaves aforesaid. Item, I give unto the said Hancock Lee my desk, book case, and clock. Item, I give to my brother Henry Lee my picture and those of my Father and mother. . . . Item, my will is that my wife sell any timber from the Lands lent her for her own use or for the payment of my debts. . . . Item, I do hereby appoint and constitute my wife Mary Lee Executrix, my brothers Richard Lee and Henry Lee, Executors, of this my last will and Testament. In Witness whereof I have hereunto set my hand and affixed my seal the twenty third day of September one thousand seven hundred and sixty five.

## "Squire" Richard Lee.

23. Richard[4], the second son of Henry Lee[3] (Richard[2], Richard[1]), and Mary Bland, his wife, was probably born at "Lee Hall," Westmoreland, about 1726. His cousin, William Lee, in 1771, wrote of him: "Richard is still living and unmarried, though forty-five years old, which is a great age for a bachelor in Virginia." Richard was always known amongst his contemporaries as the "Squire," and was constantly so named in their letters. The "Squire" bore a prominent part in the affairs of his county, representing Westmoreland almost continuously from 1757 to the time of his death. He was a Burgess in 1757–58–62–69–72–74; a member of the Conventions of 1775–76; of the House of Delegates in 1777–80–84–5–6–7–90–93. As the lists of the members of these various bodies are very incomplete, it may be assumed, as stated before, that he was in almost continuous service from 1757 to 1795. He was also a justice of the peace, one of the vestry of Cople parish (1755, 1785), and naval officer for the "port of South Potomack." One of his licenses reads thus:

> These are to Lycence and Permit William Lawrence master of the Schooner Harriet of Virginia, to break bulk, Unload and Land in any part of this District, twelve Tons of Barr and Six of Pigg-Iron, and one hh'd of New England Rum, here legally imported in the said Schooner from Annapolis, and the rates and duties imposed by Act of General Assembly on the Rum secured according to law.
>
> Given under our hands at the Custom House this 25th day of May, 1773.

Only a few of the "Squire's" letters have been found, and they are remarkable for their terseness and brevity. One, written to his friend Landon Carter, of "Sabine Hall," on the back of which Mr. Carter endorsed these words, "plurissimum in parvissimo," gave the important news of the day in these few words: "Williamsburgh, 10th May, 1777. Dear Sir, Wythe Speaker, Nicholas and Harrison Candidates; Dr. Lee at Madrid; Spain urges France to declare war, France will assist America with everything she wants. British cruisers off the Capes; Washington ten thousand strong; Carlton within thirty-five miles of Ticonderoga."

Two other letters, equally terse, read:

"To William Lee, Esqr., London. Virginia, 7th March, 1775. Dear Sir, I wrote you the 23rd of February that your Brother, the Honourable Philip Ludwell Lee, Esqr., departed this life the 21st of that month. He was interred on the 24th of February, his birthday, and a son was born the same day and at the time of his Interment. No will has yet been found. Col. Robt. Bolling at Petersburgh is dead. We are to have a Provincial Congress at Richmond the 20th of this month. Our Assembly is prorogued to the first Thursday in May. Lord Dartmouth has directed the Governor not to call an Assembly upon any account unless the Emergency of an Indian war requires it. No news of your ship."

"Richmond, 18th November, 1785. Sir, The Taxes are reduced ¼ lower than last year. No commutables to be taken. Tobacco from 25/ to 28/ per hund. Wheat at 6/ per bushel; about 80 square rigged vessels at Norfolk and in James River. Indian corn 5/6 a bushel in Madeira [?]. Please to forward the Inclosed. P. S. Jas. Mercer Judge of the Court of Appeals in the room of Mr. Blair."

No superscription.

The "Squire" seems to have been an odd character, a rather rough diamond. The following chatty letter from Alice, daughter of Richard and Grace (Ashton) Lee, of Blenheim, Charles county, Maryland, will be found of interest; it is inserted here, as it comments so strongly on the "Squire." It was written to William Lee, of London:

"Maryland, 27 September, 1772. So you threaten me if I prove deficient in the deference I owe you as a married man, with the power you have of forwarding or retarding my success in the Matrimonial Way. This would be a tremendous threat indeed were I as fond of Matrimony as my young Mistress, as you call her; but happily I am a little more than twelve years old and not so eager to tye a knot which Death alone can Dissolve. And yet I pretend not to ridicule the holy sacred institution, but have all due reverence for that and the worthy people who have entered into the Society, from good and generous motives. It is only those who chuse to be married at all events that I think deserve raillery. I was in Virginia when your letter came and complyd with your request relative to Miss Galloway's letter immediately. Your friends there are well, but I never saw Westmoreland so dull. I was at Squire Lee's when your Letter came. He is the veriest Tramontane in nature; if he ever gets married, if his wife civilizes him, she deserves to be Cannonized.

"I wish it was settled who is to be our Master here; I hear it will be soon. So you can't forbear a fling at femalities; believe me Curiosity is as imputable to the Sons as to the Daughters of Eve. Think you there was ever a Lady more Curious than our Cousin the Squire? He himself is the greatest of all curiosities; but hang him, how came he to pop twice into my head while I was writing to you.

"The Annapolis Races Commence the 6th of October, the Company is expected to be numerous and splendid. The American Comp'y of Players are there and are said to be amazingly improved. I should like to see them, as I think Theatrical Entertainments a rational amusement; but I shall not be there. I, indeed, lead rather a recluse Life, my greatest pleasure results from the Correspondence of my friends in different parts of the World, and I am very assiduous to cultivate this kind of amusement. I know your abilities will always furnish you with materials to give me this pleasure, and I hope your inclination will coincide. Mrs. Ann Lee has not yet exhibited any railling accusation against you. I thank your Mrs. Lee for her amicable wishes and desire you to greet her and Dr. Lee with my friendly Salutations."

When about sixty years old, "Squire" Lee married his first cousin, Sally, daughter of Peter Poythress, the "Antiquary," of "Branchester," Prince George's county. She was a granddaughter, and he a grandson, of Richard Bland. She was much his junior, being only sixteen when married. The "Squire" died in 1795, leaving a son and three daughters; the son died very shortly after his father; the widow married, on the 23d of May, 1798, Capt. Willoughby Newton, 3d; died on the 28th of May, 1828, and was buried at "Lee Hall." She had several children by her second husband, among them Willoughby Newton, of "Linden," who married Mary, daughter of Judge William Brockenbrough, and was the father of the Rev. John B. Newton, M. D., now assistant Bishop of Virginia.

Richard Lee's will was written the 16th of February, 1790, and probated, at Westmoreland, the 23d of March, 1795:

In the Name of God, Amen. I Richard Lee of Lee Hall, in the parish of Cople in the County of Westmoreland, Esquire, being now in perfect health and strength of Body and mind, considering the uncertainty of my life, do declare this to be my last Will and Testament. Imprimis my Soul I do entirely resign up again with all humility and sincerity my frail strength is able to express to the Lord God of the Heavens and the Earth, my Creator from whom my sinful flesh received it, in steadfast hope of mercy and forgiveness of all my offences only through the sufferings and merits of his most beloved Saviour. Amen. Amen. Amen. Item, My Body, I desire may be buried at the discretion of my Executors hereafter named. Item, I give and bequeath to my son Richard Lee and his heirs forever all my estate real and personal in possession or reversion subject to the Legacys hereafter mentioned and I desire that he may have the best Education that the Estate I have given him will afford. Item, I give and bequeath to my Wife Sally fifty pounds a year for four years after my death to be paid annually, besides her dower. Item, I give and bequeath my Lands in Hampshire and Berkeley Countys to my Executors in trust to be sold for the payment of my Debts. Item, I give to my Daughter who is not Christened and was born the Twelfth day of February 1790, One Thousand pounds sterling money of Great Britain, to be paid to her when she arrives of the age of twenty one years or the day of marriage which shall first happen and Forty pounds sterling a year for her mentainance and Education till she arrives to the age of twenty one years or day of Marriage which shall first happen. Item, I give to Mrs. Mary Graham, my niece, One hundred pounds current money. Item I give to each of my nephews and nieces a Mourning Ring of twenty shillings sterling value. Item, I desire my Estate may be kept together four years after my decease and that the profits may be applied to the Discharge of my Debts and Legacys and I desire and empower my Executors to sell any part of my personal Estate and such of the slaves as they think necessary for the payment of my Debts. Item, I give to William Watts a suit of Cloaths, shoes, stockings, hat and shirt to the value of Ten pounds sterling. I desire and order that the Minister of the Church of England that is the Incumbent of Cople parish be paid five pounds sterling a year out of my Estate untill my son Richard arrives to the age of twenty one years and in case my said son should die before that time the above Legacy be continued till he would have arrived at Lawfull age. Lastly I do hereby revoke all former Wills and Testaments before made by me and I do constitute and appoint my nephews Charles Lee Esqr., Richard Bland Lee Esqr., and my two friends Mr. Fleet Cox the elder and Mr. Fleet Cox Junior, Executors of this my last Will and Testament and Guardians to my children. In Witness whereof I have hereunto set my hand and Seal the Sixteenth day of February in the year of our Lord one thousand seven hundred and ninety and in the fourteenth year of the Commonwealth.

Richard and Sally (Poythress) Lee had four children:

i, RICHARD[5], who evidently died young and unmarried.

ii, MARY[5], who was born the 12th of February, 1790 (as stated in her father's will), and died in 1848; she married in 1804 Thomas Jones, Esq., of Chesterfield county, the son of General Joseph and Jane (Atkinson) Jones,[1] and had four sons: Joseph, Richard Lee, Thomas, and Robert Benson. Of these Judge Thomas Jones, of Richmond county, died early in 1894, aged about 80 years, leaving a son, William A. Jones, who was elected in November, 1894, for the third term, to represent the First Congressional District of Virginia in the House of Representatives.

---

[1] *Records of Bristol Parish*, 138.

Virginia ss

By the honourable Robert Dinwiddie Esquire His Majesty's Lieutenant Governor and Commander in Chief of the Colony and Dominion of Virginia

Whereas it hath been represented unto me by his Majesty's Attorney General that it would be highly serviceable for his Majesty and for the Benefit of this Colony That all penal Acts of Assembly here and all other Statutes of the Realm of Great Britain extending hereunto should be put in Execution and duly prosecuted against Offenders therein and he having intimated to me that through the Default of an Appointment of proper Persons for the Execution and due Prosecution of the same, Composition has been often made with the Informer for his Moiety, the Suit Dismist and his Majesty defrauded of his just Share of the Fines Forfeitures and Amerciaments in the several and respective County Courts of this Colony where he cannot possibly attend. For the future Prevention and Remedy whereof I do hereby authorize and Impower you Henry Lee Gent for and in his Majesty's Behalf to appear and Likewise (unless his Majesty's said Attorney General shall Personally attend) to Prosecute all Offenders against the Laws of Great Britain the particular Acts of Assembly of this Colony and all other Matters and things relating to the Crown the Dignity of his Majesty or against the Peace as shall appear to be or arise within the Cognizance or Jurisdiction of the County Court of Prince William which Court I am by his Majesty's Attorney General informed You attend And I do hereby likewise require and Command You to Take Care that the Clerk of the said Court return the Judgments and all Fines and Amerciaments which shall be Obtained in the said Court for the Use and Benefit of his Majesty into the Secretary's Office that his Majesty's Treasurer may by virtue thereof Give Orders for the due Levying of the same and Likewise to give Notice unto his said Majesty's Attorney General of any Appeals obtained upon any such Prosecution that he may be prepared to Defend the same.

Given under my hand and the Seal of the Colony at Williamsburgh the Twenty second Day of April in the XXVIIth year of the Reign of his Majesty King George the second

Robt. Dinwiddie

iii, LETTICE[5], born in 1792, and died in 1827; married in 1809 Dr. John Augustine Smith (said to have been the son of the Rev. Augustine Smith, "old Parson Smith of the Glebe," as he was styled, some time rector of Cople parish), who was formerly president of William and Mary College, and later of the "College of Physicians and Surgeons" of New York City. Their children were: Sally Poythress, who married John Campbell, of New York; Martha Burwell, who married John H. Hilchburn, of Philadelphia; Mary Dabney, who died unmarried, and Augustine, a lawyer, of New York City.

iv, RICHARDIA[5], born in 1795 and died in 1850; married in 1815, Presley Cox, and had two daughters: Elizabeth, who married E. C. Griffith, and Sarah Lee, who married Col. Thomas Broun, who purchased the old "Lee Hall" estate from Dr. Augustine Smith, and built himself a fine residence on the opposite side of the main road from the old mansion which perished by fire many years ago. The estate is now owned by his son, Thomas Broun.

## LIEUTENANT-COLONEL HENRY LEE.

24. Henry[4], the third son of Henry Lee[3] (Richard[2], Richard[1]) and Mary Bland, his wife, was born in 1729, and probably at "Lee Hall," Westmoreland. He settled in Prince William county, and lived at "Leesylvania," near the town of Dumfries. He was a Justice of the Peace in that county and first in commission. Mr. Lee represented Prince William for many years: as a Burgess in 1758–61–62–63–64–69–72, in the Conventions of 1774–75–76, and in the State Senate, 1780.

Mr. Grigsby, in his discourse on "The Virginia Convention of 1776," said: "Henry Lee, of Prince William, was an old member of the House of Burgesses, of all the Conventions, of the Declaratory Committee, and of the General Assembly. His standing was of the first, before and after the Revolution." Mr. Lee also served as County Lieutenant for Prince William, and was active in the duties of that office during the Revolutionary War. (*Va. Calendar State Papers*, I, 21, 395, etc. *Force's Tracts*, I, 1034, etc.)

On the opposite page a *fac-simile*, reduced in size, is given of his commission as attorney for Prince William county.

Very few of Henry Lee's letters have been preserved, and the larger part of those few are taken up with uninteresting business details. Writing to his cousin, William Lee, in London, on business, he closes with this bit of political gossip:

"Leesylvania, 1 April, 1775. . . . I have just returned from our Convention at Richmond Town on James River, where 118 Delegates of the People met and unanimously approved of the Proceedings of the General Congress, and thanked their Delegates. The same Delegates were appointed to represent this Colony in Continental Congress on the 10th of May next at Philadelphia. Our Militia of Independents are ordered by the Convention to be armed and well disciplined, and a great spirit of Liberty actuates every Individual. The Dutch supply us plentifully with arms and ammunition, and several large importations of oznabugs we have already had, so that we shall soon have a Plenty of Coarse linens from Holland. Your Brother, the Doctor's Conduct and Letters to the Speaker &c. are highly appreciated, and I make no Doubt of his being appointed our Agent when the Assembly meets."

Under date of 15th May, 1775, he wrote to the same as above: . . . "I humbly think your business here is really illy Conducted, and you must have an Active Agent here of Influence, who has weight with the Planters, and will Exert himself should the Tobacco trade be ever again revived; the Present Prospect being Very unbiding, for the People in the Country have already taken up arms and have Compelled Lord Dunmore to pay £350 sterling for a Quantity of Powder that he Privately in the night removed out of the magazine on board the Foye, Capt. Montague. Ten thousand riffle men are now well trained and are ready to take the field at an Hour's warning. The Die is now cast, and a blow having been struct near Boston, in w^ch^ rencounter the King's troops were beaten with the loss of 150 men, besides many wounded, and the Country People only lost 40 men. The Inhabitants have all left Boston, and that Place is now surrounded by 20,000 Provencials and 10,000 Conecticut troops are marched to the assistance of New York; also 1,500 riffle men from Fred^k^ County in Maryland under Col. Cressip, Jr., [?] to Prevent any troops landing. This is the news of the day."

To Charles Lee, Esqr., in Philadelphia: "Leesylvania, 8th September, 1779. Dear Charles: I received your agreeable Letter by Post, but without date; the best way is dating letters at the top, for fear of omitting in the hurry of conclusion. Your brother's enterprise does him signal honour, and I flatter myself it will not be in the Power of his Enemies to Pluck from him those laurels they cannot acquire, and on his conduct being enquired into his Military fame will be raised. I agree with you that the surprise of Paulus Hook casts a shade on Stony Point; the enclosed Letter to him, pray contrive safely. Vessels are daily arriving here and Gen'l Mercer is hourly Expected. Your mare is in good order at Whaley's and with foal by Magnanine; her colt is small but in good order, and a pretty Neat turned thing. I would not advise the sale of her. I saw your Letter to Col. Blackburn, and wish the war may be carried on without the aid of money Press, but borrowing, I fear from the spirit of monopoly and avidity for gain, will not be sufficient to supply the Call for the sums necessary for the great expenditures of the Army. The other States ought to follow our Example by a specific tax of grain to supply the Army with provisions. Your Mother has declined her trip to the Springs and still continues unwell; she thanks you for the shoes; she and Molly give their Loves to you."

To William Lee, in London: "Leesylvania, 1st March, 1775. Dear Sir, I have the melancholy news to Inform you of yr Brother Col. Phil's death, who died at Stratford of a nervous Pleurisy on the 21st of last month and has left Mrs. Lee his widow Very Big with Child; in him Virg'a has lost an able Judge and America a truly great Patriot; this Vacancy I hope you will use your utmost Efforts to fill up in Council with your Brother Thos. or Franc:, as the former will inherit all yr Brother's real Estate in Westmorl'd by your Father's will unless Mrs. Lee's Child should be a son, I could wish the Honour of the Family to be fixed at Stratford, as to your Bro. Col. Rich'd Henry I would by no means have him out of the House of Burgesses, as there is at Present the greatest reasons to Expect he will succeed Mr. Randolph as Speaker, who is old and infirm. I expect before this my Bill in favour of Duncan Campbell has been Presented and duly honoured for £24 sterling and that the James, Capt. Robertson has safely landed my two Hhds of Toba: and of Course to a good market, as no Toba: will after this Crop be Exported unless American Grievances are redressed as are Pointed out by the General Congress.

"We are making large Quantitys of Salt Petre from the Nitre in the Tobacco Putrified with Urine and have made some very strong well grained Powder in this County therefrom w^ch^ ketches quick and shoots with great force, so that we shall be able in Future to supply ourselves with Salt Petre and gun Powder without Importing any. Wool Cards we are making in great Quantitys and Nails will be soon made as ——— mills are Erecting thro' every Province on the Continent. The Gentlemen are training themselves thro' the Continent every week and have raised Companys who muster two days every week and emulate to Excell each other in y^e^ manual manœuvers and Evolutions as practised by the King of Prussia's Troops, for we are determined on Preserving our Libertys if necessary at the Expense of our Blood, being resolved not to survive Slavery. You may rely on it that the Continental Association will be most sacredly Kept as the

County Committee will not suffer the least breach to pass unnoticed and are very watchful, Pray Present our most aff't Compl'ts to Mrs. Lee."

Henry Lee to "Charles Lee Esqr., Student of Law in Philadelphia." Dated, "Wm'b'g. 12th June, 1779. My Dear Charles, I rec'd yours of the 1st June by Post and several others, since being on the Assembly and have regularly by every Post from this wrote you the News and Particular Occurrences from this quarter and as far as accts. from Lincolns Army, circulated from the report or lie of the day, my Ltr by the last post I yet hope you will receive, in that I gave you a Particular Account of an action reported with the Circumstances of undoubted belief to be given to the Credibility of the fact, which a few days ago was further Confirmed by two Frenchmen who left Charles town the 11th May, who said they were there at the time Provost Army attempted to take the City by Storm, and that 650 of the Enemy were killed on the spot and their whole Army routed, which I now believe to be a *Cursed lie*, for there is come to this City a deserter from the Enemy who left Charles town on the 16th, and sais no action had then happened but that it was more than Probable, without aid to effect their Escape by their shipping, which were not Arrived when he left the army, they must fall as Burgoyne did; for that the Town was too well fortified and the Garrison too strong for their force which only Consisted of 2,000 regulars and about the same number of Tory and Indians, that Gen'l Moultree who had entered the town with about 2,500 and Gen'l Williamson with about the same number were on their front and flank, and Gen'l Lincoln within eight miles in their rear with his main army, that our whole force Collected was about 8,000 and the Enemy had taken shelter in St. James Island and burnt some houses and it would be difficult for our Army to get at them, that they were short of Provisions and if Could not soon be relieved from their shipping they would be obliged to Surrender or Starve; this is nearly the Purport of his Examination before the Gov'r tho' many give no Credit to his Acc't and still believe the Frenchmens story. The truth is I believe they have had some small skirmishing and we got the better. I wrote you fully in my two last of the preditory and Cruel behaviour of the late invaders of this State, which if you have not rec'd let suffice that they far surpassed in Brutal lust the Goat or in ferocity the wild Boar, in barbarity the Savage or the vandals. Tell your Brother I will take notice of his request in two Ltrs, I have received from him and on my return write him fully as to the state of his Mares, &c. and as soon as I get home shall endeavour to Contrive you a remittance. The Expenses of your Phila. Studies when had you taken my advice might in a great measure been saved, had you applied yr hours wasted in Idle pursuits of dissipation to

Cooke, Blackstone, &c. having had a gen'l knowledge of the system of Law tracts, Possessing the fundamental Principals, you might have been now employed in reading the reports and applying the Practical Cases and digesting the reasoning of the Pleaders, and Judges on the applied maxims; my ——— this year will be near £2,000. I shall be always happy to hear from you and of yr application and frugality, w^ch^ is Commendable at all times."

Henry Lee's will, dated the 10th of August, and probated, in Prince William county, the first of October, 1787, was as follows:

In the name of God, Amen. I Henry Lee of Leesylvania in the County of Prince William, being in perfect mind and memory, but weak and infirm in body and mindful of the uncertainty of human life, do make this my last Will and Testament, hereby annulling and revoking all others heretofore by me made. First, I recommend my soul to God in Humble Hopes of his mercy through mediation and intercession of our Blessed Lord and Saviour, and my body to the earth to be interred at the discretion of my Executor hereafter mentioned. It is my will and desire that all my just debts be paid and that the estates real and personal hereafter devised and bequeathed to my sons Charles, Richard, Theodorick, and Edmund shall be subject thereto, each of my said four sons to pay an equal part thereof.

I give and devise to my beloved wife during her natural life all my houses at Leesylvania and 500 acres of land whereupon the said houses stand, being part of the Leesylvania tract of Land, to be laid off on the River Potomac and to be bounded by Neapsco creek, the River Potomac and Powell's creek and a straight line from one creek to the other so as to comprehend all the said Houses and the said quantity of 500 acres of land. Also I give and devise to her during her natural life the use of the following slaves, Alice, Beck, Racheal, Dick (the House servant) Kate, daughter of Beck, carpenter Dick, Winney, Jesse, and all Winney's children, Daniel, Tom, and old Nanny—also the use of the following horses, Diamond, Roan, Gimrack, Ranter, Flimack, and the bay mare, Famous, and the use of the black cattle, sheep, and Hogs at my mansion house farm and not those belonging to my quarters on Powell's creek or Neapsco creek, and the use of all my household Furniture except my chest of drawers and book case lately imported and whatever else may herein be particularly bequeathed, and the use of all the utensils of Husbandry used at the mansion farm and the carts and wagons there used. Also all the goods, provisions and Liquors now at Leesylvania, intended for the use and consumption of my family there, and also the annuity of one hundred pounds lawful money to be paid out of the Estates herein given to my sons Charles, Richard, Theodore and Edmund, each to be accountable for one fourth part of the said sum of £100 as the same shall in each year become due. It is my will and intention that the Devises and Bequests before mentioned to my said wife shall be to her in lieu of her dower and in full satisfaction of any claim she can have in law to any of my lands, slaves, and personal estate of any kind whatsoever. I give and devise unto my eldest and beloved son Henry all the interest I have in the lands and slaves devised to me by my brother John in his last will, and my meaning in making this devise of the said lands is to prevent all disputes that may in the future arise among those who may claim the same as heirs under me, being of the opinion I have not any interest in them tho: I have an interest in the slaves. Also I give and devise unto him and his heirs forever all my lands in the district of Kentucky whether located, surveyed or patented, also the lands I purchased of my brother Richard Lee lying in Westmoreland County near Richard Lee's mill. It is my will and desire that my son Henry shall hold all that I have given to him free and clear from any debts and legacies, but that he shall have no part of my slaves now in possession or in the possession of my sons Charles and Richard nor any part of my personal estate except the slaves, Bill, Bet and her child heretofore given to him which are to remain his forever.

I give and devise unto my second and beloved son Charles all my lands and houses in the County of Prince William known by the name of Leesylvania, being the land devised to me by my much honored Father's will and those purchased by me of Bertrand Ewell and Frances, his wife, the Hon. William Fairfax, Esquire, Thomas Chinn and Janet, his wife, and of Cuthbert Harrison containing from two to three thousand acres, a part of which lies on the west side of the main road from Colchester to Dumfries, to have and to hold the said lands and Houses, to him and his heirs forever. But that part of the said lands and the Houses herein before devised to my wife are to remain with her during her natural life. And my meaning is to include in this devise to my son Charles that tenement upon Neapsco River which I leased originally to Thomas Bookard and by him was afterwards assigned to Thomas Lawson and also to include all the lands I have a right to upon and between Neapsco and Powell's Run westward of the main road as well as those which are Eastward of said Road. Also I devise to him for love a lot of land in Dumfries not yet conveyed to me but paid for and I desire the Trustees of the said town to convey the same to him in fee simple. I give and devise to my third and beloved son Richard Bland Lee and my fourth and beloved son Theodorick Lee all my lands in Loudoun County devised to me by my Father's will and purchased by me of William and Hardage Walker and their wives, to be equally divided between them, to hold the same to them and their heirs forever respectively, my son Richard to have his choice of the dividends.

I give and devise to my youngest son Edmund all my lands in Fauquier County to hold, to him and his heirs forever, provided he arrives to the age of twenty one years or leaves lawful issue of his body which issue shall arrive at the age of twenty one years, but if he dies before that age not leaving lawful issue or having lawful issue of his body which shall not arrive at the age of twenty one years, then I devise the said lands to my son Henry Lee and his heirs forever. It is my will that my son Edmund be educated in the best manner out of the estate and property in this my will given to him.

I give to my eldest and dearly beloved Daughter Mary my square of lotts in the town of Dumfries, now in the occupation of Henderson Ferguson and Gibson, to have the same to her and her heirs forever; that in order that she may immediately be placed in an independent situation which for her dutiful and affectionate behavior she well deserves. Also I give to her the following slaves, Philis, Leb, Suiah, Betty daughter of Franklin and their future increase.

I give to my beloved Daughter Lucy the sum of one thousand pounds lawful money of Virginia, to be paid to her in spicie at marriage or the age of twenty one years, which first shall happen and in the meantime fifty pounds spicie for each year, to be paid to her guardian for her maintenance and education; also I give to her forever the following slaves, Charlotte, and Nanny daughter of Moll and their future increase.

I give and bequeath to my Daughter Nancy the sum of one thousand pounds lawful money of Virginia, to be paid to her in spicie at marriage or the age of twenty one years, which shall happen first, and in the meantime fifty pounds spicie for each year, to be paid to her Guardian for her maintenance and education. Also I give to her forever the following slaves, Alice daughter of Margery, Milly daughter of Jenny and Darby daughter of Dinah, and their increase; but if either of my daughters Lucy and Nancy shall die unmarried and before the age of twenty one years then the bequests to the person so dying shall go to the survivor.

I give and devise unto my sons Charles, Richard, Theodorick and Edmund, all the slaves and other personal estate herein before given to my wife, to be used by her during her natural life, and their increase, to be equally divided between them, forever after my wife's death. Also I give and devise to my sons Charles, Richard, Theodorick and Edmund forever all my other slaves and their increase, except what have been herein before particularly given to my eldest son and my three daughters and all the other Estate Real and Personal whatsoever and wheresoever not herein otherwise specifically disposed of, all which slaves and other Estate are to be equally divided between them as soon as can conveniently be done by my friends William Lane, Jeremiah Cockerell and John McMillion or any two of them, and it is my meaning that the slaves and stocks delivered by me at any time heretofore to my sons Charles and Richard, which are now in their possession or for which they should account to me, shall be subject to the division last mentioned. But my will further is if my son Edmund shall die before he arrives to the age of twenty one years, not leaving lawful issue of his body or leaving such Issue which shall not arrive to the age of twenty one years, then his share of my slaves and personal estate shall go to my sons Charles, Richard, Theodorick and my Daughters Mary, Lucy and Nancy or such as shall then be alive.

It is my will and desire that my Legacies to my daughters Lucy and Nancy be paid by my said sons Charles, Richard, Theodorick and Edmund and their respective heirs, each of my four said sons to pay an equal part thereof, and I appoint my son Charles Guardian to my son Edmund and daughters Lucy and Nancy till they shall respectively arrive to the age of twenty one years, and I entreat his best care and attention to their education.

And to the end that my Executor may be enabled to pay my debts and Legacies, I desire that my sons Richard, Theodorick and Edmund will punctually pay to him their several proportions as before mentioned of the sums that may become necessary from time to time to satisfy my debts and Legacies as they shall become payable and if either of them fail to do so, then and in every such case, my intention meaning and desire is that my Executor shall and may from time to time take possession of and sell for ready money so many of the slaves and stock of the person failing which shall come to such person by virtue of this my will, as shall be absolutely necessary to raise the sums that from time to time shall be lawfully demandable from such person as the proportion due according to what has been before expressed in this my last will. I appoint my son Charles Executor of this my last will and testament, and if he should die before my son Edmund shall arrive to the age of twenty one years or before my daughters Lucy and Nancy shall arrive to the age of twenty one years or be married, or before this will be fully executed in such case I appoint Ludwell Lee and my son Richard Bland Lee Executors for the completion of this my will and Guardians of such of my children as shall then be under the age of twenty one years and unmarried. In witness, &c., &c.

Henry Lee married Lucy Grymes, to whom tradition has given the name of the "Lowland Beauty," and claimed that General Washington was once a suitor for her hand. Her mother was Frances Jenings, daughter of Edmund Jenings and Frances Corbin, his wife. The following copy of Henry Lee's marriage certificate is taken from the original:

This is to certify all, whom it may concern, that I William Preston Minister of James City Parish in y[e] County of James City in the Colony of Virginia did join together in holy matrimony according to the Rites, and Ceremonies of y^e^ Church of England Henry Lee Gent: and Lucy Grymes, youngest Daughter of Charles Grymes Esq^r^ deceased, on Saturday y^e^ first Day of December in y^e^ Year of our Lord one thousand seven hundred fifty and three. (Signed) WILLIAM PRESTON.

Will and Mar: Coll: Virg: April y^e^ 26^th^ 1754.

Henry and Lucy (Grymes) Lee had eight children :

i, HENRY [5]. See 35.
ii, CHARLES [5]. See 36.
iii, RICHARD BLAND [5]. See 37.
iv, THEODORICK [5]. See 38.
v, EDMUND JENNINGS. [5] See 39.
vi, LUCY [5], born in 1774; died unmarried.
vii, MARY [5], born ——; died ——; married, about 1792, Philip Richard Fendall, of Alexandria. Mr. Fendall had previously married the widow of Philip Ludwell Lee, of Stratford; she died about 1790. By the second marriage he left a son, Philip Richard, and a daughter, Lucy Eleanor Fendall. The son, Philip R. Fendall died the 16th of February, 1868, æt. 73 years, leaving four sons and three daughters, of whom the survivors now reside at Washington.
viii, ANNE [5], born in 1776 and died in August, 1857; married, about 1793, William Byrd Page, of "Fairfield," Clarke county. (Mr. Page was the eldest son of Mann and Mary Mason (Selden) Page, of the same place; Mann Page was the eldest son of the Hon. John Page, of "North End," and Jane Byrd, his wife. The Hon. John Page was the second son of the Hon. Mann Page, of "Rosewell," and Judith Carter, his wife; the Hon. Mann Page was the son of the Hon. Matthew and Mary (Mann) Page, who was the only surviving son of Col. John Page, of England, the progenitor of the Page family of Virginia.)

William Byrd and Anne (Lee) Page had nine children:[1] 1, William Byrd, born about 1794; died unmarried. 2, Mary Anne, born about 1796 and died in December, 1873; she married, about 1816, General Roger Jones, Adjutant-General, U. S. A., and had these twelve children (Jones): William Page, Catesby ap Roger, Letitia Corbin, Mary, Dr. Eusebius Lee, Edmonia Page, Roger (Inspector-General, U. S. A.), Walter, Charles Lucian, Thomas Skelton, Virginia Byrd, and Winfield Scott Jones. 3, Rev. Charles Henry Page, the second but eldest son to have issue, married, in 1827, Gabriella Crawford, of Amherst

[1] See *Genealogy of the Page Family*, p. 100.

county. 4, Mann Randolph, born about 1803; married and had a daughter, Jane Byrd Page, who married, the 11th of May, 1854, Guerdon H. Pendleton, of Clarke county. 5, Jane Byrd, born about 1805; never married. 6, Richard Lucian, Captain, U. S. N., and Brigadier-General, C. S. A., was born about 1807; resided at Norfolk, and married, about 1832, Alexina Taylor, of that city; had a son, Walter H. Page, who was born about 1850, and a daughter who married William C. Whittle, C. S. N. 7, Cary Selden, born about 1809; never married. 8, Dr. Thomas, born about 1811; was married. 9, Edmonia Page, born about 1813; married, about 1833, Hall Neilson.

NOTE.—The General Roger Jones, Adjutant-General, U. S. A., mentioned above as having married Mary Anne Page, was the eldest son of Catesby Jones, Esq., of Westmoreland county, who married Lettice Corbin Turberville, second child of John Turberville and Martha Corbin, his wife, both of whom were grandchildren of Richard Lee and Martha Silk, his wife. (See 3, ii and iii.)

## THE GRYMES FAMILY.

Of the many influential families that once inhabited old Middlesex county, that "cradle of Virginia families," none appear to have been more prominent than that of Grymes. The first of the name in Virginia was the Rev. Charles, who was officiating in York county as early as 1642; subsequently he moved to Gloucester county, where he died. His son, John, lived at "Grimesby," near the Piankatank River. His name appeared on the vestry books of Christ Church, Lancaster, as early as 1694. This venerable church was built about midway between "Brandon," the later seat of the Grymeses, and "Rosegill," the seat of the Wormeleys. John Grymes married Alice, daughter of Lawrence Townley by his wife, Sarah, the daughter of Col. Augustine Warner. He died about 1709, and left a son, John, who was born in 1693 and died in 1748, leaving a large family. Bishop Meade has given his epitaph:

Here lies the body of the Hon. John Grymes, Esq., who for many years acted in the public affairs of this Dominion with honour, fortitude, fidelity, to their Majesties King George I. and II. Of the Council of State, of the Royal Prerogative, of the liberty and property of the subject, a zealous asserter. On the seat of Judgment, clear, sound, unbiassed. In the office of Receiver-General, punctual, approved. Of the College of William and Mary, an ornament, visitor, patron. Beneficent to all, a pattern of true piety. Respected, loved, revered. Lamented by his family, acquaintance, country. He departed this life the 2d day of November, 1748, in the 57th year of his age.

This John Grymes had a brother Charles, who married Frances Jenings, daughter of Gov. Edmund Jenings and Frances Corbin, his wife; Frances was the daughter of Henry Corbin and Alice Eltonhead, his wife, and a younger sister of Lætitia, who married Richard Lee, of "Mt. Pleasant," Westmoreland. Charles Grymes lived at "Morattico," in Richmond county; he was born about 1697, and was deceased at the date of the marriage of his daughter, Lucy, with Henry Lee, as stated in their marriage certificate. Charles Grymes was Sheriff of Richmond county, and a member of the Council in 1724–5.

## THE JENINGS FAMILY.

Arms: Argent, a chevron between three plummets, gules.

Crest: A griffin's head couped between two wings inverted or, in the beak a plummet, gules.

Peter Jenings, of Silsden in the parish of Kildnick in Craven in Comit: Ebor., married Elizabeth Parker, on the 13th of January, 1588, and had issue: Peter and William. His eldest son, Peter, who died on the 1st of September, 1651, married Anne Baldwyn and had issue: Peter, Jonathan, and Edmund. The second son, Jonathan, who died on the 24th of August, 1649, married Elizabeth, daughter and co-heir of Giles Parker, of Newly in Com: Ebor., and had issue, among others, Sir Edmund and Sir Jonathan, who married sisters; the elder, Sir Edmund (æt. 38 years on the 15th of August, 1665), born in 1627; died about 1687; married Margaret, daughter of Sir Edward Barkham, Lord Mayor of London in 1621–22; he lived at Rippon, Yorkshire; left issue: Anne, Elizabeth, Mary, Jonathan, William, and Edmund.[1] The youngest son, Edmund, was born in 1659; died in England the 5th of December, 1727; he was in Virginia at an early date; was attorney-general in 1684; "Mr. Edmund Jenings, attorney-general of Virginia" was one of the delegates from Virginia, at Albany, N. Y., on the 31st of July, 1684, at a conference with "the Oneydes, Onondages, and Cayugas Indians." (I, *Va. Cal. State Papers*, 17.) He was member of the Council, 1684, 1691, 1698, and perhaps continuously; was President of the Council, and acting governor of the State from June, 1706 to 23d of Au-

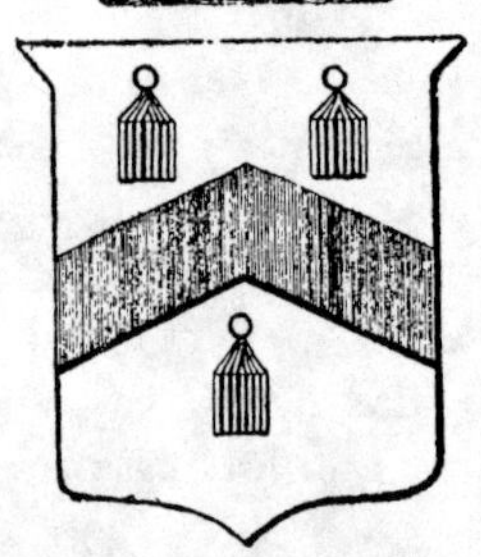

[1] This pedigree is condensed from one given in *The Curio* (of New York), p. 141.

gust, 1710. Secretary of the Colony, 1704, and revisor of its laws. (*Ibid.*, 55, 86.)

He married Frances, daughter of Henry Corbin, and Alice Eltonhead, his wife; she died at London on the 22d of November, 1713; they had several children; among them, Frances, who married Charles Grymes; Elizabeth, who married Robert Porteus, of "New Bottle," on the York River, who was member of the Council in 1715; later he removed to York, England; in the cathedral at Rippon is an inscription to his memory. He had nineteen children; next to the youngest was Beilby Porteus, born at York the 8th of May, 1731; died the 14th of May, 1808; was bishop of Chester and later of London. (*W. and M. Quarterly*, III, 38.)

Beside these daughters, Gov. Edmund Jenings had a son, Edmund, who was Secretary of the Province of Maryland; he married (in 1728) Ariana, the widow of James Frisby and of Thomas Bordley, and daughter of Matthias, and Anna Margaretta (Hermann) Vanderheyden, and had issue: Peter, Ariana, Edmund, and Charles. Ariana married John Randolph, of Williamsburg, Va., and had issue: Edmund (first Attorney-General of the U. S., and Governor of Va.), Susan Beverley, and Ariana Jenings Randolph. This Edmund Jenings died, at Bath, on the 3d of March, 1756, aged 59 years, and left a son, also Edmund Jenings, who died unmarried, 1819.

There were others of the Jenings family in Virginia; Charles, who was clerk of Elizabeth City county; John, who was clerk of Isle of Wight county, and took part in Bacon's Rebellion; and also Peter, who was once attorney-general of Virginia; he married and left descendants. (*W. and M. Quarterly*, III, 205.) The following, relating to Gov. Edmund Jenings is of interest:

To Our Trusty and Welbeloved Fran: Nicholson, Our Lieut: and Governour, &c. Trusty and Welbeloved, Wee Greet You well: Whereas the Commissioners for promoting the Trade of this Kingdom and of our Colonies and Plantations abroad, have represented to our High Treasurer here by a Memorial which hath been laid before us, that our Trusty and Welbeloved Edmund Jenings, Esqr., Secretary of the Affaires of Our Colony Of Virginia, hath for Severall months past attended them with great Diligence for Compleating the Worke of Inspecting and Amending the Laws of Our said Colony, which he (by your appointment) brought over with him from thence for that service. And in recompense of his paines and charges in this service (being about to returne again with the said Laws as Amended), They, the said Commissioners have offered their opinions, that the sume of £200 (over and above the sume of £100, which you advanced to him before his coming from thence) may be allowed him Out of Our Revenues there, To which Wee being Graciously pleased to Condescend agree, &c. &c.

(Signed)

By ye Maties Command.

GODOLPHIN.

## STRATFORD LINE, FIFTH GENERATION.

### George Fairfax Lee.

25. George Fairfax[5], eldest son of George Lee[4] (Richard[3], Richard[2], Richard[1]) and Anne (Fairfax) Washington, his second wife, was born at "Mt. Pleasant," Westmoreland county, on the 24th of February, 1754; died at same place in December, 1804; he married the widow of a Dr. Travers, of Berkeley (now Jefferson county, West Virginia), and had several children, only one of whom lived to marry; this was a daughter, Louisa. He mentioned in his will that he had had other children, who were deceased at that date. All his landed property was left to his brother, Lancelot Lee. Of his life, nothing is known; from the following letter, written to his kinsman, William Lee, then at London, it is shown that he was educated at Christ's College, Cambridge:

"Xt. College, Cambridge, Wednesday morn'g, 4th Nov'ber, 1772. Sir,—I rec'd the favour of yours, with the hampers of wine &c., and know not at this time any other way to shew my gratitude than by hasty thanks for the same. I would be much obliged to you, if you would let Dr. Shepherd provide me with a tutor, as they are all at present in College, which I imagine will take off your hands a great deal of trouble, as our lectures begin on Sunday afternoon. I will be much oblig'd to you if you will let me know, if you approve of my request, as Mr. Shepherd thinks if I had had a private tutor, when I first came to the University, it would have been of infinite service, but he says it is a thing impossible for me to do without one, during the lectures. So I hope you will write as soon as possible that I may be able to procure one before they are all engaged. I was very sorry when I read that part of your epistle which mentioned Mrs. Lee's illness, but I hope she is at this time out of all danger, and in perfect health, so as to be able to stir about again. I hope you will remember me to Mrs. Lee, Mrs. Dinwiddie, &c. I'm Sir," &c.

His will, dated 3d of December and probated the 24th of December, 1804, was as follows:

In the Name of God, Amen. I George Fairfax Lee of the County of Westmoreland and State of Virginia, being low in health but of sound mind and memory, do make and declare this to be my last will and testament, revoking all and every other heretofore made by me or in my name.

First, It is my wish to be decently interred in Mount Pleasant Garden,[1] where my

[1] This garden was probably near the house, erected by his father, on the hill further back from the river than the old mansion.

wife and children are, without pomp or parade. 2d. I wish Hugh Quinlan to pay such debts as he has assumed for me, I having acknowledged them to be just. 3d. I give unto Hugh Quinlan the amount due by William Chelton of Loudoun County being the balance of his purchase of lands from me, which I sold to discharge a debt due by John Tasker Carter to Porter Stumps.

4th. I give unto Hugh Quinlan all the lands in Loudoun county heretofore conveyed by me to him, as will appear by Deeds, in fee simple clear of all and every incumbrance whatever. This I do to prevent any dispute or censure. 5th. I give unto Tasker Quinlan, son of Hugh Quinlan, the full amount of the Debt due by his Uncle John Tasker Carter to me, which debt his father is to apply to his benefit as he may think most proper and useful.

6th. I give unto my brother Lancelot all the residue of my Estate both real and personal in fee Simple to be disposed of as he may think proper among his children. That is to say he paying the following Legacies, Viz. first to Mrs. Quinlan, for the kind and tender attention to me, three hundred dollars, which is to be applyed by her husband for the purchase of a carriage for her use. Second Legacy to be paid to my brother William five guineas for a mourning ring and thirdly five guineas to my sister for the same purpose. Given under my hand, &c.

i, LOUISA [6], married John Tasker Carter, and died without issue. On the 27th of February, 1786, George Fairfax Lee deeded two slaves to his daughter, Louisa Lee.

## LANCELOT LEE.

26. LANCELOT [5], the second son of George Lee [4] (Richard [3], Richard [2], Richard [1]) and Mrs. Anne (Fairfax) Washington, his second wife, was born at "Mt. Pleasant," Westmoreland county, the 19th of January, 1756; died ——. Mr. Lee is said to have been twice married; first to Mary Bathurst, daughter of Col. Thomas and Sallie (Skelton) Jones; after her death he married, secondly, a Miss Cockrell. By his first wife he had two sons and three daughters; by the second only a daughter, Martha, concerning whom there are no data. The issue of Lancelot and Mary Bathurst (Jones) Lee were:

i, LANCELOT BATHURST [6], who, it is said, died in Charleston, S. C., when about to embark for England; he never married.

ii, SALLIE FAIRFAX [6] married Robert Sangster, of Fairfax county, and had: Robert (who died in infancy), Mary Ann, who married a Mr. Erwin, and Thomas S. Sangster.

iii, ELIZABETH J. J. [6] married Colonel James Chipley, a lawyer of Winchester, Va., and had: William Lee, Mary Ann, Sallie Fairfax, James Monroe, Richard Henry, Ludwell Lee, and Elizabeth Washington Chipley.

iv, NANCY[6] married Richard Cockrell, of Fairfax county, and had: Mary, Sallie Lee, Richard, and Thomas Lee Cockrell.

v, THOMAS[6] married, but name of wife unknown. He is said to have had several children, of whom three sons are now living: George W., Philip De Catesby, and William F. Lee, all of whom are married and have issue. (Repeated attempts have been made to gain some reliable data concerning the issue of Lancelot Lee, but without success. The above is given on the authority of private information, based chiefly upon family tradition.)

## PHILIP THOMAS LEE.

27. PHILIP THOMAS[5], the second son of Richard Lee[4] (Philip[3], Richard[2], Richard[1]) and Grace Ashton, his wife, was born ——, and died the 28th of November, 1778, "at his father's seat on the Potomac." He married a Miss Russell, of England, who may have been a relative of the James Russell so frequently mentioned in connection with the family, and who had married Anne, daughter of Philip Lee, Sr. Miss Miller, of Washington, has in her possession a silver dish, in the centre of which are engraved the Lee arms, bearing on a shield of "pretence" the arms of "Russell of Kingseat."[1] As it seems most probable that this dish must have once belonged to Philip Thomas Lee, a print of it is given on the following page.

Philip Thomas had five children:

i, RUSSELL[6], who died in 1793, a minor, and without issue.

ii, SARAH RUSSELL[6], so named in her aunt's will. "A few days ago the Hon. Benjamin Contee, Esqr. (a delegate to Congress from this State), was married to Miss Sarah Russell Lee." (Md. *Journal*, 8th April, 1788.) They had issue: Sarah Elinor, Alice Lee, Philip Ashton Lee, and Edmund Henry Contee.

The Rev. Benjamin Contee, D. D., was born in 1755, in Prince George's county, Md.; he was appointed a second lieutenant, and served in the army during the Revolutionary War; was member of Congress in 1787–88–90–91, and later Judge of the Orphans' Court of Charles county, Md. In 1803, he was ordained to the priesthood

---

[1] Mr. J. Henry Lea employed Dr. Marshall, of the Herald's College, London, to identify the arms here borne in pretence. Dr. Marshall blazons them as: *Argent, a chevron between three tadpoles and within a bordure sable*, and once borne by the "Russells of Kingseat." This family has not been identified; but the Russells of "Ashiesteel, co. Selkirk," bear these very similar arms: *Argent on a chevron gules between three tadpoles, sable, a martin of the field, within a bordure engrailed, azure*. This dish was probably made about 1760.

in the Episcopal Church and was rector of several parishes; in 1814, he was within a few votes of receiving the election for Bishop of that diocese. Apparently he continued his duties as a judge, for he was at the time of his death, in 1816, the chief judge of the Orphans' Court of Charles county.

On the 7th December, 1790, a deed was executed between Benjamin Contee and Philip Richard Fendall, of Alexandria, for a part "of Peyton's Levels," the property of Grace Lee, late of Charles county, Md., which land had been divided between Elinor Ann Lee and the heirs of Philip Thomas Lee.

On the 5th of September, 1797, a deed was made between Philip Richard Fendall, and Mary, his wife, to Ann Lee, of Charles county, Md., for one fifth part of "Peyton's Levels" in Westmoreland and Richmond counties, which had been conveyed to Fendall by Benjamin Contee and Sarah Russell, his wife.

iii, MARGARET RUSSELL[6], married James Clerklee, and had issue: Caroline R., who married Josiah Hawkins, of Charles county, Md.; Eleanor Russell, who married Edward Henry Grette; Eliza, who married —— Lyson, and Emily, who married Thomas D. Fendall, of Charles county, Md. (See 8, i and iii.)

iv, ELINOR[6], married Dr. William Dawson, son of Ambrose Dawson, of

Yorkshire, England; they had: William, born 1798; Mary Ann, born 1799; Robert Lee, born 1801; Philips Lee, born 1803; Frederick, born 1805; Eleanor Georgiana, and Laura Dawson, who married Arch-deacon MacDonald, of Salisbury, England, and had issue. Of these, William Dawson married Sarah, daughter of Peter Augustus Jay, of New York, and had: William Pudsey (1837–1838), William Pudsey (1839–1851), and Mary Jay Dawson, born in New York, in 1842; married Colville, second son of Sir Frederick William Frankland, and had issue.

v, Ann[6], married William Gamble, no issue known.

## Governor Thomas Sim Lee.

28. Thomas Sim[5], the only son of Thomas Lee[4] (Philip[3], Richard[2], Richard[1]) and Christiana Sim, his wife, was born on the 29th of October, 1745, in Prince George's county, Md., and died on the 9th of October, 1819, at his home, "Needwood," in Frederick county, Md. Nothing is known of him until he appears in public life in 1777, as a member of the Provincial Council of Maryland. He was then only about thirty-two years old. From that date on until old age prevented, he seems to have been continually in the service of his State. The legislature elected him governor in 1779, being the second to hold that office under the State Constitution. Again in 1792 he was chosen to this position, and served the full term, but declined an election in 1798, when offered a third term. Besides these offices, he was a member of the Continental Congress in 1783–4; was elected to the Constitutional Convention of 1787, but refused to attend; later, he served in his State convention which met to ratify the Constitution, adopted at Philadelphia.

The following letter, written to the Governor of Virginia, is of some interest:

"Sir, The Marquis Lafayette has requested this State to furnish armed Vessels for the Protection of the Transports and Troops under his Command and destined for the Expedition against Portsmouth. We have only been able to procure a Brig of fourteen four-pounders, a Schooner of eight three-pounders, and a Sloop loaded and bound to sea, of three ten-pounders. From various accounts we are apprehensive this force is inferior to the Enemies Privateers in the Bay. We have wrote to the Commander of the Ships of our Ally at the Capes, and if he cannot spare one of his Vessels to convoy the Marquis, you will see the necessity of Your State immediately procuring a force, which in conjunction with ours, would certainly be superior to the enemies Cruisers. The Marquis, with the Troops, Cannon and Stores are now at the Head of Elk. We have impressed and sent to him every Vessel now at Baltimore and this place, and fear they will not be sufficient. The Marquis has requested us to procure Boats to land Cannon and Troops, which will not be in our Power, but we hope you will be able to obtain any number he may want. General Wayne, with a second Detachment from the Pennsylvania Line, is expected at the Head of Elk, and he is to join the Marquis, as soon as Vessels can be procured to transport him." (I *Va. Cal. State Papers*, 561.)

Thomas Sim Lee's will, dated the 6th of November, and probated, in Frederick county, Md., the 15th of November, 1819, was as follows:

In the Name of God, Amen. I, Thomas Sim Lee of Frederick County Maryland, being at present in full possession of my memory and understanding, but being infirm in health and considering the uncertainty of life and the certainty of death do hereby make, publish and declare this my last will and testament, hereby revoking all others by me heretofore made.

Imprimis—I direct my executors hereinafter named to bury my body decently and after the expenses of my interment are paid to discharge my just debts with honour and justice from the fund hereafter appointed.

Item—I give and devise my negroes in manner following: To my son William Lee his heirs and assigns, in addition to those I have given him during my lifetime these negroes and their increase—that is to say—Polly the daughter of Charity, and her children, Ben, Matilda and Charity—Cis the daughter of Charity and her children, John, Eliza, Jane and Sarah—Molly and her children Pris and Abraham—Nancy and Clem the children of weaver Tom and Nelly and old Michael the brother of Arom, in all fifteen negroes.

Item,—I likewise give and devise to my daughter Eliza Horsey and to her heirs and assigns in addition to those I have given her during my lifetime, these negroes and their increase namely—Anna the wife of Blacksmith Will and her children Suckey, Juliet, Nancy, Michael, Kate, Mariah and Sal,—Dick and his wife Sal and their daughter Rachael and her children, Thomas, Stephen and Betsey,—Amos the son of Charity—Isaac and his wife, Grace and their children, Isaac and Lucy—Will and his wife Fanny—Pat and his children Ignatius, Basil, Nace and John, and Polly the wife of Ignatius and their children,—and Tommy the son of Weaver Tom, and Nelly and Teresa the daughter of Molly and her daughter Nancy—together with all the future increase of the said negroes to my said daughter Eliza Horsey her heirs and assigns.

Item—I likewise give and devise to my son John Lee and to his heirs and assigns the negroes named as following: Len and his wife Peg, and their children Rachael, Philip, Suckey, Mary, Beck, Matilda and her child Betsey—Harry and his wife Mary and betsey the Mother of Mary the Children of Aaron and Poll,—Sarah and her son Aaron—Anna, Mary, Nick, and Stephen, and his wife Lucy and their children—Bistiller, Charles and his wife Betsey—Ned and John the sons of Ambrose, Thomas the son of Stephen and Lucy—Peter the son of Blacksmith Will, Aaron and his wife Rachael and their children now in the possession of my son John Lee—Beck and her two sons Robert and Henry—Jack and his wife Nancy and their daughter Nelly, Rachael the wife of Bernard and their children Stephen, Julianna Bernard and Sarah—Michael and his wife Sissey and their children, Alice, Stephen, Nancy, Kate, and Henry,—Sal the wife of house Charles—and Dick the son of Joan until his term of service expires, together with all the future increase of the said negroes to my said son John Lee and his heirs and assigns.

Item—I hereby declare it to be my will, and desire that the following named negroes shall be considered as manumitted and set free from all manner of service to my heirs—namely—Bernard the husband of Rachael—Aaron and his wife Pol—and house Charles the husband of Sal--which said last named negroes shall be maintained and taken good care of by my son John Lee during their natural lives if they think proper to live with them—also, weaver Tom and his wife Nelly who shall be maintained during their natural lives by my daughter Eliza Horsey, if they think proper to live with her—also Teresa the wife of Amos and her children—and the boy John the son of Beck whom I direct my executors to have bound to some good trade until he reaches the age of eighteen years and from that period to serve my son John Lee until he attains the age of twenty-one years that is to say, until the first day of January, in the year of our Lord, one thousand eight hundred and twenty seven from which time it is my will and desire that he be set free and manumitted.

Item—I hereby constitute aud appoint my sons William Lee and John Lee and my son-in-law Outerbridge Horsey of the State of Delaware my executors to this my last will and testament.

Item —I give and devise to my son Thomas Lee and his wife Eleanore Lee, and the survivor during their natural lives the following lots of ground in Georgetown—that is to say—one half of my lot of ground fronting on the South side of Road street containing in the whole six acres, more or less, out bounded by Road and Valley street to be laid off by my executors—Lots mentioned, one, two, three, four and twenty three fronting on Montgomery street sixty six, ninety four, ninety five and ninety six fronting on Washington street sixty seven, sixty eight and sixty nine fronting on Water Street, seventy nine and eighty fronting on Virginia Avenue, and thirty six fronting on Greene Street all the said last numbered lots of ground lying south of Bridge street and east of Jefferson street, and after the death of my son Thomas Lee and his wife Eleanore Lee I then give and bequeath the said lots of ground in Georgetown in fee simple to be divided share and share alike among the children of my said son Thomas Lee.

Item—I give and bequeath to my son Archibald Lee his heirs and assigns the following lots of ground in Georgetown—numbered thirty eight and sixty four on Washington street thirty four, thirty five and forty five on Greene street, all which lots of ground are situate between Bridge and Water streets and numbers nine and ten fronting on the south side of Needwood street as a compensation for the negroes I have given to my other children.

Item—I give and devise to my executors and to the survivors and survivor of them and to their heirs and assigns these several lots of ground in Georgetown.—Lots numbered twenty two, thirty one, and forty six fronting on Greene street, forty seven, forty eight forty nine and fifty fronting on Water street seventy four, seventy five, seventy eight, ninety one, ninety two and ninety three south of Water street and east of Washington street, and one half of my lot of ground containing in the whole six acres more or less, lying between High and Valley streets to hold the same lots of ground in trust and for the use and benefit of my son Archibald Lee; provided that my executors shall pay to my said son Archibald Lee the rents, issues and profits of the said lots of ground, and provided further if my executors shall in their discretion think proper to determine the said trust in any event, they are hereby authorized and empowered so to do,—and the fee simple in the said lots of ground shall in that case vest absolutely in my said son Archibald Lee.

Item—I give and devise to my executors and the survivors and survivor of them and their heirs and assigns these several lots of ground in Georgetown—that is to say—nineteen fronting on Needwood street, sixty three, sixty five, thirty seven, sixty, thirty and forty fronting on Washington street, south of Bridge street and all the lots numbered seventy two, seventy three, eighty one, eighty two, eighty three, eighty four, eighty five, eighty six, ninety seven, ninety eight, ninety nine and one hundred, south of Water street, to hold the same in trust and for the use and benefit of my several grandaughters the children of my daughter Mary C. Ringgold in manner following—lots numbered nineteen sixty and sixty three to Mary Digges Galloway Ringgold, lots numbered thirty nine and forty and twenty two south of Water street to Eliza Lee Ringgold, lots numbered thirty seven, sixty five, and seventy three to Anna Maria Ringgold, and the remaining lots in common among my said three grandaughters and Sarah Brooke Lee Ringgold their sister, until they shall respectively arrive at the age of twenty-five years, when it is my will and desire that this trust shall cease and the fee simple vest in my said grandaughters absolutely, provided that my said executors shall in the meantime pay to my said grandaughters, in equal portions, the rents issues and profits of the said lots of ground, and provided further if my executors shall in their discretion think proper to determine the said trust sooner in the event of marriage or other contingency they are hereby authorized and empowered so to do.

Item—I give and bequeath to my grand-son Benjamin Ringgold, the son of my daughter Mary C. Ringgold the following lots of ground in Georgetown in fee simple or when he attains the age of twenty one years—namely all my ground fronting on the north side of West street between Greene and Montgomery streets, and running back north one hundred and eighty feet.

Item—I give and devise to my grand-children Mary Digges Lee the daughter of my son Thomas Lee, Mary Digges Galloway Ringgold, Molly Digges Lee and Thomas Sim Lee the children of my son William Lee, Mary Ellen Horsey and Thomas Sim Lee Horsey to be equally divided among my said six grand-children, one half of my square of lots in Georgetown fronting on the south side of Staddart street between Greene and Montgomery streets, and running back south one hundred and eighty feet—in fee simple.

Item—I give and devise all my real estate in Frederick County State of Maryland, to my sons William Lee and John Lee and to my daughter Eliza Horsey, to them, their heirs and assigns as tenants in common and not as joint tenants, subject however to the payment of all my just debts, and in case my said sons William Lee and John Lee and my daughter Eliza Horsey should not agree concerning the division of the said estate, though it is my earnest desire they should, I nominate and appoint my friends Joseph Smith, Joseph Parson and Baker Jamison Esquires or any two of them to divide the said real estate equally between my said sons William Lee and John Lee and my said daughter Eliza Horsey having regard to quantity and quality of land; and my will and desire is that the division or allotment whereon the dwelling house and other adjacent improvements shall stand or be, shall be assigned to my son John Lee and that he shall pay an equivalent in money on reasonable credit for the improvements to my said son William Lee and my daughter Eliza Horsey, and in case the parties cannot agree concerning the value of the said improvements, my desire and request is that my said friends Joseph Smith, Joseph Parson and Baker Jamison, Esquires, or any two of them shall value the same, whose valuation shall be final and obligatory on all the parties—and whereas, it is my intention that the several devises herein contained, other than the devise of my real estate in Frederick County shall not be subject to the payment of my debts or any part of them, I hereby order and direct that all my personal estate not herein specifically bequeathed, shall be first applied to the payment of my just debts, and such portion thereof as shall remain unsatisfied out of the undevised part of my personal estate, I hereby direct to be paid out of my real estate in Frederick County aforesaid, and for this purpose charge the said real estate with the payment thereof.

Item—I give and devise two thousand dollars to my executors in trust—of which sum one thousand dollars is to be expended in the construction of a Roman Catholick church in the vicinity of my farm Needwood, and the other thousand dollars to be vested in the funds by my said executors as a support for the said church—also one hundred dollars to be distributed among the poor of this neighborhood; and also seven hundred and fifty dollars to make certain payments for which I shall leave a memorandum to govern my executors.

Item—I give and devise the debt due me on note by Mr. Tench Ringgold amounting to upwards of five hundred dollars, to my executors in trust, and for the use and benefit of my grandaughter Mary Digges Galloway Ringgold when she arrives at the age of twenty five years.

Item—I give and devise to my executors for the payment of the aforesaid legacies the following lots of ground in Georgetown—numbers thirty two—thirty three—twenty—twenty one—twenty four and twenty five, fronting on Greene, Needwood and Montgomery streets, south of Bridge Street with full power to sell said lots of ground for that purpose. Signed and sealed &c.

The following data concerning the births, deaths, marriages, etc., in the family of Governor Lee were kindly copied from his Bible by his granddaughter, Mrs. Mary Digges (Lee) Gouverneur.

Thomas Sim Lee was married, on the 27th of October, 1771, to Mary, only daughter of Ignatius Digges, of Prince George's county, Md., and Elizabeth Parkham, his wife; she was born in August, 1745, and died on the 21st of January, 1805. They had issue eight children:

i, IGNATIUS[6], born the 3d of August, 1772; he died at Liege, where he had been for several years for his education. No date.

ii, THOMAS[6]. See 40.

iii, WILLIAM[6]. See 41.

iv, MARY CHRISTIAN[6], born the 22d of February, 1777; died the 27th of November, 1813; married, the 10th of April, 1799, Tench (born 6th March, 1776), the fourth son of Thomas and Mary (Galloway) Ringgold, and had: 1, Mary Digges Galloway, born 5th of October, 1800. 2, Benjamin, born 4th of October, 1802. 3, Eliza Lee, born 11th of February, 1806. 4, Sarah Brooke, born 11th of May, 1809. 5, Anna Maria, born 29th of January, 1811. Of these children, Sarah Brooke Ringgold married, in 1828, John Moylan Thomas, of Maryland, and had eight children; one, a son, John Moylan Thomas, married Adele Ingersoll, of Philadelphia, and has two daughters. Anna Maria Ringgold, the fifth child, married, in November, 1829, Dr.

Henry Hunt, of Washington, and had Mary Lee Hunt, who married Gen. Robert Ransom, C. S. A., of North Carolina. Tench Ringgold, after his wife's death, married Mary Aylett, daughter of Thomas Ludwell and Fanny (Carter) Lee, of "Coton," Loudoun county, Va.

v, ARCHIBALD [6], born 22d of July, 1778; died 1st of April, 1781.

vi, ARCHIBALD [6], second of the name, was born 20th of April, 1781; died in July, 1839, unmarried.

vii, ELIZA [6], born the 30th of April, 1783; died the 5th of July, 1862; married, 16th of October, 1812, Outerbridge Horsey, of Delaware, and formerly U. S. Senator from that State. They had: 1, Mary Ellen, born 1813. 2, Ann Caroline, born, 1815. 3, Thomas Sim Lee, born 1817, and died aged 18. 4, William Outerbridge Horsey, born. 28th of February, 1819, and married Anna Carroll, and has issue.

viii, JOHN [6]. See 42.

## THE DIGGES FAMILY.

John Diggs, Sheriff of Kent, temp. Henry IV., bore this coat-of-arms, as may be seen in the cloisters of Christ Church, Canterbury: *Gules, on a cross argent, five eaglets sable* (Hasted's *Kent*).[1] From "Roger de Mildenhall dictus Digge," temp. King John, was descended Sir Dudley Digges, who built Chilham Castle in 1616. This Sir Dudley, once British Ambassador to Russia, M. P., and Master of the Rolls, married Mary, a daughter of Sir Thomas Kemp, of Chilham, Kent; their fourth son, Edward, who died the 15th of March, 1675–6, aged 55 years, arrived in Virginia about 1650; in the latter year, he purchased some 1,200 acres, fronting on the York River, from Captain John West. This was the famous "Bellfield" estate, which remained in the family for several generations. Here he employed two Armenians, skilled in the business, to cultivate the silk-worm.

From this Edward Digges there has descended a notable line of distinguished men. And he himself was a man of prominence, having been

[1] The print given here is a copy of the arms carved on the tomb of Dudley Digges, 1710, of "Bellfield," York county, which was kindly loaned by Mr. Lyon G. Tyler, President of William and Mary College, Williamsburg.

member of the Council, Auditor-General, and Governor (1656–68); later, he was sent as Colonial agent to England.[1] His wife, Elizabeth, is supposed to have been a sister of Col. John Page, the progenitor of that Virginia family. His tombstone states that he had six sons and seven daughters, of whom only five are known: William, Edward, Mary, Anne, and Dudley. Col. William, eldest son and heir, moved to Charles county, Md., about 1679–80, and married Mrs. Elizabeth (Sewall) Wharton, the daughter of Henry Sewall of Patuxent, Md., and Jane Lowe, his wife. Col. William became a member of the Maryland Council, and, dying in 1698, left a large family, named in his will: Edward, William, Charles, Dudley, John, Nicholas, Jane, Elizabeth, Anne, and Mary. The Maryland family are descended from these children, but they have not been clearly traced.

The Virginia branch of this family appear to be chiefly descended from Dudley, the youngest (known) son of Gov. Edward and Elizabeth (Page) Digges; he also held many positions, having been member of the Council, Auditor and Surveyor-General. He died the 18th of January, 1710–11; his wife was Elizabeth, daughter of Col. William Cole, of "Bolthorpe," Warwick county, by whom he had four children: Cole, Edward, Dudley, and Elizabeth. Of these, the eldest, Col. Cole Digges, was a Burgess and member of the Council for many years. He married Elizabeth, daughter of Dr. Henry Power, of York county, and had issue: Edward, William, Dudley, Mary, and Susannah. The eldest son, Col. Edward, was Burgess, Justice, County Lieutenant, etc.; he married Anne, "daughter of the late Nathaniel Harrison of the Council" (*Va. Gazette*), and left surviving issue: William, Cole, Edward, Mary, Thomas, Elizabeth, Hannah, Anne, Sarah, Dudley, and Charles. William inherited the family estate, "Bellfield," which he sold, in 1787, to William Waller; he was Justice and Sheriff of York county, member of the Conventions of 1775–76, later Sheriff and Delegate from Warwick. He married his cousin, Elizabeth, daughter of his uncle, William Digges, of "Denbigh," and left three children. His brother, Edward, married (11th June, 1775) Elizabeth, daughter of Col. Thomas Gaskins, Sr., of Northumberland, and sister of Anne, who was the second wife of Richard Henry Lee; he moved to Fauquier county, where he has many descendants. His eldest son, also named Edward, married Anne Eustace Gaskins, who was descended from William Eustace and Ann Lee, daughter of Hancock Lee. (Condensed from *W. and M. Quarterly*, I. 83, *et seq.*)

---

[1] For an interesting sketch of Gov. Edward Digges, by Mr. R. A. Brock, see *Virginia and Virginians*.

## Col. Philip Lee.

29. Philip[5], son of John Lee[4] (Philip[3], Richard[2], Richard[1]) and Susannah Smith, his wife, born ——; died ——; married Mary Jacqueline Smith, and had three daughters (as named in a deed of 21st November, 1801, by their aunt, Mary Smith): Mary Smith, Susannah Hancock, and "Philicia" Sally Lee. On 22d of January, 1812, Mary J. Lee deeded a slave to her grandson, Philip Lee Anthony, son of James C. Anthony and Mary Smith Anthony, of Richmond. The catalogue of the Moravian Seminary, Bethlehem, Penna., states that "Mary S. Lee, daughter of Philip Lee, of Westmoreland county, Va., was born 31st December, 1788; married, in 1808, James C. Anthony, of Richmond;" she entered the Seminary in 1799. Philip Lee lived near Nominy, Westmoreland county; he was generally styled, "Col. Phil. Lee of Nominy."

## Thomas Ludwell Lee.

30. Thomas Ludwell[5], eldest son of Thomas Ludwell Lee[4] (Thomas[3], Richard[2], Richard[1]) and Mary Aylett, his wife, was born ——; died in the fall of 1807; married Fanny, daughter of Robert W. Carter, of "Sabine Hall," Richmond county (*Critic*). Mr. Lee resided at "Coton," near Leesburg, Loudoun county. These two following letters were written by him to his kinsman and executor, George Carter, of "Oatlands," Loudoun county:

"Coton, 7th June, 1806. My dear Sir, I was delighted on going to the door to meet Solomon yesterday evening, to be told by him that he waited on you, as I was sure I should hear something certain of you, which I have not done for many months. But even now you say nothing of your health, which I was anxious to know particularly of; since I wrote you I have, thank God, recovered my strength and flesh in the most astonishing manner. I have been enabled to ride out three or four times and feel as if I should recover my former health. For four months I was lingering in a very low state of health and apprehending an affection of my Breast, when I was taken with a most violent and acute pleurisy which tho' at its height was very dangerous, yet I sincerely hope has had the effect of carrying off all those symptoms of breast complaint that threatened me before, and Doctor Sim thinks the Sweet Spring trip will place me perfectly in statu quo. I feel very grateful indeed for the pains you have taken to have my carriage made; your description of the one that can be had for 230 dollars is exactly suited to my idea of convenience. I will take the liberty of stating my choice in several respects that correspond with yours, or are not mentioned. 1st, the width to be 3 feet 2 or 3 inches, the handle plain, a glass in preference to a Blind, 2 seats, one occasionally to take out, as Mrs. Lee when I travel with my family will usually ride with me; in the spaces on each side of the door and the sunken place in the bottom of the carriage to be contrived of tin or any other material most proper for carrying provisions and liquors of different kinds, as they may be best suited to; you know the convenience of such things and of course can direct them so as that I'm sure they will suit me; the space under the drivers feet I wished to be filled by a good strong travelling trunk as large as it will admit, as it would be difficult here to get a trunk to fit it exactly; the space under his seat may be filled by a Box as you describe which will answer for carrying his baggage or anything else, this as well as the cases for carrying provisions should all take out and have locks to them. The place for carrying a Mattrass on top is such a convenience that I cannot forego it (altho' the price is high) as I entend to carry one and will thank you to let me know the size of the mattrass that it will carry as mine is to be made in the family. The axletrees to be of Iron; my harness have what are called woodcock eyes and of course the swingle trees must have Iron hooks. As to colour, any one that is likely to last well I should prefer, but that as well as everything else respecting it I am willing to abide by your discretion. Let me know the precise Sum when all my notions are complied with and when it will certainly be ready for delivery that I may be prepared. If I had written to you yesterday I should have told you that my prospect for Crop on this farm was vastly greater than ever before; there has been a worm some time discovered in the neighborhood of Leesburg, whose numbers are incredible, and destroys every field of wheat into which they enter; this was only discovered on mine yesterday evening attended by a fly that my overseer thinks is destroying the wheat also. God knows where its ravages will end; indeed the weather for several days past has been favorable for introducing the rust, to which one of my fields will be particularly liable. I have a thousand and ten thousand things to say to you, but must defer them till we meet, which I hope will be soon; spend your home with me till your house is ready for your reception. God bless you is the wish of your sincere friend."

"P. S. I must add to the trouble I have already given you by requesting you to have made for me a pair of best Calf skin Boots of British leather if it be had, if not of the best American, with white tops and such as will not soil my stockings. Solomon brings a boot for measure."

"My dear Sir, I rec'd your letter of the 12th yesterday, I am well pleased indeed to hear that you are relieved from your most terrible and painful disease, and to me, its being done without taking Physick would enhance the value of the remedy ten thousand fold, for I am tired to death of Physick except that of the kitchen, which now suits me tolerably well, for thank God I have a good appetite and am getting tolerably well. And now that we are on this subject, I must mention my particular wish that some part of the carriage may be devoted to carrying some [food], suppose the Box under the servants seat is laid off in different apartments for the purpose, as I had rather give up the well, the apartments might be lined with tin so that the grease would not penetrate; my idea is that meat, Bread, Cake and such like matters should be carried distinctly. I wish the cases to carry common quart Bottles, which in an over set would not be so likely to be broken and if broken may be easily replaced; the colour you have chosen I should prefer; if Brass clamps do not cost more than Iron for the trunk I should prefer them, with my name and Coton underneath marked with Brass nails; all these little matters you will please to direct as you see fit, but of all things it is necessary that I should receive it as early as possible. Doctor Sim is most pressing that I should set out by the 15th of July, however I must now wait for the carriage as I could no more perform the Journey on horse Back in my present situation than I could perform any other impossibility; and I have the most implicit confidence in your goodness to have it made as quickly as is possible. As to the painting I can't expect it to be done in the best manner in so short a time, but I hope he will do it as well as the time admits. Before you leave Baltimore I will thank you to know the exact sum I am to pay for the carriage, trunk, &c. I wish to God your affairs could have permitted you to have gone with me, not only for the satisfaction I should have enjoyed but it might have been of vast service to you in giving the finishing to restoring your health. Betsy is very much alarmed at the apprehension of her letter to Miss Maud having miscarried; she will with great pleasure commence a correspondence with her now altho' her letters are first to be read by the Lady Abbess. This cursed worm that alarmed the whole country so much, thank God, has scarcely injured me in the least; probably ten Bushels would cover the whole loss, which deduction from by far the best Crop I ever had is small indeed; hail storm and rust apart, I count with great certainty on 500 Barrels of Flour, exclusive of overseers share and seed. This you'll say is a very good Crop for my poor farm. . . . I wish very much to see you that we may, among other things, read my will over together that you may understand my desires as perfectly as possible."

Mr. Lee's will, dated the 8th of June, 1806, and probated in Loudoun the 14th of October, 1807, was as follows:

In the name of God, Amen. I Thomas Ludwell Lee of Coton in the county of Loudoun and state of Virginia being weak in health but of perfect disposing mind, do make and appoint this my last will and testament in the words following, to wit: It is my will and desire that my body should be decently interred by the side of my dearly loved child Thomas Ludwell Lee dec'd without any expense that is not absolutely necessary and as to my worldly estate with which it has pleased God to bless me, I give and bequeath in the following manner. 1st. I desire all my land in the county of Stafford known by the name of "Berry Hill," all my land lying on the west side of Goose Creek in the county of Loudoun, purchased of Thomas Swann who purchased of Carter's Executors, together with the mill seat appertaining thereto and 20 acres on the east side of said Creek to be laid out in the most convenient manner for the mill, all my lots in the town of Matildaville at the great falls of Potomac, devised to me by the will of my uncle Francis Lightfoot Lee, and all other property that it may hereafter appear I am entitled to, but have not now possession, to my Executrix and Executor hereinafter named, to be by them sold as soon as may be for the payment of all my just debts and the balance if any after discharging the same to be applied as is hereafter mentioned.

2d. I give and bequeath all the residue of my estate real and personal together with any balance that may arise from the sale of the property above mentioned except as hereafter excepted to my most affectionate and dearly beloved wife Fanny Lee for and during her natural life or as long as she may continue my widow for her support and that of our dear children, but should she again marry then I bequeath to her during her natural life the use of my mill property, now in the possession of Obadiah Clifford under lease, and the land on the opposite side of the Creek, which I purchased of Benjamin Edwards, but if the said mill property and land should be sold and the money placed at interest, as she is hereafter by this will authorized to do, then I give and bequeath to her for and during her natural life the whole interest arising from the sum.

3d. It is my will and desire that any time while my beloved wife remains my widow she shall have the power and is hereby authorized to sell and convey all my mill property as above described with the land I bought of Benjamin Edwards and as many as ten acres of land to be added to the lot at present laid off for Obadiah Clifford in a manner convenient for the mill, the money arising from the sale to be put to interest and well secured by mortgage on landed property; she is hereby authorized and empowered to sell all my land on the east side of Goose Creek, adjoining the land of Ludwell Lee Esqr. and my late brothers heirs as well as some other persons, on which I have lately established a farm by the name of "Forest Farm" and on which there are several leased lots, the money arising from the sale to be vested as the money arising from the mill is directed to be vested, but the principal not to be used upon any condition unless the profits of the other part of my estate should be insufficient after maintaining my family to pay my daughters when they are married £1000 which I desire may be paid to each of them as a marriage portion; she is also hereby authorized and empowered to sell any of the slaves I die possessed of and vest the money arising from the sale as is directed in the last clause, or in other slaves as she may deem most conducive to the interests of our children.

4th. My will and desire is that Coton Farm, with all the land annexed to it, except the ten acres adjoining the mill lot which my beloved wife is hereafter authorized to sell, with all the slaves, furniture, stock, farming utensils, carriages and every description of property shall be kept together for the sole use and benefit of my unmarried daughters, who are immediately on the death or marriage of their dear mother to possess and enjoy the same, but my express desire is that none of them live in the family more than one month after their marriage and from the time of their marriage that they forfeit all their rights of property in the same; after the death or marriage of my last single daughter, I desire that the whole property above mentioned should be sold and the money arising from it to be equally divided among all my daughters or their heirs.

5th. My will and desire is that if my dear wife during her life or widowhood should not have sold my mill property and land on Goose Creek, as I have authorized her to do, that then the same shall be sold by my Executor or in case of his death by the Guardians of my children, the money to be equally divided among my daughters, the married ones to be charged in the division with their marriage portion of £1000 if they have received it, or so much of it as they have rec'd.

6th. It is my will and desire that my Executrix and Executor pay to Landon Carter son of George Carter dec'd, in case he arrives at the age of twenty one years, or is married, as much money as will amount to one third of the sum arising from the sale of the land and mill seat on the west side of Goose Creek, which they are before authorized to sell for the payment of my debts, but no interest to be chargeable on the same except from the time of his coming of age or being married to the time of payment.

7th. Having made in my opinion ample provisions for the payment of all my debts, it is my desire that no Inventory or Appraisement be made of my personal estate but the same, as it is, may go immediately to the uses in the will expressed.

8th. I do hereby constitute my affectionate and dearly beloved wife Fanny Lee and my worthy friend George Carter Esqr. of Oatlands, Executrix and Executor of this my last will and testament and desire that they may be permitted to qualify to the same without giving any other security for their Execution of the trust I have reposed in them than their own Bonds. Signed, &c., &c.

Thomas Ludwell and Fanny (Carter) Lee had eight children:

i, THOMAS LUDWELL[6], who died in early infancy.

ii, ELIZABETH[6], who married her cousin, St. Leger Landon Carter, the second son of Landon Carter, of "Cleves," and Mrs. Eliza (Carter) Thornton, his wife, who was a daughter of Robert W. Carter. They apparently had no children.

iii, MARY AYLETT[6], married Tench Ringgold, being his second wife (see 28, iv); they had issue, names unknown to writer; amongst them, a daughter from whom the Hon. Edward D. White, late U. S. Senator from Louisiana and present Associate Justice of the U. S. Supreme Court, is descended.

iv, WINIFRED BEALE[6], married William Brent, Jr., of "Richland," Stafford county; he was the son of Daniel Carroll and Anne Fenton (Lee) Brent, and a first cousin of his wife. (See 17, iv.)

v, FANNY CARTER[6], died single.

vi, ANN LUCINDA[6], married John M. McCarty, son of Col. Daniel and Sarah (Mason) McCarty, of "Cedar Grove," Fairfax county.

vii, CATHARINE[6], died single.

viii, SYDNEY[6], was probably a daughter; said to have died single. There is no allusion to a second son in his father's will; he mentions one, Thomas Ludwell, deceased, but refers to his living children as if all were daughters.

## GEORGE LEE.

31. GEORGE[5], the third son of Thomas Ludwell Lee[4] (Thomas[3], Richard[2], Richard[1]) and Mary Aylett, his wife; born ——; died in 1805, probably in January; married Evelyn Byrd, daughter of Robert and Maria (Carter) Beverley, of "Wakefield," Culpeper county. His will, dated the 28th of October, 1802, and probated, in Loudoun, 11th of February, 1805, was as follows:

I George Lee of Farmwell, Loudoun county and State of Virginia, do make and ordain this my last will and testament, signed with my name and sealed and dated this 28th day of October, 1802. 1st. It is my desire that all my just debts shall be paid for which purpose I leave all the property that may come to me from the Estate of my brother Wm. A. Lee dec'd, should that property together with the rents and crops of my own estate not be sufficient to pay my debts, I empower my Executor and Executrix hereinafter mentioned to dispose of such of my property as they may think proper for that purpose. 2nd. I give to my wife Evelyn Byrd Lee all my estate both real and personal (after my just debts are paid) during her widowhood for the support of herself and my children and during her life the following negroes, Frank, Caroline, Peter, Sam, Sall, and Ned, this last bequest is made in lieu of the negroes I sold that were settled on her and as I suppose there is a difference in the value of the negroes against her, it is my desire and I hereby empower my Executor (hereinafter mentioned) to pay my wife should she marry again $500 of the first money collected from the estate left my son George.

3rd. I give and bequeath to my daughter Maria Carter Lee at the marriage of her mother or when she arrives at the age of sixteen, 1,000 acres of land in the county of Loudoun, to be laid off on the west side of the Ox Road and adjoining the land of Mr. Ludwell Lee, my brother Thomas L. Lee, to be bounded by the Ox Road as far as is necessary to give the quantity of 1,000 acres. I request my Executor to have the above land laid off as soon as is possible which survey must be binding on my heirs. I also leave her at the death of her mother my two negroes Patrick and Nelly.

4th. I give and bequeath to my son George Lee at the marriage or death of his mother all my lands in the county of Loudoun not settled on her, or given to his sister; and at his mother's death I give and bequeath to my son George Lee the whole of the property settled on his mother, both real and personal (except the negroes I sold and the household and kitchen furniture which I leave to his mother) and I also leave my son George Lee the six negroes left to his mother during her life; after her death, I leave my son George residuary legatee of this my last will and testament. I leave my brother Thomas L. Lee of Coton as Executor and my wife Evelyn B. Lee as Executrix to this will and leave the two above named persons guardians to my children until my son George Lee arrives at the age of seven

**years, then it is my will and desire that my Brother Thos. L. Lee should have entire direction of him, signed, sealed and dated the day and year above mentioned.**

George and Evelyn Byrd (Beverley) had, as mentioned in his will, only two children; apparently the daughter was the elder.

i, MARIA CARTER[6], was not 16 in 1802.

ii, GEORGE[6]. See 43.

## THE BEVERLEYS.

The Beverleys are traced back as far as the time of King John, in the records of the town of Beverley in Yorkshire. In 14 Edward III., Thomas de Beverley was appointed to superintend the fortifications of the town; many other references show the prominence of this family in that county. About 1662, Robert Beverley sold his estate near Beverley and emigrated to Virginia. He arrived about 1663, and settled in Middlesex county, of which he was a Justice in 1673, and perhaps earlier. Before that time (in 1670) he had been elected Clerk of the House of Burgesses, and seems to have held the position, almost continuously, until his death, which occurred on the 16th of March, 1787. Evidently he soon became a man of great influence in the Colony, especially with the Burgesses and the people; on the other hand he appears to have been continually at feud with the governors after Berkeley's departure.

While Berkeley was governor, Beverley was a staunch friend and supporter of his government; assisting him with a strong hand, in suppressing "Bacon's Rebellion." Though his conduct pleased the governor, it did not meet with the approval of the people, among whom his troops were quartered; they were very emphatic in their complaints against his conduct. Berkeley issued a commission, on the 13th of November, 1676, to Beverley, in which it was stated: "Whereas by many frequent and successful services to his Sacred Majesty, this Countrey and me, his Majesties Governor of it, Major Robert Beverley hath approved himself to be most loyall, circumspect and curagious in his Majesties service for the good of his countrey and the suppressing this late horrid Rebellion, began by Bacon," etc. One of the English commissioners, sent over to suppress the rebellion and to investigate its causes, was Francis Moryson, who seems to have been rancorous against Philip Ludwell and Robert Beverley, whom he declared were the chief causes of the rebellion. Yet they had both supported Berkeley in suppressing it. Later, Moryson wrote to Wiseman: "I send you Jeffrey's letter wherein you will find that Beverley and Ludwell still continue the same mutineers, as wee left them, and will never be other, but will undoubtedly cause new disturbances in the country as soon as the soldiers are gone."

Beside his lands in Middlesex, Robert Beverley owned "Beverley Park," in King and Queen county, and also lands in other counties, amounting in all, it is said, to about 50,000 acres. He was twice married; his first wife's name was Mary, surname not known. His second, was Catharine, daughter of Major Theophilus Hone, of James City county. After Beverley's death, she married Christopher Robinson, as shown by documents recorded in Middlesex. He left issue: Robert, Peter, Henry, John, and William; also two daughters, Mary and Catharine. The latter married John Robinson, once president of the Council, who died the 5th of September, 1749, and was succeeded in that position by Thomas Lee.

Robert, his son, the well known historian of Virginia, lived and died on his estate in King and Queen county; he married Ursula, daughter of the first William Byrd, of "Westover;" their son, William, married Elizabeth, daughter of Richard and Elizabeth (Randolph) Bland, of "Jordans" (her elder sister married Henry Lee, of "Lee Hall," Westmoreland), and had a son, Robert, who married Maria, daughter of Col. Landon and Maria (Byrd) Carter, of "Sabine Hall;" they lived at "Wakefield" in Culpeper county. Robert died in 1800, leaving thirteen children; his tenth child, Evelyn Byrd, married George Lee, as stated; after his death, she married, secondly, Dr. Patrick Hume Douglas.

## Thomas Lee.

32. Thomas[5], the eldest son of Richard Henry Lee[4], (Thomas[3], Richard[2], Richard[1]), and Anne Aylett, his first wife, was born at "Chantilly," on "Friday the 20th day of October, 1758, at 11 o'clock at night, and was christened by the Rev. Mr. Charles Ross on the 26th day of November, 1758. His sponsors were the Honourable Philip Ludwell Lee, Gawen Corbin, Esq., Capt. William Allerton, Miss Alice Lee, Mr. Allerton, and Miss Mary Aylett." (Family Bible of R. H. Lee.)

Thomas Lee was sent to England to school; as he was there in 1776, he must have gone over when quite young. The biographer of his father, R. H. Lee[1], has stated that Ludwell Lee was at "a school in St. Bees, in England," at the time of the moving of the Declaration of Independence.

---

[1] *Life of R. H. Lee*, 178.

It is probable that his elder brother was there with him. Arthur Lee[1] wrote from France to R. H. Lee, under date of 25th of December, 1776, " . . . I have sent for your sons hither. I mean to keep Ludwell with me, and if his genius suits to train him to arms, chiefly in the engineering line. Tom I will send to you with our dispatches, when they are of importance. He is now of an age to be useful to you in Virginia, from whence your absence must greatly damage your affairs." It appears that "Tom" did not go to Virginia soon, but entered the office of a merchant, who had dealings for the commissioners of Congress. Under date of 15th of February, 1778, Arthur Lee wrote from Paris: " . . . Tom is still with Mr. Schweighauser, and appears to be improving: Ludwell has left his school, lives with me, and I shall soon make him begin reading law." Later still, Arthur Lee wrote, from Virginia, to the Marquis of Lansdown (under date of the 3d of March, 1786) " . . . My nephew, Thomas Lee, will have the honour of presenting this letter to your lordship. He comes to finish his law studies at the Temple. Your lordship's patronage of him will be a singular happiness to him and a favour to me. I hope you will find him intelligent and capable of giving your lordship a satisfactory account of this country." Thomas Lee lived at "Park Gate," near Dumfries, in Prince William county, where he farmed and practiced law. He died between the last of July and the first of October, 1805. Was twice married; first, about the 15th of October, 1788, to Mildred, daughter of John Augustine and Hannah (Bushrod) Washington; after her death, he married, secondly, Eliza Ashton Brent. His will mentions two children, a son and a daughter; both were probably the issue of his second marriage. General Washington, in writing to Sir Isaac Heard, of the Herald's Office, London, of his family, said: "John Augustine Washington, son of Augustine and Mary (Ball) Washington, married Hannah Bushrod, and had, Bushrod, Corbin, and Mildred; Corbin married a daughter of the Honourable Richard Henry Lee; Mildred married Thomas Lee, son of the said R. H. Lee." (Sparks, 508.) A marriage bond was filed on the 13th of October, 1788, at Westmoreland, between Thomas Lee and Mildred Washington, spinster; it was signed by Thomas Lee, Sr.. and William Aliett Lee.

NOTE. This connection of Thomas Lee with a mercantile house that had dealings with the American commissioners, was used as an evidence of some intrigue on the part of the two Lees, Arthur and William, by their enemies. Deane wrote to the President of Congress, under date of 12th

---

[1] *Life of Arthur Lee*, II, pp. 110, 135, 169.

October, 1778, that "Mr. Lee's Nephew, a son of the honourable Richard Henry Lee, is in the house of Mons. Schweighauser, at Nantes, as a clerk or as a partner—I am informed the latter. Commercial affairs and the disposition of prizes are put into the care of this house, while a near connection of Mr. Schweighauser, at Guernsey or Jersey, is employing himself in sending out cruisers on our commerce."[1] John Adams said:[2] "Mr. Schweighauser was a very solid merchant, highly esteemed by everybody, and highly approved by the Court" (French).

Thomas Lee's will was dated the 15th of January, and probated, in Prince Willliam, the 7th of October, 1805. It reads:

In the name of God, Amen. I Thomas Lee, Sen., of Prince William county and Commonwealth of Virginia being at present low in health but of sound disposing mind, I return humble thanks to the almighty ruler of human events and considering the uncertainty of life, do constitute and make this my last Will and Testament, hereby revoking all others which I may have made and declaring this to be my last, as follows Viz. In the first place I do desire that my body may be decently and without parade interred and laid on the left side of my late ever dear wife, between her remains and those of my dear little infant, so that his grave may be between mine and that of his blessed dear mother when it may please our good God to take her out of this World, should it be her pleasure to be buried there, and as it is my present intention, if God spares my life long enough, to have the grave yard enclosed with a good substantial brick or stone wall; should it not be done I do require my Executors and Executrix, hereafter to be named, to have it done at the expense of my estate.

Secondly, I desire that my just debts may be paid without any unnecessary delay by my Executors, hereby authorising them to sell whatever part of my estate, real or personal, they may think most to the advantage of my estate. Thirdly. (This section was torn out during the late war.) Fourthly, I do give and bequeath to my only child and affectionate daughter Ellinor Lee all the residue of my estate real and personal in possession, reversion or remainder to her and her heirs forever.

Fifthly, If my dear wife should choose it I desire the dwelling house should be allotted on her half of the Land. Sixthly, I do constitute and appoint my ever dear Brothers and sincere friends Ludwell Lee and Francis L. Lee Executors and my beloved wife and dear daughter Eliza Ashton Lee and Ellinor Lee Executrixes to this my last Will and Testament, hereby declaring that these my Executors shall not be subject to any suit or suits for the management of my said estate by my heirs under a forfeiture of the whole estate to my said Executors, convinced of their friendship and integrity. The whole of this Will I have written with my own hand without any interlineation or erasure and pray that full faith may be given to it as such by all courts and signed this 15th day of January, one thousand eight hundred and five.

Codicil. As I know it was the earnest wish of my dear and beloved sister, Hannah Washington, that her two Daughters Jane and Molly Washington should be brought up under the care of my ever dear wife, it is my desire that they continue to live with her until they are of age and that she expend such part of their fortunes as she finds necessary in pro-

---

[1] *Letters of William Lee*, 358.
[2] *Life and Works of John Adams*, III, 129.

**viding them with a governess and such other instruction as she may judge proper for them. 23d July, 1805.**

Thomas Lee had only one surviving child:

i, ELEANOR[6], born the 13th of August, 1783; entered the Moravian Seminary, at Bethlehem, Pa., in 1796, "recommended by George Washington." (Seminary Catalogue.) Died Nov., 1807; married, —— Girard Alexander, son of Col. William Alexander, of "Effingham," Prince William county; he was born the 25th of June, 1784, and died the 2d of July, 1834; they had one son, Thomas Ludwell Alexander, colonel U. S. A., born the 26th of October, 1807; died the 11th of March, 1881, and left issue.

## LUDWELL-LEE.

33. LUDWELL[5], the second son of Richard Henry Lee[4] (Thomas[3], Richard[2], Richard[1]), and of Anne Aylett, his first wife, was born at "Chantilly" on "Monday the 13th of October, 1760, at 12 o'clock in the night, and was christened by the Rev. Mr. Ross on Sunday, the 26th of October, 1760. His proxies were Richard Lee, Esq., Doctor Arthur Lee, and Miss Elizabeth Steptoe." (Family Bible of R. H. Lee.) He died at his home, "Belmont," in Loudoun, on the 23d of March, 1836.

Ludwell Lee was educated in England and France, as shown by the extracts from the letters of his uncle, Dr. Arthur Lee, given in connection with Ludwell's older brother, Thomas Lee. His son, R. H. Lee (the biographer of his grandfather, Richard Henry Lee), has given this anecdote of Ludwell, from whom he had heard it:[1]

"A son of Mr. Lee was, at the time of the Declaration of Independence, at school in St. Bees, in England. . . . One day, as this youth was standing near one of the professors of the academy, who was conversing with a gentleman of the neighboring county, he heard the question asked, 'What boy is this?' to which the professor answered, 'He is a son of Richard Henry Lee, of America.' The gentleman, upon hearing this, put his hand upon his head and said, 'We shall yet see your father's head upon Tower Hill,' to which the boy answered, 'You may have it when you can get it.'"

Under date of the 30th of June, 1777, R. H. Lee wrote to his brother Arthur: " . . . I have written by this opportunity to our Brother William, supposing him to be in France. I told him that the times prevent

---

[1] *Life of R. H. Lee*, 178.

me from making remittance, and therefore that my sons must be sent to me by the first good opportunity if he cannot continue to advance for their frugal maintenance in France a small time longer. I wish Ludwell to go deep into the study of Natural and Civil Law and Eloquence, as well as to obtain the military improvement you put him on, my desire being that he may be able to turn either to the Law or the sword here, as his genius or his interest and service of his country might point out. I want Tom to possess himself of the knowledge of business either in Mr. Schweighauser's counting house or under his uncle, if he should go into business that may be entrusted to his care. But all or any part of this plan depends, I apprehend, entirely on their uncle William. Should any unhappy accident have befallen him and thereby prevented him from coming to France, I must rely on you to direct them to be sent over to me by the first opportunity." (*Southern Literary Messenger*, Vol. 28, No. 6, p. 429.)

After his death this sketch was published in the Leesburg paper by Mr. R. H. Henderson, of that place:

"Departed this life, on the night of Wednesday the 23d ult., at his residence in this County, Ludwell Lee, Esq., in the 76th year of his age. Mr. Lee, the oldest son of the illustrious orator, statesman, and patriot, Richard Henry Lee, rose into manhood during the memorable struggle in which his Father won an undying fame. True to the principles and spirit of that Father, the subject of this passing notice flew from the shades of the Academy to the standard of his country; and, as one of the military family of the heroic and generous Lafayette, followed it until it was crowned with glorious peace. Mr. Lee engaged in the profession of the law, but, blessed with an ample fortune, he withdrew from it at an early period, yet not until he had exhibited to his friends and his country those powers and attainments which would, under different circumstances, have rendered him one of its brightest ornaments.

"He was a distinguished member of the Virginia Legislature, and presided over the deliberations of the Senate with approved ability, dignity, and courtesy in the palmiest days of this once renowned commonwealth. But the strife and tumult of the political arena were as distasteful to him as were those of the bar. His character was essentially gentle, tranquil, and benevolent; and although he died, as he had lived, an unwavering disciple of our own Washington, the suavity of his manners always kept pace with the rectitude and firmness of his purpose. In the walks of private life, amid the social circle, at the sacred family hearth, Ludwell Lee shone with a mild and constant lustre:—here he displayed learning without ostentation;

wit without one solitary tincture of unkindness; affection which soothed and gladdened all around him. Not unscathed by sorrow in the evening of his life, he sought solace and support from Him who never forsakes those who cleave to Him in sincerity and humility. In a word, to the good man and the gentleman he added that better character which makes worldly merit less than dust in the balance. He breathed out his spirit, at last, without a groan; and has gone to rejoin in the realms of ceaseless peace and bliss that Lafayette under whose chivalrous eye he drew his youthful sword, and who came, after so many chances and changes, to embrace him again in the classic retirement of Belmont. His life happily illustrates the sublime truth, 'The Christian is the highest type of man.' He was a Christian in all the truth, in all the purity, in all the meekness, in all the Catholic love and charity of that endearing name. The places that knew him shall know him no more; he has gone where the approving smiles of his Heavenly Father shall succeed to the tears and sighs of his beloved children."

An old colored man, probably once a servant of Ludwell Lee's, recently told, in the graphic language of his race, of the visit of Lafayette to Loudoun; of how the mansions of Belmont and Coton were decorated, of the double line of lanterns which connected the two houses, that guests might readily pass from one to the other, either one of the mansions being too small to contain "all the country" that were bidden to meet the gallant Frenchman.

This letter to his uncle William Lee is interesting.

"Shooter's hill, 15th of Dec'r 1793. My Dear Uncle. I believe it to be a very just observation that the more we progress in error, the more difficult it is to get into the right way again. I feel and have felt this strongly in the business of writing to those who have more claims than one upon my epistolary attentions. Shame for the long delay, and an utter impossibility of framing an excuse keeps me from essaying a fulfilment of my duty. I must attempt none now, but only assure you that the *vis inertiæ* and not want of true affection has been the cause of my failures hitherto.

"I inclose you an accepted draft of Col. Lee which will be due by the time you can send it to Richmond. He assures me that the money shall be ready for you as soon as it is presented. This is the most convenient plan I could fall upon to transmit your money to you. It would give me sincere pleasure had I it in my power to discharge the principal of my bond to you, as the business of being in debt is one very disagreeable to me. But my crops have this year fallen very short of what they were last; only 2000 bushels of wheat for sale, which is appropriated to the payment of my debt to Mr. Fendall. I have a large crop in the ground, having sowed 630 bushels which with the benign assistance of heaven may enable next year to go a great way into the discharge of it.

"The truce which Portugal and Holland have made with the Algerines has let these robbers loose upon the trade of America. This will defeat in a great measure the benefits we derive from our Neutrality and I can see no way of getting out of the mischief but by purchasing their friendship as others have done. Indians and Algerines will give us our hands full without meddling with the hot headed Frenchmen's affairs.

"You have seen I suppose by the papers that Dallas, the first propagator of the story about Genet's appeal, has denied the whole business. Jay and King are in a pretty hole. However the President has given Mr. Genet a pretty decent dressing in his Letter to Congress upon the views of foreign Powers towards us. Political storms seem forming around us. The death of George Washington would let loose the Dogs of War; upon what a slender tie does the Peace of the New World depend; perhaps its hard earned Independence and the fairest prospect of human liberty and happiness. I am lost in conjecture and in apprehension. However I wish you a merry Christmas, and am ever most aff'ly yours, etc.

Ludwell Lee was twice married; first, about the 23d of January, 1788, to his first cousin, Flora, daughter of Philip Ludwell, and Elizabeth (Steptoe) Lee, of Stratford, by whom he had three children. He was married, secondly, in 1797, to Elizabeth, daughter of Bowles, and Mary (Fontaine) Armistead, by whom he had six children. He resided first at "Shooter's Hill," near Alexandria, and later at "Belmont," near Leesburg. His first wife died and was buried at "Shooter's Hill;" her "tomb was to be seen there prior to the late civil war" (Rev. Joseph Packard, D. D.). He was buried at Belmont.

Ludwell Lee made a nuncupative will, on the 18th of March, 1836, leaving some silver and a few slaves to his daughters, Ellen and Emily; some silver to his "son Dr. Lee." This will was attested by James L. McKenna and Edmund I. Lee.

By his first wife Mr. Lee had three children:

i, RICHARD HENRY[6]. See 44.

ii, CECILIA[6], born in 1790; died ——; married James L. McKenna; no issue.

iii, ELIZA MATILDA[6], born the 13th of September, 1791; died the 22d of January, 1875; was married, in 1811, to Richard H. Love, of Fairfax county, and had six children: of these, Ludwell and Thomas died young. 3, Richard Lee, born in 1815, died in 1855; entered the U. S. N.; married Martha Ann Pearson. 4, Cecilia Matilda, married, in 1844, Major Lewis Addison Armistead, U. S. A. She was born in 1823 and died in 1850. 5, The last son was General John Love, U. S. A., of Indiana, a graduate of West Point, who was born in 1820 and died in 1881; he married Mary F. Smith, and died without issue. 6, Their last child, Flora Lee Love, married the Rev. William Johnson, of the Episcopal church, at whose home Mrs. Love died.

By his marriage with Elizabeth Armistead, Ludwell Lee had six children:

iv, MARY ANN[6], born 8th of April, 1798; married General Robert B. Campbell, of South Carolina.

v, ELLEN MCMACKEN[6], born 5th of April, 1802; married twice; first, Thomas Bedford, of Kentucky, and had one child; secondly, in 1844, the Rev. Nathaniel Phippen Knapp, of Mobile, Alabama, and had: 1, Ludwell Lee, born in 1845, died in 1883. 2, Caroline Frances, born 1st of July, 1847; married, 9th of January, 1873, the Rev. John Richard Joyner.

vi, ELIZABETH ARMISTEAD[6], born 23d of March, 1804; "entered into rest at the residence of Rev. J. R. Joyner, Berlin, Worcester county, Md., 23d of May, 1887, Mrs. Elizabeth A. Selden, in the 84th year of her age; daughter of the Hon. Ludwell Lee, of 'Belmont,' Loudoun county, Va., and widow of the late Wilson Cary Selden, of 'Exeter,' near Leesburg, Va." (*Southern Churchman.*)

vii, EMILY[6], born ——; died in 1875, unmarried.

viii, FRANCIS LIGHTFOOT[6], born ——; died ——; married a Miss Rogers, of South Carolina, but had no issue.

ix, BOWLES ARMISTEAD[6], born ——; died ——, unmarried. A cadet from Virginia of his name entered West Point in 1828.

## FRANCIS LIGHTFOOT LEE.

34. FRANCIS LIGHTFOOT[5], the fourth son and youngest child of Richard Henry Lee[4] (Thomas[3], Richard[2], Richard[1]), by Anne (Gaskins) Pinckard, his second wife, was born "at 2 o'clock on the morning of the 18th of June, 1782; was christened by the Rev. Mr. Wilson; his sponsors were Thomas and Ludwell Lee, Mr. Aylett Lee, Miss Mary Lee, Miss Hannah Lee, Miss Flora Lee, and Miss Lucinda Lee." (Family Bible of R. H. Lee.)

Mr. Lee's early education was probably under a private tutor. In 1798 he entered Harvard College, was graduated an A. B. in 1802, and in 1806 received his A. M. (College records.) He was a lawyer by profession, and resided at "Sully," in Fairfax county, not far distant from Alexandria and Washington. He died on the 13th of April, 1850. He was twice married, his two wives having been sisters, and daughters of Col. John, and Jane (Digges) Fitzgerald, of Alexandria. By his first wife, Elizabeth, he had no surviving children; by his second, Jane, whom he married on the 9th of February, 1810, he had five children.

Colonel John Fitzgerald, the father of Elizabeth, and Jane Fitzgerald, was a native of Ireland, who had settled at Alexandria some time before the Revolution, and had become a prosperous merchant of that town. During the war he served for some time upon General Washington's staff, and the friendship begun at that time appears to have continued throughout their lives. Very frequent mention is made in Washington's diary of visits paid to Col. Fitzgerald at Alexandria. He was at one time Mayor of that town. Francis Lightfoot Lee had by his second wife these five children:

i, JANE ELIZABETH[6], born in 1811 and died in 1837; married in 1832 Henry T. Harrison, of Loudoun county, and left a daughter, who died in 1870, unmarried. Henry T. Harrison married, secondly, in 1841, Elizabeth Mary Jones, daughter of Walter and Anne Lucinda (Lee) Jones (see 36, i).

ii, SAMUEL PHILLIPS[6]. See 45.

iii, JOHN FITZGERALD[6]. See 46.

iv, ARTHUR[6], born ——; died unmarried at Louisville, Ky., on the 7th of August, 1841. In an obituary notice of him the writer says: ". . . Possessed of a high order of intelligence, deeply imbued with a love of letters, and rich in acquisitions of knowledge, he might have shone in the walks of literature and won reputation among men; but, with instinctive diffidence, he shrank from the public gaze, and deaf to the loud calls of ambition and attentive only to the 'still small voice' of conscience, he chose rather to employ his talents and acquirements in the humble but holy office of a Sunday-school teacher."

v, FRANCES ANNE[6], born at Bladensburg, Prince George's county, Md., on the 30th of June, 1816; died on the 5th of December, 1889; was twice married: first, on the 6th of September, 1842, to Goldsborough Robinson, who died on the 5th of August, 1844, leaving two sons: 1, Arthur Lee Robinson, born the 27th of December, 1843; was married on the 16th of January, 1868, to Norborne Alexina, daughter of

Norborne Alexander Galt and Elizabeth Mildred Thompson Gray, his wife; Mrs. Robinson died the 4th of December, 1868, leaving a son, Alexander Galt, born the 26th of November, 1868. 2, Goldsborough Robinson, born the 25th of March, 1845; died the 29th of March, 1887; was married on the 8th of January, 1867, to Matilda Nicholas, daughter of William, and Penelope (Pope) Prather, and had these eight children: Frances Lee, Alexander Humphrey, Julia Prather, Arthur Lee, Phillips Lee, Martha Pope, Matilda Goldsborough, and Penelope Prather Robinson. Of these Frances Lee was married on the 6th of February, 1890, to Frederick Daniel Hussey; Alexander Humphrey was married on the 9th of June, 1891, to Catharine Nelson Ficklen; Julia Prather was married on the 6th of November, 1893, to William Beynroth Hardy.

Mrs. Anne Frances (Lee) Robinson was married, secondly, on the 6th of November, 1846, to William Frederick Pettit, and had one son, William Frederick, born the 5th and died the 23d of December, 1848.

## Major-General Henry Lee.

35. Henry[5], the second child and eldest son of Henry Lee[4] (Henry[3], Richard[2], Richard[1]) and Lucy Grymes, his wife, was born at "Leesylvania," his father's home, near Dumfries, in Prince William county, on the 29th of January, 1756; he died at Cumberland Island, Georgia, the home of his old commander, General Greene, on the 25th of March, 1818.

After receiving the usual rudimentary education at home, Henry was sent to Princeton College, where he graduated in 1773. Dr. William Shippen wrote to R. H. Lee, in 1770: "Your cousin, Henry Lee, is in college and will be one of the first fellows in this country. He is more than strict in his morality, has fine genius and is diligent. Charles is in the grammar school, but Dr. Witherspoon expects much from his genius and application." (Dr. Witherspoon was then the president of Princeton College.) On leaving college, Henry was for some time employed in looking after the private affairs of his father, who was absent from home engaged in negotiating a treaty with some Indian tribes on behalf of the colony of Virginia. The next year he was intending to embark for England to pursue the study of the law; but the dark shadows of war were already threatening, and changed the prospective lawyer into an actual soldier. His later career seems to have proven him well qualified for the profession of the law, and it is probable that, had he entered the political arena, he would have made for himself a reputation of no mean proportion as an orator and legislator.

Henry Lee was foremost among those who took an active part in organizing and drilling the militia of Virginia; in consequence, he was appointed, in 1776, by Patrick Henry, then governor of the State, a captain of one of the companies of cavalry in the Virginia regiment commanded by Colonel Theodorick Bland. Lee soon distinguished himself by his thorough discipline of his troopers, as well as by the care and attention given to their horses and equipment. He wrote his colonel, under date of 13th of April, 1777, ". . . How happy would I be, if it was possible for my men to be furnished with caps and boots, prior to my appearance at head-quarters! You know, my dear Colonel, that, justly, an officer's reputation depends not only on the discipline, but appearance of his men. Could the articles mentioned be allowed my troop, their appearance into Morris [Morristown] would secure me from the imputation of carelessness as their captain, and I have vanity enough to hope would assist in procuring some little credit to the colonel and regiment. Pardon my solicitations on any head respecting the condition of my troop; my sole object is the credit of the regiment."

At the time this letter was written, Colonel Bland's regiment had joined the Army under Washington, and Lee was about to make his first appearance "at head-quarters." His appearance must have been such as he desired, or his subsequent behaviour in active service must have been successful, for he appears to have won the esteem and affection of Washington very early in the war. It is certain that he was frequently employed by his commander on confidential missions and in hazardous expeditions. "He was favorably noticed by Washington throughout the war," wrote Irving. At one time the General wrote to Lee, ". . . You may in future or while on your present command, mark your letters *private;*" this to an officer only twenty-three years old surely indicated confidence and esteem. In fact, his extreme youth seems to have been the sole reason why due rank was not awarded his military merit. He was too youthful to be elevated over the heads of men much his senior in years, though probably inferior in military talent.

This letter attests the kind feeling of appreciation in which Lee was held by his great chief:

"My dear Lee,—Although I have given you my thanks in the general orders of this day, for the late instance of your gallant behaviour, I cannot resist the inclination I feel to repeat them again in this manner. I needed no fresh proofs of your merit, to bear you in remembrance. I waited only for the proper time and season to show it; those, I hope, are not far off. I shall also think of and will reward the merit of Lindsay, when an opening presents, as far as I can consistently; and I shall not forget the corporal, whom you have recommended to my notice. Offer my sincere thanks to the whole of your gallant party, and assure them that no one felt pleasure more sensibly, or rejoiced more sincerely for your and their escape, than your affectionate," etc.

The skirmish referred to by Washington was an attempt on the part of the British to capture Lee. They attached sufficient importance to making him their prisoner to send a troop of 200 horse to secretly surround his headquarters, when they had ascertained he was near their lines and accompanied by only ten men. The Americans manned the windows of the house and succeeded in beating off their assailants. Lee reported, "The contest was very warm; the British dragoons trusting to their vast superiority in number, attempted to force their way into the house. In this they were baffled by the bravery of my men. After having left two killed and four wounded, they desisted and sheered off."

The skill and daring of Lee soon won such favor in the eyes of his chief that Washington urged Congress to give him the command of an independent corps, for scouting and foraging. In a letter to the President of Congress, he wrote:

"Captain Lee of the light dragoons, and the officers under his command, having uniformly distinguished themselves by a conduct of exemplary zeal, prudence, and bravery, I took occasion, on a late signal instance of it, to express the high sense I entertained of their merit, and to assure him, that it should not fail of being properly noticed. I was induced to give this assurance from a conviction, that it is the wish of Congress to give every encouragement to merit, and that they would cheerfully embrace so favorable an opportunity of manifesting this disposition. I had it in contemplation at the time, in case no other method more eligible could be adopted, to make an offer of a place in my family. I have consulted the committee of Congress upon the subject, and we are mutually of the opinion, that giving Captain Lee the command of two troops of horse on the proposed establishment, with the rank of major, to act as an independent corps, would be a mode of rewarding him very advantageous to the service. Captain Lee's genius particularly adapts him to command of this nature; and it will be the most agreeable to him of any station in which he could be placed."

Shortly after this, Lee was given the command of three companies each of cavalry and of infantry, to operate as an independent corps. By the attention he gave to the discipline of his men, and the care of their horses, he kept his troopers so well mounted and so effective that they were able to move with great rapidity and daring. In consequence of their dash and bravery in scouting and foraging they acquired quite a reputation, and he, the soubriquet of "Light-Horse Harry," a name which has ever clung to him. On the 19th of July, 1779, at the head of 300 men, Lee surprised and captured Paulus Hook, New Jersey, securing some 160 prisoners, and retreated with the loss of only two killed and three wounded. For "his prudence, address, and bravery," on this and other occasions, Congress voted the following resolutions. By the act of 7th of April, 1778, it was

"Resolved, whereas Captain Henry Lee, of the Light Dragoons, by the whole tenor of his conduct during the last campaign, has proved himself a brave and prudent officer, rendered essential service to his country, and acquired to himself and the corps he commanded, distinguished honor, and it being the determination of Congress to reward merit, Resolved, that Captain Henry Lee be promoted to the rank of Major-Commandant; that he be empowered to augment his present corps by enlistment of two corps of horse, to act as a separate corps."

By the act of 24th September, 1779, it was

"Resolved, that the thanks of Congress be given to Major Lee for the remarkable prudence, address and bravery displayed in the attack on the enemy's fort and works at Paulus Hook, and that they approve the humanity shown in circumstances prompting to severity, as honorable to the arms of the United States, and correspondent to the noble principles on which they were assumed, and that a gold medal, emblematic of this affair, be struck under the direction of the Board of Treasury, and presented to Major Lee."

After serving for three years in the campaigns of the northern army, Lee was ordered south to join General Greene, with whom he served until his final retirement from the army after the surrender of Cornwallis at Yorktown. Greene commended him by declaring that "no man in the

progress of the campaign had equal merit.'' When it is remembered that Lee served there with such soldiers as Morgan, Marion, Pickens, Sumter, and other gallant officers, the full extent of this praise will be appreciated. About October, 1780, Congress proposed to reorganize the army somewhat, and among the changes considered was the placing of Lee's corps in one of the regular regiments. Washington opposed this change, and wrote (11th of October, 1780) to the President of Congress: " . . . Major Lee has rendered such distinguished services, possesses so many talents for commanding a corps of this nature, and deserves so much credit for the perfection in which he has kept his corps, as well as for the handsome exploits he has performed, that it would be a loss to the service, and a discouragement to merit, to reduce him, and I do not see how he can be introduced into one of the regiments in a manner satisfactory to himself, and which will enable him to be equally useful, without giving too much disgust to the whole line of cavalry.'' This protest had due effect, and Lee retained the command of his partisan corps, being also advanced to the rank of lieutenant-colonel. In writing to John Matthews, a member of Congress from South Carolina, Washington was even more complimentary to Lee. Under date of 23d of October, he wrote: " . . . Lee's corps will go to the southward. I believe it will be found very useful. The corps itself is an excellent one, and the officer at the head of it *has great resources of genius.*''

Colonel Charles Cornwallis Chesney, of the English army, in an article on General Robert E. Lee, speaks thus of his father: "From the very first he displayed military talent of a high order, and became before long the most noted leader of his army for dashing enterprise in separate command. A special gold medal was awarded him by Congress for his capture of the fort at Paulus Hook, and in 1781 he was sent to join the forces under General Greene, in the South, there matched against Cornwallis. That Greene failed, on the whole, in his encounter is well known. He was in fact in a position of inferiority, until Cornwallis left the South for Petersburg and the Richmond peninsula. . . . Greene, however, though defeated, never ceased to hold his own stoutly against Cornwallis for the time, and afterwards recovered the Carolinas fully for Congress. His successes were due in great part to the talents and energy of his young cavalry commander. General Henry Lee had a worthy opponent in Colonel Tarleton, a cavalry officer of no mean merit in light warfare. But the republican cavalier established his superiority very fully in the series of skirmishes that ensued. And although, in his own Memoir of the War, he had the modesty to attribute his successes over Tarleton to his superiority in horse flesh, readers of his interesting work may discern for themselves that his own skill and judgment were the prime causes of the advantage, and will be disposed to agree to the full with General Greene, who wrote in his personal thanks, 'No man in the progress of the campaign had equal merit with yourself,' an expression of strong meaning coming from a plain, blunt soldier of honest character. And this praise was fully confirmed by Washington's own words of love and thanks, in a letter of later date, written long enough after to show how strong in that great man's mind was the memory of the services of 'Light-Horse Harry,' as his contemporaries familiarly called General Henry Lee."

Shortly after the surrender of Cornwallis, Lee resigned from the army, upon which occasion General Greene wrote him this letter:

"Headquarters, 27th January, 1782. Dear Sir,—I have beheld with extreme anxiety for some time past a growing discontent in your mind, and have not been without my apprehensions that your complaints originated more in distress than in ruin of your constitution. Whatever may be the source of your wounds, I wish it was in my power to heal them. . . . From our earliest acquaintance I had a partiality for you, which progressively grew into friendship. I was under no obligation to you until I came into this country; and yet I believe you will do me the justice to say I never wanted inclination to serve you. Here I have been under the greatest obligations,—obligations I can never cancel. . . . I am far from agreeing with you in the opinion that the public will never do you justice. I believe few officers, either in Europe or America, are held in so high a point of estimation as you are.[1] Substantial service is what constitutes lasting reputation; and your reports this campaign are the best panegyric that can be given of your action. . . . It is true, there are a few of your countrymen, who from ignorance and malice are disposed to do injustice to your conduct, but it is out of their power to injure you. Indeed, you are ignorant of your own weight and influence, otherwise you would despise their spleen and malice. . . . Everybody knows I have the highest opinion of you as an officer, and you know I love you as a friend; whatever may be your determination, to retire or to continue in service, my affection will accompany you." In a parting letter Greene adds (12th February, 1782): "You are going home and you will get married, but you cannot cease to be a soldier; should the war rage here I shall call for you in a few months, unless I should find your inclination opposed to my wishes."

---

[1] " . . General Henry Lee, who, if not the foremost man of all the world of his age and rank, was certainly the second of no man, if, during seven years of service, in numberless situations requiring talents, bravery and prompt execution, the commission of no fault or the neglect of no duty, entitled him to such an appellation."—(*Vindication of John Banks, of Va.*, 83.)

General Charles Lee once said of him, that "Major Lee seemed to have come out of his mother's womb a soldier." Marshall, the early historian of Washington,[1] has written: "The continued labors and exertions of all were highly meritorious, but the successful activity of one corps will attract particular attention. The legion, from its structure, was peculiarly adapted to the partisan warfare of the Southern States, and, by being detached against weaker posts of the enemy, had opportunities for displaying with advantage all the energies it possessed. In that extensive sweep which it made from the Santee to Augusta, which employed from the 15th of April to the 8th of June, this corps, acting in conjunction first with Marion, afterward with Pickens, and sometimes alone, had constituted the principal force which carried five British posts and made upward of 1100 prisoners."

Mr. Custis[2] has declared that, "No officer in the American army could have been better fitted than Lee for the command of a partisan corps; for in the surprise of posts, in gaining intelligence, of distracting and discomforting your enemy, without bringing him to a general action, and all the strategy which belongs to the partisan warfare, few officers in any service have been more distinguished than the subject of our memoir. The legion of Lee, under the untiring labors of its active, talented commander, became one of the most efficient corps in the American army. The horsemen were principally recruited in the Southern and Middle States—countries proverbial for furnishing skilful riders; while the horses, under the inspection of the Virginian commander, were superior in bone and figure, and could many of them have boasted a lineal descent from the Godolphin Arabian.

"Among Lee's officers were the good and gallant names of Eggleston, Rudolph, Armstrong, O'Neil, and the surviving honored veterans Allen M'Lane of Delaware, and Harrison of Virginia. The arrival of the legion in the South was hailed as most auspicious to the success of our arms in that quarter; indeed, so fine a corps of horse and foot, so well disciplined, and in such gallant array, was rarely to be seen in those our days of desolation. The partisan legion did good service in the campaigns of the Carolinas, and the commander won his way to the esteem and confidence of Greene, the *well-beloved of Washington*, as he had previously done to the esteem and confidence of the great chief himself; and, as a justice to the great military sagacity of Lee, let it be remembered, that he was mainly instrumental in advising Greene to that *return to the Carolinas* which eventuated in the decisive and glorious combat of Eutaw, and the virtual liberation of the South. With the close of the campaign of 1781 ended the military services of

---

[1] *Life of Washington*, IV, p. 536.

[2] *Recollections of Washington*, by G. W. P. Custis, 1860, pp. 357–9.

Lieutenant-Colonel Lee. He retired on furlough to Virginia, and was happily present at the surrender of his old adversary, the formidable Cornwallis, 19th October. Lee married shortly afterward, and settled in the county of Westmoreland, but was permitted, by his grateful and admiring countrymen, for a short time only to enjoy the *otium cum dignitate*, being successfully chosen to the state legislature, the convention for ratifying the constitution, the gubernatorial chair, and the Congress of the United States."

During all his services in these legislative bodies, Henry Lee was an ardent federalist, ably supporting Madison and others in their efforts for securing the ratification of the Constitution by the Virginia Convention. In taking this position he was an antagonist of his cousin, Richard Henry Lee, yet the latter considered his services so valuable to the State that he was anxious for him to be in the Virginia Assembly. Under date of 14th July, 1787, R. H. Lee wrote his brother, Arthur: "I do really consider it a thing of consequence to the public interest that Col. H. Lee of Stratford should be in our next Assembly, and therefore wish you would exert yourself with the old Squire [Richard Lee] to get his resignation, or disqualification rather, so that his nephew may get early into the House of Delegates. I know it is like persuading a man to sign his own death warrant, but upon my word the state of public affairs renders the sacrifice of place and vanity, necessary."

Henry Lee was governor of Virginia for three years; while in this office, Washington appointed him to command the troops ordered out to suppress the "Whiskey Rebellion," which occurred in western Pennsylvania, in 1794; he succeeded in quelling the rebellion without bloodshed. On the 19th of July, 1798, he was appointed a major-general in the army, and was honorably discharged on the 15th of June, 1800. Being a member of Congress in 1799, when the news of the death of Washington was received by Congress, he drew up a series of resolutions, formally announcing that event, which were presented in his absence, by his colleague, John Marshall; in these resolutions occur those ever memorable words: "*First in war, first in peace, and first in the hearts of his fellow-citizens.*" Thereupon, Congress resolved that "the President of the Senate and the Speaker of the House of Representatives, be desired to request one of the members of Congress to perform and deliver" an oration. Henry Lee was selected to pay this tribute on behalf of Congress to the great Washington, and the oration was delivered before Congress on the 26th of December, 1799, at the "German Lutheran Church, in 4th street, above Arch, Philadelphia, the largest in the city."

Of this oration, Mr. Custis[1] has written, as one who had heard it: "With the advantages of a classical education, General Lee possessed taste and distinguished powers of eloquence; and was selected, on the demise of Washington, to deliver the oration in the funeral solemnities decreed by Congress in honor of the Pater Patriæ. The oration having been but imperfectly committed to memory, from the very short time in which it was composed, somewhat impaired its effect upon the auditory; but, as a composition, it has only to be read to be admired, for the purity and elegance of its language, and the powerful appeal it makes to the hearts of its readers; and we will venture to affirm, that it will rank among the most celebrated performances of those highly distinguished men who mounted the rostrum on that imposing occasion of national mourning."

Mr. Custis adds:[2] "In one particular Lee may be said to have excelled his illustrious contemporaries, Marshall, Madison, Hamilton, Gouverneur Morris and Ames. It was in a surprising quickness of talent, a genius sudden, dazzling, and always at command, with an eloquence which seemed to flow unbidden. Seated at a convivial board when the death of Patrick Henry was announced, Lee called for a scrap of paper, and in a few moments produced a striking and beautiful eulogium upon the Demosthenes of modern liberty. His powers of conversation were also fascinating in the extreme, possessing those rare and admirable qualities which seize and hold captive his hearers, delighting while they instruct. That Lee was a man of letters, a scholar who had ripened under a truly classical sun, we have only to turn to his work on the southern war, where he was, indeed, the *Magna pars fui* of all which he relates—a work which well deserves to be ranked with the commentaries of the famed master of the Roman world, who, like our Lee, was equally renowned with the pen as the sword. But there is a line, a single line, in the works of Lee which would hand him over to immortality, though he had never written another. 'First in war, first in peace, and first in the hearts of his fellow-countrymen'[3] will last while language lasts. What a sublime eulogium is pronounced in that noble line! So few words, and yet how illustrative are they of the vast and matchless character of Washington! They are words which will descend with the memory of the hero they are meant to honor, to the veneration of remotest posterity, and be graven on colossal statues of the Pater Patriæ in some future age.

---

[1] *Recollections of Washington*, by G. W. P. Custis, 360-1, 478, 615.

[2] *Ibid.*, pp. 361-2-3.

[3] In the *resolutions* presented to Congress, Lee used the phrase "fellow-citizens"; but in his *oration* he used "fellow-countrymen."

"The attachment of Lee to Washington was like that of Hamilton, pure and enthusiastic—like that of the chivalric Laurens, devotional. It was in the praise of his 'hero, his friend, and his country's preserver' that the splendid talents of Lee were often elicited, with a force and grandeur of eloquence wholly his own. The fame and memory of his chief was the fondly-cherished passion to which he clung amid the wreck of his fortunes—the hope which gave warmth to his heart when all else around him seemed cold and desolate. But shall the biographer's task be complete, when the faults of his subject are not to be taken into account? Of faults, perhaps the subject of our memoir had many; yet how admirable is the maxim handed down to us from the ancients, '*De mortuis nil, nisi bonum.*' Let the faults of Lee be buried in his distant grave—let the turf of oblivion close over the failings of him whose early devotion to liberty, in liberty's battles—whose eloquence in her senates and historical memoirs of her times of trial, shed a lustre on his country in the young days of the Republic; and when Americans of some future date shall search amid the records of their early history for the lives of illustrious men who flourished in the age of Washington, high on a brilliant scroll will they find inscribed Henry Lee, a son of Virginia—patriot, soldier, and historian of the Revolution, and orator and statesman of the Republic."

In 1801 Henry Lee retired permanently from public life, hoping to spend the remainder of his days in the peaceful quiet of a Virginia farm life. "With his congressional career, ended the better days of this highly gifted man. An unhappy rage for speculation caused him to embark upon that treacherous stream, which gently, and almost imperceptibly at first, but with sure and fearful rapidity at last, hurries its victims to the vortex of destruction. It was, indeed, lamentable to behold the venerable Morris and Lee, patriots, who, in the senates of liberty and on her battle fields, had done the 'state such service,' instead of enjoying a calm and happy evening of life, to be languishing in prison and in exile. Lee, after long struggling with adversity, sought in a foreign land a refuge from his many ills, where, becoming broken in health, he returned home to die. He reached the mansion of Greene, and fortune, relenting her frowns, lit up his few remaining days with a smile. There, amid attentions the most consoling and kindly, surrounded by recollections of his old and loved commander, the most fond and endearing, the worn and wearied spirit of the patriot, statesman, and soldier of liberty found rest in the grave."

In 1809 Henry Lee wrote his interesting *Memoirs of the War in the Southern Department of the United States.* Shortly afterward (June, 1812) he was very seriously injured by a mob at Baltimore while attempting to defend the house of a friend. Later he made a voyage to the West Indies, seeking restoration for his shattered health. On his way home he landed at Cumberland Island, on the coast of Georgia, the home of his old commander and friend, General Greene, where he died on the 25th of March, 1818, and was buried. A war vessel, happening to be anchored near by, her captain and crew assisted at his funeral, and paid the last military honors to the dead soldier. As has been said: "Fortune seems to have conducted him at the close of his life almost to the tomb of Greene; and his bones may now repose by the side of those of his beloved chief; friends in war, united in death, and partners in a never-dying fame."

As stated by Mr. Custis, Henry Lee was always an ardent admirer of Washington, and never lost an opportunity of expressing his veneration for that great man. In his last illness "a surgical operation was proposed, as offering some hope of prolonging his life; but he replied that the eminent surgeon to whose skill and care, during his sojourn in the West Indies, he was so much indebted, had disapproved a resort to the proposed operation. The surgeon in attendance still urging it, the patient put an end to the discussion by saying: 'My dear sir, were the great Washington alive and here, and joining you in advocating it, I would still resist.'"

Mr. Irving has said that Henry Lee was always a favorite with Washington, and was very often favorably noticed by him. And Lee, on his part, seems to have looked up to Washington rather as a friend or older brother, than as his military chief. In his letters he appears to have asked for advice upon any private business or public topic that interested him, and to have expressed his feelings and opinions upon current affairs with much freedom. Mr. Irving says further,[1] "Colonel Henry Lee, who used to be a favored guest at Mount Vernon, does not seem to have been much under the influence of that 'reverential awe' which Washington is said to have inspired; if we may judge from the following anecdote. Washington one day at table mentioned his being in want of carriage horses, and asked Lee if he knew where he could get a pair.

"'I have a fine pair, general,' replied Lee, 'but you cannot get them.'

"'Why not?'

"'Because you will never pay more than half price for anything; and I must have full price for my horses.'

"The bantering reply set Mrs. Washington laughing, and her parrot, perched beside her, joined in the laugh. The general took this familiar

---

[1] *Life of Washington*, IV, 440.

assault upon his dignity in great good part. 'Ah, Lee, you are a funny fellow,' said he; 'see, that bird is laughing at you.'"

The following letter of sympathy from General Washington to Henry Lee, was evidently written in response to the news of the deaths of his (first) wife and son; indeed, on the original were indorsed these words by Lee himself, "the deaths of my wife and son": [1]

"New York, Augt. 27th, 1790. My dear Sir, I have been duly favoured with the receipt of your obliging letter dated the 12th of June last. I am also indebted to you for a long letter written to me in the course of last year and should have had the pleasure sooner to express my acknowledgments for the tender interest you take on account of my health and administration, but such is the multiplicity of my avocations, and so great the pressure of public business as to leave me no leisure for the agreeable duty of answering private letters from my friends—and although I shall at all times be happy to hear from them, yet I shall be but an unprofitable correspondent, as it will not be in my power to make those returns which under other circumstances I should have real pleasure in doing.

"It is unnecessary to assure you of the interest I take in whatever nearly concerns you. I therefore very sincerely condole with you on your late, and great losses; but as the ways of Providence are as inscrutable as just, it becomes the children of it to submit with resignation and fortitude to its decrees as far as the feelings of humanity will allow, and your good sense will, I am persuaded, enable you to do this. Mrs. Washington joins me in these sentiments and with great esteem and regard, I am, my dear Sir," etc.

Henry Lee was twice married; first, in the spring of 1782,[2] to his cousin Matilda, daughter of Philip Ludwell, and Elizabeth (Steptoe) Lee, of Stratford; she died about May, 1790, having had four children; of these, Nathaniel Greene died in early infancy, and Philip Ludwell, when about seven years old; the other two, a daughter and son, survived: [3]

i, LUCY GRYMES [6], born in 1786, and died in 1860; she was married, in 1803, to Bernard Moore Carter, a son of Charles Carter, by his second wife, Anne Butler Moore; they had issue: 1, Charles Henry, who

---

[1] Copied from the original by Mr. Joseph Packard, Jr.

[2] In a deed for division of lands, dated 30th of April, 1782, she was mentioned as the wife of Henry Lee, Jr.

[3] By a deed of trust, dated the 10th of August, 1790, between Henry Lee, of Stratford, and Matilda, his wife, of the first part, and Philip Ludwell Lee, Henry Lee, and Lucy Grymes Lee, children of the said Henry and Matilda, of the second part, and Richard Bland Lee and Ludwell Lee, of the third part, it was covenanted that, at the death of said Henry and Matilda, Stratford was to go to the eldest son, Philip Ludwell Lee, and the "Sugar plantation in Loudoun" to Henry Lee, the youngest son, etc.

married Rosalie Eugenia Calvert, of Prince George's county, Md., and had issue: Eugenia, Alice, Bernard, Mildred, Annote, Ella, and Mary R. Carter. Of these, Bernard married Mary Buckner, daughter of David Ridgeley, of "White Marsh," Baltimore county, and has issue. 2, Josephine, who married Eugene Frausen, and died without issue. 3, Matilda Lee, who married Thomas M. Willing, and had six children. 4, Mildred Randolph, who married Louis de Potestad, and left a son, Louis, and other children. 5, Charlotte, who married G. W. Featherstonehaugh, of England, and left issue. 6, Bernard Moore, no issue.

ii, HENRY[6]. See 47.

After his first wife's death, Henry Lee had seriously considered the idea of going to France, where, as he wrote Washington when consulting him upon the step, a major-general's commission awaited him. Washington would give no direct advice, but discouraged the idea, saying he himself would not think of taking such a step, "because it would appear a boundless ocean I was about to embark on, from whence no land is seen. . . . Those in whose hands the government [of France] is intrusted are ready to tear each other to pieces, and will more than probably prove the worst foes the country has." This project was given up, whether through the influence of Washington or from the objection of Mr. Carter, or both, is not known. Mr. Carter would not consent to a union with his daughter until assured that the French project was abandoned. He wrote, under date of the 20th of May, 1793: "The only objection we ever had to your connection with our beloved daughter is now entirely done away. You have declared upon your honor that you have relinquished all thoughts of going to France, and we rest satisfied with that assurance. As we certainly know that you have obtained her consent, you shall have that of her parents most cordially, to be joined together in the holy bonds of matrimony, whenever she pleases; and as it is determined on, by the approbation and sincere affection of all friends, as well as of the parties immediately concerned, we think the sooner it takes place the better."

On hearing of this marriage, Washington writes to Lee, " . . . As we are told that you have exchanged the rugged and dangerous field of Mars for the soft and pleasurable bed of Venus, I do in this, as I shall in every thing you may pursue like unto it, good and laudable, wish you all imaginable success and happiness."[1]

Henry Lee married, secondly, on the 18th of June, 1793, Anne Hill, daughter of Charles Carter, of "Shirley," and Anne Butler Moore, his sec-

[1] Ford's *Writings of George Washington*, XII, 311.

ond wife; Mrs. Lee was born in 1773, and died in 1829; they had six children, the record of their ages given here is from Mrs. Lee's family Bible.

iii, ALGERNON SIDNEY[6], born 2d April, 1795; died the 9th of August, 1796.

iv, CHARLES CARTER[6]. See 48.

v, ANNE KINLOCH[6], born the 19th of June, 1800; died at Baltimore on the 20th of February, 1864; she married in 1825 Judge William Louis Marshall; born at "Buckpond," Woodford county, Kentucky, on the 26th of September, 1803; died on the 5th of October, 1869, in Southern California, where he moved after his wife's death. Judge Marshall settled in Baltimore shortly after his marriage, being at that time a minister; later he studied law, and eventually became one of the leading jurists of the State, filling several public offices. Judge Marshall was the second son of Dr. Louis Marshall and Agatha Smith, his wife, who was born at "Oakhill," Fauquier county, on the 7th of October, 1773, and died at "Buckpond," Woodford county, Kentucky, in 1866. Dr. Marshall was the eleventh child of the famous Col. Thomas Marshall, a schoolmate and life-long friend of Washington. Colonel Marshall was born in Westmoreland county on the 2d of April, 1730; removed to Kentucky in 1785, and died at Washington, Mason county, in that State, on the 22d of June, 1802. He was also the father of Chief Justice John Marshall. (See Marshall Family under 84.) Judge William Lewis and Anne Kinloch (Lee) Marshall had one son, Col. Louis Henry Marshall, who was born about 1827; graduated at West Point, and was appointed Brevet Second Lieutenant, 3d Infantry, on the 1st of July, 1849; Second Lieutenant, 5th March, 1851; First Lieutenant, 10th Infantry, 3d March, 1855; Captain, 29th December, 1860; Major, 14th Infantry, 16th October, 1863; transferred to 23d Infantry the 21st of April, 1866; resigned 23d November, 1868; Brevet Colonel, 13th March, 1865, "for meritorious and gallant service during the war." Col. Marshall has been twice married; first, on the 1st of June, 1854, to Florence Burke; secondly, on the 2d of June, 1884, to Elvira C. White. With his wife and four children, Col. Marshall has been living in Southern California.

vi, SIDNEY SMITH[6]. See 49.

vii, ROBERT EDWARD[6]. See 50.

viii, CATHARINE MILDRED[6], born the 27th of February, 1811, at Alexandria; died at Paris, France, in 1856; she married, in 1831, Edward

Vernon Childe, and had: 1, Edward Lee Childe, who is living in France; he has been twice married; first, in 1868, to Blanche de Trigueti; secondly, in 1888, to Marie de Sartiges. 2, Arthur Lee Childe, who died at Munich in 1856. 3, Florence Childe, who resides at Paris; she married in 1854, Count Henri Soltyk, and has one son, Count Stanislas Soltyk, born in 1855, and now an officer in the Austrian service. 4, Mary Custis Childe, who married in 1859, Robert Gilmor Hoffman, of Baltimore, and died in 1867, without issue.

While absent from home in the West Indies, Henry Lee wrote a series of letters to his son, Carter, which the latter declared furnished "the best history of the close of our father's life." "These letters of love and wisdom," as General Robert E. Lee called them, are certainly worthy of reproduction here:[1]

"Port-au-Prince, St. Domingo, 26th June, 1816. My dear Carter,—I have just heard by a letter from Henry that you are fixed at the University of Cambridge, the seminary of my choice. You will there have not only excellent examples to encourage your love and practice of virtue, the only real good in life, but ample scope to pursue learning to its bottom, thereby fitting yourself to be useful to your country and to be an ornament to your friends.

"You know, my dear son, the deep and affectionate interest I have taken in you from the first moment of your existence, and your kind, amiable disposition will never cease enjoying and amplifying your father's happiness to the best of your ability. You will do this by preferring the practice of virtue to all other things; you know my abhorrence of lying, and you have been often told by me that it led to every vice and cancelled every tendency to virtue. Never forget this truth, and disdain this mean and infamous practice. Epaminondas, the great Theban who defended his country when environed by powerful foes, and was the most virtuous man of his age, so abhorred lying that he would never tell one even in jest. Imitate this great man and you may equal him in goodness, infinitely to be preferred to his greatness. I am too sick to continue this discussion, though I begin to hope I may live to see you, your dear mother, and our other sweet offspring. I only write now to require that you write monthly to me. Send your letters by vessels from Boston which go to Turk's Island for salt; and inclose them to Mr. Daniel Bascombe, merchant. He will send them to me wherever I may be, though I shall not get them as expeditiously

[1] These letters are taken from General Robert E. Lee's preface to his edition of his father's Memoirs.

as my heart desires. This goes to Mr. Wm. Sullivan, a gentleman of Boston, who will send it to you, and do you any necessary favor should sickness or accident render any such favor requisite. He is, too, an exemplary gentleman, worthy of your imitation. There is a little boy, James Smith, son of a Mr. Smith of these islands, at school at Westfield, not far from Cambridge; should you ever go that way call and see this boy, and assist him by your advice and countenance. He is in a strange land and far from his relatives. My prayers are offered to Almighty God for the protection of my darling Carter, and especially for establishing in his heart and conduct virtue in all its power. I pray you never to forget that virtue is our first good and lying its deadly foe."

"Turk's Island (on my voyage to New Providence) 8th August, 1816.—My dear Carter will have received one letter written as soon as I knew he was settled at Cambridge, and which was sent to the care of Mr. Sullivan, in Boston. Having this moment an opportunity to send to New York, I use it to repeat my love and prayers for his health and advancement in the acquisition of knowledge from its foundation, not on the surface. This last turns man into a puppy, and the first fits him for the highest utility and most lasting pleasure. I requested you to write monthly to me, giving to me with clearness and brevity a narrative of your studies, recreations, and your relish for the occupations which employ you in and out of college. Never mind your style; but write your first impressions quickly, clearly and honestly. Style will come in due time, as will maturity of judgment. Above all things earthly, even love to the best of mothers and your ever-devoted father, I entreat you to cherish truth and abhor deception. Dwell on the virtues, and imitate, as far as lies in your power, the great and good men whom history presents to our view.

"'Minerva! Let such examples teach thee to beware,
Against Great God thou utter aught profane;
And, if perchance, in riches or in power
Thou shinest superior, be not insolent;
For, know, a day sufficeth to exalt
Or to depress the state of mortal man.
The wise and good are by our God beloved,
But those who practice evil he abhors.'

"You have my favorite precept, instilled from your infancy by my lips, morning, noon, and night, in my familiar talks with you, here presented to your mind in the purity and elegance of the Grecian tragedian [Sophocles]. You never, I trust, will forget to make it the cardinal rule of your life. It will, at least, arrest any tendency to imitate the low, degrading usage, too common, of swearing in conversation, especially with your inferiors. My miserable state of health improves by occasional voyaging in this fine climate, with the sage guidance of a superior physician to whom I am now returning. When Boston fails to give you opportunities to write as before directed, send your letters to Mr. William Goddard, in Providence, who will forward them to me."

"Caicos, 30th September, 1816. October is near at hand, and no letter from my beloved Carter; notwithstanding I have been writing to you ever since I learned that you were at Cambridge, and the salt vessels are weekly arriving at the adjacent islands, and I had asked my friends, Mr. Sullivan and Mr. Goddard, to forward your letters. What can this mean? Anything, I know, my dear son, but your lukewarmness of devotion and love to your father. I have been detained three months on my way to my Spanish doctor in Nassau, the chief town of Providence, where I hope to be partially restored or to die in the attempt; why, then, will you not give me the delight of reading your letters! Write, I entreat you, your thoughts just as they come, and in the order and fashion in which they arise. . . . I am very serious in this requisition; and if your letters exhibit labor, instead of negligent ease, I shall be unhappy. Never show those for me to your preceptor or any one else. Speak from your heart to my heart: that is what I want, and want only. In Barbadoes, where I landed from Alexandria, and where I resided six months, I often wrote to you and sometimes to Anne, but never heard from either. One of those letters treated on the subject of your advance and progress through life, and I will here repeat some of its contents. . . . Important as it is to understand nature in its range and bearing, it is more so to be prepared for usefulness, and to render ourselves pleasing by understanding well the religious and moral knowledge of right and wrong, to investigate thoroughly the history of mankind, and to be familiar with those examples which show loveliness of truth, and demonstrate the reasonableness of our opinions by past events. Providence and justice manifest their excellence at all times and in all places; we are called to moralize daily, but we seldom turn to geometry; with intellectual nature we have constant intercourse, but speculations upon matter are rare, and when much at leisure, we know little of the skill of our acquaintance in astronomy, though we daily see him, but his integrity, his benevolence, his truth and prudence instantly appear. Read therefore the best poets, the best orators, and the best historians; as from them you draw principles of moral truth, axioms of prudence and material for conversation. This was the opinion of the great Socrates. He labored in

Athens to turn philosophy from the study of nature to the study of life. He justly thought man's great business was to learn how to do good, and to avoid evil. Be a steady, ardent disciple of Socrates; and regard virtue, whose temple is built upon truth, as the chief good. I would rather see you unlearned and unnoticed, if virtuous in practice as well as theory, than to see you the equal in glory to the great Washington; but virtue and wisdom are not opponents; they are friends and coalesce in a few characters such as his. A foolish notion often springs up with young men as they enter life, namely, that the opinion of the world is not to be regarded; whereas, it is the true criterion, generally speaking, of all things that terminate in human life. To despise its sentence, if possible, is not just; and if just, is not possible. So think now, and be confirmed as you advance. Tell me about my dear Smith and Robert: their genius, temper, their disposition to learn, their diligence, and perseverance in doing what is assigned to them. Tell me the whole truth; and be virtuous, which will render you happy."

"Nassau, New Providence, 1 Dec. 1816. My Dear Carter has never answered one of the many letters to him, from the day I understood he was placed by his dear mother at Cambridge; my misfortune, not your fault. I have confidence in your heart, not to be shaken; and I know, ardent and constant as has been my love for you, correspondent at least has been your affection and respect for me. . . . I occasionally sent you a book, which I commended to your serious study, but whether any have ever reached you, I do not know. Now I must urge you, as the library at Cambridge will present to your discrimination a large collection, to avoid all frivolous authors; such as novel writers, and all skeptical authors, whether religious, philosophic, or moral. Adhere to history and ethical authors of unrivalled character; first of the latter description is John Locke; do not only read him, but study him; do not only study, but consult him as the Grecians did the Delphic oracle. Make him the director of your mind and the guide of your lucubrations. Francis Bacon (Viscount of St. Alban's, I believe) is wonderfully instructive; though of cowardly, despicable character. The Earl of Shaftesbury, Locke's patron, is like Locke himself, in another way. Dean Swift commands your high admiration and is truly instructive, as well as infinitely agreeable. David Hume is at the head of English historians, and his essays abound with shining information to the mind, as do Johnson's works. Among the English poets prefer Pope; he is worthy of universal applause, far superior to Milton, as his *Iliad* compared with *Paradise Lost* evinces.

"I trust you are a good classic, and then among the ancients pore over Tacitus, Xenophon, Julius Cæsar, and Polybius in prose, and Homer and Sophocles in verse. Virgil is Homer's excellent imitator, but far below the transcendant Greek. Lucretius, '*de natura rerum*,' is full of marks of superior genius; but he supports atheism, and incites in the mind wonder at his folly and compassion for his error, with indignation for the possible injury he might do to the human race. If I had not partly read him, I never could have believed there ever lived a man who was in judgment an atheist. If you have not Locke in your college library, tell me, and I will furnish you; as I will with the meditations of Marcus Aurelius, the great and good emperor, adopted by Antoninus, his equal in excellence, whose name he bears in history. In the first of his meditations, he thus speaks of himself, which I give summarily, to excite your desire to become intimate with him and to emulate him:

"'From the example of my grandfather I acquired a virtuous disposition and an habitual command over my temper. From my own father I learned to behave with modesty, yet with manly firmness on all occasions. My mother I have imitated in piety, and have been taught not only to abstain from vice, but to abhor the thought of it, and she taught me to be simple and abstemious in diet. To my grandfather I am indebted for the best masters; and from the governor of my early days I learned to avoid races, games, and such diversions; substituting for them hardships and fatigues; to reduce the conveniences of life into a narrow compass, to wait upon myself; never to listen to calumny, or to meddle with the business of others. Dignetus stopped me from pursuing trifles and from believing the vulgar tales of prodigies, spirits, and such kind of follies. He taught me to bear patiently the admonitions of my friends; to sleep on a hard couch; and, while a boy, to write dialogues. From Rusticus I learned, not to assume any state in my deportment; to write letters in a plain, unornamented style; to be readily reconciled to all who had injured me, when they seemed inclined to do right; to read with care and attention; not to be content with a general, superficial view of the subject, nor to recede from my opinion only when convinced it was error. Apollonius taught me to maintain the freedom of mind; a constancy independent of fortune; and to keep a steady eye in the most minute instances to the dictates of reason; to preserve an even temper always, even in joy or pain; and to be like him, rigid in principle, but easy and affable in manners. In Sextus I had an example of a truly benevolent disposition, and of a family governed with paternal care and affection. Like him, I determined to live according to nature, simple and unaffected; and, like him, to acquire reputation without noise, and deep learning without ostentation. I imitate my relative, Severus, in love of my relations and of truth and justice; and from Claudius I learned to be always master of myself, and never to yield to passion.

"You will agree that a boy thus reared must turn out good and great when a man; and you will, I hope, hold before your eyes as a model, Marcus Aurelius. It is a small book, and its precepts should be engraven upon your mind and habituated in your conduct. You write, I hope, regularly to your dear mother, and to Henry, also to your sister

Anne, and your brother Sydney. This will improve them and cement your mutual affection. My letters you must keep and give them to Smith to read. . . . My health is better. I hope to leave this place in April, if I live. Farewell, my dear son."

"Nassau, 9 February, 1817. My beloved Carter's letter of July 25th came to hand, not on the birth day of the great and good Washington, but in his birth month, and infused into his father's heart an overflow of delight, in defiance of the torturing pains of disease. Always dear to me, always the source of delicious anticipations, I see, from your first performance ample evidence that my fond hopes will not be disappointed. Go on in the road of truth to the temple of virtue, where dwell her handmaids, modesty, temperance, benevolence, fortitude, and justice. Fame in arms or art, however conspicuous, is naught, unless bottomed on virtue. Think, therefore, of fame only as the appendage to virtue; and be virtuous, though poor, humble, and scorned.

"Remember how often I have prayed you to imitate Epaminondas in his regard for truth, if you cannot aspire to follow him in his trail of true glory. He is my favorite Grecian; and next to him Aristides, whom you place as second to Alcibiades. To bring the reasoning home to you, your dearest mother is singularly pious from love to Almighty God and love of virtue, which are synonymous; not from fear of hell—a low, base influence. Your dear mother recalls to my mind our dear Anne, Smith, Robert, and my unknown. You ought to have said something of them all, their growth, their health, their amusements, their occupations, their progress in literature, their tempers as they open, and last, not least, their love and devotion to their good mamma. . . . Your brother delineates to me your character with all the affection of his generous heart. . . . My dear Lucy, too, her excellent husband and sweet progeny, ought not to have escaped your attention. Two sheets, instead of one and a half, might have been so employed; and the more I read from my darling son the more I feast. . . . I cannot answer your query concerning Washington's charger,[1] nor withhold my admiration for your tender regard for useful animals, with gratitude to those from whom we have derived services. You know I am almost an Egyptian in my love for the cow and ox; yet after their daily service through life, after the third year I always fatten, kill, and eat them. The subject which you touch has been decided rather from feeling than judgment; we will discuss it when we meet. Your panegyric on Shakespeare is all just, but when you read the

[1] Whether he was shot in his old age, as is said to be customary in England, or as some asserted Washington did with his war-horse.

Athenian, Sophocles, you will find his superior, at least his equal, in all the requisites of tragedy.

"Eloquence is our first gift in civic walks, nor is it without great advantage in war. To be eloquent you must understand thoroughly your subject; out of the abundance of knowledge the tongue uttereth just ideas; voice, gesticulation, manner may be acquired with care, but knowledge cannot be acquired but by labor, and that by night as well as by day. In every distinguished character nature gives the turn and scope; art and study polish and spread. . . . Tell me in your reply what are your expenses *in toto*, designating every item and the sum it demands. Tell me your diversions, amusements, and bodily exercises; whether at ball, long bullets, &c. The climate of Cambridge is much colder than that of your native country. How does it agree with you? Pray guard against cold; it is the stepping-stone to other diseases; I repeat my entreaty to save yourself from its injuries, and I pray you also to cherish your health by temperance and exercise. It is hard to say whether too much eating or too much drinking most undermines the constitution; you are addicted to neither, and will, I am sure, take care to grow up free from both. Cleanliness of person is not only comely to all beholders, but is indispensable to sanctity of body. Trained by your best of mothers to value it, you will never lose sight of it. To be plain and neat in dress conforms to good sense and is emblematic of a right mind. Many lads, who avoid the practices mentioned, fall into another habit which hurts only themselves and which certainly stupefies the senses—immoderate sleeping. You know how I love my children; and how dear Smith is to me. Give me a true description of his person, mind, temper, and habits. Tell me of Anne; has she grown tall? And how is my last in looks and understanding? Robert was always good, and will be confirmed in his happy turn of mind by his ever-watchful and affectionate mother. Does he strengthen his native tendency?

"You speak of the 'soul' in your letter. I trust you mean by the word the faculty which the Almighty has imbued us with, of thinking, reasoning, and concluding; as he has given to our eyes the faculty of seeing, our ears of hearing, and our nerves of feeling. You do not mean by the soul a being connected with the body. Mr. Locke will put you right on all subjects of this sort, and ought to be revered by all who love truth and seek knowledge. When you study natural philosophy, and admire, as you must, Sir Isaac Newton, forget not Pythagoras; he announced and taught the principle that Newton has so profoundly explained,—the earth turning on its axis and all the planets turning around the sun. I have a book which I wish to send you for your constant perusal—Bacon. It is most edifying, and worthy of your exact acquaintance: and yet superb in genius and profound in knowledge as was Sir Francis Bacon, he was almost proverbially base and mean; a rare example of debasement of mind with richness of knowledge.

"Did you ever get a gun and letters from me more than six months ago? Do you ride and shoot well? These are secondary, but they are agreeable, useful, and manly. '*Unde derivatus?*' is a scholastic interrogatory; be assured, it is all important to correct literature; and you will, I hope, thoroughly meet it. When you have the derivation of every word, you can never forget the language nor be at a loss for its purest use. Your letter has been four days in my possession, and is always before me when capable of diverting my attention from my body. Mr. McIntosh, whose father was an officer in a corps against which I was employed when in the southern war, has made my house his home, and with his daughter, bestowed every effort in their power to soften my pains. She was as kind, and as tender, and as constant as would have been my daughter, and read all the letters I have received; among them one from Henry. She admired his heart and filial love. Being here at present, I sent her your letter, acquainted as she was with my affection and hopes for my Carter. You have her note returning the letter. My Spanish doctor has done me good, and sometimes inspires hopes of partial restoration. I leave here as soon as spring arrives, whatever may be my condition, and land in the South, to graduate my experience of change of climate. . . . May God Almighty cherish, bless and guide my dear son, is and ever will be the prayer of his loving father."

"Nassau, New Providence, 19 April, 1817. I answered your second letter, my dear Carter, directly after its receipt; and now repeat, so fond am I of cultivating acquaintance with my beloved boy. In my last I told you that my disease had at length yielded in a degree, and that I hoped still to mend; but whether or not, my return home would take place in a few weeks, directing my course to the South, as a warm climate still continues necessary for me. Before this day month, I expect to find a vessel to South Carolina or Georgia, when I shall embark. Mr. Goddard will be informed where to address your letters. But at all events, after May, send them by the various vessels going to Charleston from Boston, to the care of General Pinckney; indeed you might inclose them in a short epistle, asking his attention, and telling him you took the liberty in consequence of my directions Send always by vessels, as thus General Pinckney will be put to no expense. His Christian name is Thomas, and his title Major-General. Tell me all about your dear mother and my children, for scarcely do I ever hear from Henry, although I am sure he writes every two weeks.

"I find your mind is charmed with eloquence, and I infer that the bar is the theatre selected for its display. The rank of men, as established by the concurrent judgment of ages, stands thus: heroes, legislators, orators, and poets. The most useful and, in my opinion, the most honorable is the legislator, which so far from being incompatible with the profession of law, is congenial to it Generally, mankind admire most the hero; of all, the most useless, except when the safety of a nation demands his saving arm. Confessedly. Alexander, Cæsar, and Hannibal stand on the summit, in the days of Greece and Rome. Much as the two first will be admired for their magnanimous conduct, and loved for their mental excellency, the correct mind can never applaud the object for which they wasted human life, and will ever mingle with its admiration, execrations bitter and degrading.

"Hannibal, whom I am inclined to consider the first soldier of the three, and whom I believe to be the equal of the other two in all the qualities which endear individuals to those around them, had a justifiable cause of war against the Romans. Their enmity to Carthage was known; and his father, as well as himself, and all other enlightened and honest Carthaginians, long before his crossing the Alps, had been convinced by past events that the safety of Carthage hung upon the humbling of Rome, which this prince of soldiers would have completely effected, had not Hanno's envy and malice, supported by his faction in the Senate, crossed and stunted all Hannibal's plans and means. It has ever been a cause of regret with me that the history of this superior man has never reached us. We know him only from the records of his enemies; and these, notwithstanding Roman hatred and prejudice, leave him first of antiquity in cabinet and field. Polybius, being a Grecian, may be considered impartial; but his personal intimacy and almost dependence on Scipio Africanus may justly beget suspicion that he did not display candor on the virtues and exploits of Hannibal. Lycurgus, Solon, Numa, the second King of Rome, attract universal admiration as legislators; and how can Alexander, Cæsar, and Hannibal be compared with them in the promotion of human good—the only way in which man can, however humbly, imitate Almighty God and merit our love. Greece, before the grand military exploit of taking Troy, was, like the northern nations of Europe of that day, barbarous; but after their expedition against the Trojans their advance was rapid to the high reputation which they preserved until their subjugation by the Macedonians. Petty states, always fighting with each other, with Persia, or Philip, or

Alexander, they nevertheless rose to the summit of improvement in the arts of peace and war; emphatically demonstrating that the constant exercise of the mind, struggling to maintain freedom and independence of the state, brings forth that superb display of genius which attains in a little time the highest rank in literature and the arts. This is not exemplified by Greece alone; for the same result was produced by the perpetual wars among the small states of Italy, until Rome succeeded in conquering all. From the settlement of Italy by the Pelasgi, who inhabitated Arcadia in the Peloponnesus, now Morea, nearly four centuries passed before the time of Numitor, predecessor of Romulus; but as the history of that period is traditional, we know but little save that the different republics were always contending for mastership, which at last settled on Rome. Covetous of dominion and military in habit, after having subdued Italy, they went to Africa, Asia, and the contiguous regions of Europe, in quest of additional subjugation, till they brought under their dominion nearly all the world then known to them. In such continuation of wars at home and abroad, the mind was always on the stretch, and heroes, statesmen, orators, and poets, in abundance, were the certain consequence. In England, too, we find the same cause producing the same effect. During the civil wars, when the mind was in constant excitement, genius was resplendent, especially in enjoying the tranquillity of peace, which is always the case. Refer to the history of Charles I., the Protector, and Charles II.; again to James, and the Revolution, which was achieved by his expulsion, and the elevation of William and Mary, when British liberty, always the first object of our British ancestors, was fully established. The extraordinary philosopher, Roger Bacon, a friar, flourished long before this period, having been born in 1214; but Francis, Lord Bacon, a man of singular mental powers, died not long before Charles's accession to the throne; he was followed by Harvey, who was succeeded by Boyle, after whom came Sir Isaac Newton. In poetry, Milton, Jonson, Waller, Denham, Otway, and Dryden, adorned the above-mentioned period. In our own day we have experienced the display of genius during the convulsions of France, begun for the purpose of ameliorating the political condition of the country; in which laudable work the virtuous Louis XVI. embarked with truth and zeal. Even our own country never exhibited such a display of genius before or since as she did during her eight years' war.

"It may therefore be considered as a truth demonstrated by the history of man, that a continuous and ardent excitement of the mind, especially in regaining lost or defending menaced rights, places man in that train of mind and body which brings forth the greatest display of genius; especially after the storm has subsided, and the mind, reposing with security in the sweets of tranquillity, meditates without fear.

"When you answer, be sure to tell me what is your general state of health, what your hours of sleep, whether you eat copiously or sparingly, and your age; and be sure to take up in life the custom of fasting two or three days, living on bread and water, when disordered, rather than swallow drugs. Adieu, my dear son."

"Nassau, 5 May, 1817. Having within a few days, my dear Carter, received letters from home, yours of February last was inclosed by your dear mother. Your defence of your favorite Milton is entitled to much consideration; although it approaches to literary impiety, when you approximace him so close to Homer; but it cannot remove the objections I have to your poet, nor arrest my preference of Pope. '*Homo sum; humani nihil a me alienum puto.*' Had Milton condescended to treat of men—and their history affords untried subjects fit for epic poetry in abundance—I should have perused his works with delight, though not with Homeric rapture, and might have classed him with the first of English poets; but as he has preferred angels to men, my ignorance of that order of beings and their theatre of action deprives me of the capacity to perceive the poet's beauty and to decide upon the merits of his poem. Indeed, travelling with him, *terra incognita*, I become weary, and shut up the book, to be opened only by those who can comprehend celestial personages and celestial battles.

"I never could read a novel, because it was the narrative of imaginary action; and yet I have seen many grave men and pious ladies bedew their cheeks and exclaim, 'How natural, how affecting!' with Fielding in their hand. *Paradise Lost* is to me alike distasteful; and I must adhere to Pope, because he treats of man and his ways. In one of my letters I urged you to acquire French, not only to read, but to speak; and now I renew my advice with anxious zeal. If you could only thereby be benefitted with the perusal of Racine, you would be liberally rewarded. Sophocles, Euripides, in Greek; Racine, and Voltaire's *Henriade*, in French; are enough to invest your young mind with true taste, even had the immortal Homer and his coadjutor Virgil been lost to man.

"But there is another matter which very much affects my heart, and which I have glanced at in some of my letters, the acquirement of complete self-command. It is the pivot upon which the character, fame, and independence of us mortals hang. Turn your attention steadily and closely to this cardinal quality, and habituate yourself at once to reject with disdain every temptation which may assail your self-dominion. Thus are the passions, the appetites, the cravings subjected to reason, and thus does weak man humbly assimilate himself to his Almighty Creator. Encircled as were Alexander and Scipio by the glories of the field and the cabinet, their self-command evinced on the most trying occasions—when even beauty, the most captivating, and in their power by the right of conquest, was sheltered from the rude touch of passion—threw around their names the splendor of virtue which overshadowed all their glory.

"What breast is so callous to noble feelings as not to pant to be called their rivals? In one road only is the youth to walk whose mind is thus ennobled. He must begin with himself when young, and his occupations at that period are of the inferior sort, he can only become a true disciple of future glory by watching his tongue and his purse. Let not the first utter a word injurious to truth, decency, or another's peace; and never suffer want or temptation to induce the wanton disbursement of the last, but take up the determination to spend only what is absolutely necessary, and thus assume the habit of retaining part of your pecuniary allowance for casualities to which your own body is liable, and another part to enable you to help a friend when afflicted with distress. That you may at once begin and travel on to the goal under your father's guidance, ascertain exactly the sum necessary for your next year, specifying the several items; and record from week to week every expression actuated by passion, and its consequences to truth, decorum, and another's peace. . . .

"Thank you for Henry's address to his district; it does honor to his political principles, as well as to his literary talents. By a letter lately from him, he is married and I hope happily. I shall have another daughter to embrace and admire when I get home. Lucy also wrote to me; by which I learn the fate of Woodstock, and Mr. Carter's removal to Philadelphia. But all those dear to me—all thanks to the great God—were well, unstained by follies even, much less by offences against morality. Adieu, my beloved son."

"Nassau, June 18, 1817. My dear Carter will receive this additional letter, though I never expected to write again from hence; this is, too, the day of the month when your dear mother became my wife, and it is not so hot in this tropical region as it was then at Shirley, though situated in the temperate zone. Since that happy day, marked only by the union of two humble lovers, it has become conspicuous as the day that our war with Great Britain was declared in Washington; and the one that sealed the doom of Bonaparte on the field of Waterloo. The British general, rising *gradatim* from his first blow struck in Portugal, climbed on that day to the summit of fame and became distinguished by the first of titles, 'Deliverer of the civilized world.' Alexander, Hannibal, and Cæsar, among the ancients; Marlborough, Eugene, Turenne, and Frederick among the moderns—opened their arms to receive him as a brother in glory. I scarcely believe that Hannibal and Frederick would claim him as theirs especially. There is a similitude in the leading circumstances of my three heroes: the first contended against Rome, the greatest nation then on earth; Frederick against Austria, in that day like Rome; and Wellington against France, the colossal power in late days. The first and last fought, too, at the head of troops, partly their own countrymen and partly Spaniards; Frederick may be said to have commanded Prussians only, an advantage never to be doubted in war. Frederick and Wellington succeeded completely in their objects; Hannibal was lost because the senator Hanno, great in influence in Carthage, withheld, more or less, supplies of men, money, and munitions; preferring the gratification of his personal hatred to the prosperity of his country, which in the issue became ruined. The first two resembled each other in two points of character replete with weight in all affairs of man, viz., foresight and economy; Wellington certainly equals them in the first, and, for aught I know, may in the last. Both are essential to perfection, and the last is indispensable; as without it, the first power penetrated must be crushed in its efforts for want of means, which the last affords in a constant adequate current. This admirable habit grows out of reflection and love of personal independence, and happy the youth, whether in high or low condition, who clings to it as his palladium. Frederick, whose character I so much admire, was remarkable for his frugality, or rather economy and assiduity. I wish to hold him up to your imitation. . . . He rose at four; went to bed at ten; was temperate in all things; he knew everything to be done; and saw everything done in due season. He was liberal in his gifts to the deserving, but he measured them by his fiscal ability and his fiscal wants; thus he never wanted money, never missed the opportunity of advancing his nation's prosperity because the means were not ready. He had early habituated himself to keep his wants within his means, and this habit became confirmed as he grew up, and adhered to him till his death. You may acquire the same; and in your little affairs, alike important to you as his great affairs were to him, it will be sure to produce the same effects. That it should begin at once, I learn by letters from your dear mother, is indispensable, as your expenses transcend your allowance. Do think seriously and constantly on this subject. Write to me frankly, and you shall hear from me in the spirit of love and desire to gratify all requisite claims. I find the vessel in which I expected to embark to-morrow has changed its destination. I am disappointed, and must embrace any favorable opportunity, without regard to place of arrival. Do not write to me until you hear from me after my arrival."

"Nassau, 3 September, 1817. My Dear Carter,—I wrote a few days since to the care of Mr. Goddard, to tell you that my only chance of getting to the United States is in a vessel destined for Savannah, to sail in ten or fifteen days. I conclude to embrace the opportunity, *malgre* season and distance from home. Relieved much from my long torture of pain, my mind is refreshed, and I can calmly meet difficulty. You must write from Boston, under cover to Mr. Joseph Thorne, merchant, in Savannah; and detail to me your expenses, and the sum necessary to defray them. . . . Avoid debt, the sink of mental power and the subversion of independence, which draws into debasement even virtue, in appearance certainly, if not in reality. '*A man ought not only to be virtuous in reality, but he must also always appear so;*' thus said to me the great Washington. I have the following books for you, to be sent only when I have a sure conveyance:—*Newton's Principia*, 3 vols.; *Asiatic Researches*, 5 vols., and *Quintius Curtius*, the historian of Alexander Magnus; valuable all of them, and will I trust be prized by you, not because they come from me, but for their own superior worth. I hope and beg you will read well and speak better the French language. . . . Begin with a grammar, a dictionary, and two hours per day will give you the reading; a French family's acquaintance will give you the speaking. Farewell, my ever dear son."

## THE CARTER FAMILY.

So far as known, the first of this prominent and influential family to emigrate to Virginia was John Carter, who was born in England, and settled first in Upper Norfolk, now Nansemond county, which he represented as Burgess in 1649; later he settled in Lancaster, from which county he was a Burgess in 1654, and commanded the forces sent against the Rappahannock Indians. "Both himself and his eldest son John appear on the vestry-book as members of the vestry in the year 1666, the father having been acting in that capacity before—how long not known. The father, who died in 1669, had previously built, by contract, the first church standing on the spot where Christ Church now is, and the vestry received it at the hands of his son John, in six months after his father's death. . . . The first John Carter had three wives,[1] 1st, Jane, the daughter of Morgan Glyn, by whom

[1] Mr. W. G. Stanard thinks John Carter was married five times, that the "Elenor Carter" mentioned on tombstone was his second wife, not a daughter, and that his last wife was Elizabeth Shirley whom he

he had George and Eleanor; 2d, Ann, the daughter of Cleave Carter, probably of England; 3d, Sarah, the daughter of Gabriel Ludlowe, by whom he had Sarah. All of these died before him, and he was buried with them, near the chancel, in the church which he built, and the tombstone from which we take the above, covers them all, being still in the same position in the present church." (*Old Churches, Families*, II, 110, *et seq*.

The epitaph from this stone, which still (1894) lies on the right hand of the chancel, reads:

Here lyeth buried ye body of John Carter, Esq., who died ye 10th of June, Anno Domini 1669; and also Jane, ye daughter of Mr. Morgan Glyn, and George her son, and Elenor Carter, and Ann, ye daughter of Mr. Cleave Carter, and Sarah, ye daughter of Mr. Gabriel Ludlow, and Sarah her daughter, which were all his wives successively, and died before him.

John Carter was a member of the Council in 1657, and another of the same name was a member in 1724, probably a grandson. Beside the children mentioned above, apparently he left two other sons, Robert and Charles, or three sons in all. The eldest, John, was twice married, and had issue; Charles probably left issue also, but of neither is there any accurate account. From the second surviving son, Robert, generally known as "King Carter," the Virginia family is chiefly descended. Robert Carter, of "Corotoman," Lancaster county, was born in 1663, and died in 1732; he was twice married; first, in 1688, to Judith, eldest daughter of John Armistead, "the Councillor;" she died the 23d of February, 1699, in the eleventh year of her marriage, having "borne to her husband four daughters and one son, whereof, Sarah and Judith Carter, died before and are buried near her" (tombstone). He married, secondly, in 1701, Mrs. Elizabeth Willis, a daughter of Thomas Landon, of England; she was born in 1684, and died in 1719; by these two wives he had twelve children.

From five of his daughters, so many distinguished men have descended that a brief mention of them is desirable:

---

married 24 Oct., 1668; she was not buried with her husband, but was mentioned in his will with her son, Charles. (Keith, *Ancestry of Benjamin Harrison*, etc., p. 87.)

i, ELIZABETH CARTER, married twice; first, Nathaniel Burwell, who died in 1721, aged 40 years, and had Lewis, Carter, Robert, and Elizabeth, who married William Nelson, President of the Council, and father of Thomas Nelson, the Signer; his widow, then, married George Nicholas, M. D., and had Robert Carter Nicholas, Treasurer of Va., the father of Gov. Wilson Cary Nicholas, and also of Elizabeth, who married Edmund Randolph, first Attorney-General of the United States, and also Governor of Virginia. Edmund Randolph was the eldest son of John and Ariana (Jenings) Randolph, and great-grandson of Gov. Edmund and Frances (Corbin) Jenings.

ii, JUDITH CARTER married Mann Page, of "Rosewell," Gloucester county, being his second wife, and had six children; her three surviving sons, Mann, John, and Robert, became respectively the progenitors of the three branches of that family. Judith Carter was, therefore, the ancestress of the Pages of Virginia.

iii, ANNE CARTER married Benjamin Harrison, of "Berkeley," Charles City county, and had issue: Anne (who married William Randolph, of "Wilton," and had issue), Elizabeth (who married Peyton Randolph, President of the first Continental Congress), Benjamin, the Signer (and father of General William Henry Harrison), Carter Henry (of "Clifton," who married Susannah, daughter of Isham Randolph, of "Dungeness," and had issue), Charles (who was a brigadier-general in the Revolutionary Army, married Mary, daughter of Augustine Claiborne), Nathaniel (Speaker of the State Senate, Sheriff of Prince William county, 1779, married, first, Mary, daughter of Edmund Ruffin, and next Anne, daughter of William Gilliam), Robert, who died before 1771, and two daughters, who were killed by lightning with their father.

iv, MARY CARTER married George Braxton.

v, LUCY CARTER married Col. Henry Fitzhugh, and had issue (see 2, vii).

From four sons of Robert Carter are descended the later generations of this family; these four were, John, Robert, Charles, and Landon.

i, JOHN, "Secretary," eldest son, married about 1723, Elizabeth, daughter of Edward Hill, Jr., of "Shirley," Charles City county, and had three children: 1, Elizabeth (1731–1760), who married Col. William Byrd, of "Westover," and had: William, John, Thomas, Elizabeth (who married James Parke Farley), and Ottway Byrd. 2, Charles[1]

[1] The following obituary notice of him was found among the papers of his daughter, Mrs. Henry Lee: "Died on Saturday the 28th of June, 1806, Charles Carter, Esq., of 'Shirley,' aged 70 years. His long

(1736–1806), of "Shirley," was twice married; first. in 1756, to Mary W. Carter (1736–1770. daughter of Charles. of "Cleves," and Mary Walker, his first wife); she died the 30th of January, 1770, and he married, secondly, Anne Butler Moore, daughter of Bernard and Anne Catharine (Spotswood) Moore, Sr., of "Chelsea," King William county. By his first wife he had issue: John Hill and Charles, who died without issue; George (who married Lelia Skipwith), Mary (who married Col. Robert Randolph, of "Eastern View," Fauquier county), Charles (of "Mt. Atlas," married Nancy, daughter of Robert W. Carter, of "Sabine Hall"), Edward (of "Cloverland," married Jane, daughter of John Carter, of "Sudley"), and Landon, who died without issue. By his second wife Charles Carter, of "Shirley," had: Robert Hill (who died without issue), Anne Hill (who was the second wife of General Henry Lee, see 35), Dr. Robert (who married Mary, daughter of General Thomas Nelson, of York, and had issue; among them, see 77, Note), Bernard and John, who died without issue; Kate Spotswood (who married Dr. Carter Berkeley), Bernard (who married Lucy, daughter of General Henry Lee, and had issue, see 35, i), Williams (of Hanover, who married Charlotte Foushee), Butler and Mildred, who had no issue; Lucy (who married Nathaniel Burwell), and several others who died young. 3, Edward, of "Blenheim," the second son of "Secretary" John Carter, married Sarah Champe, and had issue: John (who married Aphia Fauntleroy), Eliza (who married William Stanard, of "Roxbury," Spottsylvania, and had issue), Jane (married Major Bradford, of the British army), Sarah (married, first, George Carter, and next Dr. Cutting), Charles (of Culpeper, who married Betty Lewis), William Champe (who married Maria Farley), Edward (of "Blenheim," who married successively Mary Lewis, Lucy Wood, and ——), George and Whitaker, who died without issue; Hill (of "Mine Hill," Amherst, who married —— Coles, of Albemarle), Mary Champe (who married Judge E. T. Brooke), Nancy (married Gov. M. Troup, of Georgia).

ii, ROBERT, of "Nominy Hall," Westmoreland, the second son of "King Carter" to have issue, died about 1732; he was married about 1725 to Priscilla Bladen, and had issue: Eliza, and Robert, "the Councillor," who married Frances Anne Tasker, and had George, of "Oatlands," and many others. Of "Councillor" Carter, Bishop Meade re-

---

life was spent in the tranquility of domestic enjoyments. From the mansion of hospitality his immense wealth flowed like silent streams, enlivening and refreshing every object around. In fulfilling the duties of his station, he proved himself to be an Israelite indeed, in whom there was no guile."

marks :[1] "In Councillor Carter of Nomini, the grandson of King Carter, this peculiarity [eccentricity] was found in a large measure. Early in life his disposition was marked by a tendency to wit and humor. Afterward he was the grave Councillor and always the generous philanthropist. At a later day he became scrupulous as to the holding of slaves, and manumitted great numbers. The subject of religion then engrossed his thoughts. Abandoning the religion of his fathers, he adopted the creed of the Baptists and patronized their young preachers, having a chapel in his own house at Nomini. After a time he embraced the theory of Swedenborg, and at length died an unhappy, death-dreading Papist. All the while he was a most benevolent and amiable man."

iii, CHARLES, of "Cleves" (1707–1764), was the third son of "King Carter" to leave issue; he was married three times; first, in 1728, to Mary Walker; then, in 1742, to Anne Byrd, and lastly, in 1764 (?), to Lucy Taliaferro; his children were: Charles (of "Ludlowe," who died in 1796; married Elizabeth Chiswell, and had issue), Eliza (who married William Churchill and had issue), Judith (who married William Burnet Browne, and had issue), Mary Walker (who married Charles Carter, of "Shirley," her first cousin, as stated). By his second wife he had: Anne (who married John Champe, and then Lewis Willis, of Fredericksburg), Maria (who married William Armistead, of "Hesse," Gloucester), John (married —— Claiborne), Lucy, who left no issue; Landon (of "Cleves," 1751–1811, who married, first, Mrs. Mildred Willis, and next his cousin, Mrs. Eliza (Carter) Thornton, of "Sabine Hall," and had issue, of whom later), Jane (who married Gawin Corbin, no issue), Sarah (married William Thompson and had issue). By his third wife Charles Carter (of "Cleves") had: Anne Walker, who married John Catlett. Of these children one son, Landon, may be further traced. The Carter family record states that he married Mrs. Mildred Willis and Mrs. Eliza (Carter) Thornton. But he may have had a third wife; for Philip Ludwell Lee, writing to his brother, William, under date of the 31st of May, 1769, said: "Landon Carter son of old Charles is to be married in a little while to Miss Molly Fauntleroy of Naylor's Hole." If this statement applies to this Landon, then "Molly Fauntleroy" must have been his first wife. His children were: Mildred Anne Byrd (who married Robert Mercer, and had issue, and next, John Lewis, and had issue); Lucy (who married Gen. John Minor, of Fredericksburg, and had, among others, Mary, who married the Hon. William

[1] *Old Churches, Families*, etc., II, 111.

Blackford; Dr. Lewis W., U. S. N.; Lucius, who married Catharine Berkeley, and had, among others, Charles, who married Frances Cazenove; Launcelot, a missionary in Africa, and Dr. James Minor, U. S. N.). By his second wife, Mrs. Eliza (Carter) Thornton, Landon Carter had: Robert Charles, St. Leger Landon (who married Eliza, daughter of Thomas Ludwell and Fanny (Carter) Lee, no issue), Eliza Thornton (who married William MacFarland), and also other children.

iv, LANDON, of "Sabine Hall," Richmond county, was the youngest son of "King Carter" to leave issue; he was married three times: to Elizabeth Wormeley, to Maria Byrd, and, lastly, to a Miss Beale; his children were: Robert W. (who married and had issue, among them Fanny, who married Thomas Ludwell Lee, of "Coton," Loudoun; see 30), Eliza (married Nelson Berkeley of "Airwell"), Landon (of Pittsylvania, who married Júdith Fauntleroy), John (of "Sudley," married Janet Hamilton). By his second wife he had Maria, who married Robert Beverley, of "Wakefield," Culpeper county, whose daughter, Evelyn Byrd, married George Lee, of Loudoun (see 31). By his third wife he had: Lucy, who married William Colston, and Judith, who married Reuben Beale.

Having thus briefly sketched the children of "King Carter," a few words about the common progenitor of so many distinguished persons may be of interest. Robert Carter was generally known as "King Carter," some said from his great possessions, others on account of his handsome appearance. Of his official life his tombstone gives a fair account. It stated:

Here lies buried Robert Carter, Esq., an honourable man, who by noble endowments and pure morals gave lustre to his gentle birth. Rector of William and Mary, he sustained that institution in its most trying times. He was Speaker of the House of Burgesses, and Treasurer under the most serene Princes William, Anne, George I. and II. Elected by the House its Speaker six years, and Governor of the Colony for more than a year, he upheld equally the regal dignity and the public freedom. Possessed of ample wealth, blamelessly acquired, he built and endowed, at his own expense, this sacred edifice—a signal monument of his piety toward God. He furnished it richly. Entertaining his friends kindly, he was neither a prodigal nor a parsimonious host. His first wife was Judith, daughter of John Armistead, Esq.; his second Betty, a descendant of the noble family of Landons. By these wives he had many children, on whose education he expended large sums of money. At length, full of honours and of years, when he had performed all the duties of an exemplary life, he departed from this world on the 4th day of August, in the 69th year of his age. The unhappy lament their lost comforter, the widows their lost protector, and the orphans their lost father.

This tombstone, together with those of his two wives, was placed at the east end of old Christ Church. They were very large, handsome, and elaborately carved. All are now destroyed, and the ground around is strewn with their fragments. Bishop Meade saw that of the husband, and wrote in his report on that church in 1838: "Among the latter [tombs], at the east end of the house, within a neat inclosure, recently put up, are to be seen the tombs of Robert Carter, the builder of the house, and of his two wives. These are probably the largest and richest and heaviest tombstones in our land." Bishop Meade adds: "Tradition has it that the congregation, which doubtless consisted chiefly of his dependents, did not enter the church on Sunday until the arrival of his coach, when all followed him and his family into it." He rebuilt and enlarged the church; the walls are very thick, at least three feet, and are yet sound. It has the old-style, square, high-back pews, two of which, those nearest the chancel, are at least fifteen feet square.

## Judge Charles Lee.

36. Charles[5], the second son of Henry Lee[4] (Henry[3], Richard[2], Richard[1]) and Lucy Grymes, his wife, was born in 1758, and died the 24th of June, 1815, at his home, near Warrenton, Fauquier county. He entered Princeton College in 1770; the earliest record of him is from Dr. Shippen's letter, saying: "Charles is in the grammar school; but Dr. Witherspoon expects much from his application and genius." He graduated, taking the degree of B. A. in 1775, and M. A. in 1778; in 1777 he was naval officer of "South Potomac," as attested by his signature to clearance papers; he seems to have held this office until it was abolished in 1789. Under date of 2d of August, 1789, President Washington wrote to Richard Henry Lee: "Mr. Charles Lee will certainly be brought forward as collector of the port of Alexandria." (*Life of R. H. Lee*, II, 36.) His father addressed letters to him, in 1779, as a "student of Law in Philadelphia," where it is said he studied under Jared Ingersoll. These dates seem rather conflicting, unless he held office in Virginia at the same time he studied law in Philadelphia.

President Washington appointed Charles Lee to succeed William Bradford as Attorney-General, on the 10th of December, 1795, which office he held through the administration of John Adams, and until the inauguration, in 1801, of Thomas Jefferson. "Washington was an unusually good judge of men, and President Adams confirmed his choice, not only by continuing Mr. Lee as Att'y Gen'l through his administration, but on the 18th Feb'y, 1801, sent his name to the U. S. Senate as one of the 16 new Circuit Judges, required by the reduction of the U. S. Supreme Court to 5 Judges in 1801. These new Judges were confirmed 3rd of March, 1801,

*Charles Lee*

just before midnight, hence they were called the Midnight Judges. The act of Congress creating them was repealed the 8th April, 1802, without imputing any fault on the part of the Judges. It is said that President Adams offered Mr. Lee the appointment of Chief Justice to succeed Oliver Ellsworth, but it was declined. Judge Lee retired to his home, and practiced law in the Courts of Virginia, and at Washington, until his death." (Hayden, *Va. Genealogies*, 541.) After his retirement from office, he was engaged as counsel in many important causes in the Supreme Court of the United States, such as the famous case of Marbury *vs.* Madison, *Ex parte* Bollman and Swartwout, and others. His arguments, as preserved in the Reports of the Supreme Court, evince very high legal ability and attainments. Charles Lee was also one of the lawyers for the defense of Aaron Burr in the famous trial for treason.

Richard Henry Lee appointed Charles one of his executors, to which appointment he alludes in the following letter to W. A. Washington:

"Alexandria, 24th June, 1794. Dear Sir, When I left Chantilly, it was without hope of ever again seeing the best of men, and I have felt some consolation in learning by your letter that his last moments were free of pain.

"The steps you propose to take concerning the will meet my approbation, for in all matters, delay is apt to produce embarrassment. My desire to render every service to the members of the family will induce me to give every assistance that shall go to that object. If it should be necessary for me to qualify as executor, I can do it at any time hereafter, but I shall join you and Mr. Corbin Washington in the guardianship of the children. I wish you to proceed in all things concerning the estate, as you and the other gentlemen shall think right without waiting for my presence; it being uncertain when it will be in my power to go to Westmoreland. By this I mean to express that the examination and arrangement of the papers need not be deferred for me.

"The President is at Mount Vernon and will be there a few days; he enjoys good health. I am," &c., &c.

To Wm. Ludwell Lee, Greenspring, near Williamsburg, Va. Dated, "Philadelphia, 4th April, 1797. Dear Sir, On the 5th of last month I wrote you acknowledging the receipt of your favor of the 6th of February; since which I have received two other letters on the same subject. . . .

"After Bonaparte's complete victory Mantua has surrendered—so that in a few days the Emperor has been deprived of 50,000 men. What effect this will have on France in its conduct to America is uncertain. I wish it may not encourage that republic to continue its present hostile system toward us. Mr. Pinckney has quitted the republic in obedience to the orders of the Directory and has gone to Amsterdam, there to await the further orders of his country. Should France and America come to a rupture, miserable will be my native country in consequence of the blacks now held in bondage. An obvious expedient will be to excite and maintain an insurrection; but whatever disasters shall come from France, I am persuaded they will be properly chargeable to the politicks of Virginia, which for four years have tended to make France believe we were a nation devoted to its will and not independent enough to manage our own affairs, but in conformity to its mandates. This is the matter now to be put to trial and when France discovers how they have been deceived, by those among us who pretended to be its friends, will occasion much wrath in that republic. The prospect before the United States is very unpleasing but may be made bright by union in the national counsels and by that alone."

Charles Lee was twice married; first, "by the Rev. Mr. Wilson, at 'Chantilly,' Westmoreland Co., Va., on the 11th of February, 1789," to Anne, daughter of Richard Henry and Anne (Gaskins-Pinckard) Lee, of whose portrait a print is given; she was born the 1st of December, 1770; died on Sunday the 9th of September, 1804, "after a tedious illness, of the consumptive kind, which was sustained with fortitude and patience upwards of four years; until without a groan she passed into the presence of her God in the full and bright hope of heavenly felicity through the merits of our blessed Redeemer." (Family Bible of Charles Lee.) She was buried at Shooter's Hill, the residence of her brother, Ludwell Lee (Rev. Joseph Packard, D. D.); the following epitaph for her tombstone was written by her brother, Francis Lightfoot Lee:

Here are deposited the remains of Anne Lee, daughter of Richard Henry Lee, and wife of Charles Lee. She died the 9th September, 1804, aged 33 years.

This stone is not erected in memory of her piety and virtue, for they are registered in heaven; nor of the qualities by which she was adorned, distinguished or endeared, for of these, they who knew her have a more lasting memorial in their sorrow for her death. But it is to remind the reader that neither youth nor beauty nor any excellence of heart or mind can rescue from the grave, for the entombed possessed them all.

Charles Lee had issue by both marriages;[1] by his first wife, Anne Lee, he had six children:

i, ANNE LUCINDA[6], born at "Chantilly," Westmoreland, 5th of May, 1790, and died 15th of May, 1835; married, 17th of May, 1808, Gen-

[1] Hayden, *Va. Genealogies*, pp. 541-2-3.

MRS. CHARLES LEE.

eral Walter Jones, a distinguished lawyer, and had fourteen children (for whom see Jones Family).

ii, —— a son, born the 9th of November, 1791, and died of small-pox the 1st of January, 1792.

iii, RICHARD HENRY[6], born at Alexandria, the 5th of February, 1793; died —— March, 1793.

iv, CHARLES HENRY[6], born at Alexandria, the 25th of October, 1794; "baptized by the Rev. Mr. Parsons in my absence and the name of Henry has since been added" (Family Bible).

v, WILLIAM ARTHUR[6], born at Alexandria, the 15th of September, 1796.

vi, ALFRED[6], born at Alexandria, the 2d of July, 1799; died unmarried in 1865; lived in Fairfax county.

Charles Lee married, secondly, on the 19th of July, 1809, Mrs. Margaret C. (Scott) Peyton, the widow of Yelverton Peyton, and daughter of the Rev. John and Elizabeth (Gordon) Scott; she was born the 20th of January, 1783, and died the 11th of October, 1843. By this marriage, Mr. Lee had issue:

vii, ROBERT EDEN[6]. See 51.

viii, ELIZABETH GORDON[6], born at Alexandria, the 17th of May, 1813, and resides now near Warrenton; she married, on the 25th of November, 1835, the Rev. Abraham David Pollock, D. D., a distinguished Presbyterian divine; he was born the 22d of January, 1807, and died the 3d of May, 1890; their children were: 1, Thomas Gordon, Captain C. S. A., who was born in 1838, and was killed in Pickett's charge at Gettysburg, the 3d of July, 1863; he had taken B. L. at the University of Va., in 1859. 2, Margaret Scott, who married Dr. E. P. Moore. 3, Anne Lee, who married Charles P. Janney, a lawyer of Leesburg, and has several children. 4, Rachel Elizabeth. 5, Susan Roberta, who married Matthew Gilmour. 6, Charles Lee, who died in April, 1888.

ix, ALEXANDER[6], "born at my stone house in Fauquier, near Warrenton, the 18th of April, 1815" (Family Bible). Died in infancy.

## THE JONES FAMILY.

Arms: Sable, a fess or, between three children's heads proper (for Jones), quartered with, Azure and gules, party per pale, a chevron engrailed or, between three lions rampant, argent (for Hopkins).

Crest: on a helmet, a child's head proper.

Captain Roger Jones, the progenitor of this family, was born about 1625–35, and died at his home in Stepney, then a suburb of London, in

January, 1701–2. He married twice, but apparently had issue only by his first wife, Dorothy, daughter of John Walker, Esq., of Mansfield, county Nottingham. He came to Virginia with Lord Culpeper in 1680 and made settlements, but returned to England and died there. He left at least two sons, Frederick, who married and left issue, and Colonel Thomas, who married on the 14th of February, 1725, Elizabeth, the widow of William Pratt and daughter of Dr. William Cocke and Elizabeth Catesby, his wife. He died about 1758 in Hanover county, and left issue: Thomas, Dorothea, Catesby, Frederick, William, Jekyll, Lucy, Anne, Dr. Walter, and Elizabeth. Of these children only three, Thomas, Catesby, and Dr. Walter, need be considered here.

Thomas, the eldest son, born the 25th of December, 1726, and died in Hanover county about 1785–6; married Sally, a daughter of James Skelton and Jane, his wife, who was a daughter of Francis and Mary (Bathurst) Meriwether. Thomas Jones was for a long time Clerk of Northumberland county, until he moved to Hanover in 1781. He left nine children:

i, MAJOR THOMAS AP THOMAS, who served in the Revolutionary Army; was twice married; by his second wife, Frances, daughter of "Councillor" Robert Carter, of "Nominy Hall," Westmoreland county, he had an only son, who moved to Kentucky about 1810, and has descendants in that State.

ii, JEKYLL, was a political writer of some note; never married.

iii, BATHURST, no issue.

iv, MERIWETHER, born about 1766; married Lucy Franklin Reed, and his only son, Walter, married a Miss Taylor, of Norfolk, and left issue.

v, SKELTON, was a lawyer of Richmond, and succeeded his brother Meriwether, as editor of the Richmond *Examiner*.

vi, ELIZABETH, married, in 1776, Gawin Corbin, of "Yew Spring," Caroline county, the son of John Corbin, of "Portobago," Essex, and had issue: Elizabeth, Lætitia, Gawin, Lancelot, Sally, and George Corbin. (See Corbin Family, under 2.)

vii, MARY BATHURST, who married Lancelot Lee, and had issue (See 26).

viii, SALLY, who married Capt. Nathaniel Anderson.

ix, JANE, who married John Monroe, of "Cone Place," Westmoreland, and had issue: Sally Skelton, and Dr. Thomas Jekyll Catesby, U. S. A., who died in 1840.

Catesby, who married, about 1778, Lettice Corbin, daughter of John Turberville, of "Hickory Hill," Westmoreland, and had these seven children:[1] 1, Roger, Major-General, U. S. A., who married, about 1816, Mary Anne, daughter of William Byrd and Anne (Lee) Page, of "Fairfield," Clarke county, and had these thirteen children: William Page, Catesby ap Roger, of U. S. and C. S. Navies, Lætitia Corbin, Mary Anne, Dr. Eusebius Lee, Meriwether, Edmonia Page, Roger, Inspector-General, U. S. A., Walter, Charles Lucian, C. S. N., Capt. Thomas Skelton, U. S. N. and C. S. A., Virginia Boyd, and Winfield Scott Jones. 2, Thomas ap Catesby, Commodore, U. S. N., who married Mary Walker, daughter of Charles B. Carter, of "Richmond Hill," Richmond county, and had these four children: Meriwether Patterson, Mary Lee, Mark Catesby, and Martha Corbin Jones. 3, Philip de Catesby, born about 1792; married Ann Williams, of Winchester, and died about 1873, leaving issue: John W., Lewin T., and Elizabeth Jones. 4, Eusebius, who died young. 5, Elizabeth Lee, died unmarried. 6, Martha Corbin, who married William Gordon, of Westmoreland, and had issue: William W., Caroline Virginia, and John T. Gordon. 7, Sarah Skelton, born 5th of October, 1781; married on 9th of March, 1801, Henry Waring Ball, being his first wife, and had issue: Catesby ap Henry, Lettice Corbin, and Henry Waring Ball.

Dr. Walter Jones, the ninth child of Col. Thomas Jones and Elizabeth Cocke, his wife, was born in Virginia, the 16th of December, 1745; was educated at William and Mary College, and at Edinburgh; returned to Virginia about 1770, settled in Northumberland, and attained reputation as a scholar and physician; during the Revolution, he was "physician-general" for the hospitals of the middle department; he was member of Congress in 1797–99, and 1803–11; he died in Westmoreland on the 1st of December, 1815, leaving eight children: Walter, William, Thomas, Frederick, Lucius, Anne, Elizabeth, and Maria Jones. Of these only one, General Walter, need be noticed here. He was born the 7th of October, 1776, and died at Washington, the 14th of October, 1861; studied law with Judge Bushrod Washington, and settled at Washington, where he won a national reputation as a lawyer of the greatest ability; he married, in 1808, Anne Lucinda, eldest daughter of the Hon. Judge Charles and Anne (Lee) Lee, as stated, and had fourteen children:

i, VIRGINIA COLLINS, born in 1809, died the 5th of June, 1892; married, on the 30th of July, 1833, Dr. Thomas Miller, an eminent physician of Washington, and had issue: Walter Jones, Thomas, Anne

[1] See Turberville Family under 3.

Lee, Anna Thornton (who married Stirling Murray, of Md.), Virginia, Sarah Cornelia (who married Arthur Fendall, of Washington, and has two children), Thomas Jesup, and Dr. George Richards Miller. Of these children, three daughters are living.

ii, WALTER, born in 1811, and died in 1829, while at the University of Virginia.

iii, NANNETTE LEE, born in 1812; married, on the 18th of April, 1833, Dr. Robert Eden Peyton, of Fauquier county, a son of Dr. Chandler Peyton; he was born the 9th of February, 1804, and died the 15th of July, 1872, leaving issue: Robert Eden (7th Va. Cavalry, who married Cornelia Foster, of Fauquier, and has six children), Anne Lee, Eliza Gordon Scott, and Virginia Peyton.

iv, ROSINA, born 16th May, 1814; died the 19th of July, 1891; married, on the 23d of January, 1838, the Rev. Joseph Packard, D. D., of the Theological Seminary of Virginia, and had issue (for whom see Packard Family).

v, ELIZABETH MARY, who married, in 1840, Henry T. Harrison, of Leesburg, being his second wife (see 34, i), and had issue: 1, Anne Harriotte, who died aged 18 years. 2, Elizabeth Lee, who married George M. Grayson, of Loudoun, and died childless 2d December, 1875. 3, Walter Jones, who was twice married; first, to Anne, daughter of Dr. William Powell, by whom he had a son, Henry T.; he married, secondly, Anne, daughter of Professor Benedict, and had: Rebecca, and Maria Washington Benedict Harrison. 4, Henry, a lawyer of Leesburg, who married, in January, 1885, Anne, daughter of Major John Fitzgerald Lee (see 46, iv). 5, Maria Washington. 6, Alice Janney. 7, Bushrod Washington, died young. 8, Edward Burr. 9, Mary Jones, who married Frank Conrad, a lawyer of Leesburg, and has several children.

vi, CHARLES LEE, born 1816; died 8th March, 1889, unmarried.

vii, ALICE, died in early childhood.

viii, CATHARINE ELLA, who died the 24th of November, 1863, at Shanghai, China, while engaged in active missionary work.

ix, ANNE HARRIOTTE, who married, in 1851, Matthew Harrison, a prominent lawyer of Leesburg, M. A., and B. L., of the University of Va., a member of the Va. Legislature; Mrs. Harrison died the 3d of April, 1894. They had issue: 1, Sarah Powell, who married Dr. William R. Winchester, formerly of Maryland, now of Macon, Ga., and has several children. 2, Thomas Walter, Circuit Judge of Va., who married Julia Knight, of Maryland, and has several children. 3, Burr William, died young. 4, Ann Harriotte Harrison.

x, FRANCES LEE, who is living at Washington, unmarried.
xi, SARAH CORNELIA, who resides in Virginia, is unmarried.
xii, VIOLETTA LANSDALE, who died the 28th of August, 1875, unmarried.
xiii, LUCY, died in early childhood.
xiv, THOMAS WILLIAM, who was drowned in 1853, while serving on the Mexican Boundary Commission; never married.

## THE PACKARD FAMILY.

The Rev. Joseph Packard, D. D., born on the 23d of December, 1812, the beloved and venerable Dean of the Theological Seminary of Virginia, son of the Rev. Hezekiah Packard, D. D., of Wiscasset, Me., is descended from Samuel, of New Hingham, Mass., 1638, thus: Joseph[6], Hezekiah[5], Jacob[4], Solomon[3], Zaccheus[2], Samuel[1], 1638–1684. He graduated A. B., at Bowdoin College, in 1831; A. M., in 1834; Kenyon College conferred upon him the honorary degree of D. D. in 1847; he was a professor in Bristol College, Pa., in 1834–36; and has been professor of Sacred Literature, etc., in the Virginia Seminary since 1836; was ordained Deacon by Bishop Griswold on the 17th of July, 1836; Priest by Bishop Meade on the 29th of September, 1837; was a member of the American Bible Revision committee, in 1872–1885; a collaborator of Robinson's Lexicon of the Greek of the New Testament.[1] Dr. Packard has had the following children:

i, ANNE L. LEE, who was born on the 27th of December, 1838, and died unmarried, on 18th of May, 1873.
ii, WALTER JONES, born the 10th of July, 1840; died the 13th of August, 1862; was a Lieutenant of Infantry in the Va. provisional army, and a private in the famous Rockbridge Artillery, C. S. A.
iii, JOSEPH, born the 10th of April, 1842; was graduated A. B., Kenyon College, 1860, and A. M. in 1867; served as a private in the Rockbridge Artillery, C. S. A.; afterward Lieutenant of Artillery for ordnance duty; is now practicing law at Baltimore; to whom many thanks are due for efficient assistance in preparing this volume. Mr. Packard has been twice married; first, on the 13th of April, 1868, to Laura, daughter of William Bennett, of Georgia, who died on the 28th of September, 1876, leaving two children; he married, secondly, on the 27th of December, 1882, Meta M., daughter of F. W. Hanewinckel, of Richmond; he has these children: Laura Lee, Elise Prioleau, Margaret, Emilie, Josephine, and Charles Lee.

---

[1] Hayden, *Va. Genealogies*, 542.

iv, WILLIAM, born the 9th of December, 1843, and died while a prisoner of war at Point Lookout, on the 11th of November, 1863; he served in the 7th Va. Cavalry, C. S. A.

v, ROSA JONES, born the 1st of September, 1845; died the 28th of August, 1892; married, on the 31st of August, 1869, the Rev. William H. Laird, and left a large family.

vi, MARY, who died in 1850.

vii, CHARLES LEE, who died in 1850.

viii, CORNELIA, who was born the 28th of September, 1851, and resides with her father at the Theological Seminary.

ix, MARY, born the 10th of April, 1853, and is now engaged in teaching in connection with the Episcopal Mission in Brazil.

x, THOMAS JONES, born the 22d of August, 1854; was educated at the Episcopal High School, the University of Va., and the Episcopal Theological Seminary, where he was graduated and ordained Deacon in June 1880; the next June, he was advanced to the Priesthood; has been rector of Christ Church, Mt. Laurel, Va., of St. Thomas Parish, Prince George's county, and of Christ Church, West River, Md. He was married, on the 3d of June, 1885, to Mattie, daughter of John W. Cuningham, of Person county, N. C., and has several children.

xi, CATHARINE, born 1856, and died in 1862.

## RICHARD BLAND LEE.

37. RICHARD BLAND[5], the third son of Henry Lee[4] (Henry[3], Richard[2], Richard[1]) and Lucy Grymes, his wife, was born at "Leesylvania," Prince William county, on the 20th of January, 1761, and died on the 12th of March, 1827. He was married on the 19th of June, 1794, to Elizabeth, daughter of Stephen and Mary (Parish) Collins, of Philadelphia; she died on the 24th of June, 1858, in her 91st year. Mr. John Adams has made this mention of Stephen Collins in his "Diary:"[1] "We dined at Friend Collins's, Stephen Collins, with Governor Hopkins, Governor Ward, Mr. Galloway, Mr. Rhoades, &c. . . . This gentleman is of fine figure and eminence, as well as fortune, in this place. He is of the profession of the Friends, but not stiff nor rigid. He is a native of Lynn, in New England, a brother of Ezra Collins in Boston. I have been treated by him in this city, both in the former Congress and the present, with unbounded civility and friendship. His house is open to every New England man. I never knew a more agreeable instance of hospitality."

---

[1] *Life and Works of John Adams*, II, 361.

Rich: Bland Lee.

Richard Bland Lee served in the Virginia Assembly as early as 1784, and probably many other years; he was also member of Congress in 1789 to 1795 and 1825–27. The following letter from him to "Roger Weightman, Esq., Mayor of Washington," tells something of Lafayette's visit. Writing from Baltimore, under date of the 8th of October, 1824, he said:

"I was presented to Gen. Lafayette to-day and delivered the message of the committee, together with a copy of your proposed address. He received with great politeness and cordiality my communication, and informed me that he had sent by Mr. Secretary Adams his reply to the invitation of the city which had been delivered to him at Boston—in which I understood him to say that he had noted that he would be on Monday evening at the house of a friend near Bladensburg, whom I understood to be Mr. Calvert. On Monday evening and Tuesday morning he would be ready to conform to any arrangements which might be communicated to him at that time. I collected from him that Virginia would send a steamboat to conduct him from Alexandria or Mount Vernon to Yorktown, and his probable stay in Washington would be three or four days.

"I have in vain endeavored to find Mr. French. I have visited every principal tavern and can hear nothing of him. I presume he is doing his duty.

"The Philadelphians have acknowledged that the military exhibition yesterday and the illumination last night surpassed theirs. I did not see the first, but the last exceeded anything which I had ever seen. The devices and transparencies were most appropriate and elegant. The illumination seemed to throw in a shade the brightness of the moon. Ingenuity seems to have been exhausted in emblems and gratitude in respect to Washington, Franklin, Lafayette, Adams, Jefferson, Madison, Hamilton, Jay, and Monroe—nor were De Kalb, Steuben, and Rochambeau forgotten. I shall return to-morrow. This city is filled with deputations from Alexandria and various parts of Virginia and Maryland."

Richard Bland[5] and Elizabeth (Collins) Lee had the following named children:

i, MARY ANN[6], born on the 11th of May, 1795; died on the 21st of June, 1796.

ii, RICHARD BLAND[6]. See 52.

iii, ANN MATILDA[6], born the 13th of July, 1799; died the 20th of December, 1880; married Dr. Bailey Washington, Surgeon U. S. N., eldest son of Bailey Washington, of "Windsor Forest," Stafford county, and Euphan Wallace, his wife. He was born in Westmoreland county in 1787; died at Washington, D. C., on the 14th of August, 1854. They had four children: 1, Fannie Wallace, who married Major Pierson Barton Reading, who served in the Mexican war, was with Fremont in the West, and also one of the early pioneers of California. He left these six children: Anna Washington, Alice Matilda, Pierson Barton (now deceased), Richard Washington, Robert Lee, and Fannie Collins Reading (now deceased). Mrs. Reading resides now at Washington. 2, Richard Bland Washington. 3, Anna Louisa Washington, who married Walter Dorsey Davidge, a distinguished lawyer, and had these seven children: Maud Lee, Walter Dorsey, Anna Washington, William Fendall, Francis Stuart, Edith Hathorn, and John Washington Davidge. 4, Elizabeth Lee Washington.

iv, MARY COLLINS[6], born the 6th of May, 1801; died on the 22d of February, 1805.

v, CORNELIA[6], born the 20th of March, 1804; died the 26th of December, 1876; married Dr. James W. F. Macrae, of Virginia, and had four children: 1, Collins Lee, who married Maria Thompson, and had issue: Collins Lee, Cornelia Lee, and Howard Macrae. 2, Elizabeth Westwood, who was twice married; first, to W. A. Bradley, Surgeon, U. S. A., and had Powell Macrae, Frederick William, and Maria Gillis Bradley; she married, secondly, C. C. Woolcot, U. S. N., and had William Stanton and Cornelia Lee Woolcot.

vi, ZACCHEUS COLLINS[6]. See 53.

## THEODORIC LEE.

38. THEODORIC[5], the fourth son of Henry Lee[4] (Henry[3], Richard[2], Richard[1]) and Lucy Grymes, his wife, was born on the 3d of September, 1766; died on the 10th of April, 1849, at "Eckington," the country seat, near Washington, of his son-in-law, Joseph Gales. Of Mr. Lee, his granddaughter writes: "Theodoric Lee was a gentleman in the highest sense of the word; conspicuous for benevolence and truth of character, and strong practical sense; of fine, intellectual countenance, with most kindly expressive dark gray eyes. He was given to agricultural pursuits, and was possessed of a fair fortune. . . . He married Catharine Hite, of Winchester, the youngest of the three daughters of Mr. John Hite of that place; like her sisters, Miss Hite was not only distinguished for intelligence, and beauty of person, but possessed unusual accomplishments for that day, having acquired a thorough knowledge of French and music. Mr. John Hite,

THEODORIC LEE.

her father, was the son of Jacob Hite and grandson of Baron Jost Hite, of Germany, who came to this country during the Revolutionary war, and settled on a large tract of land in Pennsylvania; his son Jacob moved to Berkeley county, Va., and purchased 3,000 acres of General Charles Lee; later he sold this property and removed to South Carolina, where subsequently some of the family were massacred by the Indians. . . . The first wife of Jacob Hite[1] was a sister of President Madison's father."

Theodoric Lee had one son and three daughters:

i, CAROLINE HITE[6], married Samuel Purviance Walker, of Baltimore. Mr. Walker was of Irish birth, was educated abroad, came to America with his cousins, John, Robert, and Samuel Purviance; located at Baltimore, where he became a successful merchant. He moved to Washington about 1829–30, and resided there until his death; he had these thirteen children: William McCreery, Samuel Purviance, Sarah Catharine, Frances Caroline, Juliana Gales, Jane Josephine, John Hite, Rosa Lee, Theodoric Lee, Isabella, Elizabeth Agg, Letitia McCreery, Emily Montoya. Of these children only one survives, Juliana Gales, to whose kindness these notes are due. Of the sons, William McCreery was a lieutenant in the U. S. Navy, and was with the Wilkes exploring expedition, in his Antarctic cruise. Mrs. Walker lived till her 86th year in full possession of her faculties.

ii, JOHN HITE[6]. See 54.

iii, SARAH JULIANA MARIA[6], "beautiful, intellectual, and accomplished, noted for deeds of charity; she was for many years at the head of the most elegant society of the national capital;" she was also noted for her great administrative ability. She married, in 1813, Joseph Gales, Jr., the editor of the *National Intelligencer*, of Washington, which was a journal of great influence in its day. Mr. Gales was for several terms the mayor of Washington, and had been acquainted, during his long residence at the capital, with all the Presidents from Madison to Buchanan; he died, honored and beloved, in July, 1860; was buried in the Congressional Cemetery, where a noble monument, erected by the leading journalists of the country, rises to mark his grave. Mr. and Mrs. Gales had no issue, but adopted their niece, Juliana Gales Walker, who now survives and resides at Washington, known by her adopted name, Gales.

iv, CATHARINE HITE[6], "was like her sisters distinguished for beauty,

---

[1] Major Isaac Hite, who married Eleanor, sister of President Madison, was of a younger generation.

benevolence, and intellect." She married Dr. George May, a graduate of Harvard, and a Bostonian by birth; he was for years one of the leading physicians of Washington city; they had two daughters: Sophia Catharine, who died on the 5th of July, 1894, unmarried, and Juliana Gales May, who resides at Washington, and is unmarried.

## Edmund Jennings Lee.

39. Edmund Jennings[5], the fifth son of Henry Lee[4], (Henry[3], Richard[2], Richard[1]) and Lucy Grymes, his wife, was born at "Leesylvania," Prince William county, on the 20th of May, 1772; died at his home in Alexandria, on the 30th of May, 1843; he married, about 1796, Sarah, the youngest daughter of Richard Henry Lee, of "Chantilly," by his second wife, Mrs. Anne (Gaskins) Pinckard. She was born at "Chantilly," on the 27th of November, 1775; died at Alexandria, on the 8th of May, 1837.

Of Edmund I. Lee, his son, Charles H. Lee, has written:[1]

"In the great undertaking, so successfully and wonderfully accomplished, of the restoration of the Episcopal Church in Virginia, attention is usually concentrated upon those who, as clergymen, wrought this great result. It has not, perhaps, been definitely recognized that there was a lay nucleus, from which many of these clerical workers were drawn, which sustained and aided their undertaking. One who will run over an old journal will find certain names of prominent laymen, from year to year, present and taking part in all the important measures under discussion. Prominent among these names, as a member of Diocesan and General Convention, trustee of Education Society, vestryman and delegate of Christ Church, and member of Standing Committee, was that of Edmund I. Lee, of Alexandria. His work for the diocese and the congregation, with which he was connected, was one of a peculiarly interesting character.

"Edmund Jennings Lee died in Alexandria in 1843 in the 72d year of his age. Early in life he became a member of the Episcopal Church, with which until his death he was identified in everything that concerned its welfare. He lived to see all of his children, who attained the age of maturity, members of the Church he loved so well, and one of them among her clergy. Deeply interested in the cause of religion in general, as in that of his own Church, he exhibited this interest in efforts for her benefit and welfare.

"As the first illustration of such effort may be mentioned his undertaking, successfully carried out, to resist and defeat the execution of the

---

1 *The Virginia Seminary Magazine*, July, 1888.

Edmund J. Lee

confiscation act in regard to church property. Before the Revolution of 1776, the Episcopal Church was established in Virginia. Each parish, under English law, held and owned a *Glebe*, that is land allotted as the 'dowry of the church;' or, in plainer language, property held for the support of the Rector and for parish uses. By an act of the Virginia Legislature, this was confiscated, and donated to the several counties for the use of their poor. This act was passed in January, 1802. It was stoutly resisted in some of the parishes, and among others, in Fairfax Parish, Alexandria county, of which the present old Christ Church was the Parish Church. The Courts of Virginia sustained this confiscation act; and thus all the Glebe lands succumbed to this process of political piracy, except those in Fairfax Parish. This property was saved by the perseverance and legal ability of Mr. Lee, and in this wise: The county of Alexandria was in 1801 made a part of the District of Columbia, and was thus brought within Federal jurisdiction. Mr. Lee had all along maintained the unconstitutionality of the confiscation law, and wrote a very able and exhaustive review of Judge Tucker's opinion on that subject. The Virginia act authorizing the sale of the Glebe lands was not passed till Alexandria county had become a part of the District of Columbia. The wardens and vestry of the church desired to dispose of the Glebe lands; but were impeded by the claims of the overseers of the poor of Fairfax county, who asserted their rights under the act of the Legislature. Mr. Lee, therefore, advised a suit in the Federal Courts, to enjoin these overseers from interference with the church property.

"This suit was argued for the church by Mr. Lee and Mr. Swann. The result was a decision by the Court that the acts under which the overseers of the poor claimed, 'so far as they go to divest the Episcopal Church of the property acquired, &c., . . . were unconstitutional and inoperative.'

"But the controversy did not end here. The vestry having, after the decision, sold the Glebe, the purchaser, becoming dissatisfied with the title, brought suit in the United States Courts to rescind the sale. This was resisted by the vendors, and the Supreme Court of the United States decided that the sale by the church authorities conveyed a good title. It was argued, as was the former suit, by Mr. Lee and Mr. Swann for the church.

"In this way Christ Church retained possession of its Glebe, which was sold, and the proceeds applied to the erection of the present commanding steeple and to the purchase of the fine toned bell that for so many years has faithfully recalled the 'sweet hour of prayer' to those who worship in that venerable sanctuary. Nor was this all. The vestry were also able to purchase the comfortable house on Washington Street, which has ever since been occupied as a rectory, besides building a substantial fence round the time-honored churchyard. All this was the result of Mr. Lee's persevering devotion and legal ability.

"It is hardly necessary to say that for many years Mr. Lee was warden and vestryman of old Christ Church, from the duties and services of which he was never absent save by compulsion. He was also long a member of the Standing Committee of the Diocese. He was from the first a trustee of the Education Society, and aided in its organization. He attended all the conventions, in which he maintained an useful and conspicuous part, his advice being sought on all important occasions.

"To Mr. Lee is entirely due the existence of the present '*Bishop's fund*' in Virginia. At one time the scarcity of money induced the Bishop and some members of the Standing Committee to think a resort to the principal of this fund necessary. This Mr. Lee steadily opposed. He was a trustee of the fund, and could not be induced to allow the appropriation even of the annual interest. He insisted, in the face of all argument to the contrary, 1st, that the object of the trust was the establishment of a permanent fund, and that to use either principal or interest at that time would be a breach of trust; and 2d, that so long as the fund remained *in statu quo*, there were reasonable hopes of additions to the principal by subscriptions, as well as by the accumulation of interest. These views, after much controversy, prevailed, and the Bishop's fund to-day remains a memento of the faithfulness, or, as Bishop Meade would pleasantly say, the 'obstinacy' of Edmund I. Lee.

"Still another instance of this useful firmness: the Town Council of Alexandria conceived the idea of widening and extending Cameron Street. The church grounds to the north of the building would necessarily be taken in by any such improvement. The Council acted under the advice of one of the best citizens and ablest lawyers that Alexandria ever produced, Robert I. Taylor, an intimate friend of Mr. Lee. The latter, however, procured an injunction against the Council, which, on argument before Judge Scott, was finally perpetuated. Thus the 'old Kirk yard' was happily preserved to the satisfaction of the people of Alexandria, and doubtless of the country generally. Mr. Lee was for several years the Mayor of Alexandria, and took special pains to enforce the proper observance of the Sabbath. As in public, so in private, he insisted on this duty. One or two illustrations of this will suffice. He was educated principally at Princeton, and imbibed many of the ideas of that excellent man, the Rev. Dr. Witherspoon, who was then at the head of that institution. While at college he had formed many warm associations. Not long before his death he received a cordial invitation from a friend in Alexandria to meet at his house at dinner two of his old Princeton classmates, and who, on hearing their former friend was then living in Alexandria, expressed a great desire to see him. Unfortunately the day appointed was Sunday. Very few, perhaps, would have resisted such an opportunity, and some may now characterize Mr. Lee's course as puritanical. He wrote a kind note to his friend, cordially thanking him for his invitation, but excusing his absence on the ground that he had made it a rule never to dine from home, except under necessity, on the Sabbath-day; but that, if possible, he would see his friends on the following day and give them a cordial welcome, and that if they should have left Alexandria too soon for this, he would call on them in Washington. Mr. Lee's rigid observance of the Sabbath may also be further illustrated by the manner in which he required those about him to respect it. Sometimes his wagon and horses from his farm in Loudoun would be detained till Saturday, but he invariably held them over until Monday at an additional expense, so as to avoid their being on the public road on the Sabbath-day. Mr. Lee was the brother of Light Horse Harry of the Revolution, and, therefore, uncle of General Robert E. Lee. Another of his brothers was Charles Lee, Attorney-General of the United States under John Adams. One of his sons was Rev. William F. Lee, a graduate of the Virginia Seminary, first editor and proprietor of the *Southern Churchman*. Three of his grandsons are now laboring in the ministry in the Diocese of Virginia.

"The writer would crave indulgence for the following letter from Bishop Moore and an extract from Bishop Meade's work on the *Old Churches and Families in Virginia*:

"'Richmond, October 23, 1817. Dear Sir:—The information you have received relative to a correspondence between Mr. Jefferson and myself is without foundation. I cordially concur with you in your views of church discipline, and am fully of the opinion that we may, with equal propriety, attempt to serve God and mammon, as to reconcile an indulgence in fashionable amusements with the divine life, but the remedy, the *remedy*, how is it to be applied? In this city, much as I wish to check the evil, I confess myself at a loss how to proceed.

"'A tender father will use every persuasion with a disobedient child, and will bear long with his perverseness before he will turn him out of doors. His affection for his children makes him tremble at the effects which austerity might produce. He is afraid that an expulsion from his society would expose his offspring to evils incalculably great. A minister of the Gospel is enjoined to instruct with *meekness* those who oppose themselves; and it is his duty, "knowing the terrors of the Lord to *persuade* men." Although he is bound to be thus prudent, he is equally obliged to guard the altar, to inspect the conduct of his members, and to see that none of them bring a reproach upon the cross of Christ. In New York the relinquishment of balls, the theatre and card table formed the *sine qua non* of admission to the communion in my church, but whether the temper of my present flock would submit to the same rule of conduct, God only knows. I am apprehensive it would produce a commotion overwhelming in its effects and desolating to our interest. Were there a few laymen in this place who would sanction the attempt and enforce it with their influence, perhaps it might succeed; but in all my conversations upon the subject with some truly excellent men belonging to my church they express the greatest apprehension, and I do not know at present of any who would uphold me in the conflict. I hope you will continue to reflect upon the subject. It is, indeed, of great moment, and merits the most pious and serious consideration. I have just returned from a long tour through the western part of the diocese, and shall leave Richmond in a few days in order to explore the countries between York and Rappahannock rivers. I could wish some plan devised for the support of two or more missionaries. The money might be raised either by subscription or sermons in our churches. Present me very respectfully and affectionately to Mrs. Lee, and believe me

" 'Your sincere friend and pastor,

" 'RICHARD CHANNING MOORE.

" 'EDMUND I. LEE, ESQ.

" 'P. S.—Do attend our next Convention, and let us endeavor to ascertain how far discipline may be exercised with prudence. I could wish you to bring the question before the Standing Committee in order to know their opinion.' "

Bishop Meade writes thus:

"Concerning two of the above-mentioned vestrymen, I may be permitted to say a few words. Mr. George Taylor and Edmund I. Lee were church wardens when I took charge of the church in 1811, and so continued until the removal of one by change of residence and the other by death after a long term of service. They were both members of the Standing Committee during the same period. I think I knew them well, and knew them to be sincere Christians and useful, punctual business men. . . . Mr. Lee generally attended on State Conventions and sometimes the General Convention. He was a man of great decision and perseverance in what he deemed right—obstinate, some of us thought, even to a fault, when we differed from him. There was no compromise at all in him with anything which he thought wrong. He was as fearless as Julius Cæsar. On a certain

Sabbath, while I was performing service in Christ Church, a certain person in the gallery disturbed myself and the congregation by undue vociferation in the responses, and also at the opening of the sermon. I paused, and requested him to desist, and was proceeding, but Mr. Lee, who was near him, arose and asked me to suspend the sermon. Walking toward the offender, he told him that he must leave the house. As he approached to enforce it, the person raised a loaded whip and struck at him. Mr. Lee, nothing moved, took him by the arms and led him out of the house, and deposited him in the town jail. When mayor of the town, he was a terror to evil-doers. Ascertaining that there was much gambling going on among the gentlemen of the place, and some of the principal ones, he took effective measures for their discovery, brought between thirty and forty before the court, and had them fined. The prosecuting attorney was his particular friend, and was slightly implicated in the evil practice; but he did not spare him. Nor did he wish to be spared; but, coming forward and paying his fine, then did his duty with all the rest. Mr. Lee was of course not a popular man, nor did he seek or care to be; but did his duty entirely regardless of others. He kept our Conventions in good order, by always insisting upon the observance of rules, of which the clergy are not always mindful. He was the great advocate of our Bishop's fund, and defended it from all invasions. I not only knew Mr. Lee from my youth up, but I saw him in his last moments, and heard him with great humility speak of himself as a poor sinner, whose only hope was in Christ. And can I speak of him without remembering that meek and holy woman to whom he was so long a most affectionate husband? She was the daughter of that Christian patriot, Richard Henry Lee. For more than thirty years she was gradually dying of consumption, and yet in such a way as to admit of the exhibition of all her Christian graces in the various relations of life. By universal consent she was one of the purest specimens of humanity sanctified by the grace of God." (*Old Churches, Families, etc.*, II, 268–69.)

At the opening of the U. S. Circuit Court, Alexandria county, 5th June, 1843, Christopher Neale, Esq., thus addressed the Court:

"I am requested by the gentlemen of the Bar of this Court to bring to the notice of your Honors certain resolutions, which were *unanimously* adopted, on Thursday last, in reference to the demise of our lamented friend, the late Edmund I. Lee.

"In performing this duty, I need scarcely remark to your Honors, how truly we deplore the loss of one, with whom most of us have been so long and so intimately acquainted, and who deservedly ranked so very high in our respect and best and warmest affections.

"In the death of Mr. Lee, the public, as well as the profession to which he belonged, have sustained the loss of one whose mind was most deeply and thoroughly imbued with the abstruse principles and learning of his profession, with varied talent, and great compass of thought.

"He was at all times the perfect gentleman, the kind neighbor, the tender parent, social companion—and last, but not least, the steady and unwavering *Christian.*

"But a little while ago, and he was in our midst, ably expounding the Law and zealously maintaining and defending his clients' rights; and yet, but a little thereafter, and we see him no more forever!

"Still we have the consoling reflection, that he is now at rest; that his cares, his toils, his anxieties, and his sorrows, are all ended, and that his Christian spirit, has ere this, commingled with the spirits of the just made perfect in a better and happier world."

To which Judge Cranch replied:

"The Court has received, with deep sensibility, the information of the death of Mr. Lee, the oldest member of this bar, and the last survivor of those who were counsellors of this Court at the time of its erection in 1801.

"The Court not only sympathizes with the bar and with the relatives of the deceased, in the great loss they have sustained, but it deplores the loss which the Court itself has suffered in being deprived of the benefit of his counsel, learning, and research in preparing his causes for the consideration of the Court, and in assisting the Judges by his able arguments.

"In the long period of our association with him in the administration of Justice, a friendship has been formed, which cannot be severed without a wound. We bear testimony to the truth of his character as portrayed in the resolutions presented to us by his brethren of the bar, and most willingly permit them to be entered upon the minutes of the Court."

Of Mrs. Lee, her pastor wrote, adding his testimony to that of the Bishop, already quoted: "In youth she acknowledged the obligations that rested upon her to dedicate all her faculties to the glory of her Creator and Redeemer. Through all her future life it was her earnest exertion to live up to her high and holy privileges as a Christian, and to recommend the religion of her Saviour to all who came under her influence. Through a long and painful illness, its abundant consolations were her support, and in the last trying hour, when flesh and heart fail, the Redeemer she had so long served did not forsake her. Faithful to His promises, the dark valley was made light by His presence. She has gone to the rest prepared for the people of God; but her bright example, as a rich legacy, she has left to her surviving friends."

Edmund I. and Sarah Lee had the following named children:

i, EDMUND JENNINGS[6]. See 55.

ii, ANNE HARRIOTTE[6], born the 6th of March, 1799; died the 10th of September, 1863; married, on the 2d of November, 1820, John Lloyd, Esq., of Alexandria; he was born the 16th of November, 1775; died the 22d of July, 1854. They had six children (Lloyd): 1, Edmund Jennings, born the 27th of August, 1822; died the 1st of October, 1889, unmarried. 2, Rebecca, born the 7th of June, 1824; died on the 17th of July, 1873; married, on 2d of May, 1844, Dr. John Prosser Tabb, of Gloucester county, and had five children: John, Matilda Prosser, John Lloyd, John Prosser, and Rebecca Lloyd Tabb. (See Tabb Family.) 3, Anne Harriotte, born the 7th of January, 1826; died the 23d of June, 1888; married the Rev. John Stearns and left issue: Mary, who married William Hoge; John, Rebecca, who married William Hastings; and Lawrence Stearns. 4, George Francis, born the 28th of October, 1828; died the 1st of October, 1866; married Mary Pindle Hammond, and had three children: Nelson, who married a Miss Morris; Nannie, who married Robert Hare Delafield; Francis Frederick, who married a Miss Taylor. 5, Jean Charlotte Washington, who married, in 1867, Captain Philip Tabb Yeatman, C. S. A., and now resides at Alexandria. 6, Mary Lee Lloyd, who is unmarried.

iii, SARAH[6], died unmarried, 14th of April, 1879, aged 78.

iv, WILLIAM FITZHUGH[6]. See 56.

v, HANNAH[6], born about 1806; died 9th of May, 1872, at Lewes, Delaware; married, on the 5th of May, 1840, at Alexandria, the Rev. Kensey Johns Stewart, D. D., of the Episcopal Church; they had the following named children: 1, Sally Lee, born 10th April and died 25th August, 1841. 2, David, born 6th April, 1842; died 8th July, 1847. 3, Hannah Philippa Lee, born 7th September, 1844; died 21st August, 1845. 4, Mary Eliza Kennedy, born 31st January, 1847. 5, Edmund Lee, born 30th January, 1851; died 21st May, 1857. 6, James Van Dyke, born 30th April, 1853; died 14th May, 1857. Of these children, Mary Eliza Kennedy Stewart married, on 28th of October, 1869, at Gordonsville, Warner Minor Woodward, of Richmond, and has the following children: Stewart Minor, Edmund Lee,

Mary Stewart, John Douglas (born 10th August, 1879; died 15th June, 1880), Mildred Minor, and Lettice Lee Woodward.

WOODWARD—John Lee, son of Philip, of Maryland, moved to Virginia and settled in Essex county; he married Susannah Smith (see 14) and had eight children, among them a daughter, Lettice Lee, who married (in 1783?) Captain John Whiting, of Gloucester; they had four children, of whom Lettice Lee Whiting married, 22d of June, 1822, Richard Woodward, and had one son, John Pitt Lee Woodward, now living, the father of the above-mentioned Warner Minor Woodward.

vi, CASSIUS FRANCIS[6]. See 57.
vii, SUSAN MEADE[6], born 26th March, 1814; died 15th of February, 1815.
viii, CHARLES HENRY[6]. See 58.
ix, RICHARD HENRY[6]. See 59.

## THE TABB FAMILY.

Though the Tabbs appear to have been long seated in Gloucester county, one of the name appearing on the vestry books of old Kingston Parish as early as 1677, the first of the family (of whom there is any record now extant in that county) was Philip Tabb, who came from Amelia county to reside with his maternal uncle, Todd, of "Toddsbury." This Philip appears to have inherited the estates of his uncle, and to have lived at "Toddsbury;" he served in the Revolutionary war as a lieutenant, and left issue: John, Edward, Henry A., and Thomas Tabb. All of these sons married and have left descendants. The two oldest, John and Edward, made considerable fortunes, trading as flour merchants from Norfolk, especially during the war of 1812, when they were very successful. After the war, both then very rich, settled in Gloucester; John resided at "White Marsh," and Edward at "Waverly," on the North River. Thomas, the youngest brother, owned "Toddsbury," and lived there until his death.

John Tabb married, on the 18th of December, 1817, Evelina Matilda, daughter of William Prosser; he is said to have been descended from Parson Prosser, one of the early rectors of York Hampton Parish. The wife of this William Prosser, after his death, married a Rootes, of "White Marsh," from whom, it is supposed, the Prossers inherited or purchased that estate. Two other daughters of William Prosser married two Lees: Julia Anna Marion, Richard Bland Lee, and Elizabeth, John Hite Lee.

John Tabb had by his marriage with Miss Prosser several children, but only two, John Prosser and Philip, survived. Dr. John Prosser Tabb inherited "White Marsh," a very elegant estate, and married, on the 2d of May, 1844, Rebecca, the eldest daughter of John and Anne Harriotte (Lee)

Lloyd, of Alexandria, as stated; they had five children: 1, John, who has been twice married; first, to Judith Coleman, of Halifax county, by whom he had issue: John, Alice, and Rebecca; he married, secondly, Mary James, of Gloucester, and had: Judith (who died), Joseph, Mary Lee, and Warner Tabb. They reside in Gloucester. 2, Matilda Prosser, who married John Tayloe Perrin, of "Goshen," Gloucester county, and had issue: Annie Lee, Rebecca Lloyd, Maud Tabb, and Elinor Perrin; they reside now at Baltimore, Md. 3, John Lloyd, who married Susan Selden, a daughter of Robert C. Selden, of "Sherwood," Gloucester county, and had issue: Warner Lewis, Maud, and Lloyd Tabb; they also reside at Baltimore, Md. 4, John Prosser, who married Nellie McKenzie, of Baltimore, and had issue: McKenzie, Prosser, and Nellie Tabb; they, too, reside, at Baltimore. 5, Rebecca, who married Samuel G. Brent, of Alexandria, and had two children.

Dr. John Prosser Tabb was compelled, after the late war, to sell "White Marsh;" he then removed to a smaller plantation, on the North River, which he named "Ditchley." He died there; also his wife and her mother, Mrs. Lloyd. Lately, his brother, Philip Tabb, has purchased "White Marsh," and now resides there. He married a Miss Morris, of New York, and had two daughters: Evelina Matilda, who married a Mr. Balliére, and has children: Catharine, who is unmarried. "Toddsbury," which may be called the cradle of the Gloucester Tabbs, has also passed into other hands.

## STRATFORD LINE, SIXTH GENERATION.

### Thomas Lee.

40. Thomas[6], the second son of Thomas Sim Lee[5] (Thomas[4], Philip[3], Richard[2], Richard[1]), and Mary Digges, his wife, was born the 2d of February, 1774; died in October, 1826; he was married, in October, 1797, to Eleanor, the only daughter of Richard Cromwell.

His will was dated the 3d of May, 1826, with two codicils added; was probated, in Anne Arundel county, Md., the 23d of October, 1826.

In the name of God, Amen. I Thomas Lee of Anne Arundel County and State of Maryland, being in perfect health of body and of sound and disposing mind, memory and understanding, Considering the certainty of death and the uncertainty of the time thereof and being desirous to settle my worldly affairs and thereby be better prepared to leave this world when it shall please God to call me hence, do therefore make and publish this my last Will and Testament in manner and form following, that is to say:

First and principally I commit my soul into the hands of Almighty God and my Body to the Earth to be decently buried at the discretion of my Executrix here after named and after my debts and funeral charges are paid I devise and bequeath as follows—

Item, I give and bequeath my farm on Elm Ridge, called Clarier Hill, together with all stock and utensils of farming now thereon, to my wife Eleanor Lee and her heirs forever in fee simple. Item, I give, will, bequeath and devise to my said wife Eleanor Lee all my right estate and interest both in law and Equity to all property or possessions, real, personal and mixed, which I in any way hold or claim title to in the State of Louisanna for and during her natural life and from and after her decease to all my children share and share alike their heirs and assigns forever; with the exception, at her own request, of my daughter Mary who was intermarried with Charles Carroll, Jr., Esq; provided also and it is my will and intention by this my last will and testament to empower, authorize and appoint my said wife Eleanor at any time when she may so elect to sell, transfer, alien and convey all my right, title, interest, estate and claims of whatsoever nature I hold in, possess or claim to possess in the aforesaid State of Louisanna as aforesaid and to invest the proceeds of such sale in any publick stock which she in her discretion may elect or prefer and to take, receive and enjoy all the interests, emoluments and rents arising therefrom, for and during her natural life and after her decease, it is my will and intention and I do hereby devise and bequeath and direct that the stock so purchased and invested by her to be equally divided between all my Children, their heirs and assigns, with the exception of my daughter mentioned as aforesaid.

Item, I devise and bequeath all the rest and residue of my Estate, real, personal and mixed to my said wife Eleanor Lee during her natural life and from and after her decease to all my children, their heirs and assigns, to be equally divided among said children share and share alike.

Lastly, I do hereby constitute and appoint Eleanor Lee, my wife, to be my Lawful Executrix of this my last will and testament, revoking and annulling all former wills by me heretofore made, ratifying and Confirming this and none other to be my last will and testament. In testimony whereof &c.

1st. Codicil. I, the above named testator do make and declare and publish this my Codicil to the above will and testament. It is my will and intention and I do hereby order and direct that in consideration of the advances already made to my son Richard Lee, now in the State of Louisanna, that he take no faith of the provision and property to be enjoyed by my children after the death of my wife Eleanor Lee, which I have directed and bequeathed in the above will and testament, to which this is a Codicil; it is also my will and I do hereby in this Codicil declare and publish it, that my servant Thomas Brent, now in the State of Louisanna, aged about fifty years, to be manumitted and that provided with a suitable support from the profits of my estate in Louisanna, 3rd of May, 1826.

2d. Codicil. I, Thomas Lee, of Anne Arundel County & State of Maryland, do make, declare and publish this my second Codicil to my last will and testament. Item, I give and bequeath to my son Thomas Lee all my right, estate and interest both in law & Equity to all property in possession, real, personal and mixed, which I any way claim title to of what my late Grandfather Ignatius Diggs of Prince Georges County died possessed of, on Condition that he the said Thomas Lee shall sell and dispose of the same to the best advantage and as speedily as possible and appropriate the proceeds thereof to the payment of all my just debts as far as the amount will extend and should there be any surplus after this object shall be accomplished, he shall place any such surplus in the hands of his mother my wife Eleanor Lee, to be disposed of by her as is directed for my other property in my will to which this is a Codicil. Item, I hereby declare & make known that the person designated in my first Codicil to my will annexed is my son Richard Henry Lee. Dated 8th of May, 1826.

On the 23d of May, 1831, his widow, Eleanor Lee, made the following renunciation of her guardianship:

To the Honourable, the Judges of the Orphans' Court of Anne Arundel County:—The subscriber, Widow of the late Thomas Lee, of Anne Arundel County, hereby renounces the right to be the Guardian to her two minor Children, William and Charles Lee, and requests that John J. Donaldson be appointed in her Stead.

Thomas and Eleanor (Cromwell) Lee had the following eleven children, only two of whom left descendants:

i, RICHARD HENRY [7], born the 31st of July, 1798; died without issue.
ii, MARY DIGGES [7], born the 9th of June, 1800; died ——; was married in October, 1825, to Charles, son of Charles Carroll and Harriet Chew, his wife, and grandson of Charles Carroll, the Signer. They had nine children. (See Carroll Family.)
iii, GEORGIANA WASHINGTON [7], born the 27th of May, 1802; no issue.
iv, THOMAS [7]. See 60.
v, ELEANOR CROMWELL [7], born the 5th of April, 1805; married and had issue, all of whom died young.
vi, JOHN CARROLL [7], born the 19th of June, 1807; no issue.
vii, HENRY POUGH [7], born the 3d of March, 1809; no issue.
viii, WILLIAM [7], born the 15th of December, 1811; no issue.
ix, SOPHIA [7], born the 1st of December, 1813; no issue.
x, CHARLES LANCELOT [7]; died in infancy.
xi, CHARLES ARTHUR [7], born in 1817; died in 1837.

## THE CARROLL FAMILY.

This distinguished Maryland family derive their descent from an ancient and honorable family of Ireland; one that is said to be descended from the ancient kings of Munster, and to have intermarried with the noble houses of Ormond and Desmond in Ireland and with that of Argyll of Scotland. Early Irish history tells much of the wealth, power, and influence of this family. Records in the possession of the Maryland branch show that the "Sept of O'Carroll was early established in Lowth, being then popularly styled Princes of Orgeil. Previous to the English invasion, immediately after the great Synod of Mellifont in 1152, is recorded the expulsion of their chief from that country, of which he had been the acknowledged lord from Drogheda to Asigh in the County of Meath." "The death of Amergin Carroll, Lord of Ely, is recorded in 1033. In 1327 John Carroll became Archbishop of Cashel. In 1349

Thomas Carroll became Bishop of Tuam." Many similar extracts might be given, but these few are sufficient to show the prominence of this family in their native land. About 1689 Charles Carroll, son of Daniel, of Littalouna, King's county, Ireland, emigrated to America and settled in the Province of Maryland. He was a Judge, Register of the Land Office, and an agent for Lord Baltimore. At his death he left a son, Charles, who was born in 1702 and died in 1782. He, too, became prominent in the province and a leader of the Roman Catholic party. He married Elizabeth Brooke (who may have been related to the first wife of Philip Lee), and had a son, Charles, afterward famous as "Charles Carroll of Carrollton." He was born at Annapolis on the 20th of September, 1737, and lived to an advanced age, to be the last survivor of those who signed the Declaration of Independence, dying at Baltimore on the 14th of November, 1832. When only eight years old he was sent to France, to be taught by the English Jesuits at St. Omer's. After six years with them he went to the Jesuit College at Rheims; next he spent two years at the College of Louis le Grand. After studying law, first in France and later at the Middle Temple, at London, he returned to Maryland in 1761. Charles Carroll was, therefore, only twenty-four when he entered upon his public career, one that was to be so useful and so brilliant. At the time of his return the Province of Maryland, in common with her sister colonies, was greatly excited over the famous "Stamp Act" and the other encroachments which it foreshadowed. Mr. Carroll immediately interested himself in the contest, and by his pen and his voice greatly aided and encouraged patriotic citizens. Space will not allow, nor is it necessary in this place, to attempt a complete sketch of Charles Carroll's career. Suffice it to say, that he was always an able, active, and fearless patriot; that he held many very prominent positions, and in all of them served his country with marked ability and success. He was at different times a member of the Provincial Assembly, of the Continental Congress, and held other similar responsible positions.

In the year 1768, he married Mary Darrall, by whom he had one son and two daughters. The son, also named Charles, married, in 1793, the celebrated beauty, Harriet Chew, a daughter of Judge Benjamin Chew, of Germantown, Penna.; she was born the 22d of October, 1775, and died the 8th of April, 1861. From this union were born one son and four daughters; the daughters were: 1, Elizabeth, who married Dr. Aaron Tucker, and had two sons. 2, Mary Sophia, who married the Hon. Richard H. Bayard, of Delaware, and had issue. 3, Harriet, who married Col. John Lee, of "Needwood" (see 42). 4, Louisa, who married Isaac Rand Jackson, of Newburyport, Mass., and left issue. The son, Charles, the fifth of the name, married Mary Digges Lee, as stated, and had these nine children (Carroll):

i, MARY, born the 10th of September, 1826; married Dr. Eleazer Acosta, of Paris, and had one daughter.

ii, CHARLES, born in October, 1828, and died in February, 1895, without issue; he married, on the 24th of June, 1857, Caroline Thompson, of Staunton, Va., who survives him.

iii, THOMAS SIM LEE, was born in 1829, and died in 1833.

iv, JOHN LEE, was born in 1830, and still survives; he has been twice married; first, on the 24th of April, 1856, to Anita, daughter of Royal Phelps, of New York, by whom he had these nine children: 1, Charles Lee, born at New York, the 5th of October, 1857, and died in 1858. 2, Mary Louisa, born the 26th of May, 1859; married, on the 3d of December, 1886, Comte Jean de Kergorlay, of France, and had issue. 3, Anita Maria, born the 28th of March, 1861; married, on the 14th of October, 1886, Baron Louis de la Grange, of France, and has issue. 4, Royal Phelps, born the 29th of October, 1862; married, on the 3d of March, 1890, Marion Langdon, of New York, and has issue. 5, Charles, born at Baltimore, the 12th of January, 1865; married, in November, 1887, Susanne Bancroft, and has issue. 6, Albert Henry, born at New York, the 6th of October, 1866; died in August, 1867. 7, Mary Irene, born the 3d of March, 1869, and died the 8th of November, 1888. 8, John Lee, born at New York, the 26th of February, 1871. 9, Mary Helen, born at New York, the 24th of March, 1873. Mr. Carroll was married, secondly, on the 14th of May, 1877, to Mary Carter Thompson, of Staunton, Va., and has one son, Philip Acosta, born the 10th of May, 1879. Mr. Carroll has been a member of the Maryland State Senate, 1867–72; Governor of the State in 1875. He now resides at Washington.

v, vi, vii, LOUISA, THOMAS SIM LEE (2d), and OSWALD, the next three children of Charles and Mary Digges (Lee) Carroll, died in early infancy.

viii, ALBERT HENRY married, on the 4th of May, 1858, Mary Cornelia, daughter of William George Read, and Sophia Catharine Howard, his wife, of Baltimore, and had issue: Mary Sophia, Mary Elinor, and Agnes Carroll. Mr. Carroll was killed on the 7th of September, 1862, near Martinsburg, West Va., while serving in the Confederate army. Mrs. Carroll married, secondly, on the 25th of June, 1866, Col. James Fenner Lee, son of Stephen S. and Sarah F. (Mallet) Lee, formerly of South Carolina, now of Baltimore.

ix, ROBERT GOODLOW HARPER, born in 1840; has been twice married; first, in 1862, to Ella Thompson, of Staunton, Va., who died without issue; he was married, secondly, in 1872, to Mary Digges Lee, daughter of Thomas Sim Lee, and Josephine O'Donnell, his wife (see 61, ii), and has two sons: 1, Charles, born the 12th of August, 1873. 2, Albert Henry, born in October, 1874.

Charles Carroll, the Signer, owned a very extensive estate, known as "Doughoregan Manor," situated in the present county of Howard, Md. This estate was devised to his grandson, and is now owned by the Hon. John Lee Carroll. "The Manor house is a large and very handsome residence of the old colonial style, with chapel annexed, built about the year 1717." His other estate, "Carrollton Manor," was situated in Frederick county, Md., and contained about 10,000 acres; it was granted by Lord Baltimore to the first Charles Carroll.

"Charles Carroll of Carrollton was not the only one of his name living in Maryland from 1737 to 1782. There were: First, his father, Charles Carroll, who died in 1782; second, his cousin, Charles Carroll, *barrister*, born 22d of March, 1723, thus by fourteen years his senior; an eminent lawyer, educated at Eton and at Cambridge University, England, studied law in the Temple, was author of the Maryland 'Declaration of Rights,' President of the Maryland Convention, member of the U. S. Congress, first Chief Justice of Maryland, &c., &c.; third, the 'Signer,' and fourth, his son, Charles." (Rev. Horace E. Hayden.) It was to avoid any confusion of names that Charles Carroll always signed "of Carrollton" after his name.

## WILLIAM LEE.

41. WILLIAM [6], the third son of Thomas Sim Lee [5] (Thomas [4], Philip [3], Richard [2], Richard [1]) and Mary Digges, his wife, was born 23d of June,

1775; died 8th of July, 1845. He married, on the 2d of October, 1809, Mary Lee, the fifth daughter of Robert Hollyday; she died the 23d of August, 1818, leaving five daughters and an infant son.

His will, dated the 8th of December, 1842, probated in Frederick county, Md., the 15th of July, 1845, was as follows:

In the name of God, Amen. I, William Lee, of Frederick County, State of Maryland, being in a state of feeble health of body but of sound and disposing mind, do declare the following to be my last Will and Testament. Imprimis, I direct my Executrix hereafter named to bury my body decently and after the expenses of my interment are paid to discharge my just debts with honor and justice from the fund hereafter appointed.

Item—I give and bequeath my negroes in manner following: to my daughter Mary Digges, her heirs and assigns these negroes and their increase, that is to say,—Henny and her child Henry, William son of Suckey Sall, Robert, Maria and her four children, William, Rachael, Alfred and Lery, Charles and his wife Prissy and their two children Edward and Philip, Joan the daughter of Lucy and Othello, in all sixteen negroes. And it is my desire and will that my said daughter in consideration of the said servant Othello, pay the sum of $400 to be added to the fund hereafter provided for the payment of debts and to be subject to all the uses and limitations which are hereinafter imposed upon that fund.

Item—I give and devise to the Trustee hereinafter appointed and his heirs forever, these following negroes and their increase, that is to say: John, Mary, and Bernard, the children of Charles and Prissy, Abraham, Mary, the daughter of Suckey Sall, and her two children Susanna and Andrew, Mary Ann the daughter of Lucy, Ben, John and Polly the children of Bob and Sall,—Babtiste, Treasy and her child, in all, fourteen negroes, the said trustee to hold the said negroes and their increase to himself and his heirs in trust, nevertheless for the sole use and benefit of my son Thomas and his heirs for ever, my son Thomas to have the power to dispose of any of the said negroes with the approval and with the written consent of said trustee, and the proceeds of said sale to be held by said trustee and invested by him for the use and benefit of the said Thomas and his heirs.

Item—I give and devise to the said trustee and his heirs forever, these following negroes and their increase, that is to say: Lucy and her five children, Margary, Isaac, and Dick, Cornelius and Thomas, Aaron the son of Bob and Sall, Daniel the son of Charles and Prissy the said trustee to have the said negroes and their increase to himself and his heirs forever, in trust, nevertheless, for the sole and separate use and benefit of my daughter Ellen Lynch of the State of Virginia and her issue, which, together with those negroes, I have heretofore in my life time, given in trust to my daughter Ellen amount to sixteen negroes.

Item—I hereby declare it to be my will and desire that the following named negroes shall be considered as manumitted and set free from all manner of service to my heirs, namely, Bob and his wife Sall, old Henny and little Will, which said last named negroes shall be maintained and taken good care of by my daughter Mary Diggs, during their natural lives, if they think proper to live with her—also Suckey Sall and Molly who shall be maintained and taken good care of during their natural lives by my son Thomas if they think proper to live with him—also Charity, who shall be maintained and taken good care of during her natural life by my daughter Ellen Lynch, if she think proper to live with her—also my faithful servant Jack who shall be maintained and taken good care of during his natural life by all or any of my said children and the said Jack shall have a right to live with or be supported by any of them with whom he may think proper to live—also Suckey and her daughter Matilda and the children of Matilda and their increase—and it is my will and desire that my said executrix, as soon as possible after my decease, shall if practicable and with the consent of the said negroes send the last named negroes, that is to say, Suckey and her family to the Roman Catholic settlement in Liberia and pay the expenses of their transportation.

Item—It is my will and desire that all the personal property on my said farm in Frederick County and State of Maryland, other than the negroes aforesaid shall be divided by my executrix, into three equal shares according to the legal appraised value thereof, which said shares I give and bequeath to my three children, one share to each; and in case they be dissatisfied with the division made by my executrix, then it is my desire that the said property be divided in the manner aforesaid by my friend and relative Col. John R. Dall whose division shall be final and binding on my said children.

Item—I hereby constitute and appoint my daughter Mary Diggs the sole executrix of this my last will and testament.

Item—I give and bequeath to my executrix aforesaid and to her heirs forever all my real estate in Montgomery County of this State, called "Burgundy," and it is my desire that my executrix should as soon as practicable sell the said "Burgundy" and appropriate the proceeds of said sale to the purposes hereinafter mentioned also all my right, title or interest in and to my Bonds, notes, money or negroes now in the State of Louisiana, belonging to me or due me from any person or persons in said State; said Bonds, notes or negroes to be converted into money as soon as practicable by my said executrix and the proceeds thereof appropriated to the purposes hereinafter mentioned.

Item—It is my will and desire that the fund created by the preceding clause should be appropriated in manner following:

1st. To pay all my just debts which are not otherwise provided for by this my last will.

2d. The balance to be paid over to the said trustee to be hereinafter appointed to be held by him to himself and his heirs, in trust nevertheless to and for the uses and purposes following, that is to say:—that he the said trustee divide the said sum so received from my executrix into two equal shares or portions, and it is my desire that he hold *one* of the said shares or portions for the use and benefit of my son Thomas and his heirs forever, with power to invest and change the investments of the same as often as the said trustee may deem it advisable to do so,—And it is my desire that he hold the other share aforesaid together with the negroes hereinbefore devised to the said trustee for the use of the said Ellen, to the sole and separate use and benefit of my said daughter Ellen and her issue forever, and in case of her dying without issue then to and for the sole use and benefit of the said Mary Diggs and the said Thomas and the survivor of them and their heirs and the heirs of the survivor of them, the said trustee to have the power to invest said share of money and change the investment thereof as he may deem the most advisable and proper, and it is my desire that the said Ellen and her husband during her life shall have the power to sell and dispose of any of said slaves hereinbefore devised to said trustee for the use of the said Ellen provided the said trustee shall approve and give his written consent thereto and in case of said sale, then the proceeds thereof shall be invested and held in trust by said trustee in manner and as last above stated.

Item—I give and bequeath to my son Thomas and his heirs and assigns the reversion of a negro girl Ellen and her increase who was by deed recorded in Washington City, D. C., given by me to a certain Mary Tritt until the said Ellen should arrive at the age of twenty-seven years.

Item—I give devise and bequeath to my daughter Mary Diggs and her heirs forever in fee simple all my land and real estate lying in Frederick County and State of Maryland on which I now reside and it is my will and desire that any sum or sums of money which I may owe the heirs of the late Dr. Clement Smith and Henry Warring shall be charged upon said real estate and be paid by my said daughter Mary Diggs.

Item—It is my will and desire that all my silver should be appraised according to law and that my daughter Mary Diggs should have the choice of taking the said silver at the appraised value: but in case she does not chuse to do so then I give the next choice to my daughter Ellen Lynch and if she does not *chuse* to do so then to my son Thomas if he will pay the appraised value thereof—which said equivalent shall be distributed as the other personal property is directed to be distributed by this will.

Item—I hereby constitute and appoint my friend Dr. Horatio Claggett of Washington County as the trustee as hereinbefore referred to, with all the powers conferred on said trustee by this my last will and testament.

Item—Finally I give and bequeath to my executrix afores'd all my property, real, personal and mixed, which is not hereinbefore specifically devised to be by her converted into money and the proceeds thereof to be paid over to the s'd trustee for the uses and purposes before specified—that is, he shall divide the same into two shares and hold the two shares for the use of Thomas and Ellen as is provided as to the fund heretofore created. Signed, etc.

Codicil. I, William Lee of Frederick County and State of Maryland desiring for good reasons to make certain changes in my last will and testament, do hereby constitute and appoint this as my codicil to my said last will and testament executed on the twenty-eighth day of December 1842, and I hereby revoke and declare null and void all parts of my said last will and testament which may be in any manner inconsistent with this my codicil:

1st. In consequence of the widowhood of my daughter Ellen the lot of servants named in my said will, as left to a trustee for her benefit, the same lot and their increase I now leave to my daughter Ellen her heirs and assigns forever.

2d. I hereby direct my executrix named in my said last will to distribute the fund raised by the sale of the residue of "Burgundy" and the property in Louisiana, as stated in my said will, in manner following: To pay all my just debts which are not otherwise provided for by my last will not excepting any balance which may be due the estate of the late Dr. Smith, which debt is now in a state of liquidation.

3d. To divide the residue into three equal shares, one of which I desire my said executrix to retain to herself and her heirs and assigns, another of which she is to pay over to my daughter Ellen her heirs and assigns, and the balance she is to pay over to the trustee in my said will named to be held by him to the use of my son Thomas, under the uses, limitations and powers in my said will particularly set forth and specified.

4th. I hereby give and bequeath to my daughter Ellen during her natural life, an annuity of three hundred dollars per annum and direct my executrix to pay or cause to be paid to my said daughter Ellen the said annuity semi-annually, that is to say, one-half thereof on the first day of January and on the First day of June—and I hereby will and direct that the said annuity shall be a charge on the real estate on which I now live and which is devised by my last will to my daughter Mary Diggs, and the said real estate shall always be bound for the said annuity during the life time of the said Ellen. Signed and sealed this 11th day of November, 1843.

William and Mary Lee (Hollyday) Lee had the following issue:

i, Mary Digges[7], born the 20th of June, 1810; was married on the 2d of September, 1851, to Samuel L. Gouverneur, of New York, no issue; Mrs. Gouverneur still survives and resides at "Needwood," Frederick county, Maryland. Almost all the data concerning the family of her grandfather, Gov. Thomas Sim Lee, have been furnished by this venerable lady, to whom many thanks are most heartily rendered.

ii, Sarah Brooke[7], born 29th of September, 1811, and died in infancy.

iii, Eliza Horsey[7], born the 25th of January, 1813; died in 1838, unmarried.

iv, Eleanor[7], born the 5th of May, 1814; married, in 1840, Eugene H. Lynch; died 7th of July, 1873, without issue.

v, Anna Gaston[7], born 25th of August, 1816; died when quite young.

vi, Thomas Sim[7]. See 61.

## Colonel John Lee.

42. John[6], the youngest child of Thomas Sim Lee[5] (Thomas[4], Philip[3], Richard[2], Richard[1]) and Mary Digges, his wife, was born the 30th of January, 1788, and died the 17th of May, 1871; he was married, on the 5th of June, 1832, to Harriet, daughter of Charles and Harriet (Chew) Carroll.

Col. John Lee, as he was always known in his latter years, was educated at Harvard, and later studied law. He resided in Washington during his last years. A writer in one of the papers of that city has said of him: "Colonel Lee was a warm Federalist in early life. After the war of 1812, he united himself with Adams and subsequently with the Whig party. He served in Congress from the Frederick, Md., district in 1823–5, and was the chairman of the House committee appointed to escort the Marquis de Lafayette from Frederick City to Washington. He was then thirty-seven years of age, and one of the most elegant men in America. As master of ceremonies in the festivities which ensued upon the arrival of the Marquis in Washington, Colonel Lee was especially distinguished. Col. Lee, during his service in Congress, became warmly attached to Mr. Clay and followed his fortunes with devotion until the last. He was his trusted and confidential friend, and in that capacity made frequent journeys throughout the country. In 1860, he supported Bell and Everett. In later years of his life he espoused the cause of the Conservatives and never ceased to feel a deep interest in their success. Colonel Lee was a most delightful companion; his conversational powers were of the first order—his memory strong and accurate. His life, extending from the adoption of the Constitution to the present day, covered one of the most remarkable eras in the history of the world. He remembered the last years of the administration of Washington—the campaigns of Suwarrow and Napoleon in Italy—Marengo, Arcola, and the battle of the Pyramids; the days of non-intercourse and embargo; the death of Hamilton; the trial of Burr. His temper was admirable; adversity could not sour him nor freeze the genial current of his soul. In religion he was a Roman Catholic and a sincere worshipper at its ancient altars. A native of the South, there was no provincialism in his composition. Col. Lee was one of the pioneers of the Chesapeake and Ohio Canal and of the Baltimore & Ohio Railroad, and never ceased, even at the advanced age of four score, to evince a deep interest in all the internal improvements of his native State."

John and Harriet (Carroll) Lee had four children:

i, MARY DIGGES[7], born —— 1834; married Dr. Jonathan Letterman, U. S. Army, and had: Mary Catharine and Ann Madeleine.

ii, HARRIET CHEW[7], died in early infancy.

iii, CHARLES CARROLL[7]. See 62.

iv, THOMAS SIM[7], born —— 1842; lives in Washington, and is rector of the Roman Catholic Church of St. Matthias.

## DR. GEORGE LEE.

43. GEORGE[6], the only son of George Lee[5] (Thomas Ludwell[4], Thomas[3], Richard[2], Richard[1]) and Eveline Byrd Beverley, his wife, was born about 1796, for his father (in his will dated the 28th of October, 1802) desired his own brother, Thomas Ludwell Lee, should assume the guardianship of George when he "arrives at the age of seven years." Dr. Lee died in 1858, probably in February of that year; he resided at Leesburg. He was married, on the 19th of July, 1827, to Sarah Moore, the daughter of Richard H. and Orra (Moore) Henderson, a lawyer of Leesburg; Mrs. Lee died at that place the 16th of February, 1888.

George Lee's will was dated the 13th of November, 1851, and probated, in Loudoun county, on the 9th of March, 1858.

I, George Lee, of the town of Leesburg in the county of Loudoun and State of Virginia, do declare this to be my last will, hereby revoking all former wills made by me. 1st. I direct that all my just debts be paid and to accomplish this object I direct my Executrix hereinafter mentioned to sell such portions of my real estate as she may think proper; after applying to the said debts the proceeds of such portions of my personal estate as she may not wish to retain, and I give her full power and authority to retain or sell such parts of my personal estate as she may think proper. 2nd. After the payment of my debts I devise and bequeath to my beloved wife Sally M. Lee all my estate of every description during her widowhood, and if she marries again it shall be divided as follows: one third shall be held by the same Sally during her lifetime, and the other two thirds shall be equally divided among my children, who may be alive and the descendants of such of them as may be dead; said descendants to have such share as their parents would have taken if alive; the third given to my wife, in the event of her marriage, shall at her death be divided in like manner, with the two thirds given in this clause to my children and their descendants. 3rd. And if my wife should remain a widow till the period of her death, I direct that all of my estate of every description shall be then equally divided among my children who shall then be alive and the descendants of such as may be dead, the said descendants to take such share as their parents would have taken if alive. 4th. I hereby empower and authorize my Executrix to sell and convey whensoever she may deem it expedient to do so, the whole or any part of my real estate and invest the proceeds in stocks of the United States or the State of Virginia, or loan them upon good real estate security if no such stocks can be obtained on what she may deem reasonable terms; and the said proceeds shall be held and enjoyed by the same persons and for the same interests as is hereinbefore directed in regard to my estate in the second and third clauses of this will. But the purchasers of said real estate shall not in any event be responsible for the application or investment of the purchase money. 5th. I constitute and appoint my said wife Sally M. Lee sole Executrix of this my last will and direct that she may be permitted to qualify without giving security. In witness whereof, etc.

Dr. George and Sally Moore (Henderson) Lee had a very large family, numbering, it is said, twenty-three children. Of these, a daughter, Orra, married John M. Orr; another, Maria, died single, as did also a third, Elizabeth Clagett; Evelyn Byrd married Thomas Delany. No dates of births, etc., known. Besides these daughters, Dr. George Lee left:

i, GEORGE[7]. See 63.
ii, ARCHIBALD HENDERSON[7], who died unmarried.

## REV. RICHARD HENRY LEE.

44. RICHARD HENRY[6], the eldest son of Ludwell Lee[5] (Richard Henry[4], Thomas[3], Richard[2], Richard[1]) and Flora Lee, his first wife, was born the 23d of June, 1794, and died at Washington, Pa., the 3d of January, 1865. He was twice married, and had issue by each marriage. Mr. Lee was educated at Dickinson College, Pa., where he graduated with the honors of his class. He then studied law with the late Judge Thomas Duncan, of Carlisle, Pa., and began the practice of his profession in Loudoun county. While residing at Leesburg he edited the Memoirs of his grandfather, Richard Henry Lee, and of his great-uncle, Dr. Arthur Lee, which were issued in 1825 and 1829 respectively. He was also at one time Mayor of Leesburg. Mr. Lee was a scholar, especially accomplished in classical literature and belles-lettres; he read Greek and Latin authors with ease, and, having a fine memory, treasured up their beauties for frequent reference. In 1833 he was called to the Chair of Languages at Washington College, Pennsylvania, and in 1837 was transferred to that of Belles-

Lettres. During his occupancy of these professorships he continued the practice of law. But in 1854 he gave up the law and resigned his professorship to begin the study of theology, with a view to entering the ministry of the Episcopal Church, which he did in 1858, and assumed charge of Trinity Church, Washington, Pa. He was in charge of that church at the time of his death.

Writing to the late Cassius F. Lee, Jr., under date of 18th of November, 1861, Mr. Lee told of his disposal of the various MSS. used by him in the preparation of the Memoirs. He wrote:

"My Dear Cousin: When your letter of the 24th ult. reached here I was in Philadelphia, and since my return I have been suffering from a severe cold, which, together with current duties, has delayed this reply.

"I am happy to see from your letter that you are cherishing a veneration for the great and wise patriots of the Revolution, and greatly regret it is out of my power to gratify your desire to possess their autographs. I presented to the Athenæum in Pha. all the MSS. from which I composed our Grandfather's Life; and to the University of Cambridge all those I used in the Life of our Uncle Arthur. Some years after I presented to the University of Virginia all the rest. I had selected some for my sons; but the many applications continually made to me, from every part of this country and Europe, led me to give away, one after another, every MSS., until I have *not one* left, to the excessive regret, now, of my sons and myself.

"Present my affectionate regards to your Father and Uncle Charles. You will greatly oblige me by letting me hear about Cousin Edmund I. Lee and his family, and of Cousin R. H. Lee. In these deplorable times I am anxious to hear of them. I hope your mother has recovered. I heard in Trenton, N. J., of her illness."

Richard Henry Lee had by Mary Duncan Mahon, his first wife, the following issue:

i, Mary Ann[7], born in 1819; died the 13th of March, 1856; married in 1854 Isaac Winston, but had no issue.

ii, Flora[7], born ——, 1821; died —— November, 1863; unmarried.

iii, Richard Henry[7]; died in infancy.

iv, Frances Hayne[7], born ——, 1823; died the 28th of July, 1885; married Isaac Winston; no issue.

Richard Henry Lee had by his second wife, Anna Eden Jordan, of St. Mary's, Maryland, the following five children:

v, Samuel A.[7], born ——, 1829; died in early infancy.

vi, RICHARD HENRY[7]. See 64.
vii, PHILIP LUDWELL[7], born the 3d of July, 1835; died unmarried on the 25th of December, 1889; was a Captain in U. S. Army.
viii, JOHN LLEWELLYN[7], born the 4th of July, 1838; died the 13th of January, 1870.
ix, FRANCIS LIGHTFOOT[7]. See 65.

## REAR-ADMIRAL SAMUEL PHILLIPS LEE.

45. SAMUEL PHILLIPS[6], the eldest son of Francis Lightfoot Lee[5] (Richard Henry[4], Thomas[3], Richard[2], Richard[1]) and Jane Fitzgerald, his second wife, was born at "Sully," Fairfax county, the 13th of February, 1812, and still survives, residing with his wife, at Silver Spring, Md., near Washington City. Entering the Navy at an early age, he has spent almost his entire life in the service of his country; a brief *résumé* can only be given here:

He was "appointed *Midshipman* from Virginia, November 22, 1825; ordered to sloop-of-war 'Hornet,' West India Station, February 7, 1827; ordered to line-of-battle-ship 'Delaware,' and transferred in the Mediterranean as Captain's Aid to frigate 'Java,' August 24, 1827; ordered to Norfolk School, Virginia, October 16, 1830. Promoted to *Passed Midshipman*, June 4, 1831, and ordered to Navy Yard, Boston, July 28, 1831. Ordered to frigate 'Brandywine,' Pacific Squadron, as Second Master, and transferred to the 'Vincennes' as Acting Lieutenant and additional navigator, April 17, 1834. Promoted to *Lieutenant*, February 9, 1837; ordered to Exploring Expedition, July 19, 1837; ordered to West India Squadron, December 13, 1839; ordered to receiving-ship at Alexandria, Virginia, December 8, 1841; ordered to Coast Survey, April 10, 1842; ordered to command Coast Survey schooner 'Vanderbuilt,' August 4, 1844; ordered to Navy Yard, Pensacola, Florida, November 11, 1844; ordered to command Coast Survey schooner 'Nautilus,' March 9, 1846; ordered to command Coast Survey brig 'Washington,' December 29, 1846, on his own application to participate in the Mexican war; was present at the capture of Tobasco, and subsequently transferred to the command of the Coast Survey steamer 'Legare.' He always considered coast-survey duty as one of the best schools of naval practice, and advocated its return to the administration of the Navy Department. Ordered to command the brig 'Dolphin' on special service, to make deep-sea soundings, try currents, search for vigias, etc. (report published by Congress, 1854), July 3, 1851. Detached and ordered to duty on wind- and current-charts, July 7, 1852.

S. P. Lee

MRS. S. PHILLIPS LEE.

Promoted to *Commander*, September 14, 1855. Ordered as member of Examining Board, March 12, 1858; ordered to command sloop-of-war 'Vandalia,' with orders to the East Indies, November 1, 1860. When he learned, at the Cape of Good Hope, of the rebellion, assuming the risk of acting against orders, he brought his ship back, and was assigned to the blockade off Charleston, South Carolina, where he succeeded in maintaining it with the 'Vandalia,' a sailing vessel, when her steam consort was blown off. Before the return of the consort, a British steam-gunboat ventured in to inspect the blockade, and finding it, under such conditions of weather, actual and close, foreign scrutiny was terminated. Ordered to command the sloop of-war 'Oneida,' January 20, 1862, and to report to Admiral Farragut. In the expedition against New Orleans, he commanded the advance division below the forts, Jackson and St. Philip. In the gunboat actions, when the gunboats took part in the bombardment, to draw the fire from the bomb-vessels, the 'Oneida' was at one time engaged alone with both forts. In the action of the passage of the forts, the 'Oneida' was one of the three vessels first to encounter the enemy's fleet, and she relieved the 'Varuna' by driving off the two rams which had rammed her, forcing their burning and captured the commander of the 'Governor Moore.' The 'Oneida' participated in the capture of the Chalmette batteries below New Orleans; became advance guard above the city. For a time Lee commanded the advance division below Vicksburg and participated in both passages of the Vicksburg batteries, the 'Oneida' being the second in line on each occasion. Promoted to *Captain*, July 16, 1862. Appointed *Acting Rear-Admiral*, September 2, 1862, and ordered to the command of the North Atlantic Blockading Squadron. Was engaged in blockading the coasts of Virginia and North Carolina, and zealously co-operating with armies in defense of Norfolk, Newbern, and Washington, fighting with their iron-clads and heavy fortifications in Trent's Reach, and their field-batteries along Grant's line of communications on the James River, always securely held while Admiral Lee was in command. For two years he fulfilled the arduous duties of his command, perfecting and maintaining a vast blockade.

"The dangerous navigation of the North Carolina coast, owing to the long shoals of Cape Fear, between the two ports into Wilmington; the nearness of the British ports of Bermuda and Nassau, from which steamers of excellent form and great speed, of low build and gray color, ran at night; the immense profits tempting the risks, made the blockade an undertaking of the greatest difficulty, and yet the Confederacy was, in effect, isolated, by several girdles of cruisers (a system originated by Rear-Admiral Lee), from foreign recruits, supplies, and munitions of war. Of the total number of blockade-running steamers captured or destroyed by this squadron, sixty-five in all, fifty-four were captured or destroyed by the fleet under Admiral Lee's command. Besides blockading, the main duty of the squadron, it, independently or in co-operation with the army, was engaged in ninety-one actions and expeditions during this period. The efficiency and importance of this service, together with the small loss from shipwreck on so dangerous a coast, have excited the approving comment of foreign military observers. Detached and ordered to command of Mississippi Squadron, October 21, 1864. The efficiency of this squadron was maintained, notwithstanding the withdrawal of a large number of experienced officers. Lee's movement up the Cumberland to support General Thomas was in co-operation with the army against the apprehended crossing of the river by Hood and his marching to the Ohio. The flag-ship was stopped at Clarksville by the low stage of water, which was still falling on Harpeth Shoals; the river rising barely enough in time to allow Fitch to move the gunboats at Nashville and participate in the defeat of Hood, but not enough to make Harpeth Shoals passable until three days later. Army communications were kept open and operations supported with vigor and effect, and the lower Mississippi was vigilantly guarded against the intervention of the trans-Mississippi Confederate forces. The operation of the squadron on the Tennessee River prevented Hood on his retreat from crossing where the Tennessee was navigable, forcing him to cross six miles above the head of navigation on Muscle Shoals, the rocky barrier that effectually closes navigation for thirty miles above the close piers of Florence Bridge, where he had previously crossed. Detached from the Mississippi Squadron, August 14, 1865, which, after much arduous labor, had been disbanded, vessels laid up or sent to other squadrons, officers and men discharged or transferred. Promoted to *Commodore*, July 25, 1866; ordered as President of Examining Board, August 7, 1866; ordered as member of Examining Board to meet at Philadelphia, March 6, 1868; ordered as President of Examining Board, April 17, 1868; ordered as President of Court-Martial at New York, May 29, 1868; ordered as President of Board of Examiners, February 13, 1869; ordered as member of a Board to examine the Atlantic Navy Yards and was author of the report to improve them, March 10, 1869; ordered in charge of Signal Service, Washington, D. C., October 13, 1869. Promoted *Rear-Admiral*, April 22, 1870; ordered to special duty at Navy Department, June 27, 1870; ordered to special duty at Navy Department, June 27, 1870; ordered to command North Atlantic Squadron, August 9, 1870; detached, August 15, 1872. Retired, February 13, 1873." (Hamersley, *Records of Living Officers of the U. S. Navy and Marine Corps.* 1890.)

Sincerely Yours,

S. P. Lee

Admiral Lee was married, on the 27th of April, 1843, to Elizabeth, daughter of Francis Preston Blair, and Eliza Violet Gist, his wife, who was a daughter of Col. Nathaniel Gist. Francis Preston Blair was born at Abingdon, Va., the 12th of April, 1791, and died at Silver Spring, Md., the 18th of October, 1876; of his long and well-known career as lawyer, politician, and statesman, it is unnecessary to allude in this place. His eldest son, Montgomery Blair, was born in Franklin county, Kentucky, the 10th of May, 1813, and died at Silver Spring, Md., the 27th of July, 1883; he graduated at West Point, served in the Seminole war, resigned in 1836 to take up the study of the law, settled at St. Louis, was Mayor of that city in 1842, Judge of Court of Common Pleas in 1843, removed to Maryland in 1852, and served as Postmaster-General from 1861 to 1864. The second son, Francis Preston, Jr., was born at Lexington, Ky., the 19th of February, 1821, and died at St. Louis, Mo., the 8th of July, 1875; was a prominent politician, served in volunteer forces during late civil war, rising to the rank of Brigadier-General, and was U. S. Senator from Missouri in 1871.

Admiral Lee has only one child, a son:

i, FRANCIS PRESTON BLAIR[7]. See 66.

## MAJOR JOHN FITZGERALD LEE.

46. JOHN FITZGERALD[6], the second son of Francis Lightfoot Lee[5] (Richard Henry[4], Thomas[3], Richard[2], Richard[1]), and Jane Fitzgerald, his second wife, was born at "Sully," Fairfax county, the 5th of May, 1813; died at St. Louis, Mo., the 17th June, 1884, and was buried in the Catholic cemetery in that city. He was married, on the 29th of April, 1845, to Eleanor Anne, daughter of William M. and Anne Darnall (Smith) Hill, of Prince George's county, Md., where she was born; she died the 24th of April, 1891.

John Fitzgerald Lee entered West Point as a cadet on 1st of July, 1830, and graduated in 1834; was appointed brevet 2d lieutenant, 1st artillery, on 1st of July, 1834; 2d lieutenant on 23d of July, 1835; served in Florida against the Seminole Indians, as captain in the regiment of mounted Creek volunteers; made 1st lieutenant 1st artillery, 17th of December, 1836; brevet captain, 27th of January, 1837, "for gallantry and good conduct in the war against the Florida Indians;" 1st lieutenant of ordnance, 9th of July, 1838; served as ordnance officer at Little Rock, 1838–40; at Washington, 1841–42; commanded the arsenal at Fort Monroe, 1846–47, the Washington arsenal, 1847–48, and later at St. Louis; was made captain of ordnance, 3d of March, 1847; appointed Judge Advocate of the Army with headquarters at Washington, 1849–62, with brevet rank of major of staff.

Such is the condensed official record of his army life; from a member of his family a few further details have been gathered. While stationed at Fort Macon, N. C., he devoted himself zealously to the study of the law, for which he had a marked aptitude; later, his proficiency in the law, especially in all questions that pertained to courts-martial, became generally recognized and indicated him as the officer best fitted for the position of Judge Advocate of the Army, when that office was created. This post he filled with signal ability, untiring zeal, and industry, making every effort to enforce discipline with firmness and strict attention to the rules and regulations of the service, but never with undue harshness; always doing his best to promote the efficiency and maintain the honor of the army, in which he took great pride. The outbreak of the Civil War found him in this post, which was greatly to his taste and pleasure, living at his own home in Washington, and at a convenient distance from his tobacco plantations in Calvert and Prince George's counties, Md.; to these plantations he made frequent visits, supervising the farming operations, and caring for the welfare of his slaves. After the struggle actually began between the sections, his sympathies and affection went with the South, though his judgment convinced him from the outset of the hopelessness of its contest against the greatly superior numbers and resources of the North. In 1862, he retired to the "Lodge," in Prince George's county, Md., which estate had been in his wife's family since it was granted them by the first Lord Baltimore and is still owned by his children. During the war, the negroes of Maryland could readily leave their masters, but, of Major Lee's slaves, not one old servant deserted him; the young men ran away, leaving their wives, children or aged parents to be cared for by the kind old master, and, after the war, even they returned to the old plantation. In 1867, Major Lee was chosen a member of the Maryland Constitutional Convention, and was a member of the State Senate in the next Assembly. In 1873, he removed to Washington for the winters. About a year before his death, he removed with his wife and daughter to St. Louis, where three of his sons were already residing.

Major Lee was a man above the middle height, of good physique, and erect military carriage. His complexion was ruddy, his head large, and covered with a thick suit of curly hair, which was always closely cut, and which in his youth was red, but later on was brown. His manner was prompt and decisive, and his language singularly terse and vigorous. His intellect was clear; and he had the prudence which his family motto enjoins; but he was extremely generous, and his sympathies were of the quickest and tenderest character; impulsive, but reliable. No man had a heartier aversion for a mean, a cruel, or a dishonorable action. His fondness for litera-

JOHN FRITZGERALD LEE.

ture was something very genuine and keen, especially for the classical models. His reading was very extensive, and a memory such as is rarely met with placed a large part of what he had read at his command in the words of the author. He was an easy, forcible writer; and a most charming, instructive, and witty conversationalist, absolutely free from ostentation, pedantry, and superciliousness; alike considerate and kind to gentle and simple, clerk and clown. His attainments and his natural gifts were accompanied by such kindness and sympathy as never to produce a depressing effect on the dullest or most envious. In fact, there were scarcely any persons so inferior that his appreciative nature could not find some merit in them; and his cheery laugh, and cordial while dignified manner, brought a glow of liveliness and pleasure to all who were thrown in contact with him, no matter how different might be their temperaments or conditions.

The following notice of Major Lee, written by an old army friend, appeared in one of the St. Louis papers:

"The grave will close to-day over the remains of this gifted man. He was little known in St. Louis, where he died, but for nearly fifty years he has been a prominent member of society in Washington City, and his name is a household word with all the other officers of the United States Army.

"He was born May 5th, 1813. He was a grandson of Richard Henry Lee, the colleague and almost the equal in eloquence of Patrick Henry in the Congress of 1776. He was admitted into the United States Military Academy as a cadet from Virginia in 1830, and graduated with distinguished honor in 1834. Commissioned a lieutenant of artillery, he was afterward attached to the ordnance corps, and stationed at various fortresses and arsenals, according to the exigencies of the service, until 1849. During this interval he served one campaign in Florida, in the Seminole War.

"He had repeatedly been detailed as Judge Advocate, and had manifested signal capacity for the duties of that detail in courts-martial and courts of inquiry. In 1849 the office of Judge Advocate of the Army of the United States, with the rank of major of cavalry, was created by the act of March 2d, and with the unanimous approval of his brother officers, he was appointed to fill that office. The important and delicate duties thus confided to him were discharged in an exemplary and most acceptable manner until July, 1862. Only those who were conversant with military affairs can estimate the services he thus rendered to the discipline and moral tone of the army.

"When the civil war broke out, Major Lee was placed in a painful and delicate situation. He condemned secession unreservedly, both as a political heresy and a blunder in statesmanship; but he could not make up his mind to bear arms against his friends and relatives in Virginia. While he disapproved of their views and their conduct, he could not divest himself of some sympathy for their persons. He was, therefore, entirely out of harmony with those who regarded any such sentiments as a crime, and by the act of the 17th of July, 1862, he was legislated out of office. He thereupon retired from the army and has since resided in Washington City or its neighborhood. He had a farm in Prince George's county, Md., and there he passed all but the winter months of each year. Those he spent in Washington City with his family. He married in 1845 Miss Hill, a lady of Prince George's county, who survives him, and of this marriage there were five children, a daughter and four sons, who also survive. Of these sons, the three eldest, William H. Lee, Arthur Lee, and John F. Lee, Jr., are, and have long been well-known and respected citizens of St. Louis.

"Maj. Lee was a man of unusual capacity, improved by extensive and well-directed reading. His vivacity, wit, and cheerfulness rendered him a delightful companion, and these qualities, with his elevated and generous spirit, made him a cherished friend to all who had the privilege of friendship with him. Seldom is a man of equal ability to be seen more entirely free from ambition. He was a man of most scrupulous integrity. He loved his family and his friends and found his happiness in their service and society; but from all the weakness of vanity he seems to have been altogether free. Like many who have been in military life until past middle age, he considered himself unfit for civil pursuits when he left the army. Only by an irksome effort did he imagine that he could succeed in the attempt to form new habits of life, and as in one sense no necessity existed for overcoming his aversion to these new methods the effort was not made.

"His departure makes in his family circle a void which is unspeakable and irreparable. To his few surviving contemporaries, while it renders their remaining days more dreary, it is at the same time a warning that he has only by a brief interval preceded them to the silent shore. One who has for more than fifty years known and loved him offers this tribute to his memory."

"St. Louis, June 18, 1884."

NOTE.—"This account is tinged by Col. Gantt's own views, but does my dear brother great injustice through misapprehension of his opinion and, indeed, intentions. He wrote me at the time: 'Maryland will secede, and I am waiting till then to resign and join her forces; but I shall give our people the same advice Robert is giving the Virginians, to act wholly on the defensive till such time as the Southern Army is strong enough to measure itself with the Northern.'

"And often did he dispute this point with our beloved Phill, when his brother would tell him: 'There was no Virginia in my commission, but only the United States.' So differently did the same subject strike minds of equal vigor, and unselfish souls moved only by the highest considerations of honor and patriotism.

(Signed) "FRANCES LEE PETTIT."

John Fitzgerald and Eleanor Ann (Hill) Lee had five children:

i, WILLIAM HILL[7]. See 67.

ii, ARTHUR[7], born the 1st of June, 1847; is unmarried; practices law at St. Louis.

iii, JOHN FITZGERALD[7], born the 29th of June, 1848; is unmarried; practices law at St. Louis, being in partnership with his brother.

iv, ANNE[7], born the 24th of April, 1851; was married on the 8th of January, 1885, to Henry Harrison, of Leesburg; son of Henry T. and Elizabeth Mary (Jones) Harrison. (See 34, i; 36, i.)

v, FRANCIS PHILLIPS[7], born the 8th of May, 1856; resides at Boston; is unmarried.

### MAJOR HENRY LEE.

47. HENRY[6], the eldest surviving son of Henry Lee[5] (Henry[4], Henry[3], Richard[2], Richard[1]) and Matilda Lee, his first wife, was born at Stratford, Westmoreland county, the 28th of May, 1787; died at Paris, France, on the 30th of January, 1837; married, about 30th of March, 1817, Anne R., daughter of Daniel McCarty, of Westmoreland county;[1] he graduated at William and Mary College in 1808; was appointed Major of the 36th Regiment by President Madison the 8th of April, 1813; served on the Canadian frontier on the staff of General James Wilkinson, and later on that of General George Izard. "On his return from Canada he met in New York Lord Jeffrey, the 'Edinburgh' reviewer, and both men were much sought after in society on account of their brilliant conversational powers." Major Lee was an ardent and influential supporter of General Jackson in his canvass for the Presidency, in whose behalf he wrote several essays, and was rewarded with the appointment of Consul to Algiers. But, as his ap-

[1] Anne R. McCarty made a marriage contract on the 29th of March, 1817, with Henry Lee, Jr. The contract mentions that Anne and Elizabeth were co-heirs of their father, Daniel McCarty. (Westmoreland records.)

pointment was rejected by the Senate, Major Lee left Algiers after a short residence and travelled through Italy on his way to Paris. While on this trip he met "Madame Mère," the mother of Napoleon, for whom he entertained an extravagant admiration, as shown in the following note to Madame Bonaparte:

"Rome, 2d April, 1830. As I feel the most profound respect for Madame, the Mother of Napoleon, that one being can entertain for another, I beg leave to offer for her acceptance the inclosed autograph letter from Gen'l Washington to my Father, considering this precious memorial of the American hero and patriot well bestowed in being placed in the hands of a lady great in her own character and illustrious in her offspring; especially in having given birth to the greatest warrior and the most generous conqueror and friend that ever existed."

Besides his review of Jefferson's writings, Major Lee began, while residing at Paris, a history of Napoleon's Italian campaign, but completed only one volume, which was published after his death.

## Charles Carter Lee.

48. Charles Carter[6], the second son of Henry Lee[5] (Henry[4], Henry[3], Richard[2], Richard[1]) and Anne Hill Carter, his second wife, was born at Stratford, Westmoreland county, on the 8th of November, 1798; he died the 21st of March, 1871, and was buried at his home, "Windsor Forest," in Powhatan county. Carter Lee entered Harvard College in 1816, and graduated second in his class in 1819; he possessed a mind of a very superior order, had a thorough classical education, a most retentive memory, and a keen wit. Being an omnivorous reader, a brilliant conversationalist, his society was most entertaining, and in consequence he was greatly sought after at all social gatherings. He was a lawyer by profession and practiced first at Washington City, then in Floyd county, Va., next in Mississippi, where he resided for several years; later he removed to Hardy county, and finally settled in Powhatan. Some verses of his, known as the *Virginia Georgics*, written for the "Hole and Corner Club of Powhatan," were published by the club in 1858.

Mr. Lee was married, on the 13th of May, 1847, to Lucy Penn, daughter of George Taylor, of "Horn Quarter," King William county, and Catharine Randolph, his wife. George Taylor was of the same family as President Taylor. The first of this family to settle in Virginia was James Taylor, who came from Carlisle, England, and settled on the shores of the Chesapeake in 16—. By his second wife, Mary Gregory, James Taylor had three daughters and two sons. John, his youngest child, married Catharine Pendleton, and had ten children; of these, James Taylor married Ann Pollard, and was the father of the well-known Hon. John Taylor, of Caroline. The Hon. John Taylor married his cousin, Lucy, daughter of John Penn (the Signer of the Declaration of Independence from North Carolina), who was born in Caroline county, Virginia, and was the only son of Moses Penn and Caroline Taylor, his wife; she was a daughter of the John Taylor and Catharine Pendleton above mentioned. George Taylor was the second son of the Hon. John Taylor. The first Taylor, in Virginia, had by his first wife a son, James, who married Martha Thompson, and had nine children; among these was a son, Zachary Taylor, who married Elizabeth, daughter of Hancock Lee by his second wife, Sarah Allerton; from this union came the father of President Taylor. A further notice of the Taylors is given under Hancock Lee[2].

Charles Carter and Lucy Penn (Taylor) had the following named children:

i, GEORGE TAYLOR[7]. See 68.
ii, HENRY[7]. See 69.
iii, ROBERT RANDOLPH[7]. See 70.
iv, WILLIAMS CARTER[7], born the 8th of September, 1852; died, unmarried, on the 21st of June, 1882. A life of promise suddenly cut off by a railroad accident.
v, MILDRED[7], born on the 20th of November, 1857; was married, on the 4th of February, 1888, to Dr. John Taylor Francis, who died ——, leaving one daughter, Mildred Lee Francis. Dr. Francis graduated in 1883 at the Medical School of the University of New York, and practiced his profession at Norfolk.
vi, CATHARINE RANDOLPH[7], born the 27th of August, 1865; was married, on the 10th of July, 1892, to Dr. John Guerrant, of Franklin county, and has a daughter, Elizabeth Moore Guerrant.
vii, JOHN PENN[7], born 11th of September, 1867, is a lawyer by profession, being a member of the firm of Dillard & Lee, of Rocky Mount, Va.

Mr. Lee is the fortunate possessor of the old family portraits of the first three generations in Virginia; Colonel Richard and his wife; Richard, Jr., and his wife, and Thomas, of Stratford and his wife. He kindly allowed them to be photographed for use in this volume.

## THE RANDOLPH FAMILY.

Arms: Gules, on a cross or, five mullets of the field.
Crest: An antelope's head erased or, in its mouth a baton.

Of the many distinguished families of Virginia, perhaps none has produced more men of marked and brilliant abilities than that of Randolph. They are descended from William Randolph, of "Turkey Island," who was a member of the House of Burgesses, of the Council, and a person of great influence in the Colony; he was born in Yorkshire, England, in the year 1651, and came to Virginia about 1674; married, about 1680, Mary, the daughter of Henry Isham, of Bermuda Hundred, James River. Col. Randolph died the 10th of April, 1711, leaving seven sons and two daughters. From these sons a very numerous family has descended, of whom only a brief outline can be given in this connection. Of the two daughters, Elizabeth married Richard Bland, and was the mother of Mary Bland, who married Henry Lee, of "Lee Hall," Westmoreland; the other daughter, Mary Randolph, married William Stith, and was the mother of William Stith, the early historian of Virginia, and once President of William and Mary College. From the five older sons are descended the later Randolphs of Virginia:

i, WILLIAM, of "Turkey Island," also known as "Councillor Randolph," married Elizabeth, daughter of Peter Beverley, of Gloucester, and Eliza Peyton, his wife, and had issue: Beverley, Peter, William, and Elizabeth. Of these, Peter (1708–1768) married Lucy, daughter of Robert Bolling, settled at "Chatsworth," Henrico county, and had issue: William, Beverley, Robert, and Anne, who married William Fitzhugh, of "Chatham," and were the parents of Mary Lee Fitzhugh, who married George Washington Parke Custis, of Arlington. The third son, William, also of "Wilton," married Anne, eldest daughter of Benjamin and Anne (Carter) Harrison, and had five children, among them Peyton (second of the name), who married his first cousin, Lucy Harrison, a daughter of Governor Benjamin Harrison, the Signer, and Elizabeth Bassett, his wife; their daughter, Catharine Randolph, married George Taylor, whose daughter, Lucy Penn Taylor, married Charles Carter Lee, as stated. Mrs. Lee was descended from two Signers of the Declaration of Independence—John Penn and Benjamin Harrison, while her husband was related to two others.

ii, THOMAS, of "Tuckahoe," the second son, married (it is said) Judith Churchill, and had one son and two daughters; the youngest daughter, Mary, married William Keith, from which union came the mother of the great Chief Justice, John Marshall. The son, William Randolph, married Maria Judith, daughter of the Hon. Mann Page, of "Rosewell;" they were the grandparents of Thomas Mann Randolph, Governor of Virginia, 1819–21, who married Martha, daughter of Thomas Jefferson, of "Monticello," and has a large number of descendants.

iii, ISHAM, of "Dungeness," was the third son of the immigrant; he married Jane Rogers, of London, and had a daughter, Jane, who married (1738) Peter Jefferson, and was the mother of President Thomas Jefferson, of "Monticello;" another daughter, Susannah, married, about 1777, Carter Harrison, the ancestor of the late mayor of Chicago.

iv, SIR JOHN was the fourth son of the immigrant; he was born in 1693, and died on the 15th of March, 1757; married Susannah, a daughter of Peter Beverley, of Gloucester county, and had: Beverley, Peyton, and John. Sir John was educated abroad, studied law at Gray's Inn; was later the Speaker of the House of Burgesses. His son, Peyton, one of the most prominent patriots of the Revolution, was born at "Tazewell Hall," near Williamsburg, in 1721, and died at Philadelphia, while attending Congress, on the 22d of October, 1775; he had been educated at William and Mary, studied law at the Inner Temple, London, and was appointed Attorney-General for Virginia in 1748; was chairman of the committee of correspondence for Virginia; presided over the Convention of 1774; was elected to the first Continental Congress, which met that year, and was chosen its presiding officer; had been Speaker of the House of Burgesses. He married Elizabeth Harrison, second daughter of Benjamin and Anne (Carter) Harrison, but had no children. His brother, John Randolph, succeeded him in the office of attorney-general; he was also educated at William and Mary; was a lawyer of great ability; he espoused the cause of England against the colonies and went to England to live, where he died; he married Ariana, a daughter of Edmund Jenings, of

Annapolis, Md., and at one time attorney-general for that province; his son, Edmund Randolph, was the first Attorney-General of the United States, and also Governor of Virginia; he married Elizabeth, a daughter of Robert Carter Nicholas, and left issue.

v, RICHARD, of "Curl's Neck," the fifth son of the immigrant to leave issue in Virginia, married Jane, a daughter of John Bolling, and Mary Kennon, his wife; Jane Bolling was fourth in descent from Pocahontas. Richard Randolph had: Richard, Mary, Jane, and John. Of these John married Frances, daughter of Theodorick Bland, and was the father of the celebrated John Randolph of "Roanoke." The latter was born on the 3d of June, 1773, and died, unmarried, at Philadelphia, on the 24th of May, 1833. His remains were interred at Hollywood Cemetery, Richmond.

## CAPTAIN SYDNEY SMITH LEE.

49. SYDNEY SMITH $^{6}$, third son of Henry Lee $^{5}$ (Henry $^{4}$, Henry $^{3}$, Richard $^{2}$, Richard $^{1}$) and Anne Hill Carter, his second wife, was born the 2d of September, 1802, at Camden, New Jersey, where his mother happened to be visiting a friend; he died on the 22d of July, 1869. Upon graduating at the naval academy, he was appointed a midshipman, 30th of December, 1820; promoted lieutenant, 17th of May, 1828; a commander on 4th ot June, 1850, and *resigned*[1] on the 28th of April, 1861, to enter the service of the Confederate States.

A daughter of General Robert E. Lee has thus written of him:[2] "No one who ever saw him can forget his beautiful face, charming personality, and grace of manner, which, joined to a nobility of character and goodness of heart, attracted all who came into contact with him, and made him the most generally beloved and popular of men. This was especially so with regard to women, to whom his conduct was that of a *preux chevalier*, the most chivalric and courteous; and, having no daughters of his own, he turned with the tenderest affection to the daughters of his brother Robert. His public service of more than thirty years in the navy of the United States is well known. He entered it as a boy of fifteen, and faithfully served his country by land and sea in many climes and on many oceans. He was in Japan with Commodore Perry, commanding his flagship, when that inaccessible country was practically opened to the commerce of the

[1] The official record states that he was "dismissed" from the service, thus intending to imply disgrace. As no officer of the army or navy can be dismissed excepting upon the proper judgment of a court-martial, this record is simply an exhibition of petty malice.

[2] *General Lee*, by Fitzhugh Lee, pp. 18, 19.

world. He was Commandant of the Naval Academy at Annapolis, and afterward in command of the navy yard at Philadelphia. When the war of secession began he was stationed at Washington, but when Virginia seceded he did not hesitate to abandon the comforts and security of the present and ambitions of the future, and cast his lot with his native State in a war in which, from the very nature of things, there could be but little hope for a naval officer. Uninfluenced, then, by hope of either fame or fortune, he sadly parted with the friends and comrades of a lifetime, including General Scott, who had been likewise devoted to him as he was to his brother, and for four years served the Southern Confederacy with the same ardor and energy and unselfishness that he had previously given to the whole country. When the end came he accepted the situation with characteristic resignation and fortitude."

During the Mexican war, Sydney Smith met his brother, Robert, at Vera Cruz; in a letter home, the soldier told of his work in placing a battery in position, and added: "The first day this battery opened, Smith served one of the guns. I had constructed the battery, and was there to direct its fire. No matter where I turned, my eyes reverted to him, and I stood by his gun whenever I was not wanted elsewhere. Oh! I felt awfully, and am at a loss what I should have done, had he been cut down before me. I thank God that he was saved. He preserved his usual cheerfulness, and I could see his white teeth through all the smoke and din of the fire. I had placed three 32 and three 68-pound guns in position. . . . Their fire was terrific, and the shells thrown from our battery were constant and regular discharges, so beautiful in their flight and so destructive in their fall. It was awful! My heart bled for the inhabitants. The soldiers I did not care so much for, but it was terrible to think of the women and children. . . . I heard from Smith to-day; he is quite well, and recovered from his fatigue."[1]

Sydney Smith Lee was married in 1834 to Anna Maria, daughter of the Hon. John and Anna Maria (Murray) Mason, of "Clermont," Fairfax county. She was born the 26th of February, 1811, and still survives. Of the wedding General Long has given this bit of information:[2] "Lieutenant Sydney Smith Lee married Miss Mason in old Christ Church at Alexandria. The party were first entertained at General John Mason's house at Clermont. They then went to Arlington, where the festivities were continued. Lieutenant Robert Lee and his friends took part in this old Virginia

---

[1] *General Lee*, by Fitzhugh Lee, p. 36.
[2] *Memoirs of General Robert E. Lee*, by General A. L. Long, p. 38.

frolic. Seven young men were bivouacked in one room at Arlington. Captain Canfield, one of the number, made much fun for the party. In the morning the negro servant made so much noise on the bare floor, bringing wood and making fires, that Canfield called out, 'Moses, why not come up on a pony?' At this point Mr. Custis threw wide open the door and called out, 'Sleep no more; Macbeth hath murdered sleep.' Every night, before the party retired, punch was bounteously dispensed from a punch-bowl which had belonged to General Washington. In the bottom of the bowl was a painting of a ship, the hull resting on the bottom, the mast projecting to the brim. The rule was to drink down to the hull—a rule strictly observed. As this bowl has a history, it may be stated that it was presented to General Washington by Colonel Fitzhugh, a former aide-de-camp, who afterward left Virginia and settled in the Genesee Valley, in Western New York."

Captain Sydney Smith and Anna Maria (Mason) Lee had seven children, all sons excepting one daughter, who died in infancy. They were:

i, FITZHUGH$^{7}$. See 71.

ii, SYDNEY SMITH$^{7}$, born at Georgetown, D. C., the 10th of February, 1837; died the 15th of April, 1888. Was in the navy; served on the Confederate cruiser "Shenandoah" under Captain Waddell. He never married.

iii, JOHN MASON$^{7}$. See 72.

iv, HENRY CARTER$^{7}$. See 73.

v, DANIEL MURRAY$^{7}$. See 74.

vi, ROBERT CARTER$^{7}$; was born at "Clermont," Fairfax county, the 17th of November, 1848; is still living and unmarried.

vii, ELIZABETH MASON$^{7}$, was born at "Clermont," Fairfax county, on the 17th of February, 1853, and died at the age of seven months.

## THE MASON FAMILY.

Arms: Azure, a point with three embattlements, argent, charged with fleur-de-lis, gules, on the middle battlement a dove with wings displayed, ppr.

Crest: A talbot passant, regardant, arg., eared sa., holding in his mouth a hart's horn, or.

Motto: Pro Patria [illegible]er.[1]

Colonel George Mason, the great-grandfather of the celebrated patriot and statesman of the Revolution and the first of that name in Virginia, is

---

[1] These arms are those of the Masons of Stratford-upon-Avon, Warwickshire, England, and were those used by the Virginia family. After the Revolution George Mason changed the motto to "Pro Republica Semper."

said to have commanded a troop of horse at the battle of Worcester, and after that disastrous defeat of the royalists to have emigrated, as did so many of his party, to Virginia. His arrival has been placed in the year 1651, and very promptly does he appear, from even the meagre records left, to have taken a prominent part in the civil and military affairs of the Colony. Especially as a "great Indian fighter" was he known, and his son after him. He was a Burgess and also Sheriff for Stafford. At his death in 1686 he left a son, George Mason, also a Justice, Sheriff, and Burgess, who by his first wife, Mary, the daughter of Col. Gerard Fowke, an intimate friend of the elder Mason, had George Mason (1690–1735), who, like his father and grandfather, was an influential man, and took an active part in county and colonial affairs. By his second wife, Anna, daughter of Stevens Thomson, the latter had the patriot, George Mason, of "Gunston Hall," Fairfax county, a near neighbor to "Belvoir" and Mt. Vernon.

"George Mason, Esq., statesman and planter of 'Gunston Hall,' Fairfax county, Va., was born in 1725 on his father's estate situated in 'Dogue's Neck,' known also as 'Mason's Neck,' then in Stafford county, and died at his residence, 'Gunston Hall,' October 7, 1792. His education, which was good, was mainly received at home from private tutors. He was twice married; first, April, 1750, to Ann, daughter of Col. William Eilbeck, of Charles county, Md., by whom he had five sons and four daughters; second, to Sarah, daughter of George Brent, of 'Woodstock,' Va. Shortly after his marriage he built 'Gunston Hall' on his paternal landed inheritance. He took an active and interested part in church affairs, and in 1765 was elected, together with George Washington, a vestryman of Pohick Church. He was a man of good habits, strong mind, retentive memory, and strict attention to business, with a special aptness for system and the formulation of legal documents and bills for enactment of laws. In 1769 he drew up the non-importation resolutions which were presented by Washington in the Virginia Assembly and which were unanimously adopted. One of these pledged the Virginia planters to purchase no slaves brought into the country after November 1 of that year. In support of the rights of Virginia, Mr. Mason printed a pamphlet with the title 'Extracts from the Virginia Charter, with some remarks upon them.' At a meeting of the people of Fairfax county, July 18, 1774, presided over by George Washington, he presented a series of twenty-four resolutions reviewing the whole ground of controversy between Great Britain and the Colonies, recommending a congress of all the Colonies and urging non-intercourse with the mother country. Later the same principles were fully affirmed by the Continental Congress.

He declined a seat in Congress but served on the Committee of Safety, which was charged with the executive government of Virginia. In 1776 he drafted the famous bill of rights and also the Constitution of Virginia. Madison said that Mason was the ablest debater he had ever heard. In 1777 he was elected to Congress, but declined. Ten years later he was a member of the committee that drafted the Constitution of the United States, but did not sign it because, as he said, it endangered the sovereignty of the States. He was also a member of the Convention of the State which adopted the Constitution, and again opposed its adoption. He was elected the first United States Senator from Virginia, but declined. He was referred to by Thomas Jefferson as a man of the first order of wisdom. Certainly George Mason deserves to be remembered as one of the purest of patriots and wisest of statesmen."

Of his children, General John Mason, a son, married Anna Maria Murray, of Maryland, and was the father of the Hon. James Murray Mason, U. S. Senator, and later Confederate Commissioner with John Slidell to England. General John Mason had also Sarah, who married General Samuel Cooper, and Anna Maria, who married Sydney Smith Lee, as stated, and who still survives.

A very interesting life of George Mason has recently been written by Miss Kate Mason Rowland, of Baltimore.

## General Lee.

50. Robert Edward[6], the fourth son of Henry Lee[5] (Henry[4], Henry[3], Richard[2], Richard[1]) and Anne Hill Carter, his second wife, was born at Stratford, Westmoreland county, the 19th of January, 1807, and died, at his home in Lexington, the 12th of October, 1870. When Robert Lee was about four years old, his father removed with his family to Alexandria, where they lived, first, on Cameron street near old Christ Church, next on Orinoco street, and, lastly, in the house on north Washington street now used as the parsonage of Christ Church. When only eleven years old he lost his father, who, prior to his death, had been absent from home for several years, so Robert Lee was reared almost entirely under the watchful and loving care of his mother. It is said she taught him, from his earliest childhood, to "practise self-denial and self-control, as well as the strictest economy in all financial concerns," traits which he ever exhibited throughout life.

Miss Emily V. Mason, in her *Popular Life of General Lee,* tells this of his loving care for his mother: "This good mother was a great invalid;

R E Lee

one of his sisters was delicate, and many years absent in Philadelphia, under the care of physicians. The eldest son, Carter, was at Cambridge, Sydney Smith in the navy, and the other sister too young to be of much aid in household matters. So Robert was the housekeeper, carried the keys, attended to the marketing, managed all of the out-door business, and took care of his mother's horses.

"At the hour when other school-boys went to play, he hurried home to order his mother's drive, and would there be seen carrying her in his arms to the carriage, and arranging her cushions with the gentleness of an experienced nurse. One of his relatives, who was often the companion of these drives, still lives. She tells us of the exertions he would make on these occasions to entertain and amuse his mother, assuring her, with the gravity of an old man, that unless she was cheerful the drive would not benefit her. When she complained of cold or 'draughts,' he would pull from his pocket a great jack-knife and newspapers, and make her laugh with his efforts to improvise curtains, and shut out the intrusive wind, which whistled through the crevices of the old family coach.

"When he left her to go to West Point, his mother was heard to say: 'How can I live without Robert? He is both son and daughter to me.'

"Years after, when he came home from West Point, he found one of the chief actors of his childhood's drama—his mother's old coachman, 'Nat'—ill, and threatened with consumption. He immediately took him to the milder climate of Georgia, nursed him with the tenderness of a son, and secured him the best medical advice. But the spring-time saw the faithful old servant laid in the grave by the hands of his kind young master."

Robert Lee was educated at private schools in Alexandria, and prepared for entrance into the military school at West Point, for from earliest youth he seems to have desired to enter the army. His first teacher was Mr. William B. Leary, an Irishman, who lived to meet his pupil after the war. Next, he went to the once famous mathematical school kept by Benjamin Hallowell; of his school days, Mr. Hallowell has left this memorandum:

"Robert E. Lee entered my school in Alexandria, Va., in the winter of 1824–25, to study mathematics, preparatory to his going to West Point. He was a most exemplary student in every respect. He was never behind time at his studies, never failed in a single recitation, was perfectly observant of the rules and regulations of the institution; was gentlemanly, unobtrusive, and respectful in all his deportment to teachers and fellow-students.

His specialty was finishing up. He imparted a neatness and finish to everything he undertook. One of the branches of mathematics he studied with me was conic sections, in which some of the diagrams were very complicated. He drew the diagrams on a slate, and although he well knew that the one he was drawing would have to be removed to make room for the next, he drew each one with as much accuracy and finish, lettering and all, as if it were to be engraved and printed. The same traits he exhibited at my school he carried with him to West Point, where, I have been told, he never received a mark of demerit, and graduated at the head of his class.''

General Lee entered West Point in 1825, and graduated, second (not first, as frequently stated) in his class, in 1829. He received an appointment as second lieutenant in the corps of military engineers; in 1835, he served upon a commission for settling the boundary lines between Ohio and Michigan; was made first lieutenant in 1836, and captain in 1838. In 1846, he was appointed chief engineer on the staff of General Wool, in Mexico, and the next year was brevetted major for gallantry at the battle of Cerro Gordo, and, for services at Contreras and Churubusco, was brevetted lieutenant-colonel in 1847. At the battle of Chapultepec he was wounded and brevetted colonel. After this war was over, he was appointed superintendent of the Military Academy at West Point, and filled this position from 1852 to 1855. In 1858, he was with Albert Sydney Johnston, fighting the Indians in Texas. His last service in the "old army" was the capture of John Brown and his band, at Harper's Ferry, at the close of 1859.

It is useless and unnecessary to describe in this connection the military life of General Lee during the thirty years he served in the United States army; it is sufficient to say that every duty was fulfilled with scrupulous fidelity, and that he rose steadily from grade to grade, rewarded at each promotion by the encomiums of his superior officers. General Scott entertained the greatest admiration for him as a man and a soldier. A gentleman has stated[1] that he had frequently heard him speak "in the very highest terms of Robert E. Lee as a soldier and Christian gentleman, but that on one occasion, when in the course of a confidential interview, he asked the direct question: 'General, whom do you regard as the greatest living soldier?' Without hesitation, and with marked emphasis, General Scott replied: '*Colonel Robert E. Lee* is not only the greatest soldier of America, but the greatest soldier now living in the world. This is my de-

[1] *Reminiscences of General Robert E. Lee*, by Rev. J. William Jones, p. 482. From this interesting volume, many of General Lee's letters, given in this sketch, have been taken.

liberate conviction, from a full knowledge of his extraordinary abilities, and, if the occasion ever arises, Lee will win this place in the estimation of the whole world.' The general then went into a detailed sketch of Lee's services, and a statement of his ability as an engineer, and his capacity not only to plan campaigns, but also to command large armies in the field, and concluded by saying: '*I tell you, sir, Robert E. Lee is the greatest soldier now living, and if he ever gets the opportunity he will prove himself the great captain of history.*' "

General Lee took no part in the political discussions which agitated the country prior to the outbreak of hostilities between the States. He was opposed to secession, but promptly resigned from the old army when it became a question as to whether he should fight for or against his native State. On that issue, he had no doubts. Consequently, upon the secession of Virginia, and the firing upon Fort Sumter, he handed in his resignation, and offered his sword to defend his native Virginia. His father before him, ardent Federalist as he was, had said: "Virginia is my country; her will I obey, however lamentable the fate to which it may subject me." Again, this father had declared that "no consideration on earth could induce me to act a part, however gratifying to me, which could be construed into disregard or faithlessness to this Commonwealth." The son therefore acted in strict accordance with the principles of the father, which, it would be safe to say, had been shared by the majority of the patriots of the Revolution.

When testifying before a committee of Congress, after the war, General Lee stated that he had resigned because he believed that "the act of Virginia in withdrawing herself from the United States carried me along with it as a citizen of Virginia, and that her laws and acts were binding upon me." Though his own duty in this crisis was clearly marked out for him in his own conscience, he never sought to decide for others, not even for his own son. In writing to his wife from Richmond, under date of the 13th of May, 1861, he wrote: ". . . Tell Custis he must consult his own judgment, reason, and conscience as to the course he may take. I do not wish him to be guided by my wishes or example. If I have done wrong, let him do better. The present is a momentous question, which every man must settle for himself and upon principle."

In a letter to the Hon. Reverdy Johnson, under date of 25th February, 1868, General Lee stated clearly his position and his sentiments, which led him to resign from the army and to refuse the most tempting offers. He used these words:

"I never intimated to any one that I desired the command of the United States army, nor did I ever have a conversation with but one gentleman, Mr. Francis Preston Blair, on the subject, which was at his invitation, and, as I understood, at the instance of the President. After listening to his remarks I declined the offer he made me to take command of the army that was to be brought into the field, stating, as candidly and as courteously as I could, that, though opposed to secession and deprecating war, I could take no part in an invasion of the Southern States.

"I went directly from the interview with Mr. Blair to the office of General Scott—told him of the proposition that had been made to me and my decision. Upon reflection after returning home, I concluded that I ought no longer to retain any commission I held in the United States army, and on the second morning thereafter I forwarded my resignation to General Scott." This latter was as follows:

"Arlington, Va., 20th April, 1861. General,—Since my interview with you on the 18th inst., I have felt that I ought no longer to retain my commission in the army. I therefore tender my resignation, which I request you will recommend for acceptance. It would have been presented at once, but for the struggle it has cost me to separate myself from a service to which I have devoted all the best years of my life, and all the ability I possessed. During the whole of that time, more than a quarter of a century, I have experienced nothing but kindness from my superiors, and the most cordial friendship from my comrades. To no one, General, have I been as much indebted as to yourself for uniform kindness and consideration; and it has always been my ardent desire to merit your approbation. I shall carry to the grave the most grateful recollections of your kind consideration, and your name and fame will always be dear to me. Save in the defense of my native State, I never desire again to draw my sword. Be pleased to accept my most earnest wishes for the continuance of your happiness and prosperity, and believe me most truly yours," &c.

"To Lieut-General Winfield Scott, Commanding U. S. Army."

In casting his lot with his native State General Lee acted with full consciousness of the gravity of the crisis. He entertained no illusions, such as some on each side professed to hold, that the war would be brief and of little importance; nor did he believe that a civil war could be avoided. Writing to his wife from Richmond, under date of 13th May, 1861, he warned her: "Do not put faith in rumors of adjustment. I see no prospect for it. It cannot be while the passions on both sides are so infuriated. Make your plans for several years of war." At another time he said: " . . . Both sides forget that we are all Americans, and that it must be a terrible struggle if it comes to war."

The following correspondence has never been published. It is very interesting. Dr. May was a Pennsylvanian by birth, but had been many

*Mary Custis Lee*

years a professor of the Theological Seminary of the Episcopal Church in Virginia, situated near Alexandria:

"Alexandria, 23d April, 1861. My dear Robert,—The inclosed letter was written to me, as you will see, in consequence of a remark I made to Dr. Sparrow, which he reported to the writer, Dr. May, that I hoped your connection with the Virginia forces, if you concluded to accept the command, might lead to some peaceful settlement of our difficulties. I hoped this from the friendship between yourself and General Scott. I have only time now to inclose you Dr. May's letter, and to offer my earnest prayer that God may make you instrumental in saving our land from this dreadful strife. In haste. Yours truly, Cassius F. Lee."

"Col. Lee."

"Theological Seminary of Va., 22d April, 1861. My dear Sir,—I am sure of your sympathy with me in the motive of what I now write, even though you may think me presumptuous and lacking in judgment. Two considerations prompt me; one, an Editorial in the *National Intelligencer* of to-day, placed by yourself in Dr. Sparrow's hands and read by him to me a few minutes ago, the other a suggestion that Col. Lee, now to be put in command of the Virginia troops, might, by God's blessing, bring peace to our distracted country. O, how my heart leaped at the thought! How many thousands, yea millions, would rise up to bless the man that should bring this to pass!

"I may be stepping out of my line in offering a word on the subject. But my heart is full, and I know you at least are willing to give me your attention. Who knows but that your cousin may be raised up by God for such a time as this? Could he bring about, at least, an armistice, preparatory to a National Assembly for a peaceful settlement of our troubles, how many hearts would he relieve and how large his share in the blessedness of peacemakers! I do not enter into the political considerations of the matter. That is not my province. It may suffice to say that, so far as became me, whether in the North or in the South, I always gave my opinion against the organization and the proposed measures of the party now controlling the General Administration. I always held that organization to be not only needless, but mischievous. When it became so sectionally dominant, I hoped still that the more thoughtful members of it would shape its course. They seem to have been overborne. The unfortunate Proclamation of the President, and the measures which were its immediate antecedents, have utterly disappointed me and saddened me. But as I said, I do not enter into the political aspect of the great question now before us. I would regard it as a Christian should and especially a Christian minister.

"My feeble voice I lift for peace. I have often turned my thoughts to Col. Lee. The world knows his services in the Mexican war. Years ago I asked my brother-in-law, Major A. H. Bowman (now of West Point), what army officers thought of him as a soldier? I remember well his emphatic answer. If those who were with him (Col. Lee) in Mexico should answer, they would unanimously declare him to be, in all military qualifications, without a rival in the service. But my interest in him was quickened by hearing of his Christian character. During his absence in Mexico I visited his family at Arlington, and heard from Mrs. Lee allusions to his private letters. I received then my opinion of him as a Christian, and have had my eye on him ever since. May we not hope that God has put him in his present position to be an instrument of abating the storm which now threatens shipwreck to the whole country? It is sad that so few of our public men are Christians. Col. Lee is a grand exception. I know, in an official post, which is not that of head of the government, he would find it difficult to follow the private promptings of his own Christian mind, for a soldier's business is not to advise his superiors, but to obey. But great respect would be shown to the judgment and Christian spirit of one so distinguished as he. Virginia gave us our original Independence through her Washington. She gave us our National Constitution through Jefferson, Madison and others. Can she not now, while we are threatened with the immeasurable evils of civil war, give us through Col. Lee peace? In common with other States, she may justly complain of wrongs. But will civil war repair them? Christianity teaches not only the duty, but the wisdom of patience and forgiveness. Virginia, from her geographical position, from her glorious share in the past and from her great political weight, has it in her power (am I presumptuous in saying it?) to come in as a mediator, rather as an *umpire* and settle the question, not only for the happiness of the whole country, but for her own special prosperity. Should Col. Lee be a leader in this matter and place his native State in this grand position (which I must think she can hold), he will have an honor never reached by Napoleon or Wellington. If Virginia may not call back the people of the continent to union, she yet may to peace. Standing apart from others, she would not, could not be invaded. She could be a healer or a peacemaker, and have all the blessedness of such an office. The wisdom of seniors has not been allowed its part in our great questions. Young, impetuous spirits seem to be leading the mind of the country. Especially has not the Christian mind, the Church, been heard. Its voice must be for peace. Our sins may be too great to allow us to have again the blessedness of a united country, but may we not have peace? Is there not moral power in the Christian mind of the country to stay the hand of fraternal strife? How many wives, mothers, widows, sisters, how many quiet, peaceful citizens of all classes, sigh for peace? How many families, now separated by wide geographical distances, would be divided in a way far more painful and dreadful by civil war? No quiet citizen, no Christian, can think of it without a fainting heart. During the civil wars of England, in the times of the Commonwealth, Lord Falkland was known in all Britain as one of the bravest men ever born in that land. After he had seen the indescribable wretchedness of the people of his native country in the strife of brothers, he would sit abstracted among his friends, and, sighing from the depths of his heart, exclaim, 'Peace, Peace.' I dare not say Col. Lee may bring us peace. The Lord can only do that. We may have so sinned that the wrath of God must lie upon us and make us suffer the awful judgment now threatening. How do all Christian sentiments, how do all the interests of the Christian Church, how do all our interests cry for peace!

"I do not say the Gospel forbids war absolutely. Its direct, primary call is to peace: 'Blessed are the peacemakers, for they shall be called the children of God.' From my inmost soul, I pray that in this our day of trial, that blessedness may be enjoyed by Col. Lee. In thus writing, do I seem to be a meddler? I am not so in purpose and motive. Perhaps I mistake my calling. I think, as a Christian and a Christian minister, I cannot err in wishing and praying for peace. Our great national questions cannot be settled except in time of peace. O, may that peace come now, at the beginning, instead of the end of a fearful conflict. So praying, I am sure of your sympathy, and subscribe myself, most sincerely your friend,

James May."

"C. F. Lee, Esqr."

"Richmond, 25 April, 1861. My dear Cassius,—I have received your letter of the 23d. I am sorry your nephew has left his College and become a soldier. It is necessary that persons on my staff should have a knowledge of their duties and experience of the wants of the service, to enable me to attend to other matters. It would otherwise give me great pleasure to take your nephew. I shall remember him if anything can be done.

"I am much obliged to you for Dr. May's letter. Express to him my gratitude for his sentiments, and tell him that no earthly act would give me so much pleasure, as to restore peace to my country. But I fear it is now out of the power of man, and in God alone must be our trust. I think our policy should be purely on the defensive. To resist aggression and allow time to allay the passions and reason to resume her sway. Virginia has to-day, I understand, joined the Confederate States. Her policy will doubtless therefore be shaped by united counsels. I cannot say what it will be. But trust that a merciful Providence will not turn his face entirely from us and dash us from the height to which his smiles had raised us.

"I wanted to say many things to you before I left home. But the event was rendered so imperatively speedy that I could not. May God preserve you and yours. Very truly, R. E. Lee."

So, failing to secure peace, General Lee prepared for war with all the ability he possessed. How well he served his State, it is not necessary to describe in a sketch of this nature; as Dr. Field has said, "The world knows it by heart."

Colonel Chesney, of the English army, believes: "The day will come when the evil passions of the great civil war will sleep in oblivion, and the North and South do justice to each other's motives, and forget each other's wrongs. Then history will speak with clear voice of the deeds done on either side, and the citizens of the whole Union do justice to the memories of the dead, and place above all others the name of the great chief of whom we have written. In strategy, mighty; in battle, terrible; in adversity, as in prosperity, a hero indeed; with the simple devotion to duty and the rare purity of the ideal Christian knight,—he joined all the kingly qualities of a leader of men. It is a wondrous future indeed that lies before America; but in her annals of the years to come, as in those of the past, there will be found few names that can rival in unsullied lustre that of the heroic defender of his native Virginia,—Robert Edward Lee."

Leaving Lee the *general* to the historian, it is the design of this brief sketch to tell something of the personal characteristics of the *man*. In pursuance of this purpose, some few of his letters, written in the confidence of friendship, or with the love of the parent, are quoted, whole or in part, as best fulfills this idea. Extracts might be taken from some of the numerous and most eloquent eulogies that have been paid General Lee, since his death, by the most gifted orators of the South. Any one of these would furnish a complete and eloquent sketch of the man and the soldier. Yet they might all be considered the biased opinions of personal friends, or due to sectional pride. It seems better therefore to give the impression of a stranger, of one not partial through friendship or sectional pride. In the summer of 1889, the Rev. Henry M. Field,[1] a Northern man, the gifted editor of the *New York Evangelist*, visited Lexington, and wrote two letters to his paper, giving fully the impression he had gathered there of General Lee's personality from the lips of those who knew him most intimately. Extracts from these two letters are given; parts being omitted which are less closely connected with General Lee. The first letter is headed:

"*The Last Years of General Lee.*"

"'The last hope of the Confederacy was dead when Stonewall Jackson was laid in his grave at Lexington!' So said the Major after he had taken the greater part of a day in detailing to me, to my intense interest, the marvellous career of the great soldier. But not so reasoned all those who had fought by Jackson's side. Not so Jackson himself; for when, on hearing of his wound, Lee wrote to him, 'Could I have directed events, I should have chosen, for the good of the country, to have been disabled in your stead,' he answered, 'No, No! Better lose twenty Jacksons than one Lee!' And now, though Jackson was dead, Lee still lived, and hope lived with him; victory was still possible; and in that faith, and under that leadership, the Confederates fought on for two years more. (Jackson died on the 10th of May, 1863; but Lee did not surrender till the 9th of April, 1865.) How well they fought is matter of history. They fought as they could *not* have fought, had they not been led by a great Commander.[2] Some, I know, assume to criticise the strategy shown in his campaigns. To such I have only to say that it is a very poor compliment to *our* leaders and *our* armies, to question the abilities of one who, with less than half the numbers, kept back for two years the tremendous forces of the North that were pressing in on every side. Whatever others may say of General Lee, the great soldiers who fought against him fully concede his splendid military genius. But it is not the purpose of this letter to speak of his military career.

"That belongs to history. 'The world knows it by heart.' But there

---

1 The Rev. Dr. Henry Martyn Field, the writer here quoted, is the youngest of the four distinguished sons of the Rev. David Dudley Field, who was born at East Guilford, Conn , the 20th of May, 1781, and died at Stockbridge, Mass., on the 15th of April, 1867; he was a son of Captain Timothy Field, an officer of the Revolutionary army. The four sons were: David Dudley, the eminent jurist; Stephen Johnson, lawyer and Justice of the Supreme Court; Cyrus West, the originator of the Atlantic cables; and lastly, Henry Martyn, who was born at Stockbridge, on the 3d of April, 1822, and still survives; an able writer, editor, and distinguished Presbyterian divine.—EDITOR.

2 With this opinion of Dr. Field, General Hooker appears to have agreed; for he said, before the Congressional Committee on the conduct of the war: "With rank and file vastly inferior to our own, intellectually and physically, that army has, by discipline alone, acquired a character for steadiness and efficiency unsurpassed, in my judgment, in ancient or modern times. We have not been able to rival it, nor has there been any near approximation to it in the other rebel armies."—EDITOR.

is a chapter in that life which the world does not know so well, which ought to be told, to the greater honor of the illustrious dead. The war was over The Northern armies had returned victorious, while the veterans of the South, defeated, but not dishonored, took their way back to their desolate homes. The army disbanded and dispersed, what should its leader do? His old ancestral home, standing on that noble height which looks down on the Potomac and across to the dome of the Capitol, was in the hands of those against whom he had been fighting for four years, and had even been turned into a national cemetery, in which slept thousands of the Union dead, whose very ghosts might rise up against his return. But if he was an exile from his own home, there were thousands of others open to him all over the South, and across the sea, where his fame had gone before him, and would have made him a welcome guest in princely halls. But such a flight from his country (for so he would have regarded it) was impossible to one of his chivalrous spirit. He had cast in his lot with his people; they had believed in him and had followed him, as they thought, to certain triumph; he would not desert them in the day of their adversity.

"Of course, had he been willing to listen to them, he could have received any number of 'business' proposals. Rich, moneyed corporations would have been glad to 'retain' him at any price as President or Director, so that they could have the benefit of his great name. One, it is said, offered him $50,000 a year. But he was not to be allured by such temptations. The very fact that they were coupled with offers of money was reason enough why he should reject them all, as he did, without a moment's hesitation. Nor could he be allured by any military proposals. Maximilian offered to place him at the head of his army if he would go to Mexico, thinking that his genius might save the fortunes of the falling empire. But he would not accept any exile, however splendid. His answer was, 'I love the mountains of Virginia still.' His work must be at home, for work he must have. After his active life, he would not sink down into idleness. With his military career ended, he must find a new career in civil life. Besides, he had a proud spirit of independence, which would not permit him to live on the bounty of the rich at home or the titled abroad. 'He would work for a living,' like the poorest of his soldiers. At length came a proposal that seemed most alien to his former pursuits; that the Commander of the Southern Armies should become the President of a College! And yet this change from a military to an academic career was not so violent as it might seem. He had been for three years Superintendent of the Military Academy at West Point, where he was associated with young men. He had been himself a student there, and had been through all the stages of scholarly discipline. Besides, the position of the College to which he was invited, in Lexington, Virginia, was attractive to him. It was remote from cities, among the mountains, and yet within the limits of that 'Old Dominion' which he looked upon as his mother.

"When it was known that he had accepted the position, his coming was looked for with great eagerness by the people of Lexington; but he did not fix the time, as he wished to avoid any public demonstration. But it had been arranged that *when* he came, he should spend a few days in the hospitable dwelling in which I was so fortunate as to be a guest. While thus in expectancy, the Professor was one day taking a walk, when he saw riding up the street, a figure that he instantly recognized as the same he had so often seen at the head of the army; and to make the picture perfect, he was mounted on his old war-horse—a magnificent iron-gray called 'Traveler'—that had so often borne his master through the smoke of battle. He wore no military uniform, nor sign of rank, but a light summer dress, while a broad Panama hat shaded a face that no one could mistake. Advancing toward him, the Professor told of the arrangements for his entertainment till he could be established in a house for himself, and led the way to his home. Naturally my friend's family were at first somewhat awed by the presence of their illustrious guest. But this was soon dissipated by his simple and unaffected manner. What 'broke the ice' most completely was his manner with the children. He was always very fond of little people, and as soon as they appeared, 'Uncle Robert,' as he was affectionately called in the army, had them in his arms and on his knees, till they soon felt perfectly at home with him. They 'captured' him at once, and he 'captured' them, and in this captured their parents also. From that moment all constraint disappeared, though nothing could ever take from the profound respect and veneration with which they looked up to 'General Lee.'

"This was in September, 1865, and on the 2d of October, after solemn prayer by the venerable Dr. White, he took the oath of office, as required by the laws of the College, and thus became its President. Naturally his name drew great numbers of students, not only from Virginia, but from all parts of the South, who were eager to 'serve' under such a leader, and the number of undergraduates rose from one hundred and fifty to over four hundred. . . . In one respect his influence was immeasurable. Every man in the South looked up to General Lee as the highest type of manhood, and his very presence was an inspiration. This is the influence which young men feel more than any other—that inspired by intense admiration—an influence that would have been very potent if the object of their admiration had been merely a great soldier, dazzling them by his genius, but destitute of high principle. Had that been the case, his influence would have been demoralizing as now it was elevating, since his superiority in all other respects was united with a character that was so gentle and so good. That he might reach the young, he sought their acquaintance, instead of standing apart in icy dignity. Professor White tells me that, if they were walking together in the College grounds, and a student was seen approaching, he would ask who he was, and when he came up, instead of passing him with a stiff and stately bow, would stop and call him by name, and ask about his family and his studies, and speak a few words of encouragement, which the young man would not forget to his dying day. To be under the authority and influence of such a man was an education in manliness. There was not a student who did not feel it, and to whom it was not the highest ambition to be guided by such a leader, to be infused with his spirit, and to follow his example. . . .

"He knew that whatever fell from his lips would be repeated, and not always as he had said it, but with a change of words, or in a different tone of voice, that might give it quite another meaning. Indeed, with all his caution, he was often quoted as saying what he did not say. As an illustration, Professor White told me that a story had gone the rounds of the papers to the effect that in a conversation Gen. Lee had brought his clenched hand down on the table, to give emphasis to his utterance, as he said, 'If I had had Stonewall Jackson with me I should have won the battle of Gettysburg and established the Southern Confederacy!' 'Now,' said the Professor, 'without ever asking him, I *know* that such an occurrence never took place, for in the first place General Lee "never brought his hand down on the table"—he was not that sort of a man—it is impossible to conceive of him as using any violence of gesture or of language. And as to Stonewall Jackson, while he did feel keenly the absence of that great corps commander, he was not the man to indulge in sweeping and positive statements; he never spoke with such absolute assurance of anything, but always with a degree of reserve, as once, when we were riding together, he said in his usual guarded and cautious manner: "If I had had Stonewall Jackson with me—*so far as man can see*—I should have won the battle of Gettysburg." So careful was he to put in this qualification: for he always recognized an overruling Power that may disappoint the wisest calculations, and defeat the most careful combinations of courage and skill.'" . . .

### "*The Character of General Lee.*"

"My last letter left us in the College Chapel at Lexington, gazing upon the recumbent statue of General Lee. While standing here, in the very presence of the dead, I am moved to say a few words in regard to the life that ended in this tomb, and the character of the man whose name is carved upon this stone. As I read history, and compare the men who have figured in the events that make history—in wars and revolutions—it seems to me that General Lee was not only a great soldier, but a great man, one of the greatest that our country has produced. After his death, the College which had hitherto borne the name of Washington, by whom it was endowed, was re-christened 'Washington *and Lee* University'—a combination which suggests a comparison of the two men whose names are here brought together. Can we trace any likeness between them? At first it seems as if no characters, as well as no careers, could be more alien to each other than those of the two great leaders, one of whom was the Founder of the Government which the other did his utmost to destroy. But nature brings forth her children in strange couples, with resemblances in some cases as marked, and as yet unexpected, as are contrasts in others. Washington and Lee, though born in different centuries, were children of the same mother, Old Virginia, and had her best blood in their veins. Descended from the stock of the English Cavaliers, both were born 'gentlemen,' and never could be anything else. Both were trained in the school of war, and as leaders of armies it would not be a violent assumption to rank Lee as the equal of Washington. But it is not in the two soldiers, but in the two men, that the future historian will find points of resemblance.

"Washington was not a brilliant man; not 'a man of genius,' such as now and then appears to dazzle mankind; but he had what was far better than genius—a combination of all the qualities that win human trust; in which intelligence is so balanced by judgment and exalted by character as to constitute a natural superiority; indicating one who is born to command, and to whom all men turn, when their hearts are 'failing them for fear,' as a leader. He was great not only in action, but in repose; great in his very calm—in the fortitude with which he bore himself through all changes of fortune, through dangers and disasters, neither elated by victory nor depressed by defeat—mental habitudes which many will recognize as reappearing in the one who seems to have formed himself upon that great model. Washington was distinguished for his magnanimity. Was not Lee also? Men in public station are apt to be sensitive to whatever concerns their standing before the world; and so, while taking to themselves the credit of success, they are strongly tempted to throw upon others the blame of failure. Soldiers especially are jealous of their reputation; and if a commander loses a battle his first impulse is to cast the odium of defeat upon some unfortunate officer. Somebody blundered; this or that subordinate did not do his duty. Military annals are filled with these recriminations. If Napoleon met with a check in his mighty plans he had no scruple in laying it to the misconduct of some lieutenant; unless, as in Russia, he could throw it upon the elements, the wintry snows and the frozen rivers—anything to relieve himself from the imputation of the want of foresight or provision for unexpected dangers. At Waterloo it was not *he* that failed in his strategy, but Marshal Ney that failed in the execution. In this respect General Lee was exactly his opposite. If he suffered a disaster he never sought to evade responsibility by placing it upon others. Even in the greatest reverse of his life, the defeat at Gettysburg, when he saw the famous charge of Pickett melt away under the terrible fire that swept the field, till the ranks were literally torn in pieces by shot and shell, he did not vent his despair in rage and reproaches, but rushing to the front, took the blame upon himself, saying, '*It is all my fault.*' Perhaps no incident of his life showed more the nobility of his nature.

"When the war was over General Lee had left to him at Lexington about the same number of years that Napoleon had at St. Helena; and if he had had the same desire to pose for posterity in the part of an illustrious exile, his mountain home would have furnished as picturesque a background as the rocky island in the South Atlantic, from which he could have dictated 'Conversations' that should furnish the materials of history. He need not have written or published a single line if he had only been willing to let others do it for him. By their pens he had opportunity to tell of the great part he had acted in the war in a way to make the whole chain of events contribute to his fame. But he seemed to care little for fame, and, indeed, was unmoved when others claimed the credit of his victories. If it be, as Pascal says, 'the truest mark of a great mind to be born without envy,' few men in history have shown more of this greatness than he And when, as was sometimes the case, old companions-in-arms reflected upon him to excuse their own mistakes, he had only to lift the veil from the secrets of history to confound them. But under all temptations he was dumb. Nothing that he *did* or *said* was more truly grand than the *silence* with which he bore the misrepresentations of friend or foe.[1] This required

[1] General Lee absolutely refused to allow any one to write in his defense, or to repeat any information received from him in private conversation. On the 22d of August, 1866, he wrote to an English gentleman who desired to write something in his behalf: " . . . What I stated to you in conversation during the visit which you did me the honor to pay me in November last was entirely for your own information, and was in no way intended for publication. . . . I have an objection to the publication of my private conversations, which are never intended but for those to whom they are addressed. . . . Though fully appreciating your kind wish to correct certain erroneous statements as regards myself, I prefer to remain silent rather than to do anything that might excite angry discussion at this time. . . . " (Jones' *Reminiscences of General Lee*, 218.)—EDITOR.

a self-command such as Washington had not to exercise at the end of his military career: for he retired from the scene crowned with victory, with a whole nation at his feet ready to do him honor, while Lee had to bear the reproach of the final disaster—a reproach in which friends sometimes joined with foes. Yet to both he answered only with the same majestic calm, the outward sign of his magnificent self-control. Such magnanimity belongs to the very highest order of moral qualities, and shows a character rare in any country or any age.

"This impression of the man does not grow less with closer observation. With the larger number of 'great men' the greatness is magnified by distance and separation. As we come nearer they dwindle in stature, till, when we are in their very presence and look them squarely in the face, they are found to be but men like ourselves, and sometimes very ordinary men—with some special ability, perhaps, which gives them success in the world, but who for all that are full of selfishness, which is the very essence of meanness, and puffed up with paltry conceit and vanity that stamps them as little rather than great. Far different was the impression made by General Lee upon those who saw him in the freedom of private intercourse. It might be expected that the soldiers who fought under him should speak with pride and admiration of their old commander; but how did he appear to his neighbors? Here in Lexington everybody knew him, at least by sight. They saw his manner of life from day to day, in his going out and his coming in, and on all the impression was the same: the nearer he came to them the greater he seemed. Every one has some anecdote to tell of him, and it is always of something that was noble and lovable. Those who knew him best loved him most and revered him most. This was not a greatness that was assumed, that was put on like a military cloak; it was in the man, and could not be put on or off; it was the greatness which comes from the very absence of pretension. And those who came closest to him give us a still further insight into his nature by telling us that what struck them most was the extent of his sympathy. Soldiers are commonly supposed to be cold and hard—a temper of mind to which they are inured by their very profession. Those whose business is the shedding of blood are thought to delight in human suffering. It is hard to believe that a soldier can have a very tender heart. Yet few men were more sensitive to others' pain than General Lee. All who came near him perceived that with his manly strength there was united an almost womanly sweetness. It was this gentleness which made him great, and which has enshrined him in the hearts of his people forever.

"This sympathy for the suffering showed itself, not in any public act so much as in a more private and delicate office which imposed upon him a very heavy burden—one that he might have declined, but the taking of which showed the man. He had an unlimited correspondence. Letters poured in upon him by the hundred and the thousand. They came from all parts of the South, not only from his old companions-in-arms, but from those he had never seen or heard of. Every mother that had lost a son in the war felt that she had a right to pour her sorrow into the ear of one who was not insensible to her grief. Families left in utter poverty appealed to him for aid. Most men would have shrunk from a labor so great as that of answering these letters. Not so General Lee. He read them, not only patiently, as a man performs a disagreeable duty, but with a tender interest, and so far as was possible, he returned the kindest answers. If he had little money to give, he could at least give sympathy, and to his old soldiers and their wives and children, it was more than money to know that they had a place in that great heart.

"While thus ministering to his stricken people, there is one public benefit which he rendered that ought never to be forgotten. Though the war was over he still stood in public relations in which he could render an immeasurable service to the whole country. There are no crises in a nation's life more perilous than those following civil war. The peace that comes after it, is peace only in name, if the passions of the war still live. After our great struggle, the South was full of inflammable materials. The fires were but smouldering in ashes and might break out at any minute, and rage with destructive fury. If the spirit of some had had full swing, the passions of the Civil War would have been not only perpetuated, but increased, and have gone down as an inheritance of bitterness from generation to generation. This stormy sea of passion but one man could control. He had no official position, civil or military. But he was the representative of the 'Lost Cause.' He had led the Southern armies to battle, and he still had the unbounded confidence of millions; and it was his attitude and his words that did more than anything else to still the angry tempest that the war had left behind. It was the sight of their great chieftain, so calm, so ready to bear the burden with his people, that soothed their anger and their pride; and made the old soldiers of the Confederacy feel that they could accept what had been accepted by their leader; and that, as he had set the example, it was no unworthy sacrifice to become loyal supporters of the restored American Union. It is therefore not too much to say that it is owing in great measure to General Lee that the Civil War has not left a lasting division between the North and the South, and that they form to-day one United Country.

"These are the grateful memories to be recalled now that he who was so mighty in war, and so gentle in peace, has passed beyond the reach of praise or blame. Do you tell me he was an 'enemy,' and that by as much as we love our country we ought to hate its enemies? But there are no enemies among the dead. When the grave closes over those with whom we have been at strife, we can drop our hatreds, and judge of them without passion, and even kindly, as we wish those who come after us to judge of us. In a few years all the contemporaries of General Lee will be dead and gone; the great soldiers that fought with him and that fought against him, will alike have passed to the grave; and then perhaps there will be a nearer approach of feeling between friend and foe.

"'Ah, yes,' say some who admit his greatness as a soldier and leader, 'if it were not for his ambition, that stopped not at the ruin of his country!' Such is the fatal accusation:

> "'Cæsar was ambitious:
> If it were so, it was a grievous fault,
> And grievously hath Cæsar answered it.'

"But was that ambition in him which was patriotism in us? How is it that *we* who were upborne for four years by a passion for our country, that stopped at no sacrifices, cannot understand that other men, of the same race and blood, could be inspired with the same passion for what they looked upon as their country, and fight for it with the same heroic devotion that we fought for ours? They as well as we were fighting for an idea: we for union, and they for independence—a cause which was as sacred to them as ours to us. Is it that what was patriotism on one side was only ambition on the other? No; it was not disappointed ambition that cut short that life, but a wound that struck far deeper. One who watched by him in those long night hours, tells me that he died of a broken heart! This is the most touching aspect of the great warrior's death; that he did not fall on the field of battle, either in the hour of defeat or victory, but in silent grief for sufferings which he could not relieve. There is something infinitely pathetic in the way that he entered into the condition of a whole people, and gave his last strength to comfort those who were fallen and cast down. It was this constant strain of hand and brain and heart that finally snapped the strings of life; so that the last view of him as he passes out of our sight, is one of unspeakable sadness. The dignity is preserved, but it is the dignity of woe. It is the same tall and stately form, yet not wearing the robes of a conquerer, but bowed with sorrows not his own. In this mournful majesty, silent with a grief beyond words, this great figure passes into history.

'There we leave him to the judgment of another generation, that standing afar off' may see some things more clearly than we. When the historian of future ages comes to write the History of the Great Republic, he will give the first place to that War of the Revolution by which our country gained its independence, and took its place among the nations of the earth; and the second to the late Civil War, which, begun for separation, ended in a closer and consolidated union. That was the last act in the great drama of our nation's life, in which history cannot forget the part that was borne by him whose silent form lies within this sepulchre.

"As I took a last look at the sarcophagus, I observed that it bore no epitaph; no words of praise were carved upon the stone; only a name, with two dates:

Robert Edward Lee,
Born January 19, 1807,
Died October 12, 1870.

"That is all; but it is enough: all the rest may be left to the calm, eternal judgment of history."

So very many of General Lee's letters have been published that it is a difficult task to select a few for renewed publication, or to choose a few as being the best. However, those to the members of his own immediate family certainly give the closest insight into the true character of the man. Writing to his two eldest sons, from,

"Ship Massachusetts, off Lobos, 27th February, 1847.

"My dear Boys: I have received your letters with the greatest pleasure, and, as I always like to talk to you both together, I will not separate you in my letters, but write one to you both. I was much gratified to hear of your progress at school, and hope that you will continue to advance, and that I shall have the happiness of finding you much improved in all your studies on my return. I shall not feel my long separation from you, if I find that my absence has been of no injury to you, and that you have both grown in goodness and knowledge, as well as stature. But, ah! how much I will suffer on my return, if the reverse has occurred! You enter all my thoughts, into all my prayers; and on you, in part, will depend whether I shall be happy or miserable, as you know how much I love you. You must do all in your power to save me from pain.

"You will learn, by my letter to your grandmother, that I have left Tampico. I saw many things to remind me of you, though that was not necessary to make me wish you were with me. The river was so calm and beautiful, and the boys were playing about in boats, and swimming their ponies. Then there were troops of donkeys carrying water through the streets. They had a kind of saddle, something like a cart-saddle, though larger, that carried two ten-gallon kegs on each side, which was a load for a donkey. They had no bridles on, but would come along in strings to the river, and, as soon as their kegs were filled, start off again. They were fatter and sleeker that any donkeys I had ever seen before, and seemed to be better cared for. I saw a great many ponies, too. They were larger than those in the upper country, but did not seem so enduring. I got one to ride around the fortifications. He had a Mexican bit and saddle, and paced delightfully, but, every time my sword struck him in the flanks, would jump and try to run off. Several of them had been broken to harness by Americans, and I saw some teams, in wagons, driven four-in-hand, well matched and trotting well.

"We had a grand parade on General Scott's arrival. The troops were all drawn up on the river bank, and fired a salute as he passed them. He landed at the market, where lines of sentinels were placed to keep off the crowd. In front of the landing the artillery was drawn up, which received him in the centre of the column, and escorted him through the streets to his lodgings. They had provided a handsome gray horse, richly caparisoned, for him, but he preferred to walk, with his staff around him, and a dragoon led his horse behind us. The windows along the streets we passed were crowded with people, and the boys and girls were in great glee, the Governor's Island band playing all the time. There were six thousand soldiers in Tampico. Mr. Barry was the adjutant of the escort. I think you would have enjoyed with me the oranges and sweet-potatoes. Major Smith became so fond of the chocolate that I could hardly get him away from the house. We only remained there one day. I have a nice stateroom on board this ship; Joe Johnston and myself occupy it, but my poor Joe is so sick all the time I can do nothing with him. I left Jem to come on with the horses, as I was afraid they would not be properly cared for. Vessels were expressly fitted up for the horses, and parties of dragoons detailed to take care of them. I had hoped they would reach here by this time, as I wanted to see how they were fixed. I took every precaution for their comfort, provided them with bran, oats, &c., and had slings made to pass under them and attached to the coverings above, so that, if in the heavy sea they should slip, or be thrown off their feet, they could not fall. I had to sell my good old horse Jim, as I could not find room for him, or, rather, I did not want to crowd the others. I know I shall want him when I land. Creole was the admiration of every one at Brazos, and they hardly believed she had carried me so far, and looked so well. Jem says there is nothing like her in all the country, and I believe he likes her better than Tom or Jerry. The sorrel mare did not appear to be so well after I got to Brazos. I had to put one of the men on her, whose horse had given out, and the saddle hurt her back. She had gotten well, however, before I left, and I told Jem to ride her every day. I hope they may both reach shore again in safety, but I fear they will have a hard time. They will first have to be put aboard a steamboat and carried to the ship that lies about two miles out at sea, then hoisted in, and how we shall get them ashore again, I do not know. Probably throw them overboard and let them swim there. I do not think we shall remain here more than one day longer. General Worth's and General Twigg's divisions have arrived, which include the regulars, and I suppose the volunteers will be coming on every day. We shall probably go on the 1st down the coast, select a place for debarkation, and make all the arrangements preparatory to the arrival of the troops. I shall have plenty to do there, and am anxious for the time to come and hope all may be successful.

"Tell Rob he must think of me very often, be a good boy, and always love Papa. Take care of Speck and the colts. Mr. Sedwick and officers send their love to you. The ship rolls so that I can scarcely write. You must write to me very often. I am always very glad to hear from you. Be sure I am thinking of you, and that you have the prayers of your affectionate father."

To his eldest son, then a cadet at West Point, he wrote this grand letter. No apology for its republication is needed:

"Arlington House, 5th April, 1852. My Dear Son,—I am just in the act of leaving home for New Mexico. My fine old regiment has been ordered to that distant region, and I must hasten on to see that they are properly cared for. I have but little to add in reply to your letters of March 26, 27, and 28. Your letters breathe a true spirit of frankness; they have given myself and your mother great pleasure. You must study to be frank with the world. Frankness is the child of honesty and courage. Say just what you mean to do on every occasion, and take it for granted you mean to do right. If a friend asks a favor you should grant it if it is reasonable; if not, tell him plainly why you cannot. You will wrong him and wrong yourself by equivocation of any kind. Never do a wrong thing to make a friend or to keep one. The man who requires you to do so is dearly purchased at a sacrifice. Deal kindly, but firmly, with all your classmates; you will find it the policy which wears best. Above all, do not appear to others what you are not. If you have any fault to find with any one tell him, not others, of what you complain. There is no more dangerous experiment than that of undertaking to be one thing before a man's face and another behind his back. We should live, act, and say nothing to the injury of any one. It is not only best as a matter of principle, but it is the path to peace and honor.

"In regard to duty, let me, in conclusion of this hasty letter, inform you that nearly a hundred years ago there was a day of remarkable gloom and darkness, still known as the dark day—a day when the light of the sun was slowly extinguished, as if by an eclipse. The Legislature of Connecticut was in session, and, as its members saw the unexpected and unaccountable darkness coming on, they shared the general awe and terror. It was supposed by many that the last day, the day of judgment, had come. Some one, in the consternation of the hour, moved an adjournment. Then there arose an old Puritan legislator, Davenport of Stamford, and said that if the last day had come he desired to be found at his place, doing his duty, and, therefore, moved that candles be brought in, so that the House could proceed with its duty. There was quietness in that man's mind—the quietness of heavenly wisdom and inflexible willingness to obey present duty. Duty, then, is the sublimest word in our language. Do your duty in all things, like the old Puritan. You cannot do more; you should never wish to do less. Never let me or your mother wear one gray hair for any lack of duty on your part."

Mrs. Lee once stated that "*attention to 'small' matters* was pre-eminently characteristic of General Lee; and she thought his example, in this respect, might be most profitably studied by the young people of the present day." This trait he exhibited throughout life; no detail of anything he had in charge seems to have been considered too trifling to merit his care that it should be thoroughly well done. This is well illustrated in the following letter to his wife. Though a thousand miles from home, he sought to be there in counsel, and to aid her in all the petty details of her household affairs; he would save her all the worry and all the care he could:

"JEFFERSON BARRACKS, 20 Aug., 1855.

"I announced on the envelope of my letter of the 17th, dearest M., that yours of the 11th, accompanied by Fitzhugh's affectionate communication of the same date, had just reached me. I have no doubt but that my reply to his former letter was carried out by your messenger who mailed the last. I have however hastened to answer his last letter, for it deserved a prompt reply, and hope it may reach him in time before his departure.

Our mails are slow. It only goes every other day from here to St. Louis, and I find it takes a fortnight for a letter to go and come. I enclosed in my letter of the 17th to him my check No. 112, dated 1st. Sept., to his order for $200 on Bank of Commerce in New York; and to you, my check of 22 Aug., to your order on Farmers' Bk. of Va., at Alex[a] for $100, and my check of 1 Sept. to the order of Hugh W. Sheffy on same bank for $195. I repeat that you may look out for the letter, and on its non-reception, stop payment of the checks at the respective banks. With this I send my check No. 113, of 25 Aug. '55 on Bk. of Com[ce] in New York to the order of Collins & Co., Baltimore, for $200, which as you have his bill, I have thought you had better remit to him. You may tell him that I have deducted $20.00 from his original offer, as the value of the two registers not used, and the cost of workmanship thereby saved; the payment of plasterer's bill, hauling, &c., and which if not satisfactory I will arrange another time. The bricks and mortar, I was to furnish. The board of his men and hauling was not much, and was more a convenience to him than expense. Perhaps $15 would have been enough, and if he say so, I wish you would send him $5. I would rather over pay than under pay mechanics. You will have to use the $100 I sent you to pay off all your bills, get the girls to school, and Fitzhugh to C. for I am afraid he is penniless, and I will send you another in time for my dear little Rob, who shall not suffer if I have to sell the shirt from my back. I am glad he is well again. I trust he may keep so, but I fear you will all have bilious attacks. I think it is better to write for the furniture you *want* from W. P. [West Point], while Mr. Smith is there; after he goes I do not know who will attend to it. I suppose however Mr. Newlands and Mr. O'Maher will be left. The *picture* had better come by *express*. It will not be ready to varnish before next spring. I am glad you are going to have the book cases repaired. What will you do with the old harpsichord and organ? The former will not be appropriate for the room and the latter ought to give place to the hall table at W. P. Renwick could make you another pair of chairs similar to the present, and the lounge, table and four chairs would be sufficient. If you have them made, recollect to have them *oiled* before being varnished, or the color will be too light. I wish indeed I could be there to help you, but it is impossible. You must have everything nice and comfortable for your father and friends, and I will enjoy it through you. I mentioned in my last letter the necessity of paying the taxes on the Washington lot before the end of Aug., to get the benefit of the discount. The amt. under the present assessment is between $4 and $5 and is payable at the Collector's office at the City Hall. It must be paid every July or Aug., I forget which. You have not mentioned lately anything about Mary's foot. I hope therefore it is still improving. Neither did you give me the result of the consultation about the horse's eye. Sometimes an operation in those cases has to be resorted to, but it ought to be done by a skillful operator. I hope in his case it will not be necessary. Give much love to your father and the children. Tell Becky, she had better come. Goodnight, my dear M., and believe me always yours.

"(P. S.) I was very glad to see that Hill Carter, Jr. of Shirley had taken one of the honors at W$^{m}$. and Mary. Who is the A. M. Randolph of Fauquier, whose oration on 'Human Progress,' is so highly spoken of? I am very sorry to see announced this morning the death of Abbott Lawrence. He is a national loss. But his deeds live after him."

While the approaching storm of civil war was as yet hardly visible, even as a tiny cloud in the political sky, General Lee wrote to his wife of the evils of slavery and of his views as to the proper methods for their emancipation:

"Fort Brown, Texas, 27th December, 1856. The steamer has arrived from New Orleans, bringing full files of papers and general intelligence from the 'States.' I have enjoyed the former very much, and, in absence of particular intelligence, have perused with much interest the series of the Alexandria *Gazette* from the 20th of November to the 8th of December inclusive. Besides the usual good reading matter, I was interested in the relation of local affairs, and inferred, from the quiet and ordinary course of events, that all in the neighborhood was going on well. I trust it may be so, and that you and particularly all at Arlington and our friends elsewhere are well. The steamer brought the President's message to Congress and the reports of the various heads of the departments, so that we are now assured that the Government is in operation and the Union in existence. Not that I had any fears to the contrary, but it is satisfactory always to have facts to go on; they restrain supposition and conjecture, confirm faith, and bring contentment. I was much pleased with the President's message and the report of the Secretary of War. The views of the President on the domestic institutions of the South are truthfully and faithfully expressed. In this enlightened age there are few, I believe, but will acknowledge that slavery as an institution is a moral and political evil in any country. It is useless to expatiate on its disadvantages. I think it, however, a greater evil to the white than to the black race, and while my feelings are strongly interested in behalf of the latter, my sympathies are stronger for the former. The blacks are immeasurably better off here than in Africa, morally, socially, and physically. The painful discipline they are undergoing is necessary for their instruction as a race, and, I hope, will prepare and lead them to better things. How long their subjection may be necessary is known and ordered by a wise and merciful Providence. Their emancipation will sooner result from a mild and melting influence than the storms and contests of fiery controversy. This influence, though slow, is sure. The doctrines and miracles of our Saviour have required nearly two thousand years to convert but a small part of the human race, and even among Christian nations what gross errors still exist! While we see the course of final abolition of slavery is onward, and we give it the aid of our prayers and all justifiable means in our power, we must leave the progress as well as the result in His hands, who sees the end and who chooses to work by slow things, and with whom a thousand years are as but a single day; although the abolitionist must know this, and must see that he has neither the right nor the power of operating except by moral means and suasion; and if he means well to the slave he must not create angry feelings in the master. That although he may not approve the mode by which it pleases Providence to accomplish its purposes, the result will never be the same; that the reasons he gives for interference in what he has no concern holds good for every kind of interference with our neighbors when we disapprove their conduct. Is it not strange that the descendants of those Pilgrim Fathers who crossed the Atlantic to preserve the freedom of their opinion have always proved themselves intolerant of the spiritual liberty of others? I hope you had a joyous Christmas at Arlington, and that it may be long and often repeated. I thought of you all and wished to be with you. Mine was gratefully but silently passed. I endeavored to find some little presents for the children in the garrison to add to their amusement, and succeeded better than I anticipated. The stores are very barren of such things here, but by taking the week beforehand in my daily walks I picked up little by little something for all. Tell Mildred I got a beautiful Dutch doll for little Emma Jones—one of those crying babies that can open and shut their eyes, turn their head, &c. For the two other little girls, Puss Shirley and Mary Sewell, I found handsome French teapots to match cups given to them by Mrs. Waite; then by means of knives and books I satisfied the boys. After dispensing my presents I went to church. The discourse was on the birth of our Saviour. It was not as simply or touchingly told as it is in the Bible. By previous invitation I dined with Major Thomas at 2 P. M. on roast turkey and plum pudding. He and his wife were alone. I had provided a pretty singing bird for the little girl, and passed the afternoon in my room. God bless you all."

To his second son, then on duty in the West, he wrote, under date of 1st of January, 1859: "A happy New Year! and many returns of the same to you, my precious Roon! Ours has been gladdened by the reception of your letter of the 4th of December from Presidio Barracks. It is the first line that has reached us since your second letter from Fort Bridger. I am sorry you have received nothing from us. I have written often and by various routes, and the other members of the family have done the same. Those that are toiling over the plains, I suppose, will never reach you. When I first learned that the Sixth was ordered to the Pacific I sent some letters to Benicia. When your letter arrived from Fort Bridger, saying your regiment had departed from Salt Lake and that you were at Camp Floyd, I inclosed some letters to Major Porter's care. After seeing that the regiment was stopped at Carson's Valley and had sent back for animals, I conjectured that you would be pushed on with your recruits, and would labor through to the Pacific, and I resumed my direction to Benicia. Surely, some of these letters should reach you. . . . But, now that you have caught Custis, I hope you are indemnified for all your privations. I am delighted at you two being together, and nothing has occurred so gratifying to me for the past year. Hold on to him as long as you can. Kiss him for me, and sleep with him every night. He must do the same with you, and charge it all to my account. God grant that it could be my fortune to be with you both! I am glad that you stood the march so well, and are so robust and bearded. I always thought and said there was stuff in you for a good soldier, and I trust you will prove it. I cannot express the gratification I felt, in meeting Colonel May in New York, at the encomiums he passed upon your soldiership, zeal, and devotion to duty. But I was more pleased at the report of your conduct. That went nearer to my heart, and was of infinitely more comfort to me. Hold on to your purity and virtue. They will proudly sustain you in all trials and difficulties, and cheer you in every calamity. I was sorry to see, from your letter to your mother, that you smoke occasionally. It is dangerous to meddle with. You have in store so much better use for your mouth. Reserve it, Roon, for its legitimate pleasure. Do not poison and corrupt it with stale vapors or tarnish your beard with their stench."

Some of the letters, written during the trying times of the war, will show how the stern soldier threw off the grave responsibilities of his position, to indulge in a little friendly badinage, or to pour forth his sympathy with the afflicted:

"Coosawhatchie, S. C., 25th December, 1861.

"My Dear Daughter: Having distributed such poor Christmas gifts as I had to those around me, I have been looking for something for you. Trifles even are hard to get these war-times, and you must not therefore expect more. I have sent you what I thought most useful in your separation from me, and hope it will be of some service. Though stigmatized as 'vile dross,' it has never been a drug with me. That you may never want for it, restrict your wants to your necessities. Yet how little will it purchase! But see how God provides for our pleasures in every way. To compensate for such 'trash,' I send you some sweet violets, that I gathered for you this morning while covered with dense white frost, whose crystals glittered in the bright sun like diamonds, and formed a brooch of rare beauty and sweetness, which could not be fabricated by the expenditure of a world of money. May God guard and preserve you for me, my dear daughter! Among the calamities of war, the hardest to bear perhaps, is the separation of families and friends. Yet all must be endured to accomplish our independence, and maintain our self-government. In my absence from you, I have thought of you very often, and regretted I could do nothing for your comfort. Your old home, if not destroyed by our enemies, has been so desecrated that I cannot bear to think of it. I should have preferred it to have been wiped from the earth, its beautiful hill sunk, and its sacred trees buried, rather than to have been degraded by the presence of those who revel in the ill they do for their own selfish purposes. You see what a poor sinner I am, and how unworthy to possess what has been given me; for that reason it has been taken away. I pray for a better spirit, and that the hearts of our enemies may be changed. In your homeless condition, I hope you make yourself contented and useful. Occupy yourself in aiding those more helpless than yourself. . . . Think always of your father."

Of Arlington and Stratford, the two homes around which so many hallowed memories were grouped, he wrote his wife the same day:[1]

"I cannot let this day of grateful rejoicing pass without some communion with you. I am thankful for the many among the past that I have passed with you, and the remembrance of them fills me with pleasure. As to our old home, if not destroyed it will be difficult ever to be recognized. Even if the enemy had wished to preserve it, it would almost have been impossible. With the number of troops encamped around it, the change of officers, the want of fuel, shelter, etc., and all the dire ne-

---

[1] *General Lee*, by Fitzhugh Lee, 129.

cessities of war, it is vain to think of its being in a habitable condition. I fear, too, the books, furniture, and relics of Mount Vernon will be gone. It is better to make up our minds to a general loss. They cannot take away the remembrances of the spot, and the memories of those that to us rendered it sacred. That will remain to us as long as life will last and that we can preserve. In the absence of a home I wish I could purchase Stratford. It is the only other place I could go to now acceptable to us, that would inspire me with pleasure and local love. You and the girls could remain there in quiet. It is a poor place, but we could make enough corn-bread and bacon for our support, and the girls could weave us our clothes. You must not build your hopes on peace on account of the United States going to war with England. Our rulers are not entirely mad, and if they find England is in earnest, and that war or a restitution of the captives [Messrs. Mason and Slidell] must be the consequence, they will adopt the latter. We must make up our minds to fight our battles and win our independence alone. No one will help us."

To his daughter-in-law, the wife of his son, W. H. F. Lee, the three following letters were written:

"Coosawhatchie, S. C., December 29, 1861. You have no occasion to inform me, you precious Chass, that you have not written to me for a long time. That I already knew, and *you* know that the letters I am obliged to write do not prevent my reading letters from you.

"If it requires fits of indignation to cause you to ventilate your paper, I will give occasion for a series of spasms, but in the present case I am innocent, as my proposition was for you to accompany your mamma to Fayetteville, and not to run off with her son to Fredericksburg. I am afraid the enemy will catch you; and, besides, there are too many young men there. I only want you to visit the old men, your grandpapa and papa. But what has got into your heads to cause you to cut off your hair? If you will weave some delicate fabrics for the soldiers of the family out of it, I will be content with the sacrifice; or, if it is an expression of a penitential mood that has come over you young women, I shall not complain. Poor little A——! Somebody told me that a widower had been making sweet eyes at her through his spectacles. Perhaps she is preparing for caps. But you can tell her not to distress herself. Her papa is not going to give her up in that way. I am, however, so glad that you are all together that I am willing you should indulge in some extravagances if they do not result in serious hurt, as they will afford a variety to the grave occupation of knitting, sewing, spinning, and weaving. You will have to get out the old wheels and looms again, else I do not know where we poor Confederates will get clothes. I have a plenty of old ones for the present, but how are they to be renewed? And that is the condition of many others. I do not think there are manufactories sufficient in the Confederacy to supply the demand; and, as the men are all engrossed by the war, the women will have to engage in the business. Fayetteville or Stratford would be a fine position for a domestic manufactory. When you go to see your grandpa, consult him about it. I am glad to hear that he is well, and hope that he will not let these disjointed times put him out of his usual way or give him inconvenience. I would not advise him to commence building at Broadneck until he sees whether the enemy can be driven from the land, as they have a great fondness for destroying residences when they can do it without danger to themselves. . . . Do not let them get that precious baby, as he is so sweet that they would be sure to eat him. . . . Kiss Fitzhugh for me and the baby. That is the sweetest Christmas-gift I can send them. I send you some sweet violets; I hope they may retain their fragrance till you receive them. I have just gathered them for you. The sun has set, and my eyes plead for relief, for they have had no rest this holy day. But my heart with all its strength stretches toward you, and those with you, and hushes in silence its yearnings. God bless you, my daughter, your dear husband, and son! Give much love to your mamma, and may every blessing attend you all, prays your devoted father."

"Dabb's, June 22, 1862. I must take a part of this holy day, my dearest Chass, to thank you for your letter of the 14th. I am very glad that my communication after the battle reached you so opportunely, and relieved your anxiety about your Fitzhugh. He has, since that, made a hazardous scout, and been protected by that Divine Providence which, I trust and pray, may always smile on, as I know it will ever watch over, you and yours. I sent you some account of this expedition in a former letter, as well as the order of General Stuart on the subject. It was badly printed, but may serve to show you that he conducted himself well. The general deals in the flowery style, as you will perceive if you ever see his report in detail; but he is a good soldier, and speaks highly of the conduct of the two Lees, who, as far as I can learn, deserve his encomiums. Your mamma is very zealous in her attentions to your sick brother. He is reported better. I think he was a few evenings since, when I saw him, and a note this morning from her states that he slowly improves. I hope he will soon be well again. He is much reduced, and looks very feeble. I suppose he will be obliged to go to the 'North Carolina White Sulphur,' to keep you young women company. How will you like that? And now I must answer your inquiries about myself. My habiliments are not as comforta-

R E Lee

ble as yours, nor so suited to this hot weather; but they are the best I have. My coat is of gray, of the regulation style and pattern, and my pants of dark blue, as is also prescribed, partly hid by my long boots. I have the same handsome hat which surmounts my gray head (the latter is *not* prescribed in the regulations), and shields my ugly face, which is masked by a white beard as stiff and wiry as the teeth of a card. In fact, an uglier person you have never seen, and so unattractive is it to our enemies that they shoot at it whenever visible to them. But, though age with its snow has whitened my head and its frosts have stiffened my limbs, my heart, you well know, is not frozen to you, and summer returns when I see you. Having now answered your questions, I have little more to say. Our enemy is quietly working within his lines, and collecting additional forces to drive us from our capital. I hope we shall be able yet to disappoint him, and drive him back into his own country. I saw Fitzhugh the other day. He was looking very well in a new suit of gray."

This hasty note to his son, full of playful humor, is very interesting:

"My Dear Fitzhugh: . . . I wrote you a few lines the other day, and also to my daughter Charlotte. Tell her she must talk quick to you. Her time is getting short, and the soldiers complain of the officers' wives visiting them when theirs cannot. I am petitioned to send them off. Your poor mother is, I fear, no better. I received yesterday a very pleasing letter from Rev. Dr. ——, complimentary of precious ——; I have mailed it to your mother. Kiss Chass for me, and tell her that daughters are not prohibited from visiting their papas. It is only objected to wives visiting their husbands. But she and Mrs. R—— are not included in the prohibition. Your uncle Carter says that they had him, with a gun and sword buckled to him, guarding a ford on James River during Stoneman's last expedition. You and Fitz must not let them capture your uncle. I wish I could have seen your review; I hope Chass did."

After his son had been wounded, he wrote these two notes—one to the son, the other to his daughter-in-law:

"My dear Son: I send you a dispatch received from C—— last night. I hope you are comfortable this morning. I wish I could see you, but I cannot. Take care of yourself, and make haste and get well, and return. Though I scarcely ever saw you, it was a great comfort to know that you were near and with me. I could think of you and hope to see you. May we yet meet in peace and happiness! Kiss Chass for me. Tell her she must not tease you while you are sick, and she must write and let me know how you are. God bless you both, my children!"

"CULPEPER, June 11, 1863.

"I am so grieved, my dear daughter, to send Fitzhugh to you wounded. But I am so grateful that his wound is of a character to give us full hope of a speedy recovery. With his youth and strength to aid him, and your tender care to nurse him, I trust he will soon be well again. I know that you will unite with me in thanks to Almighty God, who has so often shielded him in the hour of danger, for this recent deliverance, and lift up your whole heart in praise to Him for sparing a life so dear to us, while enabling him to do his duty in the station in which He had placed him. Ask him to join us in supplication, that He may always cover him with the shadow of His almighty arm, and teach him that his only refuge is in Him, the greatness of whose mercy reacheth unto the heavens, and His truth unto the clouds. As some good is always mixed with the evil in this world, you will now have him with you for a time, and I shall look to you to cure him very soon, and send him back to me; for, though I saw him seldom, I knew he was near, and always hoped to see him. I went to-day to thank Mrs. Hill for her attention to him and kindness to you. She desired me to give her regards to you both. I must now thank you for the letter you wrote to me while at Fredericksburg. I kept it by me till preparing for the battle-field, when, fearing it might reach the eyes of General Hooker, I destroyed it. We can carry with us only our recollections. I must leave Fitzhugh to tell you about the battle, the army, and the country. . . ."

On hearing of the death of his infant granddaughter, he snatches a moment from his grave military duties, allows his horse to wait at the tent door, while he pens a few lines of tender sympathy:

"Camp, Fredericksburg, 10th December, 1862. I heard yesterday, my dear daughter, with the deepest sorrow, of the death of your infant. I was so grateful at her birth. I felt that she would be such a comfort to you, such a pleasure to my dear Fitzhugh, and would fill so full the void still aching in your hearts. But now you have two sweet angels in heaven. What joy there is in the thought! What relief to your grief! What suffering and sorrow they have escaped! I can say nothing to soften the anguish you must feel, and I know you are assured of my deep and affectionate sympathy. May God give you strength to bear the affliction He has imposed, and produce future joy out of your present misery, is my earnest prayer.

"I saw Fitzhugh yesterday. He is well, and wants to see you. When you are strong enough, cannot you come to Hickory Hill, or your grandpa's, on a little visit? My horse is waiting at my tent door, but I could not refrain from sending these few lines, to recall to you the thought and love of your devoted father."

While his son was recovering from a wound he was captured by a raiding party and taken to Fort Monroe. His wife died during his confinement. This letter was written to his son on his release and return to Richmond:

"Camp, Orange County, April 24, 1864. I received last night, my dear son, your letter of the 22d. It has given me great comfort. God knows how I loved your dear, dear wife, how sweet her memory is to me, and how I mourn her loss. My grief could not be greater if you had been taken from me. You were both equally dear to me. My heart is too full to speak on this subject, nor can I write. But my grief is for ourselves, not for her. She is brighter and happier than ever—safe from all evil, and awaiting us in our heavenly abode. May God in His mercy enable us to join her in eternal praise to our Lord and Saviour. Let us humbly bow ourselves before Him, and offer perpetual prayer for pardon and forgiveness. But we cannot indulge in grief, however mournfully pleasing. Our country demands all our strength, all our energies. To resist the powerful combination now forming against us will require every man at his place. If victorious, we have everything to hope for in the future. If defeated, nothing will be left us to live for. I have not heard what action has been taken by the department in reference to my recommendations concerning the organization of the cavalry. But we have no time to wait, and you had better join your brigade. This week will in all probability bring us active work, and we must strike fast and strong. My whole trust is in God, and I am ready for whatever He may ordain. May He guide, guard, and strengthen us, is my constant prayer."

This letter was written only a few years after his marriage; it is addressed to one of his relatives in Alexandria, an old play-fellow and school-mate:

"St. Louis, 20th August, 1838. My dear Cassius and Cousin, I believe I once spoke to you on the subject of getting for me the crest, coat of arms, &c., of the Lee family, and which sure enough you *never* did. My object in making the request is for the purpose of having a seal cut with the impression of said coat, which I think is due from a man of my *large* family to his posterity, and which, I have thought, perhaps foolishly enough, might as well be right as wrong. If therefore you can assist me in this laudable enterprise, I shall be much obliged, and by enveloping it securely, directed to me at this place, and sending it, either by mail or some safe hand, to *Gen'l Gratiot*, Eng. office, Washington City, without any word or farther direction, it will come safely to hand. I once saw in the hands of Cousin Edmund, for the only time in my life, our family *tree*, and as I begin in my old age to feel a little curiosity relative to my forefathers, their origin, whereabouts, &c., any information you can give me will increase the obligation. So sit down some of these hot evenings and write it off for me, or at any rate the substance, and tell my Cousin Philippa not to let you forget it. I wish you would at the same time undeceive her on a certain point, in which as I understand, she is labouring under a grievous error. Tell her it is the farthest from my wish to detract from any of the little Lees, but as to her little boy being equal to Mr. *Rooney*, it is a thing not to be even *supposed*, much less believed, although in a credulous country where people stick at nothing from a *Coon* story to a sea serpent! You must remember us particularly to her, to Uncle Edmund, Cousins Sally, Hannah and *all* the Lloyds.

"I believe I can tell you nothing doing here that would interest you, except that we are all well; although my Dame has been complaining for a day or two. The elections are all over. The Vanites have carried the day in the State, although the Whigs in this district carried their entire ticket, and you will have the pleasure of hearing the great expunger again thunder from his place in the Senate against Banks, bribery and corruption, and what not.

"While on the river I cannot help being on the look out for that stream of Gold that was to ascend the Mississippi, tied up in silk nett purses! It would be a pretty sight, but the tide has not yet made up here. Let me know whether you can enlighten me on the point in question. And believe me, yours very truly.[1]

"To C. F. Lee, Esqr., Alexandria, D. C."

In the recent memoir of General Lee, written by his nephew, General Fitzhugh Lee, a series of extracts are given from the General's letters to his wife. Throughout these letters, he constantly expresses anxiety for the sufferings of his soldiers from want of proper food and clothing. No one can read these extracts without perceiving one of the causes for the almost perfect adoration which his men had for "Marse Bob," as they were wont to style their commander.

Such expressions as these occur in letter after letter: . . . "We had

---

[1] Copied from the original.

quite a snow day before yesterday, and last night was very cold. It is thawing this morning, though the water was freezing as I washed. I fear it will bring much discomfort to our men who are barefooted and poorly clad. I can take but little pleasure in my comforts for thinking of them." . . . " . . . The quartermaster received the things you sent. The mitts will be very serviceable. Make as many as you can obtain good material for. I have everything I want." . . . On returning from a visit to Richmond, he brought a bag of socks with him for his men, and wrote his wife: "I arrived safely yesterday. There were sixty-seven pairs of socks in the bag I brought up instead of sixty-four, as you supposed, and I found here three dozen pairs of beautiful white-yarn socks, sent over by our kind cousin Julia and sweet little Carrie, making one hundred and three pairs; all of which I sent to the Stonewall brigade. One dozen of the Stuart socks had double heels. Can you not not teach Mildred [his youngest daughter] that stitch? They sent me also some hams, which I had rather they had eaten. I pray that you may be preserved and relieved from all your troubles, and that we may all again be united here on earth and forever in heaven."

At another date: "Your note with the socks arrived last evening. I have sent them to the Stonewall brigade; the number all right—thirty pairs. Including this last parcel of thirty pairs, I have sent to that brigade two hundred and sixty-three pairs. Still, there are about one hundred and forty whose homes are within the enemy's lines and who are without socks. I shall continue to furnish them till all are supplied. Tell the young women to work hard for the brave Stonewallers." . . . A few weeks later: "Your note with the bag of socks reached me last evening. The number was correct—thirty-one pairs. I have sent them to the Stonewall brigade, which is not yet supplied. Sixty-one pairs from the ladies in Fauquier have reached Charlottesville, and I hope will be distributed soon. Now that Miss Bettie Brander has come to the aid of my daughters, the supply will soon be increased."

From camp, under date of 24th of January, 1864, he again wrote to his wife:

"I have had to disperse the cavalry as much as possible to obtain forage for their horses, and it is that which causes trouble. Provisions for men, too, are very scarce, and with very light diet and light clothing I fear they suffer; but still they are cheerful and uncomplaining. I received a report from one division the other day in which it was stated that over four hundred men were barefooted and over a thousand without blankets. . . ."

So, too, some time later he wrote: "I received your letter some days ago, and last night your note accompanying a bag of gloves and socks and a box of coffee. Mrs. Devereux sent the coffee to you, not to me, and I shall have to send it back. It is so long since we have had the foreign bean that we no longer desire it. We have a domestic article, which we procure by the bushel, that answers very well. You must keep the good things for yourself. We have had to reduce our allowance of meat one half, and some days we have none. The gloves and socks are very acceptable, and I shall give them out this morning. The socks of Mrs. Shepherd are very nice, but I think it is better to give them to the soldiers than to dispose of them as you suggest. The soldiers are much in need. We have received some shoes lately, and the socks will be a great addition. Tell Life [his youngest daughter] I think I hear her needles rattle as they fly through the meshes."

In the winter of 1864 the following incident went the rounds of the Southern press:

"One very cold morning a young soldier on the cars to Petersburg was making fruitless efforts to put on his overcoat, with his arm in a sling. His teeth, as well as his sound arm, were brought into use to effect the object; but in the midst of his efforts an officer rose from his seat, advanced to him, and very carefully and tenderly assisted him, drawing the coat gently over his wounded arm, and buttoning it comfortably; then, with a few kind and pleasant words, returned to his seat.

"Now, the officer in question was not clad in gorgeous uniform, with a brilliant wreath upon the collar and a multitude of gilt lines upon the sleeves, resembling the famous labyrinth of Crete, but he was clad in a 'simple suit of gray,' distinguished from the garb of a civilian only by the three stars which every Confederate Colonel is, by the regulations, entitled to wear. And yet he was no other than our chief general, Robert E. Lee, who is not braver than he is good and modest."

General Fitzhugh Lee also gives this: "The cavalry, for the better subsistence of men and horses, had been moved back to Charlottesville for the winter, and, not having much to do, some of the officers proposed to dance. General Lee wrote to his son Robert, then belonging to that arm of the service, from Camp, Orange Court House, 17th January, 1864: 'I inclose a letter for you which has been sent to my care. I hope you are all well and all around you. Tell Fitz I grieve over the hardships and sufferings of the men in their late expedition. I would have preferred his waiting for more favorable weather. He accomplished much under the circumstances, but would have done much more in favorable weather. I am afraid he was anxious to get back to the ball. This is a bad time for such things. We have too grave subjects on hand to engage in such trivial amusements. I would rather his officers should entertain themselves in fattening their horses, healing their men, and recruiting their regiments. There are too many Lees on the committee. I like them all to be present at battles, but can excuse them at balls. But the saying is, "Children will be children." I think he had better move his camp farther from Charlottesville, and perhaps he will get more work and less play. He and I are too old for such assemblies. I want him to write me how his men are, his horses, and what I can do to fill up his ranks.'" (*General Lee*, 324–5.)

The Hon. B. H. Hill, in a speech, said:

"Lee sometimes indulged in satire, to which his greatness gave point and power. He was especially severe on newspaper criticisms of military movements—subjects about which the writers knew nothing.

"'We made a great mistake, Mr. Hill, in the beginning of our struggle, and I fear, in spite of all we can do, it will prove to be a fatal mistake,' he said to me, after General Bragg had ceased to command the Army of Tennessee, an event Lee deplored.

"'What mistake is that, General?'

"'Why, sir, in the beginning we appointed all our worst generals to command the armies and our best generals to edit the newspapers. As you know, I have planned some campaigns and quite a number of battles. I have given the work all the care and thought I could, and sometimes, when my plans were completed, as far as I could see, they seemed perfect. But when I have fought them through I have discovered defects, and occasionally wondered I did not see some of them in advance. When it was all over I found by reading a newspaper that these best editor generals saw all the defects plainly from the start. Unfortunately, they did not communicate their knowledge to me until it was too late.' Then, after a pause, he added, with a beautiful, grave expression I can never forget: 'I have no ambition but to serve the Confederacy, and do all I can to win our independence. I am willing to serve in any capacity to which the authorities may assign me. I have done the best I could in the field, and have not succeeded as I could wish. I am willing to yield my place to these best generals, and I will do my best for the cause editing a newspaper.'

"In the same strain he once remarked to one of his generals: 'Even as poor a soldier as I am can generally discover mistakes *after it is all over*. But if I could only induce these wise gentlemen who see them so clearly beforehand to communicate with me *in advance*, instead of waiting until the evil has come upon us, to let me know what *they knew all the time*, it would be far better for my reputation and (what is of more consequence) far better for the cause.' " [1]

"Upon one occasion, General Lee received a letter from some spirit-rappers, asking his opinion on a certain great military movement. He wrote, in reply, a most courteous letter, in which he said that the question was one about which military critics would differ; that his own judgment about such matters was but poor at best, and that inasmuch as they had the power to consult (through their mediums) Cæsar, Alexander, Napoleon, Wellington, and all of the other great captains who have ever lived, he could not think of obtruding his opinion into such company." [2]

Of the final scene in the great struggle, Horace Greeley has written:

"The parting of Lee with his devoted followers was a sad one. Of the proud army, which, dating its victories from Bull Run, had driven McClellan from before Richmond, and withstood his best efforts at Antietam, and shattered Burnside's host at Fredericksburg, and worsted Hooker at Chancellorsville, and fought Meade so stoutly, though unsuccessfully, before Gettysburg, and baffled Grant's bounteous resources and desperate efforts in the Wilderness, at Spottsylvania, on the North Anna, at Cold Harbor, and before Petersburg and Richmond—a mere wreck remained. It is said that 27,000 men were included in Lee's capitulation; but of these not more than 10,000 had been able to carry their arms thus far in their hopeless and almost foodless flight." . . . The men "crowded around their departing chief, who, with streaming eyes, grasped and pressed their outstretched hands, at length finding words to say: 'Men, we have fought through the war together. I have done the best I could for you; my heart is too full to say more.' " His last official act was to request that all his private soldiers, who owned the horses they used, might be allowed to carry them home "for the spring plowing;" so, to the last, was the commander thoughtful of the welfare of his men.

The war being over, what should General Lee do? He had no home, no fortune, no occupation. Numerous offers of high positions in various corporations, and such like business ventures, were made to him; but none were to his taste nor suited to his training. Finally, the trustees of Washington College offered him the presidency of that institution; the salary was small, the place insignificant, but a home in the mountains of Virginia suited his taste, and a desire to still be of use to his State in training her

---

[1] *Reminiscences of General Robert E. Lee*, by the Rev. J. William Jones, pp. 241–2.

[2] *Ibid.*, p. 239.

young men, decided him. He entered upon his duties there in October, 1865, and steadily performed them for five years. Then his discharge came.

Of his last illness and death, Colonel William Preston Johnston has written a most graphic account.[1] Colonel Johnston was a professor at the College, had been intimately associated with General Lee during the four years of their mutual service, and was a watcher at his death-bed:

"The death of General Lee was not due to any sudden cause, but was the result of agencies dating as far back as 1863. In the trying campaign of that year, he contracted a severe sore throat, that resulted in rheumatic inflammation of the sac inclosing the heart. There is no doubt that after this sickness his health was always more or less impaired; and, although he complained little, yet rapid exercise on foot or on horseback produced pain and difficulty of breathing. In October, 1869, he was again attacked by inflammation of the heart-sac, accompanied by muscular rheumatism of the back, right side, and arms. The action of the heart was weakened by this attack; the flush upon his face was deepened, the rheumatism increased, and he was troubled with weariness and depression."

"In March, 1870, General Lee, yielding to the solicitations of friends and medical advisers, made a six weeks' visit to Georgia and Florida. He returned greatly benefited by the influence of the genial climate, the society of friends in those States, and the demonstrations of respect and affection of the people of the South; his physical condition, however, was not greatly improved. During this winter and spring he had said to his son, General Custis Lee, that his attack was mortal; and had virtually expressed the same belief to other trusted friends. And now, with that delicacy that pervaded all his actions, he seriously considered the question of resigning the presidency of Washington College, 'fearful that he might not be equal to his duties.' After listening, however, to the affectionate remonstrances of the Faculty and board of trustees, who well knew the value of his wisdom in the supervision of the college, and the power of his mere presence and example upon the students, he resumed his labors with the resolution to remain at his post and carry forward the great work he had so auspiciously begun.

"During the summer he spent some weeks at the Hot Springs of Virginia, using the baths, and came home seemingly better in health and spirits. He entered upon the duties of the opening collegiate year in Sep-

---

[1] This description of General Lee's last days was prepared by Colonel Johnston for the *Reminiscences of General Robert E. Lee*, edited by the Rev. J. William Jones.

tember with that quiet zeal and noiseless energy that marked all his actions, and an unusual elation was felt by those about him at the increased prospect that long years of usefulness and honor would yet be added to his glorious life.

"Wednesday, the 28th of September, 1870, found General Lee at the post of duty. In the morning he was fully occupied with the correspondence and other tasks incident to his office of President of Washington College, and he declined offers of assistance from members of the Faculty, of whose services he sometimes availed himself. After dinner, at four o'clock, he attended a vestry meeting of Grace (Episcopal) Church. The afternoon was chilly and wet, and a steady rain had set in, which did not cease until it resulted in a great flood, the most memorable and destructive in this region for a hundred years. The church was rather cold and damp, and General Lee, during the meeting, sat in a pew with his military cape cast loosely about him. In a conversation that occupied the brief space preceding the call to order, he took part, and told, with marked cheerfulness and kindliness of tone, some pleasant anecdotes of Bishop Meade and Chief Justice Marshall. The meeting was protracted until after seven o'clock, by a discussion touching the rebuilding of the church edifice and the increase of the rector's salary. General Lee acted as chairman, and, after hearing all that was said, gave his own opinion, as was his wont, briefly and without argument. He closed the meeting with a characteristic act. The amount required for the minister's salary still lacked a sum much greater than General Lee's proportion of the subscription, in view of his frequent and generous contributions to the church and other charities; but just before the adjournment, when the treasurer announced the amount of the deficit still remaining, General Lee said, in a low tone: 'I will give that sum.' He seemed tired toward the close of the meeting, and, as was afterward remarked, showed an unusual flush, but at the time no apprehensions were felt.

"General Lee returned to his house, and, finding his family waiting tea for him, took his place at the table, standing to say grace. The effort was vain, the lips could not utter the prayer of the heart. Finding himself unable to speak, he took his seat quietly and without agitation. His face seemed to some of the anxious group about him to wear a look of sublime resignation, and to evince a full knowledge that the hour had come when all the cares and anxieties of his crowded life were at an end. His physicians, Drs. H. T. Barton and R. L. Madison, arrived promptly and applied the usual remedies, and placed him upon the couch from which he was to arise no more. To him henceforth the things of this world were as nothing, and he bowed with resignation to the command of the Master he had followed so long with reverence.

"The symptoms of his attack resembled concussion of the brain, without the attendant swoon. There were marked debility, a slightly impaired consciousness, and a tendency to doze; but no paralysis of motion or sensation, and no evidence of softening or inflammation of the brain. His physicians treated the case as one of venous congestion, and with apparently favorable results. Yet, despite these propitious auguries drawn from his physical symptoms, in view of the great mental strain he had undergone, the gravest fears were felt that the attack was mortal. He took without objection the medicines and diet prescribed, and was strong enough to turn in bed without aid, and to sit up and take nourishment. During the earlier days of his illness, though inclined to doze, he was easily aroused, was quite conscious and observant, evidently understood whatever was said to him, and answered questions briefly but intelligently; he was, however, averse to much speaking, generally using monosyllables, as had always been his habit when sick. When first attacked, he said to those who were removing his clothes, pointing at the same time to his rheumatic shoulder, 'You hurt my arm.' Although he seemed to be gradually improving until October 10th, he apparently knew from the first that the appointed hour had come when he must enter those dark gates that, closing, reopen no more to earth. In the words of his physician, 'he neither expected nor desired to recover.' When General Custis Lee made some allusion to his recovery, he shook his head and pointed upward. On the Monday morning before his death, Dr. Madison, finding him looking better, tried to cheer him: 'How do you feel to-day, General?' General Lee replied, slowly and distinctly: 'I feel better.' The doctor then said: 'You must make haste and get well; Traveller has been standing so long in the stable that he needs exercise.' The General made no reply, but slowly shook his head and closed his eyes. Several times during his illness he put aside his medicine, saying, 'It is of no use;' but yielded patiently to the wishes of his physicians or children, as if the slackened chords of being still responded to the touch of duty or affection.

"On October 10th, during the afternoon, his pulse became feeble and rapid, and his breathing hurried, with other evidences of great exhaustion. About midnight he was seized with a shivering from extreme debility, and Dr. Barton felt obliged to announce the danger to the family. On October 11th, he was evidently sinking; his respiration was hurried, and his pulse feeble and rapid. Though less observant, he still recognized whoever approached him, but refused to take anything unless presented by his physicians. It now became certain that the case was hopeless. His decline was rapid, yet gentle, and soon after nine o'clock, on the morning of October 12th, he closed his eyes, and his soul passed peacefully from earth.

"General Lee's physicians attributed his death in great measure to moral causes. The strain of his campaigns, the bitterness of defeat aggravated by the bad faith and insolence of the victor, sympathy with the subsequent sufferings of the Southern people, and the effort at calmness under these accumulated sorrows, seemed the sufficient and real causes that slowly but steadily undermined General Lee's health and led to his death. Yet to those who saw his composure under the greater and lesser trials of life, and his justice and forbearance with the most unjust and uncharitable, it seemed scarcely credible that his serene soul was shaken by the evil that raged around him.

"General Lee's closing hours were consonant with his noble and disciplined life. Never was more beautifully displayed how a long and severe education of mind and character enables the soul to pass with equal step through this supreme ordeal; never did the habits and qualities of a lifetime, solemnly gathered into a few last sad hours, more grandly maintain themselves amid the gloom and shadow of approaching death. The reticence, the self-contained composure, the obedience to proper authority, the magnanimity, and the Christian meekness, that marked all his actions, still preserved their sway, in spite of the inroads of disease, and the creeping lethargy that weighed down his faculties.

"As the old hero lay in the darkened room, or with the lamp and hearth-fire casting shadows upon his calm, noble front, all the massive grandeur of his form, and face, and brow, remained; and death seemed to lose its terrors, and to borrow a grace and dignity in sublime keeping with the life that was ebbing away. The great mind sank to its last repose, almost with the equal poise of health. The few broken utterances that evinced at times a wandering intellect were spoken under the influence of the remedies administered; but as long as consciousness lasted there was evidence that all the high, controlling influences of his whole life still ruled; and even when stupor was laying its cold hand on the intellectual perceptions, the moral nature, with its complete orb of duties and affections, still asserted itself. A Southern poet has celebrated in song those last significant words, 'Strike the tent;' and a thousand voices were raised to give meaning to the uncertain sound, when the dying man said, with emphasis, 'Tell Hill he *must* come up!' These sentences serve to show most touchingly through what fields the imagination was passing; but generally his words, though few, were coherent; but for the most part indeed his silence was unbroken.

"This self-contained reticence had an awful grandeur, in solemn accord with a life that needed no defense. Deeds which required no justification must speak for him. His voiceless lips, like the shut gates of some majestic temple, were closed, not for concealment, but because that within was holy. Could the eye of the mourning watcher have pierced the gloom that gathered about the recesses of that great soul, it would have perceived a Presence there full of an ineffable glory. Leaning trustfully upon the all-sustaining Arm, the man whose stature, measured by mortal standards, seemed so great, passed from this world of shadows to the realities of the hereafter."

General Lee married Mary Anne Randolph Custis, the only daughter of George Washington Parke Custis and Mary Lee Fitzhugh, his wife. Mary Custis was born at Arlington the 1st of October, 1808, and died at her home in Lexington the 5th of November, 1873. She was buried in the College chapel, with her daughter, Agnes, and her husband.

Of his wedding let another speak:[1] "He was in love from boyhood. Fate brought him to the feet of one who, by birth, education, position, and family tradition, was best suited to be his life companion. . . . They had known each other when she was a child at Arlington and he a young boy in Alexandria, some eight miles away. It is said she met and admired him when he came back to Alexandria on a furlough from the Military Academy. It was the first time any one in that vicinity had seen him in his cadet uniform. He was handsomer than ever; straight, erect, symmetrical in form, with a finely shaped head on a pair of broad shoulders. He was then twenty years old, and a fine specimen of a West Point cadet on leave of absence. The impressions produced were of an enduring nature, and the officer, upon graduation, followed up the advantage gained by the attractive cadet.

"G. W. P. Custis was the adopted son of Washington and the grandson of Mrs. Washington. Lee was, therefore, to marry a great granddaughter of Mrs. Washington, and was a fortunate man, not so much, perhaps, from these ties, but because of the great qualities of head and heart possessed by Mary Custis, his affianced bride. It is difficult to say whether she was more lovely on that memorable June evening, when the Rev. Mr. Keith asked her, 'Wilt thou take this man to be thy wedded husband?' or after many years had passed, and she was seated in her large arm-chair

---

[1] *General Lee*, by Fitzhugh Lee, pp. 25–27.

in Richmond, almost unable to move from chronic rheumatism, but busily engaged in knitting socks for the sockless Confederate soldiers. The public notice of the marriage was short:

"'Married, 30th June, 1831, at Arlington House, by the Rev. Mr. Keith, Lieutenant Robert E. Lee, of the United States Corps of Engineers, to Miss Mary A. R. Custis, only daughter of G. W. P. Custis, Esq.'

"Beautiful old Arlington was in all her glory that night. The stately mansion never held a happier assemblage. 'Its broad portico and wide-spread wings held out open arms, as it were, to welcome the coming guests. Its simple Doric columns graced domestic comforts with a classic air. Its halls and chambers were adorned with the patriots and heroes, and with illustrations and relics of the great Revolution and of the "Father of his Country." Without and within history and tradition seemed to breathe their legends upon a canvas as soft as a dream of peace.'"

The bridal attendants, on this occasion, consisted of: first, Miss Catharine Mason and Lieutenant Sydney Smith Lee; second, Miss Mary Goldsborough and Lieutenant Thomas Kennedy; third, Miss Marietta Turner and Lieutenant Chambers; fourth, Miss Angela Lewis and Mr. Tillman; fifth, Miss Julia Calvert and Lieutenant Prentiss; sixth, Miss Britannia Peter and Lieutenant Thomas Turner. This wedding occurred before the fashion of "wedding trips" came into vogue; the festivities of the evening were concluded by a handsome supper, and were continued until the evening of the following Monday (the wedding took place on Thursday).

For many years, prior to her death, Mrs. Lee suffered extremely from chronic rheumatism, which crippled her so much that she could scarcely use her hands, and confined her for years to the chair of an invalid. Yet no one could have been more cheerful or less complaining. In a letter to the late Cassius F. Lee, Sr., under date of 3d of January, 1872, she wrote of herself: "I have been intending, my dear Cassius, ever since your son Edmund came, to write to you and tell you how pleased we were to see him; but a long and severe attack of rheumatism has prevented my writing. I can only write a few lines at a time, and even now I can scarcely use my pen at all. He lives quite near us and looks remarkably well and Custis tells me is doing well, is quite studious. He comes to see us often and always looks bright and cheerful. I do hope he will fulfill all your hopes and expectations. You must give our loves to his mother and all your family. I hope you have all enjoyed this Christmas and New Year. It has been an unusually sad one to me. Besides my painful sickness, during that time Fitzhugh lost his youngest child of whooping cough, a lovely little

Mary Custis Lee

girl of one year old, whom I had been looking forward to enjoy so much this winter when I expected to go down. I do not think in all my life I ever endured so tedious and painful an attack of illness and you will see since this illness I can scarcely use my pen at all. . . .

"The weather is so uncomfortable that I have relinquished all idea of going to the White House. Agnes and Mildred went there from Bob's wedding; Mildred has been suffering much from a sprained ankle, which still continues. Mary and Custis alone are with me here. We read the genealogical book but could not add anything to it. It was much fuller than anything we have, which is mostly obtained from that letter of Mr. Thomas [William?] Lee. We have all been much disappointed at the delay in bringing out the 'Memorial' volume and fear it will not be any advantage to its circulation. Mary says she has no doubt that my aunt, Mrs. Fitzhugh, could tell you all about the connection of Fitzhughs and Lees; tell her, if you should see her, that I am waiting to get my hand steadier before I write to her. What about Arlington? Can anything be done this winter? I feel so weak and miserable that the things of earth seem passing away and losing their value and interest. I suppose, though, if God should restore me to my wonted health, the interest would return. I do not think I could write another line. Tell me of my friends, of your daughters and all. Especial love to Dr. Packard. Yours affectionately."

General Robert E. Lee had the following-named children:

i, George Washington Custis[7]. See 75.

ii, Mary Custis[7], living and unmarried.

iii, William Henry Fitzhugh[7]. See 76.

iv, Annie Carter[7], born at Arlington, the 18th of June, 1839; died at the White Sulphur Springs, Warren county, North Carolina, the 20th of October, 1862. A beautiful monument has been erected over her grave by the citizens of Warren county; it was unveiled, with appropriate ceremony, the 8th of August, 1866. General Lee was obliged to deny himself the mournful satisfaction of being present at the dedication. He wrote to the ladies having it in charge: " . . . I do not know how to express to you my thanks for your great kindness to her while living, and for your affectionate remembrance of her since dead. . . . I have always cherished the intention of visiting the tomb of her who never gave me aught but pleasure; but to afford me the satisfaction which I crave, it must be done with more privacy than I can hope for on the occasion you propose. . . . "

v, Eleanor Agnes[7], born at "Arlington" about 1842; died at Lexington, 15th October, 1873.

vi, ROBERT EDWARD[7]. See 77.
vii, MILDRED CHILDE[7], living and unmarried.

## THE CUSTIS FAMILY.

John Custis, of Irish birth, came from Rotterdam to Virginia, and settled in Northampton county as early as 1640. He left six sons: Thomas, of Baltimore, Ireland; Edward, of London; Robert, of Rotterdam; John, William, and Joseph, of Virginia. His son John was Sheriff of Northampton in 1664, and "was an active, enterprising man, engaged in making salt on one of the islands; was foremost in all civil and ecclesiastical matters; was appointed, in 1676, during Bacon's Rebellion, a major-general; was a true royalist; a law and order man; a great favorite of Lord Arlington in the time of Charles II.; he was twice married; his second wife was a daughter of Col. Edmund Scarborough. He died at an advanced age, after having been full of labours through life." This John Custis was one of the vestry of Hungars Parish, and "presented sets of heavy silver Communion service to both churches, upper and lower, of Northampton; and when the lower church was built, in 1680, near which was his residence, he promised to give the builder one hogshead of tobacco, or its equivalent, and thirty gallons of cider to put up for him the first pew (the best, I suppose) in the church." . . . "He had only one son, whom he named John. This John Custis had numerous children, whose descendants, together with those of his uncle William Custis, have filled the Eastern Shore with the name. His son John, being the fourth of the name, after being educated in England, received from his grandfather the Arlington estate. He was the John Custis who removed to Williamsburg and married the daughter of Col. Daniel Parke and was the father of the Daniel Parke Custis, who married Martha Dandridge. His tomb is at Arlington House, in Northampton, and the inscription is one of the curiosities of the Eastern Shore. It is plainly to be seen from it that he was not very happy in his matrimonial relations; for it says that he only lived seven years—those seven which he had spent as a bachelor at Arlington. His wife, it is to be feared, was too much like her brother and unlike her father." (*Old Churches, Families, &c.*, I, 257, 262.)

The will of the "Honourable John Custis, Esq., of the City of Williamsburg and County of James City in the Colony of Virginia" (dated the 14th November, 1749, proved at London on 19th November, 1753) desired his executor to lay out £100 for a handsome tombstone of the best durable marble, "very decent and handsome to lay over my body, engraved on the tombstone my coat of arms, which are three parrots, and my will is that the following inscription may also be handsomely engraved on the said stone vizt."

"Under this Marble Stone lyes the Body of the Honourable John Custis Esquire of the City of Williamsburg and parish of Bruton, formerly of Hungars Parish on the Eastern Shoar of Virginia and County of Northampton the place of his Nativity, Aged—[71] years and yet lived but seven years which was the space of time he kept a Batchelors House at Arlington on the Eastern Shoar of Virginia. This Inscription put on this Stone by his own possitive Orders."

To insure faithful observance of his orders regarding his burial and the subsequent care of the tomb, he added: "And if my heir should ingratefully or obstinately refuse or neglect to comply with what relates to my Burial in every particular then I bar and cut him off from any part of my estate." He also left to "his dear friend Thomas Lee Esquire, if living at my death, £200 to buy him any one thing he has a mind to remember me." His son, Daniel Parke Custis named as sole legatee and executor.

"The following letter of young Custis to his intended bride, written a few months before their marriage, in which, according to the custom of the time, he calls her his 'Fidelia,' is a fair specimen of passionate love letters in the old colonial days. Its tone is quite different from that which characterizes the inscription upon his tomb, in which he so pointedly, though indirectly affirms, that his life, while he lived with his 'Fidelia,' was so unhappy that he considered it a blank in his existence:

"'Williamsburg, 4th February, 1705.

"'May angels guard my dearest Fidelia and deliver her safe to my arms at our next meeting; and sure they won't refuse their protection to a creature so pure and charming, it would be easy for them to mistake her for one of themselves. If you could but believe how entirely you possess the empire of my heart, you would easily credit me, when I tell you, that I can neither think nor so much as dream of any other subject than the enchanting Fidelia. You will do me wrong if you suspect that there ever was a man created that loved with more tenderness and sincerity than I do, and I should do you wrong if I could imagine that there ever was a nymph that deserved it better than you. Take this for granted, and then fancy how uneasy I am like to be under the unhappiness of your absence. Figure to yourself what tumults there will arise in my blood, what a fluttering of the spirits, what a disorder of the pulse, what passionate wishes, what absence of thought, and what crowding of sighs, and then imagine how unfit I shall be for business; but returning to the dear cause of my uneasiness; O the torture of six months' expectation! If it must be so long and necessity will till then interpose betwixt you and my inclinations, I must submit, though it be as unwilling as pride submits to superior virtue, or envy to superior success. Pray think of me, and believe that Veramour is entirely and eternally yours.'" (*Recollections of Washington*, by G. W. P. Custis, 16, 17.)

"Fidelia" was Frances, eldest daughter of Colonel Daniel Parke, whom he married in 1706. Mrs. Custis died after a short time of small-pox, leaving two children, a son and a daughter. The father, "the Hon. Daniel Parke, whose name stands first, in 1674, on the list of the vestry of Bruton Church, at Williamsburgh, was from the county of Surry, England. A tablet to his memory was placed in the first church at Williamsburgh, and afterward transferred to the second. He appears to have been a man of worth and distinction. He married a Miss Evelyn. . . . It could be wished that the record of Daniel Parke, his son, whose name is also on the vestry book, were as worthy of notice. He was indeed more notorious than his father but for other reasons." (*Old Churches, Families, &c.*, I, 180.)

Col. Parke, the elder, was Secretary of the Colonial Council; he died in 1679, and was buried at Williamsburg. The son, here referred to by Bishop Meade, was born in York county, Virginia; he married Jane, daughter of Governor Philip Ludwell by his first wife, Lucy, daughter of Robert Higginson (and widow successively of Major Lewis Burwell and Col. William Bernard). This Daniel Parke, it is said, had a very violent temper and was of licentious habits, so much so that he was compelled to leave Virginia and settle in England; later, he was appointed an aide upon the staff of Marlborough and had the honor of conveying to London the news of the victory of Blenheim. Queen Anne rewarded him by the present of her miniature set with diamonds. Through influence at court, he was appointed governor of the Leeward Islands; while gallantly defending himself from a mob there, he lost his life, 7th December, 1710. He left two daughters; Frances married, as stated, John Custis; the other daughter, Lucy, married Col. William Byrd, of "Westover," and, curiously enough, she, too, died of small-pox, her death occurring at London, in 1716.

John and Frances (Parke) Custis had two children; the son, Daniel Parke Custis, "was born at 'Queene's Creek,' according to a record in the family Bible, at Arlington, on the 15th of October, 1711. There is also a record there that 'Governor Spottswood, the Honourable William Byrd, Esqr., and Mrs. Hannah Ludwell, were godfathers and godmother.'" In 1749, Daniel Parke Custis married the beautiful Martha Dandridge, daughter of John Dandridge, of New Kent county, and died in 1757, leaving four children: Daniel Parke, Francis Parke, John Parke, and Martha Parke Custis. The two eldest died while young; Martha died at Mt. Vernon on the 19th of June, 1773. Mrs. Custis married George Washington on the 6th of January, 1759; she was born in May, 1732, and died, at Mt. Vernon, the 22d of May, 1802.

John Parke Custis was, therefore, the only child of this marriage to leave issue; he was born at the "White House," on the Pamunkey River, in New Kent county, in 1753; died at "Eltham," the residence of his maternal uncle, Burwell Bassett, on the 5th of November, 1781. He had married, on the 3d of February, 1774, Eleanor, the second daughter of Benedict Calvert, of "Mt. Airy," Prince George's county, Md., a son of Charles Calvert, sixth Lord Baltimore, and great-grandson of Benedict Calvert, fourth Lord Baltimore, who married, in 1698, Lady Charlotte Fitzroy, daughter of Edward Henry Lee, first Earl of Litchfield.[1] The young couple lived for some time at Mt. Vernon, and then moved to "Abingdon," on the Potomac, a short distance above Alexandria, where their three older children were born. It is said that Eleanor Calvert was only sixteen at the time of her marriage; nor was the husband much older, having not yet reached his twentieth year. On the 3d of April, 1773, General Washington wrote to Mr. Calvert, entering a protest against the union of the young people: ". . . My son-in-law and ward, Mr. Custis, has, as I have been informed, paid his addresses to your second daughter, and, having made some progress in her affections, has solicited her in marriage. How far a union of this sort may be agreeable to you, you can best tell; but I should think myself wanting in candor, were I not to confess, that Miss Nelly's amiable qualities are acknowledged on all hands, and that an alliance with your family will be pleasing to his. This acknowledgement being made, you must permit me to add, sir, that at this, or in any short time, his youth, inexperience, and unripened education, are, and will be, insuperable obstacles, in my opinion, to the completion of the marriage. . . . It may be expected of me, perhaps, to say something of property; but, to descend to particulars, at this time, must seem premature. In general, therefore, I shall inform you, that Mr. Custis's estate consists of about 15,000 acres of land, a good part adjoining the city of Williamsburg, and none of it forty miles from that place; several lots in the said city; between two and three hundred negroes; and about eight or ten

---

[1] Sir Edward Henry Lee, of Ditchley, was created Earl of Litchfield in 1674; he was descended from the Lees of "Quarrendon," and was not, so far as known, in any way related to the Lees of Shropshire, from whom those of Virginia are descended.

thousand pounds upon bond, and in the hands of his merchants. This estate he now holds, independent of his mother's dower, which will be an addition to it at her death ; and, upon the whole, it is such an estate as you will readily acknowledge, ought to entitle him to a handsome portion with a wife.''

In spite of Washington's protest the young couple had their way, and were married the next year. Their union was very brief, for Mr. Custis died in 1781, leaving four young children. His widow remarried, taking for her second husband Dr. David Stuart, and died the 28th of April, 1811, having had seven children by her second husband (see p. 95). Mr. Custis' children were: Elizabeth Parke, born the 21st of August, 1776 ; she married a Mr. Law. Martha Parke, born the 31st of December, 1777 ; married early in life Mr. Thomas Peter. Eleanor Parke, born the 21st of March, 1779 ; "Nelly Custis," as she has always been known, was a great beauty, and much of a favorite with her step-father. She married on 22d of February, 1799, Lawrence Lewis, a favorite nephew of the General's, being a son of Fielding Lewis and Elizabeth Washington. Their fourth child was George Washington Parke Custis, who was born at "Mt. Airy" on the 30th of April, 1781, six months before the death of his father. General Washington, immediately on hearing of the death of the father, said: "I adopt the two younger children as my own," and Mt. Vernon was thereafter their home. Mr. Custis has always been known as "the child of Mt. Vernon," and it has been said that his "Grandmamma always spoiled" him. After the death of Mrs. Washington, in 1802, Mr. Custis moved to Arlington,[1] opposite Washington, which mansion he built. He married, in 1806, Mary Lee, daughter of Col. William and Anne (Randolph) Fitzhugh, of "Chatham," and had four children, only one of whom survived infancy. This daughter, Mary Anne Randolph Custis, married Robert E. Lee, as stated. Mrs. Custis was born the 22d of April, 1788, and died the 23d of April, 1853. Mr. Custis died the 10th of October, 1857, "known and honored by his fellow-countrymen. His departure awakened profound regret." They were buried in a beautiful grove near the Arlington House, where their remains still rest. Of Mrs. Custis, every one who knew her has spoken in the highest terms. Bishop Meade wrote: "But I must not lay down my pen, though my heart bleed at its further use, without the tribute of affection, of gratitude, and reverence to one who was to me as a sister, mother, and faithful monitor. Mrs. Mary Custis, of Arlington, the wife of Mr. Washington Custis, the grandson of Mrs. General Washington, was the

---

[1] Named after the older Custis mansion in Northampton county, on the Eastern Shore.

daughter of Mr. William Fitzhugh, of 'Chatham.' Scarcely is there a lady in our land more honored than she was, and none more loved and esteemed. For good sense, prudence, sincerity, benevolence, unaffected piety, disinterested zeal in every good work, deep humility, and retiring modesty, I never knew her superior." (*Old Families, Churches, &c.*, II, 196.)

For many years Mr. Custis dispensed a generous hospitality at Arlington, his visitors being very numerous, consisting of the most distinguished Europeans and Americans of his time. The mansion at Arlington was stored with the most precious relics of the "Pater Patriæ," some of which are yet in the possession of the family, but many of them were stolen from the house in the early days of the late civil war. The few relics that were overlooked by individual depredators were seized by government officials as the rightful spoils of war, and are still exhibited in the National Museum at Washington, labelled, "*Taken from Arlington.*" Probably Washington hardly anticipated that the time would ever come when the government he had done so much to establish would "take" the heirlooms he had bequeathed to his adopted son. On this subject General Lee wrote to a member of Congress, under date of 12th of February, 1869: " . . . Mrs. Lee has determined to act upon your suggestion, and apply to President Johnson for such of the relics from Arlington as are in the Patent Office. From what I have learned, a great many things formerly belonging to General Washington, bequeathed to her by her father, in the shape of books, furniture, camp equipage, etc., were carried away by individuals, and are now scattered over the land. I hope the possessors appreciate them, and may imitate the example of their original owner, whose conduct must at times be brought to their recollection by these silent monitors. In this way they will accomplish good to the country." Later, when Mrs. Lee's application had been refused, and styled by a committee of Congress as "an insult to the loyal people of the United States," the General wrote: " . . . Had I conceived the view taken by Congress I would have endeavored to have dissuaded Mrs. Lee from applying for them. It may be a question with some whether the retention of these articles is 'more an insult,' in the language of the Committee on Public Buildings, 'to the loyal people of the United States,' than their restoration; but of this I am willing that they should be the judge; and, since Congress has decided to keep them, she must submit."

### ROBERT EDEN LEE.

51. ROBERT EDEN[6], the sixth son of Charles Lee[5] (Henry[4], Henry[3], Richard[2], Richard[1]) and Margaret (Scott) Peyton, his second wife, was

born at "Gordonsdale," Fauquier county, the 7th of September, 1810; was killed at Warrenton, 24th of July, 1843. He was married, on the 9th of October, 1835, to Margaret Gordon, daughter of Judge John and Elizabeth (Pickett) Scott; she was born in May, 1817, and died in May, 1866. No issue.

His will, dated the 29th of March, 1842, and probated in Rankin county, Miss., was as follows:

I, Robert E. Lee, do make, declare and publish this my last Will and Testament, revoking all others. I will and bequeath to my wife Margaret Gordon Lee all my property of every kind and description, real, personal and mixed, wherever the same may be situated, to have and hold the same for her sole use and benefit, absolutely and in fee simple. I confirm to my brother Alfred Lee the Land in Fairfax County, Virginia, to which I have already made him title, in fee simple, and release him from all and any obligation he may feel under, to pay any consideration for the same; it having been my intention to give him the Land aforesaid in Fairfax. I appoint the Honorable John Scott, of Oakwood, and my wife Margaret Gordon Lee, Executor and Executrix of this my last Will and Testament, to qualify and to act jointly or separately as they may think proper; and it is my will and desire that neither of them shall be required to give bond for the performance of his or her executorial trust. All written with my own hand, and sealed, and published, &c."

Margaret Gordon Lee, in her will, of date of 20th February, and probated, in Fauquier county, 31st May, 1866, left to her nieces Ann Morson Scott and Susan Morson Scott, some money, which in case they married was to be secured "by strict settlement to their sole, separate use and enjoyment, from the debts, liabilities and contracts and control of the husband." . . . "The residue of my estate I give unto my brother, Martin P. Scott, my nephew John Scott, son of my brother Robert E. Scott, dec'd, and my nephew R. T. Scott, their heirs forever, to be equally divided. I charge my said brother and my said nephews with an annuity of five hundred dollars, to be paid by them to my brother, John Scott, as long as he shall live." She also left to her nieces "such sum or sums of money as may be received upon my claim for damages against the United States Government for injury done to my property by the Federal Armies during the late war with the Southern States, which I claim should be paid as I was always loyal and true to the United States, &c."

## Colonel Richard Bland Lee.

52. Richard Bland[6], the eldest son of Richard Bland Lee[5] (Henry[4], Henry[3], Richard[2], Richard[1]) and Elizabeth Collins, his wife, was born at "Sully," Fairfax county, the 20th of July, 1797; died at Alexandria, the 2d of August, 1875; he was married, on the 23d of November, 1826, to Julia Anna Marion, daughter of William Prosser, of "White Marsh,"

Gloucester county; Mr. Prosser had been a prosperous merchant of Richmond, but later moved to Gloucester, where he died. She was born at Richmond in 1806, and died at Washington on the 2d of July, 1882; both were buried at Alexandria.

Richard Bland Lee entered the Military Academy at West Point on the 7th of May, 1814, and graduated on the 17th of July, 1817, ninth in a class of thirty graduates; he was appointed third lieutenant in the artillery corps, on 17th of July, and second lieutenant, 24th November, 1817; first lieutenant, 3d artillery, on the reorganization of the army, 1st June, 1821; brevet captain, for ten years' faithful service in one grade, 31st October, 1829. During these years, he had been stationed on garrison duty at various forts, and at the school of artillery practice. He was invited by General Cass, then Secretary of War, to take charge, as military conductor, of the caravan of Santa Fé traders, to ascertain the condition of the tribes of Indians occupying the Rocky Mountains, and to arrange some method of communication between them and the government. Having conducted the caravan to Santa Fé, through roving bands of hostile Indians, and finding at that place no means of communicating with the tribes, nor of obtaining reliable information as to their condition, at his own expense he raised and equipped a party for the first attempt at a winter exploration of the mountains; an undertaking then considered by the most experienced hunters as very impracticable. On the 15th of November, 1832, he penetrated the northern portion of New Mexico, and explored the extensive region of the head-waters of the Rio del Norte to the South Park, and as far west as the base of Salt Mountain; crossed the Green River near its entrance into the great cañon. Thence, through the valley of the Green River, across the spur of mountains to the confluence of the Little Snake and Little Bear Rivers, both of which he explored to their head-waters. Near the head of Little Snake River, he crossed the grand divide of the eastern and western waters, striking Sweet Water River near the South Pass to great Salt Lake, and near the base of Wind River Mountain. Thence across the Platte and Medicine Bow Rivers, watering the valleys of the Black Hills, and the eastern slope of the mountains, and crossing several forks of the Platte and Arkansas Rivers, he reached Santa Fé, via Toas, on the 15th of June, 1833. He had, in the period of seven months, explored an area over 1,200 miles in extent, visited six tribes of Indians, with whom he entered into friendly relations, and arranged plans for communicating between them and the government.

On the outbreak of the "Florida War," against the Seminole Indians, Richard Bland Lee entered the field as a first lieutenant, and served successively with Generals Clinch and Scott, and Governor Call. During these campaigns, he saw more active service, was more under fire, and lost more men, killed and wounded, than any officer who served with those armies. General Clinch, on retiring from command, wrote him a complimentary letter of thanks. He was selected by General Scott to command the storming party, who were to force the passage of the Withlacooche; his party were, on this occasion, the only portion of the troops under fire; for his gallant conduct in this attack, he received the commendations of the General in the presence of the army. Under Governor Call, he was assigned to the command of Fort Micanopy, the most important barrier between the Indians and the settlers; while in command there, he had three successful encounters with the Indians led by Oceola in person. Was brevetted Major "for gallantry and good conduct," 9th June, 1836; was twice wounded and in consequence compelled to leave Florida. Governor Call wrote him a letter of thanks for his efficient services while serving in Florida.

Upon reaching Washington, by appointment of the President and in the presence of the Secretary of War, the General-in-chief, and several officers invited for the occasion, he received the compliments of President Jackson, who declared that his fights in front of Fort Micanopy were the most creditable events of the war. At the beginning of the Mexican War, Major Lee offered his services to the commissary general to take the field; but General Gibson declined the offer, preferring that he should remain on duty at St. Louis, where he could be more useful. For several years, he served as chief commissary for the Pacific division; part of the time on special service in California and Oregon. He explored the region from the head of Puget Sound to the mouth of the Columbia River; also the country from San Francisco, between the Coast Range and the ocean, to the boundary of Mexico, near the head of the Gulf of California. Having arranged a system of supply in accordance with General Persifer Smith's views, he was directed to visit the Sandwich Islands, to purchase supplies, and thence to the South American States on the Pacific. Upon returning to Washington, after completing these duties, he was complimented by General Gibson for the satisfactory manner in which he had accomplished his work.

When Virginia seceded, Major Lee resigned from the army, 9th May, 1861, and was appointed a lieutenant-colonel in the commissariat of the Confederate service; took an active part in the battle of Shiloh, under General Beauregard, where he had his horse shot under him.

Richard Bland and Julia Anna Marion (Prosser) Lee had twelve children, of whom three died young. The following are now living:

i, MARY ELIZABETH[7], born the 19th of August, 1827, at "White Marsh," Gloucester county; was married, on the 2d of June, 1847, to Dr. Robert Fleming Fleming, the eldest son of Thomas Fleming and Clarissa Tilghman Walton, of Charleston, S. C.; Dr. Fleming died at Alexandria, the 19th of August, 1871, and left these six children: 1, Richard Bland Lee, born at St. Louis, Mo., the 13th of August, 1848; married, on the 3d of January, 1882, Harriet Jane, eldest daughter of Robert Henry Downman, and Fanny Scott Horner, his wife, of Warrenton; she was born the 7th of November, 1859; they have four children: Frances Lee, Mary Elizabeth Lee, Roberta Downman, and Clarissa Walton. 2, Thomas, born at St. Louis, the 26th of January, 1851; married Grace, daughter of William H. Irwin, of Alexandria, and has five children: Thomas, W. H. Irwin, Robert Fleming, J. Paton, and Mary Lee. 3, Robert Fleming, born at St. Louis, the 20th of January, 1858; is unmarried. 4, Alfred Walton, born at Washington, D. C., the 31st of August, 1861; married Gay Bernard Robertson, of Richmond, and has one son, Alfred Walton. 5, Julia Prosser, born at St. Louis, the 1st of December, 1863; married McKenzie Goldsborough, of Maryland, and has two sons: Lee Kennedy and Philip Francis. 6, Clarissa Tilghman, born at Alexandria, the 2d of July, 1868; married Henry Herbert Balch, of New York, and has two children: Henry Herbert and Clarissa Anne.

ii, JULIA EUSTIS[7], is unmarried.

iii, EVELINA PROSSER[7], born at St. Louis, Mo., the 24th of September, 1832; was married, at Washington, D. C., on the 14th of July, 1853, to Edwin Cecil Morgan, who was born in St. Mary's county, Md., the 9th of February, 1827; died, at Washington, D. C., the 29th of July, 1867; they had six sons, four of whom died in early infancy; the two surviving are: (2) Edwin Lee, born at Washington, D. C., on the 29th of September, 1855; married, at same place, on the 10th of October, 1893, Mary Garland Van Zandt, of Washington. (5) William Prosser, born at Washington, D. C., on the 25th of May, 1861.

iv, RICHARD BLAND[7]. See 78.

v, ANNA CORNELIA[7], married, on the 19th of December, 1865, to Dr. Robert Stockton Johnston Peebles, who was born at Petersburg, Va., and was a son of Dr. John Frederick and Helena Stockton (Johnston) Peebles, of that city. He was educated at the University of Pennsylvania and at the Medical College of Virginia; served during the late civil war as a surgeon in the Confederate army, both in the field and on hospital duty; after the war he was elected professor of Materia Medica and Chemistry in the Medical College of Virginia, at Richmond, which position he resigned about a year before his death. He died at Richmond the 30th of March, 1873, aged 34 years, having had three children. Of these two daughters survive, Julia Lee and Helena Stockton Peebles.

vi, JULIAN PROSSER[7]. See 79.

vii, MYRA GAINES[7], born at St. Louis, Mo., the 9th of November, 1841; was married at Tarboro, N. C., on the 23d of August, 1864, to Charles Napoleon Civalier, of Bordeaux, France, who was born the 15th of August, 1836. Of their children, Charles Napoleon and Richard Bland Lee died in infancy; two daughters are now living: 1, Julia Anna Marion Lee, born at Jackson, N. C.; was married at Alexandria on the 23d of November, 1891, to William Pinckney Holmes, of Baltimore, Md., and has: Julia Anna Marion Lee and William Pinckney Holmes. 2, Myra Lee Civalier, their second daughter, is single.

viii, WILLIAM AUGUSTUS[7], born at St. Louis, Mo., the 30th day of January, 1846; was educated in medicine at the Medical College of Virginia, where he was graduated in 1870; he served in the Confederate navy, and is now practicing his profession at Richmond.

ix, ROBERT FLEMING[7], born at St. Louis, Mo., the 13th of February, 1849; served in the Confederate army, and is now residing at Alexandria.

## JUDGE ZACCHEUS COLLINS LEE.

53. ZACCHEUS COLLINS[6], the second son of Richard Bland Lee[5] (Henry[4], Henry[3], Richard[2], Richard[1]) and Elizabeth Collins, his wife, was born the 5th of December, 1805, and died at Baltimore, the 26th of November, 1859. Mr. Lee was educated at the University of Virginia; studied law under William Wirt, and practiced his profession at Baltimore. He was a prominent member of the bar of that city; was considered an effective and eloquent speaker; he served as United States District Attorney from 1848 to 1855; was Judge of the Superior Court of Baltimore from 1855 to the time of his death. He was married, on the 15th of June, 1837, to Martha Ann, daughter of Thomas C. Jenkins, of Baltimore; she was born the 5th of April, 1819, and died the 16th of April, 1864. They had only two children:

i, RICHARD HENRY[7]. See 80.

ii, MARY ELIZABETH[7], born the 5th of November, 1840; has been twice married; first, on the 26th of December, 1861, to William B. Perine, of "Homeland," Baltimore county, Md., and had a daughter, Martha

Lee Perine, born the 19th of September, 1862, and died the 27th of April, 1891. Mr. Perine died in May, 1863, and his widow was married, secondly, on the 15th of August, 1867, to Bernard John Cooper, Post Captain of the English Navy, who died on the 26th of July, 1889, leaving three children: 1, Mary Elizabeth Lee, born the 11th of December, 1868; 2, Mary Frances Donelan Lee, born the 23d of September, 1870; 3, Bernard John Lee, born the 26th of September, 1873. Mary Frances D. L. Cooper was married, at Rome, on the 6th of June, 1894, to Don Guiseppe, second son of Marquis Patrizi, Standard Bearer of the Holy Church; he was born on the 27th of December, 1872. Mrs. Cooper resides at Rome, Italy.

## Lieutenant John Hite Lee.

54. John Hite[6], son of Theodoric Lee[5] (Henry[4], Henry[3], Richard[2], Richard[1]) and Catharine Hite, his wife, was born the 30th of July, 1797, and died in July, 1832, at Norfolk, Va., where he was then stationed on naval duty. He married, in 1825, Elizabeth, daughter of William Prosser, of "White Marsh," Gloucester county, and a sister of the Julia Prosser who married his first cousin, Richard Bland Lee. They had three children: Theodoric, Matilda, and John Hite Lee. Of these Theodoric was born at "White Marsh" the 22d of November, 1826, and died at Media, Pa., on the 16th of September, 1867 (tombstone). He entered the navy as midshipman on the 29th of September, 1841; was made master the 14th of September, 1853; lieutenant the 15th of September, 1855, and resigned on the 25th of April, 1857, soon after his marriage to a daughter of John Grigg, a book publisher of Philadelphia, by whom he had one son, John Grigg Lee. He was born at Paris, France, the 18th of July, 1857; died at New York the 8th of September, 1891 (tombstone), and was buried beside his father at Media, Pa.

The daughter, Matilda Lee, married John Royall Holcombe, and had issue: 1, John Hite Lee, Lieutenant, U. S. N., who was born the 28th of September, 1856; was educated at Washington and Lee University and at the Naval Academy at Annapolis; was married in April, 1881, to Ida Wilton Taylor, and has one son living, John Lee, born the 11th of October, 1882. 2, Thomas Allan, born the 24th of August, 1858. 3, Joseph Gales, born the 2d of December, 1861; married Lillie Browne, of Amherst C. H., Va., and has one child, Walton Holcombe. 4, Ernest Prosser, born the 17th of January, 1864; married Susan Coombs, and has one child, Gladys Holcombe. 5, Elizabeth Prosser Holcombe, born the 19th of August, 1866.

## EDMUND JENNINGS LEE.

55. EDMUND JENNINGS[6], the eldest son of Edmund Jennings Lee[5] (Henry[4], Henry[3], Richard[2], Richard[1]) and Sarah Lee, his wife, was born at Alexandria, then in the District of Columbia, on the 3d of May, 1797, and died at his home, "Leeland," near Shepherdstown, Jefferson county, West Virginia, on the 10th of August, 1877.

Mr. Lee received his earliest educational training at the school of the Rev. Mr. Maffett, in Fairfax county, a school of high repute at that day. He subsequently graduated at Princeton College, as his father had done before him. On leaving college, he studied law with his father at Alexandria; after being admitted to the bar, he settled at Wheeling, now in West Virginia, where he remained until after his marriage with Miss Shepherd. Later, he removed to Shepherdstown, at which place he resided for the remainder of his life.

Mr. Lee was a prominent lawyer, and well-known throughout his section of the State, where for many years he enjoyed a large and lucrative practice. He possessed fine abilities, strong native sense, clear, sound judgment, was of a genial, charitable disposition, and of exalted moral character. He was diligent in attending to the various duties of life, and, being well equipped for the work of his profession, and proverbially attentive to the interests of his clients, it is not surprising that he held their confidence and esteem. He never entered public life, although frequently solicited to do so. He was a member of the Episcopal Church and devoted to her interests; for a number of years he was senior warden of the church at Shepherdstown. Though, like many others of his family and State, he was opposed to secession, he was later an ardent and warm supporter of the Southern cause. Being too far advanced in years to enter the army, he remained quietly and unobtrusively at home. Yet this did not save him. During a temporary absence, both his own residence and that of his wife, near by, were burnt by the order of the famous general of the Northern army who was so valiant and efficient in this line of service.

Mr. Lee was twice married, and had issue by both marriages; he was first married, on the 10th of October, 1823, to Eliza, daughter of Captain Abraham Shepherd, of Berkeley (now Jefferson) county, (now West) Virginia. She was born the 25th of July, 1799, and died at "Leeland," the 25th of August, 1833. Mr. Lee was married, secondly, on the 7th of September, 1835, to Henrietta, daughter of Daniel Bedinger, of "Bedford," near Shepherdstown; she was born, at "Bedford," the 7th of February,

Edmund J Lee

1810, and still lives, to the great pleasure of innumerable relatives and friends.

Edmund Jennings Lee and Eliza Shepherd, his first wife, had the two following children:

i, ELLEN[7], born the 23d of September, 1824; was married, on the 19th of September, 1844, to John Simms Powell, fourth son of Cuthbert Powell and Catharine Simms, his wife, of Loudoun county, and had the following nine children: 1, Eliza Shepherd, who died aged ten years. 2, Cuthbert, born at "Salisbury," Fairfax county, the 29th of April, 1849; was married, at Kansas City, Mo., on the 27th of July, 1886, to Lucie Sidney, daughter of Washington and Mary Davies Gill, of Richmond, Va., who was born at that city the 17th of January, 1854; they have two children: Lucie Beverley, born at Kansas City, Mo., the 13th of January, 1889, and Cuthbert, born at same city, the 6th of September, 1890. 3, Katharine Simms, born at "Salisbury," Fairfax county, the 18th of March, 1851. 4, Edmund Lee, born at "Salisbury," the 10th of May, 1852. 5, Simms, born at "Salisbury," the 3d of September, 1854; was married, at Richmond, Va., on the 2d of December, 1882, to Maria Eustace, daughter of William and Caroline Pleasants Brent, who was born the 17th of January, 1858; they have these six children, all born at Parkersburg, W. Va.: Caroline Brent, born the 9th of April, 1884; John Simms, born the 5th of April, 1886; William Brent, born the 20th of August, 1887; Ellen Lee, born the 2d of November, 1889; Edmund Lee, born the 9th of July, 1892; Lucien Ludwell, born the 29th of September, 1894. 6, Eleanor Strode, born at "Salisbury," the 14th of May, 1857; was married, at Shepherdstown, W. Va., on the 27th of September, 1881, to Henry W. Potts, of Pottstown, Pa., and has four children: Eleanor Lee, born at Shepherdstown, the 11th of November, 1884; Joseph Henry, born at Shepherdstown, the 28th of December, 1887; Margaret Annan, born at Shepherdstown, the 10th of May, 1890; Llewellyn Powell, born at Summerville, S. C., the 9th of February, 1895. 7, Laura Stuart, born at "Salisbury," the 31st of May, 1859; was married, at Shepherdstown, on the 4th of May, 1886, to the Rev. William T. Roberts, formerly of Mecklenburg county, now rector of old Bruton Parish, Williamsburg; they have four children: Ellen Lee, born at Culpeper, Va., the 7th of April, 1888; William Saunders, born at Harrisonburg, the 24th of January, 1891; Laura Powell, born in Mecklenburg county, the 13th of April, 1893;

Edmund Lee, born at Williamsburg, the 6th of December, 1894. 8, Sally Lee, born at "Bedford," Jefferson county, the 5th of August, 1861. 9, Charles Lee, born at Lexington, Va., the 19th of March, 1863; was married, at Los Angeles, California, on the 25th of January, 1893, to Laura Crane, daughter of William J. and Ada M. Haughawout, who was born at Neosha Falls, Kansas, the 7th of February, 1869.

ii, CHARLES SHEPHERD[7]. See 81.

Edmund Jennings Lee had by his second wife, Henrietta Bedinger, the following five children:

iii, EDWIN GRAY[7]. See 82.

iv, IDA[7], born at "Leeland," Jefferson county, the 14th of August, 1840, and was married, on the 19th of September, 1860, to Col. Armistead Thompson Mason Rust, of Loudoun county, being his second wife; they had these eleven children: Armistead, U. S. N. (who was married, on the 22d of June, 1887, to Anne Weems Ridout, of Annapolis, Md.), George, Henrietta Lee (who was married, on the 24th of June, 1894, to William Mead Coulling, of Richmond), Lily Southgate (who was married, on the 14th of August, 1889, to Thomas Washington Edwards), Ida Lee, Edwin Gray, Henry Bedinger, William Fitzhugh, Edmund Jennings Lee, Ellsworth Marshall, and Stirling Murray Rust.

v, HENRIETTA EDMONIA[7], born at "Leeland," Jefferson county, the 28th of February, 1844; was married, on the 7th of November, 1865, to Dr. Charles Worthington Goldsborough, now of Frederick, Md.; they had six children: Charles Henry (who was married, on the 27th of December, 1882, to Birdie, daughter of John C. Neal), Edmund Lee, Catharine D., Edwin Gray, Henrietta, and Henry Bedinger Goldsborough. Dr. Goldsborough is a son of Dr. Charles Henry and Amelia (Poe) Goldsborough, and a descendant of Charles and Anna Maria (Tilghman) Goldsborough, of "Horn Point," Dorchester county, Md., the progenitor of the Maryland Goldsboroughs.

vi, EDMUND JENNINGS[7]. See 83.

vii, HENRY BEDINGER[7]. See 84.

## THE SHEPHERD FAMILY.

Thomas Shepherd emigrated from England; settled first at Annapolis, Maryland; later near the town of Mecklenburg, now Shepherdstown, and named from this family, where he acquired a large tract of land from Lord Fairfax. The present town was laid out by Thomas Shepherd, in 1762; in his will, dated in 1776, he directed his executor to deed a lot of two acres on which "the English Church stood" for church purposes. He had five sons and four daughters; of these sons, Abraham served as a captain in the Revolutionary army; in 1775 he marched with a company from Shepherdstown to join the Continental forces around Boston; later, at the battle of "King's Bridge," in November, 1776, when his superior officers had been wounded, he commanded his regiment with great credit. Of him, Bishop Meade wrote: "Without detracting from the praise due to many others who have contributed funds and efforts to the last two churches, we must ascribe the first of them chiefly to the zeal, perseverance, and liberality of that true friend of the Church in her darkest days, Mr. Abraham Shepherd." Captain Shepherd married Eleanor Strode, who was born 27th June, 1760, and lived until the 23d of September, 1853. Captain Shepherd died on the 7th of September, 1822, in his 69th year. Their daughter, Eliza Shepherd, was born 26th of July, 1799; died the 25th of August, 1833; married Edmund Jennings Lee, on the 1st of October, 1823, as stated.

## THE BEDINGER FAMILY.

The Bedingers are of German descent; Adam Bedinger, the first of the family in America, was born in the village of Dorschell, in the principality of Liechtenstein, near the city of Strasburg in Alsace. He came to America in the year 1736, landed at Philadelphia, and for a few years lived in Lancaster county, Pennsylvania, from whence he moved into York county, where he died. He had married and had four sons in his native land, but only one son, Henry, appears to have come over with him to Pennsylvania. This son resided with his father until he was about twenty-two years old, when he married Mary von Schlegel, who was a near relative of August and Friedrich von Schlegel, German writers of note. In the spring of 1762, he moved with his family to Shepherdstown, then in Frederick county, and known as Mecklenburg. There he built himself a handsome residence, near the town, where his three youngest sons were born; he died the 22d of January, 1772, in his 42d year, leaving issue: Henry, Mary, Sally, George Michel, Daniel, and Jacob. The eldest son, Henry, served in the Revolutionary war, rising to the rank of major; he married Rachel Strode, and left three daughters. The two daughters, Mary and Sally, married, respectively, Abel and Abram Morgan, two brothers, and both have descendants. George Michel, the next child, was married twice, moved to Kentucky, where he has descendants. Of Daniel, fifth child, his daughter has written: "After the death of his mother the land and house where he was born, came, either by inheritance or purchase, into his possession. Before his mother's death the Revolutionary war began; he was then in his sixteenth year, and he *ran away* and joined the army. This was in the year 1776, and although he was taken prisoner, and for many months suffered every indignity at the hands of a merciless foe, as soon as he recovered from a severe illness, he returned to the army and served until our independence was declared. Daniel Bedinger and Sarah Rutherford were married at the 'Flowing Spring,' the home of the bride's father, on the — day of April, 1791."

Daniel Bedinger built a very handsome residence, "Bedford," near Shepherdstown, where he died about 1818, in his 57th or 58th year. Of his children, Henrietta married Edmund Jennings Lee, and has recently celebrated her 85th birthday. Elizabeth Conrad, her sister, married John Thornton Augustine Washington. Of Mr. Bedinger his nephew wrote:

"Daniel Bedinger was a model of all that was noble, generous, brave, and honorable among men. A man of true genius, with the highest order of intellect, admired and beloved by his associates, who were all gentlemen of truth and probity—for my uncle held in contempt all that was false, sordid, or dishonorable, and kept aloof from all such." His daughter, Henrietta, lived at his old home, "Bedford," until it was destroyed during the late war.

## Rev. William Fitzhugh Lee.

56. William Fitzhugh[6], second son of Edmund Jennings Lee[5] (Henry[4], Henry[3], Richard[2], Richard[1]) and Sarah Lee, his wife, was born at Alexandria, the 7th of May, 1804; died, at same place, the 19th of May, 1837; he was married, on the 27th of October, 1827, to Mary Catharine Simms Chilton, daughter of William Chilton, Esq., of Loudoun county; she was born the 16th of December, 1806, and died the 6th of March, 1884.

Bishop Moore wrote of him: "Mr. Lee was admitted to the order of Deacons in Leesburg, county of Loudoun, by Bishop Moore, on Sunday, the 21st of August, 1825, and to the order of Priests, on the 10th of May, 1828. His popularity as a preacher of the gospel rendered him universally acceptable. His first settlement in the ministry was in the counties of Amelia and Goochland; and soon after in St. John's Church, Richmond Hill, and afterward in Christ Church, both in this city [Richmond].

"His zeal in the discharge of his sacred duties was of the first order.

Naturally of a feeble constitution, but possessing a mind of the most vigorous character, and a spirit of gospel industry seldom equaled, his health soon exhibited symptoms of decline. His Bishop most earnestly and frequently entreated him to contract his labors, and to rest satisfied with the usual services of the Sabbath; but, prompted by the native energy of his mind, and influenced by his love of pastoral duty, he resisted his fatherly solicitations. He would sometimes preach three times on the Lord's day, and frequently in the week, by means of which unusual effort his lungs became affected, and the disease, which terminated his life, ob tained such a firm hold on his system, that he was obliged to relinquish his pastoral charge, and to bid adieu to the congregation he had formed, and to which he was most ardently and affectionately attached.

"Mr. Lee, upon retiring from the services of the sanctuary, became editor of the *Southern Churchman*, and soon distinguished himself in that capacity. He was a decided and firm Episcopalian, but at the same time lived in peace and friendship with other denominations of Christians. During the confinement which preceded his dissolution, he endeavored to prepare himself for that solemn hour he knew to be approaching. The attention of his clerical brethren was unwearied, and their sympathies comforted and supported him in his last hour. The Lord's Supper was administered to him by his Bishop, who, in company with his distressed wife, and those friends who were present, kneeled around his sick bed, and partook with him of that holy ordinance. . . ."

"Mr. Lee was a bright example of gospel industry, and it is the firm hope of the author of this obituary, that his clerical brethren, one and all, may take courage in the work to which they have pledged themselves; and steadily and perseveringly continue faithful unto death, that they may reap the end of their faith, the salvation of their souls. Mr. Lee preached his last sermon in the Monumental Church, from the following passage of Scripture: 'This is my beloved, and this is my friend, O ye daughters of Jerusalem.'"

"His funeral sermon was preached by the Rev. Dr. Keith, in Christ Church, Alexandria, on Trinity Sunday, from John xiv, 2, 3. On a succeeding Sunday, a discourse commemorative of his death was preached in Christ Church in this city [Richmond], by the Rector, the Rev. Mr. Woodbridge, from Heb. xi, 4: 'He being dead yet speaketh.'" (*Southern Churchman.*)

Mr. Lee established *The Southern Churchman*, and was its editor until the close of the winter previous to his death. He then removed from Richmond to Alexandria, to die amidst the friends and scenes of his youth.

Shortly before he left Richmond, he lost a child, aged fourteen months; his mother preceded him to the grave by only ten days. His wife and two children survived him:

i, WILLIAM FITZHUGH[7]. See 85.
ii, MARY MORRISON[7], born the 16th of April, 1830; died the 21st of January, 1891; married Rev. Robert Allen Castleman, of Clarke county, and left one son, the Rev. R. A. Castleman, now in charge of parishes in Fairfax county, and three daughters.

### CASSIUS FRANCIS LEE.

57. CASSIUS FRANCIS[6], the third son of Edmund Jennings Lee[5] (Henry[4], Henry[3], Richard[2], Richard[1]) and Sarah Lee, his wife, was born at Alexandria on the 22d of May, 1808, and died at the same place on the 23d of January, 1890. Mr. Lee was reared and educated, lived and died, at or near Alexandria. There the whole of his long and useful life was spent. In his earlier days he was Clerk of the U. S. Courts, and was admitted to the bar, but never practiced. Later he became a member of the mercantile house of Cazenove & Company, of that town. At his father's house he had early listened to the conversations of Bishops Moore and Meade, the patriarchs of the Episcopal Church in Virginia, and doubtless it was from such intercourse, as well as from the wise instruction of his mother, that he early became imbued with that love for the Church which ever characterized him and which ruled his whole life. Of him the *Southern Churchman* has said (under date of the 30th of January, 1890):

"On Thursday last this venerable and beloved man passed from earth into the everlasting blessedness of the saints. We had not heard of his sickness, therefore his death was unexpected, though it ought not to have been, he having passed the age allotted to men. We cannot trust ourselves to speak of his long and consistent Christian life, and of that long life devoted to the interests and welfare of the Church in this diocese. For many years before the war, as treasurer of the Theological Seminary and treasurer of the Virginia Educational Society, he gave his thoughts, his affections, his time to the Seminary without compensation. After the war, his pecuniary circumstances having changed, a small salary was given him, which he more than earned, giving nearly all his time to the Education Society and to the care and interests of the Seminary. While his health had failed during the past few years, he was always deeply interested in its welfare, full of zeal for its good, and died treasurer of both. He will be missed, not only by his sons, daughters, and grandchildren, but by the pro-

Cassius F Lee

fessors and students and by his many friends, and by the Church in this diocese. His co-workers on the boards of trustees will miss him; he was always so deeply concerned and so earnestly at work for good. His Christian character, his pious zeal, his love for what was true and just and honorable—of these no one can speak in adequate terms. His light shone unconscious to himself, and that light was bright and beautiful and affectionate. . . . He lived the Christian life and died the Christian death, full of the respect of all who knew him. While we sympathize with this diocese, we rejoice that such a man lived in it and died in it. His memory—let it continue precious. . . . He was identified with Christ Church (Alexandria) as far back as 1833, and for years represented that parish in the annual Councils, and was one of the lay deputies to the General Convention held at Cincinnati; he was a member of the Standing Committee of this diocese for over a third of a century. . . . In his work, whether as a merchant, citizen, or in any work connected with the Church, he was active and indefatigable, as those who were associated with him can testify. His end was somewhat sudden. On the Sunday previous to his death he did not go to church, though he was up and about the house. That afternoon a member of his family read to him Dr. Slaughter's Memorial of the Rev. G. A. Smith, to which he listened with interest. The day following Bishop Talbot, of Wyoming, was at Christ Church and delivered an address on his missionary work, and afterward called to see Mr. Lee, who was gratified and pleased to see the Bishop. That night he retired to bed as usual, but never rose therefrom, the sudden change taking place on Thursday, and before noon his spirit had passed away. On Saturday he was buried from Christ Church, and at the funeral the hymn sung was that which he loved to repeat, and which was his favorite hymn:

> "Just as I am, without one plea,
> But that Thy blood was shed for me,
> And that Thou bidd'st me come to Thee,
> O, Lamb of God, I come."

Cassius F. Lee was married twice; first, on the 18th of September, 1833, to Hannah Philippa Ludwell Hopkins, the second daughter of John and Cornelia (Lee) Hopkins. She was born at Alexandria "twenty minutes before 6 o'clock, Saturday morning, the 3d of August, 1811; was baptized the 14th of June, 1812, by the Rev. William Meade; her Sponsors were Mrs. Bassett, Miss Nancy Riddle, Mr. William H. Fitzhugh, Mr. John Hopkins, Jr., and Capt. Croudhill" (Hopkins Family Bible). The Cornelia Lee who married John Hopkins was the youngest daughter of William and Hannah Philippa (Ludwell) Lee, of "Greenspring;" hence her daughter married a second cousin. Mrs. Hannah Philippa L. Lee died at Alexandria the 25th of January, 1844.

Cassius F. Lee had, by his first wife, the following named children:

i, CORNELIA[7], born the 27th of November, 1835, and died, unmarried, on the 24th of June, 1890.

ii, WILLIAM LUDWELL[7], born the 28th of March, 1838, and "Died at Alexandria, on Monday, the 10th inst. [May, 1858], suddenly of disease of the heart, William Ludwell Lee, aged 20 years, the eldest son of Cassius F. Lee, Esq. The many friends of Mr. Lee will deeply sympathize with him in the loss of his son. He was a young man of great promise, with one of the sweetest and purest dispositions any young man ever had; tenderly beloved by all that knew him, and cut down in a moment. But his friends sorrow not as others who have no hope. He was a disciple of Jesus. A few months ago his father kneeled with him around the communion table, to join with him, as he for the first time partook of the symbols of a Saviour's dying love. Since that time his 'walk and conversation' were as becometh a follower of Christ."

Ludwell Lee was educated at the school of Benjamin Hallowell and was such an exemplary pupil that Mr. Hallowell once volunteered to teach him without any compensation.

iii, HARRIOTTE HOPKINS[7], born the 15th of April, 1840; married, on the 28th of November, 1860, Thomas Seddon Taliaferro, of Gloucester county, and had: Thomas Seddon, Jr., Philippa Ludwell (who married, on the 11th of December, 1894, Thomas J. Wyche, formerly of Virginia, now of Wyoming), Harriotte Lee, and Susan Seddon, who was born the 26th of December, 1862, and died the 30th of May, 1866.

iv, SARAH[7], born on the 6th of January, 1842; resides at Washington, D. C.

v, CASSIUS FRANCIS[7]. See 86.

Mr. Lee was married, secondly, on the 15th of April, 1846, to Anne Eliza, the eldest daughter of William Collins and Eliza Frances (Cazenove) Gardner; she was born at Newport, R. I., the 7th of February, 1819, Sunday morning; died at "Menokin," Fairfax county, the 5th of July, 1885, Sunday evening. The children of this second marriage were:

vi, PHILIPPA[7], born the 8th of March, 1847; died the 24th of December, 1853.

vii, CONSTANCE GARDNER[7], born the 27th of October, 1848; died, at her home at Baltimore, Md., the 8th of August, 1877; she was married, on the 29th of October, 1868, to the Rev. George William Peterkin, of Richmond, only son of the Rev. Joshua Peterkin, D. D., and Elizabeth Hanson, his wife. They had: 1, George William, born the 8th of August, 1869; died —— July, 1870. 2, Constance Lee. 3, William Gardner. 4, Elizabeth Hanson. 5, Annie Cazenove, born the 8th of August, 1877, and died ten days later. Mrs. Peterkin and her deceased children were buried at Hollywood Cemetery, Richmond.

viii, CAZENOVE GARDNER[7]. See 87.

ix, FRANCIS DUPONT[7]. See 88.

x, EDMUND JENNINGS[7]. See 89.

xi, WILLIAM GARDNER[7], born the 27th of June, 1855, and died in three days.

xii, ANNIE ELIZA[7], born the 23d of October, 1861; married, on the 28th of April, 1886, the Rev. John Thompson Cole, son of the Rev. John and Frances Eleanor (Thompson) Cole, of Culpeper county; he was born the 23d of December, 1857; was educated at the Episcopal High School, the University of Virginia, and the Virginia Theological Seminary; was ordained Deacon the 16th of May, and Priest the 3d of July, 1883, and for several years was connected with the mission of the Episcopal Church in Japan, and is now acting as general secretary of the American Church Missionary Society. They have had: Annie Lee, born at Tokio, Japan, and Eleanor Thompson Cole, who died at Washington, on the 11th of January, 1893, aged eighteen months.

## THE GARDNER FAMILY.

George Gardner (1601–1677), a grandson of Sir Thomas Gardner, emigrated from England to America about 1635–40; he is mentioned in a "catalogue of such (persons) who, by the Generall Consent of the Company were admitted to be Inhabytants of the Island now called Aqueedneck, having submitted themselves to the Government that is or shall be established, according to the Word of God, therein." He married Lydia, daughter of Robert Ballou, and left, among others, a son, Joseph Gardner (1669–1726), of Newport, R. I., who was a lieutenant of "the train band," and a deputy in "the Generall Assembly held for the Collony of Rhode Island and Providence Plantations, at War-

wick in October, 1705;" he married, on the 30th of November, 1693, Katharine, daughter of John and Frances (Holden) Holmes. Frances Holden was a daughter of Captain Randall Holden, a very influential man in the Colony; he was one of the nineteen who signed this compact, at Portsmouth, 7th March, 1738: "We whose names are underwritten, do solemnly in the presence of Jehovah, incorporate ourselves into a Body Politick, and as He shall help, will submit our persons, our lives and estates unto our Lord Jesus Christ, the King of Kings and Lord of Lords, and all those perfect and most absolute laws of His, given us in his Holy Word of Truth, to be guided and judged thereby." (Austin, *Gen. Dict. of R. I.*, 100.) On the 12th of January, 1643, Capt. Randall Holden "and ten others bought of Miantonomi for 144 fathoms of Wampum, the tract of Land called Shawomet (now Warwick)." (Austin, 100.) Joseph and Katharine (Holmes) Gardner had a numerous family; their tenth child was William (1712–1744), who married, in 1736, Mary Carr, a daughter of John and Abigail (Remington) Carr. John Carr was a grandson of Gov. Caleb Carr, and a great-grandson of Roger Williams. Caleb Gardner (1739–1806), the second son of William and Mary (Carr) Gardner, was successively captain, major, and lieut.-colonel of the first Rhode Island regiment in 1775–6; later he was, in turn, a deputy, a member of the "Council of War," and "Assistant" in 1787–88–92. He was residing in Newport, in 1778, when the French squadron under Comte d'Estaing was blockaded in the harbor of Newport by Admiral Howe; Capt. Gardner, seeing from his house-top the disposition of the two fleets, rowed off to the French admiral at night and piloted his vessels out through the British squadron, under cover of the darkness and a heavy fog. (*Appleton's Ency. of Am. Biography*, II, 597.) The following letter was written to him by Maréchal de Castries, then Minister of Marine under Louis XVI., in recognition of this service and a later one rendered the French at Yorktown:

"Versailles, 3d November, 1781. Sir: M. le Comte de Barras, commander of the King's squadron in North America, informs me, Sir, of the distinguished proofs you have given of your zeal and attachment to the common cause, and of the service you have rendered as well to his squadron as to the army of M. de Rochambeau, and formerly to the squadron commanded by M. le Ct. D'Estaing. I have given an account of it to the King and His Majesty hath ordered his Ambassador at the United States to send to you, with this letter, a present from him as a particular testimony of his satisfaction. It is with pleasure that I inform you of it. I am, Sir, wholly yours. (Signed) Castries."

"To M. Caleb Gardner, Captain of Marine, Newport."

Captain Caleb Gardner was married three times; first, in 1770, to Sarah Ann, daughter of Dr. James Robinson; he was married, secondly, in 1788, to Sarah, daughter of Samuel and Mary (Gardner) Fowler; lastly, to Mary, daughter of Gov. John Collins. Caleb Gardner died the 24th of December, 1806; he was a nephew of Chief Justice and Deputy-Governor John Gardner, who died the 29th of January, 1764; both were buried at Newport.[1] Of his second marriage was born William Collins (died 28th November, 1844, aged 54), who married, in May, 1816, Eliza Frances, daughter of Antoine Charles Cazenove, who had emigrated from Geneva, being of an ancient French Huguenot family; she was born in Alexandria, the 5th of May, 1798, and died there 2d of February, 1857. After his marriage, William C. Gardner moved from Newport to Alexandria, where both he and his wife are buried. They had issue: 1, Charles Cazenove, born 17th April, 1817; died 30th May, 1844; married, 4th August, 1840, Maria Ridgely, daughter of Dr. John Syng Dorsey, of Philadelphia, and left one son, Dorsey Gardner, who has been twice married and had issue by both marriages. 2, Anne Eliza, born 7th February, 1819; died at "Menokin," Fairfax county, 5th July, 1885; married Cassius F. Lee, as stated. 3, Constance Tabor, born 17th July, 1820; died 12th May, 1849; married, 30th of October, 1845, Henry Winter Davis, of Maryland; no issue. 4, Mary Collins, born 2d July, 1823; died 5th April, 1826. 5, William Fowler, born 27th October, 1840; married, on the 23d of April, 1868, Harriet C., daughter of John H. Rowland, of Norfolk; they have three children: Harriet Rowland, Elisa Cazenove, and William Cazenove. Mr. Gardner has charge, at present, of Trinity Episcopal Church in Howard county, Maryland.

PETERKIN. The Right Reverend George William Peterkin was born at Clear Spring, Washington county, Maryland, on the 21st of March, 1841. He was educated at the Episcopal High School and later at the University of Virginia; was in attendance at the latter institution when the late civil war began, and enlisted as a private in the Southern army, in April, 1861. Was chosen 2d lieutenant in April, 1862; adjutant of his regiment, May, 1862; and later joined the staff of General William Nelson Pendleton, and served as his "tried and trusty aide," until the end of the war. He entered the Theological Seminary, near Alexandria, and graduated there in June, 1868; was ordained Deacon by Bishop Johns, on the 24th of that month; during the year of his diaconate, he assisted his father at St. James' Church,

[1] From whose tombstone the arms, given on p. 477, were copied. The Rev. Richard Gardner, D. D., Canon of Christ Church, Oxford, who died the 20th of September, 1690, bore the same arms.

Richmond; on the 25th of June, 1869, he was ordained Priest, by Bishop Whittle; from June, 1869, to 1873, he was rector of St. Stephen's Church, Culpeper Court-house; from 1873 to 1878, he had charge of Memorial Church, Baltimore. In the latter year, he was elected Bishop of the new Diocese of West Virginia, and was consecrated at St. Matthew's Church, Wheeling, on the 30th of May, 1878. The honorary degree of D. D. was conferred upon Bishop Peterkin in 1878 by Washington and Lee University, and later by Kenyon College, Ohio. The degree of LL. D. has also been conferred upon him. On the 12th of June, 1884, Bishop Peterkin was married, for the second time, to Marion, daughter of Mr. John Stewart, of "Brook Hill," near Richmond. He resides at Parkersburg, West Virginia. During the summer of 1893, Bishop Peterkin visited the mission of the Episcopal Church in Southern Brazil.

## Charles Henry Lee.

58. Charles Henry[6], the fourth son of Edmund Jennings Lee[5] (Henry[4], Henry[3], Richard[2], Richard[1]) and Sarah Lee, his wife, was born at Alexandria, the 20th of October, 1818, and resides now chiefly at Leesburg. Mr. Lee is a lawyer by profession. For some years he has made a special study of the laws of courts-martial and has published a work on the subject. Before the late civil war, he was in the office of the Adjutant-General at Washington, serving there with Generals Roger Jones, and Samuel Cooper. During the war, he served in a similar position in the Adjutant-General's office at Richmond, with rank of major. He was married, on the 7th of November, 1844, to Elizabeth A. Dunbar, who was born at Alexandria, on the 17th of December, 1822. They had one daughter, Laura Dunbar, born in Loudoun county, the 21st of July, 1846; died at Richmond, the 25th of April, 1883; was married, on the 27th of September, 1877, to George Harrison Burwell, of "Carter Hall," Clarke county. She left a son, John Townsend Burwell, who was born in Clarke county, the 8th of July, 1878.

## Judge Richard Henry Lee.

59. Richard Henry[6], the fifth son and youngest child of Edmund Jennings Lee[5] (Henry[4], Henry[3], Richard[2], Richard[1]) and Sarah Lee, his wife, was born and reared at Alexandria, then in the District of Columbia; after completing his education, he studied law, and began its practice in Jefferson county with his elder brother, Edmund I. Lee. Just prior to the outbreak of the civil war, he had been chosen commonwealth's attorney for that county, and was holding this position when he entered the army. He

was made a lieutenant in "Botts' Grays," a company of the 2d Virginia regiment, Stonewall Brigade. During the Valley campaign under General Jackson, while bearing the colors of his regiment, the color-bearer having been shot, he received a disabling wound. Upon the organization of the military courts, he was appointed, by Mr. Davis, president of the military court of the 2d army corps, which position he held until the close of the war. Before this, he had been twice taken prisoner, and was once a prisoner at Johnson's Island; the second time he was fortunate enough to effect his escape. Since the war, Mr. Lee has been practicing his profession in Clarke and Loudoun counties, with his residence near Millwood, in the former county. He has recently been elected by the State legislature county judge for Clarke. Mr. Lee was selected as the proper representative of his grandfather, Richard Henry Lee, to read the Declaration of Independence at the old State House, Philadelphia, on the 4th of July, 1876.

He married, in June, 1848, Evelyn Byrd, daughter of William Byrd Page, of "Pagebrook," Clarke county, and Eliza Mayo Atkinson, his second wife; she was born about 1823, and died at their home in Clarke, on the 25th of October, 1889. They had these five children:

i, MARY PAGE[7], living with her father, and unmarried.

ii, WILLIAM BYRD[7]. See 90.

iii, RICHARD HENRY[7], living and unmarried.

iv, ELISE ATKINSON[7] was married at Christ Church, Millwood, on the 20th of September, 1878, to the Rev. James Ridout Winchester, D. D., and has had these children: 1, Richard Henry Lee, born the 23d of August and died the 23d of September, 1879. 2, Lucy Langhorne, born the 13th of August, 1880, and died the 4th of April, 1882. 3, James Ridout, born the 11th of January, 1883, and died the 20th of September, 1886. 4, Evelyn Lee, born the 28th of July, 1885. 5. Cassius Lee, born the 6th of April, 1888. 6, Florence Whiting, born the 18th of October, 1892. James Ridout Winchester was born at Annapolis, Md., on the 15th of March, 1852, a son of Jacob Winchester and Mary Ridout, his wife, of that place; he was educated at the Episcopal High School, and at Washington and Lee University, where he took the degree of B. A. in 1874; after graduating at the Virginia Theological Seminary, he was ordained Deacon the 29th of June, 1877, and Priest the 28th of June, 1878; his diaconate was served as assistant to the late Rev. Joshua Peterkin, D. D., at St. James' Church, Richmond. His next charge was at Uniontown, Alabama, 1878 to 1880; then at Wytheville, Va., from 1880 to 1882 He was rector of Christ Church, Macon, Ga., from 1882 to 1890, when he assumed the rectorship of Christ Church, Nashville, Tenn., of which he is now in charge. In 1893, the honorary degree of D. D. was conferred upon Mr. Winchester by the University of the South, Sewanee, Tenn.

The Winchester family came from England, and settled in Queen Anne's county, Md., about 1649, receiving a grant of land from Lord Baltimore, which remained in the family until sold, in 1845, by Jacob Winchester, who, as eldest son of the eldest son, inherited it. The Ridout family, into which they married, were of French Huguenot descent; John, the first of the name in America, was the private secretary of Governor Sharpe, and later adopted by him; he married a daughter of Governor Ogle, who, family tradition states, was at one time engaged to Governor Sharpe, but he resigned his claims in favor of his adopted son, and blessed their union by leaving them his estates.

v, CHARLES HENRY[7]. See 91.

## THE PAGE FAMILY.

"Here lieth in hope of a Joyfull Resurrection the Body of Colonel John Page, of Bruton Parish Esquire. One of their Majesties Council in the Dominion of Virginia, who departed this life the 23 of January, in the year of our Lord, 1691–2, aged 65." Such is the inscription on the tombstone of the progenitor of this justly famous Virginia family. He is said to have arrived in Virginia about 1650, being then 23 years old; he married Alice Luckin, and left two sons, Francis and Matthew. The eldest son married Mary, daughter of Edward Digges, of Hampton Parish, and had only one child, a daughter Elizabeth, who married a "John Page, of York county, Gent.," of whom nothing is known. Matthew, the second son, was born at Williamsburg, in 1659, and died the 9th of January, 1703; he is described on his tombstone as "One of Her Majesties most Honourable Councell of the Parish of Abingdon in the County of Gloucester in the Collony of Virginia," etc. He married (about 1689) Mary, the only child of John and Mary Mann, of "Timberneck," Gloucester, and settled (about 1700) at "Rosewell," on Carter's Creek, also in Gloucester, which place has ever since been famous as the old homestead of the Pages. This couple left only one surviving child, a son, Mann Page, who died the

24th of January, 1730, aged 39 years. This Matthew Page was the builder of the present "Rosewell" mansion, which he commenced about 1725; it is a very large house, and was formerly an exceedingly handsome specimen of old colonial architecture. Matthew Page was twice married, but left surviving issue by his second wife only; he married first in 1712, Judith, daughter of Ralph Wormeley, of Middlesex, who died the 12th of December, 1716, aged 22 years; he married, secondly, Judith, daughter of Robert Carter, of "Corotoman," Lancaster county, by whom he left three sons, who became respectively the progenitors of the three branches of the Page family in Virginia.

i, MANN PAGE, of "Rosewell," second of that name, was the eldest son of the Hon. Mann Page, and Judith Carter, his second wife, and the progenitor of this branch of the family. He was born about 1718; the date of his death is not known; was a member of the Continental Congress of 1777, and one of the board of Visitors of William and Mary College. He was twice married; first, in the year 1743, to Alice, third daughter of the Hon. John Grymes, of Middlesex, who died the 11th of January, 1746, leaving two sons, and a daughter; he was married, secondly, about 1748, to Anne Corbin Tayloe, of "Mt. Airy," by whom he had seven children. His eldest child by his first wife, was Governor John Page, who was born the 17th April, 1744, and died the 11th of October, 1808, at Richmond where he was buried in the churchyard of St. John's Episcopal Church. He was educated at William and Mary College, of which institution he was afterward a Visitor; was a member of the House of Burgesses, of the Continental Congress, and Governor of Virginia, 1802–5. Governor Page was married twice, had twelve children by his first wife, and eight by the second. He was married, first (about 1765) to Frances, daughter of Col. Robin Burwell, of Isle-of-Wight county, and Sallie Nelson, his wife, who was a daughter of the first Thomas Nelson of Yorktown. Col. Robin Burwell was the brother of "Betty" Burwell, the wife of "President" William Nelson. Mrs. Page died in the year 1784, aged 37, leaving nine surviving children; five of whom married sons or daughters of Governor Thomas Nelson. (These intermarriages afford an example of Virginia relationships; every one of these Nelsons and Pages were related three or four times.) Governor Page married, secondly, in 1789, at New York City, Margaret, daughter of William Lowther, of Scotland, and had issue as mentioned. Governor Page's eldest son, Mann Page, who died the 24th of August, 1813, aged 47 years, was the founder of "Shelly," another seat of the Pages, which is on the opposite side of Carter's Creek from "Rosewell." By many this is thought to have been the headquarters of Powhatan, the place made famous by the rescue of Captain John Smith by Pocahontas. Mann Page married, 5th of June, 1788, Elizabeth, daughter of Governor Thomas Nelson, and had fifteen children. His younger brother, Francis Page of "Rugswamp," Hanover county, also married a daughter of Governor Thomas Nelson, and had seven children; the eldest, Anzolette Elizabeth, born in 1807, died the 14th of January, 1884, was married, on the 15th of July, 1831, to Lieutenant William Nelson Pendleton, a graduate of West Point, who later entered the ministry of the Episcopal Church, in which he served most faithfully for over forty-five years; their eldest daughter, Susan Pendleton, married Edwin Gray Lee (82, q. v.). Francis Page's youngest son was John Page, who lived at "Oakland," Hanover county; he was married, in 1847, to Elizabeth Burwell, fourth daughter of Captain Thomas Nelson, of same place, and Judith Nelson, his wife, who was the youngest child of Governor Thomas Nelson; their eldest child is the Rev. Francis Page, of the Episcopal Church, now living in Texas; the second son, Thomas Nelson Page, so favorably known and deservedly popular as a writer, lives at Washington City; their youngest son, Rosewell Page, is a lawyer.

ii, John (1720–1780), of "North End," the second son of the Hon. Mann Page, of "Rosewell," and Judith Carter, his second wife, was the progenitor of this branch of the family. He was married, about 1741, to Jane, a daughter of Col. William E. Byrd, of "Westover," (by his second wife, Maria Taylor) by whom he had fifteen children. John Page was a member of the Council, 1768, was a Visitor of William and Mary College, and a lawyer by profession. Of his children, the eldest, Mann Page, removed to "Fairfield," Clarke county; married, about 1767, Mary Mason, a daughter of Samuel Selden, of "Salvington," Stafford county. (Mary Thomson Mason, the only sister of the famous George Mason, of "Gunston," married, on the 11th of April, 1751, Col. Samuel Selden, and had Samuel and Mary Mason.) They had two children; the eldest, William Byrd Page, married, about 1797, Anne, daughter of Henry and Lucy (Grymes) Lee, of "Leesylvania," and had issue as stated (see 24, viii).

iii, Robert (1722–1768), of "Broadneck," Hanover county, the youngest son of the Hon. Mann Page, of "Rosewell," and Judith Carter, his second wife, was the progenitor of this branch of the family. The Broadneck House is supposed to have been built about 1750; it was burned during the Revolutionary War. His eldest surviving son, Robert, probably rebuilt the mansion, while the others moved to Clarke county. Robert Page was married, on the 20th of January, 1750, to Sarah Walker, who was the daughter of an English clergyman, and had nine children, the sixth of whom was John, born at "Broadneck," the 29th of June, 1760, and died the 17th of September, 1838; he was married, in 1784, to Maria Horsemander, the daughter of Col. William E. Byrd, of "Westover," and had seven children, the eldest of whom, William Byrd Page, was twice married; first to Evelyn Byrd, a daughter of Judge William Nelson, by whom he had issue, Anne Willing Page, Dr. William Byrd Page, of Philadelphia, and John Page; he was married, secondly, to Eliza Mayo, daughter of Robert Atkinson, of "Mansfield," Dinwiddie county, by whom he had Evelyn Byrd, who married, in 1851, Richard Henry Lee, and had issue as stated; his second daughter, Mary Page, married Col. William Nelson, a great-grandson of "Secretary" Thomas Nelson, of Yorktown.[1]

## STRATFORD LINE, SEVENTH GENERATION.

### Thomas Lee.

60. Thomas[7], the second son of Thomas Lee[6] (Thomas Sim[5], Thomas[4], Philip[3], Richard[2], Richard[1]) and Eleanor Cromwell, his wife, was born the 11th of May, 1803; died ——; he married Harriet Carver, of Boston, and had issue: Charles, Mary, Rebecca, Richard, and Rosa Lee[8]. Of these, Charles married Rebecca Grant, and left a son, Charles[9], who married and had a son, Dr. Richard Lee[10]. Rosa married Lieutenant Breeze, U. S. N.

### Thomas Sim Lee.

61. Thomas Sim[7], the only son of William Lee[6] (Thomas Sim[5], Thomas[4], Philip[3], Richard[2], Richard[1]) and Mary Lee Hollyday, his wife, was born the 8th of August, 1818, and died ——; he was married, on the 7th of April, 1840, to Josephine, a daughter of General Columbus O'Donnell, and had the following named children:

i, Charles O'Donnell[8], born the 8th of February, 1841; married, 11th November, 1869, Matilda Dale Jenkins, and had Josephine Jenkins, Thomas Sim, Charles Stewart, Matilda, Samuel Gouverneur, Mary Digges, Louisa Carroll, Charles O'Donnell, Gertrude, and Adrian Iselin Lee[9]. Of these children, all are living excepting Matilda, born 1st of June, 1875; died 11th of June, 1890; and Samuel Gouverneur, born 1st of February, 1877; died 20th of June, 1892.

---

[1] This brief sketch is chiefly derived from the *Page Family in Virginia*, New York, 1883.

ii, MARY DIGGES[8], born 9th of September, 1842; married, 1872, Robert Goodlow Harper Carroll, being his second wife; they have Charles and Albert Henry Carroll.

iii, WILLIAM[8], born 12th of September, 1844; married, January, 1867, Mary Frances Matthias, and had Mary, Josephine O'Donnell (born June, 1869, and died in infancy), Ellen Lynch, William and Mildred Lee[9].

iv, COLUMBUS O'DONNELL[8], born in November, 1853; was married, on the 22d of June, 1876, to Hannah Anne Tyson, and had: James Tyson (born the 3d of May, 1879, and died the 13th of June, 1881), Josephine, Hannah, Columbus O'Donnell, Philip Francis, Jessie Tyson, Mordecai Lewis Dawson, Frederick Collins, and Edward Jackson Lee[9].

## DR. CHARLES CARROLL LEE, LL. D.

62. CHARLES CARROLL[7], the eldest son of John Lee[6] (Thomas Sim[5], Thomas[4], Philip[3], Richard[2], Richard[1]) and Harriet Carroll, his wife, was born at Philadelphia in the year 1839 and died at New York City the 10th of May, 1893. Dr. Lee spent the earlier years of his life in Maryland; was graduated from the medical department of the University of Pennsylvania in 1859; served for some time on the medical staff of the army during the late war; then settled at New York, where he practiced his profession with much success. He was professor of gynæcology in the New York Post-Graduate School, consulting surgeon to the Charity Hospital, to the Women's Hospital, the St. Elizabeth's Hospital, and to the Foundling Asylum; was a member of the American Gynæcological Society, of the Academy of Medicine, Obstetrical Society, and Pathological Society, of New York. The Board of Trustees of the New York Post-Graduate School, in their resolutions of regret at his death, said: "Dr. Lee was a teacher of the highest rank, being able to intently interest his hearers, and to convey to them a clear sense of his views upon the cases in his very important department. Dr. Lee was a Christian gentleman, who had bound himself to his associates and to those who were instructed by him by the most affectionate ties."

At the time of his death he was the President of the Medical Society of the county of New York, which society, in their resolutions, state that "the loss which we mourn is by no means limited to our society, our city, or even our country. Wherever the profession of medicine is to-day practiced as a science, there will the death of Dr. Lee be recognized as a misfortune."

Dr. Lee married Helen Parrish, of Philadelphia, and had these children: Sarah Redwood, Richard Henry (born the 26th of May, 1867, and died the 30th of March, 1868), Thomas Sim, James Parrish, Charles Carroll (born the 29th of February, 1872, and died the 18th of January, 1875), Mary Helen (born the 8th of January, 1875, and died the 8th of April, 1876), Helen, and Mary Digges Lee [8].

## George Lee.

63. George [7], the only son of George Lee [6] (George [5], Thomas Ludwell [4], Thomas [3], Richard [2], Richard [1]) and Sallie Moore Henderson, his wife, was born at Leesburg the 3d of May, 1831; died at Brooklyn, N. Y., the 14th of April, 1892. He was married, on the 27th of June, 1860, to his cousin, Laura Frances, daughter of General Asa Rogers and Eleanor Lee Orr, his wife, of Leesburg. (Eleanor Lee Orr was the daughter of Dr. John Dalrymple Orr and Lucinda Lee, his wife. Lucinda Lee was the daughter of Thomas Ludwell Lee, of "Bellvue.") George and Laura Frances (Rogers) Lee had these children, now living: Hugh Douglass, Eleanor Orr, Asa Rogers, and Arthur Lee [8]. Hugh Douglass Lee is at present the representative in the male line of Thomas Lee, of Stratford.

## Richard Henry Lee.

64. Richard Henry [7], the third son of Richard Henry Lee [6] (Ludwell [5], Richard Henry [4], Thomas [3], Richard [2], Richard [1]) and Anna Eden Jordan, his second wife, was born at Leesburg, the 22d of August, 1831; died at Lewistown, Pa., the 28th of December, 1891. Mr. Lee was educated at Washington College, Pa., from which institution he graduated, in 1849, at the age of only eighteen. He was a civil engineer by profession, but had been lately the superintendent of iron works at Lewistown, and had been for many years rector's warden of St. Mark's Episcopal Church, of that place. Mr. Lee was married, on the 24th of May, 1858, to Mary Wilson, and had:

i, Richard Henry [8], born 12th of April, 1859; married, June, 1894, Catharine M. Sheaffer, and has, Richard Henry, born 13th of March, 1895.

ii, Agnes Wilson [8], born 24th of March, 1868; married, June, 1894, Albert Ladd Colby.

## Francis Lightfoot Lee.

65. Francis Lightfoot [7], the sixth son of Richard Henry Lee [6] (Ludwell [5], Richard Henry [4], Thomas [3], Richard [2], Richard [1]) and Anna Eden Jordan, his second wife, was born at Washington, Pa., the 16th of July,

1840; died the 24th of May, 1881; was married, in 1865, to Mary Duncan Mahon, and had:

i, AGNES MARY[8], born the 17th of November, 1866; died the 15th of December, 1867.
ii, ANNA EDEN[8], born 28th of April, 1868; married Robert E. Peterson, of Philadelphia, and has two children, Robert E. and Eleanor Bouvier.
iii, MARY[8], born the 13th of May, 1871.
iv, SOPHIA MAHON[8], born the 1st of May, 1875.

## FRANCIS PRESTON BLAIR LEE.

66. FRANCIS PRESTON BLAIR[7], the only son of Samuel Phillips Lee[6] (Francis Lightfoot[5], Richard Henry[4], Thomas[3], Richard[2], Richard[1]) and Elizabeth Blair, his wife, was born at "Silver Spring," Md., the 9th of August, 1857; was married, on the 1st of October, 1891, to Anne Clymer, daughter of Edward and Anne (Clymer) Brooke, of Birdsboro, Pa. They have one son, Edward Brooke Lee, born at Washington, D. C., the 23d of October, 1892. Mr. Lee is a lawyer, and resides at Washington.

## WILLIAM HILL LEE.

67. WILLIAM HILL[7], the eldest son of John Fitzgerald Lee[6] (Francis Lightfoot[5], Richard Henry[4], Thomas[3], Richard[2], Richard[1]) and Eleanor Anne Hill, his wife, was born at Washington, D. C., the 7th of March, 1846; was married, on the 3d of November, 1869, to Julia, daughter of Henry and Julia M. (Hunt) Turner. Mr. Lee is president of the Merchants' National Bank of St. Louis, where he resides. They have had the following named children:

i, ELEANOR HILL[8], born the 6th of October, 1870; died the 18th of December, 1874.
ii, HENRY TURNER[8], born the 27th of June, 1872.
iii, JULIA HUNT[8], born the 22d of September, 1874; died the 27th of September, 1877.
iv, JANET FITZGERALD[8], born the 16th of January, 1877.
v, WILLIAM HILL[8], born the 26th of September, 1879; died the 8th of January, 1889.
vi, MARGARET LORETTO[8], born the 16th of January, 1883.
vii, MARIANNE[8], born the 25th of September, 1884.

## GEORGE TAYLOR LEE.

68. GEORGE TAYLOR[7], the eldest son of Charles Carter Lee[6] (Henry[5], Henry[4], Henry[3], Richard[2], Richard[1]) and Lucy Penn Taylor, his wife,

Fitzhugh Lee

was born at Richmond the 8th of March, 1848. He married, on the 15th of May, 1888, Mrs. Ella Marion (Goodrum) Fletcher, the widow of Dr. James Jefferson Fletcher, and daughter of William and Caroline (Townsend) Goodrum, of Lenoke, Arkansas; she was born the 30th of April, 1863. They have two children: Charles Carter and Lucy Randolph Lee[8]. Mr. Lee lives at Johnson City, Tenn., where he practices law.

### HENRY LEE.

69. HENRY[7], the second son of Charles Carter Lee[6] (Henry[5], Henry[4], Henry[3], Richard[2], Richard[1]) and Lucy Penn Taylor, his wife, was born the 9th of July, 1849; he married, on the 19th of July, 1888, Lilian Elizabeth, daughter of John Anderson and Susan Caroline (Malcolm) Woollen, and has three children: Charles Carter, Robert Henry, and Virginia Lilian Lee[8]. Mr. Lee resides at Winston, N. C.

### ROBERT RANDOLPH LEE.

70. ROBERT RANDOLPH[7], the third son of Charles Carter Lee[6] (Henry[5], Henry[4], Henry[3], Richard[2], Richard[1]) and Lucy Penn Taylor, his wife, was born the 22d of May, 1853; he married, on the 4th of February, 1886, Alice Wilkinson, and has two sons: William Carter and Robert Randolph Lee[8]. Mr. Lee resides on his father's old estate in Powhatan county.

### MAJOR-GENERAL FITZHUGH LEE.

71. FITZHUGH[7], the eldest son of Sydney Smith Lee[6] (Henry[5], Henry[4], Henry[3], Richard[2], Richard[1]) and Anna Maria Mason, his wife, was born at "Clermont," Fairfax county, the 19th of November, 1835. Of his boyhood days little is known, save that he is spoken of by friends as a bright, manly boy, full of life and fun; preferring the pleasures and exercises of the playground to the dull routine of the school-room, a trait not uncommon among boys. When sixteen he entered the Military Academy at West Point, where he was graduated in July, 1856, at the head of his class in horsemanship, and was appointed second lieutenant in the famous old Second Cavalry, which regiment furnished so many officers afterward distinguished in the civil war. His first important duty was in drilling and disciplining raw recruits at the Carlisle Barracks, in Pennsylvania, where he gave evidence of ability in organizing troops. It was probably the ability shown on this duty that led to his being appointed, a few years later, an instructor of cavalry at West Point. After leaving Carlisle, Lieutenant Lee

served upon the frontier against the Indians. The following sketch of "Fitzhugh Lee as an Indian fighter," from the pen of an old army comrade, is of interest, telling both of the adventures of the subject of this sketch, and giving the experiences of the soldiers on the "plains" in a species of warfare now happily past.[1]

"In 1859 I was a bugler of 'B' Company of the 2d U. S. Cavalry (now the 5th), having enlisted in the army at the age of thirteen years. The officers of the company were: Captain, E. Kirby Smith; 1st Lieutenant, Walter Jenifer, and 2d Lieutenant, Fitzhugh Lee.

"At the time of which I write the company formed a part of the Wichita expedition, composed of six companies of the 2d Cavalry and commanded by Brevet Major Earl Van Dorn, Captain 2d Cavalry; Lieut. Lee acting as Adjutant. This expedition was organized for the purpose of operating against the main villages of the hostile Indians, whose depredations on the people of Texas had become unbearable. These Indians, leaving their families and villages in the far-distant Indian Territory, would form into small bands and, penetrating into the very heart of the settlements, murder men, women, and children, and return in comparative safety to their villages with their spoils of scalps and horses. The few mounted troops in Texas at that time were widely scattered, the posts being from 100 to 150 miles apart, and, although the officers and men were ever on the alert, still the Indians' knowledge of the country, their plainscraft and ability to travel night and day, gave them a great advantage over the soldiers, and made the chance of overtaking and punishing them very uncertain. The object of the expedition, then, was to strike the large bands congregated in their villages, give them a chastisement they would not soon forget, and thereby put an end to the depredations on the people of Texas. . . .

"The approach to the Indians' stronghold could only be made on foot and in open or skirmish order, as the undergrowth was so thick as to be almost impenetrable. Several charges were made, one being led by Major Van Dorn in person, but all were forced back, due as much to the obstacles they encountered as to the fire of the Indians. At this juncture Lieut. Lee asked permission to lead a charge against one of the flanks of the Indians' position, which was granted, and resulted in the capture of a large number of women and children and a few warriors who were mixed up with them. In a second charge he struck the Indians within a few yards of their main body, and a desperate encounter ensued. In pressing forward in advance

[1] *The Monthly Chronicle*, VII., p. 3, *et seq.*, published by the Literary Societies of the Episcopal High School of Virginia, near Alexandria.

of his men Lieut. Lee came face to face with an Indian brave. He raised his pistol, the Indian drew his bow and both fired at the same instant. The lieutenant's bullet struck the Indian squarely between the eyes and the Indian's arrow entered his right side under his extended arm, and, passing between the ribs, penetrated the right lung. The force and shock of the wound caused Lieut. Lee to stagger for support against a tree, whence he was assisted to a place of safety by his men. It was at this time that Major Van Dorn was made aware of Lieut. Lee's accident, and, taking me with him, hastened to where he lay stretched on the ground in an apparently dying condition. He motioned me to him, and I sat down beside him, taking his head in my lap. The blood was streaming from his mouth, but not a drop came from his wound. He was unable to speak, but could, by motions, make himself understood. The surgeon was soon on the spot, and used all his skill to stop the flow of blood, which threatened to strangle the patient, but was only partially successful.

"Lieut. Lee's condition was deemed very critical—so much so that Major Van Dorn thought it advisable to take down any message he might wish to send his parents, and my recollection is that the letter, as dictated, was addressed jointly to his father and mother. It was necessarily very brief, as he could only speak with great effort, and one sentence still remains fresh in my memory. It was that 'he was dying a soldier's death, the one he preferred above all others.' In the meantime, the troops had overwhelmed the Indians, killing 55 warriors and taking numerous prisoners. In the last assault, my captain—E. Kirby Smith—was severely, but not dangerously, wounded. Now that the fight was over, the officers gathered around their wounded comrade with expressions of sympathy and sorrow. They soon dispersed, however, at the request of the surgeon, who feared bad effects for his patient from the excitement of their presence. Lieut. Lee remained perfectly still for several minutes after they left, when, looking up at me, he said: 'Jack, you are going to lose your best friend.' This caused me to feel much depressed, as I was sincerely attached to him, but an incident which took place a little later made me feel differently. At that time a Lieut. Kimmel, an old West Point comrade, who had only just heard of his friend's misfortune, being at a distant part of the field, came rushing up and, taking both of Lieut. Lee's hands, said: 'Fitz, old man, we can't afford to lose you,' together with many other expressions of love and sympathy; and as the sufferer seemed pleased and interested, continued, saying: 'I had a close call myself,' and took off his hat and showed where a bullet had passed through it. Lieut. Lee, with a faint smile on his face, turned his head toward Kimmel and said between gasps: 'Kimmel, do you wish me to believe an Indian shot that hole in your hat! Acknowledge the corn, old man; didn't you go behind a tree and shoot the hole in your hat yourself?' After that I never doubted he would get well, but he had a hard struggle, and it was many months before he entirely recovered. . . .

"Soon after our arrival at Camp Colorado, Lieut. Lee was granted permission to visit Austin, the capital of the State, to witness the inauguration of General Sam. Houston as Governor, and took me with him. We traveled by ambulance and, after taking in the inauguration, started on our return *via* San Antonio, then, as now, the liveliest city in Texas. After a few days spent in San Antonio, we started for our station, arriving there on the evening of the 12th of January, 1860, in the midst of a Texas norther and snow-storm. A short time before, two men of the company, who had been on a hunting pass, came in and reported having seen a party of Indians driving a large band of horses and mules about sixteen miles from the post. As none but hostile Indians ever visited that part of the country and then only for the purpose of murder and plunder, preparations were made at once to pursue them, and, inside of an hour from our arrival at the post, Lieut. Lee, with a detachment of twelve men, was in the saddle and riding for the place where the Indians had been seen. The wind was blowing a gale and the snow drifting so as to make our progress very slow, and, in consequence, we did not reach the point where the Indians had been seen until after daylight. Their trail was soon found, but, on account of the heavy fall of snow covering it in places and the precautions taken by the Indians to hide it, such as driving their animals in a circle and other devices, it was slow work following it for the first few miles, but after that, the Indians having become careless, we were able to follow it at a trot and kept that gait without a halt or rest until night set in and it was too dark to follow further. We then halted for the first time since leaving the post eighteen hours before, not to go into camp but to sit and walk about until it was light enough to again take up the trail. Fortunately, the norther had blown itself out during the night, but it was still very cold and, no fire being allowed, we breakfasted on hard tack and frozen pork. When the time came to mount our horses, some of the men were so stiff they had to be assisted into their saddles. We had not traveled far before we came to where the Indians had halted for a short time, killed a colt and cooked a part of it. From these indications we inferred that they could not be very far ahead of us and spurred on with renewed vigor. As the sun was out bright and strong, causing the snow to melt rapidly, the trail was now easy to follow and ran a course parallel to a ridge which extended northward for several miles. This ridge was covered by a heavy growth of cedar trees, with occasional clear spaces. Pressing forward on the trail, which was becoming fresher each mile, one of our party discovered an object in the timber to our right and I was ordered to ascertain what it was. After going about 300 yards, I was able to make out that it was a loose pony, and, turning to rejoin the command, saw the Indians going over a hill less than half a mile ahead. Luckily they did not see me, and, putting spurs to my horse, I soon joined the command and reported my discovery to Lieut. Lee, who immediately halted, ordered the men to divest themselves of their overcoats and other *impedimenta*, and carefully examine their arms. Then, drawing our pistols, we moved forward at a fast gallop, and, rising the hill, came in full view of the objects of our pursuit, who, owing to being muffled up in their blankets and robes, had not as yet seen us. Indeed, we could have gotten right on them but for the accidental discharge of a pistol by one of the men, which gave the Indians notice.

"Lieut. Lee immediately ordered the charge, and the men dashed forward with yells and cheers, following the scattering Indians, who were too much surprised to make a stand, but broke for the timber on the ridge to our right. In the pursuit I found myself with Lieut. Lee and one other man trying to intercept two of the Indians before they could reach the timber. One was killed at the edge, but the other being mounted on a remarkably fast pony not only succeeded in getting to the timber, but had the audacity to turn and fire several arrows at us before entering. But Lieut. Lee was determined he should not escape, and we followed him into the timber and for several miles along the ridge. The cedar trees grew very thick in places, and we would at times ride several hundred yards without catching sight of our Indian, and then again, striking into one of the clear spaces, we would find ourselves close upon him, when Lieut. Lee would take a snap shot at him with a carbine he had borrowed from the man with us, but without effect. This continued for about seven miles, when we came to where the ridge ended in ravines opening out into the prairie. We had lost sight of our Indian for some time, but the tracks of his pony in the melting snow were quite plain and easily followed. Presently the tracks led into a dark ravine. Here we separated, Lieut. Lee taking one side and I the other, the third man following the trail. We had only gone a few hundred yards when the lieutenant called to me to come to his side of the ravine, as he wished to speak to me, and, as I turned to comply, I saw the Indian come out of the ravine we had passed, on foot, and run over the hill toward a ravine on the other side. I instantly called out, 'There he goes, lieutenant,' and the latter turned just in time to see him disappear over the hill. We immediately galloped to the point where he disappeared, but could see nothing of him anywhere, but dismounting soon discovered his moccasin tracks leading down the hill into a thicket. Leaving our horses in charge of the other man, we entered the brush abreast, with an interval between us of about thirty yards. Lieut. Lee still wore his overcoat, made of heavy cloth with cape, and was armed with an old-fashioned muzzle-loading carbine and a Colt's revolver. I had a pistol only. After making our way cautiously into the brush for a couple of hundred yards, Lieut. Lee called to me, 'Jack, keep a good look out now, for he is not far off; here is his blanket,' which he picked up from the ground and threw across the carbine he carried on his left shoulder and started forward. At this time the Indian was only a few yards away, crouching behind a small ledge of rocks, where he remained until Lieut. Lee was almost on top of him, when, straightening up with a yell, he let drive an arrow full at his breast. This the lieutenant avoided by jumping to one side, but it was shot with such force and at such close range that, after passing through the cape and left sleeve of his coat, it struck the stock of the carbine he carried and broke in two. In jumping aside Lieut. Lee dropped the carbine and was left with his pistol only, which he thrust toward the Indian to fire, when the latter grasped it by the barrel with his left hand and turned the muzzle from him. In this position the pistol was discharged without injury to either, and, in the struggle that ensued for its possession, it fell to the ground, and for the time was lost to both of the combatants. A desperate hand-to-hand struggle now ensued, the Indian attempting to use his knife and Lieut. Lee closing with him to prevent him. The whole thing was so sudden and startling that for a moment I was powerless to move and stood still in my tracks, but, hearing the lieutenant call my name, I hurried to his assistance. The Indian was the larger and stronger man, and he flung his antagonist about with apparent ease, but could not down him. Seeing me approach with my pistol presented, he managed to place the lieutenant between him and me, and I was afraid to shoot for fear I might hit my officer. An instant later, greatly to my surprise and joy, I saw the Indian hurled to the ground, Lieut. Lee falling on top—one of the prettiest falls I have ever seen. Now one of those fortunate circumstances took place which seldom happen more than once in a lifetime. As Lieut. Lee was falling he saw his pistol, which had been dropped in the struggle, lying on the ground and within reach. With great presence of mind he managed to free his right arm, grasp and cock the pistol and fire a bullet through the Indian's cheeks, while another shot better aimed sent him to the 'happy hunting grounds.'

"As soon as he could free himself from the embrace of the Indian, he arose to his feet and commenced to feel over his body for knife or arrow wounds, but, fortunately, though his clothing was cut in many places, his skin was not touched. This was due to the heavy clothing he had on, especially to the overcoat, the material of which was unusually thick and heavy.

"I remarked to him: 'You had a pretty close call with the Indian.' He replied, at the same time extending his arms, 'Yes, he was a big fellow, but I was only getting my muscle up with him and feel now that I could get away with half a dozen just like him.' Later, on my asking him how he succeeded in throwing the Indian, he said:

"'He was very strong, as far as brute strength went, but he knew nothing of the science of wrestling. For a time, though, I thought he would get me, when I happened to think of a trick in wrestling which I learned during my school days in Virginia. It was known as the "Virginia *back heel*." I tried it on him and *fotched* him.'

"Lieut. Lee was complimented in orders by his department commander and the commanding general of the army, General Scott, but I doubt if any one ever heard him talk of his achievements as a young man on the plains of Texas, as he is altogether too modest to speak of his own exploits. E. M. HAYES, Major, 7th Cavalry."

"Fort Clark, Texas, January, 1895."

The outbreak of the civil war found Fitzhugh Lee at West Point, an instructor of cavalry tactics. Every endeavor was made to induce him to continue at his post. He was told that if he were not willing to fight against his State, he could remain during the war at West Point, where good pay and easy duty would be his portion. Rejecting these tempting offers, he promptly resigned and offered his services to his native State. Being appointed adjutant-general on the staff of General Ewell, he served in that capacity during the campaign of the first Manassas. In September, 1861, he was appointed lieutenant-colonel of the First Virginia Cavalry, of which Stuart was then colonel. On the promotion of Stuart, he was chosen colonel, and, later, brigadier-general under Stuart. When Stuart made his famous raid around McClellan, Colonel Lee accompanied him. In 1863, the cavalry of the Army of Northern Virginia were divided into two divisions; Generals Hampton and Fitzhugh Lee were appointed to command them. Some time after the death of Stuart, Fitzhugh Lee succeeded Hampton as the commander of the cavalry of the Army of Northern Virginia, with rank of major-general. So much for the various positions held by him. To give a full sketch of his army services, of the battles participated in, of the special raids, of the daring scouting parties, or of the skill with which he aided in covering movements of the army, and that, too, with such a meagre force—to tell all this would be to write a history of the achievements of the Army of Northern Virginia. Suffice it to say, that General Fitzhugh Lee was frequently commended and always trusted by his superior officers, and was the idol of his brave troopers. That the cavalry arm of the Southern armies was not able to accomplish more, or to better hold its own against the greater numbers and much better equipped troopers of the enemy, was never due to any lack of bravery on the part of the soldiers nor to want of skill and daring on the part of their officers. The Southern cavalry was never properly mounted nor armed, and seldom did man or beast receive sufficient rations. But all this is well known, and needs no further statement. After the war, General Lee retired to his desolated farm in Stafford county, and, like the rest of his brave comrades, went to work. And it was hard work! He himself has said of it: "I had been accustomed all my life to draw corn from the quartermaster, and found it rather hard now to draw it from an obstinate soil, *but I did it!*" In the autumn of 1885, General Lee was elected Governor of Virginia, thus following the footsteps of his grandfather, General Henry Lee.

General Lee was married at Alexandria, on the 19th of April, 1871, to Ellen Bernard, daughter of George D. and Sarah Ellen (Hooe) Fowle, of that place; they have five children: Ellen, Fitzhugh, George, Nannie, and Virginia Lee[8].

## Major John Mason Lee.

72. John Mason[7], the third son of Sydney Smith Lee[6] (Henry[5], Henry[4], Henry[3], Richard[2], Richard[1]) and Anna Maria Mason, his wife, was born at "Clermont," Fairfax county, the 4th of January, 1839; married, on the 25th of October, 1871, Nora, the youngest daughter of Dr. William and Dorothea (Minor) Bankhead, of Caroline county; they have five children: Nannie Mason, Dorothea Bankhead, Bessie Winston, John Mason, and William Bankhead Lee[8]. John Mason Lee served in the Confederate army, rising to the rank of major.

## Henry Carter Lee.

73. Henry Carter[7], the fourth son of Sydney Smith Lee[6] (Henry[5], Henry[4], Henry[3], Richard[2], Richard[1]) and Anna Maria Mason, his wife, was born at "Clermont," Fairfax county, the 9th of January, 1842; married, on the 24th of September, 1868, Sally Buchanan Floyd, daughter of

Geo C Lee

John Warfield Johnston and Nichetti Buchanan Floyd, his wife; they have issue: Johnston, Sydney Smith, William Floyd, and Anne Mason Lee[8]. Henry Carter Lee joined the "Richmond Howitzers" at the outbreak of the late civil war; later was transferred to the staff of General W. C. Wickham, upon which he served as adjutant-general. He died at Richmond on the 6th of June, 1889.

## Daniel Murray Lee.

74. Daniel Murray[7], the fifth son of Sydney Smith Lee[6] (Henry[5], Henry[4], Henry[3], Richard[2], Richard[1]) and Anna Maria Mason, his wife, was born at Alexandria, the 14th of July, 1843; married, on the 14th of October, 1874, Nannie E., daughter of Joseph Burwell and Ann Eliza (Fitzhugh) Ficklin, of "Belmont," near Fredericksburg; they have issue: Daniel Murray, Jr., Joseph Burwell Ficklin, Edmonia Corbin, Sydney Smith, Mary Custis, and Henry Fitzhugh Lee[8]. Daniel Murray Lee served in the Confederate navy for four years; is now farming near Fredericksburg.

## Major-General George Washington Custis Lee.

75. George Washington Custis[7], the eldest son of Robert Edward Lee[6] (Henry[5], Henry[4], Henry[3], Richard[2], Richard[1]) and Mary Anne Randolph Custis, his wife, was born at Fortress Monroe, Virginia, on the 16th of September, 1832. His earlier school days were passed at "Clarens," in Fairfax county, at the classical school of the late Rev. George A. Smith; later, he entered the celebrated mathematical school of Benjamin Hallowell, at Alexandria, where his father had studied before him. President Zachary Taylor nominated him to a cadetship at West Point, and he entered that institution in June, 1850. In June, 1854, he graduated at the head of his class, having passed the four years of study there without receiving *a single demerit*. He was then assigned to the corps of engineers with the rank of brevet second lieutenant; in 1855, he was made full second lieutenant, and in 1859, first lieutenant. During his seven years service in the U. S. army he was on duty in the engineer bureau at Washington, in Georgia, Florida, and California, engaged in harbor defenses and river improvements. On the 2d of May, 1861, he resigned from the U. S. army to enter the service of his native State; he was appointed major of engineers, and when the Virginia forces were turned over to the Confederate States government, he was commissioned a captain of engineers, C. S. A. On the last of August, 1861, he was appointed aide-de-camp to the President of the Confederate States, with rank of

colonel. During his service on the President's staff he was engaged in supervising the defenses of Richmond. Toward the end of June, 1863, he was made a brigadier-general to command troops for the defense of Richmond against cavalry raids, etc. During the summer of 1864 he was appointed a major-general to command a division which operated on the lines below Richmond, from Chaffin's Bluff northward, in which command he continued until the evacuation of Richmond and Petersburg.

In the autumn of 1865 General Lee received the appointment to the chair of Civil and Military Engineering at the Virginia Military Institute, at Lexington.

He continued in this professorship until after the death of his father, when (on the 1st of February, 1871) he was elected President of Washington and Lee University, which position he now holds.

Mr. Davis held General Custis Lee in such high estimation that he considered him the proper man to succeed his father in command of the Army of Northern Virginia should occasion for a successor arise. Of this statement the Rev. J. William Jones has given this proof: Mr. Jones writes:[1]

"I have the following from the lips of the distinguished officer who related it. When General —— was compelled by failing health to ask to be relieved from a certain important command, he went to Richmond to confer with President Davis as to his successor, and to endeavor to impress upon him the very great importance of the district, and of the commander being a man of fine abilities. Mr. Davis fully sympathized with his views, and, after reflection, said: 'I know of no better man for that position than General Custis Lee. To show you my estimate of his ability, I will say that, when some time ago I thought of sending General Robert Lee to command the Western army, I had determined that his son Custis should succeed him in command of the Army of Northern Virginia. Now I wish you to go up and see General Lee, tell him what I say, and ask him to order General Custis Lee to the command of that department. Tell him I will make his son major-general, lieutenant-general, or, if need be, full general, so that he may rank any officer likely to be sent to that department.'

"General —— promptly sought Lee's headquarters, delivered Mr. Davis' message and urged a compliance. But to all of his arguments and entreaties the old chieftain had but one reply: 'I am very much obliged to Mr. Davis for his high opinion of Custis Lee. I hope that, if he had the opportunity, he would prove himself in some measure worthy of that confi-

[1] *Personal Reminiscences of General Robert E. Lee*, pp. 182–3.

W. H. F. Lee

dence. But, he is an untried man in the field, and I cannot appoint him to that command. Very much against his wishes and my own, Mr. Davis has kept him on his personal staff, and he has had no opportunity to prove his ability to handle an army in the field. Whatever may be the opinion of others, I cannot pass by my tried officers and take for that important position a comparatively new man—especially when that man is my own son. Mr. Davis can make the assignment if he thinks proper—I shall certainly not do so.' "

When his brother, W. H. F. Lee, was a prisoner of war, and held as a hostage under sentence of death, General Custis Lee requested, under a special flag of truce, the Northern authorities to be allowed to take his brother's place as a prisoner in solitary confinement and under sentence of death, giving as his reason for the proposed exchange his desire to save from sorrow the innocent and sick wife of his wounded brother. His request was refused, on the ground that the burden of war must remain upon those on whom it had chanced to fall.

## Major-General William Henry Fitzhugh Lee.

76. William Henry Fitzhugh[7], the second son of Robert Edward Lee[6] (Henry[5], Henry[4], Henry[3], Richard[2], Richard[1]) and Mary Anne Randolph Custis, his wife, was born at Arlington, Alexandria county, the 31st of May, 1837; died at "Ravensworth," Fairfax county, the 15th of October, 1891. After a thorough preparatory course of study, first under the Rev. George A. Smith, near Alexandria, then with a Mr. McNally at Baltimore, and, lastly, under the care of a Mr. Nugent at New York City, he entered Harvard College in the autumn of 1854. One who also entered the freshman class of that year has given a sketch of him as he appeared at that time:

"My acquaintance with William Henry Fitzhugh Lee commenced in the summer of 1854, when we met at Cambridge as members of the freshman class at Harvard College. He was just then entering his eighteenth year, was well grown for his age, tall, vigorous, and robust; open and frank in his address, kind and genial in his manners. He entered upon his college life with many advantages in his favor. The name of Lee was already upon the rolls of the university, for other representatives of different branches of the family had entered and graduated in the years gone by, and had left pleasant memories behind them. His distinguished lineage made him a welcome guest in the older families of the University city, and of Boston, its near neighbor, who felt a just pride in the historic and traditional associations connected with the earlier history of the country, and many of the influential members of the class belonged to such families.

"He was rather older than the average age of his classmates, and his life had been spent amid surroundings that enabled him to see a good deal of society and the world, so that he brought with him into his college a more matured mind and a greater insight than the student usually possesses at the threshold of his career. He had enjoyed excellent advantages in preparing for the entering examinations, and was well grounded in the languages as well as mathematics, so that he entered the class well fitted for the course of study to be pursued. Thus, from the first, he was prominent in the university, and soon became popular among his classmates, and his prominence and popularity was maintained during his stay among us.

"This was due not to superior distinction in any particular study or in any one feature of college life, but rather to his general standing and characteristics. He kept pace with his classmates in the recitation-room, not so much by hard and continuous study as by his quick comprehension and ready grasp of the subject in hand and the general fund of knowledge at his command. He was of a friendly and companionable nature, and there were abundant opportunities in a large class to develop this disposition, cultivate social intercourse, and strengthen the bonds of good fellowship. He had been accustomed to an out-door life in his Virginia home, and his manly training had given him an athletic frame which required constant and vigorous exercise. This he sought in active sports on the foot-ball ground and in class and college boat clubs, where he was welcomed as a valuable auxiliary." (Extract from the remarks of Senator Samuel Pasco, U. S. Senate, 4th March, 1892.)

In 1857 Mr. Lee was appointed a lieutenant in the army at the personal request of General Scott, who wrote to the Secretary of War, urging his appointment in the following complimentary terms:

"Headquarters of the Army, 8th May, 1857. Hon. J. B. Floyd, Secretary of War, Sir: I beg to ask that one of the vacant second lieutenantcies be given to W. H. F. Lee, son of Brevet Colonel R. E. Lee, at present on duty against the Comanches. I make this application mainly on the extraordinary merits of the father, the very best soldier that I ever saw in the field. But the son is himself a very remarkable youth, now about twenty, of a fine stature and constitution, a good linguist, a good mathematician, and about to graduate at Harvard University. He is also honorable and amiable, like his father, and dying to enter the army. I do not ask this commission as a favor, though if I had influence I should be happy to exert it in this case. My application is in the name of national justice, in part payment (and but a small part) of the debt due to the invaluable services of Colonel Lee. I have the honor to be," etc.

Upon receiving his appointment to the army, Mr. Lee left Harvard to join his regiment, the Sixth Infantry. His first military service was to command a detachment of soldiers on their way to join the main body, then in Texas. Later he accompanied his regiment, then under the command of the brave and skillful Albert Sydney Johnston, in his expedition against the Mormons. After the disturbances in Utah were quieted he marched with his regiment to the Pacific coast, then a very tedious journey. Lieut. Lee soon became tired of the dull routine of garrison life, and resigned his commission in the army. Returning to Virginia, he married Miss Charlotte Wickham, and settled, as a planter, on the famous old Custis estate, the "White House," on the Pamunky river, once the home of the Widow Custis when she married George Washington.

The following extracts from some letters written by Gen. R. E. Lee to his son will show the training under which he grew up:

> I hope you will always be distinguished for your avoidance of the universal bane, whisky, and every immorality. Nor need you fear to be ruled out of the society that indulges in it, for you will acquire their esteem and respect, as all venerate, if they do not practice, virtue. I hope you will make many friends, as you will be thrown with those who deserve this feeling. But indiscriminate intimacies you will find annoying and entangling, and they can be avoided by politeness and civility. When I think of your youth, impulsiveness, and many temptations, your distance from me, and the ease (and even innocence) with which you might commence an erroneous course, my heart quails within me and my whole frame and being tremble at the possible results. May Almighty God have you in His holy keeping. To His merciful providence I commit you, and I will rely upon Him and the efficacy of the prayers that will be daily and hourly offered up by those who love you.

A year or two later, on New Year's Day, 1859, he writes:

> I always thought and said there was stuff in you for a good soldier, and I trust you will prove it. I cannot express the gratification I felt, in meeting Colonel May in New York, at the encomiums he passed upon your soldiership, zeal, and devotion to your duty. But I was more pleased at the report of your conduct; that went nearer to my heart and was of infinitely more comfort to me. Hold on to your purity and virtue; they will proudly sustain you in all trials and difficulties and cheer you in every calamity.

So, too, when the young lieutenant had married and settled down a typical Virginian farmer:

> I am glad to hear that your mechanics are all paid off and that you have managed your funds so well as to have enough for your purposes. As you have commenced, I hope you will continue never to exceed your means. It will save you much anxiety and mortification, and enable you to maintain your independence of character and feeling. It is easier to make our wishes conform to our means than to make our means conform to our wishes. In fact, we want but little. Our happiness depends upon our independence, the success of our operations, prosperity of our plans, health, contentment, and the esteem of our friends, all of which, my dear son, I hope you may enjoy to the full.

On the outbreak of the late civil war, Lieut. Lee raised a company of cavalry and joined the Virginia troops. As another has said of him, he "served in every grade, successively, from captain to major-general of cavalry; he led his regiment in the famous raid around McClellan's army, and was an active participant in all those brilliant achievements which made the cavalry service so proficient.

"In the terrible fight at Brandy Station, 10th June, 1863, he was most severely wounded, and was taken to the residence of Gen. W. C. Wickham, a relative of his wife's, where he was made prisoner by a raiding party (sent for the purpose), and was carried off, at great personal suffering, to Fortress Monroe. From the latter place he was conveyed to Fort Lafayette, where he was confined until March, 1864, and treated with great severity, being held, with Capt. R. H. Taylor, under sentence of death, as hostages for two Federal officers who were prisoners in Richmond, and whom it was thought would be executed for some retaliatory measure.

"Exchanged in the spring of 1864, he returned to find his young wife and children dead, his beautiful home burned to the ground, his whole estate devastated and laid waste by the ruthless hand of war; and yet almost his first act on reaching Richmond was to go to Libby prison, visit the two Federal officers for whom he had been held as hostage, and who, like himself, had been under apprehension of being hung, and shake hands with and congratulate them. Immediately joining his command, he led his division from the Rapidan to Appomattox, where with his father, the greatest soldier of modern times, he surrendered to the inevitable." (Extracts from the remarks of Mr. E. E. Meredith, in the House of Representatives, 6 February, 1892.)

Another member of the House of Representatives paid this tribute:

"Throughout the struggle he discharged every duty and was equal to every responsibility placed upon him. His soldiers loved and trusted him as a father, for they knew he would sacrifice no life for empty glory. The saddest chapter in all his life was when—a prisoner of war at Fort Monroe, lying desperately wounded, with the threat of a retaliatory death sentence suspended over his head, in hourly expectation of its execution—he heard of the fatal illness of his wife and two little children but a few miles away. Earnestly his friends begged that he might be allowed to go and say the last farewell to them on earth. A devoted brother came, like Damon of old, and offered himself to die in 'Rooney's' place. War, inexorable war, always stern and cruel, could not accept the substituted sacrifice, and while the sick, wounded soldier, under sentence of death, lay, himself almost dying, in the dungeon of the fort, his wife and children 'passed over the river to rest under the trees' and wait there his coming. Yet no word of reproach ever passed his gentle lips. He accepted it all as the fortune of war.

"In all the walks of life—as a student at college, as an officer in the regular army, as a planter on the Pamunky, as a leader of cavalry in the civil war, as a farmer struggling with the chaos and confusion that beset him under the new order of things following the abolition of slavery, as president of the Virginia Agricultural Society, as State Senator, and as a member of Congress—Gen. William H. F. Lee met every requirement, was equal to every emergency, and left a name for honor, truth, and virtue which should be a blessed heritage and the inspiration for a nobler and loftier life to all those who shall succeed him." (Mr. Herbert Washington.)

As has been stated, General Lee was connected with the cavalry all during the war, and, naturally, took the greatest pride in its efficiency, and was jealous of its reputation. This branch of the service seems to have been neglected by the Confederate Government, hence its inefficiency. The following letter from General Lee, on this subject, will prove of interest:

"Richmond, 29th November, 1864. Dear Sir: I have the honor to acknowledge the receipt of your letter of the 23d instant, as to the requirements and principles to be observed in the reorganization of the cavalry, and to-day comply as succinctly as possible with your wishes, relative to my ideas on the subject.

"The cavalry of the Army of Northern Virginia is composed of the best material for troopers in the world. They are intelligent men, naturally excellent riders, and mounted on good horses, and require only, to make them more efficient, organization. First, more horse feed; second, to be more thoroughly and constantly drilled mounted; third, to be better armed. As far as my observation extends, the cavalry are well drilled on foot and with the sabre, as far as laid down in the cavalry tactics, but could not be perfected in the mounted drill for the reason that the horses, from want of a sufficient supply of food, cannot stand the required work. The enemy, on the contrary, being supplied in greater abundance, their mounted drills are mere exercise for their horses; and, in this respect only (save in numbers), is their cavalry superior to ours. Here is the advantage. Badly drilled squadrons charged, the men scatter in every direction; opposing squadrons, well drilled, moving in compact mass, fall upon the isolated fragments and overwhelm them in detail. Experience teaches the proper arms for cavalry to be—a pistol (Colt's navy the best size), a breech-loading carbine (Sharp's preferred), and a sabre. The government has never been able to supply the demand for cavalry arms; they ought to be imported. Our most efficient arms have been captured from the enemy, but of course not in sufficient quantities to meet the demand.

"The government ought to furnish horses, at least to meritorious troopers who are no longer capable of furnishing their own; and next, to all cavalry serving out of their own states. Existing orders now require permanently dismounted men to be transferred to the infantry, which is manifestly unjust to the deserving, well-trained trooper, whose circumstances are reduced, in many instances, by the enemy's incursions and depredations. Cases exist, however, sometimes requiring the transfer of cavalrymen to infantry organizations; for such men, soldiers, particularly distinguished for feats of courage, should be exchanged as an equivalent. The military axiom, that in all well-disciplined, drilled commands, one soldier is as good as another, approximates to a nearer degree of truth with reference to the infantry than cavalry; for whilst the former admit of a higher state of discipline, the latter fight more detached and scattered, and individual dash has a greater influence. It generally requires, too, more courage to go into a fight on horseback than on foot. Should this principle be observed, the infantry soldier would have an incentive to deeds of valor, viz.: the reward of putting him on horseback—and cavalry be composed of men who would ride up to and over almost anything.

"There should be *prompt* and just legislation to provide payment for all horses killed or permanently disabled in the line of duty, whether in action or otherwise, as long as the ownership remains with individuals. The regimental quartermaster ought to have the authority, with the approval of the Colonel, and upon the necessary certificates, to pay all such accounts in his regiment.

"Now soldiers are paid for horses *only* when killed in battle, and the accounts have to pass through so many hands that an unnecessary delay is produced even in that payment. A courier riding his horse a given number of miles in a given time, bearing important dispatches, breaks his horse down and has to abandon him, receives nothing, although he is *ordered* to make the time. A soldier has his horse permanently disabled by a wound, probably necessitating his being left in the enemy's hands, receives nothing, and, unless he can purchase another, is transferred to the infantry.

"I have written very hastily, but think you will see what is really wanting. Whilst cavalry cannot play the important part in large combats, owing to the improved range of arms, nature of the country, etc., it formerly has done in European wars, still the demand for it everywhere is great, and unless Congress takes the matter in hand, and legislates more liberally on the subject, the enemy next spring will ride rough-shod over the whole state."

After the close of the war General Lee settled on his farm, "the White House," on the Pamunky river, which had been bequeathed to him by his grandfather, George Washington Parke Custis. The country presented one continuous scene of utter desolation. For nearly four years the tramp of armies had been to and fro over this region, and had, in consequence, left in their wake only the naked earth. Nothing daunted, he set to work to build his houses, to re-mark his farm lines with fences, to restock, and, in short, to begin again the life of a Virginia farmer. Nor was his case in the least exceptional. All through the South the same hard task confronted the returned soldiers; and with the greatest heroism did they begin life anew. General Lee married, in 1867, Mary Tabb Bolling. They removed in 1874 to "Ravensworth," an estate of the Fitzhughs in Fairfax county which he inherited under the will of his mother's uncle, William Henry Fitzhugh. This estate had been patented by the first Col. William Fitzhugh, who died in 1701. There General Lee resided until his death, pursuing the quiet life of a farmer, unless taken away by the duties of various public positions to which his countrymen elected him. He served for several years in the Virginia Senate, and was elected to the Fiftieth, Fifty-first, and Fifty-second Congresses, his death occurring a few months prior to the expiration of his second term.

In personal appearance William Henry Fitzhugh Lee was tall, well proportioned, and of easy, dignified carriage. His courtly bearing and pleasant manners clearly stamped him one of the true gentlemen of the olden time. He was very fond of the country; of its animal as well as its vegetable life, even of its sounds. He was also devoted to children, and they to him. Of him his pastor has written: "Of his home life, it is too sacred to speak. It was simply beautiful. He lived for his family. All, including the servants, were devoted to him. His reading of family prayers before breakfast was very impressive. Sunday nights, after tea, he liked to hear the old hymns sung. General Lee was charitable to an extent that no one knew. Many there are, not only among his neighbors, but in all parts of Virginia and beyond, who have been the recipients of his kindness. The mail constantly brought him requests for help, and generally, when the object was a worthy one, it was not in vain. How many poor blacks, not to mention the whites, who will miss his assistance in their need!

"To his friends, and they were a host, he was as true as steel; and if he had an enemy I do not believe it was his fault. General Lee had the best control over himself of any man I ever knew. 'Better is he that ruleth his spirit than he that taketh a city.' If misunderstood or misrepresented as a public man; if worried or annoyed about business, or if things went wrong, he ever exhibited the same courteous manner and deportment. He used to say that 'because a man was worried he had no right to be rude.' One who was an inmate of his family for years says that she 'never heard from him a cross word.' As a true Christian man in every relation of life—at home, to his neighbors, to his church, to his country—I have known no higher example than General 'Rooney' Lee."

As previously stated, William H. F. Lee was twice married; first, in 1859, to Charlotte, daughter of George Wickham, U. S. N. From this union two children were born, a boy and a girl. Both died in early infancy. Mrs. Lee died 26th December, 1863, while her husband was a prisoner. Their son was named after his grandfather—Robert Edward Lee. On hearing of the baby's christening, the grandfather wrote his son: ". . . So he is called after his grandpapa, the dear little fellow. I would wish him a better name, and hope he may be a wiser and more useful man than his namesake. Such as it is, however, I gladly place it in his keeping, and feel that he must be very little like his father if it is not elevated and ennobled by his bearing and course in life. You must teach him, then, to love his grandpapa, to bear with his failings and avoid his errors, to be to you as you have been to me, and he may then enjoy the love and confidence of his father which I feel for you, greater than which no son ever possessed."

William H. F. Lee was married, secondly, on the 28th of November, 1867, to Mary Tabb, daughter of George W. and Martha S. (Nicholls) Bolling, of Petersburg, who survives him, with two sons: Robert Edward and George Bolling Lee. The former is practicing law at Washington, D. C.; the latter is studying medicine.

Bolling: Robert Bolling (1646–1709) came to Virginia in 1660. He was twice married; first, in 1675, to Jane, daughter of Thomas Rolfe, or Rolph, and granddaughter of Pocahontas; by this marriage he left one son, John Bolling, and several daughters. One daughter married Richard Randolph; another, a Col. Fleming; a third, Dr. William Gay; the fourth, Thomas Eldridge; the last, James Murray. (*Stith's History.*) The son married a Poythress. Robert Bolling married, secondly, in 1681, Anne, daughter of John Stith, and had: Robert, John Stith, Edward, Thomas, and two daughters, Anne and Agnes Bolling. Robert, 2d, married Mary

Cocke, and had: Robert, 3d, who married Mary Marshall Tabb, and left another Robert, the 4th of the name, who was four times married. By his last wife, Anne Dade Stith, he had George W. Bolling, who married Martha S. Nicholls, of Georgetown; they were the parents of Mary Tabb Bolling, who married William H. F. Lee, as stated.

## Captain Robert Edward Lee.

77. Robert Edward[7], the youngest son of Robert Edward Lee[6], (Henry[5], Henry[4], Henry[3], Richard[2], Richard[1]), and Mary Anne Randolph Custis, his wife, was born at Arlington in Alexandria county, on the 27th of October, 1843. After a course of tuition at private schools, he entered the University of Virginia in October, 1860. Though the students of the university were exempted from army service, all the young men of suitable age hastened to join the Southern army; among them, Robert E. Lee, Jr. In February, 1862, he joined the famous "Rockbridge Artillery," as a private, and served with it until appointed a lieutenant and aide to his brother, General W. H. F. Lee. He continued with the cavalry staff until the close of the war, rising to the grade of captain.

Mrs. Lee very naturally desired that her son should be with his father. In reply to a letter on this subject, the General wrote her: " . . . In reference to Rob, his company would be a great pleasure to me, and he would be extremely useful in various ways, but I am opposed to officers surrounding themselves with their sons and relatives. It is wrong in principle, and in that case selection would be made from private and social relations rather than for the public good. There is the same objection to going with Fitz Lee. I should prefer Rob's being in the line of an independent position, where he could rise by his own merit and not through the recommendation of his relatives. I expect him here soon, when I can better see what he himself thinks. The young men have no fondness for the society of the old general. He is too heavy and sombre for them." In another letter, the General adds, "I hope our son will make a good soldier."

After the close of the war, Captain Lee settled on his farm on the Pamunky river, in King William county, where he resided until 1890, when he removed to Washington, D. C., to engage in business. He has been twice married. First, on the 16th of November, 1871, to Charlotte Taylor, daughter of R. Barton Haxall, and Octavia Robinson, his wife, of Richmond; she was born on the 23d of October, 1848; died, without issue, on the 22d of September, 1872. He was married, secondly, at Washington, D. C., on the 8th of March, 1894, to Juliet, daughter of Colonel Thomas

Hill Carter, and Susan Roy, his wife, of "Pampatike," King William county.

NOTE.—Governor Thomas Nelson (eldest son of "President" William Nelson, and grandson of Thomas Nelson, the immigrant and progenitor of the Nelsons of Virginia) married, on the 29th of January, 1762, Lucy, daughter of Philip Grymes, of Middlesex county, and Mary Randolph, his wife; their seventh child, Mary Nelson, born on the 19th of December, 1774, married (about 1792) Dr. Robert Carter, of "Shirley," on James river. This Dr. Robert Carter was a younger brother of Anne Hill Carter, the second wife of General Henry Lee, and a son of Charles and Anne Butler (Moore) Carter; he had issue: Hill Carter, of "Shirley," who married Mary B. Randolph; Anne, who married William F. Wickham; Lucy, who married Edward Wickham; Thomas Nelson Carter, who was twice married; first, to Juliette Gaines, by whom he had Thomas Hill Carter, the father of Juliet, who married Captain Lee.

## RICHARD BLAND LEE.

78. RICHARD BLAND[7], the eldest son of Richard Bland Lee[6] (Richard Bland[5], Henry[4], Henry[3], Richard[2], Richard[1]) and Julia Anna Marion Prosser, his wife, was born at Fortress Monroe, Virginia, the 9th of August, 1835; married, on the 16th of March, 1865, at New York city, Mary Alice, daughter of George Amos Butt (formerly of "Exton Hall," Rutlandshire, England, and later of New York), and Mary Elizabeth McCoskry, his wife; she was a daughter of Nathaniel McCoskry and Rachael Willets Allen, of New York. Mrs. Lee was born the 4th of November, 1838, at New York, and died the 18th of December, 1890, at her husband's home, "Buckland Hall," in Prince William county.

Mr. Lee is now residing at his home in Prince William, with his younger children. He has six children:

i, RICHARD BLAND[8], born in Howard county, Md., the 15th of April, 1867; resides now at New York, and is unmarried.

ii, FRANCIS MORRIS[8], born at Alexandria the 18th of January, 1869; is now farming at the old homestead in Prince William. Is unmarried.

iii, ROBERT MCCOSKRY[8], born at "Buckland Hall," the 14th of February, 1871; is now farming in Montana; is unmarried.

iv, MARY ELIZABETH[8], born at "Buckland Hall," the 12th of August, 1873; is unmarried.

v, PHILIP HENRY[8], born at "Buckland Hall," the 20th of March, 1877; resides at New York. Is also unmarried.

vi, GEORGE ALLEN[8], born at "Buckland Hall," the 8th of February, 1880.

## CAPTAIN JULIAN PROSSER LEE.

79. JULIAN PROSSER[7], the second son of Richard Bland Lee[6] (Richard Bland[5], Henry[4], Henry[3], Richard[2], Richard[1]) and Julia Anna Marion Prosser, his wife, was born the 27th of February, 1840; was married, on the 21st of June, 1871, to Meta Wallace, daughter of Richard Arell Weaver, and Janet Cleiland Horner, his wife; Mr. Weaver was a son of Samuel and Christiana Weaver; Mrs. Weaver was a daughter of Inman Horner and Mary Henderson, his wife; she was the youngest child of Alexander Henderson, of Dumfries, who was born in Scotland in 1737; died at Dumfries about 1815; Mary Henderson died at Warrenton the 20th of December, 1831; married Inman Horner on the 31st of December, 1815. Mr. Horner was the eldest son of William Horner and Mary Edmonds, his wife; he was born the 12th of August, 1791; died the 9th of July, 1860. Mr. Lee served in the Confederate army, entering as a private and rising to the rank of captain. He now resides at Warrenton. They have the following children: Janet Henderson, Julia Anna Marion, Arell Weaver, Richard Bland, and Julian Prosser Lee[8].

## RICHARD HENRY LEE.

80. RICHARD HENRY[7], the only son of Zaccheus Collins Lee[6] (Richard Bland[5], Henry[4], Henry[3], Richard[2], Richard[1]) and Martha Ann Jenkins, his wife, was born at Baltimore, Md., the 29th of April, 1839; died the 20th of March, 1883; married, in October, 1868, Belle Isabell Wilson, of Maryland. Mr. Lee served as a private in the Confederate army. He had four children; three, Elizabeth, Richard Henry, and Zaccheus Collins, are living; one, Robert Edward, was born in 1883 and died in June, 1890.

## CHARLES SHEPHERD LEE.

81. CHARLES SHEPHERD[7], the eldest son of Edmund Jennings Lee[6] (Edmund Jennings[5], Henry[4], Henry[3], Richard[2], Richard[1]) and Eliza Shepherd, his first wife, was born the 17th of September, 1826; married, on the 16th of May, 1849, Margaret H., daughter of Mann H. and Margaret (Beall) Page. They have the following-named children: Eliza Shepherd, Margaret Page, Charles Randolph, Edmonia Louise, Ellen Byrd, Phillips Fitzgerald, Edwin Gray, Mann Randolph Page, and Eliza Holmes Lee[8].

## Brigadier-General Edwin Gray Lee.

82. Edwin Gray[7], the second son of Edmund Jennings Lee[6] (Edmund Jennings[5], Henry[4], Henry[3], Richard[2], Richard[1]) and Henrietta Bedinger, his second wife, was born at "Leeland," Jefferson county, the 25th of May, 1835; died at the Yellow Sulphur Springs, Virginia, the 24th of August, 1870. Mr. Lee was educated, first, at Hallowell's school, at Alexandria, later at William and Mary College; he then studied law under the late Judge John W. Brockenborough, at Lexington. On the breaking out of the late civil war he entered the Confederate service as a second lieutenant in the 2d Virginia infantry; in May, 1861, he was appointed first lieutenant and aide to General Thomas J. Jackson; then major of the 33d regiment, next lieutenant-colonel, and, in August, 1862, colonel of that regiment. Forced by ill health to give up duty in the field, he resigned early in 1863, but was again assigned to active duty in the fall of that year, and served on the staff of General Robert Ransom, on the south side of James river, in May, 1864; was sent to Staunton in the following June to command the post there and to call out the reserves in the valley. When the enemy advanced in force against Staunton, Col. Lee saved all the government property and all the prisoners, losing only his own baggage. In October of 1864 he was appointed a brigadier-general, and later was sent to Canada on secret service for the Confederate government. After the war, his health being very poor, he was compelled to spend his winters in the far South. On hearing of his death General Robert E. Lee wrote: "I am truly sorry to hear of Edwin Lee's death. He was a true man, and if his health had permitted would have been an ornament, as well as a benefit, to his race. He was certainly a great credit to the name."

General Edwin Lee married, on the 17th of November, 1859, Susan, eldest child of the Rev. William Nelson Pendleton, D. D., and Anzolette Elizabeth Page, his wife. Dr. Pendleton was the third son of Edmund Pendleton, of "Edmundton," Caroline county, and Lucy Nelson, his wife. Mrs. Pendleton was the daughter of Francis Page (son of Gov. John Page) and Susan, daughter of Gov. Thomas Nelson, of Yorktown. The Lucy Nelson who married Edmund Pendleton was a daughter of Col. Hugh Nelson, of Yorktown, a younger brother of Gov. Thomas Nelson; hence Doctor and Mrs. Pendleton were second cousins. Being both endowed with rare mental abilities, enriched by thorough cultivation, they were the most charming of companions, which could only be fully appreciated by those who had an opportunity of seeing them in their daily life. Dr. Pendleton was graduated from the Military School at West Point in 1830, served on garrison

duty, and as assistant professor of mathematics until he resigned, in 1837, to assume the more congenial duties of a teacher of mathematics, which was ever a favorite study with him. While engaged in this work his attention was called to the ministry, and later he was ordained priest in the Episcopal Church. At the breaking out of the civil war he felt it his duty to use for the benefit of his State the military training which that State had aided in giving him; consequently he entered the artillery service, and became famous as the commander of the artillery corps of the Army of Northern Virginia. A most interesting Memoir of him was published in 1893, written by his daughter, Mrs. Sue P. Lee, who has now in press a school history of the United States.

## Edmund Jennings Lee.

83. Edmund Jennings[7], the third son of Edmund Jennings Lee[6] (Edmund Jennings[5], Henry[4], Henry[3], Richard[2], Richard[1]) and Henrietta Bedinger, his second wife, was born at "Leeland," Jefferson county, the 8th of October, 1845; has been twice married; first, on the 23d of September, 1875, to Rebecca Lawrence, only daughter of Colonel Armistead Thompson Mason, and Eliza Southgate (Lawrence) Rust, of "Rockland," Loudoun county. Mrs. Lee died at "Leeland," the 14th of February, 1882, leaving three sons: Lawrence Rust, Edmund Jennings, and Armistead Mason Lee[8]. Mr. Lee was married, secondly, at Trinity Church, Shepherdstown, on the 26th of September, 1893, to Bessie Read, only daughter of the Rev. William H. Neilson, D. D., rector of the parish.

Mr. Lee served in the cavalry of the Southern army during the last two years of the war. Since then he has resided near Shepherdstown, being chiefly engaged in farming. He has always been an earnest, active member of the Episcopal Church; is now junior warden of Trinity Parish; has been a frequent delegate to the Diocesan and General Conventions of the church; is a trustee of the Virginia Theological Seminary, and a member of the Standing Committee of the Diocese of West Virginia.

## Rev. Henry Bedinger Lee.

84. Henry Bedinger[7], the fourth son and youngest child of Edmund Jennings Lee[6] (Edmund Jennings[5], Henry[4], Henry[3], Richard[2], Richard[1]) and Henrietta Bedinger, his second wife, was born at "Leeland," Jefferson county, the 14th of July, 1849; studied law, and was admitted to the bar the 14th of July, 1870; entered the Theological Seminary of Virginia, September, 1872; ordained Deacon in June, 1875; and Priest, in June,

1876; has had charge of St. Paul's Church, Goochland; was assistant at St. James', Richmond; in 1877, took charge of Leeds Parish, Fauquier; April, 1886, was called to Ridley Parish, Culpeper; in 1890, became assistant to the Rev. Dr. Hanckel, at Christ Church, Charlottesville; and after the death of Dr. Hanckel, rector of the parish, in September, 1892, and continues in that charge.

Mr. Lee was married, on the 20th of September, 1877, to Lucy Johnston, daughter of James Keith and Fanny L. (Ambler) Marshall, of Fauquier county, and has had the following-named children:

i, FANNY AMBLER[8], born the 31st of August, 1878; died the 21st of August, 1879.
ii, HENRY BEDINGER[8], born the 22d of January, 1880.
iii, CLAUDE MARSHALL[8], born the 17th of June, 1882.
iv, REBECCA RUST[8], born the 31st of July, 1884.
v, EDWIN GRAY[8], born the 7th of November, 1890.
vi, JAMES KEITH MARSHALL[8], born the 28th of May, 1894.

## THE MARSHALL FAMILY.

The common tradition as to the origin of the Marshalls has given them an ancestor who came to England with William the Conqueror. After his success at Hastings the King gave lands to this William Mareschal on the border of Wales, later in the county of Pembrokeshire. Of this family was William Marshall, the Earl of Pembroke, one of the Barons who forced the Magna Charta from King John. The King, apparently, bore him no ill-will, for he named him as guardian to his son and Protector of the Kingdom. A more modern progenitor was an Irish captain, one John Marshall, who fought with King Charles at Edgehill, and after his defeat came over to Virginia. Captain John Marshall came to Virginia about 1650, settled near Dumfries, where he died; "his tombstone still stood there a few years before the war." (Thomas M. Green.) He left a son, William, a small Virginia farmer, who died in Westmoreland county in 1704. A younger son of this William Marshall was named John, known as "John of the Forest." He lived in Westmoreland; was a captain in the early Indian wars of the Colony. He was born about 1700; died in April, 1752, and married Elizabeth, daughter of John Markham; he left a large family. Two daughters, Anne and Elizabeth, married two brothers, respectively John and Augustine Smith, of that county. It is said they were the sons of John Smith by Mary Ann Adkins, his wife. He is supposed to have been a native of Bristol, England, who came to Virginia about 1700 and settled on Mattoax creek, in Westmoreland; he died there in 1725. Augustine and Elizabeth (Marshall) Smith reared three daughters and one son. Perhaps these daughters were the Smiths who married the two John Lees, of Essex. (See 14 and 22.) The eldest son of John and Elizabeth (Markham) Marshall was the famous Col. Thomas Marshall. He was born in Westmoreland on the 2d of April, 1730; died on the 22d of June, 1802, at Washington, Mason county, Kentucky; he married, in 1755, Mary Randolph, daughter of the Rev. James and Mary Isham (Randolph) Keith. Mary Isham Randolph was the daughter of Thomas Randolph, of "Tuckahoe," the second son of William Randolph, of "Turkey Island." Mary Randolph Keith was born in Fauquier county on the 28th of April, 1737; died in Kentucky on the 19th of September, 1809. "Col. Thomas Marshall is regarded by his posterity with veneration. In sound judgment and depth of native mind, he is said to have surpassed all his illustrious children." He is said to have attended, with George Washington, the school of the Rev. Archibald Campbell, rector of Washington parish, Westmoreland. They were throughout life intimate friends. Col. Marshall accompanied Washington on his surveying expeditions for Lord Fairfax and others. He removed to Fauquier county and settled at "Oakhill," where his younger children were born. He was with Braddock in his ill-fated expedition, though not present at the fight in which that officer was slain. He served during the Revolutionary war; was presented with a sword by the Virginia House of Burgesses. This sword is still preserved. He was himself a member of the House of Burgesses; of the Virginia Convention of 1776; he was taken prisoner by the British at Charleston, S. C.; after his release he rode through part of Kentucky with a party of friends; he was so well pleased with the country that he located a homestead there. This place was called "Buckpond," near Versailles. It was his home until the marriage of his son, Dr. Louis Marshall, with Agatha Smith, in 1800, when the home at "Buckpond" was given to the young couple, and the old folks went to live with their son, Thomas, at Washington, Mason county, where he died. They had fifteen children. Of these Dr. Louis has been mentioned in another connection (see 35, v, p. 342). The most famous of his children, and perhaps of the family, was Chief Justice John Marshall, the soldier, lawyer, and statesman. He was born in Fauquier county on the 24th of September, 1755; died at Philadelphia on the 6th of July, 1835; married at Yorktown, on the 3d of January, 1783, Mary Willis, daughter of Jacqueline Ambler and Rebecca L. Burwell, his wife. Jacqueline Ambler (born on the 9th of August, 1742; died on the 10th of February, 1798) was the seventh child of Richard and Elizabeth (Jacqueline)

Ambler, who came to Virginia in 1716. Mary Willis Ambler was born on the 18th of March, 1766; died on the 25th of December, 1831. Judge Marshall served in the Continental Army as captain; in 1779 he left the army to study at William and Mary College, and began his famous career as a lawyer in 1780; he was frequently a member of the Virginia Legislature; also of the Virginia Convention that ratified the Constitution; was appointed by John Adams Minister to France; entered Congress, it is said at the request of Washington, in 1799; in 1800 was Secretary of State, and in 1801 was appointed Chief Justice, and so continued until his death. Of the great abilities of Judge Marshall, as an expounder of the laws, it is not necessary to speak. His great fame, as well as his sterling character, are a part of the common history of the land.

Judge Marshall left issue: Thomas, Dr. Jacqueline, Mary, John, James Keith, and Edward Carrington Marshall. Of these James Keith, born on the 13th of February, 1800, died on the 2d of December, 1862; married, on the 22d of December, 1821, Claudia Hamilton, daughter of Nathaniel Burwell and Ann R. Willis, his wife, and left twelve children. His third son, James Keith Marshall, married Frances L. Ambler, and had: Lucy Johnston (who married the Rev. Henry B. Lee, as stated), James Keith, and Charles Edward Marshall. Of the other many illustrious members of this family it is not necessary to give an account in this work.

## Lieutenant-Colonel William Fitzhugh Lee.

85. William Fitzhugh [7], the only son of Rev. William Fitzhugh Lee [6] (Edmund Jennings [5], Henry [4], Henry [3], Richard [2], Richard [1]) and Mary Catharine Simms Chilton, his wife, was born at Richmond the 27th of April, 1832; died the 29th of July, 1861. His primary education was received at Shepherdstown; then he entered the Virginia Military Institute at Lexington, and graduated on the 4th of July, 1853, delivering the Valedictory to his class; taught school until June, 1855; was appointed second lieutenant in 2d U. S. Infantry, 30th of March, 1857; in 1861, he was arrested by his superior officer for expressing strong disapproval of the action of the government against the South; was court-martialed; after his release he resigned (30th of April, 1861), and was appointed a captain in the Virginia forces; served for several months as drill-master, and was commissioned lieutenant-colonel of the 33d Virginia regiment, and attached to the army of the Shenandoah. At the first battle of Manassas, 21st of July, 1861, he led his regiment against Rickett's battery, and captured it, but it was retaken; on the second charge against that battery, he was struck by

a piece of a shell, fell mortally wounded, and died in a few days. He was buried at Shepherdstown on the 31st of July.

William F. Lee was married, on the 15th of September, 1859, to Lillie, daughter of Dr. Richard and Laura E. (Morgan) Parran, of Shepherdstown. Dr. Parran was born in Calvert county, Md.; he married Laura E. Morgan on the 29th of November, 1832. William F. Lee left one child, a daughter, Laura Morgan, who was married, on the 14th of April, 1880, to Lieutenant William A. Simpson, of the 2d artillery, U. S. A.; they have four children: Caroline Hanson, William Fitzhugh Lee, George Wirt, and Elizabeth Parran Simpson.

## Cassius Francis Lee.

86. Cassius Francis[7], the second son of Cassius Francis Lee[6] (Edmund Jennings[5], Henry[4], Henry[3], Richard[2], Richard[1]) and Hannah P. L. Hopkins, his first wife, was born at Alexandria, the 4th of January, 1844, and died at same place, the 4th of September, 1892; was married, on the 29th of May, 1873, to Mary, daughter of Richard Henry and Mary (Fife) Lloyd, of Alexandria. She was born the 12th of July, 1845, in the town of Vermont, Fulton county, Illinois; Mrs. Lee, with two daughters, Lucy Lyons and Elizabeth Lloyd Lee[8], survives her husband.

Cassius F. Lee, Jr., as he has always been known, to distinguish him from his father, took the greatest interest in all that pertained to the history of his family, and had been for years collecting wills, deeds, letters, and all manner of genealogical data. Had his life been spared, he would have arranged all these papers for publication, and would have edited a most admirable work.

## Cazenove Gardner Lee.

87. Cazenove Gardner[7], the third son of Cassius Francis Lee[6] (Edmund Jennings[5], Henry[4], Henry[3], Richard[2], Richard[1]) and Anne Eliza Gardner, his second wife, was born at Alexandria, the 30th of May, 1850; was married, on the 20th of September, 1881, to Marguerite L., the youngest daughter of Eleuthère Irénée Dupont, of Wilmington, Delaware, and Charlotte Shepard Henderson, his wife; they have two sons: Cazenove Gardner, born the 6th of October, 1882, and Maurice Dupont, born the 10th of January, 1885.

Mr. Lee attended private schools at Alexandria, then the Episcopal High School, and lastly the University of Virginia. He is a lawyer by profession, residing at Washington City.

DUPONT—Eleuthère Irénée Dupont (1829–1877) was the eldest son of Eleuthère Irénée (1771–1834), the original founder of the great powder-making firm; the latter was the second son of Pierre Samuel Dupont de Nemours (1739–1817), who was born at Paris and died at Wilmington, Delaware. Besides being a political economist of note, Mr. Dupont held many official positions of importance in his own country, and, at one time, in Poland under Stanislas Poniatowski. It is especially interesting to note that he was employed by Vergennes to assist in drawing up the treaty with England, by which the independence of the American colonies was acknowledged. During the French Revolution, Mr. Dupont advocated reform and a constitutional monarchy as against the views of the extreme republicans. He was imprisoned and only escaped the guillotine by the death of Robespierre. Later still, his house was sacked by a mob and he himself narrowly escaped transportation. In 1799, he emigrated with his family to America, where later, his son established the great powder manufactory. He returned to France in 1802, but refused to accept any official position under Napoleon. At the request of Jefferson he published, in 1812, a small treatise on *National Education in America.* After the first downfall of Napoleon, Mr. Dupont became secretary to the Provisional Government, and on the restoration of the Bourbons, he was made Councillor of State. On the return of Napoleon in 1815, he determined to leave France to spend the remainder of his days with his sons in America. His eldest son, Victor Marie (1767–1827), was the father of the late Admiral Samuel Francis Dupont (1803–1865).

## REV. FRANCIS DUPONT LEE.

88. FRANCIS DUPONT[7], the fourth son of Cassius Francis Lee[6] (Edmund Jennings[5], Henry[4], Henry[3], Richard[2], Richard[1]) and Anne Eliza Gardner, his second wife, was born at Alexandria, the 3d of January, 1852; died at his home in Fairfax county the 14th of June, 1891; was married, on the 28th of April, 1880, to his cousin, Anne Henderson, daughter of H. Allen and Anne E. Van Ness (Henderson) Taylor, of Alexandria. Mr. Lee was educated at the Episcopal High School, the University of Virginia, and the Theological Seminary of Virginia. Had several parishes under his charge, but during the last years of his life had been incapacitated for his work by ill health. His widow and one child, Constance C. Lee[8], survive him. Two other children, both sons, are dead.

## DR. EDMUND JENNINGS LEE.

89. EDMUND JENNINGS[7], the fifth son of Cassius Francis Lee[6] (Edmund Jennings[5], Henry[4], Henry[3], Richard[2], Richard[1]) and Anne Eliza Gardner,

his second wife, was born at Alexandria, the 16th of June, 1853; was educated at the Episcopal High School, and at the Washington and Lee University; later, he studied medicine at the Universities of Virginia and of Pennsylvania. He was married, on the 9th of December, 1879, to Mary Emma, the eldest daughter of Charles Smith and Catharine Iungerich, his wife, of Philadelphia. They have four children: Constance Gardner, Charles Smith, Mildred Washington, Florence Friesen Lee[8].

### Rev. William Byrd Lee.

90. William Byrd[7], the eldest son of Richard Henry Lee[6] (Edmund Jennings[5], Henry[4], Henry[3], Richard[2], Richard[1]) and Evelyn Byrd Page, his wife, was born the 21st of March, 1851; married, on the 25th of September, 1878, Sarah Jane Blackburn, daughter of Dr. Randolph and Elizabeth Sinclair (Blackburn) Kownslar, of Berryville, Clark county; she was born the 11th of June, 1853. Mr. Lee studied theology at the Theological Seminary of Virginia, was ordained Deacon in June, 1878; Priest, in 1879; has been in charge of the old Abingdon Parish, Gloucester county. They have the following children:

i, Elizabeth Sinclair[8], born the 26th of July, 1879.
ii, Richard Henry[8], born the 20th of September, 1880, and died the 26th of September, 1881.
iii, Evelyn Byrd[8], born the 23d of September, 1881.
iv, Mary Page[8], born the 23d of September, 1881.
v, Ellen Moore[8], born the 11th of June, 1884.
vi, William Byrd[8], born the 1st of February, 1888.
vii, Jane Kownslar[8].
viii, Eliza Atkinson[8].

### Rev. Charles Henry Lee.

91. Charles Henry[7], the second son of Richard Henry Lee[6] (Edmund Jennings[5], Henry[4], Henry[3], Richard[2], Richard[1]) and Evelyn Byrd Page, his wife, was born the 20th of December, 1866; graduated at the Theological Seminary of Virginia, and was ordained Deacon, 29th of June, 1893; Priest, the 30th of June, 1894. Mr. Lee married, on the 20th of September, 1893, Susan Randolph, daughter of John Esten and Mary Frances (Page) Cooke, of Clarke county. Mr. Lee has charge of Markham Parish, Culpeper county.

## DITCHLEY LINE, SECOND GENERATION.

1. Colonel Richard Lee, the Virginia immigrant, left six sons and two daughters, whom he named in the following order in his will, which is the only reliable record of them extant: John, Richard, Francis, Hancock, Betsy, Anne, and Charles. Of these children, Hancock was the second son to leave male issue in Virginia; he has always been considered the fifth son, but the inscription on his tombstone states that he was the seventh. In naming his five younger children, Colonel Richard placed the two daughters between Hancock and Charles, so it may be fairly taken for granted that they were younger than Hancock and older than Charles. If this surmise be correct, then Hancock was the fifth son. The explanation of the apparent contradiction between the Immigrant's will and the inscription on the tombstone of his son may be that the former had lost two children previous to the making of his will; or, it may be that the daughters were older than Hancock, in which case he would have been the seventh child though not the seventh son.

The following sketches of Hancock Lee and his descendants are very meagre, incomplete, and unsatisfactory, but they are the best that can be done at present with the scanty data now obtainable.

### Captain Hancock Lee.

2. Hancock[2], the "seventh son" of Richard and Anna Lee, was born in 1653, probably at the Dividing Creeks in Northumberland county. He died the 25th of May, 1709, and was buried at "Ditchley," where his tombstone is still to be seen, with its inscription perfectly legible. This burying ground was used by this branch of the family for several generations, probably until the estate was sold in 1789, to Col. James Ball, Jr., whose descendants own it to-day.

The inscription on Hancock's tombstone, copied the 10th of May, 1894, reads as follows:

> Here Lyeth the Body of Hancock Lee, Seventh son of the Honnourable Richard Lee, Who departed this Life the 25th May, Anno Domo 1729, Æta. 56 years. Also Mary, his first Wife, only Daughter of William Kendall, Gent, Who departed this Life the 24th December, Anno Domo 1694, Æta. 33 years. And Sarah, his last wife, Daughter of Isaac Allerton Esqr. Who departed this Life the 17th May, Anno Domo, 1731, Æta. 60 years.

Although this inscription states that he died in 1729, there can be no doubt that Hancock Lee died in 1709, for these reasons: The certificate of probate on his will reads: "Die July 20: 1709. This will was proved in Northumberland County Court to be the last Will and Testament of Mr. Hancock Lee, dec'd by y[e] oaths of Thomas Knight and Mary Knight, two of y[e] witnesses thereto and is admitted to Record. (Signed) Tho: Hobson C. Cur. North'd."

The Clerk's office of Northumberland was burned the 25th of October, 1710; later all the records that could be found were recorded a second time to replace those so destroyed.[1] So, on Hancock's will there is this second note of record: "Die Martii 21, 1711, This Coppie of Mr. Hancock Lee's Will and the Codicils thereto annexed were approved by y[e] Court and upon motion of Capt. John Howson are admitted to Record. (Signed) Tho: Hobson C. Cur. North'd."

Again, an inventory of Hancock's property was filed the 21st of March, 1710, and moreover in an application for a land patent, made the 6th of March, 1709–10, it was stated that the patent was for "Hancock Lee son of Hancock Lee dec'd." These records clearly prove that Hancock was deceased in 1709. If the inscription upon his tombstone be correct, that he died in 1729, *aged 56 years*, then he was born in 1673, or about nine years after the death of his father. Whilst, if the record of his first marriage, in 1675, be correct, then he married at the early age of two or three years. A true *reductio ad absurdum*.

Hancock Lee was twice married; first, in 1675, to Mary, the only daughter of Col. William Kendall, of "Newport House," Northampton county. William Kendall was a Burgess from Northampton in 1657–62–63–66, being Speaker the last year. He married, secondly, Sarah, the daughter of Col. Isaac Allerton, of Westmoreland, the son of the Isaac Allerton who came over in the "Mayflower," and who married Fear, the daughter of Elder William Brewster, another of that famous band. (Hayden, *Va. Genealogies*, 97.)

Hancock is supposed to have settled in Northampton at the time of his first marriage (1675), and to have returned to Northumberland about 1686. The record of the public positions held by him, perhaps only partial, seems to agree with this supposition. He was a Justice for Northampton county in 1677, and held a similar position in Northumberland in 1687, 1699; was also a Burgess from Northumberland in 1688. A list of civil officers, dated the 3d of June, 1699, names him as the "Naval Officer and Collector of Virginia Dutys in Northumberland County;" another list of the date of

---

[1] The oldest records of Northumberland county are in a book which has this record written in it: "This Book Contains the Records of those papers which have been presented into the County Court of Northumberland County, and by the Justices of the said Court admitted to record *again*, they having been formerly recorded, and *the books of record in which they had been recorded burned with* this *office* the *25th* day of October Anno Domini one thousand seven hundred and ten. Teste, Tho: Hobson C. Cur."

1702, mentions him as a Justice, showing him to have been in commission at the time of his death. The following is a copy of his commission as a Justice, in 1699:

WILLIAM THE THIRD, by the Grace of God, KING of England, Scotland, France and Ireland, Defender of the faith, etc., To Samuell Griffin, Hancock Lee, Charles Lee, George Cowper, Rodham Kennor, William Jones, Peter Hack, John Harris, William Howson, Cuthbert Span, Christopher Neale, John Crawley, Peter Contancean & Thomas Winder, Gentlemen, Greeting: KNOW YEE, that WEE have assigned you, and every one of you jointly and severally, OUR Justices to KEEP OUR PEACE in the County of Nothumberland, and to keep and cause to be kept all ordinances, statutes of our Kingdome of England and Lawes of this Our Ancient and Great Colony and Dominion of Virginia, made for the good of the Peace and for the conservation of the same, and for the Quiett rule and Government of the People, in all and every the Articles thereof in said county accordinge to the force, forme and effect of the same. And to chastise and punish all persons offending against the formes of those ordinances, Statutes of Our Kingdome of England & Lawes of this our Colony and Dominion, or any of them in the County aforesaid, to cause to come before you or any of you all those persons who shall threaten any of Our Liege People, either in their bodyes or burning their houses, to find sufficient security for the Peace or for the good behavior towards Us and the People. And if they shall refuse to find such security then to cause them to be kept safe in Prison until they find such security. WEE have also assigned you, or any four or more of you whereof any of you, Samuell Griffin, Hancock Lee, Charles Lee, George Cowper, Rodham Kennor and William Jones shall be one to meet at the usuall place of holding Courts in the County afores^d^ at certain dayes according to Law, to heare & Determine all Suits, Controversies and Debates between party and party, doeing therein what to Justice appertaineth according to the Lawes of our Kingdome of England and this our Ancient and great Colony and Dominion of Virginia, with power likewise to you and every of you to take Depositions and Examinations upon oath for the better manifestation of the truth in all such matters & causes as come before you, and to keep or cause to be kept all orders of Court, Orders of Councill and Proclamations Directed to you or comeing to your hands from Us, or from Our Governour or Commander in chief for the time being, and Our Councill of State. And to punish the offenders & breakers of the same according to the Lawes of Our Kingdome of England and of this Our Colony & Dominion. And further to keep, or cause the Clerke of your Court to keep, Records of all Judgments, Rules & Orders Decided and agreed upon by you, or any four or more of you, whereof you Samuell Griffin, Hancock Lee, Charles Lee, George Cowper, Rodham Kennor, and William Jones shall be one. AND FURTHER WEE Comand you and every one of you that you diligently intend the keeping of the Peace, Statutes of Our Kingdom of England, and the Lawes of this Our Colony & Dominion. And all and singular other the Premises WEE doe by Virtue of these presents comand the Sheriff of the said County of Northumberland, that at those certain dayes and places which the law doth appoint, that he cause to come before you, or any four or more of you, whereof any of you, Samuell Griffin, Hancock Lee, Charles Lee, George Cowper, Rodham Kennor, and William Jones shall be one, & soe many good and Lawfull men of his Bayliwic by whom the matters may be the better known and Enquired of. WITNESSE Our Trusty and welbeloved Francis Nicholson, Esq'r, Our Lieutenant and Governor Gen^ll^ of This our Colony and Dominion of Virginia, at James Town, under the Seale of Our Colony, the 8th day of June, in the eleventh yeare of Our Reign, Anno q^e^ Domini 1699.[1]

[1] *Va. Magazine of History, etc.*, I, 226.

The Northern Neck land records show that Hancock patented land as follows: 1,100 acres in Richmond county, the 18th April, 1704; 570 acres on both sides of Rappahannock Horsepen Run and adjoining his own land, 21st May, 1705; 1,353 acres in Richmond county, 6th June, 1704; 460 acres on north side of the Occoquan in Stafford county, 2d November, 1707; 1,750 acres at the heads of the branches of Chapowamsic in Stafford, adjoining the land of Capt. Thomas Harrison, 10th February, 1707. Hancock Lee, son of Hancock Lee, deceased, patented 1,025 acres on Wolf Run in Stafford, for which Hancock Lee the elder had obtained a warrant, 1708, and by a codicil to his will, 31st December, 1706, gave to his son the said Hancock, 6th March, 1709–10. In 1678, Hancock Lee, gent., obtained a patent for 268 acres in Accomac county.

The land formerly included in the Ditchley estate was patented the 21st of May, 1651, as shown by this patent:

To all &c. Whereas &c now Know yee that I the said Sr William Berkeley Knight &c Do with the Consent of the Council of State accordingly give and grant unto Coll$_o$ Richard Lee Esq. Secretary of State for this Colony Eight hundred acres of Land Scituate in Northumberland County and uppon the South side of a Creeke Comonly called the Dividing Creek . . . abutting North East and Northerly uppon the said Creeke Southeast and Southerly Upon a creek which issueth forth of the said Dividing Creek Which divideth his Land and the Land of Mr. Thomas Wilson Marriner, Southwest into the maine Woods West and Northwest upon a small creek which divideth this Land and the Land of Col$_o$ Richard Lee. The said Land being due unto the said Col$^o$ Richard Lee by and for the Transportation of Sixteen persons, all whose names are in the Records mentioned under this Pattent &c To have and to hold &c To be held of Our Sovereign Lord the King his Heirs and Successors forever as of his mannor of East Greenwich in free and Comon Soccage and not in Capite nor by Knights Service Yielding and paying unto our Sovereign Lord the King his Heirs and Successors &c Which payment &c. provided &c. Given att James Citty under my hand and the Seal of this Colony the 21st day of May, 1651.

Following this patent on the records of Northumberland are these two deeds:

Know all men by these p$_r$sents that I Richard Lee of Lower Machotique in the Parish of Cople and County of Westmoreland upon the perusall of my good ffather Coll$^o$: Richard Lee dec'd his Will finding the Lands he left my Bro$^{thrs}$ Hancock and Charles Lee are in Law but an Estate for Life out of the naturall affection I beare to them and their heirs doe by these p$^r$sents as heir to my good ffather dec'd doe give the Land contained in this Pattent on the other side from me and my heirs to them and their heirs as followeth (vizt) 600 acres of the said Land to my Bro$^{thr}$ Hancock and his heirs and the other 200 acres to my Cozen [nephew] Charles Lee and his heirs acccording to the agreement made between my two Bro$^{thrs}$ Hancock and Charles and Recorded in Northumberland County Court Records, always provided that according to the Will made by my Bro$^{thr}$ Charles my Cozen Leeanna Jones Enjoy and use and occupy the sd. 200 acres called Hickory Neck during her Life and after her decease to revert to the said Charles Lee and his heirs according to the disposition of his dec'd ffather in his last Will and Testament. In witness, &c. Dated 9th September, 1701.

THIS INDENTURE made the seventeenth day of Febburarie in the sixth year of y^e^ Reign of our Sovereign Lady ANNE by y^e^ Grace of God of England Scotland ffrance and Ireland Queen Defender of the Faith &c. and in y^e^ year of our Lord God one thousand seven hundred and seven, BETWEEN Richard Lee of the County of Westmoreland Esquire of the one part and Hancock Lee of the County of Northumberland Gent: of the other part WITNESSETH That the said Richard Lee upon perusall of his good ffather Coll^o^ Richard Lee deceased his will and finding that y^e^ Lands he left to his Brothers y^e^ s^d^: Hancock Lee and Charles Lee are in Law but an Estate for Life and out of the naturall affection he beareth to them and their heirs and for Divers other good Causes and Consideracons him thereunto moving but more Especially for and in Consideracon of the sume of five pounds of good and Lawful money of England to him in hand paid by y^e^ s^d^: Hancock Lee at and before y^e^ Ensealing and Delivery of these presents, the Receipt whereof and himself therewith fully satisfyed Contented and paid he doth by these presents acknowledge HAVE Given Granted sold remised Released aliened transfered Enffeeoffed and Confirmed and by these presents as heir to his said ffather Deceased for himself his heirs and assignes Doth Give Grant sell remise Release alien Transferr Enfeeoff and Confirm unto y^e^ s^d^: Hancock Lee and to his heirs for ever He being already in full and peaceable possession of y^e^ premises hereafter menconed by virtue of a lease thereof made by y^e^ s^d^: Richard Lee unto y^e^ s^d^: Hancock Lee bearing date the day before y^e^ date of these presents ALL the Right, Title, Interest, possession Claim and Demand of him y^e^ s^d^: Richard Lee of in or to that Seat Tract plantacon or parcell of Land (whereon y^e^ s^d^: Hancock Lee now liveth) Containing Eight hundred acres be y^e^ same more or less according to an agreement made between his s^d^: two Brothers y^e^ s^d^: Hancock and Charles and Recorded in Northumberland County Court Records viz: Six hundred acres of y^e^ s^d^: land being the premises by these presents meant menconed and Intended to be given Granted sold made over and Confirmed unto y^e^ s^d^: Hancock Lee his heirs and assignes for Ever. The Remaining two hundred acres of y^e^ s^d^: Land to Remain and to be to Charles Lee youngest son of the aforesaid Charles Lee and to y^e^ heirs male of his Body Lawfully Begotten and for want of such heirs to Thomas Lee Eldest son of y^e^ s^d^: Charles Lee and to y^e^ heirs male of his Body Lawfully begotten and for want of such heirs then to Revert descend and come to y^e^ next heirs at Law to y^e^ s^d^: Richard Lee for ever always provided and it is y^e^ true intent and meaning of these presents that Leeanna Jones Daughter of the s^d^: Charles Lee occupy possess and enjoy y^e^ before menconed two hundred acres of Land (Comonly known by y^e^ name of Hickory Neck) w^th^: y^e^ appurtenances During her naturall life. The s^d^: Land Scituate Lying and being upon y^e^ south side of a Creek comonly called y^e^ Dividing Creek in Lee Parish in y^e^ County of Northumberland afores^d^: and boundeth as followeth—to wit—Abutting North East and Northerly uppon the s^d^: Dividing Creek South East and Southerly upon a Creek Issueing forth of y^e^ s^d^: Dividing Creek which Divideth this Land and y^e^ Land of Mr. Thomas Wilson marriner South West into y^e^ maine woods West and North west upon a small Creek w^ch^: divideth this Land and Coll^o^: Rich. Lee's Land WITH all messuages Tenements Houses Out-houses Gardens orchards fields woods underwoods meadows pastures feedings swamps marshes ways waters water-courses Together with y^e^ Royalties of Hunting Hawking fishing and fowling and of all mines minералls and Quarries and all other privileges advantages profitts Comodities and appurtenances whatsoever to y^e^ s^d^: Granted premises belonging or in any wise appertaining Except as before Excepted together also w^th^: all yearly Rents and profitts Reserved in any Lease or

Demise of any part of ye premises aforemenconed To Have and to Hold ye sd: Plantacon or Tract of Land messuage Tenements and all other ye premises herein before Granted Bargained and sold and every part thereof with all Rights members and appurtenances thereunto belonging according to ye sd: agreement aforemenconed that is to say the sd six hundred acres of Land (being ye premises hereby meant and intended to be bargained and sold) unto ye sd: Hancock Lee and to his heirs and assignes for ever to ye only proper use and behoof of him ye sd: Hancock Lee and to his heirs and assigns for Ever The Remaining two hundred Acres called Hickory Neck to be to ye sd: Charles Lee and to ye heirs male of his Body Lawfully begotten and for want of such heirs to ye sd: Thomas Lee and to ye heirs male of his body Lawfully begotten and upon Default of such heirs to Revert to ye next heirs at Law to ye sd: Richard Lee always provided that ye sd: Leeanna Jones possess ye sd: two hundred acres of Land During her naturall Life. To be held of our Sovereign Lady the Queen her heirs and successors as of ye manner of East Greenwich in ye County of Kent in free and Comon soccage Yielding and Paying the Quitrents due and accustomed to be paid for ye the same being one shilling for every fifty acres And the sd: Richard Lee for himself his Executors administrators and assignes and Every of them Do Covenant promise Grant and agree to and with ye sd: Hancock Lee his heirs Executors administrators and assignes and every of them in manner following that is to say That the said Richard Lee now hath and untill ye Estate hereby meant menconed and intended to be made to ye sd: Hancock Lee his heirs and assignes for ever to his and their own proper use and behoof shall be fully absolutely and lawfully Executed and Vested in ye sd: Hancock Lee his heirs and assignes for Ever as aforesd: shall continue to have hold and Enjoy a good perfect free firm and indefeasible Estate in fee simple and him and his heirs for Ever of in and unto ye premises herein before Granted and every part thereof with ye appurtenances Except before Excepted And that he hath good Right full power and lawful authority to Convey ye same in any manner herein before Expressed unto ye sd: Hancock Lee and to his heirs and assignes for Ever. And that ye sd: Granted premises and every part thereof wth ye appurtenances are free and Clear of and from all former and other Gifts Grants Bargains Sales Extents Statutes Recognizances Judgments Execucons Covenants articles and agreements Intails Wills Dowers Joyntures and of and from all and all manner of other titles troubles and Incumbrances whatsoever and shall so Remain until ye Estate hereby Intended to be made shall be fully and absolutely to all intents and purposes Vested and Confirmed unto ye sd: Hancock Lee his heirs and assignes for Ever And That ye sd: Hancock Lee his heirs and assignes for ever hereafter yielding and paying ye Quitrents for ye same as aforesaid may and shall peaceably and Quietly have hold possess occupy and Enjoy ye sd: Granted premises and every part thereof wth ye appurtenances Except before Excepted fully freely and absolutely exonorated acquitted and Discharged of and from all and all manner of former and other Bargains Sales Giffts Grants Estates Rents Releases other than those herein before Expressed and of all Joyntures Dowers Statutes Recognisances Judgments Execucons forfeitures seizures Issues Extents Escheats and all other charges titles troubles Incumbrances and Demands whatsoever had made comitted suffered acknowledged Executed or Done or hereafter to be acknowledged had made Comitted suffered Executed or done by him ye sd: Richard Lee his heirs Execut'rs administrators or assignes or by any other p'son or p'sons whatsoever and free and clear of and from any Lett Suit trouble or charge whatsoever of or by ye sd: Richard Lee his heirs Exec'rs administ's and assignes or any other p'son or p'sons whatsoever. And That he ye sd: Richard Lee his heirs Execut'rs and administrators all and singular ye herein before granted premises wth ye appurtenances Except before Excepted unto ye sd: Hancock Lee his heirs and assignes shall and will warrant and forever Defend by these p'sents against him y^e^ s^d^: Richard Lee his heirs Exect's Adm'es and assignes and Every of them and against all and Every other p'son or p'sons whatsoever AND LASTLY That from time to time and at all times within seven years now next coming after y^e^ date of these presents y^e^ s^d^: Richard Lee his heirs Execut's administ's and assignes and every of them at y^e^ reasonable Request Cost and charge in y^e^ Law of y^e^ s^d^: Hancock Lee his heirs Execut's administ's and assignes or Either of them shall and will do make suffer acknowledge Execute and p'form all and every such further and other act and acts thing and things Conveyance and Conveyances assurances and Confirmacons in Law for y^e^ better assurance and sure making of y^e^ premises herein before granted and every part thereof w^th^ y^e^ appurtenances Except before Excepted unto y^e^ s^d^: Hancock Lee his heirs and assignes for Ever as aforesd: according to y^e^ true intent and meaning of these p'sents as by y^e^ s^d^: Hancock Lee his heirs and Execut's administ's and assignes or by his or their Councill Learned in y^e^ Law shall be Reasonably Devised advised or Required. IN WITNESS whereof the said Richard Lee hath hereto set his hand and seale the Day and year first above Written.

This deed was recorded at Northumberland court-house, on the 18th of February, 1707/8. It was recorded, a second time, the 16th May, 1711.

In 1716 an accurate survey was made of this estate for Richard Lee, son and heir of Hancock. The estate was then found to contain 904 acres. The original plan of this survey is now in the possession of the owners of "Ditchley," and the lines marked out on it agree exactly with the boundaries given in the old deed of 1707. To secure a perfect title to the additional 304 acres, Richard Lee applied for this patent from the Proprietor of the Northern Neck, who at that time was Catharine, daughter of Lord Culpeper and wife of Lord Fairfax:

The Right Hon^ble^ Catharine Lady Fairfax sole Proprietor of the Northern Neck of Virginia, To all to whom this present writing shall come send greeting in our Lord God Everlasting,—Whereas Mr. Richard Lee of y^e^ Cty of North'land Gent^n^ (upon his suggestion of surplus land within the bounds of a patent formerly granted to Rich'd Lee Esq. bearing date the Twenty-first day of May one thousand six hundred and fifty one, of w^ch^ the s'd suggestor is in possession) did obtain a warrant from my office for laying out the same, and having now returned a survey thereof under the hand of Mr. Jno. Coppedge Surveyor, Know y^e^ therefore that I for and in consideration of the ——— to me paid, on the annual Rent hereafter reserved, have granted made over and confirmed and do by these presents grant make over and confirme unto the said Mr. Richard Lee nine hundred and four acres of land, six hundred, part thereof being granted in a forementioned pattent and three hundred and four the residue surplus within the antient natural and artificial bounds thereof, situate lying and being in the parish great Wiccomocoe, on the southward side of the dividing creeks in the county aforesaid and bounded, &c. &c.

Kendall Lee,[1] son and heir of the Richard Lee mentioned in this grant, petitioned the Virginia Assembly, in 1766, for power to dock the entail on certain lands. In his petition he stated that he was possessed "as tenant in fee tail" of 904 acres in Northumberland county. Col.

[1] Hening, VIII, 279.

Richard Lee, the immigrant, devised two plantations to his wife, which he described as the "plantation whereon I now dwell, . . . also the plantation Mocke Nocke." At her death this land was to go to his three younger sons, whom he mentioned by name, William, Hancock, and Charles. It seems probable that his widow resided there until her death, and that her sons only entered into possession after her death. It has usually been stated that Hancock built the old Ditchley mansion about 1687, but there is no evidence to substantiate this tradition. It is not even positively known whether the immigrant lived at "Ditchley" or "Cobb's Hall." As the two were in his day practically one estate, separated only by a narrow arm of the Dividing Creeks, it is not a matter of any importance. The Ditchley estate is located on a narrow peninsula between the north and south branches of Dividing Creek; the old mansion was situated some little distance back from the main creek, near another and smaller branch. In the rear of the mansion was a grove of trees, and near by the old burial ground, still to be seen. The present house was located about two hundred yards from the old mansion; it was built by Kendall Lee, grandson of Hancock, and was completed about 1765–70, as estimated by the late James Flexmer Ball.

Of this place Bishop Meade wrote: "In the County of Northumberland and parish of Great Wycomico, within sight of the Chesapeake Bay, there is an estate and mansion called Ditchley—an English name of note, which has probably from its settlement, more than one hundred years ago, been the favorite resort of the ministers of the Episcopal Church. Its present owner is Mr. James Flexmer Ball. His father, Mr. Joseph Ball, was one of the truest members of our church. . . . Ditchley is one of the old residences of the Lees. The mansion called Cobbs, where Colonel Richard Lee, the first of the family, lived for some time, was near Ditchley, and has only recently [1853] been removed to make place for another, although it must have been built two hundred years or more." (*Old Churches, Families, &c.*, II, 135.)

Hancock Lee's will was made the 31st of December, 1706; one codicil was added the 1st of January, 1706–7; a second the 18th of May, and a third the 20th of May, 1709. It was probated at Northumberland courthouse the 20th July, 1709:

In the name of God, Amen. I Hancock Lee of the County of Northumberland in y[e] Colony of Virginia, being of sound and perfect sense and memory and blessed be God, doe make this my last Will and Testament hereby revoking all other and former wills whatsoever by me made. Impr's I comitt and comend my soule to almighty God that gave it me hopeing through the merritts of Jesus Christ my Redeemer that after this my sinfull life is ended to enjoy Eternall life and happiness with him in Heaven and my body to the earth from whence it was taken desireing the same may have a decent buryall as my Exor's or Trustees hereafter named shall think fitt. Item I give and bequeath to my deare daughter Mrs. Anna Armstead Four pounds sterling to be paid her the next shipping after my decease, if shee survives me otherwise the s[d] four pounds to be and remaine wholie to the use and benefit of my Ex'ors hereafter named. Item I give and bequeath unto my son Richard Lee thirteen silver spoons they being sent for on purpose for him, they having engraved on the back side the handle the two first letters of his name and I doe likewise give to him the said Richard Lee my silver hilted sword and buff belt with silver buckles.

Item. I give and bequeath unto my deare loveing wife a childs part of all my personall Estate if shee will be content with itt and if shee like not that shee must be content with what the late Law of this Colony will give her (that is to say) a Third of all Lands and negroes during her life and then to whome of right in Law it doth belong and my Will is further that my wife's part be sett aside from the rest of my estate in the first place whatsoever it be whether Thirds or childs part but not if my debts be very considerable att my death which hope in God they may not, then my desire is that soe much be sett apart of my estate before anything be divided as may be thought by my Trustees to be sufficient to satisfie and pay my Just debts and after my wife's part is taken out my will is that all the rest of my Estate be divided into one part more than I have children and my son Richard Lee to have two parts upon division and his choise that is to say my will is that my son Richard Lee have a double portion of all my Estate after all my Just debts and Legacies and my wifes part out as indeed he ought to have by reason that a great part of my estate came by his mother. Item. My will is that my son Richard Lee be by my Trustees hereafter possessed of his Estate when he comes to the age of Eighteen which will be in the y[e] yeare 1709 Aug't y[e] 18th. Item. My will and desire is that my estate be divided with what possible speed may be after my death soe much first sett apart as may be sufficient to satisfie and pay my Just debts and legacies and my will is that my son Richard Lee's Estate that is to say his negroes be kept and remaine working on the Land where they then are att my death, and if any cropp then on the ground they to assist in the tending of it untill it be finished and then they to have their Equall shares for the proper use of my said son Richard and my will is that my son Richard Lee have Two thirds of all the dividend of land where I now live to work his servants upon with Two thirds of all the Houseing on s[d] Plantation except the Dwelling house Kitchen Dairy and sellars the which I give my wife the whole and sole use off untill my sone Richard Lee comes to the age of Eighteen and then he my s[d] son to have the whole use and benefitt of Two thirds of all the houses and sellarage belonging to said plantation and my will is that if my wife will not be obleidged to keep the said houseing that she has priviledge of in as good repaire as they are at my death untill my sone Richard Lee comes to the age afores[d] then my will is that shee have but one Third part assigned as speedily as may be after my death and I doe desire that soe much of my sone Richards goods as may be perishable may be sold by my Trustees hereafter named as they shall think fitt. Item, I give and bequeath unto my son Richard Lee the Dividend of land I now live on being called by the name of mancocks neck to him the said Richard Lee and his heires forever, and in case of his death before he comes to the age of one and twenty or without heires of his body lawfully begotten then the said land to him her or either of their heirs to whome of right in Law it doth belong forever and I doe humbly begg my Hon[ble] and good friend Rob't Carter Esq. my deare Bro[th] Rich[d] Lee Esq. and my Cozen Cap[t] John Howson that they would be pleased to take upon them the Trust and management of my Estate and children untill they come to lawfull age. Item, I give and bequeath unto each of the said Gentle$^{n}$ above named as trustees Twenty Shillings to buy a Ring to weare for my sake which I desire may be paid out of my estate as soon as possible after my decease. Item, my will is that my son Richard Lee have not power att all to sell any negroe without the consent of two of my Good friends above named untill he comes to the age of Twenty one hereby appointing my sone Richard Lee whole and sole Exec$^{r}$ of this my last will. In witness whereof, &c.

Be it known unto all men by these presents that whereas I Hancock Lee of Northumb$^{le}$ County in y$^{e}$ Colony of Virg$^{a}$: have made and Declared my last Will and Testament in writing bearing date the last day of December 1706 I the said Hancock Lee by this present Codicill doe confirme and ratifie my said Last Will and Testam$^{t}$ and doe give and bequeath unto my son Isaac Lee all my land which I have taken up above the falls of Rapp$^{k}$ River (that is to say) Three tracts to him and his heires forever and my will and meaning is that this Codicill or schedule be and be adjudged to be part and parcell of my s$^{d}$ last Will and Testam$^{t}$ and that all things therein contained and mentioned be faithfully and truely performed and fully and amply in every respect as if the same were soe declared and sett downe in my last Will and Testam$^{t}$. In witness, &c. 1st January, 1706-7.

Be it knowne unto all men by these presents that whereas I Hancock Lee of Northumber$^{ld}$ County in y$^{e}$ Colony of Virg$^{a}$ have made and declared my last Will and Testam$^{t}$ in writing bearing date y$^{e}$ last day of December 1706 I the said Hancock Lee by this present Codicill doe confirme and ratifie my s$^{d}$ last will and Testam$^{t}$ and doe give and bequeath unto son John Lee all that tract of land I have taken up att Chapowamsick Contayning seventeen hundred and fifty acres to him the s$^{d}$ John Lee and his heires forever and if that child that my wife is now with child of be a Boy then my will and bequest is that he have all the land I have taken up above Occoquon on Sandy River and Woolf Run to him and his heires forever but if the child my wife is now with child prove a female then my son John Lee to have all my land in Potomack to him and his heires forever and my will and meaning is that this Codicill or schedule be and be adjudged to be part and parcell of my s$^{d}$ Last Will and Testam$^{t}$ and that all things herein contained and mentioned be faithfully and truely performed and as fully and amply in every respect as if the same were sett downe and declared in my Last Will and Testam$^{t}$. In witness, &c. 18th May, 1709.

My Will and desire is that five pounds be paid out of my Estate by my Trustees to the use of the parish church for a peace of Communion Plate and my will is that Mr. Bartholomew Schriever be p'd by s$^{d}$ Trustees Three pound which I have received of his from a Gentleman in Maryland. Item, I give unto ye Reverend Mr. Joseph —— Three pound to preach my funerall Sermon in Wiccocomoco Church. In testimony &c. 20th May, 1709.

Of Hancock Lee, Bishop Meade wrote: "That he was a patron of the Church is shown by the fact that he presented a Communion Cup to the parish in 1729 [1709]. In honor either of himself or father, or the whole family, the parish was then called Lee parish, as may be seen by the inscription on the cup. It was afterward called Wycomico. After the downfall of the parish, Mr. Joseph Ball placed this and the other pieces into my hands for preservation, in hope that the day might come when the old Lee and more modern Wycomico parish might call for it again." The cup is now in use at old Wycomico Church; the inscription on it, as furnished by the rector of the parish, the Rev. E. B. Burwell, reads: "Ex Dono Hancock Lee to y$^{e}$ Parish of Lee. 1711."

Hancock Lee and Mary Kendall, his first wife, had three children:

i, WILLIAM[3], born prior to 1682, for in that year he was mentioned in a deed by his grandfather, William Kendall; it is stated that he died young and without issue; that his brother, Richard Lee, inherited his lands. (VIII, Hening, 278.) As he was not mentioned in his father's will, he probably died before 1706.

ii, ANNA[3], was born prior to the 5th of January, 1682, and was living as late as October, 1754; she was evidently twice married; first to William Armistead, grandson of William, the immigrant, by whom she had a son, John, and probably daughters, Judith, Martha, Mary, and Anne. William Armistead probably died the 13th of June, 1711, æt. 40 years (tombstone); his widow had certainly remarried in 1726, when she was called "Anne Eustace" by her brother Isaac Lee, in his will. By her marriage with William Eustace she had issue: John, William, Isaac, Hancock, and daughters, Mrs. Gaskins,[1] Mrs. Beale, Mrs. Carr, and Mrs. Lee (Hayden, *Va. Genealogies*, 261.) (See Armistead Family for further notice.)

iii, RICHARD[3]. See 3.

Hancock Lee had by his second wife, Sarah Allerton, four children:

iv, ISAAC[3], was born in 1707, as shown by the codicil to his father's will; he died in England, in 1727. An abstract of his will, made by Mr. H. F. Waters, is as follows: Isaac Lee, late of Rappahannock River in America, mariner, but now of Stepney, Middlesex, 18th November, 1726; proved 3d November, 1727. To my honoured Mother, Sarah Lee, of America, Widow, one of my best negroes, such as she shall choose. To my brother Richard Lee, of America, the next best negro, such as he shall choose. To my brothers John and Hancock Lee all my estate, such as land and houses in America, to them and the survivor of them, when they shall attain the several ages of 21 years, and to the male heirs of their bodies. If they die without male issue, then to my brother Richard and the issue male of his body; failing such issue then to the daughter or daughters of my said brothers John and Hancock Lee, during their natural lives, and after their decease to my Sisters Anne Eustace and Elizabeth Lee. If they die without issue then to the daughter or daughters of my brother Richard Lee. (Other provisions.) I hereby appoint and nominate Coll. Robert Carter and my brother Richard Lee of America, Executors, &c., relating to my estate and effects in America and William Dawkins of London, Gent.,

[1] Edward Digges, eldest son of Edward and Elizabeth (Gaskins) Digges, married (30th of March, 1798), Ann Eustace Gaskins, who was probably a daughter of this Mrs. Gaskins.

relating to my affairs in England. (*New Eng. Hist. & Gen. Register*, XLIV, 391.)

v, JOHN[3], first mentioned in the codicil to his father's will, dated 18th May, 1709, so he was probably born in the early months of that year. He died the 11th August, 1789, at the home of his nephew, John Lee, in Orange county. As his will mentioned neither wife nor children, it is probable that he was never married. After a few bequests, he left to his nephew John Lee, son of brother Hancock Lee, dec'd, the residue of his estate, and in case of his death without heirs, it was to be equally divided between nephews and nieces, children of his brother Hancock Lee. He mentioned nephews Hancock, Henry, and Richard Lee, sons of his brother Hancock Lee; nieces, Sarah Alexander Gillison and Mary Willis Madison, daughters of brother Hancock Lee. John Lee, Ex'or; will dated 8th December, 1787; probated in Orange, 22d September, 1789. This John Lee, under the second codicil to his father's will, inherited 1,750 acres in Stafford on Chapowamsick; on the 2d October, 1724, a John Lee, of "Stafford," patented 240 acres in Stafford, on Cedar Run and a branch of Chapowamsic, adjoining the land of Mr. Hancock Lee. The "Mr. Hancock Lee" here mentioned was probably the brother of John, as he too inherited land in Stafford.

vi, HANCOCK[3]. See 4.

vii, ELIZABETH[3]. If Hancock Lee died 25th May, 1709, and declared, on 18th May, 1709, that his wife was then pregnant, it seems certain that both Hancock and Elizabeth were born after his death, so they must have been born in the latter part of 1709, and were twins. Elizabeth married Zachary Taylor, son of James and Martha (Thompson) Taylor, and had: Zachary, Hancock, Richard, and Elizabeth. (See Taylor Family.)

## THE ALLERTONS.

Isaac Allerton, "Merchant Tailor," of London, was born about 1583 and died in 1659; he came over to Plymouth in the "Mayflower," in 1620 was one of the five signers of the "Plymouth Compact," and was a wealthy and very prominent member of that Colony. He was chosen deputy governor in 1621, and later made four voyages to England as agent of the Colony. Finally he fell into disfavor with the ruling powers of Plymouth and in consequence removed to Marblehead, Mass., where he built stores, owned two vessels, and traded extensively. In 1635, being compelled to leave Marblehead, he settled at New Haven; was also a resident of "New Amsterdam" for some time, and at one time a member of its Council, 1643. Later he returned to New Haven, where he died in 1659. He was married three times; first in 1611, at Leyden, Holland, to Mary Norris (or Collins); she came over with him on the "Mayflower" and died the 25th February, 1621; his children by this wife were: Bartholomew, Remember, Mary, and Sarah. He married, secondly, about 1626, Fear, a daughter of Elder William Brewster (1560–1644) of Plymouth, "the father of New England," and also one of the "Mayflower" pilgrims. She died on the 12th of December, 1643, leaving one son, Isaac. Apparently there were no children by the third wife, Johanna ——. Isaac Allerton, the son, was born about 1630, at Plymouth, and lived there for some years with his grandfather, Elder Brewster; was graduated at Harvard in 1650; is supposed to have settled in Virginia about 1654. Evidently his father had been in Virginia, probably on trading voyages, for in his will he mentioned debts due him in that Colony. Major Isaac Allerton (as he has been known) settled on the west side of the Machotick creek or river; his nearest neighbors were John Lee, Henry Corbin, and Dr. Thomas Gerrard, with whom he made an arrangement for building a banqueting house and for entertaining in 1670. Isaac Allerton was major in the militia over which John Washington was the colonel; both took an active part in the Indian wars and especially in the affair "att ye Susquihano ffort" in 1676. He died in 1702; in his will he bequeathed some lands and tobacco to his "daughter Sarah Lee," mentioned his grandson, Allerton Newton, and left the bulk of his estate to his son, Willoughby Allerton. This Willoughby Allerton, Collector of Customs for Potomac River in 1711, married Mrs. Hannah Bushrod, the widow of John Bushrod of Nominy and daughter of William Keene; they had two children: Elizabeth and Isaac. He died in 1723–4; styled himself in his will, "Willoughby Allerton, Gent. of Westmoreland county in Virginia." His son Isaac was evidently the husband of Gawin Corbin's daughter, as mentioned by Bishop Meade (*Old Churches*, etc., II, 146); in his will he named her "Anne." Their children were: Gawin, Isaac, and Willoughby. This Isaac died in 1759, and bequeathed 200 acres to his neighbor, Richard Lee, Esq$^{r}$., and £700 to Capt. Hancock Eustace.

## THE TAYLOR FAMILY.

"The Taylors of Orange trace their ancestry back to James Taylor, of Carlisle, England. The time of his emigration to Virginia is not known. It appears he settled on the Chesapeake between the North and York

Rivers." (*Old Churches, Families*, etc., II, 98.) This James Taylor married, and left several children at his death in 1698. His eldest son, James, moved to Orange county, and married Martha Thompson, by whom he had: James, Zachary, George, Erasmus, Frances (who married Ambrose Madison and was the grandmother of President James Madison), and several daughters. His youngest child, John Taylor, married Catharine, daughter of Philip and Isabella (Hart) Pendleton, and had ten children; among these was James Taylor, who married Ann Pollard, and had, among others, the Hon. John Taylor (1750–1824), of Caroline county, who was a member of the U. S. Senate at several different times, member of the Virginia Assembly, etc.; he married Lucy, daughter of John Penn, the signer of the Declaration of Independence from North Carolina; their son, George Taylor, married Catharine, daughter of Peyton and Lucy (Harrison) Randolph, and had Lucy Penn Taylor, who married Charles Carter Lee, as previously stated (p. 404).

Zachary, the second son of the above-mentioned James and Martha (Thompson) Taylor married Elizabeth, daughter of Hancock and Sarah (Allerton) Lee, by whom he had (as Bishop Meade stated) seven sons and three daughters. Their second son, Hancock Taylor, was a surveyor and one of the first white persons to penetrate into the wilds of the present state of Kentucky, where he was killed in 1774 by the Indians; was accompanied by his cousin, Willis Lee, to whom he left property. Another son, Col. Richard Taylor, of Revolutionary fame, married Sarah, daughter of William Strother, of Stafford county, and had President Zachary Taylor (1784–1850), who married Margaret, daughter of Walter Smith, of Calvert county, Maryland, and was the father of General Richard Taylor, C. S. A., and also of Sarah Knox Taylor, the first wife of Jefferson Davis. Their daughter, Elizabeth Taylor, married Thomas Bell, and had a daughter, Elizabeth, who married her cousin John Lee, son of Hancock and Mary (Willis) Lee.

The Hon. Robert Taylor, member of Virginia Senate, 1804–5–6, and presiding officer of the same; member of Congress, 1825–7, was of this family. Also Col. Francis Taylor, of the Virginia Line Continental Army.

## THE ARMISTEAD FAMILY.

Arms: Argent, a chevron gules, between points of spears azure, tasselled in the middle, or.
Crest: A dexter hand in armour embowed, proper, holding the butt end of a broken spear.

It has been a tradition that the Armisteads derived their name and origin from Darmstadt, and that their seat, "Hesse," in Gloucester county,

Virginia, also derived its name from the same source. "Without deciding when or whether in modern times they crossed the German Ocean, it is sufficient to say that they were Englishmen for several generations before William Armistead came to America, the name, with varied spelling, frequently appearing in Yorkshire records of the time of Queen Elizabeth. The emigrant to America seems, from the names of his children, Anthony and Frances, to have been the son of Anthony 'Armitstead' of Kirk Deighton, Yorkshire, and Frances Thompson, of the same place, who obtained a marriage license in the year 1608. On August 3d, 1610, 'William y^e^ son of Anthony Armsteed of Kirk Deighton' was baptized at All Saints' Church, the only church in the parish. Search for a few years later discloses the fact that this child, whom I suppose the emigrant, passed safely through the period of tender infancy; at least no burial can be found. His father continued to reside there, having other children, and a contemporary named Thomas Armsteed, who also had a family. The emigrant's marriage did not take place there, if, as I assume, it was later than 1627, and prior to 1634."[1]

Such is Mr. Keith's brief account of the origin of this Virginia family, and one that has been the parent stock of many distinguished Virginians.

William "Armestead" received a patent in 1636 from Captain John West, then Governor of Virginia, for 450 acres in Elizabeth City county; among his "head rights" was his wife, Anne. He left three sons, William, John, and Anthony; also a daughter, Frances, who was married three times: first, to the Rev. Justinian Aylmer, next to Lieut-Col. Anthony Elliott, and lastly, to Col. Christopher Wormeley. All three of his sons were members of the House of Burgesses in 1685. The eldest, William, died without issue. The second, John, the "Councillor," was Sheriff for Gloucester in 1675, Burgess in 1685, and appointed to the Council in 1687. After the accession of William and Mary to the English throne, he, with Isaac Allerton and Richard Lee, was dropped from the Council for refusing to take the oaths. He is said to have married a Bowles; he certainly had one wife whose baptismal name was Judith, but her family is not definitely known. His issue were: Judith, who married "King" Robert Carter, being his first wife (see Carter Family under Stratford Line, 35); Elizabeth, who married first Ralph Wormeley and next William Churchill; William, who married Anna Lee, as stated, and lastly, Henry, who married Martha Burwell, and had issue: William, Lucy, and Robert. Of these children, William married a daughter of James

[1] *The Ancestry of Benjamin Harrison*, etc., by Charles P. Keith, p. 12, *et seq.*, from which much of this sketch has been taken.

Bowles, who had been of the Council in Maryland; he died in 1755 (VIII, Hening, 669), leaving William, John, and Bowles; the last inherited lands in Culpeper county, and married Mary Fontaine; their daughter, Elizabeth, married, in 1797, Ludwell Lee, being his second wife (see Stratford Line, 33).

Information about the marriage, number of children, etc., of William Armistead and Anna Lee, is scanty. It is not probable that she was married as early as 1691, as shown by the following: In April of that year a town or wharf was ordered to be built "ffor Northampton county upon one of the branches of Cherry Stone Creek, on the land of Mrs. Anna Lee,[1] the daughter of Captain Hancock Lee, now in the tenure of the widow of Andrew Small." (III, Hening, 59.) This land had been given her by her grandfather, as shown in the following abstract of a petition from Hening (VI, 443–4–5):

William Kendall, dec'd. of Northampton, deeded 700 acres on Cherrystone Creek, 1st August, 1685, to Hancock Lee and Mary, his wife, for life; at their decease to Anna daughter of said Hancock and Mary; said Anna after the death of Hancock and Mary entered on the said 700 acres and married William Armistead, now deceased, and had John Armistead, also deceased, who in turn left a son, John Armistead, of Gloucester county, who after the death of his grandmother, Anna, will be entitled to the said 700 acres. The said John Armistead, the father, in his will of 9th April, 1734, gave to his daughter, Susanna, £600 to be paid at 21 or marriage; also to his son William Armistead, £600, both to be paid by his son John; said Susanna has intermarried with Moore Fauntleroy, of Richmond county, &c.

As previously mentioned, William Armistead and Anna Lee probably had these five children: John, Judith, Martha, Mary, and Anne. The above extract tells of the son's issue. Mr. Keith says he was twice married; first, to Elizabeth, whom James Burwell called "sister" in his will; he next married Susanna, the daughter of Thomas Meriwether, of Essex county. His three children—John, William, and Susanna—Mr. Keith thinks, may have been by the second wife.

Of these daughters, Judith married George Dudley; Martha, also called sister,[2] by James Burwell, may have married Lewis Burwell. Mary was twice married; first, to James Burwell, who died in 1718, aged 29, leaving two children, Nathaniel Bacon and Lucy Burwell. She married, secondly, Philip Lightfoot, of York county. In his will of 31st July, 1749, he

---

1 About a hundred and fifty years ago, and earlier, the title "Mrs." was applied impartially to unmarried as well as to married women. Even children were sometimes so styled. The burial of an infant daughter of John Milton, who died aged only five months, is recorded in the parish register of St. Margaret's, Westminster, as "Mrs Katharine Milton," followed by a small c, to indicate that a child is meant.

2 Probably meaning sister-in-law, for he also mentioned "brother John Armistead" and "Mother Ann Armistead" (*W. and M. College Quarterly*, II, 232.)

mentioned three sons: John, Armistead, and William Lightfoot. The first of these sons, Mr. Keith thinks, may have been by a previous marriage. Anne, the last child of William and Anna (Lee) Armistead, is mentioned in the (Richmond) *Standard* as the daughter of Captain William Armistead, of Eastmost River, Gloucester. She married, on the 4th of April, 1725, Anthony Walke, and left issue.

The wide distribution of this family in Virginia, even many years ago, is shown by the fact that in the County Committees of Safety of 1775–76, Robert Armistead of Louisa, John of Caroline, Henry of Charles City, and John of New Kent, were members.

## DITCHLEY LINE, THIRD GENERATION.

### Richard Lee.

3. Richard[3], the second son of Hancock Lee[2] (Richard[1]) and Mary Kendall, his first wife, was born at "Ditchley" on the 18th of August, 1691, as stated in his father's will. He died in the same place in 1740, and was buried there. Richard was a Justice and first of the "Quorum" in 1714, so had probably been some years in commission; he was Clerk of Northumberland county from 1716 to 1735. He married Judith Steptoe, and had seven children, which is proven by the manner in which his personal estate was divided. One-third was awarded the widow and the other two-thirds were divided into seven parts; of these, each child evidently received one-seventh.

The auditors, Philip Smith, Robt. Jones, and Thos. Winter report:

Northumberland SS. In obedience to an order of Court made the 11th of August 1740 wherein it was ordered that we the subscribers should meet at the house of Mrs. Judith Lee to allot her the third part of her Dec^d. Husbands Estate and Mr. Peter Conway his wifes filial part of her fathers Estate, pursuant to the said order we have mett and proceeded as followeth the amounts of the thirds of the Dec^d Estate is £299 1s 1d allotted as hereunderneath [names of articles omitted]. Mr. Peter Conway's wifes part which is the 1-7 of ⅔ amounts to £85 8s 10¾d paid him as followeth [names of articles omitted].

Northumberl^d. In obedience to an order of Court of fores^d: County made the 14 of 7^br: 1741 wherein it was ordered that we y^e: subscribers should meet and allot Mr. Charles Lee his wifes Filial part of her fathers Estate accordingly we mett at the house of Mrs. Judith Lee the 4^th: of this instant and allotted him off Eighty five pounds five shillings and four pence three farthings it being his just part.

This division applied only to the personal estate: the real estate was inherited by his son Kendall. Of these seven children the names of only five have been ascertained. The Northumberland records give the marriage contract, dated 16th of February, 1749, between Samuel Peachy, of Richmond county, and Judith Lee, widow, of Northumberland county, which was witnessed by John Leeland, Kendall Lee, Betty Lee, and Lucy Lee.

i, KENDALL[4]. See 5.

ii, ELIZABETH[4], who married Major Peter Conway, being his second wife, prior to division of her father's estate in 1740; she survived him, for he left "his loving wife Betty my Chair and two horses and also my mulatto boy Robin besides her Dower of all my Estate." (Hayden, *Va. Genealogies*, 246, foot-note.)

iii, MARY[4], who married her cousin Charles Lee, of "Cobbs Hall," prior to "the 14th of 7br: 1741"; "Mary Lee wife of Charles Lee departed this Life the 4th day of March, in the year of our Lord God 1744." (Family Bible.)

iv, JUDITH[4], born ——; died the 24th of March, 1791; married about 1745–6, David Galloway, Sr., a native of Edinburgh, Scotland, who then lived in Virginia, and had, it is said, only two children, Helen and David; Helen married a Mr. Gilmour, a Scotchman then residing in Lancaster county, Va.; David married Margaret, daughter of Capt. James Blair, of Northumberland, and had, at least, one son, Richard Lee Galloway.

v, LETTICE[4]; from her tomb at old White Chapel, Lancaster, this inscription was copied: "In memory of Lettice, 3d wife of Col. James Ball, daughter of Richard Lee of Ditchley. Died the 17th of November, 1811, in the 80th year of her age." She was married about 1753, and had issue: 1, Judith, who was twice married; first, on the 3d of November, 1772, to Leroy Griffin, and next, to —— Fauntleroy. 2, James Ball, born the 20th of February, 1755, and died the 18th of December, 1825; he married, about 1776, Frances Downman, and had Joseph (born 19th of August, 1777, and died the 19th of September, 1851), who was the father of the late James Flexmer Ball. James Ball purchased part of the Ditchley estate in 1789. 3, Anne, who married, on the 31st of May, 1779, James Wallace Ball, and had issue. 4, Sarah, who married Robert Fauntleroy and had issue. 5, Frances, who married her first cousin George Lee (9, q. v.), son of Kendall and Betty (Heale) Lee, and had issue.

Of this Mrs. Ball, Miss Julia R. Downman wrote: "I have heard my parents and others speak of her 'as old Mrs. Ball who lived at Bewdley.' After her son James' marriage she gave up the house to them, and took as her rooms a wing of the house (long since pulled down), where my father and mother well remember going in to see her whenever they went to Bewdley. She had her own servants, and superintended their needlework and spinning, work that was considered of great importance in that day. I know that old Mrs. Ball's mother was a Miss Steptoe. I have often seen a very handsome portrait of her, said to have been painted by Sir Joshua Reynolds, and which was cut out of the frame and carried off during the last war." (Hayden, *Va. Genealogies*, 95, 96.)

## Hancock Lee.

4. Hancock[3], the youngest son of Hancock Lee[2] (Richard[1]) by his second wife, Sarah Allerton, was born in the latter part of the year 1709, as proven by statements in the last codicil to his father's will. He married in 1733, Mary, daughter of Col. Henry Willis, of Fredericksburg. Of this Col. Willis, his grandson, Byrd C. Willis, wrote.[1] "It is said of my grandfather, Col. Henry Willis, that he courted his three wives when maids and married them as widows. . . . He had children by each wife. His sons by the first and second wives died without male heirs. One of them left a daughter, the late Mrs. Mary Daingerfield, of Coventry, Spottsylvania county, Va. His daughters married a Lee, a Lewis, and a Green. Mrs. Lee lived in Fauquier county, Va." Hancock Lee lived during the latter years of his life near Warrenton, in Fauquier, where he died, some time prior to August of 1789; but when he settled there is not known. In 1729, a Hancock Lee patented 393 acres in King William county, and sold 400 in 1751 for £115. One of the name was Justice for King George county, 1745 (W. G. Stanard). He left the following children:

i, Willis[4], who accompanied his cousin Hancock Taylor and his brother Hancock Lee to Kentucky in 1774. From some extracts from the old *Kentucky Gazette* this is taken: "In the year 1774 several surveyors arrived in Kentucky, amongst them were Col. John Floyd, Hancock Taylor, James Douglass, Isaac Hite, and Willis Lee. Taylor and Lee were both killed by the Indians," etc. Hancock Taylor made his will (July, 1774) a day or two before he died, and left part of the lands he had surveyed to his "cousin Hancock Lee." Willis Lee was not killed, only wounded, at that time. Gen. Robert Payne, in an application for a pension as a Revolutionary soldier, stated "During the summer

---

[1] Mr. Thomas Marshall Green, of Danville, Ky., himself a descendant of Col. Henry Willis, has devoted much time to the history of this and other families; while he has not been able to fully ascertain the names of Col. Willis' three wives, he feels confident that the first was Anne Alexander, the widow of John Smith, of Purtons; the second and third, he thinks, were both Mildred Washingtons; one the widow of Brown, the other of Roger Gregory. As to the last wife there does not seem to be any question. Mr. Green is of the opinion that the Mary Willis who married Hancock Lee must have been a daughter by the first wife. "Mrs. Mildred Gregory" was General Washington's godmother, when he was baptized, the 5th of April, 1732, so she had not married Col. Willis at that date. The date of the marriage of Hancock Lee and Mary Willis is recorded at Spottsylvania court-house.

of 1776 the Indians evinced a hostile disposition. They had killed Willis Lee, wounded Cyrus McCracken and Joseph Lindsey, and stolen some horses."[1]

ii, HANCOCK[4]. See 6.

iii, JOHN[4]. See 7.

iv, HENRY[4]. See 8.

v, RICHARD[4], died unmarried.

vi, SARAH ALEXANDER[4], married Col. John Gillison, of the 6th Va. Infantry, Continental Army.

vii, MARY WILLIS[4], born ——; died the 14th of March, 1798, and was buried at "Montpelier," Orange county, the Madison estate; she married Captain Ambrose Madison, a son of Col. James and Eleanor (Conway) Madison, of "Montpelier," and younger brother of President James Madison. Captain Madison served in the Virginia Line during the Revolution. (Hayden, *Va. Genealogies*, 225–7.) They had a daughter, Nellie Conway, who married Dr. John Willis, of "Whitehall," Gloucester county; he died in 1812 of the yellow fever, and was also buried at "Montpelier;" they had two children: Col. John Willis, of Orange, and Mary Lee, who married her cousin, John Hancock Lee (19, q. v.).

## DITCHLEY LINE, FOURTH GENERATION.

### KENDALL LEE.

5. KENDALL[4], the son of Richard Lee[3] (Hancock[2], Richard[1]) and Judith Steptoe, his wife, was born ——, and died some time in the year 1780, probably in January. He married "Betty" Heale, of Lancaster, on the 9th of July, 1749 (Lancaster records); was a vestryman of Wycomico Parish in 1777. (*Old Families, Churches*, etc., II, 469.) His will, dated the 18th of September, 1779, and probated in Northumberland the 14th of February, 1780, mentioned his wife, "Betty Lee," his sons, William, George, Kendall, Hancock, Richard Lancelot, and Arthur; his daughters, Judith, Priscilla, Betty Edwards, and also Betty and Nancy, daughters of John Kent. His wife's will, dated the 25th of November, 1789, and probated in July, 1790, mentioned their children as given in his will, and also grandsons, Archibald Campbell, William Lee Campbell, and Thomas Edwards, son-in-law.

In 1766, Kendall Lee applied to the Assembly for leave to dock the entail on some of his lands. In his petition, he stated that William Kendall, late of Northampton county, by a deed of the 20th of April, 1682,

---

[1] Kindly furnished by Mr. Green, from whom much valuable information has been received.

gave to Hancock Lee and Mary, his then wife, daughter of said William Kendall, 2,050 acres at Matchepungo, in Northampton, for their natural lives, and at their deaths to go to William Lee, his grandson and to his heirs, and in default of issue to the next male heir of Hancock and Mary Lee; and in default of such issue to his granddaughter, Anna Lee. This land at William's death fell to his brother Richard, as next heir to Hancock and Mary Lee. The petition also mentions that Kendall was "seized in fee simple of 50 acres in Northumberland adjoining a larger tract of 904 acres, whereof he is seized as tenant in fee tail" (VIII, Hening, 478), clearly proving that he had inherited the Ditchley estate.

The following record of the issue of Kendall Lee and Betty Heale, his wife, is substantially as given by Mr. Hayden (*Va. Genealogies*, 98), with a few additions and corrections; especially in the record of the son Kendall, whom Mr. Hayden's informant had confounded with another of the same name:

i, WILLIAM[5], married Jane Payne; in 1789, he sold "Ditchley" to Col. James Ball, Jr., of "Bewdley," Lancaster county, who had married his aunt, Lettice Lee; Mr. Lee afterward removed to Fauquier county.

ii, GEORGE[5]. See 9.

iii, KENDALL[5]. See 10.

iv, HANCOCK[5]. See 11.

v, RICHARD LANCELOT[5], died in Fauquier county in September or October, 1790; his will mentioned brothers, William, George, Kendall, Hancock, and Arthur; sisters, Priscilla, Betty Edwards, and Judith Pierce. Apparently he was never married.

vi, ARTHUR[5], no issue.

vii, MARY[5], married Dr. Archibald Campbell, and had: Archibald and William Lee, as named in their grandmother's will. This Dr. Campbell may have been a son or grandson of the Rev. Archibald Campbell, who was rector of old Round Hill Church, Westmoreland; he left three sons, Archibald, Alexander, and John.

viii, ELIZABETH[5], "Betty," married Thomas Edwards, a son of Thomas and Elizabeth (Fauntleroy) Edwards; he was born 28th of January, 1752; died 20th of April, 1798; was Clerk of the Northumberland courts, and a vestryman of Wycomico Parish in 1777. Their issue were: Richard, Kendall, Thomas, Lancelot, Mary Kendall, and Alice Lee Edwards. In his will he committed his two daughters "to the particular care of my two invaluable friends, Mrs. Helen Gilmour and Mrs. Judith Pierce," and his son Kendall to his brother Richard Edwards. Named his friends, William Lee, John Gordon, Presly

Thornton, and his brothers, Leroy and Griffin Edwards, together with his son, Richard Edwards, as his executors.

ix, JUDITH[5], was twice married; first, to —— Pierce, and had at least one child, a daughter, Mary Pierce, who married, in 1803–4, the Hon. Willam Lee Ball, a grandson of James Ball and Lettice Lee, his wife. In 1790 she was called "Judith Pierce" by her brother, Richard Lancelot Lee; also by her brother-in-law, Thomas Edwards, in his will dated the 13th of September, 1797. She married, secondly, General John Blackwell, and had at least two daughters, Ann Eliza and Emma Blackwell. The former was married, on the 27th of February, 1817, to Dr. James Kendall Ball, of "Edgewood," Lancaster county, and had issue: John Barton, Capt. James Kendall, Fayette, and Octavia Augusta Ball. The second daughter, Emma, was married about 1815 to George William Downman; no issue. (Hayden, *Va. Genealogies*, 98, 129.) There does not seem to be any probability that Judith Lee was married three times, as has been suggested (*Ibid.*, 265), for her brother-in-law called her "Mrs. Judith Pierce" as late as Sepber, 1797.

x, PRISCILLA[5], born 12th of June, 1770; died 27th of May, 1834; was married, on 19th of October, 1794, to Griffin Edwards, son of Thomas and Elizabeth (Fauntleroy) Edwards. Griffin Edwards was born 17th of March, 1768; they had these eight children: 1, Ann Priscilla, born 22d of July, 1795; died 17th of February, 1818; was married, on the 11th of September, 1815, to Col. Joseph Ball (his third wife), the youngest son of Capt. David Ball. Col. Joseph Ball married, fourthly, Martha Kendall, a daughter of Kendall Lee and Mary Nutt (11, Cobbs Hall Line). 2, Betty Griffin, born 8th of March, 1797; died in 187–. 3, Louise Bushrod, born 11th of April, 1799; died 28th of November, 1801. 4, Lucy Lee, born 30th of July, 1801; died 20th of December, 1837; married —— Hughlett. 5, LeRoy Griffin, born 14th of February, 1804; died 23d of August, 1866; married, in May, 1837, Fannie W. Robins, of Norfolk county. 6, William Lee, born 14th of March, 1807; died ——, 187–; married Elizabeth Garland, of Richmond county. 7, Mary Catharine, born 17th of April, 1810; died 11th of June, 1853. 8, Virginia Fauntleroy, born 16th of April, 1810; married Thomas Hughlett. (*Ibid.*, 99.)

## CAPTAIN HANCOCK LEE.

6. HANCOCK[4], the second son of Hancock Lee[3] (Hancock[2], Richard[1]) and Mary Willis, his wife, was probably born about 1736, and died

in the year 1815. Hancock Lee was evidently a civil engineer by profession. He accompanied his elder brother, Willis Lee, and his cousin, Hancock Taylor, to Kentucky in 1771. By the latter's will he inherited lands in that state. He was also employed by the Ohio Company to survey their lands. George Mason, of "Gunston," wrote: "Captain Hancock Lee and one Mr. Lee are returned from surveying the Ohio Company's 200,000 acres of land, and are now here making out their returns and settling their accounts, in assisting which I am closely engaged, as I wish to have everything as clear and as regular as possible. They have got it all in one tract, upon a large creek called Licking Creek, which falls into the Ohio river on the southeast side, about 150 miles below the Scioto river and about 60 miles above the mouth of the Kentucky river, so that it is clear both of Henderson's and the Vandalia Company's claim. By all accounts, it is equal to any land on this continent, being exceedingly rich and level." (*Life of George Mason*, I, 214.)

Of this Captain Hancock Lee, his grandson, John Hancock Lee, wrote: "My grandfather was of a roving disposition and fond of adventure. I have often heard him say he was the first white[1] man who ever entered the present limits of Kentucky, where much of his early life was spent in surveying and locating lands and in conflicts with the Indians, by whom he was several times captured, and narrowly escaped death at the stake. He has often told me that on his return from his first trip to that state he met Boone on the Allegheny mountains, making his first trip, and told him where he would find some venison that he had prepared and secreted for use on his next trip. He was a warm friend of Boone's, and was with him on many of his trips. Being a warm friend and of a modest, retiring disposition, he would never dispute with him the honour of being the first white man on that dark and bloody ground. I have been told by some of his early companions that a more fearless man than my

[1] This statement is evidently an error. It is not definitely known when the first white explorer entered the present limits of Kentucky. The first explorers, as well as the first settlers, were from Virginia, but the dates of their explorations have not been clearly proven. It is said that a Col. Wood was in Kentucky as early as 1654. The first authentic reports of an exploration are found in the manuscript journal of Dr. Thomas Walker, who was there in 1750. He was accompanied by many Virginians, but Hancock Lee would probably have been too young to have been of his party. One Lewis Evans issued an imperfect map in 1752, which included portions of that state. Boone first visited Kentucky in 1769, so he was a comparatively late explorer; consequently, if Hancock Lee met him on his return from this trip, he was certainly not the first white man to enter Kentucky. The first actual attempt to found a settlement there was made in 1774 by James Harrod and a party of about forty persons. Hancock Lee's visit was probably prior to this date. It is certain, from land records and lawsuits, that Hancock Taylor and others of his party did early survey and locate claims in that state. These claims were very easily located. Each claimant was required to make his own survey, designating thereon the bounds of the land he had taken up. This plan was then recorded and a warrant issued. So a surveyor could readily locate in a few hours a tract of 1,000 or more acres, which he could sell or hold.

grandfather they never knew. The following anecdote of him will illustrate the indomitable character of his courage: During the war of 1812 his son Hancock belonged to a volunteer company from Fauquier, then stationed at Hampton, under Gen'l Porterfield. My grandfather, then upwards of 80 years of age, determined upon making him a visit; so he mounted his noble old horse, then in his twenty-third or fourth year, which had borne him over the Allegheny on more than 20 trips to Kentucky, and which was the first saddle horse I ever saw. After slow stages he reached Hampton and was warmly received by his son and young friends of the company. In a few days after his arrival he was aroused early one morning and told that the enemy, whose ships had been lying in the offing for several days, were about to make a landing, that our command had determined to evacuate the town, and advised him to get up and go with the army. This he determined not to do. As soon as he could dress he went out, obtained a musket, and took a position near the water, behind a row of buildings, from which place he continued to fire upon the enemy all the time they were landing and until he was surrounded by a party, who, seeing him alone, an old, feeble man, and not caring to shoot him, called upon him to surrender. This he refused to do to a private, but said if an officer would receive his weapon he would surrender. Upon an officer stepping up he delivered up his weapon to him and was carried on board the Admiral's (Cockburn) vessel and kept a prisoner. He was most kindly treated, and when the fleet was about to sail he was sent ashore and his old horse given back to him. He often said the horse had been ridden nearly to death by the British officers. This story may seem Quixotic, but it is literally true, as any old volunteer, who may be living, will confirm. Please excuse my weakness in burdening you with this story. It is due to the memory of one who was literally without fear and without reproach." (MS. letter.) Hancock Lee married Winifred Beale, who (his grandson stated) was the daughter of John Beale, of Westmoreland,[1] and had ten children. Of these children very little is known, one not even by name; four others, Arthur, Pamela, Mary Frances, and Anne, died unmarried. The others were:

i, WILLIS[5]. See 12.
ii, HANCOCK[5]. See 13.
iii, THOMAS[5]. See 14.
iv, EMELINE[5], married a Mr. Richards, and died without issue.

---

[1] She might have been a daughter of John Beale, of Richmond county, whose will (dated in December, 1766, and probated in August, 1767) mentioned his wife, Elizabeth, and daughters, Ann, Sarah, Winifred, Eustace, Elizabeth, and Charlotte. (Hayden, *Va. Genealogies*, 738.)

v, ELIZABETH[5], married Captain Sangster, of Fauquier county, and died recently without issue.

## MAJOR JOHN LEE.

7. JOHN[4], the third son of Hancock Lee[3] (Hancock[2], Richard[1]) and Mary Willis, his wife, was born ——, and died in 1802; he was married about the 18th of December, 1781, to Elizabeth, daughter of Thomas Bell, and Elizabeth Taylor, his wife, who was a granddaughter of Hancock Lee and Sarah Allerton, his second wife. Their marriage bond, dated the 18th of December, 1781, stated that "there is a marriage suddenly intended to be solemnized between the above-bound John Lee and Elizabeth Bell, spinster," and under the same date Thomas Bell gave permission for a marriage license to be issued "to Major John Lee to be married to my Daughter Elizabeth Bell." The records of Orange show that Major John Lee sold his residence near the court-house and his lands in 1792, and moved to Kentucky. In 1792, John Lee, Elizabeth Bell, his wife, and Margaret Bell, "children of the late Thomas Bell, dec'd, of Orange," appointed James Bell, of Orange, their attorney to convey a tract of land to William Norris, of Fauquier county.

John Lee was appointed an ensign in 1775; captain of the 2d state regiment in 1777; major, 1st February, 1778, and was in service until 1782. He received for his military services 5,333½ acres of land.

Major John and Elizabeth (Bell) Lee had:

i, JOHN HANCOCK[5], married his cousin, Anne, daughter of Henry Lee; no issue.

ii, LEWIS[5], married but left no issue.

iii, SARAH[5], who married John Jordan Crittenden,[1] of Kentucky, and had these six children: 1, George Bibb, who was a graduate of West Point, served in the Mexican War, resigned in 1861, entered the Southern army, and rose to the rank of major-general, was state librarian after the war, and died the 27th of November, 1880, unmarried. 2, Ann Mary, who married Chapman Coleman, a merchant of Louisville, and at one time U. S. Marshal for Kentucky; they had these children: Florence (who married Patrick Joyce, a lawyer of Louisville); Crittenden; Chapman (who was until recently chief secretary of the U. S.

---

1 John Jordan Crittenden was born in Woodford county, Ky., the 10th of September. 1786, and died at Frankfort, the 26th of July, 1863. He held many distinguished offices under both state and national governments; was U. S. Senator from Kentucky, 1817–19, and again, 1835–41; was Attorney-General under President Harrison, 1841; again Senator, 1842–48; Governor of Kentucky, 1848–50; Attorney-General under President Fillmore, 1850–53; again Senator, 1855–61, and lastly a Representative from Kentucky, 1861–63.

Legation at Berlin); Eugenie (who was educated in Germany, and has translated some of Miss Muhlbach's novels); Judith (who married the Hon. Charles Adams, at one time a member of Congress from New York City), and Sarah Lee Coleman. 3, Cornelia, who married the Rev. John C. Young, D. D., LL. D., a native of Pennsylvania, a graduate of Princeton, and for many years pastor of various Presbyterian Churches; in 1830, he was elected the President of Centre College, Danville, Ky., which position he held until his death in 1857; his first wife was a daughter of Joseph Cabell Breckinridge; his second, Cornelia Crittenden, by whom he had issue: Rev. John C. Young, Jr., who was also a Presbyterian clergyman, and a brilliant orator; Rev. William C. Young, also a Presbyterian clergyman, was Moderator of the Presbyterian General Assembly at Portland, Ore., in 1892, and is now President of Centre College; their other children were: Eugenie, Zillah, Sarah Lee, and George C. Young. 4, Thomas Leonidas Crittenden, who was commonwealth's attorney at Frankfort, then aide to General Taylor at Buena Vista, next Consul at Liverpool under Taylor and Fillmore, and lastly served in the U. S. army during the late civil war, rising to the rank of major-general; he married Catharine Todd, and had Lieutenant John Crittenden, of the 20th Infantry, who was killed by the Sioux Indians at Little Big Horn, the 25th of June, 1876. 5, Robert Henry Crittenden, who was twice married, and left six children. 6, Sarah Lee Crittenden, who married Dr. Edward H. Watson, of Frankfort, Ky., and had issue: Crittenden, Captain U. S. N., George, Jane, and Annie Watson.

iv, MATILDA A.[5], was the third wife of Samuel McDowell Wallace, eldest son of Judge Caleb and Priscilla (Christian) Wallace; they had issue: 1, Thomas Henry, who married Frances Taylor, and had six children. 2, John Lee, who married Malvina Gillespie, and had several children. 3, Sarah Lee, is not married. 4, Andrew, died unmarried. 5. William Christian, married Dora Taylor, has several children; lives in Florida. 6, Cornelia, married Samuel Redd, and has five children; lives near Austin, Texas. 7, Mary Priscilla, married Charles Harvey, who died in 1888; she lives now at Lexington, Ky., no issue. 8, Elizabeth Lee, married James L. Searles, of Lexington, Ky., and had four children. 9, Caleb McDowell Wallace, married Emma Fowler; he died in 1888, leaving several children, who reside with their mother at Ocala, Florida.

v, ELIZABETH[5], married Dr. —— Wilkinson, of Frankfort, Ky., no issue.

vi, LUCINDA[5], married Dr. R. H. Call (a brother of Governor Call), who moved from Logan county, Ky., to Florida; they had two sons: General George, C. S. A., killed at the battle of "Seven Pines," and the present U. S. Senator Wilkinson Call, of Florida.

vii, ANNE[5], who married —— Price.[1]

### HENRY LEE.

8. HENRY[4], the fourth son of Hancock Lee[3] (Hancock[2], Richard[1]) and Mary Willis, his wife, was married[2] and had five children. (A writer in the (Richmond) *Critic* claims that this Henry Lee was the person of that name who was born in Virginia in 1758, and died in Mason county, Ky., in 1846; was a member of the Virginia Legislature, of the Virginia Convention of 1788, of the Kentucky Convention of 1787, and Judge of the Circuit Court. There was a "Henry Lee of Virginia" who matriculated at the Middle Temple, London, in 1773. Mr. Thomas M. Green writes that the father of the Henry Lee of Kentucky was named Stephen.)

Henry Lee's children were:

i, WILLIS[5], who died unmarried.
ii, HANCOCK[5], never married.
iii, JOHN[5], never married.
iv, —— (daughter) married a Mr. Davis.
v, ANNE[5], who married her cousin, John Hancock Lee, no issue.

## DITCHLEY LINE, FIFTH GENERATION.

### GEORGE LEE.

9. GEORGE[5], the second son of Kendall Lee[4] (Richard[3], Hancock[2], Richard[1]) and Betty Heale, his wife, was married on the 16th of February, 1787, to Frances, daughter of Col. James Ball, by Lettice Lee, his third wife, and had these children:

i, GEORGE[6], the North'd records have the marriage bond of George Lee and Mary Edwards, widow, dated the 8th of October, 1804; they are said to have had a daughter.
ii, ARTHUR[6]. See 15.
iii, BETTY[6], died unmarried.
iv, FRANCES[6], married the Rev. Mr. Seward, of Richmond county.
v, ANNA[6], was married on the 3d of September, 1829, to Col. Joseph Ball, of "Ditchley;" died without issue.

---

[1] Most of the information concerning the children and grandchildren of Major John Lee was kindly furnished by Mr. Thomas Marshall Green, Danville, Ky.

[2] The name of Henry Lee's wife is not known; she may have been Elizabeth Burwell, eldest daughter of the Rev. Richard Hewitt, of Hungars Parish, and Elizabeth Read, his wife (*W. and M. College Quarterly*, II, 232, 233.)

## THE BALL FAMILY.

Arms: Argent, a lion passant sable, on a chief of the second three mullets of the first. Crest: Out of the clouds, ppr., a demi-lion rampant sable, powdered with estoilles arg., holding a globe, or. Motto: Coelumqui tueri.

As a very complete genealogy of the Ball family has recently been published,[1] only a bare outline is given here, merely to show the relationship of the various members of this family who have married Lees.

William Ball, merchant and planter, who, tradition states, came to Virginia about 1650, with a wife and three children, was the progenitor of this large and influential family. In March, 1675–6, "Coll. William Ball and lieut. coll. John Carter, or either of them, in the county of Lancaster," were empowered by the Virginia Assembly to raise soldiers for defense against the Indians. (II, Hening, 239.) At his death in 1680, Col. Ball left a widow and these three children: William, Joseph, and Hannah. The eldest, Capt. William Ball, it is said, was three times married, and left a large family. James, his third son, was also married three times, and was the father of thirteen children. His ninth child was Col. James Ball, of "Bewdley," Lancaster, who was born the 31st of December, 1718, and died the 24th of November, 1789; he too was three times married; his third wife was Lettice Lee, daughter of Richard Lee, of "Ditchley," and Judith Steptoe, his wife; they had five children; the second was James Ball, Jr. (1755–1825), who purchased the "Ditchley" estate from his cousin William Lee, and settled there. His son, Col. Joseph Ball, was twice married; secondly, in 1829, to Anna Lee, daughter of George Lee, and Frances Ball, as just stated, but had no issue. His son, James Flexmer Ball, who was born at "Ditchley," the 30th of June, 1816, and died at the same place in October, 1894, had been twice married, and left four sons, several daughters and grandchildren to mourn his loss. To his son Horâce L. Ball many thanks are due for kind assistance in sending data. Mr. Ball possessed the original deeds,[2] surveyor's plans, etc., for the "Ditchley" estate.

Col. Joseph Ball, the second son of the immigrant, was born in England, the 24th of May, 1649, and died at his estate, "Epping Forest," Lancaster county, in June, 1711. Col. Joseph Ball had by his second wife one child, Mary Ball, justly famous as the mother of George Washington. She was born in 1707–8, and died the 25th of August, 1789; was married, on the 6th of March, 1730–1, to Augustine Washington. Her first child,

---

[1] In the *Virginia Genealogies*, by the Rev. Horace Edwin Hayden, Wilkesbarre, Penna., 1891.

[2] As given on pp. 521–22–23–24.

35

George Washington, was "Born ye 11th Day of February, 1731–2 about ten in the Morning, and was Baptiz'd the 5th of April following, Messrs. Beverly Whiting and Capt. Christopher Brooks godfathers and Mrs. Mildred Gregory godmother." Capt. William Ball, of "Millenbeck," Lancaster, a cousin of the above-mentioned Col. James Ball, married (1746–7) Lettice Lee, daughter of Col. Henry Lee, of "Lee Hall," and Mary Bland, his wife; their daughter Mary married a John Ball.

## Kendall Lee.

10. Kendall[5], the third son of Kendall Lee[4] (Richard[3], Hancock[2], Richard[1]) and Betty Heale, his wife, was born at "Ditchley," the 30th of July, 1763; died in Fluvanna county, the 9th of June, 1811; he was twice married; first to Sarah, daughter of Col. John and Lucy (Churchill) Gordon, who was born the 21st of June, 1764, and died very shortly after her marriage, without issue. He was married secondly, on the 6th of December, 1788, to Judith Burton, daughter of Col. George Payne, of Goochland county; she was born the 12th of September, 1769, and died the 29th of October, 1850. In 1794, Richard Baylor Payne conveyed 314½ acres to Kendall Lee, of Goochland county; in 1806, this tract was conveyed by Kendall Lee and Judith Burton Lee, his wife, to William Johnson, and was then described as that "tract of land generally known as Kendall Lee's former residence." In the last conveyance Kendall Lee's residence was stated to be then in Fluvanna county.

Kendall and Judith Burton (Payne) Lee had the following-named issue; names and dates from their family Bible:

i, George Kendall[6], born in 1789; died in 1859, without issue. Lived in New Orleans, where he was for many years cashier of a bank; died at Richmond, Va.
ii, Thomas[6]. See 16.
iii, Richard Henry[6], born in 1792; died in 1816, without issue.
iv, Elizabeth Kendall[6], born in 1794, and died in 1863, without issue.
v, William[6]. See 17.
vi, Hancock[6]. See 18.
vii, Virginia Payne[6], born in 1799; married, 1822, Howell Lewis, and had: Richard and Virginia Lewis.

## Hancock Lee.

11. Hancock[5], the fourth son of Kendall Lee[4] (Richard[3], Hancock[2], Richard[1]) and Betty Heale, his wife, married Sinah Ellen, daughter of

Col. Richard Chichester, of Fairfax county, and Sarah McCarty, his second wife. The will of Sinah E. Lee, dated the 12th of July, 1851, and probated at Fairfax court-house, on the 18th of August, 1851, named their children in the following order:

i, RICHARD KENDALL[6].
ii, BETTY[6], residuary legatee and executrix.
iii, SARAH MCCARTY[6], wife of James Wren, so stated in mother's will.
iv, MARY KENDALL[6], wife of —— Sangster.
v, ANN MCCARTY[6], wife of John R. Ratcliffe; issue: John R. Ratcliffe, Ann Maria Coleman, Cora L. Ratcliffe, and Laura F. Ratcliffe.
vi, CATHARINE ANN[6], wife of George W. Wren.
vii, SINAH ELLEN CHICHESTER[6], wife of —— Fitzhugh.
viii, DODRIDGE C.[6].
ix, HANCOCK[6].
x, WILLIAM L.[6].
xi, DANIEL C.[6], deceased, without issue.

## WILLIS LEE.

12. WILLIS[5], the eldest son of Hancock Lee[4] (Hancock[3], Hancock[2], Richard[1]) and Winifred Beale, his wife, married Mary Richards, and had two children:

i, JOHN HANCOCK[6]. See 19.
ii, MARY WILLIS[6], who married Thomas Scott Ashton (1803–1873), of Fauquier county, the sixth and youngest son of Major Lawrence Ashton, and Elizabeth Scott, his wife, and had eleven children, whose names have not been ascertained.

## HANCOCK LEE.

13. HANCOCK[5], the second son of Hancock Lee[4] (Hancock[3], Hancock[2], Richard[1]) and Winifred Beale, his wife, was born ——, and died the 22d of July, 1842; he was married, on the 12th of August, 1819, to Susan Richards, a cousin of his brother's wife, and daughter of William Richards and Anne Blackwell, his wife; Mrs. Lee died the 18th of August, 1873, having had nine children. Hancock Lee, though under age, served with the Virginia troops in the war of 1812.

i, ANNE[6], born the 10th of November, 1820, and died the 18th of February, 1862; she was married, on the 3d of October, 1843, to John Howison, of "Greenview," Fauquier county, and had seven children: 1, John Hancock, born the 4th of July, 1844, and was so severely wounded at Gettysburg that he died on the 18th of July, 1863. 2, Edward Moore, born in June, 1845, and was also fatally wounded in the late civil war, dying on the 24th of August, 1864, at Petersburg. 3, Hancock Lee, born the 13th of October, 1847; was married on the 13th of August, 1874, to Margaret Ann, daughter of George William Howison, of Prince William county, Va., and Mary Eliza Humphreys, of Maple Springs, Texas; she was born the 11th of November, 1856, at Bogota, Texas, where they now reside, and have issue: Robert Lee, Lucien Lee, Helen Margaret, John William, Mary Rebecca, and Sarah Ann Howison. 4, Helen McDonnell, born the 24th of October, 1850; was married, on the 7th of April, 1880, to John W. Rinehart, and resides near Alaska, Mineral county, West Va.; they have these six children: Mary Buckner, Elijah, Helen Howison, Anne Lee, John Howison, and Marion Dunnington Rinehart. 5, Ludwell Lee, born the 5th of August, 1851; was married, in December, 1877, to Annie Caroline, daughter of James A. Beckham and Emma Brent Coons, his wife, both of Harper's Ferry, West Va., and has two children: Ludwell Lee and William Hardy Howison; they reside at Socorro, New Mexico. 6, Neil McCoul, born the 7th of August, 1853, and married, on the 30th of November, 1881, Mary Frances, daughter of W. P. Clatterbuck and Elizabeth Humphreys, his wife, and has five children living: Elizabeth Payne, Anne Lee, Frances Virginia, William Clatterbuck, and Rebecca Reynolds Howison. 7, Nannie McPhail, born the 13th of December, 1856, and married, on the 9th of November, 1876, Patrick C. Waring, of Essex county, Va.

ii, FRANCES[6], born the 16th of March, 1822, and married, on the 9th of December, 1841, Robert Willis, of Orange court-house, and had four children: 1, Robert, born the 9th of October, 1843, and died unmarried. 2, Jane, born in April, 1844, and also died unmarried. 3, Hancock Lee, born the 1st of March, 1846, and has been twice married; first, to a Miss Louise Bull, and next, to a Miss Eckloff, and had issue: Robert Lee, Maud L., and Fannie Madison Willis. 4, George Willis, born the 17th of March, 1848, and was living, recently, in New Mexico, unmarried.

iii, MARY[6], born the 30th of August, 1823, and died, unmarried, on the 20th of October, 1860.

iv, VIRGINIA[6], born the 4th of December, 1824; has been twice married; first, to Smith Rixey, on the 4th of June, 1868, and next, to A. Richards, on the 21st of October, 1877.

v, LUDWELL[6], born the 6th of May, 1826, and died, unmarried, in 1855.
vi, SUSAN[6], born the 6th of June, 1830, and married Horace Dodd, of Fauquier county, and has nine children.
vii, LOUISA[6], born the 11th of September, 1832, and died unmarried.
viii, THOMAS[6], born the 19th of April, 1834, and is unmarried.
ix, HENRY HANCOCK[6]. See 20.
x, WILLIAM[6], born the 1st of August, 1840, and died the 19th of April, 1863.

### THOMAS LEE.

14. THOMAS[5], the third son of Hancock Lee[4] (Hancock[3], Hancock[2], Richard[1]) and Winifred Beale, his wife, married —— Bell, of Louisville, Ky.; he removed to Missouri, and died there in 1860. He had two daughters:

i, MATILDA[6], who married —— Gaskins, and had two sons, who were killed during the late war.
ii, JANE[6]; died unmarried.

## DITCHLEY LINE, SIXTH GENERATION.

### ARTHUR LEE.

15. ARTHUR[6], the second son of George Lee[5] (Kendall[4], Richard[3], Hancock[2], Richard[1]) and Frances Ball, his wife, married Sarah Haggeman, who died in 1883, and left issue:

i, WILLIAM KENDALL[7]. See 21.
ii, ARTHUR H.[7], died unmarried in 1891.
iii, MARY[7], married —— Locke.
iv, JOHN HAGGEMAN[7], died, without issue, in 1886; lived in Lancaster.
v, JOSEPH BALL[7], died without issue.
vi, GEORGE[7]. See 22.
vii, JAMES BALL[7], died without issue.
viii, RICHARD HENRY[7], died without issue.

### THOMAS LEE.

16. THOMAS[6], the second son of Kendall Lee[5] (Kendall[4], Richard[3], Hancock[2], Richard[1]) and Judith Burton Payne, his second wife, was born in 1791 and died in 1849; he married, on the 15th of September, 1816, Mary Pearson, and removed to Kentucky. They had the following-named issue:

i, ELIZABETH KENDALL[7], born the 14th of August, 1820; died the 3d of June, 1854; married, on the 7th of January, 1840, William P. Hahn; no issue.

ii, GEORGE THOMAS[7], born the 6th of January, 1824; died the 5th of October, 1827.

iii, MARY VIRGINIA[7], born the 10th of November, 1826; died the 26th of April, 1855; she married, the 14th of July, 1846, William B. Scott, and had: 1, Mary Florence, born the 7th of June, 1847; died the 4th of January, 1889; married E. S. St. John; no issue. 2, Martha B., born the 7th of October, 1849; died in April, 1877; married John Haines, and had Margaret Lee, who married Charles Starr. 3, Elizabeth K., born the 15th of July, 1854; died the 28th of August, 1855.

iv, JUDITH[7], born the 27th of November, 1828; married, 3d of November, 1846, John Gargan, and had: 1, Mary. 2, William Thomas, born the 14th of April, 1852; died the 8th of August, 1854. 3, John H., born the 1st of September, 1857; died the 25th of May, 1875. 4, Virginia, born the 17th of September, 1857; married J. B. Keyser. 5, Eliza C. 6, Thomas Lee. 7, Benjamin F. 8, Anna R. Gargan.

v, RICHARD HENRY[7], born the 11th of March, 1831; died the 25th of October, 1861; served in Morgan's command, C. S. A., and was killed while on service.

## WILLIAM LEE.

17. WILLIAM[6], the third son of Kendall Lee[5] (Kendall[4], Richard[3], Hancock[2], Richard[1]) and Judith Burton Payne, his second wife, was born in 1795 and died in 1874; he was twice married; first, on the 11th of December, 1823, to Eliza Wamack; secondly, on the 11th of November, 1840, to Hannah Saunders, and had two sons. Mr. Lee was a farmer in Cumberland county.

i, WILLIAM THOMAS[7]. See 23.

ii, JAMES HANCOCK[7], born the 2d of February, 1844, and died the 30th of March, 1865. Served in the Confederate army until discharged on account of ill-health.

## HANCOCK LEE.

18. HANCOCK[6], the fourth son of Kendall Lee[5] (Kendall[4], Richard[3], Hancock[2], Richard[1]) and Judith Burton Payne, his second wife, was born the 26th of July, 1797, and died the 5th of November, 1860; he was twice married; first, on the 8th of July, 1824, to Mary, daughter of Dr. James Henderson, of Manchester, Va., and Mary Ogleby, his wife; she was

born the 13th of March, 1802, and died the 29th of March, 1844. Mr. Lee married, secondly, on the 12th of August, 1847, Martha Bickerton, daughter of Carter Henry Drew and Juliet Shore, his wife, of Richmond; she was born the 17th of October, 1818, and died the 26th of December, 1892. Mr. Lee resided at Richmond, where he had been for many years the teller of the Farmers Bank of Virginia. He was highly esteemed by all; was a devoted member and elder in the Presbyterian Church. By his first marriage he had ten children, only three of whom lived to maturity; by his second he had four children, only one of whom now survives.

i, MARY HENDERSON [7], born the 29th of October, 1825; died the 18th of September, 1826.

ii, VIRGINIA PAYNE [7], born the 18th of June, 1826; died the 1st of December, 1839.

iii, FRANCES ELIZABETH [7], born the 28th of July, 1827; died the 27th of June, 1828.

iv, JAMES KENDALL [7]. See 24.

v, ELLEN [7], born the 13th of September, 1831; died the 17th of April, 1841.

vi, WILLIAM HANCOCK [7], born the 7th of September, 1834; died the 29th of April, 1835.

vii, CHARLOTTE [7], born the 11th of August, 1836; lives at Richmond.

viii, MARGARET HENDERSON [7], born the 1st of May, 1838; lives now at Richmond. To whom many thanks are most gratefully rendered for efficient assistance in gathering data for this record.

ix, JUDITH BURTON [7], born the 28th of November, and died the 1st of December, 1839.

x, JANE BARCLAY [7], born the 12th of September, 1841; died the 25th of August, 1843.

xi, JULIET [7], born the 26th of November, 1853, and resides now at Richmond.

xii, MARY RUTHERFORD [7], born the 3d of June, 1855; died the 11th of June, 1880; was married, on the 25th of May, 1879, to Robert Somerville, no issue.

xiii, —— son, who died an infant in 1857.

xiv, CARTER HENRY [7], born the 8th of January, and died the 8th of February, 1859.

## JOHN HANCOCK LEE.

19. JOHN HANCOCK [6], the only son of Willis Lee [5] (Hancock [4], Hancock [3], Hancock [2], Richard [1]) and Mary Richards, his wife, was born in

1805, died in October, 1873, and was buried at "Montpelier" in Orange county. Though born in Fauquier, Mr. Lee spent the greater part of his life in Orange, which county he represented for many years in the Virginia Assembly. He was educated at Princeton, and later studied law at the University of Virginia. Being in attendance at the latter institution when Lafayette made his visit there, he was chosen to welcome the distinguished Frenchman on the part of the students. Mr. Lee was married three times; first, when scarcely twenty-one years old, to his cousin[1] Mary Willis, a daughter of Dr. John Willis and Nellie Conway Madison, his wife; after her death he married secondly, her cousin Fannie, a daughter of Lewis Willis and Lucy Madison, his wife; for his third wife, he married Mary, daughter of Sydney Jones, of Petersburg. He left five children:

- i, LÆTITIA[7], who married Dr. Robert Madison, and had Lætitia, and Mary who died young.
- ii, NELLIE CONWAY[7], born in 1826, and died in 1875.
- iii, LEWIS HERMAN[7], born the 7th of March, 1849; died the 30th of July, 1878; married, on the 12th of October, 1876, Georgia Garland, daughter of the Rev. J. S. Hansborough, and had one daughter, Mary Madison, born the 28th of March, 1877, and resides with her mother near Orange Court-house.
- iv, LIZZIE MADISON[7], who married William Albert Bragg, of Richmond, and has three children: Hancock Lee, Elise Calvin, and Fannie Madison Bragg.
- v, NORMA OVERTON[7], who married John Brockenbrough Woodward.

## HENRY HANCOCK LEE.

20. HENRY HANCOCK[6], the third son of Hancock Lee[5] (Hancock[4], Hancock[3], Hancock[2], Richard[1]) and Susan Richards, his wife, was born the 26th of August, 1837; was married, on the 14th of June, 1860, to Olivia Nutt, the daughter of Moncure Nutt and Ann Smith, his wife; they have ten children:

- i, HENRY HANCOCK[7]. See 25.
- ii, ANNIE[7], born the 16th of October, 1864; is unmarried.
- iii, ROBERT EDWARD[7]. See 26.
- iv, MARY[7], born the 20th of October, 1867; is unmarried.
- v, LUCY[7], born the 15th of April, 1870; is unmarried.

---

[1] Mary Willis Lee, youngest child of Hancock Lee and Mary Willis, his wife, married Ambrose Madison, and had a daughter, Nellie Conway Madison, who married Dr. John Willis. (See 4, vii.)

vi, OLIVIA$^{7}$, born the 3d of May, 1872; is unmarried.
vii, FRANCES$^{7}$, born the 22d of February, 1874; is unmarried.
viii, LUDWELL$^{7}$, born the 24th of June, 1876.
ix, FRANCIS$^{7}$, born the 1st of January, 1879.
x, ALICE$^{7}$, born the 8th of March, 1882.

## DITCHLEY LINE, SEVENTH GENERATION.

### WILLIAM KENDALL LEE.

21. WILLIAM KENDALL$^{7}$, the eldest son of Arthur Lee$^{6}$ (George$^{5}$, Kendall$^{4}$, Richard$^{3}$, Hancock$^{2}$, Richard$^{1}$) and Sarah Haggeman, his wife, married a Miss Henderson, and had two sons:

i, WILLIAM HENDERSON$^{8}$, now living in Lancaster county.
ii, ARTHUR$^{8}$, also living in Lancaster county.

### GEORGE LEE.

22. GEORGE$^{7}$, the fifth son of Arthur Lee$^{6}$ (George$^{5}$, Kendall$^{4}$, Richard$^{3}$, Hancock$^{2}$, Richard$^{1}$) married Ellen, daughter of William Howson and Elvira (Henry) Clark, of Halifax county, and had four children:

i, ARTHUR$^{8}$.
ii, WILLIAM HOWSON CLARK$^{8}$.
iii, ELLEN BRUCE$^{8}$.
iv, GEORGE KENDALL$^{8}$.

### WILLIAM THOMAS LEE.

23. WILLIAM THOMAS$^{7}$, the eldest son of William Lee$^{6}$ (Kendall$^{5}$, Kendall$^{4}$, Richard$^{3}$, Hancock$^{2}$, Richard$^{1}$) and Eliza Wamack, his first wife, was born the 23d of October, 1830, and died the 19th of June, 1865; married on the 11th of July, 1860, Susan Blanton. He was a lieutenant in the 44th Virginia Infantry, C. S. A.; left one son, Elisha Kendall Lee$^{8}$, of Farmville, Va.

### CAPTAIN JAMES KENDALL LEE.

24. JAMES KENDALL$^{7}$, the eldest and only surviving son of Hancock Lee$^{6}$ (Kendall$^{5}$, Kendall$^{4}$, Richard$^{3}$, Hancock$^{2}$, Richard$^{1}$) and Mary Henderson, his first wife, was born at Richmond on the 31st of July, 1829, and died on the 2d of August, 1861, from the effects of a gunshot wound received at the first battle of Manassas. After a preliminary course at the private schools in his native city Mr. Lee entered Princeton and graduated, receiving the degree of Bachelor of Arts. He then studied law, and began

its practice at Richmond, and was succeeding, to a promising degree, when the civil war broke out. Gov. Henry A. Wise appointed him first lieutenant in the first Virginia regiment on 1st of December, 1859; on the 16th of April, 1861, Gov. John Letcher appointed him captain in the same regiment. The following notice of his death was published shortly after his decease:

"Died, near Manassas Junction, August 2d, Captain James K. Lee, of this city, from a wound received in the battle of Bull Run, July 18th.

"Captain Lee is one of the many noble victims that will be demanded by that cruel and wicked war which is now upon us. As soon as it became evident that the war was inevitable he raised a company in connection with the first regiment of this city, and whilst leading his men gallantly in the severe engagement of July 18th was struck by a minie ball, which entered his side just under the shoulder, and, passing through both lobes of the lungs, came out a little below the heart on the other side, producing a wound of the most dangerous character. From this wound he lingered in great pain for a fortnight, evincing the utmost resignation, until he fell asleep in Jesus.

"Captain Lee was a son of the late Hancock Lee, of this city, and inherited many of the amiable traits of his beloved father. He graduated at Princeton College about fourteen years ago, and after studying law in this city engaged in its practice with the most flattering hopes of success. About five years ago he joined the First Presbyterian Church of this city, and at once took his stand as an energetic working Christian. As a teacher in the Sunday-school, as a member and officer of the Y. M. C. A., and as a member of the church, he was busy and untiring in his Master's service. In all three relations his place will be hard to fill. The death of his father devolved on him much of the care of the surviving family, but he assumed it with a loving promptness that could not be exceeded, and at once began to discharge a father's duties to the little orphaned ones then left fatherless. His inestimable importance to them would have justified him in the eyes of many in remaining at home, but his heart was too noble to disregard his country's call, and he responded at once, and fell gallantly defending his native soil from rapine and murder. The vast crowd that thronged to his funeral gave token of the place he held in the public heart and the deep sense entertained by the whole city of the heroism of his career. He now sleeps calmly beside his beloved father, but the memory of his noble, Christian life and his grand, heroic death, we trust will raise up many another young man to come forward and take the place which he has vacated on earth, and prepare to stand beside him in Heaven."

At a meeting of the Bar of the city of Richmond resolutions were passed, in which it was "*Resolved*, That the Bar of the city of Richmond lament the loss of Capt. James K. Lee, one of their brethren, whose legal attainments, uprightness, and courtesy made him an ornament to the profession, while his personal virtues commanded the esteem and affection of his associates. . . ."

The two following letters were written by Captain Lee to his sisters, then at Richmond; the first just before the battle and the other, by the hand of a friend, after he had been wounded:

"Fairfax Court House, Va., 20th June, 1861. My dear Sisters, Our movements of late have been so uncertain, and my time so fully occupied, that I have thought it best and have been obliged to suspend the writing of letters, except on the most urgent business. I dropt you a line a few days ago by Mr. John Hatcher, before I received your (Mag's) last letter. Ever since, and even before that, we have been hearing of orders directing us to return to Manassas Junction, and I thought I would wait until such orders became definite before I wrote again, in order that I might give you some assurance of seeing me in Richmond shortly. We have received our orders to return there to-morrow; but such is the nature of our position that they may be countermanded before the sun rises; and I am sorry I cannot yet state when it is probable I may get a leave of absence. I cannot think of asking for it while we are here. . . .

"I wish I had time to tell you all about our sojourn here. The village itself is in the midst of a beautiful country, and though many of the inhabitants have deserted it, there remain enough, together with the officers and men (the greater part of whom are very nice gentlemen) to make it quite a sociable little place. I have visited but little, though the citizens have been very polite and attentive to us all. I ran against a relation in the street the other day, William Lee Edwards, Esqr., a resident lawyer, who took me to his office and told me all about our family in this neighborhood. The county fairly swarms with them. He and our father were first cousins; his mother was Priscilla Lee, sister to Kendall Lee, our grandfather. Many of the Lees still live about here, but of course I have had no opportunity to meet with them.

"A widow lady, named Ratcliffe, said to have two very pretty daughters, and a resident here, is also a relation; but neither she nor the pretty cousins are here. The Sangsters, and the Fitzhughs of Alexandria, are also related, I think he said. He told me a heap about them, and also about the family still in Northumberland, none of which I ever expect to remember. If the war ever ends I think I shall make a special trip in this direction, by way of setting up the old genealogical tree again. What is curious, too, there are a great many Paynes in this county, and some of them are related or connected with the Lees.

"Several of the officers, including myself, have been boarding here at a private boarding-house kept by a Mrs. Chapman. They are very pleasant people, though I think she is a Northern lady; her husband is a Virginian. All this section of the country is peopled with Yankees, and that is one reason why Lincoln has been so anxious to get a foothold here. He expects to get aid and comfort from them. There is no doubt that all the information received at Washington in reference to our forces about here has been communicated by persons residing in the county, and some near the village. The residents of the village itself are believed to be true to the State. Certainly our landlady is, else why should she take such pleasure in stuffing us with waffles reeking in rich mountain butter, biscuits so light that they fly to your head if you but touch them, eggs fresh from the hen-house, cold ham, veal, lamb, salt shad and herring, and the most delicious coffee with *cream*, and plenty of rich, yellow milk to wash it all down! Else why does she, for dinner, cook so many chickens in so many ways, serve up such nice lamb and bacon, provide so much nice lettuce, green peas, potatoes, beets, eggs if you like, hot corn bread (breakfast biscuits, too), ending either with gooseberry tarts, strawberries with cream (real cream), or perhaps all three together! Else why does she, at supper, bring out her preserved ginger and watermelon and so insidiously insist on our taking just another waffle or a glass of milk, and a few more of the strawberries! Without doubt she must be loyal! At least I can't believe otherwise until some better reason can be given for her treating us so well than the paltry compensation she receives from us for committing such damages at her table.

"I suppose you have heard about the battle at 'Vienna,' that took place at a village of that name about 5 miles from here last Monday? . . . Since then they have advanced by another road to within about 6 miles of this place. I shouldn't be surprised if we had another skirmish shortly, though no immediate or sudden attack is apprehended. Love to all. Kiss Juliet and Mary for me, also Lizzie and Lucy if they have returned, and the darling Mildred (for taking such good care of you)."

Dictated to a comrade: "Colonel Ware's, near Manassas Junction, Tuesday, July 23d. [1861] Dear Mag. I have had many offers from my friends since I was wounded to write to you all for me, the saddest of which was Edward Fontaine, who brought me a letter from you and promised to return the next day and answer it. But the morrow never came to him, as I am informed. I avail myself now of the kind offer of Mr. Stiles, merely to thank you, and, through you, all near and dear to you and to me for their kind expressions of sympathy and affection so many times made. I have consulted Drs. Cullen and Maury, our regimental surgeons, and also Dr. Brody, of General Beauregard's staff, as to the propriety of my proceeding at once to Richmond. They unite in advising me to lie quiet a few days longer, after which it will be safer to travel. My wounds are evidently healing, though I am completely prostrated. My attendants are a member of my company, who is a very good nurse, and my servant James, with whom I think I can manage to get along pretty well. I have a large house, deserted by its inmates, nearly all to myself. I have enough to do to think about myself, the scenes of the past and the hopes of the future, not to be annoyed by the calm solitude of my situation. You must try to imagine me quite comfortable. Do not be surprised to hear of my arrival any day. I am determined to take possession of your room, which you will please vacate without any further notice, and fit up in a handsome and comfortable style! Tell all the girls, my cousins and the rest, I shall want to see them all as soon as I arrive. They must be ready to talk to me, not expecting me to say a word to them. Love to Ma and the children, to Charlotte, Uncle Mat, the Grattans, Mabens, and all who have been kind enough to mention me."

## Henry Hancock Lee.

25. Henry Hancock $^{7}$, the eldest son of Henry Hancock Lee $^{6}$ (Hancock $^{5}$, Hancock $^{4}$, Hancock $^{3}$, Hancock $^{2}$, Richard $^{1}$) and Olivia Nutt, his wife, was born on the 21st of June, 1862; was married, on the 23d of December, 1891, to Maud, daughter of Henry Paine and Mary Taylor, his wife, and has two daughters: Mary Olivia Lee $^{8}$, born the 1st of January, 1893, and Norma Lee $^{8}$, born the 2d of February, 1894.

## Robert Edward Lee.

26. Robert Edward $^{7}$, the second son of Henry Hancock Lee $^{6}$ (Hancock $^{5}$, Hancock $^{4}$, Hancock $^{3}$, Hancock $^{2}$, Richard $^{1}$) and Olivia Nutt, his wife, was born the 15th of January, 1866; married Meta, daughter of John Shumate and Mary Weaver, his wife, and has one daughter, Mary Downman Lee $^{8}$, born the 2d of November, 1893.

## COBBS HALL LINE, SECOND GENERATION.

1. COLONEL RICHARD LEE's third son to leave male descendants in Virginia was his youngest child, Charles Lee, of "Cobbs Hall," whose descendants have chiefly lived in the counties of Northumberland, Lancaster, and Middlesex. Unfortunately the records of this branch of the family are even more scanty than those of the Ditchley Line. Therefore these sketches of its members are imperfect, incomplete, and very unsatisfactory. But they are the best that can be done with the data at hand.

### CAPTAIN CHARLES LEE.

2. CHARLES[2], the youngest child of Richard and Anna Lee, was probably born about 1656, and at "Cobbs Hall," where he lived, died, and was buried—according to family tradition. He married Elizabeth, daughter of Thomas Medstand, of Lancaster county, who was a Justice for that county in 1669, and died about 1675. They were probably married about 1676–78, as his eldest son was of age at the date of his will, but the other children were not. On the 10th of May, 1692, Charles Lee and Mrs. Elizabeth Lee witnessed the will of one Michael Griggs. They were certainly married and settled in Northumberland prior to 1684, as proven by this deed:

> This Indenture made the one and twentieth day of December in the thirty sixth year of the reigne of our Sovereign Lord Charles the Second by the grace of God of England, Scotland, France and Ireland King Defender of the Faith &c., and in the year of our Lord One Thousand six Hundred and Eighty & four, Between Charles Lee of the County of Northumberland in Virginia Gent. and Elizabeth his Wife, daughter and heir to one Thomas Medstand late of the County of Lancaster gentleman deceased, of the one part and Robert Scholfield of the County of Lancaster planter of the other part, Witnesseth: That the said Charles Lee and Elizabeth his wife for a good and valuable consideration to them in hand paid by the said Robert Scholfield, the receipt whereof they doe hereby acknowledge &c., . . . All that piece or parcell of land situate lying and being in the parish of Christ Church in the said County of Lancaster, Containing by estimation two hundred and three acres of land bounded as follows. . . . Said land is part and parcell of land taken up by one Epafraditus Lawson of a dividend of land Containing one thousand acres as by patent thereof bearing date the two and twentieth day of May in the year of our Lord 1650, which patent was assigned over to the said Thomas Medstand by one Robert Davis and Elizabeth his Wife, daughter of the said Epafraditus Lawson, as by record in Lancaster County bearing date the sixth and twentieth day of September in the year of our Lord 1666, and since by the said Medstand owned in his own name as by pattent bearing date the sixth and twentieth day of September in the year of our Lord 1668.

Charles Lee was a Justice for Northumberland in 1687–1699,[1] and was

[1] A copy of his commission as a Justice is given in full on p. 520.

named in a list of civil officers, dated in 1702, showing him to have been in commission at the time of his death.

As previously stated (page 53), Colonel Richard Lee had taken up two tracts of land at the Dividing Creeks, in Northumberland; the first of these contained six hundred acres, and was the plantation later known as "Cobbs Hall." The other tract contained eight hundred acres, two hundred of which were given to Charles by his brother Richard Lee, as shown by the deed given on page 521. No less than six deeds, with accompanying patents, are on record at Northumberland court-house, securing these lands to the two brothers. The following is the original patent for "Cobbs Hall."

To all &c Whereas &c now Knowe That I the said Edward Diggs Esq doe give and grant unto Collo Richard Lee six hundred Acres of Land Scituate in Northumberland County and upon the South side of the Dividing Creek abutting East upon the said Creek South East southerly upon another Parcell of Land belonging to the said Lee divided from this by a small Creek Called Andrews Creek, South West Westerly upon the Glade and high land North West northerly upon a run and small Creek Called ffreemans fford. The said Land being due unto the said Collo Richard Lee by and for the Transportation of Twelve Persons into this Collony &c To Have and To Hold &c Yielding and paying &c Which payment &c dated the 4th of March 1656.

Next after the patent, on the records, comes this brief deed:

I Richard Lee son and heir of Collo Richard Lee dec'd doe by these p'sents and out of naturall affection I beare Cozen [nephew] Charles Lee assign over all my Right and Title and Interest to the Land contained in the Pattent on the other side to my Cozen Charles Lee and his heirs for Ever, In witness, etc. Dated 9th September, 1707.

His will was dated the 13th of July, 1700, and probated at Northumberland court-house, on the 17th of December, 1701.

I Charles Lee being in perfect health and strength of memory do make this my last Will and Testament. First, I give and bequeath my soul to that good and gracious God yt gave it me and to my blessed redeemer Jesus Christ, assuredly trusting in and by his meritorious death and Passion to receive Salvation, and my Body to be disposed of as my loving Wife shall . . . [desire?] not doubting but at the last both body and soul will be reunited and gl. . . d, next I give and bequeath unto my son Thomas all my Land on Rappahannock River side had by my wife as also 500 acres left me by Walter Jenkins, to him and his heirs male forever, one feather bed and further a childs part of my negroes, Cattel and household stuff and in case of his death without heirs, to be divided amongst my other children, the Land to my son Charles and the heir male of his body. Next, I give and bequeath to my son Charles the 600 acres whereon I now am, a feather bed and furniture, a childs part of my negroes and Cattel wth other household stuff, and in case of his death before age to be equally divided among my other Children, the land to my son Thomas. Next, I give and bequeath to my daughter Lee Hannah Lee that 200 acres of land had out of Bro. Hancock's tract, a childs part of my negroes and cattle wth other houshold stuff, the sheep of her mark, which is two crops and a slit in one ear, and in case of her death before age, to be divided amongst my other Children, the land to my son Charles.

Next, I give and bequeath to my daughter Eliz: a childs part of my negroes and cattle w^th other houshold stuff, the half of my white serv^ts and in case of her death before age to be equally divided among my other children. Lastly, I give and bequeath to my loveing Wife all my bedding not set down and an equal part of my negroes and cattle and halfe of my white hands w^th a childs part of my other houshold stuff, my part of the mill and all my sheep and hoggs, whom I make Executrix of this my last Will and Testament, &c.

Die Jan^y 21st 1718. This Originall Will attested of Capt Charles Lee was presented to y^e Court by R^d Lee (& y^e records where it was recorded being burnt) & on the said R^d Lee's motion it is again admitted to record. Teste, (signed) R^d Lee Cl. Cur.

From this will it is learned that his wife survived him, and was duly granted letters of administration. His children are named in the will, and also in the deed of release (p. 523) by their uncle, Richard Lee. Charles, the younger son, inherited the family homestead, which is stated to have contained six hundred acres. Across Andrews' Creek and adjoining on the south side of the "Ditchley" estate, were the two hundred acres, "had out of Brother Hancock's tract," given to Leeanna Lee. She was mentioned as "Leeanna Jones" by her uncle in 1707. On the surveyor's plat, made in 1716, there is a "corner marked hicory by y^e end of William Jones plantation." A little further to the southeast is given "the corner marked hickory in Capt. Morris Jones cornfield." Which of these two married Leeanna Lee is uncertain, but the description of the boundaries of her 200 acres would indicate that her land was that marked on the surveyor's plat as belonging to William Jones.

The children of Charles and Elizabeth (Medstand) Lee were:

i, Thomas[3]. See 3.

ii, Charles[3]. See 4.

iii, Leeanna[3], was under age in 1700, but was married in 1707; she probably married the William Jones mentioned above, and had issue (as given in her daughter's will), a son and three daughters; one of the daughters, Leeanna, married her cousin, Charles Lee (7, q. v.); Ann married Thomas Cottrell; the third married —— Bell, and had two sons, Charles and Thomas Bell. This Jones was probably of the Roger Jones family, as they resided in this neighborhood. (See Jones Family, p. 365.)

iv, Elizabeth[3], of whom nothing is known; but it is possible that she married Capt. John Howson. John and Elizabeth Howson both died in 1714, as their wills were ordered to be recorded that year, and the next year an order was issued for the appraisement of their estates. She made Charles Lee one of her executors. Their wills cannot be found now.

# COBBS HALL LINE, THIRD GENERATION.

## THOMAS LEE.

3. THOMAS[3], the eldest son of Charles Lee[2] (Richard[1]) and Elizabeth Medstand, his wife, was born about 1679, he being the only child of age in 1700; he died some time in the year 1735. A Mr. Thomas Lee was Justice for Lancaster in 1712 and Sheriff in 1714. His will, dated the 16th of June, 1733, and probated the 11th of June, 1735, was as follows:

In the name of God, Amen. I Thomas Lee being in good health and Memory do make and appoint this my Last will and testament, Impr[s]. I give and bequeath my soul to God that gave it hoping in and through the Merrits of my blessed Lord and Saviour Jesus Christ to receive remission of all my sins, my body to y[e] ground to have a Christian and Decent burial. Item, I give my son Wm. Lee all Land where Wm. Rankins and Richard Weaver now live to him and the heirs of his body Lawfully begotten forever. Item, I give unto my sons, Thomas, Richard, and Charles all that tract of Land whereon I now live to be Equally Divided between them and the heirs of their body Lawfully begotten for ever. Item, I give and bequeath unto son John all that tract of Land on y[e] head of Corrotoman River which I had by my wife where Harvey now lives to him and the heirs of his body Lawfully begotten for ever Provided the Child my wife goes with be not a boy which if it be then my will is that the sd. Land be Equally Divided between them and the heirs of their Bodys Lawfully begotten for ever. Item, I give and bequeath unto my wife one fourth part of my personal Estate during her natural Life or Widowhood but if she should Intermarry then to have but one Childs part, also my will is that she have Liberty to dispose of her said fourth part to such of her Children as she shall think proper at her decease provided she live unmarried. Item, my will is that my Estate be kept together until my children come to Lawfull age or marriage. Item, my will and Request is that my loving Brother Major Charles Lee, my good friend Mr. Nicholas Martin and my loving Wife be Executors of this my Last Will and Testament and that my son William Lee, when he comes to the age of one and twenty be allowed to be one of my Executors. Item, my will is that my personal Estate after my Wife's part is taken out be Equally Divided between all my Children. Item, I give and bequeath unto my son William Lee my Phillip's English Dickonary. Item, I do ordain and appoint this my Last Will and Testament, Revoking all former Wills, &c.

The name of Thomas Lee's wife is not known. His children, all minors in 1733, were named in his will and in that of his second son, Thomas in 1758, with these exceptions: William, the eldest, and Richard, the third sons, are omitted, and a daughter, Elizabeth, is added; she must have been born after the making of her father's will.

Thomas Lee's children, then, were:

i, WILLIAM[4]; was not mentioned by his brother in 1758. The register of old Christ Church, Lancaster, gives, "William, son of Thomas and Ann Lee, dyed 13th January, 1735," who *might* have been this William.

ii, THOMAS[4]. See 5.

iii, RICHARD[4]; probably died unmarried, as neither he nor any children were mentioned in 1758 by his brother Thomas.

iv, CHARLES[4]. See 6.

v, JOHN[4]; was mentioned by his brother in 1758, and was apparently then unmarried.

vi, ELIZABETH[4]; was mentioned by her brother in 1758 as "sister Elizabeth Dibrell," and £40 was left to her eldest son. She was probably born in the latter half of the year 1733 and died in 1770. She married, it is said, Anthony Dibrell about 1755, and had four children; Charles, Elizabeth, Judith, and Anthony Dibrell. One of her descendants, Charles Dibrell, was a general in the Confederate army. It is a tradition in the families of Dibrell and Fearn that this Elizabeth had a sister, Leeanna, who married John Fearn, of Buckingham county, and has left a line of descendants. Unfortunately, no authentic proof of this tradition has yet been discovered. The register of old Christ Church, Lancaster, gives this: "John ffearne of Gloster and Mary Lee of this parish were married y[e] — of November, 1687."

## MAJOR CHARLES LEE.

4. CHARLES[3], the second son of Charles Lee[2] (Richard[1]) and Elizabeth Medstand, his wife, was under age at the date of his father's will; he died in 1740–1, as evidenced by the following certificate:

"Northumberland SSt. By virtue of an order of Court, dated the 11th day of May, 1741, We the subscribers met and appraised, divided and set apart the Estate of Major Charles Lee dec'd. One half to Mrs. Elizabeth Brent Guardian to Elizabeth Lee, Margaret Lee and Ann Lee, and the other half to Mr. Charles Lee Ex'or of the dec'd Major Charles Lee. Witness our hands 6th June, 1741."

Charles was mentioned by his elder brother, Thomas, as "my loving Brother Major Charles Lee," and appointed one of his executors. He was probably the "Captain Charles Lee" who was a church warden of Wycomico Parish in 1732. (*Old Churches, Families*, etc., II, 114.) The Lancaster records contain the original marriage bond, dated the 8th of November, 1721, between Charles Lee and Elizabeth Pinckard, which is signed by Charles Lee and Thomas Pinckard. The signature on this bond seems to be identical with that in the old family Bible, now in the possession of Judge Edwin Broun, from which the names and dates of birth of these children are taken. His wife had probably died prior to the division of his estate in 1741, as no share of it was allotted to her.

i, CHARLES[4]. See 7.

ii, ELIZABETH[4], born the 3d of April, 1724, and in July, 1742, she was awarded her portion of her father's estate, being then described as "Mrs. Elizabeth Lee orphan of Charles Lee Gent. dec'd." Her will, dated the 13th of October, 1775, and probated in Northumberland, on the 13th of December, 1784, mentioned her nephew, Charles Lee, and his son, Charles Lee, Jr.; also Jane Swan, Ann Taylor, niece, Charles Leland, son of John Leland, and Richard Evers Lee. Of the last mentioned no authentic data have been found; it seems probable that he was of this family, but no proof has been discovered.

iii, MARGARET[4], born the 9th of March, 1726.

iv, ANN[4], born the 5th of March, 1728.

v, LUCY[4], born the 14th of December, 1730.

vi, JUDITH[4], born the 10th of March, 1732. Neither Judith nor Lucy are mentioned in the division of their father's estate, or placed under the guardianship of Mrs. Elizabeth Brent in the above quoted order of the court. The Northumberland records state that Mrs. Elizabeth Brent, on the 9th of March, 1746, was appointed a guardian of Judith and Sally Lee, and on the 7th of September, 1747, she filed an account as guardian for the same. No clue is given as to the parentage of these two children.

## COBBS HALL LINE, FOURTH GENERATION.

### THOMAS LEE.

5. THOMAS[4], the second son of Thomas Lee[3] (Charles[2], Richard[1]) died in 1759. His will, dated the 1st of December, 1758, and probated, in Lancaster, on the 16th of March, 1759, gives all the information known concerning him and his family:

In the name of God, Amen. December the 1st, 1758. I Thomas Lee Colony of Virginia in the County of Lancaster and Parish of Christ Church being very sick and weak in Body but of Perfect mind and memory thanks be to God for it however Calling to mind the mortality of my Body and knowing that it is appointed for all men once to die do make and ordain this my last Will and Testament, that is to say Principally and first of all I Recommend my Soul into the hands of God that gave it, and my Body to the Earth to be decently Intered at the discretion of my Ex'rs hereafter named, not doubting but at the General Resurrection I shall Receive the same again by the Mighty Power of my ever blessed Redeemer and as to such worldly Estate as it hath Pleased God to bless me with in this Life I give and dispose of the same in manner and form following:

Imp[s] After my Just Debts and funeral Charges are fully paid and Satisffyed then I give and Bequeath unto my Daughter Mary Lee one negro boy named Dick that I had by my

Brother Richard Lee to her and the heirs of her Body for ever. Imprs I give and Bequeath unto Brother John Lee one negro wench named Cate that I had by my Brother Richard Lee to him and the heirs of his Body forever. And as I owe Richard Blade some money my will and Desire is it shall be paid out of the money that Wm. Grigs owes me and the remainder of the money derived from William Grigs I give and Bequeath to my Brother John Lee to him and the heirs of his Body forever. Imprs then I give and Bequeath unto my two Children Mary Lee and George Lee to them and the heirs of their Bodys forever all the rest and Residue of my Estate Both Real and Personal of what Nature and kind soever, but in case my Children should die without heirs Lawfully Begotten of their Bodys then I give and Bequeath to my Loving wife Lucy Lee all the Estate I had by her and the Increase and one negro wench named Feby and likewise my Cheer and two horses and the *Explanation of the Testament*, and in case of the death of my two Children Mary Lee and George Lee without heirs Lawfully Begotten of there Bodys I give and Bequeath to my Brother Charles Lee all the Tract of Land I now Live on to him and his heirs forever. Imprs I give and Bequeath unto my Brother John Lee all the Land [I] have in White Chapple parish, to him and his heirs forever in case my two Children Mary Lee and George Lee dies without heirs Lawfully Begotten of their Bodys. Imprs I give and Bequeath unto my Brother Charles Lee one negro fellow named Aaron in case my Children dies without heirs Lawfully Begotten of their Bodys. Imprs I give and Bequeath unto my Loving wife Lucy Lee one half of my stock and household furniture in case of the death of my Children without heirs Lawfully Begotten of their Bodys, and in case of the death of my two Children Mary Lee and George Lee without heirs Lawfully Begotten of their Bodys, I give and Bequeath all the Rest of my negroes not before mentioned to my Brother John Lee to him and the heirs of his Body, and my will and Desire is that my Brother John Lee may work the negroes he now has upon the Land I now Live on as Long as he Lives Single and have the proffits of them and in case of the death of my two Children Mary Lee and George Lee without heirs Lawfully Begotten of their Bodys my will and desire is that my Estate be kept together till forty pounds Current money of Virginia be Raised and that money I give and Bequeath to my Sister Elizabeth Debrell's Eldest son to him and his heirs Lawfully Begotten of his Body for ever and in case he dies without such heirs then the forty pounds Current money to be Equally Divided Between my two Brothers Charles Lee and John Lee. Item, I do hereby Nominate Constitute and appoint my Loving wife Luce Lee Ex'r'x as Long as she Lives a widow and no longer, also Charles Lee Eppa Lawson and George Currell Ex'rs to this my Last will and Testament, &c., &c.

The issue of Thomas and Lucy Lee were:

i, MARY[5].
ii, GEORGE[5].

### CHARLES LEE.

6. CHARLES[4], the fourth son of Thomas Lee[3] (Charles[2], Richard[1]) died in the spring of 1792. In his will he mentioned his wife, Joannah, and some negroes that she had inherited under the will of William Morgan, dec'd. She was probably his daughter. They were married on the 7th of May, 1753.

His will, dated in 1791, and probated in Lancaster the 19th of March, 1792, was as follows:

In the name of God Amen, I Charles Lee of the parish of Christ Church and County of Lancaster, being in Perfect sense and memory do make and publish this my last will and testament in manner and Form following that is to say. Imprimis I resign my soul to God who gave it me and my body to the earth to be decently buried at the discretion of my Executors hereafter named, and my worldly estate I dispose of in the following manner, Item I give to my beloved wife Joannah Lee during her life all my Land lying on the north side the bridge branch with all my houses, orchards, stocks of all kinds, household and kitchen furniture, plantation utensils and my stills, casks, and tubs. Item I give and bequeath all the remaining part of my Land lying on the south side of the bridge branch, and after the death of my said wife Joannah Lee the whole of my Land to my son Thomas Lee, provided he complies with certain conditions hereafter mentioned, to him and his Heirs forever, but in case he shall not comply with the said conditions then I give and bequeath the same as hereafter mentioned. I also give to my said son Thomas Lee after the death of my said wife, my stills, casks, tubs, my large looking glass and Philips's Dictionary. Item I give and bequeath to my son Richard Lee one negro man named Anthony, one negroe boy named Charles, one negroe man named Billy, and one negroe woman named Frank and her Future Increase, to him and his Heirs forever. Item I lend to my Daughter Elizabeth Beale during her natural life one negroe boy Spencer, and after her death to be equally divided between her children Charles and John Beale. Item I give and bequeath to my said daughter Elizabeth Beale after the death of my said wife two cows and calves the first choice and the bed and table she has now in her possession. Item I give and bequeath to my grandsons Charles and John Beale one negroe boy David, one negroe boy Hillander and negroe Cate and her future Increase to be equally divided between Charles and John Beale and if either Charles or John Beale should die before they arrive to the age of twenty one years the share of the one so dying to the survivor, and if the said Charles and John should both die before they attain the age of twenty one years, then I give and bequeath the said negroes and Increase to my son Thomas Lee and his Heirs forever. Item I give and bequeath to my Daughter Sarah Lee one negroe boy named Billy to her and her heirs. Item I give and bequeath to my Daughter Ann Lee one negroe Girl named Jenny and her Future Increase to her and her heirs. Item I give and bequeath all the remaining part of my negroes (and after the death of my said wife) all my household and kitchen furniture and stocks of all kinds not hereinafter bequeathed to be equally divided between my two Daughters Sarah and Ann Lee. Item It is my will and desire that after the death of my said wife Joannah Lee all the negroes that she holds under the last will and testament of William Morgan Decd be equally divided between my children Thomas Lee, Richard Lee, Elizabeth Beale, Sarah Lee, and Ann Lee and if my said son Thomas Lee shall not consent to have the said negroes so divided among all my said children, Then and in that case I give and bequeath all my lands to my son Richard Lee and his heirs forever and revoke and annul the conditional bequest herein before made thereof to my said son Thomas Lee. Item It is my will that my estate shall not be Inventoried or appraised. And Lastly I nominate constitute and appoint my loving wife Joannah Lee and my sons Thomas Lee and Richard Lee Executors of this my last will and testament, hereby revoking all former Wills by me made. In witness, etc.

[Codicil]. Item, It is my desire that the two negroes that I have given to my son Richard Lee in the within will, to wit, William and Anthony, shall remain the property of my loving wife Joannah Lee during her natural life and then to go to my son Richard Lee as within given.

The children of Charles and Joannah (Morgan) Lee were:

i, THOMAS[5]. See 8.

ii, RICHARD[5], probably married Lucy Drury, 18th September, 1783. (Lancaster records.) In 1788 a Richard and Lucy Lee executed a deed to William Walker. (Northumberland records.)

iii, ELIZABETH[5], married, 5th March, 1771, John Eustace Beale; her father named in his will two grandsons: Charles and John Beale.

iv, SARAH[5].

v, ANN[5].

BEALE: Thomas Beale, of Richmond county, in his will (dated 20th February, 1728; probated 4th June, 1729) mentioned sons: Thomas, William, Taverner, Charles, Richard, Reuben, and John; daughters: Ann and Elizabeth, also wife Elizabeth, whose will (dated 17th May, 1728; probated 6th June, 1729) named same children.

Charles Beale, of Richmond county, in his will (dated 2d May, 1760; probated 1st October, 1764) mentioned his wife, son Charles, nephew Thomas Beale; nieces, Susanna Beale, Ann Hamilton, John Eustace, and Charles, son of brother Taverner Beale; brother Richard Beale; nephews Thomas Beale and Austin Brockenbrough, Ex'rs.

William Beale, of Richmond county, in his will (dated 9th March, 1776; probated 6th July, 1776) mentioned sons William, Thomas, Reuben, Richard, Robert, daughter Susanna, and Mr. William Ball, who married daughter Ann Beale. (Hayden, *Va. Genealogies*, 738.)

A Beale married a daughter of William and Anna (Lee[3]–Armistead) Eustace. They may have been the parents of this John Eustace Beale.

## CHARLES LEE.

7. CHARLES[4], the eldest son of Charles Lee[3] (Charles[2], Richard[1]) and Elizabeth Pinckard, his wife, was born at "Cobbs Hall" the 2d of November, 1722, and died there about October of 1747. He was twice married, each time to a cousin; his first wife was Mary, daughter of Richard and Judith (Steptoe) Lee, of "Ditchley," who died at the birth of her son, Charles, on the 4th of March, 1744. (These dates are from his family Bible, now in the possession of Judge Edwin Broun, of Northumberland.) Charles Lee married, secondly, Leeanna, daughter of William (?) and Leeanna (Lee) Jones. (See 1, iii.)

In his will (dated the 30th of December, 1746, and probated the 9th of November, 1747) he named his wife, "Leeannah Lee," his two sons, Charles and Thomas, both minors, and "the child my wife now goes with." Peter Conway, David Galloway and Kendall Lee were appointed his executors; an appraisement of his estate was ordered the same day his will was admitted to probate.

The will of Leeanna Lee, his second wife, dated the 24th of June and probated the 10th of August, 1761, was as follows:

In the name of God, Amen. I Leeanna Lee of the parish of Wicomico and County of Northumberland being weak of body but of a sound mind purfect sence and memory and calling to remembrance the uncertainty of Life and that it is appointed for all Men once to die, Do make and ordain this to be my last Will and Testament in manner and form following. I give and bequeath unto my beloved sister Ann Cottrell my Negro Girl Sally. Also I give to my Nephue Charles Jones my Negro Girl Rachel. Also I give to my Nephew James Bell the sum of one hundred pounds current money to be paid to him at the expiration of one year after my decease. Also I give to Samuel Heath Jameson when he arrives at the age of Twenty One years the sum of Eighty Pounds current money, but it is my Will and desire that in case he the s$^{d}$ Samuel Heath Jameson shou'd die before he attains that age, or should by any means Recover the land which now belongs to my said Nephew Charles Jones, that the said Samuel Heath Jameson should not have the said Legacy of Eighty Pounds. All the rest of my Estate of any Denomination whatsoever I give equally to be divided between my Nephews Charles Bell Charles Jones and my loving sister Ann Cottrell excepting one good Feather Bed and Furniture which I give to my son in law [step son] Charles Lee. The above mentioned Charles Bell Charles Jones and Ann Cottrell paying my Debts Legaces and Funeral Expences. My will and desire is that Thomas Cottrell Husband to my sister Ann Cottrell shall never have any of the effects that I have given her, and if the Law shou'd by any means whatsoever give it to him that then it shou'd Return to Mr. David Boyd (Attorney at Law) for the use of my said sister Ann Cottrell and after the death of my said sister that all that I have given her return to her son William Nelms and if in case he shou'd die without a Lawful Heir that then the said effects return to my said Nephews Charles Bell and Charles Jones or their Lawfull Heirs. I hereby order and it is my will that the said Charles Bell Charles Jones and Ann Cottrell shall gett a Tombstone with a proper inscription thereon of the value of Ten Pounds and put the same over the Grave of my late son Thomas Lee. And I also order and it is my Will that the said Charles Bell Charles Jones and Ann Cottrell shall after my desease—procure to be built a proper Brick wall round the Burying place of myself and ancestors on this plantation where I now live in case my son in Law Charles Lee will permit the same and allow the Bricks to be made and wood to burn them off the said plantation. I do hereby appoint and ordain the said Charles Bell Charles Jones and James Bell to be the Executors of this my Will, etc. Mourning rings to the value of one Pistole each to my Nephew Thomas Bell, my Nease Mary Burnley and to my Cousin Margret Boy'd.

Apparently, Charles Lee had two children by each wife, as follows:

i, ANN[5], "the daughter of Charles and Mary Lee, was born y$^{e}$ 24th June, 1742."

ii, CHARLES[5]. See 9.

iii, THOMAS[5], was the son by the second wife, and was probably born about 1745; he died before the date of his mother's will, 24th of June, 1761.

iv, ——, born after the date of his father's will, 30th December, 1746; as the second wife left no surviving child, he probably died young.

## COBBS HALL LINE, FIFTH GENERATION.

### THOMAS LEE.

8. THOMAS[5], the only son of Charles Lee[4] (Charles[3], Charles[2], Richard[1]) and Joannah Morgan, his wife, is said to have married and left a son, Thomas[6], who was born in 1795 and died in 1851; was married, in 1818, to Margaret Ormond, and had five children: James Ormond, Elizabeth, Ann, Elizabeth Ormond, and Sarah Ann Lee[7].

### COLONEL CHARLES LEE.

9. CHARLES[5], the only son of Charles Lee[4] (Charles[3], Charles[2], Richard[1]) and Mary Lee, his first wife, was born "ye 4th March, 1744, at Cobbs Hall," Northumberland; he died about March of the year 1785. His will, dated the 17th of February and probated the 12th of April, 1785, mentioned only his wife, "Sarah Lee," son Charles, and "all the rest of my children." Their Christian names were given by their elder brother, Charles, in his will and by their own wills. Charles Lee left "the manor plantation" to his wife during her life and made provision for the education of his children; after her death the plantation was to go to son Charles. The widow was evidently living there in 1789, as the place was marked that year on the surveyor's plat as "Mrs. Lee's Land." Charles Lee was a vestryman of Wycomico Parish in 1772 (*Old Churches, Families*, etc., II, 469); Sheriff for Northumberland in 1783, as shown by his bond now on file, and a delegate to the Assembly (*Critic*) in 1780. He was the "Captain Charles Lee" who served on the court-martial (16th February, 1781) presided over by Col. Thomas Gaskins. It seems probable that he was also the naval officer for the South Potomac who signed clearance papers the 24th of March, 1777, which office has been previously ascribed to Charles Lee (Stratford Line, 36), of Alexandria.[1]

He married Sarah Hull (1747–1827), whose will, dated the 2d of June, 1823, mentioned daughter Molly McDaniel, Edwin Lee, son, and "Edwin Lee son of aforementioned Edwin Lee;" Thomas Broun, son-in-law; Sarah E. Broun, granddaughter; Sarah E. Lee (daughter of Kendall), granddaughter.

The issue of Charles and Sarah (Hull) Lee were:

i, CHARLES[6], who married, but apparently had no issue. The marriage

[1] The statement on page 362, that this office had been held by the other Charles Lee, was based upon a comparison of his well-known writing, as given in many letters, with the writing on this clearance paper. But a closer scrutiny and a comparison of dates has led to the conclusion that the previous statement was an error.

bond of Charles Lee and Elizabeth Edwards, spinster, of 20th October, 1792, was probably his. His will, dated — December, 1794, and probated the 14th of April, 1795, mentioned his mother, Sarah; brothers Richard, Edwin, and John; sisters Judith, "not yet sixteen," and Mary Lee. His wife survived him, as shown by the following deed:

In a deed from Richard Lee, of Northumberland to Kendall Lee of same county, dated 3d March, 1795, it was stated that "Whereas Charles Lee dec'd, did by his last will, bearing date 1794, give and devise to the said Richard Lee all that tract or parcell of land on which he resided at the time of his death, and which was devised to him by the last will and testament of Col. Charles Lee dec'd containing 500 acres more or less, which said tract of land the said Richard was to take possession of upon the death or marriage of the widow of the said Charles Lee and upon the death of Mrs. Sarah Lee, the widow of the late Col. Charles Lee dec'd, and whereas by another clause in the said will it was conditioned that the said Richard immediately upon his entry and enjoyment of the said land should pay to his brother Edwin Lee the sum of £100. Now this Indenture witnesseth that the said Richard Lee for and in consideration that the said Kendall do and shall pay unto the said Edwin Lee the aforesaid sum of £100 at such time as the said Richard would have to pay the same and also for and in consideration of the natural love and affection which the said Richard bears towards the said Kendall as well as for divers other good causes and considerations, hath given granted, &c."

ii, SARAH[6], died unmarried in 1813; her will mentioned Sarah Lee her mother; Martha Kendall Lee, Sarah Elizabeth Broun, and Elizabeth Hudnall Lee, nieces.

iii, RICHARD[6]. See 10.

iv, KENDALL[6]. See 11.

v, JOHN[6], moved South, married and had issue; names, etc., not known.

vi, EDWIN[6], settled near Norfolk, married and had, at least one son, Edwin Lee[7], who was named in the will of his grandmother, Mrs. Sarah Lee, of date of 2d June, 1823.

vii, ELIZABETH[6], born 12th November, 1779; died 10th March, 1839; was married, on 29th of October, 1807, to Thomas Broun, of Northumberland; they had issue: Judith, Judge Edwin (living in Northumberland), Dr. Charles Lee (died in 1855), Sarah Elizabeth, and William Broun.

viii, JUDITH[6], married —— Dismuke; lived in Kentucky.

ix, MARY[6]; her mother's will mentioned "Molly McDaniel, Daughter."

## COBBS HALL LINE, SIXTH GENERATION.

### Richard Lee.

10. Richard[6], the second son of Charles Lee[5] (Charles[4], Charles[3], Charles[2], Richard[1]) and Sarah Hull, his wife, died the 10th of March, 1824, aged 56; on the 21st of March, 1795, he married Elizabeth, daughter of Thomas Hurst, whom he mentioned in his will, dated 10th October, 1822; also mentioned Martha Lee, his grandchild and "sons and daughters," without naming them. The issue of Richard and Elizabeth (Hurst) Lee were:

i, Sarah[7], died unmarried.

ii, Charles[7], married —— Hurst; died 26th of January, 1822 (*Critic*) and left no issue.

iii, Jane[7], died unmarried; was buried at "Cobbs Hall."

iv, Martha[7], born the 26th of April, 1803; died the 6th of January, 1878; was married on the 8th of January, 1833, to Lewis G. Harvey and had two sons: William Henry Harvey, who died in early infancy; Richard L. Harvey, who was twice married; first, to Lucy E. Edwards, of Westmoreland county, by whom he had two children, who died young. He married secondly, Susan Perkins, daughter of Judge R. S. G. Perkins of Yazoo county, Miss., by whom he had: Lewis, Robert, Charles Lee, Warner Hurst, Julia, Estelle, Susan Perkins, and Mary Grayson Harvey. Martha (Lee) Harvey devised "Cobbs Hall" to her grandsons, after the death of their mother; they are therefore the heirs to the old Lee homestead, where they now reside.

v, Mary[7], married her cousin Edwin Lee; no issue. (See 11, viii.)

vi, Susan[7], married William Harvey, in 1825.

vii, Elizabeth[7] (Betsy), married —— Hughlett; no issue.

### Kendall Lee.

11. Kendall[6], the third son of Charles Lee[5] (Charles[4], Charles[3], Charles[2], Richard[1]) and Sarah Hull, his wife, died in 1815; he married Mary Nutt, "Spinster," the 4th of August, 1796; his will, dated 30th March, and probated 9th October, 1815, mentioned his "wife and children," without naming them; letters of administration were granted his wife Mary. In 1839 Edwin Lee deeded to George G. Lee all his right in the lands of Kendall Lee, dec'd, which accrued to him under the will of Mary Lee, mother of said Edwin. In same year, John L. Lee, Martha K. Lee, William H. Lee, Kendall Lee, Mary L. Lee, Sarah E. Lee, and George G. Lee executed a deed to Lewis G. Harvey, in which it was stated that their parents were Kendall Lee and Mary Nutt, his wife. Their issue were:

i, MARY LELAND[7], died unmarried; her will, dated 11th October, 1841, probated, Northumberland, on the 20th June, 1842, mentioned sister Sarah Elizabeth Lee, brother George G. Lee; nieces Mary Lee Ball and Mary Jane Lee.

ii, SARAH ELIZABETH[7], married —— Garlington; no issue.

iii, MARTHA KENDALL[7], married, on 13th November, 1819, Col. Joseph Ball, being his fourth wife; she survived him and moved, about 1830, to Missouri. They had: Thomas Kendall, William Henry Lee, James W. W., Mary Lee, David, Bruce, Josephine, Virginia Ball. Of these, Thomas Kendall Ball married Martha Gunn, but left no issue. William Henry Ball married Mary Harris, and lives in Randolph county, Mo. James W. W. Ball married Sallie E. Hull, lives at Carrollton, Mo. Mary Ball married John P. Horner, of Boone county, Mo. David Ball married Lucy Austin and has Henry Lee, Robert E., Lucy, and Jessie Ball. Bruce Ball was killed during the late war, at the battle of "Pea Ridge;" he was not married. Josephine Ball married Judge John Hull; no issue.

iv, GEORGE G.[7], married twice; first —— Carpenter; secondly, —— Sprigg; two children by each marriage; George and Leroy, by the first; Ann and Henry, by the second. In 1839 George G. Lee and Winifred Lee, his wife, signed a deed.

v, JOHN L.[7], married in 1834 Elizabeth Ball, and had: 1, Mary Jane Lee; born 7th of August, 1835; married twice; first, 29th of April, 1856, Joseph W. Brent, C. S. A., who died in camp on 22d of July, 1861, leaving George W. Brent (1860–1878). She married, secondly, in 1876, Walter Shay, C. S. A., of "Saratoga," Lancaster county. 2, Sally Ann Lee, born the 8th of March, 1838; married, 29th April, 1857, John D. Kemm, C. S. A., and had: i, Betty Alice, born 25th May, 1858. ii, William Everett, born 8th July, 1860. iii, Annie Irene, born 12th September, 1864. iv, Virgil Lee, born 10th July, 1869. v, David E. Ball, born 4th November, 1871. vi, Florence O., born 22d September, 1877. 3, Richardette Lee. (Hayden, *Va. Genealogies*, 68.)

vi, WILLIAM HENRY[7], married Henrietta R. S. Ball, daughter of Rev. David Ball, Rector of All Hallows Parish, Worcester county, Md., and Mrs. Sarah Eustace McAdams his wife; they lived in Chariton county, Mo.; left issue: David Ball Lee, John Edward Lee, and many others.

vii, EDWIN[7], married his cousin, Mary Lee, daughter of Richard and Elizabeth (Hurst) Lee[6]; no issue. In a deed of trust (1830), Edwin Lee mentioned his wife, Mary Lee, as a daughter of Richard Lee, and his own father as Kendall Lee. (Northumberland Records.)

# APPENDIX.

Some very interesting information, received too late for arrangement in its proper place, is given here, rather than have it omitted altogether.

FENDALL—The records given of the marriages between the Fendalls and the Lees has already been stated to be rather problematical (see pp. 99 and 151). The following notices of marriages and deaths, kindly furnished by Miss Kate Mason Rowland, of Baltimore, entirely changes previous statements. It was supposed (p. 99) that Eleanor Lee married P. R. Fendall, which the following shows to be an error:

On Sunday the 22d Instant, in the 49th year of her Age, after a short Illness, died Mrs. Eleanor Fendall, Wife to Benjamin Fendall, Esq: of Charles county. She was a Lady most justly and universally esteemed for every good Quality that could adorn or endear her character; exemplarily pious and charitable, without show or ostentation in the least; the lovingest Wife, the tenderest and most affectionate Mother. Not only her Family, and especially her Husband, are most disconsolate for her extraordinary Loss; but all in her Neighbourhood, or of her Acquaintance, are greatly affected by her departure. (Md. *Gazette*, 26 April, 1759.)

Mr. Fendall probably had children by this wife, for, with the following obituary notice of his second, mention was made of her being a "mother-in-law."

Piscataway, 1 September, 1763. On the 25th of August last, Mrs. Priscilla Fendall (wife of Benjamin Fendall, Esq.) of Charles county Departed this Life aged 49 years. (Md. *Gazette*, 15 September, 1763.)

Grace, the wife of Richard Lee, in her will (p. 150), appointed her "son in law Philip Richard Fendall" one of her executors. But no mention was made of his wife or any Fendall children; in light of the information then at hand, it was suggested that son in law probably meant brother in law (p. 151), but this was an erroneous supposition, as shown by the following marriage notice:

On Sunday last [i. e., 30th September] Mr. Philip Richard Fendall, Clerk of Charles County, was married to Miss Sarah Lettice Lee, eldest daughter to the Honorable Richard Lee Esq., Naval Officer of North Potowmack. A very valuable young couple! with every natural Endowment, and needful Accomplishment, to render them agreeably useful in Public, and promise their Happiness in private Life. Long may they live, and be prosperous in the world; to reap, fully, the benefit of their early and constant affection for each other. (Md. *Gazette*, 4 October, 1759.)

On Thursday, the 8th Instant, after a short Illness, Died Mrs. Sarah Lettice Fendall, Wife of Mr. Philip Richard Fendall, Clerk of Charles County. A very striking Example of the great uncertainty of all human Procurements, with what Zeal and Eagerness soever we pursue them, or Fondness we possess them with! She was a Lady very worthy our high Expectations, had God been pleased to allow her length of time to fulfil them in; but being cut off in almost the Bloom of Youth, and too, too soon from her happy Nuptials, she had but little opportunity for displaying to so full an extent that high pitch of merit in the character of *Wife*, which was justly ascribed her in her maiden condition. Her Fate was sudden and unexpected, and she has therefore the more left behind her a disconsolate Husband, most mournful Relations, and condoling Acquaintance. But her Memory is so grateful that it ought to set Bounds to our Sorrow and to mitigate all uneasiness on account of her Loss. (Md. *Gazette*, 22d January, 1761.)

PLATER—In the previous list (pp. 152–3) only two daughters of Richard and Grace (Ashton) Lee were given; it seems they had four, but two were not mentioned in their mother's will because they had died previous to its execution. The fourth daughter married and died as given in these notices:

On Sunday, the 5th Instant was married in Charles County, George Plater, of St. Mary's County Esq. to Miss Hannah Lee (Daughter of the Hon. Richard Lee Esq.), an amiable young Lady, endow'd with every Accomplishment to render the Connubial State happy. (Md. *Gazette*, 16 December, 1762.)

On Tuesday morning the 20th of this Instant, Died Mrs. Hannah Plater, the amiable and virtuous consort of George Plater Esq: of St. Mary's Co., and Daughter of Richard Lee Esq. She was in the Full Bloom of Life, and had not been Ten months married. (Md. *Gazette*, 26 September, 1763.)

In the issue of the Md. *Gazette*, April 29 to May 6, 1729, Richard Lee is mentioned as the "High Sheriff of Prince George's County, Md." Mention was also made (12th February, 1759) of the arrival from London, of Hancock Lee, merchant, and of his death, 4th November, 1759 (p. 160). The death of Arthur Lee, representative for Charles county, is stated to have occurred the 17th of July, 1760 (p. 157).

BOWIE—On page 99, it is stated that Hannah, daughter of Philip Lee, of Maryland, married a Bowie, and it was suggested that his baptismal name was "Daniel." This was an erroneous suggestion. By the kindness of Mr. Wilson Miles Cary, of Baltimore, the following abstract of the will of Thomas Bowie is given. Mr. Cary states that Thomas and James Bowie of Prince George's county were brothers; father's name not known to him. Their wills are recorded at Annapolis.

James (1744–8–28; 9–28) makes his "brother Thomas" executor, and leaves three daughters, Lucy, Eleanor and Martha Bowie.

Thomas (1758–3–20; 5–3) mentions wife Hannah and three children, Daniel, Elizabeth Lawson, and Barbara Bowie. The children were given correctly in the previous statement, with the exception of Elizabeth Lawson, who married Thomas Belt, as stated. Daniel Bowie was an officer in the Revolution, and was killed, it is said, in 1776. His will (1776–8–26; 1777–5–3) would indicate his fate. He desired his "body to be buried in a vault at my plantation near Collington [Prince George's county] about twenty yards below the vault of my deceased father, should I fall in battle and my body be attainable." Mentions brother Philip Sprigg, friend Walter Bowie, sisters Elizabeth Belt, Barbara Hall, and Lettie Sprigg; aunt Eleanor Skinner and Miss Millicent Tyler; friend Patrick Sim, Lieut. Butler, Lieut. Beans, James Mullican [ex'or], and Thomas Harwood.

SILK—The following abstract of the will of Martha Silk, who married Richard Lee, is from recent "Gleanings" by Mr. Henry F. Waters; from which it is learned that she was the widow of a Thomas Moore when she married Richard Lee:

Martha Lee of Mansel Street in Goodman's Fields in the parish of St. Mary's Matfellon *als* Whitechapel, Middlesex, widow, 26 April, 1725, proved 5 May, 1725. I give all my messuage etc. in Gracechurch Street, London, and all my lands in Cople Parish or elsewhere in the County of Westmoreland and Colony of Virginia, in parts beyond the seas, unto my son George Lee, etc., for ever. I give all my messuages, etc. in the County of Suffolk (subject to a mortgage and subject also to the payment of one hundred pounds to Daniel Watts, at one and twenty, pursuant to the will of Thomas Moore, my former husband, deceased) unto my two daughters Martha Lee and Lettice Lee, etc., share and share alike as tenants in common and not as joint tenants, etc. If all my said three children, George, Martha and Lettice Lee, shall happen to die without issue, I give and devise my said estate in the city of London unto such children of my late brother John Silk deceased and of the children of my brother Abraham Silk as shall be living, etc. To my very good friend Mr. Oliver Marton of the Temple, my brother the said Tobias Silk and William Wareham, citizen barber surgeon of London, ten pounds apiece for mourning. The residue of my personal estate to my said three children, equally to be divided among them, at the ages of one and twenty years, etc. My brother Tobias Silk and the said Mr. William Wareham to be their guardians. To Ruth Hill, widow, and Neomi Hill, her daughter, five pounds apiece to put themselves into mourning. Romney, 114. (*New England Hist. and Gen. Register*, April, 1895, pp. 263–4.)

THOMAS LEE, of Stratford—William Lee stated that his father had suffered a severe loss by fire, but did not give any clue as to the time or place where the fire occurred. It has been stated (p. 74) that this fire probably occurred at "Mt. Pleasant," and that the "burnt house field" at that place derived its name from a disastrous fire which had undoubtedly taken place there. The following notice of this fire, published by Miss Kate Mason Rowland in the (April, 1895) *William and Mary Quarterly*, seems to confirm the previous supposition:

Maryland *Gazette*, 4 February, 1729. Last Wednesday night Col. Thomas Lee's fine house in Virginia was burnt, his office, barns and out-houses, his plate, cash (to the sum of £10,000), papers and everything entirely lost. His lady and child were forced to be thrown out of a window, and he himself hardly escaped the flames, being much scorched. A white girl about twelve years old (a servant) perished in the fire. It is said Col. Lee's loss is not less than £50,000. The fine large house of Col. Carter on Rappahannock was also burnt lately. The particulars of this loss we cannot give you, but we are informed it is very great.

March 4 to 11—Stolen out of the house of Col. Thomas Lee in Virginia (some time before it was burnt) a considerable quantity of valuable plate—viz.: Two Caudle Cups, three Pints each, one Chocolate-Pot, one Coffee-Pot, one Tea-Pot, Three Castors, Four Salts, A Plate with the Corbin Arms, Pint Tumbler, ditto arms, Four Candle-sticks, one or two Pint Cans, a Funel for Quart Bottles, no Arms on it. A pair of Snuffers and Stand etc. This plate has on it the Coat-of-Arms or Crest, belonging to the name of Lee, viz: Fess Cheque between eight billets, Four and Four. The Crest is a Squirrel sitting upon end eating an Acorn off the branch of a Tree proper.

N. B. The Governor of Virginia has published a Reward of 50 Pounds, and a Pardon to any one of the Accomplices who will discover the rest (except the person who set fire to the House).

CARTER—In the same issue of the *William and Mary Quarterly* are given several letters of William Beverley, in which these Carter data are to be found: Secretary John Carter (p. 358) died the 31st of July, 1742. The position of Secretary of the Colony was then a purchasable one; Mr. Carter paid £1,500 for it, and Mr. Beverley stated he was willing to give more than £2,000 for the place. Mr. Beverley, writing (under date of 27th July, 1743) to Lord Fairfax, says: " . . . I doubt not but Col^o Fairfax has informed your L^dp of Miss Nancy Fx's being marr'd to Mr. Adju^ntt Washington, Col^o Charles Carter and Col^o Land^n Carter to y^e 2 Miss Byrds" (pp. 360, 361). Lawrence Washington married Anne Fairfax the 19th of July, 1743; after his death she married George Lee (p. 140).

On pages 104 *et seq.* is given an account of the visit to Lancaster of William Beverley and Thomas Lee to treat with the Indians of the Six Nations. Writing under date of 16th November, 1744, Mr. Beverley says:

" . . . Altho' what Col^o Lee and myself did with the Indians had the Honour of your and the other Gent^ns approbation, yet we mett not with y^e same from our Assembly, for they would not approve of the treaty, neither would they give us one Farthing nor contribute any thing to the charges, and if the King will not give us any thing, we shall have our Labour for our pains." (*William and Mary Quarterly*, April, 1895, p. 238.)

# ERRATA.

Page 95, sixth line from bottom, for *Pinkard* read *Pinckard.*

" 96, eighth line, for *Skolto* read *Sholto;* seventh line, for *has* read *have.*

" 102, twenty-ninth line, for *Charlottsville* read *Charlottesville.*

" 141, foot-note, for *side* read *site.*

" 148, twenty-sixth line, for *Gary* read *Cary.*

" 163, eleventh line, for *Matthew* read *Matthews.*

" 165, tenth line from bottom, omit *you.*

" 168, fourteenth line, for *mrs.* read *mr.s.*

" 183, fourth line of foot-note, for *was* read *were.*

" 207, line eleventh, for *Westmoreland* read *Northumberland.*

" 238, sixth line from bottom, for *show* read *shows.*

" 341, line second, the children of Charles Henry and Rosalie Eugenia (Calvert) Carter should read: Rosalie Eugenia, Alice, Bernard, Ella, Mildred, Annette, and Mary Randolph Carter.

" 362, the statement that Charles Lee was naval officer for "South Potomac" River in 1777 is probably erroneous. See page 568.

" 372, by an oversight two of the children of Cornelia Lee and Dr. James W. F. Macrae were omitted. They were: 3, Richard Bland Lee; 4, James Fitzgerald.

" 374, line eleventh, omit *Mrs.*

" 509, fourteen line from bottom, for *Belle Isabell* read *Isabella.*

# INDEX.

## IN TWO PARTS.

PART FIRST.—The Christian names of the descendants of Colonel Richard Lee bearing the name of Lee; children deceased under ten years omitted.

PART SECOND.—The descendants of Colonel Richard Lee bearing other surnames, and all others mentioned in the volume.

The names appearing in parentheses refer to the husband or wife; also place of residence, etc. Given to individualize as closely as possible.

## PART FIRST—CHRISTIAN NAMES OF LEES.

PART SECOND.—The descendants of Colonel Richard Lee bearing other surnames, and all others mentioned in the volume.

*Additions*

*and*

*Corrections*

*to*

# LEE OF VIRGINIA

# 1642-1892

**Page 51, after line 25,** add: "The first known record of Richard Lee in Virginia is his signature, May 22, 1638, in Patent Book A, Part 2, page 573. The signature is identical with one in the York County Order Book, 1640."

**Page 65, line 31,** for "vi, ELIZABETH[2], no data." read: "vi, ELIZABETH[2], probably married, first, Leonard Howson, and, second, John Turberville, and had issue by both marriages. (*Tyler's Quarterly* VIII, 44.)"

**Page 74, line 1,** for "Watts... Watts," read: "Watkins... Watkins,"

**Page 99, lines 29-36,** for "viii, ELEANOR[4], . . . a son and a daughter." read: "viii, ELEANOR[4], died 22 April 1759, married 18 November 1729 Benjamin Fendall, born 20 August 1708, son of John and Elizabeth (Hanson) Fendall, and had three children: John Fendall[5], born 28 October 1730, married 24 September 1751 Sarah Alexander, daughter of Philip and Sarah (Hooe) Alexander, and died 1763 leaving issue; Sarah Fendall[5], born 7 February 1732, died 1793, married Col. Thomas Contee of Nottingham, Prince George's County, Md.; and Philip Richard Fendall[5], born 24 November 1734, married three times. He married first, 30 September 1759, his first cousin Sarah Lettice Lee[5], daughter of Richard and Grace (Ashton) Lee[4]; she died 8 January 1761 without issue. (pp. 148-153.) Philip Richard Fendall[5] married second, between 1775 and 1780, Mrs. Elizabeth (Steptoe) Lee, born 22 November 1743, daughter of Col. James Steptoe of Hominy Hall, Westmoreland Co., Va., and widow of Philip Ludwell Lee[4] of Stratford (pp. 165-168); she died about June, 1789, without issue by this marriage. Philip Richard Fendall[5] married third, in 1791, Mary Lee[5], born 9 July 1764, daughter of Henry and Lucy (Grymes) Lee[4] (pp. 291-299); she died 10 November 1827, and had issue, Lucy Eleanor Fendall[6], died unmarried, and Philip Richard Fendall[6], born 18 December 1794, died 16 February 1868, married in 1827 Elizabeth Mary Young, daughter of Gen. Robert Young of Alexandria, and had nine sons and three daughters.

**Page 100, lines 34-35,** delete: "There seems to be considerable doubt as to the third marriage of Lettice Lee."

**Page 100, line 38,** add: "However, her will, signed 'Lettice Sim,' is in Annapolis Wills, 49-12."

**Page 148, line 26,** for "who was a Miss Gary." read "Sarah Cary."

**Page 151, lines 28-33,** for "This can only be explained . . . she died in 1759." read: "Her eldest daughter, Mrs. Sarah Lettice Lee Fendall, had died without issue in 1761."

**Page 152, after line 30,** add:

"iii, SARAH LETTICE[5], married 30 September 1759, Philip Richard Fendall[5], son of Benjamin and Eleanor (Lee) Fendall[4], and died without issue 8 January 1761. (pp. 99, 573, 574.)

"iv, HANNAH[5], married 5 December 1762, as his first wife, George Plater, and died without issue 20 September 1763. (p. 574.)

"v, ANNIE[5], mentioned on parents' tombstone, but not in mother's will."

**Page 152, line 31,** for "iii, ELEANOR ANN[5]" read "vi, ELEANOR ANN[5]"

**Page 153, line 23,** for "iv, ALICE[5]" read "vii, ALICE[5]"

**Page 153, line 28,** add: "Mrs. Alice Lee Weems died 25 July 1789 without issue."

**Page 172, line 19,** for "1759" read "1757"

**Page 207, line 28,** delete: "died in 1803-4."

**Page 254, lines 15-16,** for "died in 1815;" read "died 24 July 1818;"

**Page 254, line 24,** for "the 2d of April, 1819;" read "the 2d of April, 1818;"

**Page 298, lines 13-19,** for "vii, MARY[5], . . . reside at Washington." read "vii, MARY[5], born 9 July 1764, died 18 November 1827, married, as his third wife, Philip Richard Fendall[5], son of Benjamin and Eleanor (Lee) Fendall[4], and had issue. (p. 99.)"

**Page 304, line 3,** for "but name of wife unknown," read: "His wife's name was Harriet Hutchinson."

**Page 528, lines 7-17,** for "ii, ANNA$^3$ . . . for further notice.)" read: "ii, ANNA$^3$, was born prior to the 5th of January, 1682, and was living as late as October, 1754; she married William Armistead, grandson of William, the immigrant, by whom she had a son, John, and probably daughters, Judith, Martha, Mary, and Anne. William Armistead died the 13th of June, 1711, aet. 40 years (tombstone). (See Armistead Family for further notice.)"

**Page 528. line 19,** for "four children" read "five children".

**Page 529, after line 29,** add: "viii, ANNE$^3$, born about 1705, married before 16 February 1720/1 William Eustace, and had issue: John, William, Isaac, Hancock, Mrs. Gaskins, Mrs. Beale, Mrs. Carr, and Mrs. Lee (Hayden, *Va. Genealogies,* 261.) She was called Anne Eustace by her brother Isaac Lee, in his will, 1726. Half-sisters named Anna and Anne have led to confusion."

**Page 534, lines 37-38,** delete: "Of these seven children, the names of only five have been ascertained."

**Page 536, after line 4,** add:

"vi, ANN$^4$, born about 1733, died about 1769, married first, by 1754, George Kerr of Northumberland Co., who died about 1761; married second, 25 February 1765, Thomas Gaskins, born about 1723, died about 1785, of Northumberland Co.

"vii, LUCY$^4$, born 1735, died 30 March 1806, married first, as his second wife, Baldwin Matthews Smith of Northumberland Co., son of Philip Smith and Mary Matthews, and widower of Frances Burgess, by whom he had had four children. Baldwin Matthews and Lucy (Lee) Smith had two children, Judith Smith, who married John Leland, and Mildred Smith, who married Leroy Peachy. Mrs. Lucy Lee Smith married second, 11 December 1772, as his second wife, William Montague, born about 1728, died 1784."

**Page 560, lines 35-40,** for "iv, ELIZABETH$^3$, of whom nothing is known . . . cannot be found now." read: "iv, ELIZABETH$^3$, probably married Thomas Griffin and had issue. (*Va. Magazine of History and Biography* I, 254-256; *William and Mary Quarterly,* 2nd Series, XIV, 244.)"